Course   PRINCIPLES OF FINANCE
Finance 301

D1486623

http://create.mheducation.com

ISBN-10: 1308115555   ISBN-13: 9781308115559

Contents

Credits

PART ONE   Overview of Financial Management

Introduction to Financial Management

1

Compensation of corporate executives in the United States continues to be a hot button issue. It is widely thought that CEO pay has grown to exorbitant levels (at least in some cases). In July 2010, the Dodd-Frank *Wall Street Reform and Consumer Protection Act* became law. The "say on pay" portion of the bill requires that, beginning in January 2011, corporations with a market value over $75 million must allow a nonbinding shareholder vote on executive pay. (Note that because the bill applies to corporations, it does not give voters a "say on pay" for U.S. representatives and senators.)

Specifically, the measure allows shareholders to approve or disapprove a company's executive compensation plans. Because the bill is nonbinding, it does not permit shareholders to veto a compensation package and does not place limits on executive pay. In February 2011, the shareholders of Beazer Homes USA and Jacobs Engineering Group became the first shareholders to vote against executive compensation under the new law. Of course, these companies weren't alone. In 2011, about 50 companies received negative shareholder votes on executive compensation.

Understanding how a corporation sets executive pay, and the role of shareholders in that process, takes us into issues involving the corporate form of organization, corporate goals, and corporate control, all of which we cover in this chapter.

To begin our study of financial management, we address two central issues. First: What is corporate, or business, finance, and what is the role of the financial manager? Second: What is the goal of financial management?

1.1

Check out the companion website for this text at www. mhhe.com/rwj.

FINANCE: A QUICK LOOK

Before we plunge into our study of "corp. fin.," we think a quick overview of the finance field might be a good idea. Our goal is to clue you in on some of the most important areas in finance and some of the career opportunities available in each. We also want to illustrate some of the ways finance fits in with other areas such as marketing, management, and accounting.

The Four Basic Areas

Traditionally, financial topics are grouped into four main areas:

1. Corporate finance
2. Investments
3. Financial institutions
4. International finance

We discuss each of these next.

For job descriptions in finance and other areas, visit www .careers-in-business .com.

Corporate Finance   The first of these four areas, corporate finance, is the main subject of this book. We begin covering this subject with our next section, so we will wait until then to get into any details. One thing we should note is that the term *corporate finance* seems to imply that what we cover is only relevant to corporations, but the truth is that almost all of the topics we consider are much broader than that. Maybe *business finance* would be a little more descriptive, but even this is too narrow because at least half of the subjects we discuss in the pages ahead are really basic financial ideas and principles applicable across all the various areas of finance and beyond.

Investments   Broadly speaking, the investments area deals with financial assets such as stocks and bonds. Some of the more important questions include:

1. What determines the price of a financial asset, such as a share of stock?
2. What are the potential risks and rewards associated with investing in financial assets?
3. What is the best mixture of the different types of financial assets to hold?

Students who specialize in the investments area have various career opportunities. Being a stockbroker is one of the most common. Stockbrokers often work for large companies such as Merrill Lynch, advising customers on what types of investments to consider and helping them make buy and sell decisions. Financial advisers play a similar role, but are not necessarily brokers.

Portfolio management is a second investments-related career path. Portfolio managers, as the name suggests, manage money for investors. For example, individual investors frequently buy into mutual funds. Such funds are simply a means of pooling money that is then invested by a portfolio manager. Portfolio managers also invest and manage money for pension funds, insurance companies, and many other types of institutions.

Security analysis is a third area. A security analyst researches individual investments, such as stock in a particular company, and makes a determination as to whether the price is right. To do so, an analyst delves deeply into company and industry reports, along with a variety of other information sources. Frequently, brokers and portfolio managers rely on security analysts for information and recommendations.

These investments-related areas, like many areas in finance, share an interesting feature. If they are done well, they can be very rewarding financially (translation: You can make a lot of money). The bad news, of course, is that they can be very demanding and very competitive, so they are definitely not for everybody.

Financial Institutions Financial institutions are basically businesses that deal primarily in financial matters. Banks and insurance companies would probably be the most familiar to you. Institutions such as these employ people to perform a wide variety of finance-related tasks. For example, a commercial loan officer at a bank would evaluate whether a particular business has a strong enough financial position to warrant extending a loan. At an insurance company, an analyst would decide whether a particular risk was suitable for insuring and what the premium should be.

International Finance International finance isn't so much an area as it is a specialization within one of the main areas we described above. In other words, careers in international finance generally involve international aspects of either corporate finance, investments, or financial institutions. For example, some portfolio managers and security analysts specialize in non-U.S. companies. Similarly, many U.S. businesses have extensive overseas operations and need employees familiar with such international topics as exchange rates and political risk. Banks frequently are asked to make loans across country lines, so international specialists are needed there as well.

Why Study Finance?

Who needs to know finance? In a word, you. In fact, there are many reasons you need a working knowledge of finance even if you are not planning a finance career. We explore some of these next.

Marketing and Finance If you are interested in marketing, you need to know finance because, for example, marketers constantly work with budgets, and they need to understand how to get the greatest payoff from marketing expenditures and programs. Analyzing costs and benefits of projects of all types is one of the most important aspects of finance, so the tools you learn in finance are vital in marketing research, the design of marketing and distribution channels, and product pricing, just to name a few areas.

Financial analysts rely heavily on marketing analysts, and the two frequently work together to evaluate the profitability of proposed projects and products. As we will see in a later chapter, sales projections are a key input in almost every type of new product analysis, and such projections are often developed jointly between marketing and finance.

Beyond this, the finance industry employs marketers to help sell financial products such as bank accounts, insurance policies, and mutual funds. Financial services marketing is one of the most rapidly growing types of marketing, and successful financial services marketers are very well compensated. To work in this area, you obviously need to understand financial products.

Accounting and Finance For accountants, finance is required reading. In smaller businesses in particular, accountants are often required to make financial decisions as well as perform traditional accounting duties. Further, as the financial world continues to grow more complex, accountants have to know finance to understand the implications of many of the newer types of financial contracts and the impact they have on financial statements. Beyond this, cost accounting and business finance are particularly closely related, sharing many of the same subjects and concerns.

Financial analysts make extensive use of accounting information; they are some of the most important end users. Understanding finance helps accountants recognize what types of information are particularly valuable and, more generally, how accounting information is actually used (and abused) in practice.

Management and Finance   One of the most important areas in management is strategy. Thinking about business strategy without simultaneously thinking about financial strategy is an excellent recipe for disaster, and, as a result, management strategists must have a very clear understanding of the financial implications of business plans.

In broader terms, management employees of all types are expected to have a strong understanding of how their jobs impact profitability, and they are also expected to be able to work within their areas to improve profitability. This is precisely what studying finance teaches you: What are the characteristics of activities that create value?

You and Finance   Perhaps the most important reason to know finance is that you will have to make financial decisions that will be very important to you personally. Today, for example, when you go to work for almost any type of company, you will be asked to decide how you want to invest your retirement funds. We'll see in a later chapter that what you choose to do can make an enormous difference in your future financial well-being. On a different note, is it your dream to start your own business? Good luck if you don't understand basic finance before you start; you'll end up learning it the hard way. Want to know how big your student loan payments are going to be before you take out that next loan? Maybe not, but we'll show you how to calculate them anyway.

These are just a few of the ways that finance will affect your personal and business lives. Whether you want to or not, you are going to have to examine and understand financial issues, and you are going to have to make financial decisions. We want you to do so wisely, so keep reading.

CONCEPT QUESTIONS

1.1a   What are the major areas in finance?

1.1b   Besides wanting to pass this class, why do you need to understand finance?

1.2   BUSINESS FINANCE AND THE FINANCIAL MANAGER

Now we proceed to define business finance and the financial manager's job.

What Is Business Finance?

Imagine you were to start your own business. No matter what type you started, you would have to answer the following three questions in some form or another:

1. What long-term investments should you take on? That is, what lines of business will you be in, and what sorts of buildings, machinery, and equipment will you need?

2. Where will you get the long-term financing to pay for your investments? Will you bring in other owners, or will you borrow the money?
3. How will you manage your everyday financial activities, such as collecting from customers and paying suppliers?

These are not the only questions, but they are among the most important. Business finance, broadly speaking, is the study of ways to answer these three questions. We'll be looking at each of them in the chapters ahead.

The Financial Manager

The financial management function is usually associated with a top officer of the firm, often called the chief financial officer (CFO) or vice president of finance. Figure 1.1 is a simplified organizational chart that highlights the finance activity in a large firm. As shown, the vice president of finance coordinates the activities of the treasurer and the controller. The controller's office handles cost and financial accounting, tax payments, and management information systems. The treasurer's office is responsible for managing the firm's cash and credit, its financial planning, and its capital expenditures. These treasury activities are all related to the three general questions raised above, and the chapters ahead deal primarily with these issues. Our study thus bears mostly on activities usually associated with the treasurer's office. In a smaller firm, the treasurer and controller might be the same person, and there would be only one office.

For current issues facing CFOs, see www.cfo.com.

Financial Management Decisions

As our discussion above suggests, the financial manager must be concerned with three basic types of questions. We consider these in greater detail next.

Capital Budgeting   The first question concerns the firm's long-term investments. The process of planning and managing a firm's long-term investments is called capital budgeting. In capital budgeting, the financial manager tries to identify investment opportunities that are worth more to the firm than they cost to acquire. Loosely speaking, this means that the value of the cash flow generated by an asset exceeds the cost of that asset.

capital budgeting
The process of planning and managing a firm's long-term investments.

Regardless of the specific investment under consideration, financial managers must be concerned with how much cash they expect to receive, when they expect to receive it, and how likely they are to receive it. Evaluating the *size, timing,* and *risk* of future cash flows is the essence of capital budgeting. In fact, whenever we evaluate a business decision, the size, timing, and risk of the cash flows will be, by far, the most important things we will consider.

Capital Structure   The second question for the financial manager concerns how the firm obtains the financing it needs to support its long-term investments. A firm's capital structure (or financial structure) refers to the specific mixture of long-term debt and equity the firm uses to finance its operations. The financial manager has two concerns in this area. First: How much should the firm borrow? Second: What are the least expensive sources of funds for the firm?

capital structure
The mixture of debt and equity maintained by a firm.

In addition to deciding on the financing mix, the financial manager has to decide exactly how and where to raise the money. The expenses associated with raising long-term financing can be considerable, so different possibilities must be carefully evaluated. Also,

6   **PART 1**   Overview of Financial Management

FIGURE **1.1**

A simplified organizational chart.

The exact titles and organization differ from company to company

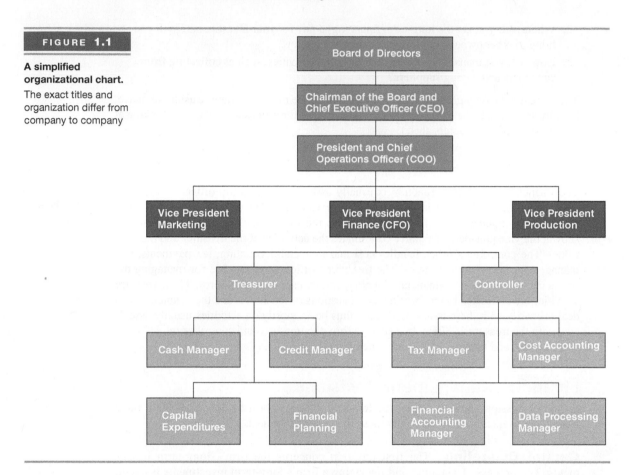

businesses borrow money from a variety of lenders in a number of different ways. Choosing among lenders and among loan types is another job handled by the financial manager.

working capital

A firm's short-term assets and liabilities.

Working Capital Management   The third question concerns **working capital** management. The term *working capital* refers to a firm's short-term assets, such as inventory, and its short-term liabilities, such as money owed to suppliers. Managing the firm's working capital is a day-to-day activity that ensures the firm has sufficient resources to continue its operations and avoid costly interruptions. This involves a number of activities related to the firm's receipt and disbursement of cash.

Some questions about working capital that must be answered are the following: (1) How much cash and inventory should we keep on hand? (2) Should we sell on credit to our customers? (3) How will we obtain any needed short-term financing? If we borrow in the short term, how and where should we do it? This is just a small sample of the issues that arise in managing a firm's working capital.

Conclusion   The three areas of corporate financial management we have described—capital budgeting, capital structure, and working capital management—are very broad categories. Each includes a rich variety of topics, and we have indicated only a few of the questions that arise in the different areas. The chapters ahead contain greater detail.

CONCEPT QUESTIONS

1.2a   What is the capital budgeting decision?

1.2b   What do you call the specific mixture of long-term debt and equity that a firm chooses to use?

1.2c   Into what category of financial management does cash management fall?

FORMS OF BUSINESS ORGANIZATION

1.3

Large firms in the United States, such as IBM and Apple, are almost all organized as corporations. We examine the three different legal forms of business organization—sole proprietorship, partnership, and corporation—to see why this is so.

Sole Proprietorship

A **sole proprietorship** is a business owned by one person. This is the simplest type of business to start and is the least regulated form of organization. For this reason, there are more proprietorships than any other type of business, and many businesses that later become large corporations start out as small proprietorships.

The owner of a sole proprietorship keeps all the profits. That's the good news. The bad news is that the owner has *unlimited liability* for business debts. This means that creditors can look to the proprietor's personal assets for payment. Similarly, there is no distinction between personal and business income, so all business income is taxed as personal income.

The life of a sole proprietorship is limited to the owner's life span, and, importantly, the amount of equity that can be raised is limited to the proprietor's personal wealth. This limitation often means that the business is unable to exploit new opportunities because of insufficient capital. Ownership of a sole proprietorship may be difficult to transfer since this requires the sale of the entire business to a new owner.

sole proprietorship
A business owned by a single individual.

For more information on forms of business organization, visit www.nolo.com.

Partnership

A **partnership** is similar to a proprietorship, except that there are two or more owners (partners). In a *general partnership*, all the partners share in gains or losses, and all have unlimited liability for all partnership debts, not just some particular share. The way partnership gains (and losses) are divided is described in the *partnership agreement*. This agreement can be an informal oral agreement, such as "let's start a lawn mowing business," or a lengthy, formal written document.

In a *limited partnership*, one or more *general partners* will run the business and have unlimited liability, but there will be one or more *limited partners* who do not actively participate in the business. A limited partner's liability for business debts is limited to the amount that partner contributes to the partnership. This form of organization is common in real estate ventures, for example.

The advantages and disadvantages of a partnership are basically the same as those for a proprietorship. Partnerships based on a relatively informal agreement are easy and inexpensive to form. General partners have unlimited liability for partnership debts, and the

partnership
A business formed by two or more individuals or entities.

partnership terminates when a general partner wishes to sell out or dies. All income is taxed as personal income to the partners, and the amount of equity that can be raised is limited to the partners' combined wealth. Ownership by a general partner is not easily transferred because a new partnership must be formed. A limited partner's interest can be sold without dissolving the partnership, but finding a buyer may be difficult.

Because a partner in a general partnership can be held responsible for all partnership debts, having a written agreement is very important. Failure to spell out the rights and duties of the partners frequently leads to misunderstandings later on. Also, if you are a limited partner, you must not become deeply involved in business decisions unless you are willing to assume the obligations of a general partner. The reason is that if things go badly, you may be deemed to be a general partner even though you say you are a limited partner.

Based on our discussion, the primary disadvantages of sole proprietorships and partnerships as forms of business organization are (1) unlimited liability for business debts on the part of the owners, (2) limited life of the business, and (3) difficulty of transferring ownership. These three disadvantages add up to a single, central problem: The ability of such businesses to grow can be seriously limited by an inability to raise cash for investment.

Corporation

corporation

A business created as a distinct legal entity owned by one or more individuals or entities.

The **corporation** is the most important form (in terms of size) of business organization in the United States. A corporation is a legal "person" separate and distinct from its owners, and it has many of the rights, duties, and privileges of an actual person. Corporations can borrow money and own property, can sue and be sued, and can enter into contracts. A corporation can even be a general partner or a limited partner in a partnership, and a corporation can own stock in another corporation.

Not surprisingly, starting a corporation is somewhat more complicated than starting the other forms of business organization. Forming a corporation involves preparing *articles of incorporation* (or a charter) and a set of *bylaws*. The articles of incorporation must contain a number of things, including the corporation's name, its intended life (which can be forever), its business purpose, and the number of shares that can be issued. This information must normally be supplied to the state in which the firm will be incorporated. For most legal purposes, the corporation is a "resident" of that state.

The bylaws are rules describing how the corporation regulates its own existence. For example, the bylaws describe how directors are elected. The bylaws may be amended or extended from time to time by the stockholders.

In a large corporation, the stockholders and the managers are usually separate groups. The stockholders elect the board of directors, who then select the managers. Management is charged with running the corporation's affairs in the stockholders' interests. In principle, stockholders control the corporation because they elect the directors.

As a result of the separation of ownership and management, the corporate form has several advantages. Ownership (represented by shares of stock) can be readily transferred, and the life of the corporation is therefore not limited. The corporation borrows money in its own name. As a result, the stockholders in a corporation have limited liability for corporate debts. The most they can lose is what they have invested.

The relative ease of transferring ownership, the limited liability for business debts, and the unlimited life of the business are the reasons why the corporate form is superior when it comes to raising cash. If a corporation needs new equity, it can sell new shares of stock and attract new investors. The number of owners can be huge; larger corporations have many thousands or even millions of stockholders. For example, the General Electric Company (better known as GE) has about 10 billion shares outstanding and 4 million shareholders.

The corporate form has a significant disadvantage. Since a corporation is a legal person, it must pay taxes. Moreover, money paid out to stockholders in the form of dividends is taxed again as income to those stockholders. This is *double taxation,* meaning that corporate profits are taxed twice: at the corporate level when they are earned and again at the personal level when they are paid out.

Today all 50 states have enacted laws allowing for the creation of a relatively new form of business organization, the limited liability company (LLC). The goal of this entity is to operate and be taxed like a partnership but retain limited liability for owners, so an LLC is essentially a hybrid of a partnership and a corporation. Although states have differing definitions for LLCs, the more important scorekeeper is the Internal Revenue Service (IRS). The IRS will consider an LLC a corporation, thereby subjecting it to double taxation, unless it meets certain specific criteria. In essence, an LLC cannot be too corporationlike, or it will be treated as one by the IRS. LLCs have become common. For example, Goldman Sachs, one of Wall Street's last remaining partnerships, decided to convert from a private partnership to an LLC (it later "went public," becoming a publicly held corporation). Large accounting firms and law firms by the score have converted to LLCs.

A Corporation by Another Name . . .

The corporate form has many variations around the world. Exact laws and regulations differ, of course, but the essential features of public ownership and limited liability remain. These firms are often called *joint stock companies, public limited companies,* or *limited liability companies.*

Table 1.1 gives the names of a few well-known international corporations, their country of origin, and a translation of the abbreviation that follows the company name.

Company	Country of Origin	Type of Company	Translation	TABLE 1.1
Bayerische Motoren Werke (BMW) AG	Germany	Aktiengesellschaft	Corporation	**International corporations**
Montblanc GmbH	Germany	Gesellschaft mit beschränkter Haftung	Company with limited liability	
Rolls-Royce PLC	United Kingdom	Public limited company	Public limited company	You can find the translation for any business type at www.corporate information.com.
Shell UK Ltd.	United Kingdom	Limited	Corporation	
Unilever NV	Netherlands	Naamloze Vennootschap	Limited liability company	
Fiat SpA	Italy	Società per Azioni	Public limited company	
Saab AB	Sweden	Aktiebolag	Joint stock company	
Peugeot SA	France	Société Anonyme	Joint stock company	

CONCEPT QUESTIONS

1.3a   What are the three forms of business organization?

1.3b   What are the primary advantages and disadvantages of sole proprietorships and partnerships?

1.3c   What is the difference between a general and a limited partnership?

1.3d   Why is the corporate form superior when it comes to raising cash?

1.4 THE GOAL OF FINANCIAL MANAGEMENT

To study financial decision making, we first need to understand the goal of financial management. Such an understanding is important because it leads to an objective basis for making and evaluating financial decisions.

Profit Maximization

Profit maximization would probably be the most commonly cited business goal, but this is not a very precise objective. Do we mean profits this year? If so, then actions such as deferring maintenance, letting inventories run down, and other short-run, cost-cutting measures will tend to increase profits now, but these activities aren't necessarily desirable.

The goal of maximizing profits may refer to some sort of "long-run" or "average" profits, but it's unclear exactly what this means. First, do we mean something like accounting net income or earnings per share? As we will see, these numbers may have little to do with what is good or bad for the firm. Second, what do we mean by the long run? As a famous economist once remarked: "In the long run, we're all dead!" More to the point, this goal doesn't tell us the appropriate trade-off between current and future profits.

The Goal of Financial Management in a Corporation

Find a business finance magazine site that discusses current issues facing the financial executive at www.business financemag.com.

The financial manager in a corporation makes decisions for the stockholders of the firm. Given this, instead of listing possible goals for the financial manager, we really need to answer a more fundamental question: From the stockholders' point of view, what is a good financial management decision?

If we assume stockholders buy stock because they seek to gain financially, then the answer is obvious: Good decisions increase the value of the stock, and poor decisions decrease it.

Given our observations, it follows that the financial manager acts in the shareholders' best interests by making decisions that increase the value of the stock. The appropriate goal for the financial manager in a corporation can thus be stated quite easily:

> **The goal of financial management is to maximize the current value per share of the existing stock.**

The goal of maximizing the value of the stock avoids the problems associated with the different goals we discussed above. There is no ambiguity in the criterion, and there is no short-run versus long-run issue. We explicitly mean that our goal is to maximize the *current* stock value. Of course, maximizing stock value is the same thing as maximizing the market price per share.

FINANCE MATTERS

◀ For the latest news on the topics covered in this chapter, scan here.

Corporate Ethics

Large companies are sometimes guilty of unethical behavior. Often this unethical behavior takes the form of false or misleading financial statements. In one of the largest corporate fraud cases in history, energy giant Enron Corporation was forced to file for bankruptcy in December 2001 amid allegations that the company's financial statements were deliberately misleading and false. Enron's bankruptcy not only destroyed that company, but its auditor Arthur Andersen as well.

Often, unethical behavior is also illegal. For example, consider insider trading, which is buying or selling stock based on information not available to the public. A recent example involved Raj Rajaratnam, the founder of the investment firm Galleon Group. He was charged with gathering inside information from friends at numerous companies. For example, a government wiretap picked up a conversation in which Rajaratnam said, "I heard yesterday from somebody who's on the board of Goldman Sachs that they are going to lose $2 per share. The street has them making $2.50." He was arrested in October 2009 and, in May 2011, was convicted of 14 counts of securities fraud and conspiracy to commit securities fraud. In December 2011, he began his 11-year prison sentence. Additionally, Rajaratnam was fined about $93 million for his actions.

The difference between ethical and unethical behavior can sometimes be murky. For example, many U.S. companies have relocated to Bermuda for reasons beyond the beautiful pink beaches; namely, Bermuda has no corporate income taxes. With a population of less than 65,000, the island is home to more than 13,000 international companies. Stanley Works, the well-known maker of Stanley tools, was among the U.S. corporations that chose to move to the island paradise. By doing so, Stanley estimated that it would save $30 million per year in taxes. Since the goal of the corporation is to maximize shareholder wealth, this would seem like a good move, and the practice is entirely legal. But is it ethical? What are the issues?

Another corporate activity that has generated much controversy is the practice of outsourcing, or offshoring, jobs to other countries. U.S. corporations engage in this practice when labor costs in another country are substantially lower than they are domestically. Again, this is done to maximize shareholder wealth. But, the ethical dilemma in this case is even trickier. Some U.S. workers do lose jobs when offshoring occurs. On the other hand, the Milken Institute estimated that every $1 spent on offshoring a service job to India generated a net value to the United States of $1.13, along with another $.33 to India. And it gets even more complicated: What about foreign companies such as BMW and Toyota who "insource" jobs by building plants in the United States? Is it unethical to outsource U.S. jobs while, at the same time, insourcing jobs from other countries?

A More General Financial Management Goal

Given our goal as stated above (maximize the value of the stock), an obvious question comes up: What is the appropriate goal when the firm has no traded stock? Corporations are certainly not the only type of business, and the stock in many corporations rarely changes hands, so it's difficult to say what the value per share is at any given time.

As long as we are dealing with for-profit businesses, only a slight modification is needed. The total value of the stock in a corporation is simply equal to the value of the owners' equity. Therefore, a more general way of stating our goal is:

> **Maximize the market value of the existing owners' equity.**

With this goal in mind, it doesn't matter whether the business is a proprietorship, a partnership, or a corporation. For each of these, good financial decisions increase the market value of the owners' equity and poor financial decisions decrease it.

Finally, our goal does not imply that the financial manager should take illegal or unethical actions in the hope of increasing the value of the equity in the firm. What we mean is that the financial manager best serves the owners of the business by identifying goods and services that add value to the firm because they are desired and valued in the free marketplace. Our nearby *Finance Matters* box discusses some recent ethical issues and problems faced by well-known corporations.

Business ethics are considered at www. thecro.com.

Sarbanes-Oxley Act

In response to corporate scandals involving companies such as Enron, WorldCom, Tyco, and Adelphia, Congress enacted the Sarbanes-Oxley Act in 2002. The Act, which is better known as "Sarbox," is intended to strengthen protection against corporate accounting fraud and financial malpractice. Key elements of Sarbox took effect on November 15, 2004.

Sarbox contains a number of requirements designed to insure that companies tell the truth in their financial statements. For example, the officers of a public corporation must review and sign the annual report. They must attest that the annual report does not contain false statements or material omissions and also that the financial statements fairly represent the company's financial results. In essence, Sarbox makes management personally responsible for the accuracy of a company's financial statements.

Because of its extensive requirements, compliance with Sarbox can be very costly, which has led to some unintended results. Since its implementation, hundreds of public firms have chosen to "go dark," meaning that their shares would no longer be traded in the major stock markets, in which case Sarbox does not apply. Most of these companies stated that their reason was to avoid the cost of compliance. Ironically, in such cases, the law had the effect of eliminating public disclosure instead of improving it.

Sarbox has also probably affected the number of companies going public in the United States. Recently, many U.S.-based companies have chosen to go public on the London Stock Exchange's Alternative Investment Market (AIM) instead. The cost savings can be enormous, especially for small companies. For example, Protonex Technologies, a fuel cell developer based in Southborough, Massachusetts, estimated that it costs about $1 million per year in compliance costs and mailings to stockholders to be listed on the AIM. In contrast, the annual cost to be listed on the NASDAQ would be about $3 million, with a large part of the increase due to Sarbox compliance costs.

To find out more about Sarbanes-Oxley, go to www.soxlaw.com.

CONCEPT QUESTIONS

1.4a   What is the goal of financial management?

1.4b   What are some shortcomings of the goal of profit maximization?

1.5

THE AGENCY PROBLEM AND CONTROL OF THE CORPORATION

We've seen that the financial manager in a corporation acts in the best interests of the stockholders by taking actions that increase the value of the firm's stock. However, we've also seen that in large corporations ownership can be spread over a huge number of stockholders. This dispersion of ownership arguably means that management effectively controls the firm. In this case, will management necessarily act in the best interests of the stockholders? Put another way, might not management pursue its own goals at the stockholders' expense? We briefly consider some of the arguments below.

Agency Relationships

The relationship between stockholders and management is called an *agency relationship*. Such a relationship exists whenever someone (the principal) hires another (the agent) to represent his or her interest. For example, you might hire someone (an agent) to sell a car that you own while you are away at school. In all such relationships, there is a possibility of conflict of interest between the principal and the agent. Such a conflict is called an **agency problem**.

Suppose you hire someone to sell your car and you agree to pay her a flat fee when she sells the car. The agent's incentive in this case is to make the sale, not necessarily to get you the best price. If you paid a commission of, say, 10 percent of the sales price instead of a flat fee, then this problem might not exist. This example illustrates that the way an agent is compensated is one factor that affects agency problems.

Management Goals

To see how management and stockholder interests might differ, imagine that a corporation is considering a new investment. The new investment is expected to favorably impact the stock price, but it is also a relatively risky venture. The owners of the firm will wish to take the investment (because the share value will rise), but management may not because there is the possibility that things will turn out badly and management jobs will be lost. If management does not take the investment, then the stockholders may lose a valuable opportunity. This is one example of an *agency cost*.

It is sometimes argued that, left to themselves, managers would tend to maximize the amount of resources over which they have control, or, more generally, business power or wealth. This goal could lead to an overemphasis on business size or growth. For example, cases where management is accused of overpaying to buy another company just to increase the size of the business or to demonstrate corporate power are not uncommon. Obviously, if overpayment does take place, such a purchase does not benefit the owners of the purchasing company.

Our discussion indicates that management may tend to overemphasize organizational survival to protect job security. Also, management may dislike outside interference, so independence and corporate self-sufficiency may be important goals.

Do Managers Act in the Stockholders' Interests?

Whether managers will, in fact, act in the best interests of stockholders depends on two factors. First, how closely are management goals aligned with stockholder goals? This question relates to the way managers are compensated. Second, can management be replaced if they do not pursue stockholder goals? This issue relates to control of the firm. As we will discuss, there are a number of reasons to think that, even in the largest firms, management has a significant incentive to act in the interests of stockholders.

Managerial Compensation   Management will frequently have a significant economic incentive to increase share value for two reasons. First, managerial compensation, particularly at the top, is usually tied to financial performance in general and oftentimes to share value in particular. For example, managers are frequently given the option to buy stock at a fixed price. The more the stock is worth, the more valuable is this option. The second incentive managers have relates to job prospects. Better performers within the firm will tend to get promoted. More generally, those managers who are successful in pursuing stockholder goals will be in greater demand in the labor market and thus command higher salaries.

In fact, managers who are successful in pursuing stockholder goals can reap enormous rewards. For example, Timothy Cook, CEO of Apple, received about $378 million in 2011 alone, which is way more than Oprah Winfrey ($165 million) and Michael Bay ($160 million). Information on executive compensation, along with a ton of other information, can be easily found on the web for almost any public company. Our nearby *Work the Web* box shows you how to get started.

agency problem
The possibility of conflict of interest between the owners and management of a firm.

WORK THE WEB

◄ To get updated data, scan here.

The web is a great place to learn about individual companies, and there are a slew of sites available to help you. Try pointing your Web browser to finance.yahoo.com. Once there, you should see something like this on the page:

To look up a company, you need its "ticker symbol" (or just ticker for short), which is a unique one-to-four letter identifier. Or, you can just type in a company's name to find the ticker. For example, we typed in "SIRI," which is the ticker symbol for Sirius XM Radio, the satellite radio provider. Here is a portion of what we got:

There is a lot of information here and a lot of other links for you to explore, so have at it. By the end of the term, we hope it all makes sense to you!

Questions

1. Go to finance.yahoo.com and find the current stock prices for Southwest Airlines (LUV), Harley-Davidson (HOG), and Starwood Hotels & Resorts (HOT).
2. Get a quote for American Express (AXP) and follow the "Key Statistics" link. What information is available on this link? What do mrq, ttm, yoy, and lfy mean?

Control of the Firm   Control of the firm ultimately rests with stockholders. They elect the board of directors, who, in turn, hires and fires management. The mechanism by which unhappy stockholders can act to replace existing management is called a *proxy fight*. A proxy is the authority to vote someone else's stock. A proxy fight develops when a group solicits proxies in order to replace the existing board, and thereby replace existing management.

Recently, proxy fights have become more civil. In 2011, just 31 percent of proxy fights went the distance, meaning they ultimately resulted in a shareholder vote. That's down from between 51 and 56 percent of proxy fights over the 2006–2010 period. Before that, it was not uncommon for 70 percent or more of proxy fights to result in shareholder votes. Companies today appear to be more willing to compromise with activist shareholders, perhaps because both companies and activist shareholders have become more concerned with the potential high costs of a long, bitter proxy fight.

Another way that management can be replaced is by takeover. Those firms that are poorly managed are more attractive as acquisitions than well-managed firms because a greater profit potential exists. Thus, avoiding a takeover by another firm gives management another incentive to act in the stockholders' interests.

For example, consider the case of Carl Icahn and his offer to buy Commercial Metals Company for $15 per share. Carl Icahn specializes in takeovers. His ownership stake in Commercial Metals reached 10 percent in 2011, making him a particularly important (and unhappy) shareholder. He offered to buy the entire company, but, in December 2011, the board of directors rejected his $1.73 billion bid, arguing that it undervalued the company and its prospects. Among other reasons, the board argued that the price offered was lower than the 52-week high stock price of $18.09 reached in February 2011 and only slightly above the stock price when Mr. Icahn announced that the company's shares were undervalued. However, at the time Mr. Icahn made his bid, the stock price was around $11.50, so the offer price was significantly above the then-current stock price.

Conclusion   The available theory and evidence are consistent with the view that stockholders control the firm and that stockholder wealth maximization is the relevant goal of the corporation. Even so, there will undoubtedly be times when management goals are pursued at the expense of the stockholders, at least temporarily.

Agency problems are not unique to corporations; they exist whenever there is a separation of ownership and management. This separation is most pronounced in corporations, but it certainly exists in partnerships and proprietorships as well.

Stakeholders

Our discussion thus far implies that management and stockholders are the only parties with an interest in the firm's decisions. This is an oversimplification, of course. Employees, customers, suppliers, and even the government all have a financial interest in the firm.

These various groups are called **stakeholders** in the firm. In general, a stakeholder is someone other than a stockholder or creditor who potentially has a claim on the cash flows of the firm. Such groups will also attempt to exert control over the firm, perhaps to the detriment of the owners.

stakeholder
Someone other than a stockholder or creditor who potentially has a claim on the cash flows of the firm.

CONCEPT QUESTIONS

1.5a   What is an agency relationship?

1.5b   What are agency problems and how do they arise? What are agency costs?

1.5c   What incentives do managers in large corporations have to maximize share value?

FINANCIAL MARKETS AND THE CORPORATION

1.6

We've seen that the primary advantages of the corporate form of organization are that ownership can be transferred more quickly and easily than with other forms and that money can be raised more readily. Both of these advantages are significantly enhanced by the existence of financial markets, and financial markets play an extremely important role in corporate finance.

Cash Flows to and from the Firm

The interplay between the corporation and the financial markets is illustrated in Figure 1.2. The arrows in Figure 1.2 trace the passage of cash from the financial markets to the firm and from the firm back to the financial markets.

FIGURE 1.2

Cash flows between the firm and the financial markets

A. Firm issues securities to raise cash.
B. Firm invests in assets.
C. Firm's operations generate cash flow.
D. Cash is paid to government as taxes. Other stakeholders may receive cash.

E. Reinvested cash flows are plowed back into firm.
F. Cash is paid out to investors in the form of interest and dividends.

Suppose we start with the firm selling shares of stock and borrowing money to raise cash. Cash flows to the firm from the financial markets (A). The firm invests the cash in current and fixed (or long-term) assets (B). These assets generate some cash (C), some of which goes to pay corporate taxes (D). After taxes are paid, some of this cash flow is reinvested in the firm (E). The rest goes back to the financial markets as cash paid to creditors and shareholders (F).

A financial market, like any market, is just a way of bringing buyers and sellers together. In financial markets, it is debt and equity securities that are bought and sold. Financial markets differ in detail, however. The most important differences concern the types of securities that are traded, how trading is conducted, and who the buyers and sellers are. Some of these differences are discussed next.

Primary versus Secondary Markets

Financial markets function as both primary and secondary markets for debt and equity securities. The term *primary market* refers to the original sale of securities by governments and corporations. The *secondary markets* are those in which these securities are bought and sold after the original sale. Equities are, of course, issued solely by corporations. Debt securities are issued by both governments and corporations. In the discussion that follows, we focus on corporate securities only.

Primary Markets   In a primary-market transaction, the corporation is the seller, and the transaction raises money for the corporation. Corporations engage in two types of primary market transactions: public offerings and private placements. A public offering, as the name suggests, involves selling securities to the general public, whereas a private placement is a negotiated sale involving a specific buyer.

By law, public offerings of debt and equity must be registered with the Securities and Exchange Commission (SEC). Registration requires the firm to disclose a great deal of information before selling any securities. The accounting, legal, and selling costs of public offerings can be considerable.

Partly to avoid the various regulatory requirements and the expense of public offerings, debt and equity are often sold privately to large financial institutions such as life insurance companies or mutual funds. Such private placements do not have to be registered with the SEC and do not require the involvement of underwriters (investment banks that specialize in selling securities to the public).

> To learn more about the SEC, visit www.sec.gov.

> To learn more about the exchanges, visit www.nyse.com and www.nasdaq.com.

Secondary Markets

A secondary-market transaction involves one owner or creditor selling to another. It is therefore the secondary markets that provide the means for transferring ownership of corporate securities. Although a corporation is only directly involved in a primary-market transaction (when it sells securities to raise cash), the secondary markets are still critical to large corporations. The reason is that investors are much more willing to purchase securities in a primary-market transaction when they know that those securities can later be resold if desired.

Dealer versus auction markets There are two kinds of secondary markets: *auction* markets and *dealer* markets. Generally speaking, dealers buy and sell for themselves, at their own risk. A car dealer, for example, buys and sells automobiles. In contrast, brokers and agents match buyers and sellers, but they do not actually own the commodity that is bought or sold. A real estate agent, for example, does not normally buy and sell houses.

Dealer markets in stocks and long-term debt are called *over-the-counter* (OTC) markets. Most trading in debt securities takes place over the counter. The expression *over the counter* refers to days of old when securities were literally bought and sold at counters in offices around the country. Today, a significant fraction of the market for stocks and almost all of the market for long-term debt have no central location; the many dealers are connected electronically.

Auction markets differ from dealer markets in two ways. First, an auction market, or exchange, has a physical location (like Wall Street). Second, in a dealer market, most of the buying and selling is done by the dealer. The primary purpose of an auction market, on the other hand, is to match those who wish to sell with those who wish to buy. Dealers play a limited role.

Trading in corporate securities The equity shares of most of the large firms in the United States trade in organized auction markets. The largest such market is the New York Stock Exchange (NYSE), which accounts for more than 85 percent of all the shares traded in auction markets. Other auction exchanges include the American Stock Exchange (AMEX) and regional exchanges such as the Chicago Stock Exchange.

In addition to the stock exchanges, there is a large OTC market for stocks. In 1971, the National Association of Securities Dealers (NASD) made available to dealers and brokers an electronic quotation system called NASDAQ (NASD Automated Quotations system, pronounced "naz-dak"). There are roughly three times as many companies on NASDAQ as there are on NYSE, but they tend to be much smaller in size and trade less actively.

> The Tokyo Stock Exchange in English: www.tse.or.jp/english.

There are exceptions, of course. Both Microsoft and Intel trade OTC, for example. Nonetheless, the total value of NASDAQ stocks is significantly less than the total value of NYSE stocks.

There are many large and important financial markets outside the United States, of course, and U.S. corporations are increasingly looking to these markets to raise cash. The Tokyo Stock Exchange and the London Stock Exchange (TSE and LSE, respectively) are two well-known examples. The fact that OTC markets have no physical location means that national borders do not present a great barrier, and there is now a huge international OTC debt market. Because of globalization, financial markets have reached the point where trading in many instruments never stops; it just travels around the world.

The London Stock Exchange: www.londonstock exchange.com.

Listing   Stocks that trade on an organized exchange (or market) are said to be *listed* on that exchange. In order to be listed, firms must meet certain minimum criteria concerning, for example, asset size and number of shareholders. These criteria differ for different exchanges.

NYSE has the most stringent requirements of the stock markets in the United States. There are minimums on earnings, assets, and number and market value of shares outstanding.

CONCEPT QUESTIONS

1.6a   What is a dealer market? How do dealer and auction markets differ?

1.6b   What is the largest auction market in the United States?

1.6c   What does *OTC* stand for? What is the large OTC market for stocks called?

SUMMARY AND CONCLUSIONS

 ◄ Think you've mastered the material? Scan here to take a chapter quiz.

www.mhhe.com/rwj

This chapter has introduced you to some of the basic ideas in business finance. In it, we saw that:

1. Business finance has three main areas of concern:
    a. Capital budgeting. What long-term investments should the firm take?
    b. Capital structure. Where will the firm get the long-term financing to pay for its investments? In other words, what mixture of debt and equity should we use to fund our operations?
    c. Working capital management. How should the firm manage its everyday financial activities?

2. The goal of financial management in a for-profit business is to make decisions that increase the value of the stock, or, more generally, increase the market value of the equity.

3. The corporate form of organization is superior to other forms when it comes to raising money and transferring ownership interests, but it has the significant disadvantage of double taxation.

4. There is the possibility of conflicts between stockholders and management in a large corporation. We called these conflicts agency problems and discussed how they might be controlled and reduced.

Of the topics we've discussed thus far, the most important is the goal of financial management. Throughout the text, we will be analyzing many different financial decisions, but we always ask the same question: How does the decision under consideration affect the value of the equity in the firm?

 connect POP QUIZ!
|FINANCE

Can you answer the following questions? If your class is using *Connect Finance,* log on to the Self-Quiz and Study feature in the Library tab to see if you know the answers to these and other questions, check out the study tools, and find out what topics require additional practice!

Section 1.2 Does business finance include determining which long-term assets a firm should purchase?

Section 1.3 Under what forms of organization does the owner have unlimited liability?

Section 1.4 What is the intent of the Sarbanes-Oxley Act of 2002?

Section 1.5 Who are the stakeholders in a firm?

Section 1.6 What are the features of a dealer market?

CRITICAL THINKING AND CONCEPTS REVIEW

LO 1 **1.1** **The Financial Management Decision Process.**   What are the three types of financial management decisions? For each type of decision, give an example of a business transaction that would be relevant.

LO 3 **1.2** **Sole Proprietorships and Partnerships.**   What are the four primary disadvantages to the sole proprietorship and partnership forms of business organization? What benefits are there to these types of business organization as opposed to the corporate form?

LO 3 **1.3** **Corporations.**   What is the primary disadvantage of the corporate form of organization? Name at least two of the advantages of corporate organization.

LO 3 **1.4** **Corporate Finance Organization.**   In a large corporation, what are the two distinct groups that report to the chief financial officer? Which group is the focus of corporate finance?

LO 2 **1.5** **Goal of Financial Management.**   What goal should always motivate the actions of the firm's financial manager?

LO 4 **1.6** **Agency Problems.**   Who owns a corporation? Describe the process whereby the owners control the firm's management. What is the main reason that an agency relationship exists in the corporate form of organization? In this context, what kinds of problems can arise?

LO 3 **1.7** **Primary versus Secondary Markets.**   You've probably noticed coverage in the financial press of an initial public offering (IPO) of a company's securities. Social networking company Facebook is a relatively recent example. Is an IPO a primary-market transaction or a secondary-market transaction?

20   PART **1**   Overview of Financial Management

www.mhhe.com/rwj

LO 3   **1.8**   **Auction versus Dealer Markets.**   What does it mean when we say the New York Stock Exchange is an auction market? How are auction markets different from dealer markets? What kind of market is NASDAQ?

LO 2   **1.9**   **Not-for-Profit Firm Goals.**   Suppose you were the financial manager of a not-for-profit business (a not-for-profit hospital, perhaps). What kinds of goals do you think would be appropriate?

LO 2   **1.10**   **Ethics and Firm Goals.**   Can our goal of maximizing the value of the stock conflict with other goals, such as avoiding unethical or illegal behavior? In particular, do you think subjects such as customer and employee safety, the environment, and the general good of society fit in this framework, or are they essentially ignored? Try to think of some specific scenarios to illustrate your answer.

LO 2   **1.11**   **International Firm Goal.**   Would our goal of maximizing the value of the stock be different if we were thinking about financial management in a foreign country? Why or why not?

LO 4   **1.12**   **Agency Problems.**   Suppose you own stock in a company. The current price per share is $25. Another company has just announced that it wants to buy your company and will pay $35 per share to acquire all the outstanding stock. Your company's management immediately begins fighting off this hostile bid. Is management acting in the shareholders' best interests? Why or why not?

LO 4   **1.13**   **Agency Problems and Corporate Ownership.**   Corporate ownership varies around the world. Historically, individuals have owned the majority of shares in public corporations in the United States. In Germany and Japan, however, banks, other large financial institutions, and other companies own most of the stock in public corporations. Do you think agency problems are likely to be more or less severe in Germany and Japan than in the United States? Why? In recent years, large financial institutions such as mutual funds and pension funds have been becoming the dominant owners of stock in the United States, and these institutions are becoming more active in corporate affairs. What are the implications of this trend for agency problems and corporate control?

LO 4   **1.14**   **Executive Compensation.**   Critics have charged that compensation to top management in the United States is simply too high and should be cut back. For example, focusing on large corporations, John Hammergren, CEO of McKesson, earned about $131 million in 2011 and about $285 million over the 2007–2011 period. Are such amounts excessive? In answering, it might be helpful to recognize that superstar athletes such as LeBron James, top entertainers such as Oprah Winfrey, and many others at the top of their respective fields earn at least as much, if not more.

LO 4   **1.15**   **Sarbanes-Oxley.**   In response to the Sarbanes-Oxley Act, many small firms in the United States have opted to "go dark" and delist their stock. Why might a company choose this route? What are the costs of "going dark"?

WHAT'S ON THE WEB?

1.1 Listing Requirements.   This chapter discussed some of the listing requirements for the NYSE and NASDAQ. Find the complete listing requirements for the New York Stock Exchange at www.nyse.com and NASDAQ at www.nasdaq.com. Which has more stringent listing requirements? Why don't they have the same listing requirements?

1.2 Business Formation.   As you may (or may not) know, many companies incorporate in Delaware for a variety of reasons. Visit BizFilings at www.bizfilings.com to find out why. Which state has the highest fee for incorporation? For an LLC? While at the site, look at the FAQ section regarding corporations and LLCs.

CHAPTER CASE
THE McGEE CAKE COMPANY

In early 2007, Doc and Lyn McGee formed the McGee Cake Company. The company produced a full line of cakes, and its specialties included chess cake,* lemon pound cake, and double-iced, double-chocolate cake. The couple formed the company as an outside interest, and both continued to work at their current jobs. Doc did all the baking, and Lyn handled the marketing and distribution. With good product quality and a sound marketing plan, the company grew rapidly. In early 2011, the company was featured in a widely distributed entrepreneurial magazine. Later that year, the company was featured in *Gourmet Desserts*, a leading specialty food magazine. After the article appeared in *Gourmet Desserts*, sales exploded, and the company began receiving orders from all over the world.

*Chess cake is quite delicious and distinct from cheesecake. The origin of the name is obscure.

Because of the increased sales, Doc left his other job, followed shortly by Lyn. The company hired additional workers to meet demand. Unfortunately, the fast growth experienced by the company led to cash flow and capacity problems. The company is currently producing as many cakes as possible with the assets it owns, but demand for its cakes is still growing. Further, the company has been approached by a national supermarket chain with a proposal to put four of its cakes in all of the chain's stores, and a national restaurant chain has contacted the company about selling McGee cakes in its restaurants. The restaurant would sell the cakes without a brand name.

Doc and Lyn have operated the company as a sole proprietorship. They have approached you to help manage and direct the company's growth. Specifically, they have asked you to answer the following questions:

QUESTIONS

1. What are the advantages and disadvantages of changing the company organization from a sole proprietorship to an LLC?

2. What are the advantages and disadvantages of changing the company organization from a sole proprietorship to a corporation?

3. Ultimately, what action would you recommend the company undertake? Why?

www.mhhe.com/rwj

2 Financial Statements, Taxes, and Cash Flow

learning objectives

After studying this chapter, you should be able to:

LO 1 Differentiate between accounting value (or "book" value) and market value.

LO 2 Distinguish accounting income from cash flow.

LO 3 Explain the difference between average and marginal tax rates.

LO 4 Determine a firm's cash flow from its financial statements.

When a company announces a "write-off," it frequently means that the value of the company's assets has declined. For example, in 2011, Hewlett-Packard (HP) announced that it was writing off $3.3 billion due to its decision to shut down the company's WebOS operating system business. What made this write-off particularly costly was that HP had acquired WebOS when it purchased Palm for $1.2 billion the previous year. So, the write-off was more than 2.5 times what HP had paid for Palm. And in the second quarter of 2011, Bank of America announced a write-off of $14 billion due to its acquisition of Countrywide. In fact, Bank of America had a series of big write-offs, including $34 billion in 2010, $33.7 billion in 2009, and $16.2 billion in 2008.

So did stockholders in these companies lose billions of dollars (or more) because of the write-offs? The answer is probably not. Understanding why ultimately leads us to the main subject of this chapter: that all-important substance known as *cash flow*.

In this chapter, we examine financial statements, taxes, and cash flow. Our emphasis is not on preparing financial statements. Instead, we recognize that financial statements are frequently a key source of information for financial decisions, so our goal is to briefly examine such statements and point out some of their more relevant features. We pay special attention to some of the practical details of cash flow.

As you read, pay particular attention to two important differences: (1) the difference between accounting value and market value and (2) the difference between accounting income and cash flow. These distinctions will be important throughout the book.

balance sheet
Financial statement showing a firm's accounting value on a particular date.

2.1 THE BALANCE SHEET

The **balance sheet** is a snapshot of the firm. It is a convenient means of organizing and summarizing what a firm owns (its *assets*), what a firm owes (its *liabilities*), and the difference between the two (the firm's *equity*) at a given point in time. Figure 2.1 illustrates how

FIGURE 2.1

The balance sheet.
Left side: Total value of assets. Right side: Total value of liabilities and shareholders' equity.

the balance sheet is constructed. As shown, the left-hand side lists the assets of the firm, and the right-hand side lists the liabilities and equity.

Assets: The Left-Hand Side

Assets are classified as either *current* or *fixed*. A fixed asset is one that has a relatively long life. Fixed assets can either be *tangible,* such as a truck or a computer, or *intangible,* such as a trademark or patent. A current asset has a life of less than one year. This means that the asset will normally convert to cash within 12 months. For example, inventory would normally be purchased and sold within a year and is thus classified as a current asset. Obviously, cash itself is a current asset. Accounts receivable (money owed to the firm by its customers) is also a current asset.

ExcelMaster
coverage online

Liabilities and Owners' Equity: The Right-Hand Side

The firm's liabilities are the first thing listed on the right-hand side of the balance sheet. These are classified as either *current* or *long-term.* Current liabilities, like current assets, have a life of less than one year (meaning they must be paid within the year), and they are listed before long-term liabilities. Accounts payable (money the firm owes to its suppliers) is one example of a current liability.

Two excellent sites for company financial information are finance.yahoo.com and money.cnn.com.

A debt that is not due in the coming year is classified as a long-term liability. A loan that the firm will pay off in five years is one such long-term debt. Firms borrow over the long term from a variety of sources. We will tend to use the terms *bonds* and *bondholders* generically to refer to long-term debt and long-term creditors, respectively.

Finally, by definition, the difference between the total value of the assets (current and fixed) and the total value of the liabilities (current and long-term) is the *shareholders' equity,* also called *common equity* or *owners' equity.* This feature of the balance sheet is intended to reflect the fact that, if the firm were to sell all of its assets and use the money to pay off its debts, then whatever residual value remained would belong to the shareholders. So, the balance sheet "balances" because the value of the left-hand side always equals the value of the right-hand side. That is, the value of the firm's assets is equal to the sum of its liabilities and shareholders' equity:[1]

Disney has a good investor site at thewaltdisney-company.com.

Assets = Liabilities + Shareholders' equity   [2.1]

---

[1] The terms *owners' equity, shareholders' equity,* and *stockholders' equity* are used interchangeably to refer to the equity in a corporation. The term *net worth* is also used. Variations exist in addition to these.

This is the balance sheet identity, or equation, and it always holds because shareholders' equity is defined as the difference between assets and liabilities.

Net Working Capital

net working capital
Current assets less current liabilities.

As shown in Figure 2.1, the difference between a firm's current assets and its current liabilities is called **net working capital**. Net working capital is positive when current assets exceed current liabilities. Based on the definitions of current assets and current liabilities, this means that the cash that will become available over the next 12 months exceeds the cash that must be paid over that same period. For this reason, net working capital is usually positive in a healthy firm.

Table 2.1 shows a simplified balance sheet for the fictitious U.S. Corporation. There are three particularly important things to keep in mind when examining a balance sheet: liquidity, debt versus equity, and market value versus book value.

EXAMPLE | **2.1**

BUILDING THE BALANCE SHEET

A firm has current assets of $100, net fixed assets of $500, short-term debt of $70, and long-term debt of $200. What does the balance sheet look like? What is shareholders' equity? What is net working capital?

In this case, total assets are $100 + 500 = $600 and total liabilities are $70 + 200 = $270, so shareholders' equity is the difference: $600 − 270 = $330. The balance sheet would thus look like:

Assets		Liabilities and Shareholders' Equity	
Current assets	$100	Current liabilities	$ 70
Net fixed assets	500	Long-term debt	200
		Shareholders' equity	330
		Total liabilities and	
Total assets	$600	shareholders' equity	$600

Net working capital is the difference between current assets and current liabilities, or $100 − 70 = $30.

Liquidity

Annual and quarterly financial statements (and lots more) for most public U.S. corporations can be found in the EDGAR database at www.sec.gov.

Liquidity refers to the speed and ease with which an asset can be converted to cash. Gold is a relatively liquid asset; a custom manufacturing facility is not. Liquidity really has two dimensions: ease of conversion versus loss of value. Any asset can be converted to cash quickly if we cut the price enough. A highly liquid asset is therefore one that can be quickly sold without significant loss of value. An illiquid asset is one that cannot be quickly converted to cash without a substantial price reduction.

Assets are normally listed on the balance sheet in order of decreasing liquidity, meaning that the most liquid assets are listed first. Current assets are relatively liquid and include cash and those assets that we expect to convert to cash over the next 12 months. Accounts receivable, for example, represent amounts not yet collected from customers on sales already made. Naturally, we hope these will convert to cash

U.S. CORPORATION Balance Sheets as of December 31, 2013 and 2014 ($ in Millions)					
	2013	2014		2013	2014
Assets			**Liabilities and Owners' Equity**		
Current assets			Current liabilities		
Cash	$ 104	$ 160	Accounts payable	$ 232	$ 266
Accounts receivable	455	688	Notes payable	196	123
Inventory	553	555	Total	$ 428	$ 389
Total	$1,112	$1,403			
Fixed assets					
Net fixed assets	$1,644	$1,709	Long-term debt	$ 408	$ 454
			Owners' equity		
			Common stock and paid-in surplus	600	640
			Retained earnings	1,320	1,629
			Total	$1,920	$2,269
			Total liabilities and		
Total assets	$2,756	$3,112	owners' equity	$2,756	$3,112

TABLE 2.1

Balance sheets for U.S. Corporation

in the near future. Inventory is probably the least liquid of the current assets, at least for many businesses.

Fixed assets are, for the most part, relatively illiquid. These consist of tangible things such as buildings and equipment that don't convert to cash at all in normal business activity (they are, of course, used in the business to generate cash). Intangible assets, such as a trademark, have no physical existence but can be very valuable. Like tangible fixed assets, they won't ordinarily convert to cash and are generally considered illiquid.

Liquidity is valuable. The more liquid a business is, the less likely it is to experience financial distress (that is, difficulty in paying debts or buying needed assets). Unfortunately, liquid assets are generally less profitable to hold. For example, cash holdings are the most liquid of all investments, but they sometimes earn no return at all—they just sit there. There is therefore a trade-off between the advantages of liquidity and forgone potential profits.

Debt versus Equity

To the extent that a firm borrows money, it usually gives first claim to the firm's cash flow to creditors. Equity holders are only entitled to the residual value, the portion left after creditors are paid. The value of this residual portion is the shareholders' equity in the firm, which is just the value of the firm's assets less the value of the firm's liabilities:

Shareholders' equity = Assets − Liabilities

This is true in an accounting sense because shareholders' equity is defined as this residual portion. More importantly, it is true in an economic sense: If the firm sells its assets and pays its debts, whatever cash is left belongs to the shareholders.

The use of debt in a firm's capital structure is called *financial leverage*. The more debt a firm has (as a percentage of assets), the greater is its degree of financial leverage. As we discuss in later chapters, debt acts like a lever in the sense that using it can greatly magnify

The home page for the Financial Accounting Standards Board (FASB) is www.fasb.org.

FINANCE MATTERS

 ◀ For the latest news on the topics covered in this chapter, scan here.

Fairly Accurate Financial Accounting?

A major objective of the Financial Accounting Standards Board (FASB) is to create rules that provide users of financial statements with information that can be used to make investment, credit, and other similar decisions. For example, beginning in September of 2007, FASB required banks to use fair value accounting, which only seems fair to us. However, this requirement proved to be controversial in the economic downturn of 2008 and 2009.

Under fair value accounting, banks have to value certain assets on their balance sheets according to what they could be sold for in the open market. This process is relatively simple for a security that is frequently traded. However, during 2008 and into 2009, trading essentially ground to a halt in many types of assets that banks held in great quantity. So, how do you price an asset for the value at which it could be sold when no one will buy it?

Banks argued that market prices for much of what they held were, in essence, fire sale prices and that the assets were actually worth more than they would fetch in such a distress sale. Using fair value accounting, they said, was really unfair because prices were so distorted. Proponents of fair value accounting argued that removing or relaxing fair value accounting would weaken the value of financial statements.

In the end, the fair value accounting issue ended up at a hearing at the U.S. House of Representatives, which, we should note, is not known for its financial accounting prowess. At the hearing, members of the House panel suggested that FASB modify its stance. In the end, the chair of FASB agreed to relax fair value accounting to provide banks with more flexibility in valuing their assets.

---

both gains and losses. So, financial leverage increases the potential reward to shareholders, but it also increases the potential for financial distress and business failure.

Market Value versus Book Value

The true value of any asset is its *market* value, which is simply the amount of cash we would get if we actually sold it. In contrast, the values shown on the balance sheet for the firm's assets are *book values* and generally are not what the assets are actually worth. Under **Generally Accepted Accounting Principles (GAAP)**, audited financial statements in the United States generally show assets at *historical cost*. In other words, assets are "carried on the books" at what the firm paid for them (minus accumulated depreciation), no matter how long ago they were purchased or how much they are worth today.

Generally Accepted Accounting Principles (GAAP)
The common set of standards and procedures by which audited financial statements are prepared.

For current assets, market value and book value might be somewhat similar since current assets are bought and converted into cash over a relatively short span of time. In other circumstances, they might differ quite a bit. Moreover, for fixed assets, it would be purely a coincidence if the actual market value of an asset (what the asset could be sold for) were equal to its book value. For example, a railroad might own enormous tracts of land purchased a century or more ago. What the railroad paid for that land could be hundreds or thousands of times less than what it is worth today. The balance sheet would nonetheless show the historical cost. There are exceptions to this practice. See our nearby *Finance Matters* box for some discussion.

Managers and investors will frequently be interested in knowing the market value of the firm. This information is not on the balance sheet. The fact that balance sheet assets are listed at cost means that there is no necessary connection between the total assets shown and the market value of the firm. Indeed, many of the most valuable assets that a firm might have—good management, a good reputation, talented employees—don't appear on the balance sheet at all. To give one example, one of the most valuable assets for many well-known companies is their brand name. According to one source, the names "Coca-Cola," "Microsoft," and "IBM" are all worth in excess of $50 billion.

Similarly, the owners' equity figure on the balance sheet and the true market value of the equity need not be related. For financial managers, then, the accounting value of the equity is not an especially important concern; it is the market value that matters. Henceforth, whenever we speak of the value of an asset or the value of the firm, we will normally mean its *market value*. So, for example, when we say the goal of the financial manager is to increase the value of the stock, we mean the market value of the stock.

MARKET VERSUS BOOK VALUES

EXAMPLE 2.2

The Klingon Corporation has fixed assets with a book value of $700 and an appraised market value of about $1,000. Current assets are $400 on the books, but approximately $600 would be realized if they were liquidated. Klingon has $500 in long-term debt, both book value and market value, and no current liabilities of any kind. What is the book value of the equity? What is the market value?

We can construct two simplified balance sheets, one in accounting (book value) terms and one in economic (market value) terms:

KLINGON CORPORATION Balance Sheets Market Value versus Book Value					
Assets	Book	Market	**Liabilities and Shareholders' Equity**	Book	Market
Current assets	$ 400	$ 600	Long-term debt	$ 500	$ 500
Net fixed assets	700	1,000	Shareholders' equity	600	1,100
	$1,100	$1,600		$1,100	$1,600

In this example, shareholders' equity is actually worth almost twice as much as what is shown on the books. The distinction between book and market values is important precisely because book values can be so different from true economic values.

CONCEPT QUESTIONS

2.1a   What is the balance sheet identity?

2.1b   What is liquidity? Why is it important?

2.1c   What do we mean by financial leverage?

2.1d   Explain the difference between accounting value and market value. Which is more important to the financial manager? Why?

THE INCOME STATEMENT

2.2

The **income statement** measures performance over some period of time, usually a quarter or a year. The income statement equation is:

Revenues – Expenses = Income   [2.2]

If you think of the balance sheet as a snapshot, then you can think of the income statement as a video recording covering the period between a before and an after picture. Table 2.2 gives a simplified income statement for U.S. Corporation.

income statement
Financial statement summarizing a firm's performance over a period of time.

TABLE 2.2	U.S. CORPORATION 2014 Income Statement ($ in Millions)		
Income statement for U.S. Corporation	Net sales		$1,509
	Cost of goods sold		750
	Depreciation		65
	Earnings before interest and taxes		$ 694
	Interest paid		70
	Taxable income		$ 624
	Taxes		212
	Net income		$ 412
	Dividends	$103	
	Addition to retained earnings	309	

ExcelMaster
coverage online

The first thing reported on an income statement would usually be revenue and expenses from the firm's principal operations. Subsequent parts include, among other things, financing expenses such as interest paid. Taxes paid are reported separately. The last item is *net income* (the so-called bottom line). Net income is often expressed on a per-share basis and called *earnings per share (EPS)*.

As indicated, U.S. paid cash dividends of $103. The difference between net income and cash dividends, $309, is the addition to retained earnings for the year. This amount is added to the cumulative retained earnings account on the balance sheet. If you look back at the two balance sheets for U.S. Corporation, you'll see that retained earnings did go up by this amount, $1,320 + 309 = $1,629.

EXAMPLE 2.3

EARNINGS AND DIVIDENDS PER SHARE

Suppose U.S. had 200 million shares outstanding at the end of 2014. Based on the income statement in Table 2.2, what was EPS? What were dividends per share?

From the income statement, U.S. had a net income of $412 million for the year. Total dividends were $103 million. Since 200 million shares were outstanding, we can calculate earnings per share and dividends per share as follows:

Earnings per share = Net income/ Total shares outstanding
= $412/200 = $2.06 per share

Dividends per share = Total dividends/ Total shares outstanding
= $103/200 = $.515 per share

When looking at an income statement, the financial manager needs to keep three things in mind: GAAP, cash versus noncash items, and time and costs.

GAAP and the Income Statement

An income statement prepared using GAAP will show revenue when it accrues. This is not necessarily when the cash comes in. The general rule (the recognition principle) is to recognize revenue when the earnings process is virtually complete and the value of an exchange of goods or services is known or can be reliably determined. In practice, this principle usually means that revenue is recognized at the time of sale, which need not be the same as the time of collection.

Expenses shown on the income statement are based on the matching principle. The basic idea here is to first determine revenues as described above and then match those revenues with the costs associated with producing them. So, if we manufacture a product and then sell it on credit, the revenue is recognized at the time of sale. The production and other costs associated with the sale of that product would likewise be recognized at that time. Once again, the actual cash outflows may have occurred at some very different times. Thus, as a result of the way revenues and expenses are reported, the figures shown on the income statement may not be at all representative of the actual cash inflows and outflows that occurred during a particular period.

Noncash Items

A primary reason that accounting income differs from cash flow is that an income statement contains **noncash items**. The most important of these is *depreciation*. Suppose a firm purchases a fixed asset for $5,000 and pays in cash. Obviously, the firm has a $5,000 cash outflow at the time of purchase. However, instead of deducting the $5,000 as an expense, an accountant might depreciate the asset over a five-year period.

noncash items
Expenses charged against revenues that do not directly affect cash flow, such as depreciation.

If the depreciation is straight-line and the asset is written down to zero over that period, then $5,000/5 = $1,000 would be deducted each year as an expense.[2] The important thing to recognize is that this $1,000 deduction isn't cash—it's an accounting number. The actual cash outflow occurred when the asset was purchased.

The depreciation deduction is simply another application of the matching principle in accounting. The revenues associated with an asset would generally occur over some length of time. So, the accountant seeks to match the expense of purchasing the asset with the benefits produced from owning it.

As we will see, for the financial manager, the actual timing of cash inflows and outflows is critical in coming up with a reasonable estimate of market value, so we need to learn how to separate the cash flows from the noncash accounting entries. In reality, the difference between cash flow and accounting income can be pretty dramatic. For example, in January 2012, aluminum manufacturer Alcoa reported a loss of $193 million. Sounds bad, but Alcoa reported a *positive* cash flow of $656 million! In large part, the loss was due to noncash restructuring charges and other special items.

Time and Costs

It is often useful to think of the future as having two distinct parts: the short run and the long run. These are not precise time periods. The distinction has to do with whether costs are fixed or variable. In the long run, all business costs are variable. Given sufficient time, assets can be sold, debts can be paid, and so on.

If our time horizon is relatively short, however, some costs are effectively fixed—they must be paid no matter what (property taxes, for example). Other costs such as wages to laborers and payments to suppliers are still variable. As a result, even in the short run, the firm can vary its output level by varying expenditures in these areas.

The distinction between fixed and variable costs is important, at times, to the financial manager, but the way costs are reported on the income statement is not a good guide as to which costs are which. The reason is that, in practice, accountants tend to classify costs as either product costs or period costs.

Product costs include such things as raw materials, direct labor expense, and manufacturing overhead. These are reported on the income statement as costs of goods sold, but they include both fixed and variable costs. Similarly, period costs are incurred during a particular time period and might be reported as selling, general, and administrative

---

[2] By "straight-line," we mean that the depreciation deduction is the same every year. By "written down to zero," we mean that the asset is assumed to have no value at the end of five years.

WORK THE WEB

◄ To get
updated data,
scan here.

The U.S. Securities and Exchange Commission (SEC) requires that most public companies file regular reports, including annual and quarterly financial statements. The SEC has a public site named EDGAR that makes these reports available free at www.sec.gov. We went to "Search for Company Filings" and searched for "Microsoft." When we got our results, we limited our search to Form 10-K. Here is what we got:

MICROSOFT CORP CIK#: 0000789019 (see all company filings)			Business Address: ONE MICROSOFT WAY REDMOND WA 98052-6399 425-882-8080	Mailing Address: ONE MICROSOFT WAY REDMOND WA 98052-6399
SIC: 7372 - SERVICES-PREPACKAGED SOFTWARE State location: WA	State of Inc.: WA	Fiscal Year End: 0630 (Assistant Director Office: 3) Get insider transactions for this issuer Get insider transactions for this reporting owner				

Filter Results: Filing Type: 10-K   Prior to: (YYYYMMDD)   Ownership? ○ include ● exclude ○ only   Limit Results Per Page: 40 Entries   [Search] [Show All]

Items 1 - 18   RSS Feed

Filings	Format	Description	Filing Date	File/Film Number
10-K	Documents / Interactive Data	Annual report [Section 13 and 15(d), not S-K Item 405] Acc-no: 0001193125-11-200680 (34 Act) Size: 16 MB	2011-07-28	000-14278 11960292
10-K	Documents / Interactive Data	Annual report [Section 13 and 15(d), not S-K Item 405] Acc-no: 0001193125-10-171791 (34 Act) Size: 29 MB	2010-07-30	000-14278 10980074
10-K	Documents	Annual report [Section 13 and 15(d), not S-K Item 405] Acc-no: 0001193125-09-158735 (34 Act) Size: 1 MB	2009-07-30	000-14278 09971624
10-K	Documents	Annual report [Section 13 and 15(d), not S-K Item 405] Acc-no: 0001193125-08-162768 (34 Act) Size: 1 MB	2008-07-31	000-14278 08962715
10-K	Documents	Annual report [Section 13 and 15(d), not S-K Item 405] Acc-no: 0001193125-07-170817 (34 Act) Size: 1 MB	2007-08-03	000-14278 071124629
10-K	Documents	Annual report [Section 13 and 15(d), not S-K Item 405] Acc-no: 0001193125-06-169006 (34 Act) Size: 1 MB	2006-09-25	000-14278 061058640
10-K	Documents	Annual report [Section 13 and 15(d), not S-K Item 405] Acc-no: 0001193125-05-174826 (34 Act) Size: 1 MB	2005-09-01	000-14278 051050609
10-K	Documents	Annual report [Section 13 and 15(d), not S-K Item 405] Acc-no: 0001193125-04-150699 Size: 1 MB	2004-09-01	000-14278 041011640
10-K	Documents	Annual report [Section 13 and 15(d), not S-K Item 405] Acc-no: 0001193125-03-045032 Size: 1 MB	2003-09-05	000-14278 03693340
10-K	Documents	Annual report [Section 13 and 15(d), not S-K Item 405] Acc-no: 0001032210-02-001351 Size: 1 MB	2002-09-06	000-14278 02757959
10-K	Documents	Annual report [Section 13 and 15(d), not S-K Item 405] Acc-no: 0001032210-01-501009 Size: 261 KB	2001-09-18	000-14278 1739790
10-K	Documents	Annual report [Section 13 and 15(d), not S-K Item 405] Acc-no: 0001032210-00-001851 Size: 457 KB	2000-09-28	000-14278 731256
10-K	Documents	Annual report [Section 13 and 15(d), not S-K Item 405] Acc-no: 0001032210-99-001375 Size: 269 KB	1999-09-28	000-14278 99710734
10-K	Documents	Annual report [Section 13 and 15(d), not S-K Item 405] Acc-no: 0001032210-98-001057 Size: 178 KB	1998-09-25	000-14278 98715634
10-K	Documents	Annual report [Section 13 and 15(d), not S-K Item 405] Acc-no: 0001017062-97-001764 Size: 186 KB	1997-09-29	000-14278 97687684
10-K	Documents	Annual report [Section 13 and 15(d), not S-K Item 405] Acc-no: 0000891020-96-001138 Size: 147 KB	1996-09-27	000-14278 96635660
10-K	Documents	Annual report [Section 13 and 15(d), not S-K Item 405] Acc-no: 0000891020-95-000433 Size: 189 KB	1995-09-25	000-14278 95575909
10-K	Documents	Annual report [Section 13 and 15(d), not S-K Item 405] Acc-no: 0000891020-94-000175 Size: 443 KB	1994-09-27	000-14278 94550472

As of the date of this search, EDGAR had 18 of these reports for Microsoft available for downloading. The 10-K is the annual report filed with the SEC. It includes, among other things, the list of officers and their salaries, financial statements for the previous fiscal year, and an explanation by the company for the financial results. Here is an exercise for you: Go to the "Descriptions of SEC Forms" page and find the different forms companies must file with the SEC. What is a 10-Q report?

Questions

1. As you can imagine, electronic filing of documents with the SEC has not been around for very long. Go to www.sec.gov and find the filings for General Electric. What is the date of the oldest 10-K available on the website for General Electric? Look up the 10-K forms for IBM and Apple to see if the year of the first electronic filing is the same for these companies.
2. Go to www.sec.gov and find out when the following forms are used: Form DEF 14A, Form 8-K, and Form 6-K.

expenses. Once again, some of these period costs may be fixed and others may be variable. The company president's salary, for example, is a period cost and is probably fixed, at least in the short run.

The balance sheets and income statement we have been using thus far are hypothetical. Our nearby *Work the Web* box shows how to find actual balance sheets and income statements online for almost any company.

Earnings Management

The way that firms are required by GAAP to report financial results is intended to be objective and precise. In reality, there is plenty of wiggle room, and, as a result, companies have significant discretion over their reported earnings. For example, corporations frequently like to show investors that they have steadily growing earnings. To do this, they might take steps to overstate or understate earnings at various times to smooth out dips and surges. Doing so is called *earnings management,* and it is a controversial practice.

With the increasing globalization of business, accounting standards need to be more alike across countries. In recent years, U.S. accounting standards have increasingly become more closely tied to International Financial Reporting Standards (IFRS). In particular, the Financial Accounting Standards Board (in charge of U.S. GAAP) and the IASB (in charge of IFRS), have been working toward a convergence of policies, although a final decision has not yet been reached as this is written.

For more information about IFRS, check out the website www.ifrs .org

---

CONCEPT QUESTIONS

2.2a   What is the income statement equation?

2.2b   What are the three things to keep in mind when looking at an income statement?

2.2c   Why is accounting income not the same as cash flow?

TAXES

2.3

Taxes can be one of the largest cash outflows that a firm experiences. For example, for the fiscal year 2011, Walmart's earnings before taxes were about $24.4 billion. Its tax bill, including all taxes paid worldwide, was a whopping $7.9 billion, or about 32.4 percent of its pretax earnings. The size of the tax bill is determined through the tax code, an often-amended set of rules. In this section, we examine corporate tax rates and how taxes are calculated. Taxes for partnerships and proprietorships are computed using the personal income tax schedules; we don't discuss these here, but the general procedures are the same as for corporate taxes.

ExcelMaster coverage online

If the various rules of taxation seem a little bizarre or convoluted to you, keep in mind that the tax code is the result of political, not economic, forces. As a result, there is no reason why it has to make economic sense.

Corporate Tax Rates

Corporate tax rates in effect for 2012 are shown in Table 2.3. A peculiar feature is that corporate tax rates are not strictly increasing. As shown, corporate tax rates rise from 15 percent to 39 percent, but they drop back to 34 percent on income over $335,000. They then rise to 38 percent and subsequently fall to 35 percent.

The IRS has a great website! (www.irs.gov)

According to the originators of the current tax rules, there are only four corporate rates: 15 percent, 25 percent, 34 percent, and 35 percent. The 38 and 39 percent brackets arise because of "surcharges" applied on top of the 34 and 35 percent rates. A tax is a tax is a tax, however, so there are really six corporate tax rates, as we have shown.

32   **PART 2**   Understanding Financial Statements and Cash Flow

TABLE 2.3	Taxable Income	Tax Rate
Corporate tax rates	$ 0– 50,000	15%
	50,001– 75,000	25
	75,001– 100,000	34
	100,001– 335,000	39
	335,001–10,000,000	34
	10,000,001–15,000,000	35
	15,000,001–18,333,333	38
	18,333,334+	35

Average versus Marginal Tax Rates

average tax rate
Total taxes paid divided by total taxable income.

marginal tax rate
Amount of tax payable on the next dollar earned.

In making financial decisions, it is frequently important to distinguish between average and marginal tax rates. Your average tax rate is your tax bill divided by your taxable income, in other words, the percentage of your income that goes to pay taxes. Your marginal tax rate is the extra tax you would pay if you earned one more dollar. The percentage tax rates shown in Table 2.3 are all marginal rates. Put another way, the tax rates in Table 2.3 apply to the part of income in the indicated range only, not all income.

The difference between average and marginal tax rates can be best illustrated with a simple example. Suppose our corporation has a taxable income of $200,000. What is the tax bill? From Table 2.3, we can figure our tax bill as:

$$
\begin{array}{lll}
.15(\$\ 50,000) & = \$\ 7,500 \\
.25(\$\ 75,000 - 50,000) & = \ \ \ 6,250 \\
.34(\$100,000 - 75,000) & = \ \ \ 8,500 \\
.39(\$200,000 - 100,000) & = \ \underline{\ \ 39,000} \\
& \ \ \ \underline{\$61,250}
\end{array}
$$

Our total tax is thus $61,250.

In our example, what is the average tax rate? We had a taxable income of $200,000 and a tax bill of $61,250, so the average tax rate is $61,250/200,000 = 30.625\%$. What is the marginal tax rate? If we made one more dollar, the tax on that dollar would be 39 cents, so our marginal rate is 39 percent.

Table 2.4 summarizes some different taxable incomes, marginal tax rates, and average tax rates for corporations. Notice how the average and marginal tax rates come together at 35 percent.

TABLE 2.4	(1) Taxable Income	(2) Marginal Tax Rate	(3) Total Tax	(3)/(1) Average Tax Rate
Corporate taxes and tax rates	$ 45,000	15%	$ 6,750	15.00%
	70,000	25	12,500	17.86
	95,000	34	20,550	21.63
	250,000	39	80,750	32.30
	1,000,000	34	340,000	34.00
	17,500,000	38	6,100,000	34.86
	50,000,000	35	17,500,000	35.00
	100,000,000	35	35,000,000	35.00

DEEP IN THE HEART OF TAXES   EXAMPLE 2.4

Algernon, Inc., has a taxable income of $85,000. What is its tax bill? What is its average tax rate? Its marginal tax rate?

From Table 2.3, the tax rate applied to the first $50,000 is 15 percent; the rate applied to the next $25,000 is 25 percent; and the rate applied after that up to $100,000 is 34 percent. So, Algernon must pay .15 × $50,000 + .25 × 25,000 + .34 × (85,000 − 75,000) = $17,150. The average tax rate is thus $17,150/85,000 = 20.18%. The marginal rate is 34 percent since Algernon's taxes would rise by 34 cents if it had another dollar in taxable income.

With a *flat-rate* tax, there is only one tax rate, and this rate is the same for all income levels. With such a tax, the marginal tax rate is always the same as the average tax rate. As it stands now, corporate taxation in the United States is based on a modified flat-rate tax, which becomes a true flat rate for the highest incomes.

In looking at Table 2.4, notice that the more a corporation makes, the greater is the percentage of taxable income paid in taxes. Put another way, under current tax law, the average tax rate never goes down, even though the marginal tax rate does. As illustrated, for corporations, average tax rates begin at 15 percent and rise to a maximum of 35 percent.

It will normally be the marginal tax rate that is relevant for financial decision making. The reason is that any new cash flows will be taxed at that marginal rate. Since financial decisions usually involve new cash flows or changes in existing ones, this rate will tell us the marginal effect on our tax bill.

There is one last thing to notice about the tax code as it affects corporations. It's easy to verify that the corporate tax bill is just a flat 35 percent of taxable income if our taxable income is more than $18.33 million. Also, for the many midsize corporations with taxable incomes in the $335,000 to $10,000,000 range, the tax rate is a flat 34 percent. Since we will usually be talking about large corporations, you can assume that the average and marginal tax rates are 35 percent unless we explicitly say otherwise.

We should note that we have simplified the U.S. tax code in our discussions. In reality, the tax code is much more complex, and it is riddled with various tax deductions and loopholes allowed for certain industries. As a result, the average corporate tax rate can be far from 35 percent for many companies. Table 2.5 displays average tax rates for various industries.

As you can see, the average tax rate ranges from 33.8 percent for electric utilities to 4.5 percent for biotechnology firms. For a discussion of one of the complexities of the tax code, see our nearby *Finance Matters* box.

Industry	Number of Companies	Average Tax Rate
Electric utilities (Eastern U.S.)	24	33.8%
Trucking	33	32.7
Railroad	15	27.4
Securities brokerage	30	20.5
Banking	481	17.5
Medical supplies	264	11.2
Internet	239	5.9
Pharmaceutical	337	5.6
Biotechnology	121	4.5

TABLE 2.5

Average tax rates for various industries

FINANCE MATTERS

◄ For the latest news on the topics covered in this chapter, scan here.

What Is Warren Buffett's Tax Rate?

In 2011, famed investor Warren Buffett, one of the wealthiest individuals in the world, created a stir when he publicly stated that his tax rate was lower than the tax rate paid by his secretary. The previous year, Buffet's gross income was about $63 million, on which he paid only a 15 percent tax rate. His secretary (with a substantially lower income) had a 31 percent marginal tax rate. Also in 2011, when Republican presidential contender Mitt Romney released his income taxes, it was revealed that he too paid an income tax rate of only 15 percent on his $21 million annual income.

Why do Buffett's and Romney's tax rates appear so low? Currently, under the U.S. tax system, wage income is taxed at a much higher rate than dividends and long-term capital gains. In fact, in the highest tax bracket, wage income is taxed at 35 percent, while dividends and long-term capital gains are taxed at 15 percent. For Buffett and Romney, most of their annual income comes from their investments, not wages, hence the 15 percent rate.

So do rich guys get all the (tax) breaks? U.S. President Barack Obama seems to think so. In his 2012 State of the Union Address, with Buffett's secretary Debbie Bosanek joining First Lady Michelle Obama in her box as a special guest, he called for the creation of a "Buffett tax." As he described it, such a tax would be an extra tax paid by very high-income individuals. Maybe President Obama was mad about the fact that he and the first lady paid (in 2009) $1.7 million in federal taxes on their joint income of $5.5 million, implying an average tax rate of 31 percent.

Of course, you know that income received from dividends is already taxed. Dividends are paid from corporate income, which is taxed at 35 percent for larger dividend-paying companies. Effectively, any tax on dividends is double taxation on that money. The tax code realizes this. The lower tax rate on dividends simply lowers the double tax rate. The same thing is true for capital gains; taxes are paid on the money before the investment is made.

In Buffett's case, most of his wealth stems from his approximately 30 percent ownership of Berkshire Hathaway Corporation. Based on its 14,097 (no typo!)-page tax return, Berkshire's 2010 corporate tax bill was $5.6 billion on income of $19 billion, a 29 percent average rate. Buffett's share of Berkshire's tax bill therefore amounts to something on the order of $1.68 billion! If we include Berkshire's corporate taxes, Buffett's average tax rate is more like 29 + 15 = 44 percent.

To give another example, consider the situation described by N. Gregory Mankiw, the well-known economist and textbook author. Mankiw considers taking a writing job for $1,000. He figures that if he earns an 8 percent return and there are no taxes, he would be able to leave his children about $10,000 in 30 years when he passes on. However, because of federal, state, and Medicare taxes, he would receive only about $523 after taxes today. And because of corporate taxes and personal income taxes, his return on the same investment would be only about 4 percent, which will result in a balance of $1,700 in 30 years. When he dies, his account will be taxed using the marginal estate tax rate, which is as high as 55 percent. As a result, his children will receive only about $1,000, implying a tax rate of 90 percent!

CONCEPT QUESTIONS

2.3a What is the difference between a marginal and an average tax rate?
2.3b Do the wealthiest corporations receive a tax break in terms of a lower tax rate? Explain.

2.4 CASH FLOW

At this point, we are ready to discuss perhaps one of the most important pieces of financial information that can be gleaned from financial statements: *cash flow*. By cash flow, we simply mean the difference between the number of dollars that came in and the number that went out. For example, if you were the owner of a business, you might be very interested in how much cash you actually took out of your business in a given year. How to determine this amount is one of the things we discuss next.

There is no standard financial statement that presents this information in the way that we wish. We will therefore discuss how to calculate cash flow for U.S. Corporation and point out how the result differs from that of standard financial statement calculations. Important note: There is a standard financial accounting statement called the *statement of cash flows,* but it is concerned with a somewhat different issue that should not be confused with what is discussed in this section.

From the balance sheet identity, we know that the value of a firm's assets is equal to the value of its liabilities plus the value of its equity. Similarly, the cash flow from the firm's assets must equal the sum of the cash flow to creditors and the cash flow to stockholders (or owners, if the business is not a corporation):

Cash flow from assets = Cash flow to creditors   [2.3]
+ Cash flow to stockholders

This is the cash flow identity. What it reflects is the fact that a firm generates cash through its various activities, and that cash either is used to pay creditors or else is paid out to the owners of the firm. We discuss the various things that make up these cash flows next.

Cash Flow from Assets

Cash flow from assets involves three components: operating cash flow, capital spending, and change in net working capital. **Operating cash flow** refers to the cash flow that results from the firm's day-to-day activities of producing and selling. Expenses associated with the firm's financing of its assets are not included since they are not operating expenses.

In the normal course of events, some portion of the firm's cash flow is reinvested in the firm. *Capital spending* refers to the net spending on fixed assets (purchases of fixed assets less sales of fixed assets). Finally, *the change in net working capital* is the amount spent on net working capital. It is measured as the change in net working capital over the period being examined and represents the net increase or decrease in current assets over current liabilities. The three components of cash flow are examined in more detail below. In all our examples, all amounts are in millions of dollars.

ExcelMaster
coverage online

cash flow from assets
The total of cash flow to creditors and cash flow to stockholders, consisting of the following: operating cash flow, capital spending, and change in net working capital.

operating cash flow
Cash generated from a firm's normal business activities.

Operating Cash Flow   To calculate operating cash flow (OCF), we want to calculate revenues minus costs, but we don't want to include depreciation since it's not a cash outflow, and we don't want to include interest because it's a financing expense. We do want to include taxes because taxes are, unfortunately, paid in cash.

If we look at U.S. Corporation's income statement (Table 2.2), we see that earnings before interest and taxes (EBIT) are $694. This is almost what we want since it doesn't include interest paid. We need to make two adjustments. First, recall that depreciation is a noncash expense. To get cash flow, we first add back the $65 in depreciation since it wasn't a cash deduction. The other adjustment is to subtract the $212 in taxes since these were paid in cash. The result is operating cash flow:

U.S. CORPORATION 2014 Operating Cash Flow	
Earnings before interest and taxes	$694
+ Depreciation	65
− Taxes	212
Operating cash flow	$547

U.S. Corporation thus had a 2014 operating cash flow of $547.

Operating cash flow is an important number because it tells us, on a very basic level, whether or not a firm's cash inflows from its business operations are sufficient to cover its everyday cash outflows. For this reason, a negative operating cash flow is often a sign of trouble.

There is an unpleasant possibility for confusion when we speak of operating cash flow. In accounting practice, operating cash flow is often defined as net income plus depreciation. For U.S. Corporation, this would amount to $412 + 65 = $477. The accounting definition of operating cash flow differs from ours in one important way: Interest is deducted when net income is computed. Notice that the difference between the $547 operating cash flow we calculated and this $477 is $70, the amount of interest paid for the year. This definition of cash flow thus considers interest paid to be an operating expense. Our definition treats it properly as a financing expense. If there were no interest expense, the two definitions would be the same.

To finish our calculation of cash flow from assets for U.S. Corporation, we need to consider how much of the $547 operating cash flow was reinvested in the firm. We consider spending on fixed assets first.

Capital Spending   Net capital spending is just money spent on fixed assets less money received from the sale of fixed assets. At the end of 2013, net fixed assets for U.S. Corporation (Table 2.1) were $1,644. During the year, we wrote off (depreciated) $65 worth of fixed assets on the income statement. So, if we didn't purchase any new fixed assets, net fixed assets would have been $1,644 − 65 = $1,579 at year's end. The 2014 balance sheet shows $1,709 in net fixed assets, so we must have spent a total of $1,709 − 1,579 = $130 on fixed assets during the year:

Ending net fixed assets	$1,709
− Beginning net fixed assets	1,644
+ Depreciation	65
Net investment in fixed assets	$ 130

This $130 is our net capital spending for 2014.

Could net capital spending be negative? The answer is yes. This would happen if the firm sold off more assets than it purchased. The *net* here refers to purchases of fixed assets net of any sales of fixed assets.

Change in Net Working Capital   In addition to investing in fixed assets, a firm will also invest in current assets. For example, going back to the balance sheet in Table 2.1, we see that at the end of 2014, U.S. had current assets of $1,403. At the end of 2013, current assets were $1,112, so, during the year, U.S. invested $1,403 − 1,112 = $291 in current assets.

As the firm changes its investment in current assets, its current liabilities will usually change as well. To determine the change in net working capital, the easiest approach is just to take the difference between the beginning and ending net working capital (NWC) figures. Net working capital at the end of 2014 was $1,403 − 389 = $1,014. Similarly, at the end of 2013, net working capital was $1,112 − 428 = $684. So, given these figures, we have:

Ending NWC	$1,014
− Beginning NWC	684
Change in NWC	$ 330

Net working capital thus increased by $330. Put another way, U.S. Corporation had a net investment of $330 in NWC for the year.

Conclusion   Given the figures we've come up with, we're ready to calculate cash flow from assets. The total cash flow from assets is given by operating cash flow less the amounts invested in fixed assets and net working capital. So, for U.S., we have:

U.S. CORPORATION 2014 Cash Flow from Assets	
Operating cash flow	$547
− Net capital spending	130
− Change in NWC	330
Cash flow from assets	$ 87

From the cash flow identity above, this $87 cash flow from assets equals the sum of the firm's cash flow to creditors and its cash flow to stockholders. We consider these next.

It wouldn't be at all unusual for a growing corporation to have a negative cash flow. As we shall see below, a negative cash flow means that the firm raised more money by borrowing and selling stock than it paid out to creditors and stockholders that year.

A Note on "Free" Cash Flow   Cash flow from assets sometimes goes by a different name, **free cash flow**. Of course, there is no such thing as "free" cash (we wish!). Instead, the name refers to cash that the firm is free to distribute to creditors and stockholders because it is not needed for working capital or fixed asset investments. We will stick with "cash flow from assets" as our label for this important concept because, in practice, there is some variation in exactly how free cash flow is computed; different users calculate it in different ways. Nonetheless, whenever you hear the phrase "free cash flow," you should understand that what is being discussed is cash flow from assets or something quite similar.

free cash flow
Another name for cash flow from assets.

Cash Flow to Creditors and Stockholders

The cash flows to creditors and stockholders represent the net payments to creditors and owners during the year. They are calculated in a similar way. **Cash flow to creditors** is interest paid less net new borrowing; **cash flow to stockholders** is dividends paid less net new equity raised.

cash flow to creditors
A firm's interest payments to creditors less net new borrowings.

cash flow to stockholders
Dividends paid out by a firm less net new equity raised.

Cash Flow to Creditors   Looking at the income statement in Table 2.2, we see that U.S. paid $70 in interest to creditors. From the balance sheets in Table 2.1, long-term debt rose by $454 − 408 = $46. So, U.S. Corporation paid out $70 in interest, but it borrowed an additional $46. Net cash flow to creditors is thus:

U.S. CORPORATION 2014 Cash Flow to Creditors	
Interest paid	$70
− Net new borrowing	46
Cash flow to creditors	$24

Cash flow to creditors is sometimes called *cash flow to bondholders*; we will use these terms interchangeably.

TABLE 2.6
Cash flow summary

I. The cash flow identity

Cash flow from assets = Cash flow to creditors (bondholders)
+ Cash flow to stockholders (owners)

II. Cash flow from assets

Cash flow from assets = Operating cash flow
− Net capital spending
− Change in net working capital (NWC)

where

Operating cash flow = Earnings before interest and taxes (EBIT)
+ Depreciation − Taxes
Net capital spending = Ending net fixed assets − Beginning net fixed assets
+ Depreciation
Change in NWC = Ending NWC − Beginning NWC

III. Cash flow to creditors (bondholders)

Cash flow to creditors = Interest paid − Net new borrowing

IV. Cash flow to stockholders (owners)

Cash flow to stockholders = Dividends paid − Net new equity raised

Cash Flow to Stockholders From the income statement, dividends paid to stockholders amount to $103. To get net new equity raised, we need to look at the common stock and paid-in surplus account. This account tells us how much stock the company has sold. During the year, this account rose by $40, so $40 in net new equity was raised. Given this, we have:

U.S. CORPORATION 2014 Cash Flow to Stockholders	
Dividends paid	$103
− Net new equity raised	40
Cash flow to stockholders	$ 63

The cash flow to stockholders for 2014 was thus $63.

Conclusion

The last thing that we need to do is to verify that the cash flow identity holds to be sure that we didn't make any mistakes. From above, cash flow from assets is $87. Cash flow to creditors and stockholders is $24 + 63 = $87, so everything checks out. Table 2.6 contains a summary of the various cash flow calculations for future reference.

An Example: Cash Flows for Dole Cola

This extended example covers the various cash flow calculations discussed in the chapter. It also illustrates a few variations that may arise.

Operating Cash Flow During the year, Dole Cola, Inc., had sales and cost of goods sold of $600 and $300, respectively. Depreciation was $150, and interest paid was $30. Taxes were calculated at a straight 34 percent. Dividends were $30. (All figures are in millions of dollars.) What was operating cash flow for Dole? Why is this different from net income?

The easiest thing to do here is to go ahead and create an income statement. We can then pick up the numbers we need. Dole Cola's income statement is given below:

DOLE COLA 2014 Income Statement	
Net sales	$600
Cost of goods sold	300
Depreciation	150
Earnings before interest and taxes	$150
Interest paid	30
Taxable income	$120
Taxes	41
Net income	$ 79
Dividends	$30
Addition to retained earnings	49

Net income for Dole was thus $79. We now have all the numbers we need. Referring back to the U.S. Corporation example and Table 2.6, we have:

DOLE COLA 2014 Operating Cash Flow	
Earnings before interest and taxes	$150
+ Depreciation	150
− Taxes	41
Operating cash flow	$259

As this example illustrates, operating cash flow is not the same as net income, because depreciation and interest are subtracted out when net income is calculated. If you recall our earlier discussion, we don't subtract these out in computing operating cash flow because depreciation is not a cash expense and interest paid is a financing expense, not an operating expense.

Net Capital Spending   Suppose beginning net fixed assets were $500 and ending net fixed assets were $750. What was the net capital spending for the year?

From the income statement for Dole, depreciation for the year was $150. Net fixed assets rose by $250. Dole thus spent $250 along with an additional $150, for a total of $400.

Change in NWC and Cash Flow from Assets   Suppose Dole Cola started the year with $2,130 in current assets and $1,620 in current liabilities. The corresponding ending figures were $2,260 and $1,710. What was the change in NWC during the year? What was cash flow from assets? How does this compare to net income?

Net working capital started out as $2,130 − 1,620 = $510 and ended up at $2,260 − 1,710 = $550. The change in NWC was thus $550 − 510 = $40. Putting together all the information for Dole Cola, we have:

DOLE COLA 2014 Cash Flow From Assets	
Operating cash flow	$259
− Net capital spending	400
− Change in NWC	40
Cash flow from assets	−$181

Dole had a cash flow from assets of −$181. Net income was positive at $79. Is the fact that cash flow from assets was negative a cause for alarm? Not necessarily. The cash flow here is negative primarily because of a large investment in fixed assets. If these are good investments, then the resulting negative cash flow is not a worry.

Cash Flow to Creditors and Stockholders

We saw that Dole Cola had cash flow from assets of −$181. The fact that this is negative means that Dole raised more money in the form of new debt and equity than it paid out for the year. For example, suppose we know that Dole didn't sell any new equity for the year. What was cash flow to stockholders? To creditors?

Since it didn't raise any new equity, Dole's cash flow to stockholders is just equal to the cash dividend paid:

DOLE COLA	
2014 Cash Flow to Stockholders	
Dividends paid	$30
− Net new equity	0
Cash flow to stockholders	$30

Now, from the cash flow identity, the total cash paid to creditors and stockholders was −$181. Cash flow to stockholders is $30, so cash flow to creditors must be equal to −$181 − 30 = −$211:

Cash flow to creditors + Cash flow to stockholders = −$181
Cash flow to creditors + $30   = −$181
Cash flow to creditors   = −$211

Since we know that cash flow to creditors is −$211 and interest paid is $30 (from the income statement), we can now determine net new borrowing. Dole must have borrowed $241 during the year to help finance the fixed asset expansion:

DOLE COLA	
2014 Cash Flow to Creditors	
Interest paid	$ 30
− Net new borrowing	241
Cash flow to creditors	−$211

CONCEPT QUESTIONS

2.4a   What is the cash flow identity? Explain what it says.

2.4b   What are the components of operating cash flow?

2.4c   Why is interest paid not a component of operating cash flow?

SUMMARY AND CONCLUSIONS

This chapter has introduced you to some of the basics of financial statements, taxes, and cash flow. In it, we saw that:

◄ Think you've mastered the material? Scan here to take a chapter quiz.

1. The book values on an accounting balance sheet can be very different from market values. The goal of financial management is to maximize the market value of the stock, not its book value.

2. Net income as it is computed on the income statement is not cash flow. A primary reason is that depreciation, a noncash expense, is deducted when net income is computed.

3. Marginal and average tax rates can be different, and it is the marginal tax rate that is relevant for most financial decisions.

4. The marginal tax rate paid by the corporations with the largest incomes is 35 percent.

5. There is a cash flow identity much like the balance sheet identity. It says that cash flow from assets equals cash flow to creditors and stockholders.

The calculation of cash flow from financial statements isn't difficult. Care must be taken in handling noncash expenses, such as depreciation, and in not confusing operating costs with financing costs. Most of all, it is important not to confuse book values with market values and accounting income with cash flow.

connect POP QUIZ!

|FINANCE

Can you answer the following questions? If your class is using *Connect Finance*, log on to the Self-Quiz and Study feature in the Library tab to see if you know the answers to these and other questions, check out the study tools, and find out what topics require additional practice!

Section 2.1 Brown Stone Mills has total assets of $43,200, total equity of $25,600, net fixed assets of $31,700, and long-term debt of $11,500. What is the net working capital?

Section 2.2 Last year, Denver Mountain Gear had net income of $132,800. The firm had 60,000 shares of stock outstanding and added $56,400 to its retained earnings. What was the dividend per share?

Section 2.3 Gladiators, Inc. has a marginal tax rate of 34 percent and an average tax rate of 23 percent. How much additional tax will the firm owe if its taxable income increases by $20?

Section 2.4 At the beginning of the year, a firm had total assets of $360,000, current liabilities of $28,700, and total equity of $229,000. At the end of the year, the total assets were $411,000, current liabilities were $31,600, and total equity was $246,000. The firm paid $6,800 in interest expense. What is the cash flow to creditors for the year?

www.mhhe.com/rwj

CHAPTER REVIEW AND SELF-TEST PROBLEM

2.1 Cash Flow for Rasputin Corporation. This problem will give you some practice working with financial statements and figuring cash flow. Based on the following information for Rasputin Corporation, prepare an income statement for 2014 and balance sheets for 2013 and 2014. Next, following our U.S. Corporation examples in the chapter, calculate cash flow from assets for Rasputin, cash flow to creditors, and cash flow to stockholders for 2014. Use a 34 percent tax rate throughout. You can check your answers below. (See Problem 21.)

	2013	2014
Sales	$3,790	$3,990
Cost of goods sold	2,043	2,137
Depreciation	975	1,018
Interest	225	267
Dividends	200	225
Current assets	2,140	2,346
Net fixed assets	6,770	7,087
Current liabilities	994	1,126
Long-term debt	2,869	2,956

■ Answer to Chapter Review and Self-Test Problem

2.1 In preparing the balance sheets, remember that shareholders' equity is the residual. With this in mind, Rasputin's balance sheets are as follows:

RASPUTIN CORPORATION
Balance Sheets as of December 31, 2013 and 2014

	2013	2014		2013	2014
Current assets	$2,140	$2,346	Current liabilities	$ 994	$1,126
Net fixed assets	6,770	7,087	Long-term debt	2,869	2,956
			Equity	5,047	5,351
			Total liabilities and		
Total assets	$8,910	$9,433	shareholders' equity	$8,910	$9,433

The income statement is straightforward:

RASPUTIN CORPORATION
2014 Income Statement

Sales	$3,990
Cost of goods sold	2,137
Depreciation	1,018
Earnings before interest and taxes	$ 835
Interest paid	267
Taxable income	$ 568
Taxes (34%)	193
Net income	$ 375
Dividends	$225
Addition to retained earnings	150

Notice that we've used a flat 34 percent tax rate. Also, notice that the addition to retained earnings is just net income less cash dividends.

We can now pick up the figures we need to get operating cash flow:

RASPUTIN CORPORATION 2014 Operating Cash Flow	
Earnings before interest and taxes	$ 835
+ Depreciation	1,018
− Current taxes	193
Operating cash flow	$1,660

Next, we get the capital spending for the year by looking at the change in fixed assets, remembering to account for the depreciation:

Ending fixed assets	$7,087
− Beginning fixed assets	6,770
+ Depreciation	1,018
Net investment in fixed assets	$1,335

After calculating beginning and ending NWC, we take the difference to get the change in NWC:

Ending NWC	$1,220
− Beginning NWC	1,146
Change in NWC	$ 74

We now combine operating cash flow, net capital spending, and the change in net working capital to get the total cash flow from assets:

RASPUTIN CORPORATION 2014 Cash Flow from Assets	
Operating cash flow	$1,660
− Net capital spending	1,335
− Change in NWC	74
Cash flow from assets	$ 251

To get cash flow to creditors, notice that long-term borrowing increased by $87 during the year and that interest paid was $267, so:

RASPUTIN CORPORATION 2014 Cash Flow to Creditors	
Interest paid	$267
− Net new borrowing	87
Cash flow to creditors	$180

Finally, dividends paid were $225. To get net new equity, we have to do some extra calculating. Total equity was up by $5,351 − 5,047 = $304. Of this increase, $150 was from additions to retained earnings, so $154 in new equity was raised during the year. Cash flow to stockholders was thus:

RASPUTIN CORPORATION 2014 Cash Flow to Stockholders	
Dividends paid	$225
− Net new equity	154
Cash flow to stockholders	$ 71

As a check, notice that cash flow from assets ($251) does equal cash flow to creditors plus cash flow to stockholders ($180 + 71 = $251).

CRITICAL THINKING AND CONCEPTS REVIEW

LO 1 2.1 **Liquidity.**   What does liquidity measure? Explain the trade-off a firm faces between high-liquidity and low-liquidity levels.

LO 2 2.2 **Accounting and Cash Flows.**   Why is it that the revenue and cost figures shown on a standard income statement may not be representative of the actual cash inflows and outflows that occurred during a period?

LO 1 2.3 **Book Values versus Market Values.**   In preparing a balance sheet, why do you think standard accounting practice focuses on historical cost rather than market value?

LO 2 2.4 **Operating Cash Flow.**   In comparing accounting net income and operating cash flow, what two items do you find in net income that are not in operating cash flow? Explain what each is and why it is excluded in operating cash flow.

LO 1 2.5 **Book Values versus Market Values.**   Under standard accounting rules, it is possible for a company's liabilities to exceed its assets. When this occurs, the owners' equity is negative. Can this happen with market values? Why or why not?

LO 4 2.6 **Cash Flow from Assets.**   Suppose a company's cash flow from assets was negative for a particular period. Is this necessarily a good sign or a bad sign?

LO 4 2.7 **Operating Cash Flow.**   Suppose a company's operating cash flow was negative for several years running. Is this necessarily a good sign or a bad sign?

LO 4 2.8 **Net Working Capital and Capital Spending.**   Could a company's change in NWC be negative in a given year? (Hint: Yes.) Explain how this might come about. What about net capital spending?

LO 4 2.9 **Cash Flow to Stockholders and Creditors.**   Could a company's cash flow to stockholders be negative in a given year? (Hint: Yes.) Explain how this might come about. What about cash flow to creditors?

LO 4 2.10 **Firm Values.**   Referring back to the examples used at the beginning of the chapter, note that we suggested that stockholders probably didn't suffer as a result of the reported loss. What do you think was the basis for our conclusion?

QUESTIONS AND PROBLEMS

LO 1
1. **Building a Balance Sheet.** Kroeger, Inc., has current assets of $1,970, net fixed assets of $9,650, current liabilities of $1,520, and long-term debt of $4,370. What is the value of the shareholders' equity account for this firm? How much is net working capital?

Basic
(Questions 1–13)

LO 2
2. **Building an Income Statement.** Draiman, Inc., has sales of $795,000, costs of $345,000, depreciation expense of $76,000, interest expense of $41,000, and a tax rate of 35 percent. What is the net income for this firm?

LO 2
3. **Dividends and Retained Earnings.** Suppose the firm in Problem 2 paid out $56,000 in cash dividends. What is the addition to retained earnings?

LO 2
4. **Per-Share Earnings and Dividends.** Suppose the firm in Problem 3 had 60,000 shares of common stock outstanding. What is the earnings per share, or EPS, figure? What is the dividends per share figure?

LO 1
5. **Market Values and Book Values.** Klingon Widgets, Inc., purchased new cloaking machinery three years ago for $8 million. The machinery can be sold to the Romulans today for $6.7 million. Klingon's current balance sheet shows net fixed assets of $3.1 million, current liabilities of $790,000, and net working capital of $145,000. If all the current assets were liquidated today, the company would receive $865,000 cash. What is the book value of Klingon's total assets today? What is the market value?

LO 3
6. **Calculating Taxes.** The SGS Co. had $215,000 in taxable income. Using the rates from Table 2.3 in the chapter, calculate the company's income taxes.

LO 3
7. **Tax Rates.** In Problem 6, what is the average tax rate? What is the marginal tax rate?

LO 2
8. **Calculating OCF.** Hammett, Inc., has sales of $34,630, costs of $10,340, depreciation expense of $2,520, and interest expense of $1,750. If the tax rate is 35 percent, what is the operating cash flow, or OCF?

LO 4
9. **Calculating Net Capital Spending.** Rotweiler Obedience School's December 31, 2013, balance sheet showed net fixed assets of $1,635,000, and the December 31, 2014, balance sheet showed net fixed assets of $1,976,000. The company's 2014 income statement showed a depreciation expense of $305,000. What was Rotweiler's net capital spending for 2014?

LO 4
10. **Calculating Additions to NWC.** The December 31, 2013, balance sheet of Maria's Tennis Shop, Inc., showed current assets of $1,045 and current liabilities of $960. The December 31, 2014, balance sheet showed current assets of $1,310 and current liabilities of $1,090. What was the company's 2014 change in net working capital, or NWC?

LO 4
11. **Cash Flow to Creditors.** The December 31, 2013, balance sheet of Schism, Inc., showed long-term debt of $1,280,000, and the December 31, 2014, balance sheet showed long-term debt of $1,410,000. The 2014 income statement showed an interest expense of $93,400. What was the firm's cash flow to creditors during 2014?

LO 4
12. **Cash Flow to Stockholders.** The December 31, 2013, balance sheet of Schism, Inc., showed $120,000 in the common stock account and $2,120,000 in the additional paid-in surplus account. The December 31, 2014, balance sheet showed $135,000 and $2,380,000 in the same two accounts, respectively. If the company paid out $135,000 in cash dividends during 2014, what was the cash flow to stockholders for the year?

LO 4   **13. Calculating Cash Flows.**   Given the information for Schism, Inc., in Problems 11 and 12, suppose you also know that the firm's net capital spending for 2014 was $640,000, and that the firm reduced its net working capital investment by $105,000. What was the firm's 2014 operating cash flow, or OCF?

LO 4   **14. Calculating Cash Flows.**   Weiland Co. shows the following information on its 2014 income statement: sales = $167,000; costs = $88,600; other expenses = $4,900; depreciation expense = $11,600; interest expense = $8,700; taxes = $18,620; dividends = $9,700. In addition, you're told that the firm issued $2,900 in new equity during 2014, and redeemed $4,000 in outstanding long-term debt.

Intermediate
(Questions 14–23)

    a.   What is the 2014 operating cash flow?

    b.   What is the 2014 cash flow to creditors?

    c.   What is the 2014 cash flow to stockholders?

    d.   If net fixed assets increased by $23,140 during the year, what was the addition to NWC?

LO 2   **15. Using Income Statements.**   Given the following information for Sookie's Cookies Co., calculate the depreciation expense: sales = $55,000; costs = $43,200; addition to retained earnings = $2,600; dividends paid = $1,150; interest expense = $1,670; tax rate = 40 percent.

LO 1   **16. Preparing a Balance Sheet.**   Prepare a balance sheet for Alaskan Orange Corp. as of December 31, 2014, based on the following information: cash = $197,000; patents and copyrights = $863,000; accounts payable = $288,000; accounts receivable = $265,000; tangible net fixed assets = $5,300,000; inventory = $563,000; notes payable = $194,000; accumulated retained earnings = $4,586,000; long-term debt = $1,450,000.

LO 1   **17. Residual Claims.**   Chevelle, Inc., is obligated to pay its creditors $7,800 during the year.

    a.   What is the value of the shareholders' equity if assets equal $9,300?

    b.   What if assets equal $6,900?

LO 3   **18. Marginal versus Average Tax Rates.**   (Refer to Table 2.3.) Corporation Growth has $83,000 in taxable income, and Corporation Income has $8,300,000 in taxable income.

    a.   What is the tax bill for each firm?

    b.   Suppose both firms have identified a new project that will increase taxable income by $10,000. How much in additional taxes will each firm pay? Why is this amount the same?

LO 2   **19. Net Income and OCF.**   During the year, Belyk Paving Co. had sales of $2,600,000. Cost of goods sold, administrative and selling expenses, and depreciation expense were $1,535,000, $465,000, and $520,000, respectively. In addition, the company had an interest expense of $245,000 and a tax rate of 35 percent. (Ignore any tax loss carryback or carryforward provisions.)

    a.   What is Belyk's net income?

    b.   What is its operating cash flow?

    c.   Explain your results in (a) and (b).

LO 2   **20. Accounting Values versus Cash Flows.**   In Problem 19, suppose Belyk Paving Co. paid out $420,000 in cash dividends. Is this possible? If net capital spending was zero, no new investments were made in net working capital, and no new stock was issued during the year, what do you know about the firm's long-term debt account?

LO 4

21. Calculating Cash Flows. Titan Football Manufacturing had the following operating results for 2014: sales = $23,730; cost of goods sold = $16,780; depreciation expense = $2,840; interest expense = $414; dividends paid = $616. At the beginning of the year, net fixed assets were $16,560, current assets were $2,940, and current liabilities were $2,592. At the end of the year, net fixed assets were $18,840, current assets were $3,528, and current liabilities were $2,484. The tax rate for 2014 was 35 percent.

a. What is net income for 2014?

b. What is the operating cash flow for 2014?

c. What is the cash flow from assets for 2014? Is this possible? Explain.

d. If no new debt was issued during the year, what is the cash flow to creditors? What is the cash flow to stockholders? Explain and interpret the positive and negative signs of your answers in (a) through (d).

LO 4

22. Calculating Cash Flows. Consider the following abbreviated financial statements for Cabo Wabo, Inc.:

CABO WABO, INC.
Partial Balance Sheets as of December 31, 2013 and 2014

Assets	2013	2014	Liabilities and Owners' Equity	2013	2014
Current assets	$ 3,198	$ 3,389	Current liabilities	$1,381	$2,030
Net fixed assets	14,826	15,500	Long-term debt	8,086	9,434

CABO WABO, INC.
2014 Income Statement

Sales	$47,842
Costs	23,992
Depreciation	4,040
Interest paid	750

a. What is owners' equity for 2013 and 2014?

b. What is the change in net working capital for 2014?

c. In 2014, Cabo Wabo purchased $8,424 in new fixed assets. How much in fixed assets did Cabo Wabo sell? What is the cash flow from assets for the year? (The tax rate is 40 percent.)

d. During 2014, Cabo Wabo raised $2,535 in new long-term debt. How much long-term debt must Cabo Wabo have paid off during the year? What is the cash flow to creditors?

LO 4

23. Cash Flow Identity. Graffiti Advertising, Inc., reported the following financial statements for the last two years. Construct the cash flow identity for the company. Explain what each number means.

2014 Income Statement

Sales	$621,720
Cost of goods sold	334,427
Selling & administrative	137,206
Depreciation	60,033
EBIT	$ 90,054
Interest	21,226
EBT	$ 68,828
Taxes	27,531
Net income	$ 41,297
Dividends	$ 15,600
Addition to retained earnings	$ 25,697

www.mhhe.com/rwj

GRAFFITI ADVERTISING, INC.
Balance Sheet as of December 31, 2013

Cash	$ 14,652	Accounts payable	$ 10,535
Accounts receivable	20,893	Notes payable	15,858
Inventory	15,173	Current liabilities	$ 26,393
Current assets	$ 50,718	Long-term debt	$150,500
Net fixed assets	$378,869	Owners' equity	$252,694
		Total liabilities and	
Total assets	$429,587	owners' equity	$429,587

GRAFFITI ADVERTISING, INC.
Balance Sheet as of December 31, 2014

Cash	$ 15,737	Accounts payable	$ 11,563
Accounts receivable	23,209	Notes payable	18,113
Inventory	25,029	Current liabilities	$ 29,676
Current assets	$ 63,975	Long-term debt	$167,200
Net fixed assets	$446,942	Owners' equity	$314,041
		Total liabilities and	
Total assets	$510,917	owners' equity	$510,917

LO 4

Challenge
(Questions 24–25)

24. Net Fixed Assets and Depreciation.   On the balance sheet, the net fixed assets (NFA) account is equal to the gross fixed assets (FA) account (which records the acquisition cost of fixed assets) minus the accumulated depreciation (AD) account (which records the total depreciation taken by the firm against its fixed assets). Using the fact that NFA = FA − AD, show that the expression given in the chapter for net capital spending, $NFA_{end} - NFA_{beg} + D$ (where D is the depreciation expense during the year), is equivalent to $FA_{end} - FA_{beg}$.

LO 3

25. Tax Rates.   Refer to the corporate marginal tax rate information in Table 2.3.

   a.   Why do you think the marginal tax rate jumps up from 34 percent to 39 percent at a taxable income of $100,001, and then falls back to a 34 percent marginal rate at a taxable income of $335,001?

   b.   Compute the average tax rate for a corporation with exactly $335,001 in taxable income. Does this confirm your explanation in part (a)? What is the average tax rate for a corporation with exactly $18,333,334? Is the same thing happening here?

   c.   Both the 39 percent and 38 percent tax rates represent what is called a tax "bubble." Suppose the government wanted to lower the upper threshold of the 39 percent marginal tax bracket from $335,000 to $200,000. What would the new 39 percent bubble rate have to be?

WHAT'S ON THE WEB?

2.1 Change in Net Working Capital.   Visit Alcoa at www.alcoa.com. Find the most recent annual report and locate the balance sheets for the past two years. Use these balance sheets to calculate the change in net working capital. How do you interpret this number?

2.2 Book Values versus Market Values.   The home page for Coca-Cola Company can be found at www.coca-cola.com. Locate the most recent annual report, which contains a balance sheet for the company. What is the book value of equity for Coca-Cola? The

www.mhhe.com/rwj

market value of a company is the number of shares of stock outstanding times the price per share. This information can be found at finance.yahoo.com using the ticker symbol for Coca-Cola (KO). What is the market value of equity? Which number is more relevant for shareholders?

2.3 Net Working Capital. Duke Energy is one of the world's largest energy companies. Go to the company's home page at www.dukeenergy.com, follow the link to the investor's page, and locate the annual reports. What was Duke Energy's net working capital for the most recent year? Does this number seem low to you given Duke's current liabilities? Does this indicate that Duke Energy may be experiencing financial problems? Why or why not?

2.4 Cash Flows to Stockholders and Creditors. Cooper Tire and Rubber Company provides financial information for investors on its website at www.coopertires.com. Follow the "Investors" link and find the most recent annual report. Using the consolidated statement of cash flows, calculate the cash flow to stockholders and the cash flow to creditors.

EXCEL *MASTER IT!* PROBLEM

Using Excel to find the marginal tax rate can be accomplished using the VLOOKUP function. However, calculating the total tax bill is a little more difficult. Below we have shown a copy of the IRS tax table for an individual from a recent year. Often, tax tables are presented in this format.

If taxable income is over . . .	But not over . . .	The tax is:
$ 0	$7,825	10% of the amount over $0
7,825	31,850	$782.50 plus 15% of the amount over $7,825
31,850	77,100	$4,386.25 plus 25% of the amount over $31,850
77,100	160,850	$15,698.75 plus 28% of the amount over $77,100
160,850	349,700	$39,148.75 plus 33% of the amount over $160,850
349,700		$101,469.25 plus 35% of the amount over $349,700

In reading this table, the marginal tax rate for taxable income less than $7,825 is 10%. If the taxable income is between $7,825 and $31,850, the tax bill is $782.50 plus the marginal taxes. The marginal taxes are calculated as the taxable income minus $7,825 times the marginal tax rate of 15%.

Below, we have the corporate tax table as shown in the textbook, as well as a taxable income.

Taxable income is greater than or equal to . . .	But less than . . .	Tax rate
$ 0	$50,000	15%
50,001	75,000	25
75,001	100,000	34
100,001	335,000	39
335,001	10,000,000	34
10,000,001	15,000,000	35
15,000,001	18,333,333	38
18,333,334		35

a. Create a tax table in Excel for corporate taxes similar to the individual tax table shown above. Your spreadsheet should then calculate the marginal tax rate, the average tax rate, and the tax bill for any level of taxable income input by a user.

b. For a taxable income of $1,350,000, what is the marginal tax rate?

c. For a taxable income of $1,350,000, what is the total tax bill?

d. For a taxable income of $1,350,000, what is the average tax rate?

CHAPTER CASE
CASH FLOWS AND FINANCIAL STATEMENTS AT SUNSET BOARDS, INC.

Sunset Boards is a small company that manufactures and sells surfboards in Malibu. Tad Marks, the founder of the company, is in charge of the design and sale of the surfboards, but his background is in surfing, not business. As a result, the company's financial records are not well maintained.

The initial investment in Sunset Boards was provided by Tad and his friends and family. Because the initial investment was relatively small, and the company has made surfboards only for its own store, the investors haven't required detailed financial statements from Tad. But thanks to word of mouth among professional surfers, sales have picked up recently, and Tad is considering a major expansion. His plans include opening another surfboard store in Hawaii, as well as supplying his "sticks" (surfer lingo for boards) to other sellers.

Tad's expansion plans require a significant investment, which he plans to finance with a combination of additional funds from outsiders plus some money borrowed from banks. Naturally, the new investors and creditors require more organized and detailed financial statements than Tad has previously prepared. At the urging of his investors, Tad has hired financial analyst Paula Wolfe to evaluate the performance of the company over the past year.

After rooting through old bank statements, sales receipts, tax returns, and other records, Paula has assembled the following information:

	2013	2014
Cost of goods sold	$169,969	$214,607
Cash	24,524	26,056
Depreciation	47,980	54,230
Interest expense	10,442	11,954
Selling & administrative expenses	33,425	43,626
Accounts payable	43,344	48,090
Net fixed assets	211,680	264,021
Sales	333,426	406,427
Accounts receivable	17,378	22,542
Notes payable	19,757	21,571
Long-term debt	106,848	119,976
Inventory	36,570	50,185
New equity	0	20,160

Sunset Boards currently pays out 50 percent of net income as dividends to Tad and the other original investors, and has a 20 percent tax rate. You are Paula's assistant, and she has asked you to prepare the following:

1. An income statement for 2013 and 2014.
2. A balance sheet for 2013 and 2014.
3. Operating cash flow for each year.
4. Cash flow from assets for 2014.
5. Cash flow to creditors for 2014.
6. Cash flow to stockholders for 2014.

www.mhhe.com/rwj

QUESTIONS

1. How would you describe Sunset Boards' cash flows for 2014? Write a brief discussion.

2. In light of your discussion in the previous question, what do you think about Tad's expansion plans?

3

Working with Financial Statements

learning objectives

After studying this chapter, you should be able to:

LO 1 Standardize financial statements for comparison purposes.

LO 2 Compute and, more important, interpret some common ratios.

LO 3 Assess the determinants of a firm's profitability and growth.

LO 4 Identify and explain some of the problems and pitfalls in financial statement analysis.

In April 2012, shares of famed orange shoe company Crocs, Inc., were trading for about $20. At that price, Crocs had a price-earnings, or PE, ratio of 16, meaning that investors were willing to pay $16 for every dollar in income earned by Crocs. At the same time, investors were willing to pay $140 for each dollar earned by online seller Amazon.com, but only a meager $8 and $9 for each dollar earned by Capital One Financial and Dell, respectively. And then there were stocks like Motorola Mobility, which, despite having no earnings (a loss actually), had a stock price of about $39 per share. Meanwhile, the average stock in the Standard and Poor's (S&P's) 500 index, which contains 500 of the largest publicly traded companies in the United States, had a PE ratio of about 16, so Crocs was average in this regard.

As we look at these numbers, an obvious question arises: Why were investors willing to pay so much for a dollar of Amazon.com earnings but so much less for a dollar earned by Dell? To understand the answer, we need to delve into subjects such as relative profitability and growth potential, and we also need to know how to compare financial and operating information across companies. By a remarkable coincidence, that is precisely what this chapter is about.

The PE ratio is just one example of a financial ratio. As we will see in this chapter, there are a wide variety of such ratios, all designed to summarize specific aspects of a firm's financial position. In addition to discussing financial ratios and what they mean, we will have quite a bit to say about who uses this information and why.

Everybody needs to understand ratios. Managers will find that almost every business characteristic, from profitability to employee productivity, is summarized in some kind of ratio. Marketers examine ratios dealing with costs, markups, and margins. Production personnel focus on ratios dealing with issues such as operating efficiency. Accountants need to understand ratios because, among other things, ratios are one of the most common and important forms of financial statement information.

In fact, regardless of your field, you may very well find that your compensation is tied to some ratio or group of ratios. Perhaps that is the best reason to study up!

In Chapter 2, we discussed some of the essential concepts of financial statements and cash flows. This chapter continues where our earlier discussion left off. Our goal here is to expand your understanding of the uses (and abuses) of financial statement information.

A good working knowledge of financial statements is desirable simply because such statements, and numbers derived from those statements, are the primary means of communicating financial information both within the firm and outside the firm. In short, much of the language of business finance is rooted in the ideas we discuss in this chapter.

In the best of all worlds, the financial manager has full market value information about all of the firm's assets. This will rarely (if ever) happen. So, the reason we rely on accounting figures for much of our financial information is that we are almost always unable to obtain all (or even part) of the market information that we want. The only meaningful yardstick for evaluating business decisions is whether or not they create economic value (see Chapter 1). However, in many important situations, it will not be possible to make this judgment directly because we can't see the market value effects.

We recognize that accounting numbers are often just pale reflections of economic reality, but they frequently are the best available information. For privately held corporations, not-for-profit businesses, and smaller firms, for example, very little direct market value information exists at all. The accountant's reporting function is crucial in these circumstances.

Clearly, one important goal of the accountant is to report financial information to the user in a form useful for decision making. Ironically, the information frequently does not come to the user in such a form. In other words, financial statements don't come with a user's guide. This chapter is a first step in filling this gap.

Company financial information can be found in many places on the web, including www.financials.com and finance.google.com.

STANDARDIZED FINANCIAL STATEMENTS

One obvious thing we might want to do with a company's financial statements is to compare them to those of other, similar companies. We would immediately have a problem, however. It's almost impossible to directly compare the financial statements for two companies because of differences in size.

For example, Ford and GM are obviously serious rivals in the auto market, but GM was historically much larger (in terms of assets), so it was difficult to compare them directly. For that matter, it's difficult to even compare financial statements from different points in time for the same company if the company's size has changed. The size problem is compounded if we try to compare GM and, say, Toyota. If Toyota's financial statements are denominated in yen, then we have a size *and* a currency difference.

ExcelMaster
coverage online

TABLE 3.1	PRUFROCK CORPORATION Balance Sheets as of December 31, 2013 and 2014 ($ in millions)		
		2013	2014
Assets			
Current assets			
Cash		$ 84	$ 98
Accounts receivable		165	188
Inventory		393	422
Total		$ 642	$ 708
Fixed assets			
Net plant and equipment		$2,731	$2,880
Total assets		$3,373	$3,588
Liabilities and Owners' Equity			
Current liabilities			
Accounts payable		$ 312	$ 344
Notes payable		231	196
Total		$ 543	$ 540
Long-term debt		$ 531	$ 457
Owners' equity			
Common stock and paid-in surplus		$ 500	$ 550
Retained earnings		1,799	2,041
Total		$2,299	$2,591
Total liabilities and owners' equity		$3,373	$3,588

To start making comparisons, one obvious thing we might try to do is to somehow standardize the financial statements. One very common and useful way of doing this is to work with percentages instead of total dollars. The resulting financial statements are called **common-size statements**. We consider these next.

common-size statement
A standardized financial statement presenting all items in percentage terms. Balance sheet items are shown as a percentage of assets and income statement items as a percentage of sales.

Common-Size Balance Sheets

For easy reference, Prufrock Corporation's 2013 and 2014 balance sheets are provided in Table 3.1. Using these, we construct common-size balance sheets by expressing each item as a percentage of total assets. Prufrock's 2013 and 2014 common-size balance sheets are shown in Table 3.2.

Notice that some of the totals don't check exactly because of rounding errors. Also notice that the total change has to be zero since the beginning and ending numbers must add up to 100 percent.

In this form, financial statements are relatively easy to read and compare. For example, just looking at the two balance sheets for Prufrock, we see that current assets were 19.7 percent of total assets in 2014, up from 19.1 percent in 2013. Current liabilities declined from 16.0 percent to 15.1 percent of total liabilities and equity over that same time. Similarly, total equity rose from 68.1 percent of total liabilities and equity to 72.2 percent.

Overall, Prufrock's liquidity, as measured by current assets compared to current liabilities, increased over the year. Simultaneously, Prufrock's indebtedness diminished as a percentage of total assets. We might be tempted to conclude that the balance sheet has grown "stronger."

IBM's website has a good guide to reading financial statements. Visit www.ibm.com/investor.

PRUFROCK CORPORATION Common-Size Balance Sheets December 31, 2013 and 2014				TABLE 3.2
	2013	2014	Change	
Assets				
Current assets				
Cash	2.5%	2.7%	+ .2%	
Accounts receivable	4.9	5.2	+ .3	
Inventory	11.7	11.8	+ .1	
Total	19.1	19.7	+ .7	
Fixed assets				
Net plant and equipment	80.9	80.3	− .7	
Total assets	100.0%	100.0%	0%	
Liabilities and Owners' Equity				
Current liabilities				
Accounts payable	9.2%	9.6%	+ .3%	
Notes payable	6.8	5.5	− 1.4	
Total	16.0	15.1	− 1.0	
Long-term debt	15.7	12.7	− 3.0	
Owners' equity				
Common stock and paid-in surplus	14.8	15.3	+ .5	
Retained earnings	53.3	56.9	+ 3.5	
Total	68.1	72.2	+ 4.1	
Total liabilities and owners' equity	100.0%	100.0%	0%	

PRUFROCK CORPORATION 2014 Income Statement ($ in millions)		TABLE 3.3
Sales	$2,311	
Cost of goods sold	1,344	
Depreciation	276	
Earnings before interest and taxes	$ 691	
Interest paid	141	
Taxable income	$ 550	
Taxes (34%)	187	
Net income	$ 363	
Dividends	$121	
Addition to retained earnings	242	

Common-Size Income Statements

A useful way of standardizing the income statement shown in Table 3.3 is to express each item as a percentage of total sales, as illustrated for Prufrock in Table 3.4.

This income statement tells us what happens to each dollar in sales. For Prufrock, interest expense eats up $.061 out of every sales dollar, and taxes take another $.081. When all is said and done, $.157 of each dollar flows through to the bottom line (net income), and that amount is split into $.105 retained in the business and $.052 paid out in dividends.

56   **PART 2**   Understanding Financial Statements and Cash Flow

TABLE 3.4

PRUFROCK CORPORATION Common-Size Income Statement 2014		
Sales		100.0%
Cost of goods sold		58.2
Depreciation		11.9
Earnings before interest and taxes		29.9
Interest paid		6.1
Taxable income		23.8
Taxes (34%)		8.1
Net income		15.7%
Dividends	5.2%	
Addition to retained earnings	10.5	

These percentages are very useful in comparisons. For example, a very relevant figure is the cost percentage. For Prufrock, $.582 of each $1.00 in sales goes to pay for goods sold. It would be interesting to compute the same percentage for Prufrock's main competitors to see how Prufrock stacks up in terms of cost control.

CONCEPT QUESTIONS

3.1a   Why is it often necessary to standardize financial statements?

3.1b   Describe how common-size balance sheets and income statements are formed.

3.2

RATIO ANALYSIS

financial ratios
Relationships determined from a firm's financial information and used for comparison purposes.

ExcelMaster
coverage online

Another way of avoiding the problems involved in comparing companies of different sizes is to calculate and compare **financial ratios**. Such ratios are ways of comparing and investigating the relationships between different pieces of financial information. We cover some of the more common ratios next, but there are many others that we don't touch on.

One problem with ratios is that different people and different sources frequently don't compute them in exactly the same way, and this leads to much confusion. The specific definitions we use here may or may not be the same as ones you have seen or will see elsewhere. If you are ever using ratios as a tool for analysis, you should be careful to document how you calculate each one, and, if you are comparing your numbers to those of another source, be sure you know how their numbers are computed.

We will defer much of our discussion of how ratios are used and some problems that come up with using them until a bit later in the chapter. For now, for each of the ratios we discuss, several questions come to mind:

1. How is it computed?
2. What is it intended to measure, and why might we be interested?
3. What is the unit of measurement?
4. What might a high or low value be telling us? How might such values be misleading?
5. How could this measure be improved?

Financial ratios are traditionally grouped into the following categories:

1. Short-term solvency, or liquidity, ratios.
2. Long-term solvency, or financial leverage, ratios.
3. Asset management, or turnover, ratios.
4. Profitability ratios.
5. Market value ratios.

We will consider each of these in turn. In calculating these numbers for Prufrock, we will use the ending balance sheet (2014) figures unless we explicitly say otherwise. Also notice that the various ratios are color keyed to indicate which numbers come from the **income statement** and which come from the **balance sheet**.

Short-Term Solvency, or Liquidity, Measures

As the name suggests, short-term solvency ratios as a group are intended to provide information about a firm's liquidity, and these ratios are sometimes called *liquidity measures*. The primary concern is the firm's ability to pay its bills over the short run without undue stress. Consequently, these ratios focus on current assets and current liabilities.

For obvious reasons, liquidity ratios are particularly interesting to short-term creditors. Since financial managers are constantly working with banks and other short-term lenders, an understanding of these ratios is essential.

One advantage of looking at current assets and liabilities is that their book values and market values are likely to be similar. Often (though not always), these assets and liabilities just don't live long enough for the two to get seriously out of step. On the other hand, like any type of near-cash, current assets and liabilities can and do change fairly rapidly, so today's amounts may not be a reliable guide to the future.

Current Ratio   One of the best-known and most widely used ratios is the *current ratio*. As you might guess, the current ratio is defined as:

$$\text{Current ratio} = \frac{\text{Current assets}}{\text{Current liabilities}} \qquad\qquad [3.1]$$

For Prufrock, the 2014 current ratio is:

$$\text{Current ratio} = \frac{\$708}{\$540} = 1.31 \text{ times}$$

Because current assets and liabilities are, in principle, converted to cash over the following 12 months, the current ratio is a measure of short-term liquidity. The unit of measurement is either dollars or times. So, we could say Prufrock has $1.31 in current assets for every $1 in current liabilities, or we could say Prufrock has its current liabilities covered 1.31 times over.

To a creditor, particularly a short-term creditor such as a supplier, the higher the current ratio, the better. To the firm, a high current ratio indicates liquidity, but it also may indicate an inefficient use of cash and other short-term assets. Absent some extraordinary circumstances, we would expect to see a current ratio of at least 1, because a current ratio of less than 1 would mean that net working capital (current assets less current liabilities) is negative. This would be unusual in a healthy firm, at least for most types of businesses.

The current ratio, like any ratio, is affected by various types of transactions. For example, suppose the firm borrows over the long term to raise money. The short-run effect would be an increase in cash from the issue proceeds and an increase in long-term debt. Current liabilities would not be affected, so the current ratio would rise.

Finally, note that an apparently low current ratio may not be a bad sign for a company with a large reserve of untapped borrowing power.

| EXAMPLE 3.1 | **CURRENT EVENTS** |

Suppose a firm were to pay off some of its suppliers and short-term creditors. What would happen to the current ratio? Suppose a firm buys some inventory. What happens in this case? What happens if a firm sells some merchandise?

The first case is a trick question. What happens is that the current ratio moves away from 1. If it is greater than 1 (the usual case), it will get bigger, but if it is less than 1, it will get smaller. To see this, suppose the firm has $4 in current assets and $2 in current liabilities for a current ratio of 2. If we use $1 in cash to reduce current liabilities, then the new current ratio is ($4 − 1)/($2 − 1) = 3. If we reverse the original situation to $2 in current assets and $4 in current liabilities, then the change will cause the current ratio to fall to 1/3 from 1/2.

The second case is not quite as tricky. Nothing happens to the current ratio because cash goes down while inventory goes up—total current assets are unaffected.

In the third case, the current ratio would usually rise because inventory is normally shown at cost, and the sale would normally be at something greater than cost (the difference is the markup). The increase in either cash or receivables is therefore greater than the decrease in inventory. This increases current assets, and the current ratio rises.

Quick (or Acid-Test) Ratio   Inventory is often the least liquid current asset. It's also the one for which the book values are least reliable as measures of market value since the quality of the inventory isn't considered. Some of the inventory may later turn out to be damaged, obsolete, or lost.

More to the point, relatively large inventories are often a sign of short-term trouble. The firm may have overestimated sales and overbought or overproduced as a result. In this case, the firm may have a substantial portion of its liquidity tied up in slow-moving inventory.

To further evaluate liquidity, the *quick*, or *acid-test, ratio* is computed just like the current ratio, except inventory is omitted:

$$\text{Quick ratio} = \frac{\text{Current assets} - \text{Inventory}}{\text{Current liabilities}} \qquad [3.2]$$

Notice that using cash to buy inventory does not affect the current ratio, but it reduces the quick ratio. Again, the idea is that inventory is relatively illiquid compared to cash. For Prufrock, this ratio in 2014 was:

$$\text{Quick ratio} = \frac{\$708 - 422}{\$540} = .53 \text{ times}$$

The quick ratio here tells a somewhat different story than the current ratio, because inventory accounts for more than half of Prufrock's current assets. To exaggerate the point, if this inventory consisted of, say, unsold nuclear power plants, then this would be a cause for concern.

To give an example of current versus quick ratios, based on recent financial statements, Walmart and Manpower, Inc., had current ratios of .88 and 1.32, respectively. However, Manpower carries no inventory to speak of, whereas Walmart's current assets are virtually all inventory. As a result, Walmart's quick ratio was only .22, whereas Manpower's was 1.32, the same as its current ratio.

Cash Ratio   A very short-term creditor might be interested in the *cash ratio*.

$$\text{Cash ratio} = \frac{\text{Cash}}{\text{Current liabilities}} \qquad [3.3]$$

You can verify that this works out to be .18 times for Prufrock.

Long-Term Solvency Measures

Long-term solvency ratios are intended to address the firm's long-run ability to meet its obligations, or, more generally, its financial leverage. These ratios are sometimes called *financial leverage ratios* or just *leverage ratios*. We consider three commonly used measures and some variations.

Total Debt Ratio   The *total debt ratio* takes into account all debts of all maturities to all creditors. It can be defined in several ways, the easiest of which is:

$$\text{Total debt ratio} = \frac{\text{Total assets} - \text{Total equity}}{\text{Total assets}}$$

$$= \frac{\$3,588 - 2,591}{\$3,588} = .28 \text{ times} \qquad [3.4]$$

In this case, an analyst might say that Prufrock uses 28 percent debt.[1] Whether this is high or low or whether it even makes any difference depends on whether or not capital structure matters, a subject we discuss in a later chapter.

Prufrock has $.28 in debt for every $1 in assets. Therefore, there is $.72 in equity (=$1 − .28) for every $.28 in debt. With this in mind, we can define two useful variations on the total debt ratio, the *debt-equity ratio* and the *equity multiplier:*

$$\text{Debt-equity ratio} = \text{Total debt}/\text{Total equity}$$

$$= \$.28/\$.72 = .39 \text{ times} \qquad [3.5]$$

$$\text{Equity multiplier} = \text{Total assets}/\text{Total equity}$$

$$= \$1/\$.72 = 1.39 \text{ times} \qquad [3.6]$$

The fact that the equity multiplier is 1 plus the debt-equity ratio is not a coincidence:

$$\text{Equity multiplier} = \text{Total assets}/\text{Total equity} = \$1/\$.72 = 1.38 \text{ times}$$

$$= (\text{Total equity} + \text{Total debt})/\text{Total equity}$$

$$= 1 + \text{Debt-equity ratio} = 1.38 \text{ times}$$

The thing to notice here is that given any one of these three ratios, you can immediately calculate the other two, so they all say exactly the same thing.

Times Interest Earned   Another common measure of long-term solvency is the *times interest earned* (TIE) *ratio*. Once again, there are several possible (and common) definitions, but we'll stick with the most traditional:

$$\text{Times interest earned ratio} = \frac{\text{EBIT}}{\text{Interest}}$$

$$= \frac{\$691}{\$141} = 4.9 \text{ times} \qquad [3.7]$$

As the name suggests, this ratio measures how well a company has its interest obligations covered, and it is often called the interest coverage ratio. For Prufrock, the interest bill is covered 4.9 times over.

Cash Coverage   A problem with the TIE ratio is that it is based on EBIT, which is not really a measure of cash available to pay interest. The reason is that depreciation, a

---

[1] Total equity here includes preferred stock (discussed in Chapter 7), if there is any. An equivalent numerator in this ratio would be (Current liabilities + Long-term debt).

noncash expense, has been deducted out. Since interest is most definitely a cash outflow (to creditors), one way to define the *cash coverage ratio* is:

$$\text{Cash coverage ratio} = \frac{\text{EBIT + Depreciation}}{\text{Interest}}$$

$$= \frac{\$691 + 276}{\$141} = \frac{\$967}{\$141} = 6.9 \text{ times}$$

[3.8]

The numerator here, EBIT plus depreciation, is often abbreviated EBITD (earnings before interest, taxes, and depreciation—say "ebbit-dee"). It is a basic measure of the firm's ability to generate cash from operations, and it is frequently used as a measure of cash flow available to meet financial obligations.

A common variation on EBITD is earnings before interest, taxes, depreciation, and amortization (EBITDA—say "ebbit-dah"). Here *amortization* refers to a noncash deduction similar conceptually to depreciation, except it applies to an intangible asset (such as a patent) rather than a tangible asset (such as a machine). Note that the word *amortization* here does not refer to the repayment of debt, a subject we discuss in a later chapter.

Asset Management, or Turnover, Measures

We next turn our attention to the efficiency with which Prufrock uses its assets. The measures in this section are sometimes called *asset utilization ratios*. The specific ratios we discuss can all be interpreted as measures of turnover. What they are intended to describe is how efficiently, or intensively, a firm uses its assets to generate sales. We first look at two important current assets: inventory and receivables.

Inventory Turnover and Days' Sales in Inventory

During the year, Prufrock had a cost of goods sold of $1,344. Inventory at the end of the year was $422. With these numbers, *inventory turnover* can be calculated as:

$$\text{Inventory turnover} = \frac{\text{Cost of goods sold}}{\text{Inventory}}$$

$$= \frac{\$1,344}{\$422} = 3.2 \text{ times}$$

[3.9]

In a sense, we sold off, or turned over, the entire inventory 3.2 times. As long as we are not running out of stock and thereby forgoing sales, the higher this ratio is, the more efficiently we are managing inventory.

If we know that we turned our inventory over 3.2 times during the year, then we can immediately figure out how long it took us to turn it over on average. The result is the average *days' sales in inventory:*

$$\text{Days' sales in inventory} = \frac{365 \text{ days}}{\text{Inventory turnover}}$$

$$= \frac{365}{3.2} = 114 \text{ days}$$

[3.10]

This tells us that, roughly speaking, inventory sits 114 days on average before it is sold. Alternatively, assuming we used the most recent inventory and cost figures, it will take about 114 days to work off our current inventory.

For example, in December 2011, the auto industry had a 49-day supply of cars and trucks. Of course, not all manufacturers had the same inventory level. At that same time, General Motors had a 67-day supply. This inventory level means that at the then current rate of sales, it would have taken General Motors 67 days to deplete the available supply, or, equivalently, that General Motors had 67 days of vehicle sales in inventory. At the same time, Mitsubishi had an 111-day supply of cars, while BMW had a mere 26-day supply. The car with the fewest days in inventory was the 2012 Nissan Leaf at four days. This type of information is useful to auto manufacturers in planning future marketing and production decisions. Historically, a 60-day supply of inventory has been considered normal in the automobile industry, so these figures pointed to manufacturing continuing at the same level, or increasing slightly, in 2012.

It might make more sense to use the average inventory in calculating turnover. Inventory turnover would then be $1,344/[($393 + 422)/2] = 3.3 times.[2] It depends on the purpose of the calculation. If we are interested in how long it will take us to sell our current inventory, then using the ending figure (as we did initially) is probably better.

In many of the ratios we discuss in the following pages, average figures could just as well be used. Again, it depends on whether we are worried about the past, in which case averages are appropriate, or the future, in which case ending figures might be better. Also, using ending figures is common in reporting industry averages; so, for comparison purposes, ending figures should be used in such cases. In any event, using ending figures is definitely less work, so we'll continue to use them.

Receivables Turnover and Days' Sales in Receivables

Our inventory measures give some indication of how fast we can sell products. We now look at how fast we collect on those sales. The *receivables turnover* is defined in the same way as inventory turnover:

$$\text{Receivables turnover} = \frac{\text{Sales}}{\text{Accounts receivable}}$$

$$= \frac{\$2,311}{\$188} = 12.3 \text{ times}$$

[3.11]

Loosely speaking, we collected our outstanding credit accounts and reloaned the money 12.3 times during the year.[3]

This ratio makes more sense if we convert it to days, so the *days' sales in receivables* is:

$$\text{Days' sales in receivables} = \frac{365 \text{ days}}{\text{Receivables turnovers}}$$

$$= \frac{365}{12.3} = 30 \text{ days}$$

[3.12]

Therefore, on average, we collect on our credit sales in 30 days. For obvious reasons, this ratio is very frequently called the *average collection period* (ACP).

Also note that if we are using the most recent figures, we can also say that we have 30 days' worth of sales currently uncollected. We will learn more about this subject when we study credit policy in a later chapter.

PAYABLES TURNOVER   EXAMPLE 3.2

Here is a variation on the receivables collection period. How long, on average, does it take for Prufrock Corporation to *pay* its bills? To answer, we need to calculate the accounts payable turnover rate using cost of goods sold. We will assume that Prufrock purchases everything on credit.

The cost of goods sold is $1,344, and accounts payable are $344. The turnover is therefore $1,344/$344 = 3.9 times. So, days' costs in payables was about 365/3.9 = 94 days. On average, then, Prufrock takes 94 days to pay. As a potential creditor, we might take note of this fact.

---

[2] Notice that we calculated the average as (Beginning value + Ending value)/2.

[3] Here we have implicitly assumed that all sales are credit sales. If they were not, then we would simply use total credit sales in these calculations, not total sales.

Total Asset Turnover   Moving away from specific accounts like inventory or receivables, we can consider an important "big picture" ratio, the *total asset turnover* ratio. As the name suggests, total asset turnover is:

$$\text{Total asset turnover} = \frac{\text{Sales}}{\text{Total assets}}$$

$$= \frac{\$2,311}{\$3,588} = .64 \text{ times}$$

[3.13]

In other words, for every dollar in assets, we generated $.64 in sales.

A closely related ratio, the *capital intensity ratio,* is simply the reciprocal of (that is, 1 divided by) total asset turnover. It can be interpreted as the dollar investment in assets needed to generate $1 in sales. High values correspond to capital-intensive industries (such as public utilities). For Prufrock, total asset turnover is .64, so, if we flip this over, we get that capital intensity is $l/.64 = $1.56. That is, it takes Prufrock $1.56 in assets to create $1 in sales.

It might seem that a high total asset turnover ratio is always a good sign for a company, but it isn't necessarily. Consider a company with old assets. The assets would be almost fully depreciated and might be very outdated. In this case, the book value of assets is low, contributing to a higher asset turnover. Plus, the high turnover might also mean that the company will need to make major capital outlays in the near future. A low asset turnover might seem bad, but it could indicate the opposite: The company could have just purchased a lot of new equipment, which implies that the book value of assets is relatively high. These new assets could be more productive and efficient than those used by the company's competitors.

The eXtensible Business Reporting Language (XBRL) is designed to make extracting EDGAR data easier. You can learn more about it at www.xbrl.org.

EXAMPLE | 3.3

MORE TURNOVER

Suppose you find that a particular company generates $.40 in sales for every dollar in total assets. How often does this company turn over its total assets?

The total asset turnover here is .40 times per year. It takes 1/.40 = 2.5 years to turn assets over completely.

Profitability Measures

The three measures we discuss in this section are probably the best known and most widely used of all financial ratios. In one form or another, they are intended to measure how efficiently the firm uses its assets and how efficiently the firm manages its operations. The focus in this group is on the bottom line—net income.

Profit Margin   Companies pay a great deal of attention to their *profit margin:*

$$\text{Profit margin} = \frac{\text{Net income}}{\text{Sales}}$$

$$= \frac{\$363}{\$2,311} = 15.7\%$$

[3.14]

This tells us that Prufrock, in an accounting sense, generates a little less than 16 cents in profit for every dollar in sales.

All other things being equal, a relatively high profit margin is obviously desirable. This situation corresponds to low expense ratios relative to sales. However, we hasten to add that other things are often not equal.

For example, lowering our sales price will usually increase unit volume, but will normally cause profit margins to shrink. Total profit (or, more importantly, operating cash flow) may go up or down, so the fact that margins are smaller isn't necessarily bad. After all, isn't it possible that, as the saying goes, "Our prices are so low that we lose money on everything we sell, but we make it up in volume!"?[4]

Return on Assets *Return on assets* (ROA) is a measure of profit per dollar of assets. It can be defined several ways, but the most common is:

$$\text{Return on assets} = \frac{\text{Net income}}{\text{Total assets}}$$

$$= \frac{\$363}{\$3,588} = 10.12\% \qquad \qquad [3.15]$$

Return on Equity *Return on equity* (ROE) is a measure of how the stockholders fared during the year. Since benefiting shareholders is our goal, ROE is, in an accounting sense, the true bottom-line measure of performance. ROE is usually measured as:

$$\text{Return on equity} = \frac{\text{Net income}}{\text{Total equity}}$$

$$= \frac{\$363}{\$2,591} = 14\% \qquad \qquad [3.16]$$

Therefore, for every dollar in equity, Prufrock generated 14 cents in profit, but, again, this is only correct in accounting terms.

Because ROA and ROE are such commonly cited numbers, we stress that it is important to remember they are accounting rates of return. For this reason, these measures should properly be called *return on book assets* and *return on book equity*. In addition, ROE is sometimes called *return on net worth*. Whatever it's called, it would be inappropriate to compare the result to, for example, an interest rate observed in the financial markets.

The fact that ROE exceeds ROA reflects Prufrock's use of financial leverage. We will examine the relationship between these two measures in more detail below.

Market Value Measures

Our final group of measures is based, in part, on information not necessarily contained in financial statements—the market price per share of the stock. Obviously, these measures can be calculated directly only for publicly traded companies.

We assume that Prufrock has 33 million shares outstanding and the stock sold for $88 per share at the end of the year. If we recall that Prufrock's net income was $363 million, then we can calculate that its earnings per share were:

$$\text{EPS} = \frac{\text{Net income}}{\text{Shares outstanding}} = \frac{\$363}{33} = \$11 \qquad \qquad [3.17]$$

Price-Earnings Ratio The first of our market value measures, the *price-earnings*, or PE, *ratio* (or multiple), is defined as:

$$\text{PE ratio} = \frac{\text{Price per share}}{\text{Earnings per share}}$$

$$= \frac{\$88}{\$11} = 8 \text{ times} \qquad \qquad [3.18]$$

In the vernacular, we would say that Prufrock shares sell for eight times earnings, or we might say that Prufrock shares have, or "carry," a PE multiple of 8.

Since the PE ratio measures how much investors are willing to pay per dollar of current earnings, higher PEs are often taken to mean that the firm has significant prospects for future growth. Of course, if a firm had no or almost no earnings, its PE would probably be quite large; so, as always, care is needed in interpreting this ratio.

---

[4]No, it's not; margins can be small, but they do need to be positive!

Price-Sales Ratio   In some cases, companies will have negative earnings for extended periods, so their PE ratios are not very meaningful. A good example is a recent start-up. Such companies usually do have some revenues, so analysts will often look at the *price-sales ratio:*

$$\text{Price-sales ratio} = \text{Price per share/Sales per share} \qquad [3.19]$$

In Prufrock's case, sales were $2,311, so here is the price-sales ratio:

$$\text{Price-sales ratio} = \$88/(\$2,311/33) = \$88/\$70 = 1.26$$

As with PE ratios, whether a particular price-sales ratio is high or low depends on the industry involved.

Market-to-Book Ratio   A second commonly quoted measure is the *market-to-book ratio:*

$$\text{Market-to-book ratio} = \frac{\text{Market value per share}}{\text{Book value per share}}$$

$$= \frac{\$88}{2,591/33} = \frac{\$88}{\$78.5} = 1.12 \text{ times} \qquad [3.20]$$

Notice that book value per share is total equity (not just common stock) divided by the number of shares outstanding.

Since book value per share is an accounting number, it reflects historical costs. In a loose sense, the market-to-book ratio therefore compares the market value of the firm's investments to their cost. A value less than 1 could mean that the firm has not been successful overall in creating value for its stockholders.

Enterprise Value–EBITDA Ratio   A company's enterprise value is an estimate of the market value of the company's operating assets. By operating assets, we mean all the assets of the firm except cash. Of course, it's not practical to work with the individual assets of a firm because market values would usually not be available. Instead, we can use the right-hand side of the balance sheet and calculate the enterprise value as

$$\begin{aligned}\text{Enterprise value} = \ &\text{Total market value of the stock} \\ &+ \text{Book value of all liabilities} - \text{Cash}\end{aligned} \qquad [3.21]$$

We use the book value for liabilities because we typically can't get the market values, at least not for all of them. However, book value is usually a reasonable approximation for market value when it comes to liabilities, particularly short-term debts. Notice that the sum of the value of the market values of the stock and all liabilities equals the value of the firm's assets from the balance sheet identity. Once we have this number, we subtract the cash to get the enterprise value.

Enterprise value is frequently used to calculate the EBITDA ratio (or multiple):

$$\text{EBITDA ratio} = \text{Enterprise value/EBITDA} \qquad [3.22]$$

This ratio is similar in spirit to the PE ratio, but it relates the value of all the operating assets (the enterprise value) to a measure of the operating cash flow generated by those assets (EBITDA).

This completes our definition of some common ratios. We could tell you about more of them, but these are enough for now. We'll leave it here and go on to discuss some ways of using these ratios instead of just how to calculate them. Table 3.5 summarizes the ratios we've discussed. Table 3.6 provides some information for the well-known home supply stores Lowe's and Home Depot for their fiscal years ending in 2011. As you can see, Home

TABLE 3.5	**Common financial ratios**

I. Short-term solvency, or liquidity, ratios

$$\text{Current ratio} = \frac{\text{Current assets}}{\text{Current liabilities}}$$

$$\text{Quick ratio} = \frac{\text{Current assets} - \text{Inventory}}{\text{Current liabilities}}$$

$$\text{Cash ratio} = \frac{\text{Cash}}{\text{Current liabilities}}$$

II. Long-term solvency, or financial leverage, ratios

$$\text{Total debt ratio} = \frac{\text{Total assets} - \text{Total equity}}{\text{Total assets}}$$

$$\text{Debt-equity ratio} = \text{Total debt} / \text{Total equity}$$

$$\text{Equity multiplier} = \text{Total assets} / \text{Total equity}$$

$$\text{Times interest earned ratio} = \frac{\text{EBIT}}{\text{Interest}}$$

$$\text{Cash coverage ratio} = \frac{\text{EBIT} + \text{Depreciation}}{\text{Interest}}$$

III. Asset utilization, or turnover, ratios

$$\text{Inventory turnover} = \frac{\text{Cost of goods sold}}{\text{Inventory}}$$

$$\text{Days' sales in inventory} = \frac{365 \text{ days}}{\text{Inventory turnover}}$$

$$\text{Receivables turnover} = \frac{\text{Sales}}{\text{Accounts receivable}}$$

$$\text{Payables turnover} = \frac{\text{Cost of goods sold}}{\text{Accounts payable}}$$

$$\text{Days' sales in receivables} = \frac{365 \text{ days}}{\text{Receivables turnover}}$$

$$\text{Days' costs in payables} = \frac{365 \text{ days}}{\text{Payables turnover}}$$

$$\text{Total asset turnover} = \frac{\text{Sales}}{\text{Total assets}}$$

$$\text{Capital intensity} = \frac{\text{Total assets}}{\text{Sales}}$$

IV. Profitability ratios

$$\text{Profit margin} = \frac{\text{Net Income}}{\text{Sales}}$$

$$\text{Return on assets (ROA)} = \frac{\text{Net income}}{\text{Total assets}}$$

$$\text{Return on equity (ROE)} = \frac{\text{Net income}}{\text{Total equity}}$$

$$\text{ROE} = \frac{\text{Net income}}{\text{Sales}} \times \frac{\text{Sales}}{\text{Assets}} \times \frac{\text{Assets}}{\text{Equity}}$$

V. Market value ratios

$$\text{Price-earnings ratio} = \frac{\text{Price per share}}{\text{Earnings per share}}$$

$$\text{Price-sales ratio} = \frac{\text{Price per share}}{\text{Sales per share}}$$

$$\text{Market-to-book ratio} = \frac{\text{Market value per share}}{\text{Book value per share}}$$

$$\text{EBITDA ratio} = \frac{\text{Enterprise value}}{\text{EBITDA}}$$

Depot has a slightly higher current ratio, debt-equity ratio, and total asset turnover. Home Depot also has higher profitability ratios. Because of its increased use of leverage and better profitability, Home Depot has a higher ROE, something we will discuss in the next section.

The price-earnings ratio is similar for Lowe's and Home Depot, although Home Depot's market-to-book ratio is almost twice as large as Lowe's. Overall, Home Depot appears to be performing better than Lowe's based on this abbreviated financial analysis. Of course, if we really want to examine these two companies, we would want to look at more ratios than the ones presented here.

CONCEPT QUESTIONS

3.2a What are the five groups of ratios? Give two or three examples of each kind.

3.2b Turnover ratios all have one of two figures as numerators. What are these two figures? What do these ratios measure? How do you interpret the results?

3.2c Profitability ratios all have the same figure in the numerator. What is it? What do these ratios measure? How do you interpret the results?

3.2d Given the total debt ratio, what other two ratios can be computed? Explain how.

	Lowe's	Home Depot
Sales	$50,208	$70,395
Net income	1,839	3,883
Current assets	10,072	14,520
Current liabilities	7,891	9,376
Total assets	33,559	40,518
Total debt	17,026	22,620
Total equity	16,533	17,898
Price per share	27.20	44.50
Book value per share	13.78	11.78
Earnings per share	1.53	2.55
Current ratio	1.28	1.55
Debt-equity ratio	1.03	1.26
Total asset turnover	1.50	1.74
Profit margin	3.66%	5.52%
ROE	11.12%	21.70%
ROA	5.48%	9.58%
Market-to-book ratio	1.97	3.78
Price-earnings ratio	17.75	17.42

TABLE 3.6

Financial information from 2011 for Lowe's and Home Depot (numbers in millions except for per-share data)

3.3 THE DUPONT IDENTITY

ExcelMaster
coverage online

As we mentioned in discussing ROA and ROE, the difference between these two profitability measures is a reflection of the use of debt financing, or financial leverage. We illustrate the relationship between these measures in this section by investigating a famous way of decomposing ROE into its component parts.

To begin, let's recall the definition of ROE:

$$\text{Return on equity} = \frac{\text{Net income}}{\text{Total equity}}$$

If we were so inclined, we could multiply this ratio by Assets/Assets without changing anything:

$$\text{Return on equity} = \frac{\text{Net income}}{\text{Total equity}} = \frac{\text{Net income}}{\text{Total equity}} \times \frac{\text{Assets}}{\text{Assets}}$$

$$= \frac{\text{Net income}}{\text{Assets}} \times \frac{\text{Assets}}{\text{Total equity}}$$

Notice that we have expressed the ROE as the product of two other ratios—ROA and the equity multiplier:

$$\text{ROE} = \text{ROA} \times \text{Equity multiplier} = \text{ROA} \times (1 + \text{Debt-equity ratio})$$

Looking back at Prufrock, for example, we see that the debt-equity ratio was .39 and ROA was 10.12 percent. Our work here implies that Prufrock's ROE, as we previously calculated, is:

$$\text{ROE} = 10.12\% \times 1.39 = 14\%$$

We can further decompose ROE by multiplying the top and bottom by total sales:

$$\text{ROE} = \frac{\text{Sales}}{\text{Sales}} \times \frac{\text{Net income}}{\text{Assets}} \times \frac{\text{Assets}}{\text{Total equity}}$$

If we rearrange things a bit, ROE is:

$$\text{ROE} = \underbrace{\frac{\text{Net income}}{\text{Sales}} \times \frac{\text{Sales}}{\text{Assets}}}_{\text{Return on assets}} \times \frac{\text{Assets}}{\text{Total equity}}$$

[3.23]

$$= \text{Profit margin} \times \text{Total asset turnover} \times \text{Equity multiplier}$$

What we have now done is to partition ROA into its two component parts, profit margin and total asset turnover. This last expression is called the **DuPont identity**, after the DuPont Corporation, which popularized its use.

We can check this relationship for Prufrock by noting that the profit margin was 15.7 percent and the total asset turnover was .64. ROE should thus be:

> **ROE = Profit margin × Total asset turnover × Equity multiplier**
>
> = .157 × .64 × 1.39
>
> = .14 = 14%

DuPont identity
Popular expression breaking ROE into three parts: operating efficiency, asset use efficiency, and financial leverage.

This 14 percent ROE is exactly what we had before.

The DuPont identity tells us that ROE is affected by three things:

1. Operating efficiency (as measured by profit margin).
2. Asset use efficiency (as measured by total asset turnover).
3. Financial leverage (as measured by the equity multiplier).

Weakness in either operating or asset use efficiency (or both) will show up in a diminished return on assets, which will translate into a lower ROE.

Considering the DuPont identity, it appears that a firm could leverage up its ROE by increasing its amount of debt. It turns out this will only happen if the ratio of EBIT to total assets is greater than the interest rate. More importantly, the use of debt financing has a number of other effects, and, as we discuss at some length in later chapters, the amount of leverage a firm uses is governed by its capital structure policy.

The decomposition of ROE we've discussed in this section is a convenient way of systematically approaching financial statement analysis. If ROE is unsatisfactory by some measure, then the DuPont identity tells you where to start looking for the reasons. To give an example, take a look at the information about Internet companies Yahoo! and Google in Table 3.7. As you can see, in 2011, Yahoo! had an ROE of 8.4 percent, up from its ROE in 2009 of 4.8 percent. In contrast, also in 2011, Google had an ROE of 16.7 percent, up from its ROE in 2009 of 15 percent. Given this information, why is Google's ROE so much higher than Yahoo!'s over this period of time, and what accounts for the increase in Yahoo!'s ROE?

Looking at the DuPont breakdown, we see that Yahoo!'s profit margin increased dramatically, from 9.3 percent to 21 percent. Google's profit margin was 25.7 percent in 2011, an increase from the level two years before. Google's total asset turnover declined, as did Yahoo!'s. Finally, Google's leverage rose slightly, while Yahoo!'s was almost constant.

Taken together, the numbers paint a relatively clear picture. Yahoo!'s ROE rose mostly because of a sharp increase in profit margins, which was offset somewhat by slight decreases in total asset turnover and leverage. Google's ROE was relatively steady. The most

Yahoo!							
Year	**ROE**	**=**	**Profit margin**	**×**	**Total asset turnover**	**×**	**Equity multiplier**
2011	8.4%	=	21.0%	×	0.337	×	1.18
2010	9.8%	=	19.5%	×	0.424	×	1.19
2009	4.8%	=	9.3%	×	0.433	×	1.20
Google							
Year	**ROE**	**=**	**Profit margin**	**×**	**Total asset turnover**	**×**	**Equity multiplier**
2011	16.7%	=	25.7%	×	0.522	×	1.25
2010	18.4%	=	29.0%	×	0.507	×	1.25
2009	15.0%	=	19.4%	×	0.686	×	1.12

TABLE 3.7

DuPont analysis for Yahoo! and Google

TABLE 3.8

FINANCIAL STATEMENTS FOR DUPONT
12 months ending December 31, 2011
(All numbers are in millions)

Income Statement		Balance Sheet			
Sales	$38,719	Current assets		Current liabilities	
CoGS	27,814	Cash	$ 4,841	Accounts payable	$ 4,816
Gross profit	$10,905	Accounts receivable	6,022	Notes payable	817
SG&A expense	4,220	Inventory	7,195	Other	5,552
R&D expense	1,956	Total	$18,058	Total	$11,185
EBIT	$ 4,729	Fixed assets	$30,434	Total long-term debt	$28,245
Interest	447			Total equity	$ 9,062
EBT	$ 4,282	Total assets	$48,492	Total liabilities and equity	$48,492
Taxes	772				
Net income	$ 3,510				

noticeable difference between the companies is Google's much higher profit margin and total asset turnover, suggesting that Google is able to generate revenues at far lower cost than Yahoo! and use its assets more efficiently, which results in a much higher ROE.

An Expanded DuPont Analysis

The regulatory filings of publicly traded corporations may be found at www.sec.gov.

So far, we've seen how the DuPont equation lets us break down ROE into its basic three components: profit margin, total asset turnover, and financial leverage. We now extend this analysis to take a closer look at how key parts of a firm's operations feed into ROE. To get going, we went to the SEC website (www.sec.gov) and found the 10-K for chemical products giant DuPont. In the 10-K, we located the financial statements for 2011. What we found is summarized in Table 3.8.

Using the information in Table 3.8, Figure 3.1 shows how we can construct an expanded DuPont analysis for DuPont and present that analysis in chart form. The advantage of the extended DuPont chart is that it lets us examine several ratios at once, thereby getting a better overall picture of a company's performance and also allowing us to determine possible items to improve.

Looking at the left-hand side of our DuPont chart in Figure 3.1, we see items related to profitability. As always, profit margin is calculated as net income divided by sales. But, as our chart emphasizes, net income depends on sales and a variety of costs, such as cost of goods sold (CoGS) and selling, general, and administrative expenses (SG&A expense). DuPont can increase its ROE by increasing sales and also by reducing one or more of these costs. In other words, if we want to improve profitability, our chart clearly shows us the areas on which we should focus.

Turning to the right-hand side of Figure 3.1, we have an analysis of the key factors underlying total asset turnover. Thus, for example, we see that reducing inventory holdings through more efficient management reduces current assets, which reduces total assets, which then improves total asset turnover.

CONCEPT QUESTIONS

3.3a   Return on assets, or ROA, can be expressed as the product of two ratios. Which two?

3.3b   Return on equity, or ROE, can be expressed as the product of three ratios. Which three?

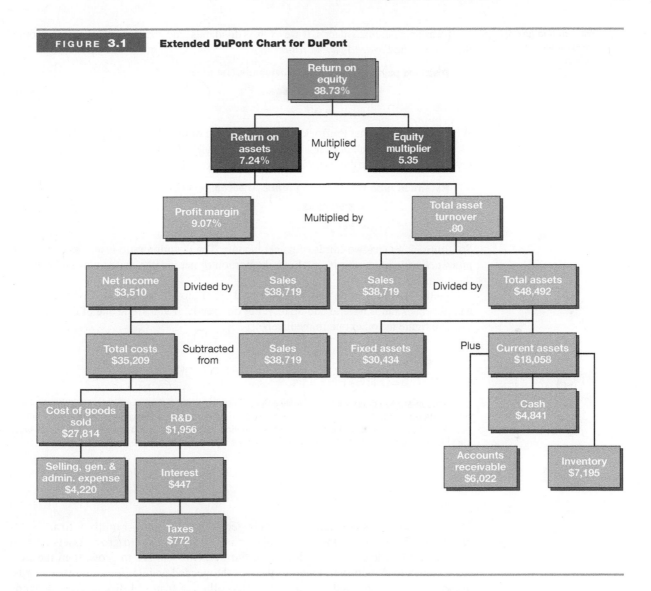

FIGURE 3.1 Extended DuPont Chart for DuPont

INTERNAL AND SUSTAINABLE GROWTH

3.4

A firm's return on assets and return on equity are frequently used to calculate two additional numbers, both of which have to do with the firm's ability to grow. We examine these next, but first we introduce two basic ratios.

Dividend Payout and Earnings Retention

As we have seen in various places, a firm's net income gets divided into two pieces. The first piece is cash dividends paid to stockholders. Whatever is left over is the addition to retained earnings. For example, from Table 3.3, Prufrock's net income was $363, of which

You can find growth rates under the research links at finance.yahoo.com.

$121 was paid out in dividends. If we express dividends paid as a percentage of net income, the result is the *dividend payout ratio:*

$$\text{Dividend payout ratio} = \text{Cash dividends/Net income}$$

$$= \$121/\$363 \qquad\qquad\qquad \textbf{[3.24]}$$

$$= 33\tfrac{1}{3}\%$$

What this tells us is that Prufrock pays out one-third of its net income in dividends.

Anything Prufrock does not pay out in the form of dividends must be retained in the firm, so we can define the *retention ratio* as:

$$\text{Retention ratio} = \text{Addition to retained earnings/Net income}$$

$$= \$242/\$363 \qquad\qquad\qquad \textbf{[3.25]}$$

$$= 66\tfrac{2}{3}\%$$

So, Prufrock retains two-thirds of its net income. The retention ratio is also known as the *plowback ratio* because it is, in effect, the portion of net income that is plowed back into the business.

Notice that net income must be either paid out or plowed back, so the dividend payout and plowback ratios have to add up to 1. Put differently, if you know one of these figures, you can figure the other one immediately.

EXAMPLE 3.4

PAYOUT AND RETENTION

The Manson-Marilyn Corporation routinely pays out 40 percent of net income in the form of dividends. What is its plowback ratio? If net income was $800, how much did stockholders actually receive?

If the payout ratio is 40 percent, then the retention, or plowback, ratio must be 60 percent since the two have to add up to 100 percent. Dividends were 40 percent of $800, or $320.

ROA, ROE, and Growth

Investors and others are frequently interested in knowing how rapidly a firm's sales can grow. The important thing to recognize is that if sales are to grow, assets have to grow as well, at least over the long run. Further, if assets are to grow, then the firm must somehow obtain the money to pay for the needed acquisitions. In other words, growth has to be financed, and as a direct corollary, a firm's ability to grow depends on its financing policies.

A firm has two broad sources of financing: *internal* and *external*. Internal financing simply refers to what the firm earns and subsequently plows back into the business. External financing refers to funds raised by either borrowing money or selling stock.

The Internal Growth Rate   Suppose a firm has a policy of financing growth using only internal financing. This means that the firm won't borrow any funds and won't sell any new stock. How rapidly can the firm grow? The answer is given by the **internal growth rate:**

internal growth rate

The maximum possible growth rate for a firm that relies only on internal financing.

$$\text{Internal growth rate} = \frac{\text{ROA} \times b}{1 - \text{ROA} \times b} \qquad\qquad \textbf{[3.26]}$$

where ROA is, as usual, return on assets, and b is the retention, or plowback, ratio we just discussed.

For example, for the Prufrock Corporation, we earlier calculated ROA as 10.12 percent. We also saw that the retention ratio is $66\frac{2}{3}$ percent, or $\frac{2}{3}$, so the internal growth rate is:

$$\text{Internal growth rate} = \frac{\text{ROA} \times b}{1 - \text{ROA} \times b}$$

$$= \frac{.1012 \times \frac{2}{3}}{1 - .1012 \times \frac{2}{3}}$$

$$= 7.23\%$$

Thus, if Prufrock relies solely on internally generated financing, it can grow at a maximum rate of 7.23 percent per year.

The Sustainable Growth Rate   If a firm only relies on internal financing, then, through time, its total debt ratio will decline. The reason is that assets will grow, but total debt will remain the same (or even fall if some is paid off). Frequently, firms have a particular total debt ratio or equity multiplier that they view as optimal (why this is so is the subject of Chapter 13).

With this in mind, we now consider how rapidly a firm can grow if (1) it wishes to maintain a particular total debt ratio and (2) it is unwilling to sell new stock. There are various reasons why a firm might wish to avoid selling stock, and equity sales by established firms are actually a relatively rare occurrence. Given these two assumptions, the maximum growth rate that can be achieved, called the **sustainable growth rate**, is:

$$\text{Sustainable growth rate} = \frac{\text{ROE} \times b}{1 - \text{ROE} \times b} \qquad [3.27]$$

Notice that this is the same as the internal growth rate, except that ROE is used instead of ROA.

Looking at Prufrock, we earlier calculated ROE as 14 percent, and we know that the retention ratio is $\frac{2}{3}$, so we can easily calculate sustainable growth as:

$$\text{Sustainable growth rate} = \frac{\text{ROE} \times b}{1 - \text{ROE} \times b}$$

$$= \frac{.14 \times \frac{2}{3}}{1 - .14 \times \frac{2}{3}}$$

$$= 10.29\%$$

sustainable growth rate
The maximum possible growth rate for a firm that maintains a constant debt ratio and doesn't sell new stock.

If you compare this sustainable growth rate of 10.29 percent to the internal growth rate of 7.23 percent, you might wonder why it is larger. The reason is that, as the firm grows, it will have to borrow additional funds if it is to maintain a constant debt ratio. This new borrowing is an extra source of financing in addition to internally generated funds, so Prufrock can expand more rapidly.

Determinants of Growth   In our previous section, we saw that the return on equity, or ROE, could be decomposed into its various components using the DuPont identity. Since ROE appears so prominently in the determination of the sustainable growth rate, the factors important in determining ROE are also important determinants of growth.

As we saw, ROE can be written as the product of three factors:

ROE = Profit margin × Total asset turnover × Equity multiplier

If we examine our expression for the sustainable growth rate, we see that anything that increases ROE will increase the sustainable growth rate by making the top bigger and the bottom smaller. Increasing the plowback ratio will have the same effect.

FINANCE MATTERS

◀ For the latest news on the topics covered in this chapter, scan here.

How Fast Is Too Fast?

Growth rates are an important tool for evaluating a company, and, as we will see later, an important tool for valuing a company's stock. When thinking about (and calculating) growth rates, a little common sense goes a long way. For example, in 2011, retailing giant Walmart had about 1.02 billion square feet of stores, distribution centers, and so forth. The company expected to expand its square footage by a little less than 5 percent over the next year. This increase doesn't sound too outrageous, but can Walmart grow its square footage at 5 percent indefinitely?

We'll get into the calculation in our next chapter, but if you assume that Walmart grows at 5 percent per year over the next 245 years, the company will have about 100 trillion square feet of property, which is about the total land mass of the entire United States! In other words, if Walmart keeps growing at 5 percent, the entire country will eventually be one big Walmart. Scary.

Research in Motion, the manufacturer of the Blackberry, is another example. The company had total revenues of about $3 billion in 2006 and $19.5 billion in 2011. This represents an annual rate of increase of 64 percent! How likely do you think it is that the company can continue this growth rate? If this growth continued, the company would have revenues of about $19.85 trillion in just 14 years, which exceeds the gross domestic product (GDP) of the United States. Obviously, Research in Motion's growth rate will slow substantially in the next several years.

What about growth in cash flow? As of the beginning of 2012, cash flow for Internet travel booking website Priceline. com grew at an annual rate of about 60 percent for the past five years. The company generated about $1.4 billion in cash flow for 2011. If Priceline.com's cash flow grew at the same rate for the next 15 years, the company would generate about $1.65 trillion dollars per year, or more than the $1.07 trillion of U.S. currency circulating in the world.

As these examples show, growth rates can be deceiving. It is fairly easy for a small company to grow very fast. If a company has $100 dollars in sales, it only has to increase sales by another $100 to have a 100 percent increase in sales. If the company's sales are $10 billion, it has to increase sales by another $10 billion to achieve the same 100 percent increase. So, long-term growth rate estimates must be chosen very carefully. As a rule of thumb, for really long-term growth estimates, you should probably assume that a company will not grow much faster than the economy as a whole, which is about 1 to 3 percent (inflation-adjusted).

Putting it all together, what we have is that a firm's ability to sustain growth depends explicitly on the following four factors:

1. **Profit margin.** An increase in profit margin will increase the firm's ability to generate funds internally and thereby increase its sustainable growth.

2. **Total asset turnover.** An increase in the firm's total asset turnover increases the sales generated for each dollar in assets. This decreases the firm's need for new assets as sales grow and thereby increases the sustainable growth rate. Notice that increasing total asset turnover is the same thing as decreasing capital intensity.

3. **Financial policy.** An increase in the debt-equity ratio increases the firm's financial leverage. Since this makes additional debt financing available, it increases the sustainable growth rate.

4. **Dividend policy.** A decrease in the percentage of net income paid out as dividends will increase the retention ratio. This increases internally generated equity and thus increases internal and sustainable growth.

The sustainable growth rate is a very useful number. What it illustrates is the explicit relationship between the firm's four major areas of concern: its operating efficiency as measured by profit margin, its asset use efficiency as measured by total asset turnover, its financial policy as measured by the debt-equity ratio, and its dividend policy as measured by the retention ratio. If sales are to grow at a rate higher than the sustainable growth rate, the firm must increase profit margins, increase total asset turnover, increase financial leverage, increase earnings retention, or sell new shares.

The two growth rates, internal and sustainable, are summarized in Table 3.9. The *Finance Matters* box above discusses some issues related to growth rates.

I. **Internal growth rate**

TABLE 3.9

Summary of internal and sustainable growth rates

Internal growth rate $= \dfrac{\text{ROA} \times b}{1 - \text{ROA} \times b}$

where

ROA = Return on assets = Net income/Total assets

b = Plowback (retention) ratio

= Addition to retained earnings/Net income

= 1 − Dividend payout ratio

The internal growth rate is the maximum growth rate that can be achieved with no external financing of any kind.

II. **Sustainable growth rate**

Sustainable growth rate $= \dfrac{\text{ROE} \times b}{1 - \text{ROE} \times b}$

where

ROE = Return on equity = Net income/Total equity

b = Plowback (retention) ratio

= Addition to retained earnings/Net income

= 1 − Dividend payout ratio

The sustainable growth rate is the maximum growth rate that can be achieved with no external equity financing while maintaining a constant debt-equity ratio.

A Note on Sustainable Growth Rate Calculations Very commonly, the sustainable growth rate is calculated using just the numerator in our expression, ROE × b. This causes some confusion, which we can clear up here. The issue has to do with how ROE is computed. Recall that ROE is calculated as net income divided by total equity. If total equity is taken from an ending balance sheet (as we have done consistently, and is commonly done in practice), then our formula is the right one. However, if total equity is from the beginning of the period, then the simpler formula is the correct one.

In principle, you'll get exactly the same sustainable growth rate regardless of which way you calculate it (as long as you match up the ROE calculation with the right formula). In reality, you may see some differences because of accounting-related complications. By the way, if you use the average of beginning and ending equity (as some advocate), yet another formula is needed. Also, all of our comments here apply to the internal growth rate as well.

A simple example is useful to illustrate these points. Suppose a firm has a net income of $20 and a retention ratio of .60. Beginning assets are $100. The debt-equity ratio is .25, so beginning equity is $80.

If we use beginning numbers, we get the following:

ROE = $20/80 = .25 = 25%
Sustainable growth = .25 × .60 = .15 = 15%

For the same firm, ending equity is $80 + .60 × $20 = $92. So, we can calculate this:

ROE = $20/92 = .2174 = 21.74%
Sustainable growth = .2174 × .60/(1 − .2174 × .60) = .15 = 15%

These growth rates are exactly the same (after accounting for a small rounding error in the second calculation). See if you don't agree that the internal growth rate is 12%.

CONCEPT QUESTIONS	
3.4a	What does a firm's internal growth rate tell us?
3.4b	What does a firm's sustainable growth rate tell us?
3.4c	Why is the sustainable growth rate likely to be larger than the internal growth rate?

3.5 | USING FINANCIAL STATEMENT INFORMATION

ExcelMaster
coverage online

Our last task in this chapter is to discuss in more detail some practical aspects of financial statement analysis. In particular, we will look at reasons for doing financial statement analysis, how to go about getting benchmark information, and some of the problems that come up in the process.

Why Evaluate Financial Statements?

As we have discussed, the primary reason for looking at accounting information is that we don't have, and can't reasonably expect to get, market value information. It is important to emphasize that, whenever we have market information, we will use it instead of accounting data. Also, if there is a conflict between accounting and market data, market data should be given precedence.

Financial statement analysis is essentially an application of "management by exception." In many cases, such analysis will boil down to comparing ratios for one business with some kind of average or representative ratios. Those ratios that seem to differ the most from the averages are tagged for further study.

Internal Uses   Financial statement information has a variety of uses within a firm. Among the most important of these is performance evaluation. For example, managers are frequently evaluated and compensated on the basis of accounting measures of performance such as profit margin and return on equity. Also, firms with multiple divisions frequently compare the performance of those divisions using financial statement information.

Another important internal use of financial statement information involves planning for the future. Historical financial statement information is very useful for generating projections about the future and for checking the realism of assumptions made in those projections.

External Uses   Financial statements are useful to parties outside the firm, including short-term and long-term creditors and potential investors. For example, we would find such information quite useful in deciding whether or not to grant credit to a new customer.

We would also use this information to evaluate suppliers, and suppliers would use our statements before deciding to extend credit to us. Large customers use this information to decide if we are likely to be around in the future. Credit-rating agencies rely on financial statements in assessing a firm's overall creditworthiness. The common theme here is that financial statements are a prime source of information about a firm's financial health.

We would also find such information useful in evaluating our main competitors. We might be thinking of launching a new product. A prime concern would be whether the competition would jump in shortly thereafter. In this case, we would be interested in our competitors' financial strength to see if they could afford the necessary development.

Finally, we might be thinking of acquiring another firm. Financial statement information would be essential in identifying potential targets and deciding what to offer.

Choosing a Benchmark

Given that we want to evaluate a division or a firm based on its financial statements, a basic problem immediately comes up. How do we choose a benchmark, or a standard of comparison? We describe some ways of getting started in this section.

Time-Trend Analysis   One standard we could use is history. Suppose we found that the current ratio for a particular firm is 2.4 based on the most recent financial statement information. Looking back over the last 10 years, we might find that this ratio has declined fairly steadily over that period.

Based on this, we might wonder if the liquidity position of the firm has deteriorated. It could be, of course, that the firm has made changes that allow it to use its current assets more efficiently, that the nature of the firm's business has changed, or that business practices have changed. If we investigate, we might find any of these possible explanations. This is an example of what we mean by management by exception—a deteriorating time trend may not be bad, but it does merit investigation.

Peer Group Analysis   The second means of establishing a benchmark is to identify firms similar in the sense that they compete in the same markets, have similar assets, and operate in similar ways. In other words, we need to identify a *peer group*. There are obvious problems with doing this since no two companies are identical. Ultimately, the choice of which companies to use as a basis for comparison is subjective.

One common way of identifying potential peers is based on **Standard Industrial Classification (SIC) codes**. These are four-digit codes established by the U.S. government for statistical reporting purposes. Firms with the same SIC code are frequently assumed to be similar.

The first digit in an SIC code establishes the general type of business. For example, firms engaged in finance, insurance, and real estate have SIC codes beginning with 6. Each additional digit narrows down the industry. So, companies with SIC codes beginning with 60 are mostly banks and banklike businesses; those with codes beginning with 602 are mostly commercial banks; and SIC code 6025 is assigned to national banks that are members of the Federal Reserve system. Table 3.10 is a list of selected two-digit codes (the first two digits of the four-digit SIC codes) and the industries they represent.

Standard Industrial Classification (SIC) code
U.S. government code used to classify a firm by its type of business operations.

Agriculture, Forestry, and Fishing	Retail Trade	**TABLE 3.10**
01 Agriculture production—crops	54 Food stores	
02 Forestry	55 Auto dealers and gas stations	**Selected two-digit SIC codes**
Mining	58 Eating and drinking places	
10 Metal mining	Finance, Insurance, and Real Estate	
13 Oil and gas extraction	60 Banking	
Construction	63 Insurance	
15 Building construction	65 Real Estate	
16 Construction other than building	Services	
Manufacturing	78 Motion pictures	
28 Chemicals and allied products	80 Health services	
29 Petroleum refining	82 Educational services	
35 Machinery, except electrical		
37 Transportation equipment		
Transportation, Communication, Electric, Gas, and Sanitary Service		
45 Transportation by air		
49 Electric, gas, and sanitary services		

Learn more about
NAICS at
www.naics.com.

Beginning in 1997, a new industry classification system was instituted. Specifically, the North American Industry Classification System (NAICS, pronounced "nakes") is intended to replace the older SIC codes, and it probably will eventually. Currently, however, SIC codes are widely used.

SIC codes are far from perfect. For example, suppose you were examining financial statements for Walmart, the largest retailer in the United States. In a quick scan of the nearest financial database, you might find about 20 large, publicly owned corporations with this same SIC code, but you might not be too comfortable with some of them. Target would seem to be a reasonable peer, but Neiman-Marcus also carries the same industry code. Are Walmart and Neiman-Marcus really comparable?

As this example illustrates, it is probably not appropriate to blindly use SIC code-based averages. Instead, analysts often identify a set of primary competitors and then compute a set of averages based on just this group. Also, we may be more concerned with a group of the top firms in an industry, not the average firm. Such a group is called an *aspirant group,* because we aspire to be like them. In this case, a financial statement analysis reveals how far we have to go.

We can now take a look at a specific industry. Suppose we are in the retail hardware business. Table 3.11 contains some condensed common-size financial statements for this industry from RMA, one of many sources of such information. Table 3.12 contains selected ratios from the same source.

There is a large amount of information here, most of which is self-explanatory. On the right in Table 3.11, we have current information reported for different groups based on sales. Within each sales group, common-size information is reported. For example, firms with sales in the $10 million to $25 million range have cash and equivalents equal to 6.5 percent of total assets. There are 36 companies in this group, out of 369 in all.

On the left, we have three years' worth of summary historical information for the entire group. For example, operating expenses rose from 34.7 percent of sales to 36.4 percent over that time.

Table 3.12 contains some selected ratios, again reported by sales groups on the right and time period on the left. To see how we might use this information, suppose our firm has a current ratio of 2. Based on the ratios, is this value unusual?

Looking at the current ratio for the overall group for the most recent year (third column from the left in Table 3.12), we see that three numbers are reported. The one in the middle, 2.8, is the median, meaning that half of the 369 firms had current ratios that were lower and half had bigger current ratios. The other two numbers are the upper and lower quartiles. So, 25 percent of the firms had a current ratio larger than 4.5 and 25 percent had a current ratio smaller than 1.6. Our value of 2 falls comfortably within these bounds, so it doesn't appear too unusual. This comparison illustrates how knowledge of the range of ratios is important in addition to knowledge of the average. Notice how stable the current ratio has been for the last three years.

EXAMPLE | 3.5

MORE RATIOS

Take a look at the most recent numbers reported for Sales/Receivables and EBIT/Interest in Table 3.12 What are the overall median values? What are these ratios?

If you look back at our discussion, you will see that these are the receivables turnover and the times interest earned, or TIE, ratios. The median value for receivables turnover for the entire group is 45.6 times. So, the days in receivables would be 365/45.6 = 8, which is the bold-faced number reported. The median for the TIE is 3.0 times. The number in parentheses indicates that the calculation is meaningful for, and therefore based on, only 336 of the 369 companies. In this case, the reason is that only 336 companies paid any significant amount of interest.

TABLE 3.11	Selected financial statement information

RETAIL—Hardware Stores   NAICS 444130

Comparative Historical Data				Current Data Sorted by Sales					

			Type of Statement				1	2	7
12	6	10	Unqualified				1	2	7
33	48	33	Reviewed		4	3	5	16	5
83	64	88	Compiled	6	37	14	20	7	4
106	121	134	Tax Returns	29	63	15	25	2	
103	98	104	Other	14	39	22	12	9	8

				43 (4/1–9/30/10)			326 (10/1/10–3/31/11)		

4/1/08–3/31/09 ALL 337	4/1/09–3/31/10 ALL 337	4/1/10–3/31/11 ALL 369	NUMBER OF STATEMENTS	0-1 MM 49	1-3MM 143	3-5MM 54	5-10MM 63	10-25MM 36	25MM & OVER 24
			Assets						
6.4%	7.2%	6.8%	Cash & Equivalents	7.0%	7.1%	6.7%	7.3%	6.5%	3.4%
10.3	10.0	8.5	Trade Receivables (net)	7.3	6.6	9.6	10.1	11.8	11.1
53.7	51.0	53.1	Inventory	55.7	55.3	47.6	52.8	48.2	54.7
2.6	1.7	2.1	All Other Current	1.2	2.1	3.0	1.6	2.5	2.2
73.0	69.9	70.4	Total Current	71.1	71.1	67.0	71.8	69.0	71.3
14.4	15.3	15.0	Fixed Assets (net)	12.9	13.7	17.4	15.1	15.9	20.0
2.3	3.9	2.7	Intangibles (net)	1.6	3.0	2.4	2.9	3.1	3.5
10.2	10.9	11.8	All Other Non-Current	14.3	12.2	13.2	10.3	12.0	5.2
100.0	100.0	100.0	Total	100.0	100.0	100.0	100.0	100.0	100.0
			Liabilities						
12.1	8.9	8.4	Notes Payable-Short Term	6.4	8.6	8.5	6.4	9.9	14.7
3.0	3.5	2.8	Cur. Mat.-L.T.D.	3.0	2.8	3.1	2.4	2.6	2.9
13.2	12.0	12.9	Trade Payables	13.4	11.2	13.2	14.8	11.9	18.6
.1	.2	.1	Income Taxes Payable	.2	.1	.1	.1	.3	.0
7.0	6.5	6.9	All Other Current	6.5	7.2	7.1	7.2	5.3	7.6
35.4	30.9	31.2	Total Current	29.5	29.9	31.9	31.0	30.0	43.8
19.8	22.7	21.0	Long-Term Debt	33.8	23.1	20.3	15.3	13.2	11.4
.1	.1	.1	Deferred Taxes	.0	.0	.1	.1	.3	.3
7.8	9.5	11.5	All Other Non-Current	27.4	12.5	4.0	7.5	8.1	5.3
36.9	36.7	36.1	Net Worth	9.2	34.5	43.6	46.2	48.4	39.2
100.0	100.0	100.0	Total Liabilities & Net Worth	100.0	100.0	100.0	100.0	100.0	100.0
			Income Data						
100.0	100.0	100.0	Net Sales	100.0	100.0	100.0	100.0	100.0	100.0
36.4	38.9	38.0	Gross Profit	41.4	38.7	39.7	34.7	36.3	34.2
34.7	37.2	36.4	Operating Expenses	42.8	37.0	37.2	32.4	34.5	32.2
1.7	1.7	1.6	Operating Profit	−1.4	1.7	2.6	2.3	1.8	2.0
.0	.0	−.2	All Other Expenses (net)	−.7	−.1	−.2	−.3	−.2	.6
1.7	1.8	1.8	Profit Before Taxes	−.7	1.8	2.7	2.7	2.1	1.4

M = $ thousand; MM = $ million.

Interpretation of Statement Studies Figures: RMA cautions that the studies be regarded only as a general guideline and not as an absolute industry norm. This is due to limited samples within categories, the categorization of companies by their primary NAICS code only, and different methods of operations by companies within the same industry. For these reasons, RMA recommends that the figures be used only as general guidelines in addition to other methods of financial analysis.

TABLE 3.12   Selected ratios

Retail—Hardware Stores   NAICS 444130

Comparative Historical Data			Type of Statement	Current Data Sorted by Sales					
12	6	10	Unqualified				1	2	7
33	48	33	Reviewed		4	3	5	16	5
83	64	88	Compiled	6	37	14	20	7	4
106	121	134	Tax Returns	29	63	15	25	2	
103	98	104	Other	14	39	22	12	9	8
				43 (4/1–9/30/10)		326 (10/1/10–3/31/11)			
4/1/08–3/31/09 ALL 337	4/1/09–3/31/10 ALL 337	4/1/10–3/31/11 ALL 369	NUMBER OF STATEMENTS	0-1MM 49	1-3MM 143	3-5MM 54	5-10MM 63	10-25MM 36	25MM & OVER 24
			Ratios						
4.2	4.9	4.5	Current	5.4	5.0	4.5	4.3	4.4	2.5
2.6	2.8	2.8		2.4	3.5	2.7	2.6	2.9	1.6
1.6	1.6	1.6		1.6	1.8	1.6	1.8	1.5	1.4
1.0	1.1	1.0	Quick	1.2	1.0	1.0	1.2	1.2	.5
.5	.5	.5		.5	.5	.4	.6	.6	.2
.2	.2	.2		.1	.2	.3	.2	.3	.1
4 81.5	5 78.7	4 98.1	Sales/ Receivables	2 146.6	3 114.4	5 80.2	4 99.2	5 79.6	4 85.4
9 39.4	10 36.7	8 45.6		10 35.8	7 50.4	8 43.7	9 41.8	9 39.3	13 27.8
22 16.4	20 18.0	18 19.9		17 21.8	13 28.3	23 15.7	27 13.5	24 15.5	20 18.7
94 3.9	95 3.8	100 3.6	Cost of Sales/ Inventory	116 3.2	110 3.3	94 3.9	87 4.2	66 5.5	90 4.1
138 2.7	141 2.6	141 2.6		191 1.9	160 2.3	121 3.0	123 3.0	118 3.1	134 2.7
185 2.0	200 1.8	187 1.9		297 1.2	207 1.8	169 2.2	153 2.4	172 2.1	168 2.2
14 26.4	14 26.6	15 24.2	Cost of Sales/ Payables	10 35.4	12 30.5	16 23.1	16 23.3	15 24.0	26 13.8
24 15.0	24 15.4	26 13.9		33 11.1	22 16.4	26 13.8	26 14.3	23 15.9	37 9.9
38 9.5	37 9.8	43 8.4		88 4.2	37 9.8	45 8.1	44 8.3	36 10.1	47 7.7
3.8	3.7	3.7	Sales/Working Capital	3.1	3.5	4.0	4.4	4.1	6.7
5.6	5.5	5.4		4.2	4.5	6.2	6.1	6.0	8.5
10.5	9.2	10.1		9.4	8.6	10.0	11.6	12.5	17.4
6.5	6.7	6.6	EBIT/Interest	5.1	6.0	10.2	7.2	7.1	7.8
(306) 2.4	(295) 2.6	(336) 3.0		(44) 1.6	(127) 3.0	(49) 3.8	(58) 3.3	(34) 3.2	2.2
.9	.5	1.0		−1.4	.7	1.2	1.7	1.9	.7
4.1	4.2	5.5	Net Profit + Depr., Dep., Amort./Cur. Mat. L/T/D		4.7				
(54) 1.7	(50) 1.6	(44) 1.6			(11) 1.4				
.4	.5	.4			.9				
.1	.1	.1	Fixed/Worth	.1	.1	.1	.1	.1	.2
.3	.3	.3		.6	.3	.3	.2	.2	.4
1.1	1.6	1.1		−.8	3.3	.7	.6	.7	1.0
.6	.6	.6	Debt/Worth	.9	.5	.4	.6	.6	1.0
1.6	1.7	1.5		5.9	1.5	1.3	1.0	1.2	1.8
4.6	7.3	5.6		−14.5	32.4	3.0	3.2	2.4	3.5
25.4	26.9	23.9	% Profit Before Taxes/ Tangible Net Worth	20.9	21.1	42.3	34.7	16.1	15.6
(289) 12.2	(280) 11.0	(311) 11.2		(30) 9.4	(112) 11.2	(50) 13.2	(61) 12.5	(35) 8.4	(23) 12.6
1.5	1.9	2.1		.4	.8	2.2	3.5	3.1	−.1

(continued)

TABLE 3.12   *(continued)*

4/1/08– 3/31/09 ALL 337	4/1/09– 3/31/10 ALL 337	4/1/10– 3/31/11 ALL 369	NUMBER OF STATEMENTS	43 (4/1–9/30/10)			326 (10/1/10–3/31/11)		
				0-1MM 49	1-3MM 143	3-5MM 54	5-10MM 63	10-25MM 36	25MM & OVER 24
9.8 4.2 −.2	9.9 4.1 −.5	9.9 4.1 .0	% Profit Before Taxes/ Total Assets	9.5 2.8 −3.9	9.0 4.4 −1.1	13.3 6.1 .3	12.2 4.8 1.3	6.8 3.5 1.1	8.1 2.4 −.9
73.0 26.0 10.2	56.5 24.4 9.7	64.1 25.3 9.8	Sales/Net Fixed Assets	79.7 31.4 9.8	68.6 26.1 9.5	61.1 17.7 8.7	49.3 25.3 12.4	33.5 23.1 10.2	37.2 21.6 9.2
3.0 2.4 1.8	2.9 2.2 1.7	2.8 2.3 1.7	Sales/Total Assets	2.4 1.9 1.3	2.8 2.3 1.7	3.0 2.3 1.7	3.0 2.5 2.0	3.0 2.3 1.9	2.8 2.6 1.7
.6 (269) 1.2 2.0	.6 (270) 1.3 2.2	.7 (283) 1.2 2.1	% Depr., Dep., Amort./ Sales	.8 (32) 1.9 3.7	.7 (103) 1.2 2.4	.7 (40) 1.2 2.0	.5 (57) 1.0 1.5	.8 (29) 1.0 1.4	.7 (22) 1.4 1.9
1.7 (197) 3.1 5.4	1.9 (201) 3.5 5.6	1.6 (220) 3.4 5.6	% Officers', Directors', Owners' Comp/Sales	4.0 (26) 6.8 9.7	1.8 (90) 3.9 5.7	1.7 (36) 3.3 4.3	1.5 (46) 2.3 5.0	1.2 (15) 2.0 3.2	
5286386M	3234499M	3274629M	Net Sales ($)	31281M	275677M	205299M	428265M	553714M	1780393M
2072674M	1496318M	1464549M	Total Assets ($)	18939M	134776M	101186M	176737M	257734M	775177M

M = $ thousand; MM = $ million.

There are many sources of ratio information in addition to the one we examine here. The *Work the Web* box on the next page shows how to get this information for just about any company, along with some very useful benchmarking information. Be sure to look it over and then benchmark your favorite company.

Problems with Financial Statement Analysis

We close out our chapter on working with financial statements by discussing some additional problems that can arise in using financial statements. In one way or another, the basic problem with financial statement analysis is that there is no underlying theory to help us identify which items or ratios to look at and to guide us in establishing benchmarks.

As we discuss in other chapters, there are many cases where financial theory and economic logic provide guidance in making judgments about value and risk. Very little such help exists with financial statements. This is why we can't say which ratios matter the most and what a high or low value might be.

One particularly severe problem is that many firms, such as General Electric (GE), are conglomerates owning more or less unrelated lines of business. The consolidated financial statements for such firms don't really fit any neat industry category. More generally, the kind of peer group analysis we have been describing is going to work best when the firms are strictly in the same line of business, the industry is competitive, and there is only one way of operating.

80   PART **2**   Understanding Financial Statements and Cash Flow

WORK THE WEB

◄ To get updated data, scan here.

As we discussed in this chapter, ratios are an important tool for examining a company's performance, but gathering the necessary information can be tedious and time consuming. Fortunately, many sites on the web provide this information for free. One of the best is investing .businessweek.com. We went there, entered the ticker symbol "GPS" (for The Gap), and then went to the ratio page. Here is an abbreviated look at the results:

CONSUMER DISCRETIONARY SECTOR | SPECIALTY RETAIL INDUSTRY   January 21, 2012 3:33 PM ET

GAP INC/THE (GPS:New York)

LAST **$18.63** USD   CHANGE TODAY **-0.74 -3.82%**   VOLUME **11.0M**   GPS On Other Exchanges ▼

As of 8:04 PM 01/20/12 All times are local (Market data is delayed by at least 15 minutes).

| Snapshot | News | Charts | Financials | Earnings | People | Ownership | Transactions | Options |

Financial Statements   Ratios   Pensions & Options   SEC Filings

Ratio data TTM as of 10/29/2011   ☐ GPS

PROFITABILITY - GAP INC/THE (GPS)

Return on Assets	13.52%	Return on Equity	27.99%
Industry Comparison		Industry Comparison	
Return on Capital	24.02%		
Industry Comparison			

Source: Reprinted by permission of *BusinessWeek*. Copyright © 2012 by the McGraw-Hill Companies, Inc.

This website is unique in that it shows the ratios compared to the industry quintile ratios. As you can see, The Gap is in the top 20th percentile for its return on assets, return on capital, and return on equity.

Questions

1. Go to *investing.businessweek.com* and find the major ratio categories listed on this website. How do the categories differ from the categories listed in the textbook?
2. Go to *investing.businessweek.com* and find all the ratios for The Gap. How is the company performing in each ratio category presented on this website?

Other websites provide different information about a company's ratios. For example, www.reuters.com provides some ratio analyses for five-year periods.

Another problem that is becoming increasingly common is that major competitors and natural peer group members in an industry may be scattered around the globe. The automobile industry is an obvious example. The problem here is that financial statements from outside the United States do not necessarily conform at all to GAAP (more precisely, different countries can have different GAAPs). The existence of different standards and procedures makes it very difficult to compare financial statements across national borders.

Even companies that are clearly in the same line of business may not be comparable. For example, electric utilities engaged primarily in power generation are all classified in the same group (SIC 4911). This group is often thought to be relatively homogeneous. However, utilities generally operate as regulated monopolies, so they don't compete with each other. Many have stockholders, and many are organized as cooperatives with no stockholders. There are several different ways of generating power, ranging from hydroelectric to nuclear, so the operating activities can differ quite a bit. Finally, profitability is strongly

FINANCE MATTERS

◄ For the latest news on the topics covered in this chapter, scan here.

What's in a Ratio?

Abraham Briloff, a well-known financial commentator, famously remarked that "financial statements are like fine perfume; to be sniffed but not swallowed." As you have probably figured out by now, his point is that information gleaned from financial statements—and ratios and growth rates computed from that information—should be taken with a grain of salt.

For example, looking back at our chapter opener regarding PE ratios, investors must really think that Amazon.com will have extraordinary growth. After all, they are willing to pay about $140 for every dollar the company currently earns, which definitely makes it look like a growth company. Looking back, from 2006 to 2011, Amazon.com's revenue increased by 28.5 percent per year, and its net income increased by 24.5 percent per year. More important, looking ahead, the well-known independent investment research company Value Line projected revenue growth of 28 percent per year and earnings growth of 27.5 percent per year over the next five years for Amazon.com.

Another problem that can occur with ratio analysis is negative equity. Let's look at corporate communications company Standard Register, for example. The company reported a loss of about $88 million dollars during 2011, and its book value of equity was negative $99 million. If you calculate the ROE for the company, you will find that it is about 89 percent, which is outstanding. Unfortunately, if

you examine the ROE a little closer you will find something unusual: The more the company loses, the higher the ROE becomes. Also, in this case, both the market-to-book and PE ratios are negative. How do you interpret a negative PE? We're not really sure either. Whenever a company has a negative book value of equity, it means the losses for the company have been so large that they have erased all the book equity. In this case, ROE, PE ratios, and market-to-book ratios are usually not reported because they lack meaning.

Even if a company's book equity is positive, you still have to be careful. For example, consider Philip Morris, which had a market-to-book ratio of about 670 at the end of the company's 2011 fiscal year. Since this ratio measures the value created by the company for shareholders, things look pretty good for the company. But a closer look shows that Philip Morris's book value of equity per share was $2.04 in 2010, but it dropped to $0.13 in 2011 even though the company posted a positive net income for the year. As it happens, the drop was due to accounting changes made by the company, not economic gains or losses, but it nonetheless dramatically increased the market-to-book ratio during this period.

Financial ratios are important tools used in evaluating companies of all types, but you cannot simply take a number as given. Instead, before doing any analysis, the first step is to ask whether the number actually makes sense.

affected by regulatory environment, so utilities in different locations can be very similar but show very different profits.

Several other general problems frequently crop up. First, different firms use different accounting procedures—for inventory, for example. This makes it difficult to compare statements. Second, different firms end their fiscal years at different times. For firms in seasonal businesses (such as a retailer with a large Christmas season), this can lead to difficulties in comparing balance sheets because of fluctuations in accounts during the year. Finally, for any particular firm, unusual or transient events, such as a one-time profit from an asset sale, may affect financial performance. In comparing firms, such events can give misleading signals. Our nearby *Finance Matters* box discusses some additional issues.

CONCEPT QUESTIONS

3.5a What are some uses for financial statement analysis?

3.5b What are SIC codes and how might they be useful?

3.5c Why do we say that financial statement analysis is management by exception?

3.5d What are some of the problems that can come up with financial statement analysis?

PRINCIPLES OF FINANCE Finance 301

SUMMARY AND CONCLUSIONS

◀ Think you've mastered the material? Scan here to take a chapter quiz.

This chapter has discussed aspects of financial statement analysis, including:

1. Standardized financial statements. We explained that differences in firm size make it difficult to compare financial statements, and we discussed how to form common-size statements to make comparisons easier.

2. Ratio analysis. Evaluating ratios of accounting numbers is another way of comparing financial statement information. We therefore defined and discussed a number of the most commonly reported and used financial ratios. We also discussed the famous DuPont identity as a way of analyzing financial performance, and we examined the connection between profitability, financial policy, and growth.

3. Using financial statements. We described how to establish benchmarks for comparison purposes and discussed some of the types of information that are available. We then examined some of the potential problems that can arise.

After you have studied this chapter, we hope that you will have some perspective on the uses and abuses of financial statements. You should also find that your vocabulary of business and financial terms has grown substantially.

 ≣connect POP QUIZ!

|FINANCE

Can you answer the following questions? If your class is using *Connect Finance,* log on to the Self-Quiz and Study feature in the Library tab to see if you know the answers to these and other questions, check out the study tools, and find out what topics require additional practice!

Section 3.1 A common-size balance sheet expresses all accounts as a percentage of what?

Section 3.2 Hahn's Pianos has a profit margin of 6.65 percent on sales of $23,200,000. Assume the firm has debt of $9,000,000 and total assets of $15,600,000. What is the firm's ROA?

Section 3.3 The Delson Company has an ROA of 8.8 percent, an 8.50 percent profit margin, and an ROE of 14.50 percent. What is the company's total asset turnover?

Section 3.4 Assume Mudvayne Inc. has a 7.1 percent ROA and a 23 percent payout ratio. What is the internal growth rate?

Section 3.5 What term applies to the comparison of a current financial ratio to the historical values of that ratio?

CHAPTER REVIEW AND SELF-TEST PROBLEMS

3.1   **Common-Size Statements.** Below are the most recent financial statements for Wildhack. Prepare a common-size income statement based on this information. How do you interpret the standardized net income? What percentage of sales goes to cost of goods sold? (See Problem 15.)

www.mhhe.com/rwj

WILDHACK CORPORATION
2014 Income Statement
($ in millions)

Sales	$3,756
Cost of goods sold	2,453
Depreciation	490
Earnings before interest and taxes	$ 813
Interest paid	613
Taxable income	$ 200
Taxes (34%)	68
Net income	$ 132

Dividends	$46
Addition to retained earnings	86

WILDHACK CORPORATION
Balance Sheets as of December 31, 2013 and 2014
($ in millions)

Assets	2013	2014	Liabilities and Owners' Equity	2013	2014
Current assets			Current liabilities		
Cash	$ 120	$ 88	Accounts payable	$ 124	$ 144
Accounts receivable	224	192	Notes payable	1,412	1,039
Inventory	424	368	Total	$1,536	$1,183
Total	$ 768	$ 648	Long-term debt	$1,804	$2,077
Fixed assets			Owners' equity		
Net plant			Common stock		
and equipment	$5,228	$5,354	and paid-in surplus	$ 300	$ 300
			Retained earnings	2,356	2,442
Total assets	$5,996	$6,002	Total	$2,656	$2,742
			Total liabilities		
			and owners' equity	$5,996	$6,002

3.2 Financial Ratios. Based on the balance sheets and income statement in the previous problem, calculate the following ratios for 2014: (See Problem 35.)

Current ratio	_____
Quick ratio	_____
Cash ratio	_____
Inventory turnover	_____
Receivables turnover	_____
Days' sales in inventory	_____
Days' sales in receivables	_____
Total debt ratio	_____
Times interest earned ratio	_____
Cash coverage ratio	_____

www.mhhe.com/rwj

3.3   ROE and the DuPont Identity.   Calculate the 2014 ROE for the Wildhack Corporation and then break down your answer into its component parts using the DuPont identity. (See Problem 36.)

3.4   Sustainable Growth.   Based on the following information, what growth rate can Corwin maintain if no external financing is used? What is the sustainable growth rate? (See Problems 20, 21.)

CORWIN COMPANY
Financial Statements

Income Statement		Balance Sheet			
Sales	$2,750	Current assets	$ 600	Long-term debt	$ 200
Cost of sales	2,400	Net fixed assets	800	Equity	1,200
Tax (34%)	119	Total	$1,400	Total	$1,400
Net income	$ 231				
Dividends	$ 77				

■ Answers to Chapter Review and Self-Test Problems

3.1   We've calculated the common-size income statement below. Remember that we simply divide each item by total sales.

WILDHACK CORPORATION
2014 Common-Size Income Statement

Sales	100.0%
Cost of goods sold	65.3
Depreciation	13.0
Earnings before interest and taxes	21.6
Interest paid	16.3
Taxable income	5.3
Taxes (34%)	1.8
Net income	3.5%
Dividends	1.2%
Addition to retained earnings	2.3

Net income is 3.5 percent of sales. Since this is the percentage of each sales dollar that makes its way to the bottom line, the standardized net income is the firm's profit margin. Cost of goods sold is 65.3 percent of sales.

3.2   We've calculated the ratios below based on the ending figures. If you don't remember a definition, refer back to Table 3.5.

Current ratio	$648/$1,183	= .55 times
Quick ratio	$280/$1,183	= .24 times
Cash ratio	$88/$1,183	= .07 times
Inventory turnover	$2,453/$368	= 6.7 times
Receivables turnover	$3,756/$192	= 19.6 times
Days' sales in inventory	365/6.7	= 54.5 days
Days' sales in receivables	365/19.6	= 18.6 days

Total debt ratio	$3,260/$6,002	= 54.3%
Times interest earned ratio	$813/$613	= 1.33 times
Cash coverage ratio	$1,303/$613	= 2.13 times

3.3 The return on equity is the ratio of net income to total equity. For Wildhack, this is $132/$2,742 = 4.8%, which is not outstanding. Given the DuPont identity, ROE can be written as:

ROE = Profit margin × Total asset turnover × Equity multiplier

= $132/$3,756 ×	$3,756/$6,002 ×	$6,002/$2,742
= 3.5% ×	.626 ×	2.19
= 4.8%		

Notice that return on assets, ROA, is 3.5% × .626 = 2.2%.

3.4 Corwin retains $b = (1 - .33) = \frac{2}{3} \approx .67$ of net income. Return on assets is $231/$1,400 = 16.5%. The internal growth rate is:

$$\frac{\text{ROA} \times b}{1 - \text{ROA} \times b} = \frac{.165 \times \frac{2}{3}}{1 - .165 \times \frac{2}{3}} = 12.36\%$$

Return on equity for Corwin is $231/$1,200 = 19.25%, so we can calculate the sustainable growth rate as:

$$\frac{\text{ROE} \times b}{1 - \text{ROE} \times b} = \frac{.1925 \times \frac{2}{3}}{1 - .1925 \times \frac{2}{3}} = 14.72\%$$

CRITICAL THINKING AND CONCEPTS REVIEW

LO 2 **3.1** **Current Ratio.**   What effect would the following actions have on a firm's current ratio? Assume that net working capital is positive.

    a. Inventory is purchased.

    b. A supplier is paid.

    c. A short-term bank loan is repaid.

    d. A long-term debt is paid off early.

    e. A customer pays off a credit account.

    f. Inventory is sold at cost.

    g. Inventory is sold for a profit.

LO 2 **3.2** **Current Ratio and Quick Ratio.**   In recent years, Dixie Co. has greatly increased its current ratio. At the same time, the quick ratio has fallen. What has happened? Has the liquidity of the company improved?

LO 2 **3.3** **Current Ratio.**   Explain what it means for a firm to have a current ratio equal to .50. Would the firm be better off if the current ratio were 1.50? What if it were 15.0? Explain your answers.

LO 2 **3.4** **Financial Ratios.**   Fully explain the kind of information the following financial ratios provide about a firm:

    a. Quick ratio

    b. Cash ratio

    c. Capital intensity ratio

    d. Total asset turnover

    e. Equity multiplier

www.mhhe.com/rwj

PART **2** Understanding Financial Statements and Cash Flow

f. Times interest earned ratio

g. Profit margin

h. Return on assets

i. Return on equity

j. Price-earnings ratio

LO 1 3.5 **Standardized Financial Statements.** What types of information do common-size financial statements reveal about the firm? What is the best use for these common-size statements?

LO 2 3.6 **Peer Group Analysis.** Explain what peer group analysis means. As a financial manager, how could you use the results of peer group analysis to evaluate the performance of your firm? How is a peer group different from an aspirant group?

LO 3 3.7 **DuPont Identity.** Why is the DuPont identity a valuable tool for analyzing the performance of a firm? Discuss the types of information it reveals as compared to ROE considered by itself.

LO 2 3.8 **Industry-Specific Ratios.** Specialized ratios are sometimes used in specific industries. For example, the so-called book-to-bill ratio is closely watched for semiconductor manufacturers. A ratio of .93 indicates that for every $100 worth of chips shipped over some period, only $93 worth of new orders were received. In December 2011, the North American semiconductor equipment industry's book-to-bill ratio was .88, with orders of $1.298 billion and billings of $1.512 billion. The most recent peak in the book-to-bill ratio was in February 2010 when it reached 1.23. The most recent low occurred in January 2009 when it reached .47. What is this ratio intended to measure? Why do you think it is so closely followed?

LO 2 3.9 **Industry-Specific Ratios.** So-called same-store sales are a very important measure for companies as diverse as McDonald's and Sears. As the name suggests, examining same-store sales means comparing revenues from the same stores or restaurants at two different points in time. Why might companies focus on same-store sales rather than total sales?

LO 2 3.10 **Industry-Specific Ratios.** There are many ways of using standardized financial information beyond those discussed in this chapter. The usual goal is to put firms on an equal footing for comparison purposes. For example, for auto manufacturers, it is common to express sales, costs, and profits on a per-car basis. For each of the following industries, give an example of an actual company and discuss one or more potentially useful means of standardizing financial information:

a. Public utilities

b. Large retailers

c. Airlines

d. Online services

e. Hospitals

f. College textbook publishers

LO 2 3.11 **Financial Statement Analysis.** You are examining the common-size income statements for a company for the past five years and have noticed that the cost of goods as a percentage of sales has been increasing steadily. At the same time, EBIT as a percentage of sales has been decreasing. What might account for the trends in these ratios?

LO 2 3.12 **Financial Statement Analysis.** In the previous question, what actions might managers take to improve these ratios?

QUESTIONS AND PROBLEMS

FINANCE

Select problems are available in McGraw-Hill *Connect.* Please see the packaging options section of the preface for more information.

LO 2   **1. Calculating Liquidity Ratios.**   SDJ, Inc., has net working capital of $1,730, current liabilities of $5,140, and inventory of $2,170. What is the current ratio? What is the quick ratio?

Basic
(Questions 1–26)

LO 2   **2. Calculating Profitability Ratios.**   Remi, Inc., has sales of $15 million, total assets of $9 million, and total debt of $3.7 million. If the profit margin is 7 percent, what is net income? What is ROA? What is ROE?

LO 2   **3. Calculating the Average Collection Period.**   Pujols Lumber Yard has a current accounts receivable balance of $527,167. Credit sales for the year just ended were $5,938,261. What is the receivables turnover? The days' sales in receivables? How long did it take on average for credit customers to pay off their accounts during the past year?

LO 2   **4. Calculating Inventory Turnover.**   Bobaflex Corporation has ending inventory of $426,163 and cost of goods sold for the year just ended was $6,238,615. What is the inventory turnover? The days' sales in inventory? How long on average did a unit of inventory sit on the shelf before it was sold?

LO 2   **5. Calculating Leverage Ratios.**   Allen, Inc., has a total debt ratio of .34. What is its debt-equity ratio? What is its equity multiplier?

LO 2   **6. Calculating Market Value Ratios.**   Rossdale, Inc., had additions to retained earnings for the year just ended of $575,000. The firm paid out $140,000 in cash dividends, and it has ending total equity of $7.3 million. If the company currently has 490,000 shares of common stock outstanding, what are earnings per share? Dividends per share? What is book value per share? If the stock currently sells for $47 per share, what is the market-to-book ratio? The price-earnings ratio? If total sales were $15.4 million, what is the price-sales ratio?

LO 3   **7. DuPont Identity.**   If jPhone, Inc., has an equity multiplier of 1.65, total asset turnover of 1.8, and a profit margin of 6 percent, what is its ROE?

LO 3   **8. DuPont Identity.**   Jiminy Cricket Removal has a profit margin of 8 percent, total asset turnover of 1.24, and ROE of 14.30 percent. What is this firm's debt-equity ratio?

LO 2   **9. Calculating Average Payables Period.**   For the past year, Hero, Inc., had a cost of goods sold of $75,382. At the end of the year, the accounts payable balance was $15,732. How long on average did it take the company to pay off its suppliers during the year? What might a large value for this ratio imply?

LO 2   **10. Equity Multiplier and Return on Equity.**   Rainbow Company has a debt-equity ratio of .95. Return on assets is 7.5 percent, and total equity is $735,000. What is the equity multiplier? Return on equity? Net income?

LO 3   **11. Internal Growth.**   If Nuber, Inc., has an ROA of 8 percent and a payout ratio of 25 percent, what is its internal growth rate?

LO 3   **12. Sustainable Growth.**   If the Crash Davis Driving School has an ROE of 14.5 percent and a payout ratio of 30 percent, what is its sustainable growth rate?

LO 3   **13. Sustainable Growth.**   Based on the following information, calculate the sustainable growth rate for Northern Lights Co.:

$$
\begin{aligned}
\text{Profit margin} &= 10.4\% \\
\text{Capital intensity ratio} &= .60 \\
\text{Debt-equity ratio} &= .55 \\
\text{Net income} &= \$115{,}000 \\
\text{Dividends} &= \$55{,}000
\end{aligned}
$$

LO 3

14. Sustainable Growth. Assuming the following ratios are constant, what is the sustainable growth rate?

$$\text{Total asset turnover} = 1.35$$
$$\text{Profit margin} = 5.7\%$$
$$\text{Equity multiplier} = 1.47$$
$$\text{Payout ratio} = 40\%$$

Bethesda Mining Company reports the following balance sheet information for 2013 and 2014. Use this information to work Problems 15 through 17.

BETHESDA MINING COMPANY
Balance Sheets as of December 31, 2013 and 2014

Assets	2013	2014	Liabilities and Owners' Equity	2013	2014
Current assets			Current liabilities		
Cash	$ 21,396	$ 24,385	Accounts payable	$214,414	$192,480
Accounts receivable	51,552	58,318	Notes payable	99,022	134,508
Inventory	121,807	143,615	Total	$313,436	$326,988
Total	$194,755	$226,318	Long-term debt	$271,700	$285,300
			Owners' equity		
			Common stock and paid-in surplus	$200,000	$200,000
Fixed assets			Accumulated retained earnings	132,481	171,358
Net plant and equipment	$722,862	$757,328	Total	$332,481	$371,358
Total assets	$917,617	$983,646	Total liabilities and owners' equity	$917,617	$983,646

LO 1   **15. Preparing Standardized Financial Statements.** Prepare the 2013 and 2014 common-size balance sheets for Bethesda Mining.

LO 2   **16. Calculating Financial Ratios.** Based on the balance sheets given for Bethesda Mining, calculate the following financial ratios for each year:

    a. Current ratio

    b. Quick ratio

    c. Cash ratio

    d. Debt-equity ratio and equity multiplier

    e. Total debt ratio

LO 3   **17. DuPont Identity.** Suppose that the Bethesda Mining Company had sales of $2,945,376 and net income of $89,351 for the year ending December 31, 2014. Calculate the DuPont identity.

LO 3   **18. DuPont Identity.** The Cavo Company has an ROA of 9 percent, a profit margin of 6 percent, and an ROE of 17 percent. What is the company's total asset turnover? What is the equity multiplier?

LO 2   **19. Return on Assets.** Beckinsale, Inc., has a profit margin of 5.8 percent on sales of $16,000,000. If the firm has debt of $7,900,000 and total assets of $14,000,000, what is the firm's ROA?

LO 3   **20. Calculating Internal Growth.** The most recent financial statements for Shinoda Manufacturing Co. are shown below:

Income Statement		Balance Sheet			
Sales	$75,300	Current assets	$ 27,000	Debt	$ 37,200
Costs	55,380	Fixed assets	89,300	Equity	79,100
Taxable income	$19,920	Total	$116,300	Total	$116,300
Tax (35%)	6,972				
Net Income	$12,948				

Assets and costs are proportional to sales. Debt and equity are not. The company maintains a constant 40 percent dividend payout ratio. No external financing is possible. What is the internal growth rate?

LO 3 **21. Calculating Sustainable Growth.** For Shinoda Manufacturing in Problem 20, what is the sustainable growth rate?

LO 2 **22. Total Asset Turnover.** Kaleb's Karate Supply had a profit margin of 8.5 percent, sales of $16 million, and total assets of $6.8 million. What was total asset turnover? If management set a goal of increasing total asset turnover to 2.75 times, what would the new sales figure need to be, assuming no increase in total assets?

LO 2 **23. Return on Equity.** Martinez, Inc., has a total debt ratio of .65, total debt of $345,000, and net income of $31,280. What is the company's return on equity?

LO 2 **24. Market Value Ratios.** Mustaine, Inc., has a current stock price of $54. For the past year, the company had net income of $7,900,000, total equity of $26,300,000, sales of $50,500,000, and 4.1 million shares of stock outstanding. What are earnings per share (EPS)? Price-earnings ratio? Price-sales ratio? Book value per share? Market-to-book ratio?

LO 3 **25. Profit Margin.** Dimeback Co. has total assets of $8,500,000 and a total asset turnover of 1.8 times. If the return on assets is 8.5 percent, what is its profit margin?

LO 2 **26. Enterprise Value–EBITDA Multiple.** The market value of the equity of Thompson, Inc., is $580,000. The balance sheet shows $35,000 in cash and $190,000 in debt, while the income statement has EBIT of $91,000 and a total of $135,000 in depreciation and amortization. What is the enterprise value–EBITDA multiple for this company?

LO 3 **27. Using the DuPont Identity.** Y3K, Inc., has sales of $9,310, total assets of $4,390, and a debt-equity ratio of .25. If its return on equity is 15 percent, what is its net income?

Intermediate
(Questions 27–46)

LO 2 **28. Ratios and Fixed Assets.** The Hooya Company has a long-term debt ratio (i.e., the ratio of long-term debt to long-term debt plus equity) of .45 and a current ratio of 1.30. Current liabilities are $2,435, sales are $11,610, profit margin is 9 percent, and ROE is 12.8 percent. What is the amount of the firm's net fixed assets?

LO 2 **29. Profit Margin.** In response to complaints about high prices, a grocery chain runs the following advertising campaign: "If you pay your child $2 to go buy $50 worth of groceries, then your child makes twice as much on the trip as we do." You've collected the following information from the grocery chain's financial statements:

(millions)	
Sales	$840.00
Net income	16.80
Total assets	385.00
Total debt	263.50

Evaluate the grocery chain's claim. What is the basis for the statement? Is this claim misleading? Why or why not?

LO 3

30. Using the DuPont Identity. The Rose Company has net income of $153,210. There are currently 28.32 days' sales in receivables. Total assets are $863,000, total receivables are $157,310, and the debt-equity ratio is .35. What is the company's profit margin? Its total asset turnover? Its ROE?

LO 2

31. Calculating the Cash Coverage Ratio. Delectable Turnip, Inc.'s, net income for the most recent year was $7,638. The tax rate was 34 percent. The firm paid $3,816 in total interest expense and deducted $4,873 in depreciation expense. What was the company's cash coverage ratio for the year?

LO 2

32. Calculating the Times Interest Earned Ratio. For the most recent year, Seether, Inc., had sales of $465,000, cost of goods sold of $208,730, depreciation expense of $60,400, and additions to retained earnings of $72,800. The firm currently has 20,000 shares of common stock outstanding, and the previous year's dividends per share were $1.35. Assuming a 34 percent income tax rate, what was the times interest earned ratio?

LO 2

33. Return on Assets. A fire has destroyed a large percentage of the financial records of the Inferno Company. You have the task of piecing together information in order to release a financial report. You have found the return on equity to be 14.3 percent. Sales were $1,840,000, the total debt ratio was .45, and total debt was $673,000. What is the return on assets (ROA)?

LO 2

34. Ratios and Foreign Companies. Prince Albert Canning PLC had a net loss of £32,817 on sales of £512,621. What was the company's profit margin? Does the fact that these figures are quoted in a foreign currency make any difference? Why? In dollars, sales were $785,802. What was the net loss in dollars?

Some recent financial statements for Smolira Golf, Inc., follow. Use this information to work Problems 35 through 38.

SMOLIRA GOLF, INC.
Balance Sheets as of December 31, 2013 and 2014

	2013	2014		2013	2014
Assets			**Liabilities and Owners' Equity**		
Current assets			Current liabilities		
Cash	$ 4,607	$ 4,910	Accounts payable	$ 3,413	$ 3,846
Accounts receivable	6,702	8,149	Notes payable	2,768	3,416
Inventory	17,357	19,350	Other	138	165
Total	$28,666	$ 32,409	Total	$ 6,319	$ 7,427
			Long-term debt	$22,500	$ 19,000
			Owners' equity		
			Common stock		
			and paid-in surplus	$38,000	$ 38,000
Fixed assets			Accumulated retained earnings	20,535	44,792
Net plant and equipment	58,688	76,810	Total	$58,535	$ 82,792
Total assets	$87,354	$109,219	Total liabilities and owners' equity	$87,354	$109,219

SMOLIRA GOLF, INC.
2014 Income Statement

Sales	$205,227
Cost of goods sold	138,383
Depreciation	5,910
EBIT	$ 60,934
Interest paid	1,617
Taxable income	$ 59,317
Taxes	20,760
Net income	$ 38,557

Dividends	$14,300	
Retained earnings	24,257	

LO 2

35. Calculating Financial Ratios. Find the following financial ratios for Smolira Golf (use year-end figures rather than average values where appropriate):

Short-term solvency ratios

   a. Current ratio _____

   b. Quick ratio _____

   c. Cash ratio _____

Asset utilization ratios

   d. Total asset turnover _____

   e. Inventory turnover _____

   f. Receivables turnover _____

Long-term solvency ratios

   g. Total debt ratio _____

   h. Debt-equity ratio _____

   i. Equity multiplier _____

   j. Times interest earned ratio _____

   k. Cash coverage ratio _____

Profitability ratios

   l. Profit margin _____

   m. Return on assets _____

   n. Return on equity _____

LO 3

36. DuPont Identity. Construct the DuPont identity for Smolira Golf.

LO 2

37. Market Value Ratios. Smolira Golf has 10,000 shares of common stock outstanding, and the market price for a share of stock at the end of 2014 was $73. What is the price-earnings ratio? What is the price-sales ratio? What are the dividends per share? What is the market-to-book ratio at the end of 2014?

LO 2

38. Interpreting Financial Ratios. After calculating the ratios for Smolira Golf, you have uncovered the following industry ratios for 2014:

	Lower Quartile	Median	Upper Quartile
Current ratio	1.3	2.6	5.3
Total asset turnover	2.1	2.7	4.1
Debt-equity ratio	.25	.50	.60
Profit margin	8.4%	11.9%	16.3%

PART 2   Understanding Financial Statements and Cash Flow

How is Smolira Golf performing based on these ratios?

LO 3   **39. Growth and Profit Margin.**   Fulkerson Manufacturing wishes to maintain a sustainable growth rate of 8 percent a year, a debt-equity ratio of .65, and a dividend payout ratio of 30 percent. The ratio of total assets to sales is constant at 1.25. What profit margin must the firm achieve?

LO 2   **40. Market Value Ratios.**   Abercrombie & Fitch and ANN, INC., owner of Ann Taylor stores, reported the following numbers (in millions) for fiscal year 2011. Calculate the earnings per share, market-to-book ratio, and price-earnings ratio for each company.

	Abercrombie	**ANN, INC.**
Net income	$ 127.658	$ 86.566
Shares outstanding	84.72	48.34
Stock price	$ 47.06	$ 24.43
Total equity	$1,862.456	$363.877

LO 3   **41. Growth and Assets.**   A firm wishes to maintain an internal growth rate of 7.1 percent and a dividend payout ratio of 25 percent. The current profit margin is 5.7 percent and the firm uses no external financing sources. What must total asset turnover be?

LO 3   **42. Sustainable Growth.**   Based on the following information, calculate the sustainable growth rate for Perks, Inc.:

Profit margin = 5.2%

Total asset turnover = 1.90

Total debt ratio =   .30

Payout ratio = 15%

What is the ROA here?

LO 3   **43. Sustainable Growth and Outside Financing.**   You've collected the following information about Erna, Inc.:

Sales = $275,000

Net income = $19,000

Dividends = $8,100

Total debt = $67,000

Total equity = $91,000

What is the sustainable growth rate for the company? If it does grow at this rate, how much new borrowing will take place in the coming year, assuming a constant debt-equity ratio? What growth rate could be supported with no outside financing at all?

LO 4   **44. Constraints on Growth.**   High Flyer, Inc., wishes to maintain a growth rate of 13 percent per year and a debt-equity ratio of .35. The profit margin is 6 percent, and total asset turnover is constant at 1.10. Is this growth rate possible? To answer, determine what the dividend payout ratio must be. How do you interpret the result?

LO 3   **45. Internal and Sustainable Growth Rates.**   Best Buy reported the following numbers (in millions) for the years ending February 2011 and 2012. What are the internal and sustainable growth rates? What are the internal and sustainable growth rates using ROE × b and (ROA × b) and the end of period equity (assets)? What are the growth rates if you use the beginning of period equity in this equation? Why aren't the growth rates the same? What is your best estimate of the internal and sustainable growth rates?

	2011	2012
Net income		$ 1,277
Dividends		237
Total assets	$18,302	17,849
Total equity	6,302	6,602

LO 3

46. Expanded DuPont Identity. Hershey Co. reported the following income statement and balance sheet (in millions) for 2011. Construct the expanded DuPont identity similar to Figure 3.1. What is the company's return on equity?

Income Statement

Sales	$6,080.788
CoGS	3,548.896
Other costs	1,288.373
Depreciation	188.491
EBIT	$1,055.028
Interest	92.183
EBT	$ 962.845
Taxes	333.883
Net income	$ 628.962

Balance Sheet

Assets		Liabilities & Equity	
Current assets		Current liabilities	$1,173.775
Cash	$ 693.686		
Accounts receivable	703.919	Long-term debt	$3,539.551
Inventory	648.953		
Total	$2,046.558	Shareholders'	
Fixed assets	$3,539.416	equity	$ 872.648
		Total liabilities and	
		shareholders'	
Total assets	$5,585.974	equity	$5,585.974

3.1 DuPont Identity. You can find financial statements for Walt Disney Company at Disney's home page, thewaltdisneycompany.com. For the three most recent years, calculate the DuPont identity for Disney. How has ROE changed over this period? How have changes in each component of the DuPont identity affected ROE over this period?

3.2 Ratio Analysis. You want to examine the financial ratios for Dell Inc. Go to www.reuters.com and type in the ticker symbol for the company (DELL). Next, go to the financials link. You should find financial ratios for Dell and the industry, sector, and S&P 500 averages for each ratio.

a. What do TTM and MRQ mean?

b. How do Dell's recent profitability ratios compare to their values over the past five years? To the industry averages? To the sector averages? To the S&P 500 averages? Which is the better comparison group for Dell: the industry, sector, or S&P 500 averages? Why?

c. In what areas does Dell seem to outperform its competitors based on the financial ratios? Where does Dell seem to lag behind its competitors?

d. Dell's inventory turnover ratio is much larger than that for all comparison groups. Why do you think this is?

WHAT'S ON THE WEB?

www.mhhe.com/rwj

3.3 Standardized Financial Statements.   Go to www.att.com and find the income statements and balance sheets for the two most recent years at this link. Using this information, prepare the common-size income statements and balance sheets for the two years.

3.4 Asset Utilization Ratios.   Find the most recent financial statements for Walmart at www.walmart.com and Boeing at www.boeing.com. Calculate the asset utilization ratio for these two companies. What does this ratio measure? Is the ratio similar for both companies? Why or why not?

EXCEL *MASTER IT!* PROBLEM

The exTensible Business Reporting Language (XBRL) is likely the future of financial reporting. XBRL is a computer language that "tags" each item and specifies what that item is. XBRL reporting has already been adopted for use in Australia, Japan, and the United Kingdom. As of early 2009, a Securities and Exchange Commission advisory committee has recommended that U.S. companies be required to submit financial reports to the SEC in XBRL format. It has been suggested to require that XBRL be gradually implemented, so it could be several years before we see all companies file XBRL financial reports. All listed U.S. companies file electronic reports with the SEC, but the reports are only available in html or text format. XBRL reporting will allow investors to quickly download financial statements for analysis.

Currently, several companies voluntarily submit financial statements in XBRL format. For this assignment, go to the SEC website at www.sec.gov. Once there, find the link that says "Interactive Data (XBRL)," and follow the link. Now follow the "Interactive Data Viewers" link, then "Interactive Financial Reports." Download the income statement and balance sheet from the annual report for the company you chose. Using these reports, calculate the financial ratios for the company from the data available, typically two or three years. Do you notice any changes in these ratios that might indicate further investigation?

CHAPTER CASE
RATIOS AND FINANCIAL PLANNING AT S&S AIR, INC.

Chris Guthrie was recently hired by S&S Air, Inc., to assist the company with its financial planning, and to evaluate the company's performance. Chris graduated from college five years ago with a finance degree. He has been employed in the finance department of a Fortune 500 company since then.

S&S Air was founded 10 years ago by friends Mark Sexton and Todd Story. The company has manufactured and sold light airplanes over this period, and the company's products have received high reviews for safety and reliability. The company has a niche market in that it sells primarily to individuals who own and fly their own airplanes. The company has two models, the Birdie, which sells for $53,000, and the Eagle, which sells for $78,000.

While the company manufactures aircraft, its operations are different from commercial aircraft companies. S&S Air builds aircraft to order. By using prefabricated parts, the company is able to complete the manufacture of an airplane in only five weeks. The company also receives a deposit on each order, as well as another partial payment before the order is complete. In contrast, a commercial airplane may take one and one-half to two years to manufacture once the order is placed.

Mark and Todd have provided the following financial statements. Chris has gathered the industry ratios for the light airplane manufacturing industry.

S&S Air, Inc.
2014 Income Statement

Sales	$24,092,400
Cost of goods sold	17,982,000
Other expenses	2,878,800
Depreciation	786,000
EBIT	$ 2,445,600
Interest	434,400
Taxable income	$ 2,011,200
Taxes (40%)	804,480
Net income	$ 1,206,720

Dividends	$246,000	
Add. to retained earnings	$960,720	

S&S Air, Inc.
2014 Balance Sheet

Assets		Liabilities & Equity	
Current assets		Current liabilities	
Cash	$ 438,048	Accounts payable	$ 858,816
Accounts receivable	1,841,616	Notes payable	1,735,680
Inventory	1,486,200	Total current liabilities	$ 2,594,496
Total current assets	$ 3,765,864		
Fixed assets		Long-term debt	$ 4,590,000
Net plant and equipment	$14,778,816	Shareholder equity	
		Common stock	$ 180,000
		Retained earnings	$11,180,184
		Total equity	$11,360,184
Total assets	$18,544,680	Total liabilities & equity	$18,544,680

www.mhhe.com/rwj

Light Airplane Industry Ratios			
	Lower Quartile	Median	Upper Quartile
Current ratio	0.50	1.43	1.89
Quick ratio	0.64	0.84	1.05
Cash ratio	0.08	0.21	0.39
Total asset turnover	0.68	0.85	1.28
Inventory turnover	4.89	6.15	10.89
Receivables turnover	6.27	9.82	11.51
Total debt ratio	0.31	0.52	0.61
Debt-equity ratio	0.58	1.08	1.56
Equity multiplier	1.58	2.08	2.56
Times interest earned	5.18	8.06	9.83
Cash coverage ratio	5.84	8.43	10.27
Profit margin	4.05%	5.15%	6.47%
Return on assets	6.05%	10.53%	13.21%
Return on equity	9.93%	16.54%	26.15%

QUESTIONS

1. Calculate the ratios for S&S Air that are shown for the industry.

2. Mark and Todd agree that a ratio analysis can provide a measure of the company's performance. They have chosen Boeing as an aspirant company. Would you choose Boeing as an aspirant company? Why or why not?

3. Compare the performance of S&S Air to the industry. For each ratio, comment on why it might be viewed as positive or negative relative to the industry. Suppose you create an inventory ratio calculated by inventory divided by current liabilities. How do you think S&S Air's ratio would compare to the industry average?

4. Calculate the internal growth rate and sustainable growth rate for S&S Air. What do these numbers mean?

Introduction to Valuation: The Time Value of Money

4

As you are probably aware, the United States government has a significant amount of debt. That debt, which is widely owned by investors, comes in different varieties, including Series EE U.S. Treasury savings bonds. With a Series EE bond, you pay a particular amount today of, say, $25, and the bond accrues interest over the time you hold it. In early 2012, the U.S. Treasury promised to pay .60 percent per year on EE savings bonds. In an interesting (and important) wrinkle, if you hold the bond for 20 years, the Treasury promises to "step up" the value to double your cost. That is, if the $25 bond you purchased and all the accumulated interest earned is worth less than $50, the Treasury will automatically increase the value of the bond to $50.

Is giving up $50 in exchange for $100 in 20 years a good deal? On the plus side, you get back $2 for every $1 you put up. That probably sounds good, but, on the downside, you have to wait 20 years to get it. What you need to know is how to analyze this trade-off. This chapter gives you the tools you need.

Specifically, our goal here is to introduce you to one of the most important principles in finance, the time value of money. What you will learn is how to determine the value today of some cash flow to be received later. This is a very basic business skill, and it underlies the analysis of many different types of investments and financing arrangements. In fact, almost all business activities, whether they originate in marketing, management, operations, or strategy, involve comparing outlays made today to benefits projected for the future. How to do this comparison is something everyone needs to understand; this chapter gets you started.

learning objectives

After studying this chapter, you should be able to:

LO 1 Determine the future value of an investment made today.

LO 2 Determine the present value of cash to be received at a future date.

LO 3 Calculate the return on an investment.

LO 4 Predict how long it takes for an investment to reach a desired value.

O ne of the basic problems faced by the financial manager is how to determine the value today of cash flows expected in the future. For example, the jackpot in a PowerBall™ lottery drawing was $110 million. Does this mean the winning ticket was worth $110 million? The answer is no because the jackpot was actually going to pay out over a 20-year period at a rate of $5.5 million per year. How much was the ticket worth then? The answer depends on the time value of money, the subject of this chapter.

In the most general sense, the phrase *time value of money* refers to the fact that a dollar in hand today is worth more than a dollar promised at some time in the future. On a practical level, one reason for this is that you could earn interest while you waited; so, a dollar today would grow to more than a dollar later. The trade-off between money now and money later thus depends on, among other things, the rate you can earn by investing. Our goal in this chapter is to explicitly evaluate this trade-off between dollars today and dollars at some future time.

A thorough understanding of the material in this chapter is critical to understanding material in subsequent chapters, so you should study it with particular care. We will present a number of examples in this chapter. In many problems, your answer may differ from ours slightly. This can happen because of rounding and is not a cause for concern.

To find out more about U.S. savings bonds and other government securities, go to www. treasurydirect.gov.

4.1   FUTURE VALUE AND COMPOUNDING

future value (FV)
The amount an investment is worth after one or more periods.

The first thing we will study is future value. **Future value (FV)** refers to the amount of money an investment will grow to over some period of time at some given interest rate. Put another way, future value is the cash value of an investment at some time in the future. We start out by considering the simplest case, a single-period investment.

ExcelMaster
coverage online

Investing for a Single Period

Suppose you were to invest $100 in a savings account that pays 10 percent interest per year. How much would you have in one year? You would have $110. This $110 is equal to your original *principal* of $100 plus $10 in interest that you earn. We say that $110 is the future value of $100 invested for one year at 10 percent, and we simply mean that $100 today is worth $110 in one year, given that 10 percent is the interest rate.

In general, if you invest for one period at an interest rate of r, your investment will grow to $(1 + r)$ per dollar invested. In our example, r is 10 percent, so your investment grows to $1 + .10 = 1.1$ dollars per dollar invested. You invested $100 in this case, so you ended up with $100 \times 1.10 = $110.

Investing for More than One Period

Going back to our $100 investment, what will you have after two years, assuming the interest rate doesn't change? If you leave the entire $110 in the bank, you will earn $110 \times .10 = $11 in interest during the second year, so you will have a total of $110 + 11 = $121. This $121 is the future value of $100 in two years at 10 percent. Another way of looking at it is that one year from now you are effectively investing $110 at 10 percent for a year. This is a single-period problem, so you'll end up with $1.1 for every dollar invested, or $110 \times 1.1 = $121 total.

This $121 has four parts. The first part is the $100 original principal. The second part is the $10 in interest you earn in the first year, and the third part is another $10 you earn in the second year, for a total of $120. The last $1 you end up with (the fourth part) is interest you earn in the second year on the interest paid in the first year: $10 × .10 = $1.

This process of leaving your money and any accumulated interest in an investment for more than one period, thereby reinvesting the interest, is called **compounding**. Compounding the interest means earning **interest on interest**, so we call the result **compound interest**. With **simple interest**, the interest is not reinvested, so interest is earned each period only on the original principal.

compounding
The process of accumulating interest in an investment over time to earn more interest.

INTEREST ON INTEREST | EXAMPLE 4.1

Suppose you locate a two-year investment that pays 14 percent per year. If you invest $325, how much will you have at the end of the two years? How much of this is simple interest? How much is compound interest?

At the end of the first year, you will have $325 × (1 + .14) = $370.50. If you reinvest this entire amount, and thereby compound the interest, you will have $370.50 × 1.14 = $422.37 at the end of the second year. The total interest you earn is thus $422.37 − 325 = $97.37. Your $325 original principal earns $325 × .14 = $45.50 in interest each year, for a two-year total of $91 in simple interest. The remaining $97.37 − 91 = $6.37 results from compounding. You can check this by noting that the interest earned in the first year is $45.50. The interest on interest earned in the second year thus amounts to $45.50 × .14 = $6.37, as we calculated.

We now take a closer look at how we calculated the $121 future value. We multiplied $110 by 1.1 to get $121. The $110, however, was $100 also multiplied by 1.1. In other words:

$121 = $110 × 1.1
= ($100 × 1.1) × 1.1
= $100 × (1.1 × 1.1)
= $100 × 1.1²
= $100 × 1.21

interest on interest
Interest earned on the reinvestment of previous interest payments.

compound interest
Interest earned on both the initial principal and the interest reinvested from prior periods.

At the risk of belaboring the obvious, let's ask: How much would our $100 grow to after three years? Once again, in two years, we'll be investing $121 for one period at 10 percent. We'll end up with $1.1 for every dollar we invest, or $121 × 1.1 = $133.1 total. This $133.1 is thus:

$133.1 = $121 × 1.1
= ($110 × 1.1) × 1.1
= ($100 × 1.1) × 1.1 × 1.1
= $100 × (1.1 × 1.1 × 1.1)
= $100 × 1.1³
= $100 × 1.331

simple interest
Interest earned only on the original principal amount invested.

You're probably noticing a pattern to these calculations, so we can now go ahead and state the general result. As our examples suggest, the future value of $1 invested for t periods at a rate of r per period is:

Future value = $1 × $(1 + r)^t$ [4.1]

The expression $(1 + r)^t$ is sometimes called the *future value interest factor* (or just *future value factor*) for $1 invested at r percent for t periods. It can be abbreviated as FVIF(r, t).

	Year	Beginning Amount	Interest Earned	Ending Amount
TABLE 4.1	1	$100.00	$10.00	$110.00
	2	110.00	11.00	121.00
Future value of	3	121.00	12.10	133.10
$100 at 10 percent	4	133.10	13.31	146.41
	5	146.41	14.64	161.05
			Total interest $61.05	

In our example, what would your $100 be worth after five years? We can first compute the relevant future value factor as:

$$(1 + r)^t = (1 + .10)^5 = 1.1^5 = 1.6105$$

Your $100 will thus grow to:

$$\$100 \times 1.6105 = \$161.05$$

The growth of your $100 each year is illustrated in Table 4.1. As shown, the interest earned in each year is equal to the beginning amount multiplied by the interest rate of 10 percent.

In Table 4.1, notice that the total interest you earn is $61.05. Over the five-year span of this investment, the simple interest is $100 × .10 = $10 per year, so you accumulate $50 this way. The other $11.05 is from compounding.

A brief introduction to key financial concepts is available at www. teachmefinance.com.

Figure 4.1 illustrates the growth of the compound interest in Table 4.1. Notice how the simple interest is constant each year, but the compound interest you earn gets bigger every year. The size of the compound interest keeps increasing because more and more interest builds up and there is thus more to compound.

Future values depend critically on the assumed interest rate, particularly for long-lived investments. Figure 4.2 illustrates this relationship by plotting the growth of $1 for

FIGURE 4.1

Future value, simple interest, and compound interest

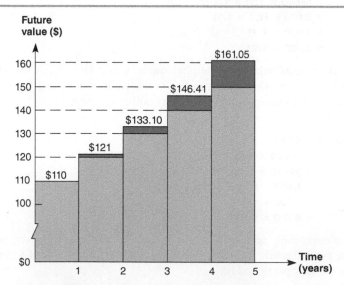

Growth of $100 original amount at 10% per year. Blue shaded area represents the portion of the total that results from compounding of interest.

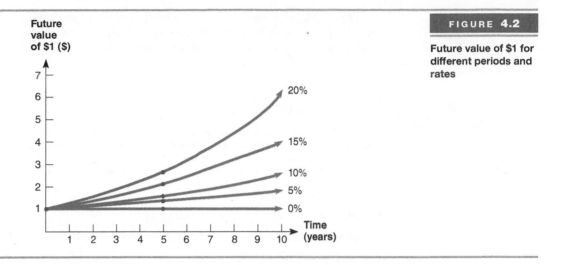

FIGURE 4.2

Future value of $1 for different periods and rates

different rates and lengths of time. Notice that the future value of $1 after 10 years is about $6.20 at a 20 percent rate, but it is only about $2.60 at 10 percent. In this case, doubling the interest rate more than doubles the future value.

To solve future value problems, we need to come up with the relevant future value factors. There are several different ways of doing this. In our example, we could have multiplied 1.1 by itself five times. This would work just fine, but it would get to be very tedious for, say, a 30-year investment.

Fortunately, there are several easier ways to get future value factors. Most calculators have a key labeled "y^x." You can usually just enter 1.1, press this key, enter 5, and press the "=" key to get the answer. This is an easy way to calculate future value factors because it's quick and accurate.

Alternatively, you can use a table that contains future value factors for some common interest rates and time periods. Table 4.2 contains some of these factors. Table A.1 in Appendix A at the end of the book contains a much larger set. To use the table, find the column that corresponds to 10 percent. Then look down the rows until you come to five periods. You should find the factor that we calculated, 1.6105.

Tables such as Table 4.2 are not as common as they once were because they predate inexpensive calculators and are only available for a relatively small number of rates. Interest rates are often quoted to three or four decimal places, so the tables needed to deal with these accurately would be quite large. As a result, the "real world" has moved away from using them. We will emphasize the use of a calculator in this chapter.

Number of	Interest Rates				TABLE 4.2
Periods	5%	10%	15%	20%	Future value
1	1.0500	1.1000	1.1500	1.2000	interest factors
2	1.1025	1.2100	1.3225	1.4400	
3	1.1576	1.3310	1.5209	1.7280	
4	1.2155	1.4641	1.7490	2.0736	
5	1.2763	1.6105	2.0114	2.4883	

These tables still serve a useful purpose. To make sure you are doing the calculations correctly, pick a factor from the table and then calculate it yourself to see that you get the same answer. There are plenty of numbers to choose from.

EXAMPLE 4.2

COMPOUND INTEREST

You've located an investment that pays 12 percent. That rate sounds good to you, so you invest $400. How much will you have in three years? How much will you have in seven years? At the end of seven years, how much interest have you earned? How much of that interest results from compounding?

Based on our discussion, we can calculate the future value factor for 12 percent and three years as:

$$(1 + r)^t = 1.12^3 = 1.4049$$

Your $400 thus grows to:

$$\$400 \times 1.4049 = \$561.97$$

After seven years, you will have:

$$\$400 \times 1.12^7 = \$400 \times 2.2107 = \$884.27$$

Thus, you will more than double your money over seven years.

Since you invested $400, the interest in the $884.27 future value is $884.27 − 400 = $484.27. At 12 percent, your $400 investment earns $400 × .12 = $48 in simple interest every year. Over seven years, the simple interest thus totals 7 × $48 = $336. The other $484.27 − 336 = $148.27 is from compounding.

How much do you need at retirement? Locate the "Retirement Planning" link at www.about.com.

The effect of compounding is not great over short time periods, but it really starts to add up as the horizon grows. To take an extreme case, suppose one of your more frugal ancestors had invested $5 for you at a 6 percent interest rate 200 years ago. How much would you have today? The future value factor is a substantial $1.06^{200} = 115,125.90$ (you won't find this one in a table), so you would have $5 × 115,125.90 = $575,629.50 today. Notice that the simple interest is just $5 × .06 = $.30 per year. After 200 years, this amounts to $60. The rest is from reinvesting. Such is the power of compound interest!

EXAMPLE 4.3

HOW MUCH FOR THAT ISLAND?

To further illustrate the effect of compounding for long horizons, consider the case of Peter Minuit and the Indians. In 1626, Minuit bought all of Manhattan Island for about $24 in goods and trinkets. This sounds cheap, but the Indians may have gotten the better end of the deal. To see why, suppose the Indians had sold the goods and invested the $24 at 10 percent. How much would it be worth today?

Roughly 388 years have passed since the transaction. At 10 percent, $24 will grow by quite a bit over that time. How much? The future value factor is approximately:

$$(1 + r)^t = 1.1^{388} \approx 11,000,000,000,000,000$$

That is, 11 followed by 15 zeroes. The future value is thus on the order of $24 × 11 quadrillion, or about $264 *quadrillion* (give or take a few hundreds of trillions).

Well, $264 quadrillion is a lot of money. How much? If you had it, you could buy the United States. All of it. Cash. With money left over to buy Canada, Mexico, and the rest of the world, for that matter.

This example is something of an exaggeration, of course. In 1626, it would not have been easy to locate an investment that would pay 10 percent every year without fail for the next 388 years.

Using a Financial Calculator

CALCULATOR HINTS

Although there are the various ways of calculating future values we have described so far, many of you will decide that a financial calculator is the way to go. If you are planning on using one, you should read this extended hint; otherwise, skip it.

A financial calculator is simply an ordinary calculator with a few extra features. In particular, it knows some of the most commonly used financial formulas, so it can directly compute things like future values.

Financial calculators have the advantage that they handle a lot of the computation, but that is really all. In other words, you still have to understand the problem; the calculator just does some of the arithmetic. In fact, there is an old joke (somewhat modified) that goes like this: Anyone can make a mistake on a time value of money problem, but to really screw one up takes a financial calculator! We therefore have two goals for this section. First, we'll discuss how to compute future values. After that, we'll show you how to avoid the most common mistakes people make when they start using financial calculators.

How to Calculate Future Values with a Financial Calculator   Examining a typical financial calculator, you will find five keys of particular interest. They usually look like this:

For now, we need to focus on four of these. The keys labeled **PV** and **FV** are just what you would guess: present value and future value. The key labeled **N** refers to the number of periods, which is what we have been calling *t*. Finally, **I/Y** stands for the interest rate, which we have called *r*.[1]

If we have the financial calculator set up right (see our next section), then calculating a future value is very simple. Take a look back at our question involving the future value of $100 at 10 percent for five years. We have seen that the answer is $161.05. The exact keystrokes will differ depending on what type of calculator you use, but here is basically all you do:

1. Enter −100. Press the **PV** key. (The negative sign is explained below.)
2. Enter 10. Press the **I/Y** key. (Notice that we entered 10, not .10; see below.)
3. Enter 5. Press the **N** key.

Now we have entered all of the relevant information. To solve for the future value, we need to ask the calculator what the **FV** is. Depending on your calculator, you either press the button labeled "CPT" (for compute) and then press **FV**, or else you just press **FV**. Either way, you should get 161.05. If you don't (and you probably won't if this is the first time you have used a financial calculator!), we will offer some help in our next section.

Before we explain the kinds of problems that you are likely to run into, we want to establish a standard format for showing you how to use a financial calculator. Using the example we just looked at, in the future, we will illustrate such problems like this:

Enter   5   10   −100

Solve for   161.05

---

[1] The reason financial calculators use N and I/Y is that the most common use for these calculators is determining loan payments. In this context, N is the number of payments and I/Y is the interest rate on the loan. But, as we will see, there are many other uses of financial calculators that don't involve loan payments and interest rates.

(continued)

Here is an important tip: Appendix D in the back of the book contains some more detailed instructions for the most common types of financial calculators. See if yours is included, and, if it is, follow the instructions there if you need help. Of course, if all else fails, you can read the manual that came with the calculator.

How to Get the Wrong Answer Using a Financial Calculator   There are a couple of common (and frustrating) problems that cause a lot of trouble with financial calculators. In this section, we provide some important *dos* and *don'ts*. If you just can't seem to get a problem to work out, you should refer back to this section.

There are two categories we examine: three things you need to do only once and three things you need to do every time you work a problem. The things you need to do just once deal with the following calculator settings:

1. *Make sure your calculator is set to display a large number of decimal places.* Most financial calculators only display two decimal places; this causes problems because we frequently work with numbers—like interest rates—that are very small.

2. *Make sure your calculator is set to assume only one payment per period or per year.* Some financial calculators assume monthly payments (12 per year) unless you say otherwise.

3. *Make sure your calculator is in "end" mode.* This is usually the default, but you can accidently change to "begin" mode.

If you don't know how to set these three things, see Appendix D or your calculator's operating manual. There are also three things you need to do *every time you work a problem*:

1. *Before you start, completely clear out the calculator.* This is very important. Failure to do this is the number one reason for wrong answers; you simply must get in the habit of clearing the calculator every time you start a problem. How you do this depends on the calculator (see Appendix D), but you must do more than just clear the display. For example, on a Texas Instruments BA II Plus, you must press **2nd** then **CLR TVM** for *clear time value of money*. There is a similar command on your calculator. Learn it!

    Note that turning the calculator off and back on won't do it. Most financial calculators remember everything you enter, even after you turn them off. In other words, they remember all your mistakes unless you explicitly clear them out. Also, if you are in the middle of a problem and make a mistake, *clear it out and start over.* Better to be safe than sorry.

2. *Put a negative sign on cash outflows.* Most financial calculators require you to put a negative sign on cash outflows and a positive sign on cash inflows. As a practical matter, this usually just means that you should enter the present value amount with a negative sign (because normally the present value represents the amount you give up today in exchange for cash inflows later). You enter a negative value on the BA II Plus by first entering a number and then pressing the **+/−** key. By the same token, when you solve for a present value, you shouldn't be surprised to see a negative sign.

3. *Enter the rate correctly.* Financial calculators assume that rates are quoted in percent, so if the rate is .08 (or 8 percent), you should enter 8, not .08.

If you follow these guidelines (especially the one about clearing out the calculator), you should have no problem using a financial calculator to work almost all of the problems in this and the next few chapters. We'll provide some additional examples and guidance where appropriate.

PRESENT VALUE AND DISCOUNTING

4.2

When we discuss future value, we are thinking of questions such as the following: What will my $2,000 investment grow to if it earns a 6.5 percent return every year for the next six years? The answer to this question is what we call the future value of $2,000 invested at 6.5 percent for six years (verify that the answer is about $2,918).

There is another type of question that comes up even more often in financial management that is obviously related to future value. Suppose you need to have $10,000 in 10 years, and you can earn 6.5 percent on your money. How much do you have to invest today to reach your goal? You can verify that the answer is $5,327.26. How do we know this? Read on.

ExcelMaster
coverage online

The Single-Period Case

We've seen that the future value of $1 invested for one year at 10 percent is $1.10. We now ask a slightly different question: How much do we have to invest today at 10 percent to get $1 in one year? In other words, we know the future value here is $1, but what is the **present value (PV)**? The answer isn't too hard to figure out. Whatever we invest today will be 1.1 times bigger at the end of the year. Since we need $1 at the end of the year:

present value (PV)
The current value of future cash flows discounted at the appropriate discount rate.

Present value × 1.1 = $1

Or, solving for the present value:

Present value = $1/1.1 = $.909

In this case, the present value is the answer to the following question: What amount, invested today, will grow to $1 in one year if the interest rate is 10 percent? Present value is thus just the reverse of future value. Instead of compounding the money forward into the future, we **discount** it back to the present.

discount
Calculate the present value of some future amount.

SINGLE-PERIOD PV   **EXAMPLE** **4.4**

Suppose you need $800 to buy textbooks next year. You can earn 7 percent on your money. How much do you have to put up today?

We need to know the PV of $800 in one year at 7 percent. Proceeding as above:

Present value × 1.07 = $800

We can now solve for the present value:

Present value = $800 × (1/1.07) = $747.66

Thus, $747.66 is the present value. Again, this just means that investing this amount for one year at 7 percent will result in a future value of $800.

From our examples, the present value of $1 to be received in one period is generally given as:

PV = $1 × [1/(1 + r)] = $1/(1 + r)

We next examine how to get the present value of an amount to be paid in two or more periods into the future.

Present Values for Multiple Periods

Suppose you need to have $1,000 in two years. If you can earn 7 percent, how much do you have to invest to make sure that you have the $1,000 when you need it? In other words, what is the present value of $1,000 in two years if the relevant rate is 7 percent?

Based on your knowledge of future values, you know that the amount invested must grow to $1,000 over the two years. In other words, it must be the case that:

$$\$1,000 = PV \times 1.07 \times 1.07$$
$$= PV \times 1.07^2$$
$$= PV \times 1.1449$$

Given this, we can solve for the present value:

Present value = $1,000/1.1449 = $873.44

Therefore, $873.44 is the amount you must invest in order to achieve your goal.

EXAMPLE 4.5

SAVING UP

You would like to buy a new automobile. You have $50,000, but the car costs $68,500. If you can earn 9 percent, how much do you have to invest today to buy the car in two years? Do you have enough? Assume the price will stay the same.

What we need to know is the present value of $68,500 to be paid in two years, assuming a 9 percent rate. Based on our discussion, this is:

PV = $68,500/1.09² = $68,500/1.1881 = $57,655.08

You're still about $7,655 short, even if you're willing to wait two years.

As you have probably recognized by now, calculating present values is quite similar to calculating future values, and the general result looks much the same. The present value of $1 to be received *t* periods into the future at a discount rate of *r* is:

PV = $1 × [1/(1 + r)ᵗ] = $1/(1 + r)ᵗ [4.2]

discount rate
The rate used to calculate the present value of future cash flows.

The quantity in brackets, $1/(1 + r)^t$, goes by several different names. Since it's used to discount a future cash flow, it is often called a *discount factor*. With this name, it is not surprising that the rate used in the calculation is often called the **discount rate**. We will tend to call it this in talking about present values. The quantity in brackets is also called the *present value interest factor* (or just *present value factor*) for $1 at *r* percent for *t* periods and is sometimes abbreviated as PVIF(*r, t*). Finally, calculating the present value of a future cash flow to determine its worth today is commonly called **discounted cash flow (DCF) valuation**.

discounted cash flow (DCF) valuation
Valuation calculating the present value of a future cash flow to determine its value today.

To illustrate, suppose you need $1,000 in three years. You can earn 15 percent on your money. How much do you have to invest today? To find out, we have to determine the

| Number of | Interest Rates | | | | TABLE 4.3 |
Periods	5%	10%	15%	20%	Present value interest factors
1	.9524	.9091	.8696	.8333	
2	.9070	.8264	.7561	.6944	
3	.8638	.7513	.6575	.5787	
4	.8227	.6830	.5718	.4823	
5	.7835	.6209	.4972	.4019	

present value of $1,000 in three years at 15 percent. We do this by discounting $1,000 back three periods at 15 percent. With these numbers, the discount factor is:

$$1/(1 + .15)^3 = 1/1.5209 = .6575$$

The amount you must invest is thus:

$$\$1,000 \times .6575 = \$657.50$$

We say that $657.50 is the present, or discounted, value of $1,000 to be received in three years at 15 percent.

There are tables for present value factors just as there are tables for future value factors, and you use them in the same way (if you use them at all). Table 4.3 contains a small set of these factors. A much larger set can be found in Table A.2 in Appendix A.

In Table 4.3, the discount factor we just calculated, .6575, can be found by looking down the column labeled "15%" until you come to the third row. Of course, you could use a financial calculator, as we illustrate nearby.

As the length of time until payment grows, present values decline. As Example 4.6 illustrates, present values tend to become small as the time horizon grows. If you look out

---

CALCULATOR HINTS

You solve present value problems on a financial calculator just like you do future value problems. For the example we just examined (the present value of $1,000 to be received in three years at 15 percent), you would do the following:

Enter	3	15			1,000
	N	1/Y	PMT	PV	FV
Solve for				−657.50	

Notice that the answer has a negative sign; as we discussed above, that's because it represents an outflow today in exchange for the $1,000 inflow later.

DECEPTIVE ADVERTISING   **EXAMPLE 4.6**

Recently, some businesses have been saying things like "Come try our product. If you do, we'll give you $100 just for coming by!" If you read the fine print, what you find out is that they will give you a savings certificate that will pay you $100 in 25 years or so. If the going interest rate on such certificates is 10 percent per year, how much are they really giving you today?

What you're actually getting is the present value of $100 to be paid in 25 years. If the discount rate is 10 percent per year, then the discount factor is:

$$1/1.1^{25} = 1/10.8347 = .0923$$

This tells you that a dollar in 25 years is worth a little more than nine cents today, assuming a 10 percent discount rate. Given this, the promotion is actually paying you about .0923 × $100 = $9.23. Maybe this is enough to draw customers, but it's not $100.

FIGURE 4.3

Present value of $1 for different periods and rates

far enough, they will always get close to zero. Also, for a given length of time, the higher the discount rate is, the lower is the present value. Put another way, present values and discount rates are inversely related. Increasing the discount rate decreases the PV and vice versa.

The relationship between time, discount rates, and present values is illustrated in Figure 4.3. Notice that by the time we get to 10 years, the present values are all substantially smaller than the future amounts.

CONCEPT QUESTIONS

4.2a   What do we mean by the present value of an investment?

4.2b   The process of discounting a future amount back to the present is the opposite of doing what?

4.2c   What do we mean by discounted cash flow, or DCF, valuation?

4.2d   In general, what is the present value of $1 to be received in t periods, assuming a discount rate of r per period?

4.3

MORE ON PRESENT AND FUTURE VALUES

If you look back at the expressions we came up with for present and future values, you will see there is a very simple relationship between the two. We explore this relationship and some related issues in this section.

For a downloadable, Windows-based financial calculator, go to www.calculator.org.

Present versus Future Value

What we called the present value factor is just the reciprocal of (that is, 1 divided by) the future value factor:

Future value factor $= (1 + r)^t$

Present value factor $= 1/(1 + r)^t$

In fact, the easy way to calculate a present value factor on many calculators is to first calculate the future value factor and then press the **1/X** key to flip it over.

If we let FV_t stand for the future value after t periods, then the relationship between future value and present value can be written very simply as one of the following:

$$PV \times (1 + r)^t = FV_t$$
$$PV = FV_t / (1 + r)^t = FV_t \times [1/(1 + r)^t] \qquad [4.3]$$

We will call this last result the *basic present value equation*. We will use it throughout the text. There are a number of variations that come up, but this simple equation underlies many of the most important ideas in finance.

ExcelMaster
coverage online

EVALUATING INVESTMENTS

EXAMPLE 4.7

To give you an idea of how we will be using present and future values, consider the following simple investment. Your company proposes to buy an asset for $335. This investment is very safe. You will sell off the asset in three years for $400. You know you could invest the $335 elsewhere at 10 percent with very little risk. What do you think of the proposed investment?

This is not a good investment. Why not? Because you can invest the $335 elsewhere at 10 percent. If you do, after three years it will grow to:

$$\$335 \times (1 + r)^t = \$335 \times 1.1^3$$
$$= \$335 \times 1.331$$
$$= \$445.89$$

Since the proposed investment only pays out $400, it is not as good as other alternatives we have. Another way of saying the same thing is to notice that the present value of $400 in three years at 10 percent is:

$$\$400 \times [1/(1 + r)^t] = \$400/1.1^3 = \$400/1.331 = \$300.53$$

This tells us that we only have to invest about $300 to get $400 in three years, not $335. We will return to this type of analysis later on.

Determining the Discount Rate

It will turn out that we will frequently need to determine what discount rate is implicit in an investment. We can do this by looking at the basic present value equation:

$$PV = FV_t / (1 + r)^t$$

There are only four parts to this equation: the present value (PV), the future value (FV_t), the discount rate (r), and the life of the investment (t). Given any three of these, we can always find the fourth.

FINDING *r* FOR A SINGLE-PERIOD INVESTMENT

EXAMPLE 4.8

You are considering a one-year investment. If you put up $1,250, you will get back $1,350. What rate is this investment paying?

First, in this single-period case, the answer is fairly obvious. You are getting a total of $100 in addition to your $1,250. The implicit rate on this investment is thus $100/1,250 = 8 percent.

More formally, from the basic present value equation, the present value (the amount you must put up today) is $1,250. The future value (what the present value grows to) is $1,350. The time involved is one period, so we have:

$$\$1,250 = \$1,350/(1 + r)^t$$
$$1 + r = \$1,350/1,250 = 1.08$$
$$r = 8\%$$

In this simple case, of course, there was no need to go through this calculation, but, as we describe below, it gets a little harder when there is more than one period.

To illustrate what happens with multiple periods, let's say that we are offered an investment that costs us $100 and will double our money in eight years. To compare this to other investments, we would like to know what discount rate is implicit in these numbers. This discount rate is called the *rate of return,* or sometimes just *return,* on the investment. In this case, we have a present value of $100, a future value of $200 (double our money), and an eight-year life. To calculate the return, we can write the basic present value equation as:

$$PV = FV_t/(1 + r)^t$$
$$\$100 = \$200/(1 + r)^8$$

It could also be written as:

$$(1 + r)^8 = \$200/100 = 2$$

We now need to solve for r. There are three ways we could do it:

1. Use a financial calculator. (See below.)
2. Solve the equation for $1 + r$ by taking the eighth root of both sides. Since this is the same thing as raising both sides to the power of ⅛, or .125, this is actually easy to do with the ⎡ y^x ⎤ key on a calculator. Just enter 2, then press ⎡ y^x ⎤, enter .125, and press the ⎡ = ⎤ key. The eighth root should be about 1.09, which implies that r is 9 percent.
3. Use a future value table. The future value factor for eight years is equal to 2. If you look across the row corresponding to eight periods in Table A.1, you will see that a future value factor of 2 corresponds to the 9 percent column, again implying that the return here is 9 percent.

Why does the Rule of 72 work? See www.moneychimp.com.

Actually, in this particular example, there is a useful "back of the envelope" means of solving for r—the Rule of 72. For reasonable rates of return, the time it takes to double your money is given approximately by $72/r\%$. In our example, this means that $72/r\% = 8$ years, implying that r is 9 percent as we calculated. This rule is fairly accurate for discount rates in the 5 percent to 20 percent range.

The nearby *Finance Matters* box provides some examples of rates of return on collectibles. See if you can verify the numbers reported there.

EXAMPLE 4.9   **DOUBLE YOUR FUN**

You have been offered an investment that promises to double your money every 10 years. What is the approximate rate of return on the investment?

From the Rule of 72, the rate of return is given approximately by $72/r\% = 10$, so the rate is approximately $72/10 = 7.2\%$. Verify that the exact answer is 7.177 percent.

A slightly more extreme example involves money bequeathed by Benjamin Franklin, who died on April 17, 1790. In his will, he gave 1,000 pounds sterling to Massachusetts and the city of Boston. He gave a like amount to Pennsylvania and the city of Philadelphia. The money was paid to Franklin when he held political office, but he believed that politicians should not be paid for their service (it appears that this view is not widely shared by modern-day politicians).

Franklin originally specified that the money should be paid out 100 years after his death and used to train young people. Later, however, after some legal wrangling, it was agreed that the money would be paid out in 1990, 200 years after Franklin's death. By that time, the

FINANCE MATTERS

◀ For the latest news on the topics covered in this chapter, scan here.

Collectibles as Investments?

It used to be that trading in collectibles such as baseball cards, art, and old toys occurred mostly at auctions, swap meets, and collectible shops, all of which were limited to regional traffic. However, with the growing popularity of online auctions such as eBay, trading in collectibles has expanded to an international arena. The most visible form of collectible is probably the baseball card, but Furbies, Beanie Babies, and Pokémon cards have been extremely hot collectibles in the recent past. However, it's not just fad items that spark interest from collectors; virtually anything of sentimental value from days gone by is considered collectible, and, more and more, collectibles are being viewed as investments.

Collectibles typically provide no cash flows until they are sold, and condition and buyer sentiment are the major determinants of value. The rates of return have been amazing at times, but care is needed in interpreting them. For example, in 2011, an 1855-S Indian Head gold $3 coin sold for $1,322,500. While that looks like a whopping price increase to the untrained eye, check for yourself that the actual return on the investment was only about 8.69 percent per year. Not too bad, but nowhere near the return most people expect from looking at the sales price.

Comic books have recently grown in popularity among collectors. Spiderman, who first appeared in *Amazing Fantasy* No. 15, is an extremely popular superhero. The comic book sold in August 1963 at a cover price of 12 cents. In 2011, a copy of this issue had mutated to a price of $1.1 million at auction, the first Marvel Comics superhero to hit the million dollar mark. This seems like a very high return to the untrained eye, and indeed it is! Check for yourself that the return was about 39.65 percent per year.

Stamp collecting (or philately) is a another popular activity. Possibly the most desirable stamp in the world is the Mauritius "Post Office" stamp, issued in 1847. One thousand of the stamps were originally printed, and many were used on invitations by the wife of the Governor of Mauritius for a ball she was holding. Only 27 of the stamps are confirmed to remain in existence. In 2011, a blue two pence version of the stamp sold for £1,053,090 (about $1,645,000). Assuming two pence is equal to two cents, see for yourself that this represents an annual return of about 11.75 percent.

Pennsylvania bequest had grown to about $2 million; the Massachusetts bequest had grown to $4.5 million. The money was used to fund the Franklin Institutes in Boston and Philadelphia. Assuming that 1,000 pounds sterling was equivalent to 1,000 dollars, what rate of return did the two states earn (the dollar did not become the official U.S. currency until 1792)?

For Pennsylvania, the future value is $2 million and the present value is $1,000. There are 200 years involved, so we need to solve for r in the following:

$$\$1{,}000 = \$2 \text{ million}/(1 + r)^{200}$$
$$(1 + r)^{200} = 2{,}000$$

Solving for r, we see that the Pennsylvania money grew at about 3.87 percent per year. The Massachusetts money did better; verify that the rate of return in this case was 4.3 percent. Small differences can add up!

We can illustrate how to calculate unknown rates using a financial calculator with these numbers. For Pennsylvania, you would do the following:

CALCULATOR HINTS

Enter	200			−1,000	2,000,000
	N	I/Y	PMT	PV	FV
Solve for		3.87			

As in our previous examples, notice the minus sign on the present value, representing Franklin's outlay made many years ago. What do you change to work the problem for Massachusetts?

EXAMPLE | **4.10**

SAVING FOR COLLEGE

You estimate that you will need about $80,000 to send your child to college in eight years. You have about $35,000 now. If you can earn 20 percent per year, will you make it? At what rate will you just reach your goal?

If you can earn 20 percent, the future value of your $35,000 in eight years will be:

$$FV = \$35,000 \times 1.20^8 = \$35,000 \times 4.2998 = \$150,493.59$$

So, you will make it easily. The minimum rate is the unknown r in the following:

$$FV = \$35,000 \times (1 + r)^8 = \$80,000$$
$$(1 + r)^8 = \$80,000/35,000 = 2.2857$$

Therefore, the future value factor is 2.2857. Looking at the row in Table A.1 that corresponds to eight periods, we see that our future value factor is roughly halfway between the ones shown for 10 percent (2.1436) and 12 percent (2.4760), so you will just reach your goal if you earn approximately 11 percent. To get the exact answer, we could use a financial calculator or we could solve for r:

$$(1 + r)^8 = \$80,000/35,000 = 2.2857$$
$$1 + r = 2.2857^{(1/8)} = 2.2857^{.125} = 1.1089$$
$$r = 10.89\%$$

EXAMPLE | **4.11**

ONLY 18,262.5 DAYS TO RETIREMENT

You would like to retire in 50 years as a millionaire. If you have $10,000 today, what rate of return do you need to earn to achieve your goal?

The future value is $1,000,000. The present value is $10,000, and there are 50 years until retirement. We need to calculate the unknown discount rate in the following:

$$\$10,000 = \$1,000,000/(1 + r)^{50}$$
$$(1 + r)^{50} = 100$$

The future value factor is thus 100. You can verify that the implicit rate is about 9.65 percent.

Finding the Number of Periods

Suppose we were interested in purchasing an asset that costs $50,000. We currently have $25,000. If we can earn 12 percent on this $25,000, how long until we have the $50,000? Finding the answer involves solving for the last variable in the basic present value equation, the number of periods. You already know how to get an approximate answer to this particular problem. Notice that we need to double our money. From the Rule of 72, this will take about $72/12 = 6$ years at 12 percent.

To come up with the exact answer, we can again manipulate the basic present value equation. The present value is $25,000, and the future value is $50,000. With a 12 percent discount rate, the basic equation takes one of the following forms:

$$\$25,000 = \$50,000/1.12^t$$
$$\$50,000/25,000 = 1.12^t = 2$$

We thus have a future value factor of 2 for a 12 percent rate. We now need to solve for t. If you look down the column in Table A.1 that corresponds to 12 percent, you will see that a future value factor of 1.9738 occurs at six periods. It will thus take about six years, as we calculated. To get the exact answer, we have to explicitly solve for *t* (or use a financial calculator). If you do this, you will find that the answer is 6.1163 years, so our approximation was quite close in this case.

If you do use a financial calculator, here are the relevant entries:

Enter		12		−25,000	50,000
	N	I/Y	PMT	PV	FV

Solve for   6.1163

WAITING FOR GODOT

You've been saving up to buy the Godot Company. The total cost will be $10 million. You currently have about $2.3 million. If you can earn 5 percent on your money, how long will you have to wait? At 16 percent, how long must you wait?

At 5 percent, you'll have to wait a long time. From the basic present value equation:

$2.3 = $10/1.05^t$

$1.05^t = 4.35$

$t = 30$ years

At 16 percent, things are a little better. Verify for yourself that it will take about 10 years.

This example finishes our introduction to basic time value of money concepts. Table 4.4 on page 114 summarizes present value and future value calculations for future reference. As the *Work the Web* box in this section shows, online calculators are widely available to handle these calculations, but it is still important to know what is going on.

Using a Spreadsheet for Time Value of Money Calculations

More and more, businesspeople from many different areas (and not just finance and accounting) rely on spreadsheets to do all the different types of calculations that come up in the real world. As a result, in this section, we will show you how to use a spreadsheet to handle the various time value of money problems we presented in this chapter. We will use Microsoft Excel™, but the commands are similar for other types of software. We assume you are already familiar with basic spreadsheet operations.

As we have seen, you can solve for any one of the following four potential unknowns: future value, present value, the discount rate, or the number of periods. With a spreadsheet, there is a separate formula for each. In Excel, these are as follows:

Learn more about using Excel for time value of money and other calculations at www.studyfinance.com.

To Find	Enter This Formula
Future value	= FV (rate,nper,pmt,pv)
Present value	= PV (rate,nper,pmt,fv)
Discount rate	= RATE (nper,pmt,pv,fv)
Number of periods	= NPER (rate,pmt,pv,fv)

(continued)

In these formulas, pv and fv are present and future value, nper is the number of periods, and rate is the discount, or interest, rate.

There are two things that are a little tricky here. First, unlike a financial calculator, the spreadsheet requires that the rate be entered as a decimal. Second, as with most financial calculators, you have to put a negative sign on either the present value or the future value to solve for the rate or the number of periods. For the same reason, if you solve for a present value, the answer will have a negative sign unless you input a negative future value. The same is true when you compute a future value.

To illustrate how you might use these formulas, we will go back to an example in the chapter. If you invest $25,000 at 12 percent per year, how long until you have $50,000? You might set up a spreadsheet like this:

	A	B	C	D	E	F	G	H
1								
2	Using a spreadsheet for time value of money calculations							
3								
4	If we invest $25,000 at 12 percent, how long until we have $50,000? We need to solve for the							
5	unknown number of periods, so we use the formula NPER (rate, pmt, pv, fv).							
6								
7	Present value (pv):	$25,000						
8	Future value (fv):	$50,000						
9	Rate (rate):	.12						
10								
11	Periods:	6.116255						
12								
13	The formula entered in cell B11 is =NPER(B9,0,-B7,B8); notice that pmt is zero and that pv has a							
14	negative sign on it. Also notice that the rate is entered as a decimal, not a percentage.							

TABLE 4.4

Summary of time value of money calculations

I. **Symbols**

PV = Present value, what future cash flows are worth today
FV_t = Future value, what cash flows are worth in the future
r = Interest rate, rate of return, or discount rate per period—typically, but not always, one year
t = Number of periods—typically, but not always, the number of years
C = Cash amount

II. **Future value of C invested at r percent per period for t periods**

$$FV_t = C \times (1 + r)^t$$
The term $(1 + r)^t$ is called the *future value factor*.

III. **Present value of C to be received in t periods at r percent per period**

$$PV = C/(1 + r)^t$$
The term $1/(1 + r)^t$ is called the *present value factor*.

IV. **The basic present value equation giving the relationship between present and future value is**

$$PV = FV_t/(1 + r)^t$$

WORK THE WEB

How important is the time value of money? A recent search on one web engine returned over 600 million hits! It is important to understand the calculations behind the time value of money, but the advent of financial calculators and spreadsheets has eliminated the need for tedious calculations. In fact, many websites offer time value of money calculators. The following is an example from Moneychimp's website, www.moneychimp.com. You need $125,000 in 20 years and will invest your money at 9.8 percent. How much do you need to deposit today? To use the calculator, you simply enter the values and hit "Calculate." The results look like this:

◄ To get updated data, scan here.

Inputs		
Future Value:	$	125,000.00
Years:		20
Discount Rate:		9.8 %
	Calculate	
Results		
Present Value:	$	19,269.18

Who said time value of money calculations are hard?

Questions

1. *Use the present value calculator on this website to answer the following: Suppose you want to have $140,000 in 25 years. If you can earn a 10 percent return, how much do you have to invest today?*
2. *Use the future value calculator on this website to answer the following question: Suppose you have $8,000 today that you plan to save for your retirement in 40 years. If you earn a return of 10.8 percent per year, how much will this account be worth when you are ready to retire?*

CONCEPT QUESTIONS

4.3a   What is the basic present value equation?

4.3b   What is the Rule of 72?

SUMMARY AND CONCLUSIONS

◄ Think you've mastered the material? Scan here to take a chapter quiz.

This chapter has introduced you to the basic principles of present value and discounted cash flow valuation. In it, we explained a number of things about the time value of money, including:

1. For a given rate of return, the value at some point in the future of an investment made today can be determined by calculating the future value of that investment.

2. The current worth of a future cash flow can be determined for a given rate of return by calculating the present value of the cash flow involved.

3. The relationship between present value and future value for a given rate, r, and time, t, is given by the basic present value equation:

$$PV = FV_t/(1 + r)^t$$

As we have shown, it is possible to find any one of the four components (PV, FV_t, r, or t) given the other three.

The principles developed in this chapter will figure prominently in the chapters to come. The reason for this is that most investments, whether they involve real assets or financial assets, can be analyzed using the discounted cash flow, or DCF, approach. As a result, the DCF approach is broadly applicable and widely used in practice. Before going on, therefore, you might want to do some of the problems below.

 connect POP QUIZ!
|FINANCE

Can you answer the following questions? If your class is using *Connect Finance,* log on to the Self-Quiz and Study feature in the Library tab to see if you know the answers to these and other questions, check out the study tools, and find out what topics require additional practice!

Section 4.1 If you deposit $4,500 in an IRA, earn a 10.55 percent rate of return, and make no additional contributions, how much will that account be worth in 44 years?

Section 4.2 If you want to be a millionaire upon your retirement in 45 years, how much do you need to invest today? Assume an 11.20 percent annual return, and no additional contributions.

Section 4.3 At 4.75 percent interest, how long does it take to double your money?

CHAPTER REVIEW AND SELF-TEST PROBLEMS

4.1 **Calculating Future Values.** Assume you deposit $1,000 today in an account that pays 8 percent interest. How much will you have in four years? (See Problem 2.)

4.2 **Calculating Present Values.** Suppose you have just celebrated your 19th birthday. A rich uncle set up a trust fund for you that will pay you $100,000 when you turn 25. If the relevant discount rate is 11 percent, how much is this fund worth today? (See Problem 3.)

4.3 **Calculating Rates of Return.** You've been offered an investment that will double your money in 12 years. What rate of return are you being offered? Check your answer using the Rule of 72. (See Problem 4.)

4.4   Calculating the Number of Periods.   You've been offered an investment that will pay you 7 percent per year. If you invest $10,000, how long until you have $20,000? How long until you have $30,000? (See Problem 5.)

■ **Answers to Chapter Review and Self-Test Problems**

4.1   We need to calculate the future value of $1,000 at 8 percent for four years. The future value factor is:

$1.08^4 = 1.3605$

The future value is thus $1,000 \times 1.3605 = \$1,360.50$.

4.2   We need the present value of $100,000 to be paid in six years at 11 percent. The discount factor is:

$1/1.11^6 = 1/1.8704 = .5346$

The present value is thus about $53,460.

4.3   Suppose you invest, say, $100. You will have $200 in 12 years with this investment. So, $100 is the amount you have today, the present value, and $200 is the amount you will have in 12 years, or the future value. From the basic present value equation, we have:

$$\$200 = \$100 \times (1 \times r)^{12}$$
$$2 = (1 \times r)^{12}$$

From here, we need to solve for r, the unknown rate. As shown in the chapter, there are several different ways to do this. We will take the 12th root of 2 (by raising 2 to the power of 1/12):

$$2^{(1/12)} = 1 + r$$
$$1.0595 = 1 + r$$
$$r = 5.95\%$$

Using the Rule of 72, we have $72/t = r\%$, or $72/12 = 6\%$, so our answer looks good (remember that the Rule of 72 is only an approximation).

4.4   The basic equation is:

$$\$20,000 = \$10,000 \times (1 + .07)^t$$
$$2 = (1 + .07)^t$$

If we solve for t, we get that $t = 10.24$ years. Using the Rule of 72, we get $72/7 = 10.29$ years, so, once again, our answer looks good. To get $30,000, verify for yourself that you will have to wait 16.24 years.

CRITICAL THINKING AND CONCEPTS REVIEW

LO 1   **4.1   Compounding.**   What is compounding? What is discounting?

LO 1   **4.2   Compounding and Periods.**   As you increase the length of time involved, what happens to future values? What happens to present values?

LO 1   **4.3   Compounding and Interest Rates.**   What happens to a future value if you increase the rate, r? What happens to a present value?

LO 1   **4.4**   **Future Values.** Suppose you deposit a large sum in an account that earns a low interest rate and simultaneously deposit a small sum in an account with a high interest rate. Which account will have the larger future value?

LO 3   **4.5**   **Ethical Considerations.**   Take a look back at Example 4.6. Is it deceptive advertising? Is it unethical to advertise a future value like this without a disclaimer?

On March 28, 2008, Toyota Motor Credit Corporation (TMCC), a subsidiary of Toyota Motor, offered some securities for sale to the public. Under the terms of the deal, TMCC promised to repay the owner of one of these securities $100,000 on March 28, 2038, but investors would receive nothing until then. Investors paid TMCC $24,099 for each of these securities; so they gave up $24,099 on March 28, 2008, for the promise of a $100,000 payment 30 years later.

LO 2   **4.6**   **Time Value of Money.**   Why would TMCC be willing to accept such a small amount today ($24,099) in exchange for a promise to repay about 4 times that amount ($100,000) in the future?

LO 3   **4.7**   **Call Provisions.**   TMCC has the right to buy back the securities on the anniversary date at a price established when the securities were issued (this feature is a term of this particular deal). What impact does this feature have on the desirability of this security as an investment?

LO 3   **4.8**   **Time Value of Money.**   Would you be willing to pay $24,099 today in exchange for $100,000 in 30 years? What would be the key considerations in answering yes or no? Would your answer depend on who is making the promise to repay?

LO 3   **4.9**   **Investment Comparison.**   Suppose that when TMCC offered the security for $24,099, the U.S. Treasury had offered an essentially identical security. Do you think it would have had a higher or lower price? Why?

LO 3   **4.10**   **Length of Investment.**   The TMCC security is bought and sold on the New York Stock Exchange. If you looked at the price today, do you think the price would exceed the $24,099 original price? Why? If you looked in the year 2018, do you think the price would be higher or lower than today's price? Why?

QUESTIONS AND PROBLEMS

Select problems are available in McGraw-Hill *Connect*. Please see the packaging options section of the preface for more information.

LO 1   **1. Simple Interest versus Compound Interest.**   First City Bank pays 6 percent simple interest on its savings account balances, whereas Second City Bank pays 6 percent interest compounded annually. If you made a deposit of $7,500 in each bank, how much more money would you earn from your Second City Bank account at the end of 10 years?

Basic
(Questions 1–15)

LO 1   **2. Calculating Future Values.**   For each of the following, compute the future value:

Present Value	Years	Interest Rate	Future Value
$ 3,150	6	13%	
8,453	19	7	
89,305	13	9	
227,382	21	5	

LO 2   **3. Calculating Present Values.**   For each of the following, compute the present value:

Present Value	Years	Interest Rate	Future Value
	15	4%	$ 17,328
	8	9	41,517
	13	12	790,382
	25	11	647,816

LO 3   **4. Calculating Interest Rates.**   Solve for the unknown interest rate in each of the following:

Present Value	Years	Interest Rate	Future Value
$ 715	9		$ 1,381
905	6		1,718
15,000	21		141,832
70,300	18		312,815

LO 4   **5. Calculating the Number of Periods.**   Solve for the unknown number of years in each of the following:

Present Value	Years	Interest Rate	Future Value
$ 195		9%	$ 1,105
2,105		7	3,700
47,800		12	387,120
38,650		19	198,212

LO 3   **6. Calculating Rates of Return.**   Assume the total cost of a college education will be $280,000 when your child enters college in 18 years. You presently have $45,000 to invest. What annual rate of interest must you earn on your investment to cover the cost of your child's college education?

LO 4   **7. Calculating the Number of Periods.**   At 5 percent interest, how long does it take to double your money? To quadruple it?

LO 3   **8. Calculating Rates of Return.**   In 2011, an 1880-O Morgan silver dollar sold for $13,113. What was the rate of return on this investment?

LO 4   **9. Calculating the Number of Periods.**   You're trying to save to buy a new $150,000 Ferrari. You have $35,000 today that can be invested at your bank. The bank pays 3.2 percent annual interest on its accounts. How long will it be before you have enough to buy the car?

LO 2   **10. Calculating Present Values.**   Imprudential, Inc., has an unfunded pension liability of $675 million that must be paid in 25 years. To assess the value of the firm's stock, financial analysts want to discount this liability back to the present. If the relevant discount rate is 6 percent, what is the present value of this liability?

LO 2   **11. Calculating Present Values.**   You have just received notification that you have won the $2 million first prize in the Centennial Lottery. However, the prize will be awarded on your 100th birthday (assuming you're around to collect), 80 years from now. What is the present value of your windfall if the appropriate discount rate is 10 percent?

www.mhhe.com/rwj

LO 1

12. Calculating Future Values. Your coin collection contains 50 1952 silver dollars. If your grandparents purchased them for their face value when they were new, how much will your collection be worth when you retire in 2058, assuming they appreciate at annual rate of 6.1 percent?

LO 1   **LO 3**

13. Calculating Growth Rates and Future Values. In 1895, the first U.S. Open Golf Championship was held. The winner's prize money was $150. In 2011, the winner's check was $1,440,000. What was the annual percentage increase in the winner's check over this period? If the winner's prize increases at the same rate, what will it be in 2045?

LO 3

14. Calculating Rates of Return. In 2011, an *Action Comics* No. 1, featuring the first appearance of Superman, was sold at auction for $2,161,000. The comic book was originally sold in 1938 for $.10. What was the annual increase in the value of this comic book?

LO 3

15. Calculating Rates of Return. In October 2011, the average house price in the United States was $242,300. In October 2004, the average price was $289,600. What was the annual change in the average selling price?

LO 3

16. Calculating Rates of Return. Refer back to the Series EE savings bonds we discussed at the very beginning of the chapter.

Intermediate
(Questions 16–25)

   a. Assuming you purchased a $50 face value bond, what rate of return would you earn if you held the bond for 20 years until it doubled in value?

   b. If you purchased a $50 face value bond in early 2012 at the then current interest rate of .60 percent per year, how much would the bond be worth in 2022?

   c. In 2022, instead of cashing the bond in for its then current value, you decide to hold the bond until it doubles in face value in 2032. What rate of return will you earn over the last 10 years?

LO 2

17. Calculating Present Values. Suppose you are still committed to owning a $150,000 Ferrari (see Question 9). If you believe your mutual fund can achieve a 10.25 percent annual rate of return, and you want to buy the car in 10 years on the day you turn 30, how much must you invest today?

LO 1

18. Calculating Future Values. You have just made your first $5,000 contribution to your individual retirement account. Assuming you earn a 10.1 percent rate of return and make no additional contributions, what will your account be worth when you retire in 45 years? What if you wait 10 years before contributing? (Does this suggest an investment strategy?)

LO 1

19. Calculating Future Values. You are scheduled to receive $15,000 in two years. When you receive it, you will invest it for six more years at 8 percent per year. How much will you have in eight years?

LO 4

20. Calculating the Number of Periods. You expect to receive $25,000 at graduation in two years. You plan on investing it at 9 percent until you have $150,000. How long will you wait from now? (Better than the situation in Question 9, but still no Ferrari.)

LO 1

21. Calculating Future Values. You have $7,000 to deposit. Regency Bank offers 12 percent per year compounded monthly (1 percent per month), while King Bank offers 12 percent but will only compound annually. How much will your investment be worth in 20 years at each bank?

LO 3

22. Calculating Rates of Return. An investment offers to triple your money in 24 months (don't believe it). What rate per three months are you being offered?

LO 4

23. Calculating the Number of Periods. You can earn .43 percent per month at your bank. If you deposit $1,800, how long must you wait until your account has grown to $3,100?

LO 2

24. Calculating Present Values. You need $75,000 in 10 years. If you can earn .57 percent per month, how much will you have to deposit today?

LO 2

25. Calculating Present Values. You have decided that you want to be a millionaire when you retire in 45 years. If you can earn an annual return of 10 percent, how much do you have to invest today? What if you can earn 5 percent?

LO 1

26. Calculating Future Values. You have $20,000 you want to invest for the next 40 years. You are offered an investment plan that will pay you 7 percent per year for the next 20 years and 11 percent per year for the last 20 years. How much will you have at the end of the 40 years? Does it matter if the investment plan pays you 11 percent per year for the first 20 years and 7 percent per year for the next 20 years? Why or why not?

Challenge
(Question 26)

4.1 Calculating Future Values. Go to www.dinkytown.net and find the "Savings Calculator" calculator. If you currently have $10,000 and invest this money at 9 percent, how much will you have in 30 years? Assume you will not make any additional contributions. How much will you have if you can earn 11 percent?

4.2 Calculating the Number of Periods. Go to www.dinkytown.net and find the "Cool Million" calculator. You want to be a millionaire. You can earn 11.5 percent per year. Using your current age, at what age will you become a millionaire if you have $25,000 to invest, assuming you make no other deposits (ignore inflation)?

4.3 Calculating the Number of Periods. Go to www.moneychimp.com and find the "Compound Interest" calculator. You want to buy a Lamborghini Murciélago. Assume the price of the car is $330,000 and you have $35,000. If you can earn an 11 percent return, how long must you wait to buy this car (assuming the price stays the same)?

4.4 Calculating Rates of Return. Use the Return Rate calculator at www.moneychimp.com to solve the following problem. You still want to buy the Lamborghini Murciélago, but you have $60,000 to invest and want to buy the car in 15 years. What interest rate do you have to earn to accomplish this (assuming the price stays the same)?

4.5 Future Values and Taxes. Taxes can greatly affect the future value of your investment. The Financial Calculators website at www.fincalc.com has a financial calculator that adjusts your return for taxes. Go to this page and find this calculator. Suppose you have $50,000 to invest today. If you can earn a 12 percent return, and you have no additional savings, how much will you have in 20 years? (Enter 0 percent as the tax rate.) Now, assume that your marginal tax rate is 27.5 percent. How much will you have at this tax rate?

WHAT'S ON THE WEB?

www.mhhe.com/rwj

EXCEL *MASTER IT!* PROBLEM

Before the advent of financial calculators (and Excel), tables were often used in the calculation of present values and future values. Using a two-way data table, create a future value table and a present value table. To make the table a little more interesting, make sure the table will calculate the future values and present values for different dollar amounts. One thing we should note here is that you will not be able to simply copy and paste the tables presented earlier in this workbook. When a data table is created, you cannot insert or delete rows or columns at a later point in time.

5 | Discounted Cash Flow Valuation

learning objectives

After studying this chapter, you should be able to:

LO 1 Determine the future and present value of investments with multiple cash flows.

LO 2 Calculate loan payments and find the interest rate on a loan.

LO 3 Describe how loans are amortized or paid off.

LO 4 Explain how interest rates are quoted (and misquoted).

What do professional baseball players Rod Barajas, Prince Fielder, and Albert Pujols have in common? All three athletes signed big contracts in 2011 or early 2012. The contract values were reported as $7.5 million, $214 million, and $240 million, respectively. That's definitely major league money, but, even so, reported numbers like these can be misleading. For example, in November 2011, Barajas signed with the Pittsburgh Pirates. His contract called for a salary of $4 million with a club option for $3.5 million for 2013, for a total of $7.5 million. Not Fielder's or Pujol's money, but still not too shabby for someone who makes a living using the "tools of ignorance" (jock jargon for a catcher's equipment).

A closer look at the numbers shows that Rod, Prince, and Albert did pretty well, but nothing like the quoted figures. Using Albert's contract as an example, although the value was reported to be $240 million, it was actually payable over several years. It consisted of $12 million in 2012, $16 million in 2013, $23 million in 2014, then a $1 million annual salary increase for the next seven years until 2021. Because the payments were spread out over time, we must consider the time value of money, which means his contract was worth less than reported. How much did he really get? This chapter gives you the "tools of knowledge" to answer this question.

In our previous chapter, we learned how to examine single, lump-sum future payments to determine their current, or present, value. This is a useful skill, but we need to go further and figure out how to handle multiple future payments because that is the much more common situation. For example, most loans (including student loans) involve receiving a lump sum today and making future payments.

More generally, most types of business decisions, including decisions concerning marketing, operations, and strategy, involve the comparison of costs incurred today with cash inflows hoped for later. Evaluating the cost-benefit trade-off requires the tools that we develop in this chapter.

Because discounted cash flow valuation is so important, students who learn this material well will find that life is much easier down the road. Getting it straight now will save you a lot of headaches later.

I n our previous chapter, we covered the basics of discounted cash flow valuation. However, so far, we have only dealt with single cash flows. In reality, most investments have multiple cash flows. For example, if Sears is thinking of opening a new department store, there will be a large cash outlay in the beginning and then cash inflows for many years. In this chapter, we begin to explore how to value such investments.

When you finish this chapter, you should have some very practical skills. For example, you will know how to calculate your own car payments or student loan payments. You will also be able to determine how long it will take to pay off a credit card if you make the minimum payment each month (a practice we do not recommend). We will show you how to compare interest rates to determine which are the highest and which are the lowest, and we will also show you how interest rates can be quoted in different, and at times deceptive, ways.

FUTURE AND PRESENT VALUES OF MULTIPLE CASH FLOWS

5.1

Thus far, we have restricted our attention to either the future value of a lump-sum present amount or the present value of some single future cash flow. In this section, we begin to study ways to value multiple cash flows. We start with future value.

Future Value with Multiple Cash Flows

Suppose you deposit $100 today in an account paying 8 percent. In one year, you will deposit another $100. How much will you have in two years? This particular problem is relatively easy. At the end of the first year, you will have $108 plus the second $100 you deposit, for a total of $208. You leave this $208 on deposit at 8 percent for another year. At the end of this second year, the account is worth:

ExcelMaster
coverage online

$208 × 1.08 = $224.64

Figure 5.1 is a *time line* that illustrates the process of calculating the future value of these two $100 deposits. Figures such as this one are very useful for solving complicated problems. Anytime you are having trouble with a present or future value problem, drawing a time line will usually help you to see what is happening.

In the first part of Figure 5.1, we show the cash flows on the time line. The most important thing is that we write them down where they actually occur. Here, the first cash flow occurs today, which we label as Time 0. We therefore put $100 at Time 0 on the time line. The second $100 cash flow occurs one year from today, so we write it down at the point labeled as Time 1. In the second part of Figure 5.1, we calculate the future values one period at a time to come up with the final $224.64.

FIGURE **5.1**	**A.** The time line:

Drawing and using a time line

B. Calculating the future value:

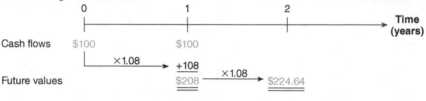

EXAMPLE 5.1	### SAVING UP REVISITED

You think you will be able to deposit $4,000 at the end of each of the next three years in a bank account paying 8 percent interest. You currently have $7,000 in the account. How much will you have in three years? In four years?

At the end of the first year, you will have:

$7,000 × 1.08 + 4,000 = $11,560

At the end of the second year, you will have:

$11,560 × 1.08 + 4,000 = $16,484.80

Repeating this for the third year gives:

$16,484.80 × 1.08 + 4,000 = $21,803.58

Therefore, you will have $21,803.58 in three years. If you leave this on deposit for one more year (and don't add to it), at the end of the fourth year, you'll have:

$21,803.58 × 1.08 = $23,547.87

When we calculated the future value of the two $100 deposits, we simply calculated the balance as of the beginning of each year and then rolled that amount forward to the next year. We could have done it another, quicker way. The first $100 is on deposit for two years at 8 percent, so its future value is:

$100 × 1.08² = $100 × 1.1664 = $116.64

The second $100 is on deposit for one year at 8 percent, and its future value is thus:

$100 × 1.08 = $108.00

The total future value, as we previously calculated, is equal to the sum of these two future values:

$116.64 + 108 = $224.64

FIGURE 5.2

Time line for $2,000 per year for five years

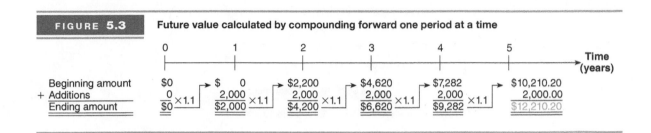

FIGURE 5.3   Future value calculated by compounding forward one period at a time

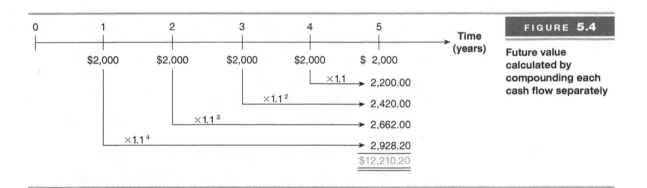

FIGURE 5.4

Future value calculated by compounding each cash flow separately

Based on this example, there are two ways to calculate future values for multiple cash flows: (1) compound the accumulated balance forward one year at a time or (2) calculate the future value of each cash flow first and then add these up. Both give the same answer, so you can do it either way.

To illustrate the two different ways of calculating future values, consider the future value of $2,000 invested at the end of each of the next five years. The current balance is zero, and the rate is 10 percent. We first draw a time line as shown in Figure 5.2.

On the time line, notice that nothing happens until the end of the first year when we make the first $2,000 investment. This first $2,000 earns interest for the next four (not five) years. Also notice that the last $2,000 is invested at the end of the fifth year, so it earns no interest at all.

Figure 5.3 illustrates the calculations involved if we compound the investment one period at a time. As illustrated, the future value is $12,210.20.

Figure 5.4 goes through the same calculations, but it uses the second technique. Naturally, the answer is the same.

EXAMPLE 5.2

SAVING UP ONCE AGAIN

If you deposit $100 in one year, $200 in two years, and $300 in three years, how much will you have in three years? How much of this is interest? How much will you have in five years if you don't add additional amounts? Assume a 7 percent interest rate throughout.

We will calculate the future value of each amount in three years. Notice that the $100 earns interest for two years, and the $200 earns interest for one year. The final $300 earns no interest. The future values are thus:

$$
\begin{aligned}
\$100 \times 1.07^2 &= \$114.49 \\
\$200 \times 1.07 &= 214.00 \\
+\$300 &= \underline{300.00} \\
\text{Total future value} &= \underline{\underline{\$628.49}}
\end{aligned}
$$

The future value is thus $628.49. The total interest is:

$$\$628.49 - (100 + 200 + 300) = \$28.49$$

How much will you have in five years? We know that you will have $628.49 in three years. If you leave that in for two more years, it will grow to:

$$\$628.49 \times 1.07^2 = \$628.49 \times 1.1449 = \$719.56$$

Notice that we could have calculated the future value of each amount separately. Once again, be careful about the lengths of time. As we previously calculated, the first $100 earns interest for only four years, the second deposit earns three years' interest, and the last earns two years' interest:

$$
\begin{aligned}
\$100 \times 1.07^4 = \$100 \times 1.3108 &= \$131.08 \\
\$200 \times 1.07^3 = \$200 \times 1.2250 &= 245.01 \\
+\$300 \times 1.07^2 = \$300 \times 1.1449 &= \underline{343.47} \\
\text{Total future value} &= \underline{\underline{\$719.56}}
\end{aligned}
$$

Present Value with Multiple Cash Flows

It will turn out that we will very often need to determine the present value of a series of future cash flows. As with future values, there are two ways we can do it. We can either discount back one period at a time, or we can just calculate the present values individually and add them up.

Suppose you need $1,000 in one year and $2,000 more in two years. If you can earn 9 percent on your money, how much do you have to put up today to exactly cover these amounts in the future? In other words, what is the present value of the two cash flows at 9 percent?

The present value of $2,000 in two years at 9 percent is:

$2,000/1.09² = $1,683.36

The present value of $1,000 in one year is:

$1,000/1.09 = $917.43

Therefore, the total present value is:

$1,683.36 + 917.43 = $2,600.79

To see why $2,600.79 is the right answer, we can check to see that after the $2,000 is paid out in two years, there is no money left. If we invest $2,600.79 for one year at 9 percent, we will have:

$2,600.79 × 1.09 = $2,834.86

We take out $1,000, leaving $1,834.86. This amount earns 9 percent for another year, leaving us with:

$1,834.86 × 1.09 = $2,000

This is just as we planned. As this example illustrates, the present value of a series of future cash flows is simply the amount that you would need today in order to exactly duplicate those future cash flows (for a given discount rate).

An alternative way of calculating present values for multiple future cash flows is to discount back to the present one period at a time. To illustrate, suppose we had an investment that was going to pay $1,000 at the end of every year for the next five years. To find the present value, we could discount each $1,000 back to the present separately and then add the results up. Figure 5.5 illustrates this approach for a 6 percent discount rate. As shown, the answer is $4,212.37 (ignoring a small rounding error).

Alternatively, we could discount the last cash flow back one period and add it to the next-to-the-last cash flow:

$1,000/1.06 + 1,000 = $943.40 + 1,000 = $1,943.40

We could then discount this amount back one period and add it to the Year 3 cash flow:

$1,943.40/1.06 + 1,000 = $1,833.40 + 1,000 = $2,833.40

This process could be repeated as necessary. Figure 5.6 illustrates this approach and the remaining calculations.

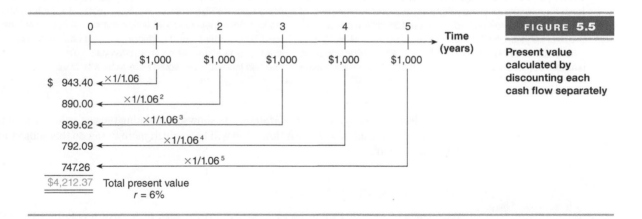

FIGURE 5.5

Present value calculated by discounting each cash flow separately

FIGURE 5.6

Present value calculated by discounting back one period at a time

FINANCE MATTERS

◀ For the latest news on the topics covered in this chapter, scan here.

Jackpot!

If you, or someone you know, is a regular lottery player, you probably already understand that you are 20 times more likely to be killed by a lightning bolt than to win a big lottery jackpot. How bad are the odds? Nearby you will find a table comparing your chances of winning the Mega Millions Lottery to other events.

Big Game: Is It Worth the Gamble?	
Odds of winning Mega Millions jackpot	1:135,145,920*
Odds of being killed by a venomous spider	1:57,018,763
Odds of being killed by a dog bite	1:11,403,753
Odds of being killed by lightning	1:6,479,405
Odds of being killed by drowning	1:690,300
Odds of being killed by falling from a bed or other furniture	1:388,411
Odds of being killed in a car crash	1:6,029

Source: Virginia Lottery Web site. All other odds from the National Safety Council.

Sweepstakes may have different odds than lotteries, but the odds may not be much better. Probably the largest advertised grand prize ever was Pepsi's "Play for a Billion," which, you guessed it, had a $1 billion (*billion!*) prize. Not bad for a day's work, but you still have to read the fine print. It turns out that the winner would be paid $5 million per year for the next 20 years, $10 million per year for years 21 to 39, and a lump sum of $710 million in 40 years. From what you have learned, you know the value of the sweepstakes wasn't even

close to $1 billion. In fact, at an interest rate of 10 percent, the present value was about $70.7 million.

Lottery jackpots are often paid out over 20 or more years, but the winner can usually choose to take a lump sum cash payment instead. For example, in November 2011, three investment advisers from Connecticut won the $245 million Powerball lottery. The group had the option of a single cash payment of $146.2 million or payments over the next 30 years, which is what the group chose to accept.

Some lotteries make your decision a little tougher. The Ontario Lottery will pay you either $2,000 a week for the rest of your life or $1.3 million now. (That's in Canadian dollars, by the way.) Of course, there is the chance you might die in the near future, so the lottery guarantees that your heirs will collect the $2,000 weekly payments until the 20th anniversary of the first payment, or until you would have turned 91, whichever comes first. This payout scheme complicates your decision quite a bit. If you live for only the 20-year minimum, the break-even interest rate between the two options is about 5.13 percent per year, compounded weekly. If you expect to live longer than the 20-year minimum, you might be better off accepting $2,000 per week for life. Of course, if you manage to invest the $1.3 million lump sum at a rate of return of about 8 percent per year (compounded weekly), you can have your cake and eat it too since the investment will return $2,000 at the end of each week forever! Taxes complicate the decision in this case because the lottery payments are all on an aftertax basis. Thus, the rates of return in this example would have to be aftertax as well.

As the accompanying *Finance Matters* box shows, calculating present values is a vital step in comparing alternative cash flows. We will have much more to say on this subject in subsequent chapters.

EXAMPLE 5.3   HOW MUCH IS IT WORTH?

You are offered an investment that will pay you $200 in one year, $400 the next year, $600 the next year, and $800 at the end of the next year. You can earn 12 percent on very similar investments. What is the most you should pay for this one?

We need to calculate the present value of these cash flows at 12 percent. Taking them one at a time gives:

$$\$200 \times 1/1.12^1 = \$200/1.1200 = \$\ \ 178.57$$
$$\$400 \times 1/1.12^2 = \$400/1.2544 = \ \ 318.88$$
$$\$600 \times 1/1.12^3 = \$600/1.4049 = \ \ 427.07$$
$$+\$800 \times 1/1.12^4 = \$800/1.5735 = \ \ \underline{508.41}$$
$$\text{Total present value} = \underline{\$1,432.93}$$

(continued)

If you can earn 12 percent on your money, then you can duplicate this investment's cash flows for $1,432.93, so this is the most you should be willing to pay.

HOW MUCH IS IT WORTH? PART 2   EXAMPLE 5.4

You are offered an investment that will make three $5,000 payments. The first payment will occur four years from today. The second will occur in five years, and the third will follow in six years. If you can earn 11 percent, what is the most this investment is worth today? What is the future value of the cash flows?

We will answer the questions in reverse order to illustrate a point. The future value of the cash flows in six years is:

$$\$5,000 \times 1.11^2 + 5,000 \times 1.11 + 5,000 = \$6,160.50 + 5,550 + 5,000$$
$$= \$16,710.50$$

The present value must be:

$$\$16,710.50/1.11^6 = \$8,934.12$$

Let's check this. Taking them one at a time, the PVs of the cash flows are:

$$\$5,000 \times 1/1.11^6 = \$5,000/1.8704 = \$2,673.20$$
$$\$5,000 \times 1/1.11^5 = \$5,000/1.6851 = \ \ 2,967.26$$
$$+\$5,000 \times 1/1.11^4 = \$5,000/1.5181 = \ \ \underline{3,293.65}$$
$$\text{Total present value} = \underline{\$8,934.12}$$

This is as we previously calculated. The point we want to make is that we can calculate present and future values in any order and convert between them using whatever way seems most convenient. The answers will always be the same as long as we stick with the same discount rate and are careful to keep track of the right number of periods.

How to Calculate Present Values with Multiple Future Cash Flows Using a Financial Calculator   CALCULATOR HINTS

To calculate the present value of multiple cash flows with a financial calculator, we will simply discount the individual cash flows one at a time using the same technique we used in our previous chapter, so this is not really new. There is a shortcut, however, that we can show you. We will use the numbers in Example 5.3 to illustrate.

To begin, of course, we first remember to clear out the calculator! Next, from Example 5.3, the first cash flow is $200 to be received in one year and the discount rate is 12 percent, so we do the following:

Now, you can write down this answer to save it, but that's inefficient. All calculators have a memory where you can store numbers. Why not just save it there? Doing so cuts way down on mistakes because you don't have to write down and/or rekey numbers, and it's much faster.

Next, we value the second cash flow. We need to change N to 2 and FV to 400. As long as we haven't changed anything else, we don't have to reenter I/Y or clear out the calculator, so we have:

Enter 2   400

Solve for   −318.88

You save this number by adding it to the one you saved in our first calculation, and so on for the remaining two calculations.

As we will see in a later chapter, some financial calculators will let you enter all of the future cash flows at once, but we'll discuss that subject when we get to it.

A Note on Cash Flow Timing

In working present and future value problems, cash flow timing is critically important. In almost all such calculations, it is implicitly assumed that the cash flows occur at the end of each period. In fact, all the formulas we have discussed, all the numbers in a standard present value or future value table, and, very importantly, all the preset (or default) settings on a financial calculator or spreadsheet assume that cash flows occur at the end of each period. Unless you are very explicitly told otherwise, you should always assume that this is what is meant.

As a quick illustration of this point, suppose you are told that a three-year investment has a first-year cash flow of $100, a second-year cash flow of $200, and a third-year cash flow of $300. You are asked to draw a time line. Without further information, you should always assume that the time line looks like this:

On our time line, notice how the first cash flow occurs at the end of the first period, the second at the end of the second period, and the third at the end of the third period.

We will close out this section by answering the question we posed at the beginning of the chapter concerning baseball player Albert Pujols's contract. Remember that the contract called for $12 million in 2012, $16 million in 2013, $23 million in 2014, and then a $1 million annual salary increase for the next seven years until 2021. If 12 percent is the appropriate discount rate, what kind of deal did the Los Angeles Angel's first baseman field?

To answer, we can calculate the present value by discounting each year's salary back to the present as follows (notice we assumed the future salaries will be paid at the end of the year):

Year 1: $12,000,000 × 1/1.12 = $10,714,285.71
Year 2: $16,000,000 × 1/1.12² = $12,755,102.04

Year 10: $30,000,000 × 1/1.12¹⁰ = $9,659,197.10

If you fill in the missing rows and then add (do it for practice), you will see that Pujols's contract had a present value of about $126.09 million, or only about 53 percent of the $240 million reported value, but still pretty good.

How to Calculate Present Values with Multiple Future Cash Flows Using a Spreadsheet

SPREADSHEET
STRATEGIES

Just as we did in our previous chapter, we can set up a basic spreadsheet to calculate the present values of the individual cash flows as follows. Notice that we have simply calculated the present values one at a time and added them up.

	A	B	C	D	E	F
1						
2		Using a spreadsheet to value multiple cash flows				
3						
4	What is the present value of $200 in one year, $400 the next year, $600 the next year, and					
5	$800 the last year if the discount rate is 12 percent?					
6						
7	Rate:	.12				
8						
9	Year	Cash flows	Present values	Formula used		
10	1	$200	$178.57	=PV($B$7, A10,0,-B10)		
11	2	$400	$318.88	=PV($B$7, A11,0,-B11)		
12	3	$600	$427.07	=PV($B$7, A12,0,-B12)		
13	4	$800	$508.41	=PV($B$7, A13,0,-B13)		
14						
15		Total PV:	**$1,432.93**	=SUM(C10:C13)		
16						
17	Notice the negative signs inserted in the PV formulas. These just make the present values have					
18	positive signs. Also, the discount rate in cell B7 is entered as $B$7 (an "absolute" reference)					
19	because it is used over and over. We could have just entered ".12" instead, but our approach is					
20	more flexible.					
21						
22						

5.1a   Describe how to calculate the future value of a series of cash flows.

5.1b   Describe how to calculate the present value of a series of cash flows.

5.1c   Unless we are explicitly told otherwise, what do we always assume about the timing of cash flows in present and future value problems?

5.2

VALUING LEVEL CASH FLOWS: ANNUITIES AND PERPETUITIES

We will frequently encounter situations where we have multiple cash flows that are all the same amount. For example, a very common type of loan repayment plan calls for the borrower to repay the loan by making a series of equal payments for some length of time. Almost all consumer loans (such as car loans) and home mortgages feature equal payments, usually made each month.

More generally, a series of constant, or level, cash flows that occur at the end of each period for some fixed number of periods is called an ordinary **annuity**; or, more correctly, the cash flows are said to be in ordinary annuity form. Annuities appear very frequently in financial arrangements, and there are some useful shortcuts for determining their values. We consider these next.

annuity
A level stream of cash flows for a fixed period of time.

Present Value for Annuity Cash Flows

ExcelMaster
coverage online

Suppose we were examining an asset that promised to pay $500 at the end of each of the next three years. The cash flows from this asset are in the form of a three-year, $500 ordinary annuity. If we wanted to earn 10 percent on our money, how much would we offer for this annuity?

From the previous section, we know that we can discount each of these $500 payments back to the present at 10 percent to determine the total present value:

Present value = $500/1.1¹ + 500/1.1² + 500/1.1³
= $500/1.10 + 500/1.21 + 500/1.331
= $454.55 + 413.22 + 375.66
= $1,243.43

This approach works just fine. However, we will often encounter situations where the number of cash flows is quite large. For example, a typical home mortgage calls for monthly payments over 30 years, for a total of 360 payments. If we were trying to determine the present value of those payments, it would be useful to have a shortcut.

Since the cash flows on an annuity are all the same, we can come up with a very useful variation on the basic present value equation. It turns out that the present value of an annuity of C dollars per period for t periods when the rate of return, or interest rate, is r is given by:

$$\text{Annuity present value} = C \times \left(\frac{1 - \text{Present value factor}}{r} \right)$$
$$= C \times \left\{ \frac{1 - [1/(1 + r)^t]}{r} \right\} \qquad [5.1]$$

The term in parentheses on the first line is sometimes called the present value interest factor for annuities and abbreviated PVIFA(r, t).

The expression for the annuity present value may look a little complicated, but it isn't difficult to use. Notice that the term in square brackets on the second line, $1/(1 + r)^t$, is the same present value factor we've been calculating. In our example just above, the interest rate is 10 percent and there are three years involved. The usual present value factor is thus:

Present value factor = 1/1.1³ = 1/1.331 = .75131

To calculate the annuity present value factor, we just plug this in:

Annuity present value factor = (1 − Present value factor)/r

= (1 − .75131)/.10

= .248685/.10 = 2.48685

Just as we calculated before, the present value of our $500 annuity is then:

Annuity present value = $500 × 2.48685 = $1,243.43

HOW MUCH CAN YOU AFFORD?

EXAMPLE 5.5

After carefully going over your budget, you have determined you can afford to pay $632 per month toward a new sports car. You call up your local bank and find out that the going rate is 1 percent per month for 48 months. How much can you borrow?

To determine how much you can borrow, we need to calculate the present value of $632 per month for 48 months at 1 percent per month. The loan payments are in ordinary annuity form, so the annuity present value factor is:

Annuity PV factor = (1 − Present value factor)/r

$$= [1 − (1/1.01^{48})]/.01$$

$$= (1 − .6203)/.01 = 37.9740$$

With this factor, we can calculate the present value of the 48 payments of $632 each as:

Present value = $632 × 37.9740 = $24,000

Therefore, $24,000 is what you can afford to borrow and repay.

Annuity Tables Just as there are tables for ordinary present value factors, there are tables for annuity factors as well. Table 5.1 contains a few such factors; Table A.3 in Appendix A contains a larger set. To find the annuity present value factor we just calculated, look for the row corresponding to three periods and then find the column for 10 percent. The number you see at that intersection should be 2.4869 (rounded to four decimal places), as we calculated. Once again, try calculating a few of these factors yourself and compare your answers to the ones in the table to make sure you know how to do it. If you are using a financial calculator, just enter $1 as the payment and calculate the present value; the result should be the annuity present value factor.

Number of Periods	Interest Rates				
	5%	10%	15%	20%	
1	.9524	.9091	.8696	.8333	
2	1.8594	1.7355	1.6257	1.5278	
3	2.7232	2.4869	2.2832	2.1065	
4	3.5460	3.1699	2.8550	2.5887	
5	4.3295	3.7908	3.3522	2.9906	

TABLE 5.1

Annuity present value interest factors

CALCULATOR HINTS

Annuity Present Values

To find annuity present values with a financial calculator, we need to use the **PMT** key (you were probably wondering what it was for). Compared to finding the present value of a single amount, there are two important differences. First, we enter the annuity cash flow using the **PMT** key, and, second, we don't enter anything for the future value, **FV** . So, for example, the problem we have been examining is a three-year, $500 annuity. If the discount rate is 10 percent, we need to do the following (after clearing out the calculator!):

Enter	3	10	500		
	N	**I/Y**	**PMT**	**PV**	**FV**
Solve for				−1,243.43	

As usual, we get a negative sign on the PV.

SPREADSHEET STRATEGIES

Annuity Present Values

Using a spreadsheet to work the same problem goes like this:

	A	B	C	D	E	F	G
1							
2	Using a spreadsheet to find annuity present values						
3							
4	What is the present value of $500 per year for 3 years if the discount rate is 10 percent?						
5	We need to solve for the unknown present value, so we use the formula PV(rate, nper, pmt, fv).						
6							
7	Payment amount per period:	$500					
8	Number of payments:	3					
9	Discount rate:	.1					
10							
11	Annuity present value:	$1,243.43					
12							
13	The formula entered in cell B11 is =PV(B9, B8, −B7, 0); notice that fv is zero and that pmt has a						
14	negative sign on it. Also notice that the discount rate is entered as a decimal, not a percentage.						
15							

Finding the Payment   Suppose you wish to start up a new business that specializes in the latest of health food trends, frozen yak milk. To produce and market your product, the Yakee Doodle Dandy, you need to borrow $100,000. Because it strikes you as unlikely that this particular fad will be long-lived, you propose to pay off the loan quickly by making five equal annual payments. If the interest rate is 18 percent, what will the payments be?

In this case, we know that the present value is $100,000. The interest rate is 18 percent, and there are five years to make payments. The payments are all equal, so we need to find the relevant annuity factor and solve for the unknown cash flow:

$$\text{Annuity present value} = \$100,000 = C \times (1 - \text{Present value factor})/r$$
$$\$100,000 = C \times (1 - 1/1.18^5)/.18$$
$$= C \times (1 - .4371)/.18$$
$$= C \times 3.1272$$
$$C = \$100,000/3.1272 = \$31,978$$

Therefore, you'll make five payments of just under $32,000 each.

Annuity Payments

CALCULATOR
HINTS

Finding annuity payments is easy with a financial calculator. In our example just above, the PV is $100,000, the interest rate is 18 percent, and there are five years. We find the payment as follows:

Enter	5	18		100,000	
	N	**I/Y**	**PMT**	**PV**	**FV**
Solve for			−31,978		

Here we get a negative sign on the payment because the payment is an outflow for us.

Annuity Payments

SPREADSHEET
STRATEGIES

Using a spreadsheet to work the same problem goes like this:

	A	B	C	D	E	F	
1							
2		Using a spreadsheet to find annuity payments					
3							
4	What is the annuity payment if the present value is $100,000, the interest rate is 18 percent, and						
5	there are 5 periods? We need to solve for the unknown payment in an annuity, so we use the						
6	formula PMT(rate, nper, pv, fv)						
7							
8	Annuity present value:	$100,000					
9	Number of payments:	5					
10	Discount rate:	.18					
11							
12	Annuity payment:	($31,977.78)					
13							
14	The formula entered in cell B12 is =PMT(B10, B9, B8); notice that the						
15	payment has a negative sign because it is an outflow to us.						

EXAMPLE 5.6

FINDING THE NUMBER OF PAYMENTS

You ran a little short on your spring break vacation, so you put $1,000 on your credit card. You can only afford to make the minimum payment of $20 per month. The interest rate on the credit card is 1.5 percent per month. How long will you need to pay off the $1,000?

What we have here is an annuity of $20 per month at 1.5 percent per month for some unknown length of time. The present value is $1,000 (the amount you owe today). We need to do a little algebra (or else use a financial calculator):

$$\$1,000 = \$20 \times (1 - \text{Present value factor})/.015$$

$$(\$1,000/20) \times .015 = 1 - \text{Present value factor}$$

$$\text{Present value factor} = .25 = 1/(1 + r)^t$$

$$1.015^t = 1/.25 = 4$$

At this point, the problem boils down to asking the following question: How long does it take for your money to quadruple at 1.5 percent per month? Based on our previous chapter, the answer is about 93 months:

$$1.015^{93} = 3.99 \approx 4$$

It will take you about 93/12 = 7.75 years at this rate.

CALCULATOR HINTS

Finding the Number of Payments

To solve this one on a financial calculator, do the following:

Enter	1.5	−20	1,000	
N	**I/Y**	**PMT**	**PV**	**FV**

Solve for 93.11

Notice that we put a negative sign on the payment you must make, and we have solved for the number of months. You still have to divide by 12 to get our answer. Also, some financial calculators won't report a fractional value for N; they automatically (without telling you) round up to the next whole period (not to the nearest value). With a spreadsheet, use the function =NPER(rate,pmt,pv,fv); be sure to put in a zero for fv and to enter −20 as the payment.

Finding the Rate   The last question we might want to ask concerns the interest rate implicit in an annuity. For example, an insurance company offers to pay you $1,000 per year for 10 years if you pay $6,710 up front. What rate is implicit in this 10-year annuity?

In this case, we know the present value ($6,710), we know the cash flows ($1,000 per year), and we know the life of the investment (10 years). What we don't know is the discount rate:

$$\$6,710 = \$1,000 \times (1 - \text{Present value factor})/r$$

$$\$6,710/1,000 = 6.71 = \{1 - [1/(1 + r)^{10}]\}/r$$

So, the annuity factor for 10 periods is equal to 6.71, and we need to solve this equation for the unknown value of r. Unfortunately, this is mathematically impossible to do directly. The only way to do it is to use a table or trial and error to find a value for r.

If you look across the row corresponding to 10 periods in Table A.3, you will see a factor of 6.7101 for 8 percent, so we see right away that the insurance company is offering just about 8 percent. Alternatively, we could just start trying different values until we got very close to the answer. Using this trial-and-error approach can be a little tedious, but, fortunately, machines are good at that sort of thing.[1]

To illustrate how to find the answer by trial and error, suppose a relative of yours wants to borrow $3,000. She offers to repay you $1,000 every year for four years. What interest rate are you being offered?

The cash flows here have the form of a four-year, $1,000 annuity. The present value is $3,000. We need to find the discount rate, r. Our goal in doing so is primarily to give you a feel for the relationship between annuity values and discount rates.

We need to start somewhere, and 10 percent is probably as good a place as any to begin. At 10 percent, the annuity factor is:

Annuity present value factor = (1 − 1/1.10⁴)/.10 = 3.1699

The present value of the cash flows at 10 percent is thus:

Present value = $1,000 × 3.1699 = $3,169.90

You can see that we're already in the right ballpark.

Is 10 percent too high or too low? Recall that present values and discount rates move in opposite directions: Increasing the discount rate lowers the PV and vice versa. Our present value here is too high, so the discount rate is too low. If we try 12 percent:

Present value = $1,000 × (1 − 1/1.12⁴)/.12 = $3,037.35

Now we're almost there. We are still a little low on the discount rate (because the PV is a little high), so we'll try 13 percent:

Present value = $1,000 × (1 − 1/1.13⁴)/.13 = $2,974.47

This is less than $3,000, so we now know that the answer is between 12 percent and 13 percent, and it looks to be about 12.5 percent. For practice, work at it for a while longer and see if you find that the answer is about 12.59 percent.

Finding the Rate

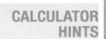

Alternatively, you could use a financial calculator to do the following:

Enter	4		1,000	−3,000	
	N	**I/Y**	**PMT**	**PV**	**FV**
Solve for		12.59			

Notice that we put a negative sign on the present value (why?). With a spreadsheet, use the function =RATE(nper,pmt,pv,fv); be sure to put in a zero for fv and to enter 1,000 as the payment and −3,000 as the present value.

---

[1] Financial calculators rely on trial and error to find the answer. That's why they sometimes appear to be "thinking" before coming up with the answer. Actually, it is possible to directly solve for r if there are fewer than five periods, but it's usually not worth the trouble.

Future Value for Annuities

On occasion, it's also handy to know a shortcut for calculating the future value of an annuity. As you might guess, there are future value factors for annuities as well as present value factors. In general, the future value factor for an annuity is given by:

$$\text{Annuity FV factor} = (\text{Future value factor} - 1)/r$$
$$= [(1 + r)^t - 1]/r \qquad\qquad [5.2]$$

To see how we use annuity future value factors, suppose you plan to contribute $2,000 every year into a retirement account paying 8 percent. If you retire in 30 years, how much will you have?

The number of years here, t, is 30, and the interest rate, r, is 8 percent, so we can calculate the annuity future value factor as:

$$\text{Annuity FV factor} = (\text{Future value factor} - 1)/r$$
$$= (1.08^{30} - 1)/.08$$
$$= (10.0627 - 1)/.08$$
$$= 113.2832$$

The future value of this 30-year, $2,000 annuity is thus:

$$\text{Annuity future value} = \$2,000 \times 113.2832$$
$$= \$226,566.42$$

CALCULATOR HINTS

Future Values of Annuities

Of course, you could solve this problem using a financial calculator by doing the following:

Enter   30   8   −2,000

| N | I/Y | PMT | PV | FV |

Solve for   226,566.42

Notice that we put a negative sign on the payment (why?). With a spreadsheet, use the function =FV(rate,nper,pmt,pv); be sure to put in a zero for pv and to enter −2,000 as the payment.

A Note on Annuities Due

So far, we have only discussed ordinary annuities. These are the most important, but there is a variation that is fairly common. Remember that with an ordinary annuity, the cash flows occur at the end of each period. When you take out a loan with monthly payments, for example, the first loan payment normally occurs one month after you get the loan. However, when you lease an apartment, the first lease payment is usually due immediately. The second payment is due at the beginning of the second month, and so on. A lease is an example of an **annuity due**. An annuity due is an annuity for which the cash flows occur at the beginning of each period. Almost any type of arrangement in which we have to prepay the same amount each period is an annuity due.

annuity due
An annuity for which the cash flows occur at the beginning of the period.

There are several different ways to calculate the value of an annuity due. With a financial calculator, you simply switch it into "due" or "beginning" mode. It is very important to remember to switch it back when you are finished! Another way to calculate the present value of an annuity due can be illustrated with a time line. Suppose an annuity due has five payments of $400 each, and the relevant discount rate is 10 percent. The time line looks like this:

Notice how the cash flows here are the same as those for a *four*-year ordinary annuity, except that there is an extra $400 at Time 0. For practice, verify that the present value of a four-year $400 ordinary annuity at 10 percent is $1,267.95. If we add on the extra $400, we get $1,667.95, which is the present value of this annuity due.

There is an even easier way to calculate the present or future value of an annuity due. If we assume that cash flows occur at the end of each period when they really occur at the beginning, then we discount each one by one period too many. We could fix this by simply multiplying our answer by $(1 + r)$, where r is the discount rate. In fact, the relationship between the value of an annuity due and an ordinary annuity with the same number of payments is just:

Annuity due value = Ordinary annuity value × (1 + *r*)   [5.3]

This works for both present and future values, so calculating the value of an annuity due involves two steps: (1) calculate the present or future value as though it were an ordinary annuity and (2) multiply your answer by $(1 + r)$.

Perpetuities

We've seen that a series of level cash flows can be valued by treating those cash flows as an annuity. An important special case of an annuity arises when the level stream of cash flows continues forever. Such an asset is called a **perpetuity** since the cash flows are perpetual. Perpetuities are also called **consols**, particularly in Canada and the United Kingdom. See Example 5.7 for an important example of a perpetuity.

Since a perpetuity has an infinite number of cash flows, we obviously can't compute its value by discounting each one. Fortunately, valuing a perpetuity turns out to be the easiest possible case. The present value of a perpetuity is simply:

PV for a perpetuity = *C*/*r* [5.4]

For example, an investment offers a perpetual cash flow of $500 every year. The return you require on such an investment is 8 percent. What is the value of this investment? The value of this perpetuity is:

Perpetuity PV = *C*/*r* = $500/.08 = $6,250

This concludes our discussion of valuing investments with multiple cash flows. For future reference, Table 5.2 contains a summary of the annuity and perpetuity basic calculations we described. By now, you probably think that you'll just use online calculators to handle annuity problems. Before you do, see our nearby *Work the Web* box.

Time value applications abound on the web. See, for example, www.collegeboard.com and personal.fidelity.com.

perpetuity
An annuity in which the cash flows continue forever.

consol
A type of perpetuity.

TABLE 5.2

Summary of annuity and perpetuity calculations

I. **Symbols**
   PV = Present value, what future cash flows are worth today
   FV_t = Future value, what cash flows are worth in the future at time t
   r = Interest rate, rate of return, or discount rate per period—typically, but not always, one year
   t = Number of periods—typically, but not always, the number of years
   C = Cash amount

II. **Future value of C invested per period for t periods at r percent per period**
   $FV_t = C \times [(1 + r)^t - 1]/r$
   A series of identical cash flows paid for a set number of periods is called an annuity, and the term $[(1 + r)^t - 1]/r$ is called the *annuity future value factor*.

III. **Present value of C per period for t periods at r percent per period**
   $PV = C \times \{1 - [1/(1 + r)^t]\}/r$
   The term $\{1 - [1/(1 + r)^t]\}/r$ is called the *annuity present value factor*.

IV. **Present value of a perpetuity of C per period**
   $PV = C/r$
   A perpetuity has the same cash flow every period forever.

WORK THE WEB

◀ To get updated data, scan here.

As we discussed in our previous chapter, many websites have financial calculators. One of these sites is Calculatoredge, which is located at www.calculatoredge.com. Suppose you retire with $1,000,000 and want to withdraw an equal amount each year for the next 30 years. If you can earn a 9 percent return, how much can you withdraw each year? Here is what Calculatoredge says:

Enter your values:

Currency:	US Dollars ▼	
Starting Principal:	1000000	US Dollars
Annual Interest Rate:	9	%
Repayment Period:	30	Years

[Calculate]   [Clear]

Results:

Annuity Payment: 89299.40   US Dollars / Year

According to the Calculatoredge calculator, the answer is $89,299.40. How important is it to understand what you are doing? Calculate this one for yourself, and you should get $97,336.35. Which one is right? You are, of course! What's going on is that Calculatoredge assumes (but tells you on a different page) that the annuity is in the form of an annuity due, not an ordinary annuity. Recall that with an annuity due the payments occur at the beginning of the period rather than at the end of the period. The moral of the story is clear: *Caveat calculator.*

Questions

1. *Go to the calculator at www.calculatoredge.com and find out how much the website says you could withdraw each year if you have $2,500,000, earn an 8 percent interest rate, and make annual withdrawals for 35 years. How much more are the withdrawals if they are in the form of an ordinary annuity?*

2. *Suppose you have $500,000 and want to make withdrawals each month for the next 10 years. The first withdrawal is today and the appropriate interest rate is 9 percent compounded monthly. Using this website, how much are your withdrawals?*

PREFERRED STOCK

EXAMPLE 5.7

Preferred stock (or preference stock) is an important example of a perpetuity. When a corporation sells preferred stock, the buyer is promised a fixed cash dividend every period (usually every quarter) forever. This dividend must be paid before any dividend can be paid to regular stockholders, hence the term *preferred*.

Suppose the Fellini Co. wants to sell preferred stock at $100 per share. A very similar issue of preferred stock already outstanding has a price of $40 per share and offers a dividend of $1 every quarter. What dividend will Fellini have to offer if the preferred stock is going to sell?

The issue that is already out has a present value of $40 and a cash flow of $1 every quarter forever. Since this is a perpetuity:

Present value = $40 = $1 $\times$ (1/r)

$r = 2.5\%$

To be competitive, the new Fellini issue will also have to offer 2.5 percent *per quarter;* so, if the present value is to be $100, the dividend must be such that:

Present value = $100 = C \times (1/.025)$

C = $2.5 (per quarter)

CONCEPT QUESTIONS

5.2a   In general, what is the present value of an annuity of C dollars per period at a discount rate of r per period? The future value?

5.2b   In general, what is the present value of a perpetuity?

COMPARING RATES: THE EFFECT OF COMPOUNDING PERIODS

The last issue we need to discuss has to do with the way interest rates are quoted. This subject causes a fair amount of confusion because rates are quoted in many different ways. Sometimes the way a rate is quoted is the result of tradition, and sometimes it's the result of legislation. Unfortunately, at times, rates are quoted in deliberately deceptive ways to mislead borrowers and investors. We will discuss these topics in this section.

ExcelMaster
coverage online

Effective Annual Rates and Compounding

If a rate is quoted as 10 percent compounded semiannually, then what this means is that the investment actually pays 5 percent every six months. A natural question then arises: Is 5 percent every six months the same thing as 10 percent per year? It's easy to see that it is not. If you invest $1 at 10 percent per year, you will have $1.10 at the end of the year. If you invest at 5 percent every six months, then you'll have the future value of $1 at 5 percent for two periods, or:

$1 $\times$ 1.05² = $1.1025

This is $.0025 more. The reason is very simple. What has occurred is that your account was credited with $1 $\times$ .05 = 5 cents in interest after six months. In the following six months, you earned 5 percent on that nickel, for an extra .05 $\times$ .05 = .0025 = .25 cents.

As our example illustrates, 10 percent compounded semiannually is actually equivalent to 10.25 percent per year. Put another way, we would be indifferent between 10 percent compounded semiannually and 10.25 percent compounded annually. Anytime we have compounding during the year, we need to be concerned about what the rate really is.

stated interest rate
The interest rate expressed in terms of the interest payment made each period. Also, quoted interest rate.

In our example, the 10 percent is called a stated, or quoted, interest rate. Other names are used as well. The 10.25 percent, which is actually the rate that you will earn, is called the effective annual rate (EAR). To compare different investments or interest rates, we will always need to convert to effective rates. Some general procedures for doing this are discussed next.

Calculating and Comparing Effective Annual Rates

effective annual rate (EAR)
The interest rate expressed as if it were compounded once per year.

To see why it is important to work only with effective rates, suppose you've shopped around and come up with the following three rates:

Bank A: 15 percent, compounded daily
Bank B: 15.5 percent, compounded quarterly
Bank C: 16 percent, compounded annually

Which of these is the best if you are thinking of opening a savings account? Which of these is best if they represent loan rates?

To begin, Bank C is offering 16 percent per year. Since there is no compounding during the year, this is the effective rate. Bank B is actually paying .155/4 = .03875, or 3.875 percent, per quarter. At this rate, an investment of $1 for four quarters would grow to:

$$\$1 \times 1.03875^4 = \$1.1642$$

The EAR, therefore, is 16.42 percent. For a saver, this is much better than the 16 percent rate Bank C is offering; for a borrower, it's worse.

Bank A is compounding every day. This may seem a little extreme, but it is very common to calculate interest daily. In this case, the daily interest rate is actually:

$$.15/365 = .000411$$

This is .0411 percent per day. At this rate, an investment of $1 for 365 periods would grow to:

$$\$1 \times 1.000411^{365} = \$1.1618$$

The EAR is 16.18 percent. This is not as good as Bank B's 16.42 percent for a saver, and not as good as Bank C's 16 percent for a borrower.

This example illustrates two things. First, the highest quoted rate is not necessarily the best. Second, compounding during the year can lead to a significant difference between the quoted rate and the effective rate. Remember that the effective rate is what you get or what you pay.

If you look at our examples, you see that we computed the EARs in three steps. We first divided the quoted rate by the number of times that the interest is compounded. We then added 1 to the result and raised it to the power of the number of times the interest is compounded. Finally, we subtracted the 1. If we let m be the number of times the interest is compounded during the year, these steps can be summarized simply as:

$$EAR = (1 + Quoted\ rate/m)^m - 1 \qquad [5.5]$$

For example, suppose you were offered 12 percent compounded monthly. In this case, the interest is compounded 12 times a year, so m is 12. You can calculate the effective rate as:

EAR = (1 + Quoted rate/m)^m − 1

$= (1 + .12/12)^{12} − 1$

$= 1.01^{12} − 1$

$= 1.126825 − 1$

$= 12.6825\%$

WHAT'S THE EAR?   EXAMPLE | 5.8

A bank is offering 12 percent compounded quarterly. If you put $100 in an account, how much will you have at the end of one year? What's the EAR? How much will you have at the end of two years?

The bank is effectively offering 12%/4 = 3% every quarter. If you invest $100 for four periods at 3 percent per period, the future value is:

Future value = $100 × 1.03^4

$= $100 × 1.1255$

$= 112.55

The EAR is 12.55 percent: $100 × (1 + .1255) = $112.55.

We can determine what you would have at the end of two years in two different ways. One way is to recognize that two years is the same as eight quarters. At 3 percent per quarter, after eight quarters, you would have:

$100 × 1.03^8 = $100 × 1.2668 = $126.68

Alternatively, we could determine the value after two years by using an EAR of 12.55 percent; so after two years you would have:

$100 × 1.1255^2 = $100 × 1.2668 = $126.68

Thus, the two calculations produce the same answer. This illustrates an important point. Anytime we do a present or future value calculation, the rate we use must be an actual or effective rate. In this case, the actual rate is 3 percent per quarter. The effective annual rate is 12.55 percent. It doesn't matter which one we use once we know the EAR.

QUOTING A RATE   EXAMPLE | 5.9

Now that you know how to convert a quoted rate to an EAR, consider going the other way. As a lender, you know you want to actually earn 18 percent on a particular loan. You want to quote a rate that features monthly compounding. What rate do you quote?

In this case, we know that the EAR is 18 percent, and we know that this is the result of monthly compounding. Let q stand for the quoted rate. We thus have:

EAR = (1 + Quoted rate/m)^m − 1

$.18 = (1 + q/12)^{12} − 1$

$1.18 = (1 + q/12)^{12}$

We need to solve this equation for the quoted rate. This calculation is the same as the ones we did to find an unknown interest rate in Chapter 4:

$1.18^{(1/12)} = 1 + q/12$

$1.18^{.08333} = 1 + q/12$

(continued)

$$1.0139 = 1 + q/12$$
$$q = .0139 \times 12$$
$$= 16.68\%$$

Therefore, the rate you would quote is 16.68 percent, compounded monthly.

EARs and APRs

annual percentage rate (APR)

The interest rate charged per period multiplied by the number of periods per year.

Sometimes it's not altogether clear whether a rate is an effective annual rate or not. A case in point concerns what is called the **annual percentage rate (APR)** on a loan. Truth-in-lending laws in the United States require that lenders disclose an APR on virtually all consumer loans. This rate must be displayed on a loan document in a prominent and unambiguous way.[2]

Given that an APR must be calculated and displayed, an obvious question arises: Is an APR an effective annual rate? Put another way: If a bank quotes a car loan at 12 percent APR, is the consumer actually paying 12 percent interest? Surprisingly, the answer is no. There is some confusion over this point, which we discuss next.

The confusion over APRs arises because lenders are required by law to compute the APR in a particular way. By law, the APR is simply equal to the interest rate per period multiplied by the number of periods in a year. For example, if a bank is charging 1.2 percent per month on car loans, then the APR that must be reported is $1.2\% \times 12 = 14.4\%$. So, an APR is in fact a quoted, or stated, rate in the sense we've been discussing. For example, an APR of 12 percent on a loan calling for monthly payments is really 1 percent per month. The EAR on such a loan is thus:

$$\text{EAR} = (1 + \text{APR}/12)^{12} - 1$$
$$= 1.01^{12} - 1 = 12.6825\%$$

EXAMPLE 5.10 WHAT RATE ARE YOU PAYING?

A typical credit card agreement quotes an interest rate of 18 percent APR. Monthly payments are required. What is the actual interest rate you pay on such a credit card?

Based on our discussion, an APR of 18 percent with monthly payments is really $.18/12 = .015$, or 1.5 percent, per month. The EAR is thus:

$$\text{EAR} = (1 + .18/12)^{12} - 1$$
$$= 1.015^{12} - 1$$
$$= 1.1956 - 1$$
$$= 19.56\%$$

This is the rate you actually pay.

The difference between an APR and an EAR probably won't be all that great (as long as the rates are relatively low), but it is somewhat ironic that truth-in-lending laws sometimes require lenders to be *un*truthful about the actual rate on a loan.

---

[2] By law, lenders are required to report the APR on all consumer loans. We normally compute the APR as the interest rate per period multiplied by the number of periods in a year. According to federal law, the APR is a measure of the cost of consumer credit expressed as a yearly rate, and it includes interest and certain noninterest charges and fees. In practice, the APR can be much higher than the interest rate on the loan if the lender charges substantial fees that must be included in the federally mandated APR calculation.

There can be a huge difference between the APR and EAR when interest rates are large. For example, consider "payday loans." Payday loans are short-term loans made to consumers, often for less than two weeks, and are offered by companies such as AmeriCash Advance and National Payday. The loans work like this: You write a check today that is postdated (i.e., the date on the check is in the future) and give it to the company. They give you some cash. When the check date arrives, you either go to the store and pay the cash amount of the check, or the company cashes it (or else automatically renews the loan).

For example, as of 2012 in one particular state, Check Into Cash allows you to write a check for $115 dated 14 days in the future, for which they give you $100 today. So what are the APR and EAR of this arrangement? First, we need to find the interest rate, which we can find by the FV equation as follows:

$$FV = PV \times (1 + r)^1$$
$$\$115 = \$100 \times (1 + r)^1$$
$$1.15 = (1 + r)$$
$$r = .15, \text{ or } 15\%$$

That doesn't seem too bad until you remember this is the interest rate for *14 days*! The APR of the loan is:

$$APR = .15 \times 365/14$$
$$APR = 3.9107, \text{ or } 391.07\%$$

And the EAR for this loan is:

$$EAR = (1 + \text{Quoted rate}/m)^m - 1$$
$$EAR = (1 + .15)^{365/14} - 1$$
$$EAR = 37.2366, \text{ or } 3,723.66\%$$

Now that's an interest rate! Just to see what a difference a small difference in fees can make, Check 'n Go will make you write a check for $117.64 for the same amount. Check for yourself that the APR of this arrangement is 459.90 percent and the EAR is 6,809.87 percent.

EARs, APRs, Financial Calculators, and Spreadsheets

A financial calculator will convert a quoted rate (or an APR) to an EAR and back. Unfortunately, the specific procedures are too different from calculator to calculator for us to illustrate in general terms; you'll have to consult Appendix D or your calculator's operating manual. Typically, however, what we have called EAR is labeled "EFF" (for *effective*) on a calculator. More troublesome is the fact that what we have called a quoted rate (or an APR) is labeled "NOM" (for *nominal*). Unfortunately, the term *nominal rate* has come to have a different meaning that we will see in our next chapter. So, just remember that *nominal* in this context means quoted or APR.

With a spreadsheet, we can easily do these conversions. To convert a quoted rate (or an APR) to an effective rate in Excel, for example, use the formula EFFECT(nominal_rate,npery), where nominal_rate is the quoted rate or APR and npery is the number of compounding periods per year. Similarly, to convert an EAR to a quoted rate, use NOMINAL(effect_rate,npery), where effect_rate is the EAR.

146   **PART 3**   Valuation of Future Cash Flows

5.4

ExcelMaster
coverage online

LOAN TYPES AND LOAN AMORTIZATION

Whenever a lender extends a loan, some provision will be made for repayment of the principal (the original loan amount). A loan might be repaid in equal installments, for example, or it might be repaid in a single lump sum. Because the way that the principal and interest are paid is up to the parties involved, there are actually an unlimited number of possibilities.

In this section, we describe a few forms of repayment that come up quite often; more complicated forms can usually be built up from these. The three basic types of loans are pure discount loans, interest-only loans, and amortized loans. Working with these loans is a very straightforward application of the present value principles that we have already developed.

Pure Discount Loans

The pure discount loan is the simplest form of loan. With such a loan, the borrower receives money today and repays a single lump sum at some time in the future. A one-year, 10 percent pure discount loan, for example, would require the borrower to repay $1.1 in one year for every dollar borrowed today.

Because a pure discount loan is so simple, we already know how to value one. Suppose a borrower was able to repay $25,000 in five years. If we, acting as the lender, wanted a 12 percent interest rate on the loan, how much would we be willing to lend? Put another way, what value would we assign today to that $25,000 to be repaid in five years? Based on our work in Chapter 4, we know that the answer is just the present value of $25,000 at 12 percent for five years:

$$\text{Present value} = \$25,000/1.12^5$$
$$= \$25,000/1.7623$$
$$= \$14,186$$

Pure discount loans are very common when the loan term is short, say, a year or less. In recent years, they have become increasingly common for much longer periods.

EXAMPLE 5.11

TREASURY BILLS

When the U.S. government borrows money on a short-term basis (a year or less), it does so by selling what are called *Treasury bills,* or *T-bills* for short. A T-bill is a promise by the government to repay a fixed amount at some time in the future, for example, 3 months or 12 months.

Treasury bills are pure discount loans. If a T-bill promises to repay $10,000 in 12 months, and the market interest rate is 7 percent, how much will the bill sell for in the market?

Since the going rate is 7 percent, the T-bill will sell for the present value of $10,000 to be paid in one year at 7 percent, or:

Present value = $10,000/1.07 = $9,345.79

Interest-Only Loans

A second type of loan has a repayment plan that calls for the borrower to pay interest each period and to repay the entire principal (the original loan amount) at some point in the future. Such loans are called *interest-only loans.* Notice that if there is just one period, a pure discount loan and an interest-only loan are the same thing.

For example, with a three-year, 10 percent, interest-only loan of $1,000, the borrower would pay $1,000 × .10 = $100 in interest at the end of the first and second years. At the end of the third year, the borrower would return the $1,000 along with another $100 in interest for that year. Similarly, a 50-year interest-only loan would call for the borrower to pay interest every year for the next 50 years and then repay the principal. In the extreme, the borrower pays the interest every period forever and never repays any principal. As we discussed earlier in the chapter, the result is a perpetuity.

Most corporate bonds have the general form of an interest-only loan. Because we will be considering bonds in some detail in the next chapter, we will defer a further discussion of them for now.

Amortized Loans

With a pure discount or interest-only loan, the principal is repaid all at once. An alternative is an *amortized loan,* with which the lender may require the borrower to repay parts of the loan amount over time. The process of paying off a loan by making regular principal reductions is called *amortizing* the loan.

A simple way of amortizing a loan is to have the borrower pay the interest each period plus some fixed amount. This approach is common with medium-term business loans. For example, suppose a business takes out a $5,000, five-year loan at 9 percent. The loan agreement calls for the borrower to pay the interest on the loan balance each year and to reduce the loan balance each year by $1,000. Since the loan amount declines by $1,000 each year, it is fully paid in five years.

In the case we are considering, notice that the total payment will decline each year. The reason is that the loan balance goes down, resulting in a lower interest charge each year, while the $1,000 principal reduction is constant. For example, the interest in the first year will be $5,000 × .09 = $450. The total payment will be $1,000 + 450 = $1,450. In the second year, the loan balance is $4,000, so the interest is $4,000 × .09 = $360, and the total payment is $1,360. We can calculate the total payment in each of the remaining years by preparing a simple *amortization schedule* as follows:

Year	Beginning Balance	Total Payment	Interest Paid	Principal Paid	Ending Balance
1	$5,000	$1,450	$ 450	$1,000	$4,000
2	4,000	1,360	360	1,000	3,000
3	3,000	1,270	270	1,000	2,000
4	2,000	1,180	180	1,000	1,000
5	1,000	1,090	90	1,000	0
Totals		$6,350	$1,350	$5,000	

Notice that, in each year, the interest paid is just given by the beginning balance multiplied by the interest rate. Also, notice that the beginning balance is given by the ending balance from the previous year.

Probably the most common way of amortizing a loan is to have the borrower make a single, fixed payment every period. Almost all consumer loans (such as car loans) and mortgages work this way. For example, suppose our five-year, 9 percent, $5,000 loan was amortized this way. How would the amortization schedule look?

We first need to determine the payment. From our discussion earlier in the chapter, we know that this loan's cash flows are in the form of an ordinary annuity. In this case, we can solve for the payment as follows:

$$\$5{,}000 = C \times (1 - 1/1.09^5)/.09$$
$$= C \times (1 - .6499)/.09$$

This gives us:

$$C = \$5{,}000/3.8897$$
$$= \$1{,}285.46$$

The borrower will therefore make five equal payments of $1,285.46. Will this pay off the loan? We will check by filling in an amortization schedule.

In our previous example, we knew the principal reduction each year. We then calculated the interest owed to get the total payment. In this example, we know the total payment. We will thus calculate the interest and then subtract it from the total payment to get the principal portion in each payment.

In the first year, the interest is $450, as we calculated before. Since the total payment is $1,285.46, the principal paid in the first year must be:

Principal paid = $1,285.46 − 450 = $835.46

The ending loan balance is thus:

Ending balance = $5,000 − 835.46 = $4,164.54

The interest in the second year is $4,164.54 × .09 = $374.81, and the loan balance declines by $1,285.46 − 374.81 = $910.65. We can summarize all of the relevant calculations in the following schedule:

Year	Beginning Balance	Total Payment	Interest Paid	Principal Paid	Ending Balance
1	$5,000.00	$1,285.46	$ 450.00	$ 835.46	$4,164.54
2	4,164.54	1,285.46	374.81	910.65	3,253.88
3	3,253.88	1,285.46	292.85	992.61	2,261.27
4	2,261.27	1,285.46	203.51	1,081.95	1,179.32
5	1,179.32	1,285.46	106.14	1,179.32	.00
Totals		$6,427.31	$1,427.31	$5,000.00	

You can find a good loan amortization schedule online at www.myamortization chart.com.

Since the loan balance declines to zero, the five equal payments do pay off the loan. Notice that the interest paid declines each period. This isn't surprising since the loan balance is going down. Given that the total payment is fixed, the principal paid must be rising each period.

If you compare the two loan amortizations in this section, you will see that the total interest is greater for the equal total payment case, $1,427.31 versus $1,350. The reason for this is that the loan is repaid more slowly early on, so the interest is somewhat higher. This doesn't mean that one loan is better than the other; it simply means that one is effectively paid off faster than the other. For example, the principal reduction in the first year is $835.46 in the equal total payment case compared to $1,000 in the first case. Many websites offer loan amortization schedules. See our nearby *Work the Web* box for an example.

Loan Amortization Using a Spreadsheet

SPREADSHEET STRATEGIES

Loan amortization is a very common spreadsheet application. To illustrate, we will set up the problem that we have just examined, a five-year, $5,000, 9 percent loan with constant payments. Our spreadsheet looks like this:

	A	B	C	D	E	F	G	H
1								
2			Using a spreadsheet to amortize a loan					
3								
4			Loan amount:	$5,000				
5			Interest rate:	.09				
6			Loan term:	5				
7			Loan payment:	$1,285.46				
8				Note: payment is calculated using PMT(rate,nper,-pv,fv).				
9			Amortization table:					
10								
11			Year	Beginning	Total	Interest	Principal	Ending
12				Balance	Payment	Paid	Paid	Balance
13		1	$5,000.00	$1,285.46	$450.00	$835.46	$4,164.54	
14		2	4,164.54	1,285.46	374.81	910.65	3,253.88	
15		3	3,253.88	1,285.46	292.85	992.61	2,261.27	
16		4	2,261.27	1,285.46	203.51	1,081.95	1,179.32	
17		5	1,179.32	1,285.46	106.14	1,179.32	.00	
18		Totals		$6,427.31	$1,427.31	$5,000.00		
19								
20		Formulas in the amortization table:						
21								
22			Year	Beginning	Total	Interest	Principal	Ending
23				Balance	Payment	Paid	Paid	Balance
24		1	=+D4	=$D$7	=+$D$5*C13	=+D13-E13	=+C13-F13	
25		2	=+G13	=$D$7	=+$D$5*C14	=+D14-E14	=+C14-F14	
26		3	=+G14	=$D$7	=+$D$5*C15	=+D15-E15	=+C15-F15	
27		4	=+G15	=$D$7	=+$D$5*C16	=+D16-E16	=+C16-F16	
28		5	=+G16	=$D$7	=+$D$5*C17	=+D17-E17	=+C17-F17	
29								
30		Note: totals in the amortization table are calculated using the SUM formula.						
31								

We close out this discussion by noting that one type of loan may be particularly important to you. Student loans are an important source of financing for many college students, helping to cover the cost of tuition, books, new cars, condominiums, and many other things.

WORK THE WEB

 ◄ To get updated data, scan here.

Preparing an amortization table is one of the more tedious time value of money applications. Using a spreadsheet makes it relatively easy, but there are also websites available that will prepare an amortization table very quickly and simply. One such site is Bankrate.com. The website at www .bankrate.com has a mortgage calculator for home loans, but the same calculations apply to most other types of loans such as car loans and student loans. College graduates in 2011 left school with an average of $22,900 in student loans. Suppose you graduate with the average student loan and decide to pay the loan off over the next 15 years at 6.8 percent, the maximum interest rate for unsubsidized Stafford loans. What are your monthly payments? Using the calculator, for the first year, we get:

	Amortization Table for $22,900.00 Borrowed on Jun. 01, 2012				
Month / Year	Payment	Principal Paid	Interest Paid	Total Interest	Balance
July 2012	$203.28	$73.51	$129.77	$129.77	$22,826.49
Aug. 2012	$203.28	$73.93	$129.35	$259.12	$22,752.56
Sept. 2012	$203.28	$74.35	$128.93	$388.05	$22,678.21
Oct. 2012	$203.28	$74.77	$128.51	$516.56	$22,603.44
Nov. 2012	$203.28	$75.19	$128.09	$644.64	$22,528.25
Dec. 2012	$203.28	$75.62	$127.66	$772.30	$22,452.63
Jan. 2013	$203.28	$76.05	$127.23	$899.54	$22,376.58
Feb. 2013	$203.28	$76.48	$126.80	$1,026.34	$22,300.10
Mar. 2013	$203.28	$76.91	$126.37	$1,152.70	$22,223.19
April 2013	$203.28	$77.35	$125.93	$1,278.63	$22,145.84
May 2013	$203.28	$77.79	$125.49	$1,404.13	$22,068.05

As you can see, the monthly payment will be $203.28. The first payment will consist of $73.51 in principal and $129.77 in interest. Over the life of the loan you will pay a total of $13,690.33 in interest.

Questions

1. *Suppose you take out a 30-year mortgage for $250,000 at an interest rate of 6.8 percent. Use this website to construct an amortization table for the loan. What are the interest payment and principal amounts in the 110th payment? How much in total interest will you pay over the life of the loan?*

2. *You take out a 30-year mortgage for $275,000 at an interest rate of 7.3 percent. How much will you pay in interest over the life of this loan? Now assume you pay an extra $100 per month on this loan. How much is your total interest now? How much sooner will the mortgage be paid off?*

Sometimes students do not seem to fully realize that such loans have a serious drawback: They must be repaid. See our nearby *Finance Matters* box for a discussion.

CONCEPT QUESTIONS

5.4a   What is a pure discount loan?

5.4b   What does it mean to amortize a loan?

FINANCE MATTERS

◀ For the latest news on the topics covered in this chapter, scan here.

An Unwelcome Christmas Present

If you are reading this, we can assume that you are a college student. While you will receive an education in college, and studies show that college graduates earn higher salaries on average than nongraduates, you might receive an unwelcome Christmas present if you graduate in May: student loan payments. About one-half of all college students graduate with student loans, and over 90 percent of the loans are Stafford loans. Stafford loans are available through lenders such as Sallie Mae, online lenders, or, in some cases, your college. Stafford loans must be paid off in 10 years, but there is a six-month grace period from the time you graduate until the first payment must be made. The interest rate on unsubsidized Stafford loans made after July 1, 2006, is 6.8 percent.

If you have student loans, you went through an introductory program. Just in case you forgot, here are several of the repayment options. First, you can make equal monthly payments like most other loans. A second option is to pay only the interest on the loan for up to four years, and then begin making principal and interest payments. This means your payments at the end of the loan are higher than the equal payment option. A third option is to make payments based on a percentage of your salary. A fourth option is a graduated payment option that increases your monthly payments on a predetermined schedule. Finally, you can consolidate your loans one time. If the loan balance is high enough, you may be able to extend your payment for up to 30 years.

So how do student loans work in practice? A recent graduate from the University of Maryland with a master's degree in creative writing graduated with $40,000 in student loans. Her loan payments were $442 a month, a payment that was difficult to make on her salary as a fundraiser. She considered the percentage of salary option, which would have lowered her monthly payments to about $200 per month. However, she realized that this was just putting off the inevitable, so she took a second job to make up the difference.

A recent master's graduate from law school took a different route. His student loans totaled $109,000 and required monthly payments of $1,200 per month for 10 years. The option chosen by this lawyer was to consolidate his loans and extend his payments to 30 years. This reduced his monthly payments to about $640 per month.

A Chicago couple is using a third solution. Both the husband and wife are doctors. The wife is out of her residency and employed full time, while the husband is finishing his last year of residency. What is most unusual about this couple is the amount of student loan debt. The wife's student loan balance is $234,000, the husband's student loan balance is $310,000, and the couple has a $156,000 mortgage! The wife's student loan repayments have already started and amount to $1,750 per month. So how is the couple handling this? They are paying a total of $2,250 per month towards the wife's student loans. This will reduce the repayment period from 22 years to 13 years. The couple is also paying an additional $100 per month on their $1,500 mortgage payment. Fortunately, when the husband's residency ends, he expects his salary to triple. The couple will need it. His loan payments will be $2,349 per month. And you thought your student loan was high! Maybe MD stands for "mucho debt"!

SUMMARY AND CONCLUSIONS

This chapter rounds out your understanding of fundamental concepts related to the time value of money and discounted cash flow valuation. Several important topics were covered, including:

◀ Think you've mastered the material? Scan here to take a chapter quiz.

1. There are two ways of calculating present and future values when there are multiple cash flows. Both approaches are straightforward extensions of our earlier analysis of single cash flows.

2. A series of constant cash flows that arrive or are paid at the end of each period is called an ordinary annuity, and we described some useful shortcuts for determining the present and future values of annuities.

3. Interest rates can be quoted in a variety of ways. For financial decisions, it is important that any rates being compared be first converted to effective rates.

The relationship between a quoted rate, such as an annual percentage rate, or APR, and an effective annual rate, or EAR, is given by:

$$EAR = (1 + \text{Quoted rate}/m)^m - 1$$

where *m* is the number of times during the year the money is compounded, or, equivalently, the number of payments during the year.

4. Many loans are annuities. The process of paying off a loan gradually is called amortizing the loan, and we discussed how amortization schedules are prepared and interpreted.

---

 connect POP QUIZ!
|FINANCE

Can you answer the following questions? If your class is using *Connect Finance,* log on to the Self-Quiz and Study feature in the Library tab to see if you know the answers to these and other questions, check out the study tools, and find out what topics require additional practice!

Section 5.1 You want to buy a new car for $39,500. The contract is in the form of a 48-month annuity due at a 6.85 percent APR. What will your monthly payment be?

Section 5.2 You want to buy a new car for $74,400, and the finance office at the dealership has quoted you a 6.8 percent APR loan for 48 months to buy the car. What is the effective annual rate on this loan?

Section 5.3 What is the effective rate of a loan with a stated rate (APR) of 14 percent, compounded monthly?

Section 5.4 For a three-year loan of $63,000, given an annual interest rate of 10 percent and equal annual payments, how much interest is paid over the life of the loan?

CHAPTER REVIEW AND SELF-TEST PROBLEMS

5.1   Present Values with Multiple Cash Flows.   A first-round draft choice quarterback has been signed to a three-year, $10 million contract. The details provide for an immediate cash bonus of $1 million. The player is to receive $2 million in salary at the end of the first year, $3 million the next, and $4 million at the end of the last year. Assuming a 10 percent discount rate, is this package worth $10 million? How much is it worth? (See Problem 1.)

5.2   Future Value with Multiple Cash Flows.   You plan to make a series of deposits in an interest-bearing account. You will deposit $1,000 today, $2,000 in two years, and $8,000 in five years. If you withdraw $3,000 in three years and $5,000 in seven years, how much will you have after eight years if the interest rate is 9 percent? What is the present value of these cash flows? (See Problem 3.)

5.3   Annuity Present Value.   You are looking into an investment that will pay you $12,000 per year for the next 10 years. If you require a 15 percent return, what is the most you would pay for this investment? (See Problem 2.)

5.4   **APR versus EAR.**   The going rate on student loans is quoted as 9 percent APR. The terms of the loan call for monthly payments. What is the effective annual rate, or EAR, on such a student loan? (See Problem 14.)

5.5   **It's the Principal That Matters.**   Suppose you borrow $10,000. You are going to repay the loan by making equal annual payments for five years. The interest rate on the loan is 14 percent per year. Prepare an amortization schedule for the loan. How much interest will you pay over the life of the loan? (See Problem 55.)

5.6   **Just a Little Bit Each Month.**   You've recently finished your MBA at the Darnit School. Naturally, you must purchase a new BMW immediately. The car costs about $42,000. The bank quotes an interest rate of 15 percent APR for a 72-month loan with a 10 percent down payment. What will your monthly payment be? What is the effective interest rate on the loan? (See Problem 20.)

■ Answers to Chapter Review and Self-Test Problems

5.1   Obviously, the package is not worth $10 million because the payments are spread out over three years. The bonus is paid today, so it's worth $1 million. The present values for the three subsequent salary payments are:

$$\$2/1.1 + 3/1.1^2 + 4/1.1^3 = \$2/1.1 + 3/1.21 + 4/1.331$$
$$= \$7.3028$$

The package is worth a total of $8.3028 million.

5.2   We will calculate the future value for each of the cash flows separately and then add the results up. Notice that we treat the withdrawals as negative cash flows:

$$\begin{aligned}
\$1,000 \times 1.09^8 &= &\$1,000 \times 1.9926 &= &\$ 1,992.60 \\
\$2,000 \times 1.09^6 &= &\$2,000 \times 1.6771 &= &3,354.20 \\
-\$3,000 \times 1.09^5 &= &-\$3,000 \times 1.5386 &= &-4,615.87 \\
\$8,000 \times 1.09^3 &= &\$8,000 \times 1.2950 &= &10,360.23 \\
-\$5,000 \times 1.09^1 &= &-\$5,000 \times 1.0900 &= &\underline{-5,450.00} \\
& & \text{Total future value} &= &\underline{\$ 5,641.12}
\end{aligned}$$

This value includes a small rounding error.

To calculate the present value, we could discount each cash flow back to the present or we could discount back a single year at a time. However, since we already know that the future value in eight years is $5,641.12, the easy way to get the PV is just to discount this amount back eight years:

$$\begin{aligned}
\text{Present value} &= \$5,641.12/1.09^8 \\
&= \$5,641.12/1.9926 \\
&= \$2,831.03
\end{aligned}$$

We again ignore a small rounding error. For practice, you can verify that this is what you get if you discount each cash flow back separately.

5.3   The most you would be willing to pay is the present value of $12,000 per year for 10 years at a 15 percent discount rate. The cash flows here are in ordinary annuity form, so the relevant present value factor is:

$$\begin{aligned}
\text{Annuity present value factor} &= [1 - (1/1.15^{10})]/.15 \\
&= (1 - .2472)/.15 \\
&= 5.0188
\end{aligned}$$

The present value of the 10 cash flows is thus:

Present value = $12,000 × 5.0188
= $60,225

This is the most you would pay.

5.4 A rate of 9 percent with monthly payments is actually 9%/12 = .75% per month. The EAR is thus:

$$EAR = (1 + .09/12)^{12} - 1 = 9.38\%$$

5.5 We first need to calculate the annual payment. With a present value of $10,000, an interest rate of 14 percent, and a term of five years, the payment can be determined from:

$10,000 = Payment × (1 − 1/1.14^5)/.14
= Payment × 3.4331

Therefore, the payment is $10,000/3.4331 = $2,912.84 (actually, it's $2,912.8355; this will create some small rounding errors in the schedule below). We can now prepare the amortization schedule as follows:

Year	Beginning Balance	Total Payment	Interest Paid	Principal Paid	Ending Balance
1	$10,000.00	$ 2,912.84	$1,400.00	$ 1,512.84	$8,487.16
2	8,487.16	2,912.84	1,188.20	1,724.63	6,762.53
3	6,762.53	2,912.84	946.75	1,966.08	4,796.45
4	4,796.45	2,912.84	671.50	2,241.33	2,555.12
5	2,555.12	2,912.84	357.72	2,555.12	.00
Totals		$14,564.17	$4,564.17	$10,000.00	

5.6 The cash flows on the car loan are in annuity form, so we only need to find the payment. The interest rate is 15%/12 = 1.25% per month, and there are 72 months. The first thing we need is the annuity factor for 72 periods at 1.25 percent per period:

Annuity present value factor = (1 − Present value factor)/r
= [1 − (1/1.0125^{72})]/.0125
= [1 − (1/2.4459)]/.0125
= (1 − .4088)/.0125
= 47.2925

The present value is the amount we finance. With a 10 percent down payment, we will be borrowing 90 percent of $42,000, or $37,800.

So, to find the payment, we need to solve for *C* in the following:

$37,800 = C × Annuity present value factor
= C × 47.2925

Rearranging things a bit, we have:

C = $37,800 × (1/47.2925)
= $37,800 × .02115
= $799.28

Your payment is just under $800 per month.

The actual interest rate on this loan is 1.25 percent per month. Based on our work in the chapter, we can calculate the effective annual rate as:

$$EAR = 1.0125^{12} - 1 = 16.08\%$$

The effective rate is about one point higher than the quoted rate.

CRITICAL THINKING AND CONCEPTS REVIEW

LO 1   **5.1**   **Annuity Period.**   As you increase the length of time involved, what happens to the present value of an annuity? What happens to the future value?

LO 1   **5.2**   **Interest Rates.**   What happens to the future value of an annuity if you increase the rate, r? What happens to the present value?

LO 1   **5.3**   **Annuity Present Values.**   Tri-State Megabucks Lottery advertises a
LO 2 $10 million grand prize. The winner receives $500,000 today and 19 annual payments of $500,000. A lump sum option of $5 million payable immediately is also available. Is this deceptive advertising?

LO 1   **5.4**   **Annuity Present Values.**   Suppose you won the Tri-State Megabucks Lottery in the previous question. What factors should you take into account in deciding whether you should take the annuity option or the lump sum option?

LO 1   **5.5**   **Present Value.**   If you were an athlete negotiating a contract, would you want a big signing bonus payable immediately and smaller payments in the future, or vice versa? How about looking at it from the team's perspective?

LO 1   **5.6**   **Present Value.**   Suppose two athletes sign 10-year contracts for $80 million. In one case, we're told that the $80 million will be paid in 10 equal installments. In the other case, we're told that the $80 million will be paid in 10 installments, but the installments will increase by 5 percent per year. Who got the better deal?

LO 4   **5.7**   **APR and EAR.**   Should lending laws be changed to require lenders to report EARs instead of APRs? Why or why not?

LO 3   **5.8**   **Time Value.**   On subsidized Stafford loans, a common source of financial aid for college students, interest does not begin to accrue until repayment begins. Who receives a bigger subsidy, a freshman or a senior? Explain.

LO 3   **5.9**   **Time Value.**   In words, how would you go about valuing the subsidy on a subsidized Stafford loan?

LO 3   **5.10**   **Time Value.**   Eligibility for a subsidized Stafford loan is based on current financial need. However, both subsidized and unsubsidized Stafford loans are repaid out of future income. Given this, do you see a possible objection to having two types?

QUESTIONS AND PROBLEMS

   Select problems are available in McGraw-Hill *Connect*. Please see the packaging options section of the preface for more information.

LO 1   1. **Present Value and Multiple Cash Flows.**   Rooster Co. has identified an investment project with the following cash flows. If the discount rate is 10 percent, what is the present value of these cash flows? What is the present value at 18 percent? At 24 percent?

Basic
(Questions 1–28)

Year	Cash Flow
1	$ 830
2	610
3	1,140
4	1,390

LO 1

2. Present Value and Multiple Cash Flows. Investment X offers to pay you $3,700 per year for nine years, whereas Investment Y offers to pay you $5,500 per year for five years. Which of these cash flow streams has the higher present value if the discount rate is 6 percent? If the discount rate is 22 percent?

 LO 1

3. Future Value and Multiple Cash Flows. Havana, Inc., has identified an investment project with the following cash flows. If the discount rate is 8 percent, what is the future value of these cash flows in Year 4? What is the future value at an interest rate of 11 percent? At 24 percent?

Year	Cash Flow
1	$ 1,075
2	1,235
3	1,510
4	1,965

 LO 1

4. Calculating Annuity Present Values. An investment offers $6,700 per year for 15 years, with the first payment occurring 1 year from now. If the required return is 8 percent, what is the value of the investment? What would the value be if the payments occurred for 40 years? For 75 years? Forever?

LO 1

5. Calculating Annuity Cash Flows. For each of the following annuities, calculate the annual cash flow.

Present Value	Years	Interest Rate
$ 36,800	6	11%
27,500	8	7
145,000	15	8
215,000	20	6

LO 1

6. Calculating Annuity Values. For each of the following annuities, calculate the present value.

Annuity Payment	Years	Interest Rate
$ 2,100	7	8%
1,095	9	7
11,000	18	9
30,000	28	11

LO 1 **7. Calculating Annuity Cash Flows.** For each of the following annuities, calculate the annual cash flow.

Future Value	Years	Interest Rate
$ 25,000	8	5%
1,000,000	40	7
750,000	25	8
135,000	13	4

LO 1 **8. Calculating Annuity Values.** For each of the following annuities, calculate the future value.

Annual Payment	Years	Interest Rate
$1,500	10	8%
5,000	40	9
3,200	9	6
7,500	30	10

LO 1 **9. Calculating Annuity Values.** If you deposit $5,000 at the end of each of the next 20 years into an account paying 10.8 percent interest, how much money will you have in the account in 20 years? How much will you have if you make deposits for 40 years?

LO 1 **10. Calculating Perpetuity Values.** Curly's Life Insurance Co. is trying to sell you an investment policy that will pay you and your heirs $25,000 per year forever. If the required return on this investment is 6 percent, how much will you pay for the policy?

LO 1 **11. Calculating Perpetuity Values.** In the previous problem, suppose Curly's told you the policy costs $450,000. At what interest rate would this be a fair deal?

LO 4 **12. Calculating EAR.** Find the EAR in each of the following cases:

Stated Rate (APR)	Number of Times Compounded	Effective Rate (EAR)
10%	Quarterly	
17	Monthly	
13	Daily	
9	Semiannually	

LO 4 **13. Calculating APR.** Find the APR, or stated rate, in each of the following cases:

Stated Rate (APR)	Number of Times Compounded	Effective Rate (EAR)
	Semiannually	14%
	Monthly	9
	Weekly	8
	Daily	13

www.mhhe.com/rwj

LO 4   **14. Calculating EAR.**   First National Bank charges 10.9 percent compounded monthly on its business loans. First United Bank charges 11.1 percent compounded semiannually. As a potential borrower, which bank would you go to for a new loan?

LO 4   **15. Calculating APR.**   Magnus Credit Corp. wants to earn an effective annual return on its consumer loans of 17 percent per year. The bank uses daily compounding on its loans. What interest rate is the bank required by law to report to potential borrowers? Explain why this rate is misleading to an uninformed borrower.

LO 4   **16. Calculating Future Values.**   What is the future value of $1,270 in 16 years assuming an interest rate of 9 percent compounded semiannually?

LO 4   **17. Calculating Future Values.**   Bucher Credit Bank is offering 4.7 percent compounded daily on its savings accounts. If you deposit $4,500 today, how much will you have in the account in five years? In 10 years? In 20 years?

LO 4   **18. Calculating Present Values.**   An investment will pay you $75,000 in nine years. If the appropriate discount rate is 6 percent compounded daily, what is the present value?

LO 4   **19. EAR versus APR.**   Ricky Ripov's Pawn Shop charges an interest rate of 17 percent per month on loans to its customers. Like all lenders, Ricky must report an APR to consumers. What rate should the shop report? What is the effective annual rate?

LO 2   **20. Calculating Loan Payments.**   You want to buy a new sports coupe for $68,500, and the finance office at the dealership has quoted you a loan with an APR of 5.9 for 60 months to buy the car. What will your monthly payments be? What is the effective annual rate on this loan?

LO 2   **21. Calculating Number of Periods.**   One of your customers is delinquent on his accounts payable balance. You've mutually agreed to a repayment schedule of $500 per month. You will charge 1.4 percent per month interest on the overdue balance. If the current balance is $17,340, how long will it take for the account to be paid off?

LO 4   **22. Calculating EAR.**   Friendly's Quick Loans, Inc., offers you "Five for four, or I knock on your door." This means you get $4 today and repay $5 when you get your paycheck in one week (or else). What's the effective annual return Friendly's earns on this lending business? If you were brave enough to ask, what APR would Friendly's say you were paying?

LO 1   **23. Valuing Perpetuities.**   Maybepay Life Insurance Co. is selling a perpetual annuity contract that pays $2,500 monthly. The contract currently sells for $265,000. What is the monthly return on this investment vehicle? What is the APR? The effective annual return?

LO 1   **24. Calculating Annuity Future Values.**   You are to make monthly deposits of $500 into a retirement account that pays 10.3 percent interest compounded monthly. If your first deposit will be made one month from now, how large will your retirement account be in 35 years?

LO 1   **25. Calculating Annuity Future Values.**   In the previous problem, suppose you make $6,000 annual deposits into the same retirement account. How large will your account balance be in 35 years?

LO 1   **26. Calculating Annuity Present Values.**   Beginning three months from now, you want to be able to withdraw $2,100 each quarter from your bank account to cover college expenses over the next four years. If the account pays .45 percent interest per quarter, how much do you need to have in your bank account today to meet your expense needs over the next four years?

LO 1
27. Discounted Cash Flow Analysis.   If the appropriate discount rate for the following cash flows is 7.3 percent, what is the present value of the cash flows?

Year	Cash Flow
1	$1,200
2	1,100
3	800
4	600

LO 1
28. Discounted Cash Flow Analysis.   If the appropriate discount rate for the following cash flows is 9.29 percent per year, what is the present value of the cash flows?

Year	Cash Flow
1	$1,400
2	1,900
3	3,400
4	4,300

LO 4
29. Simple Interest versus Compound Interest.   First Simple Bank pays 6 percent simple interest on its investment accounts. If First Complex Bank pays interest on its accounts compounded annually, what rate should the bank set if it wants to match First Simple Bank over an investment horizon of 10 years?

Intermediate
(Questions 29–56)

LO 2
30. Calculating Annuities Due.   You want to buy a new sports car from Muscle Motors for $52,500. The contract is in the form of a 60-month annuity due at a 6.25 percent APR. What will your monthly payment be?

LO 4
31. Calculating Interest Expense.   You receive a credit card application from Shady Banks Savings and Loan offering an introductory rate of 1.8 percent per year, compounded monthly for the first six months, increasing thereafter to 18 percent compounded monthly. Assuming you transfer the $10,000 balance from your existing credit card and make no subsequent payments, how much interest will you owe at the end of the first year?

LO 4
32. Calculating the Number of Periods.   You are saving to buy a $195,000 house. There are two competing banks in your area, both offering certificates of deposit yielding 5.5 percent. How long will it take your initial $85,000 investment to reach the desired level at First Bank, which pays simple interest? How long at Second Bank, which compounds interest monthly?

LO 4
33. Calculating Future Values.   You have an investment that will pay you 1.13 percent per month. How much will you have per dollar invested in one year? In two years?

LO 4
34. Calculating Annuity Interest Rates.   Although you may know William Shakespeare from his classic literature, what is not well-known is that he was an astute investor. In 1604, when he was 40 and writing *King Lear*, Shakespeare grew worried about his eventual retirement. Afraid that he would become like King Lear in his retirement and beg hospitality from his children, he purchased grain "tithes," or shares in farm output, for 440 pounds. The tithes paid him 60 pounds per year for 31 years. Even though he died at the age of 52, his children received the remaining payments. What interest rate did the Bard of Avon receive on this investment?

LO 1 35. **Comparing Cash Flow Streams.** You've just joined the investment banking firm of Dewey, Cheatum, and Howe. They've offered you two different salary arrangements. You can have $6,100 per month for the next two years, or you can have $4,800 per month for the next two years, along with a $25,000 signing bonus today. If the interest rate is 7 percent compounded monthly, which do you prefer?

LO 1 36. **Calculating Present Value of Annuities.** Peter Lynchpin wants to sell you an investment contract that pays equal $15,000 amounts at the end of each of the next 20 years. If you require an effective annual return of 7 percent on this investment, how much will you pay for the contract today?

LO 4 37. **Calculating Rates of Return.** You're trying to choose between two different investments, both of which have up-front costs of $45,000. Investment G returns $75,000 in six years. Investment H returns $105,000 in 9 years. Which of these investments has the higher return?

LO 1 38. **Present Value and Interest Rates.** What is the relationship between the value of an annuity and the level of interest rates? Suppose you just bought a 10-year annuity of $10,000 per year at the current interest rate of 10 percent per year. What happens to the value of your investment if interest rates suddenly drop to 5 percent? What if interest rates suddenly rise to 15 percent?

LO 1 39. **Calculating the Number of Payments.** You're prepared to make monthly payments of $250, beginning at the end of this month, into an account that pays 8 percent interest compounded monthly. How many payments will you have made when your account balance reaches $50,000?

LO 2 40. **Calculating Annuity Present Values.** You want to borrow $85,000 from your local bank to buy a new sailboat. You can afford to make monthly payments of $1,800, but no more. Assuming monthly compounding, what is the highest rate you can afford on a 60-month APR loan?

LO 1 41. **Calculating Present Values.** In January 2012, the Texas Rangers signed Yu Darvish, formerly of the Nippon-Ham Fighters, to a contract reportedly worth $60.8 million. Yu's salary (including roster bonus) was to be paid as $6.3 million in 2012, $10.3 million in 2013, $10.8 million in 2014 to 2016, and $11.8 million in 2017. If the appropriate interest rate is 11 percent, what kind of deal did the pitcher snag? Assume all payments are paid at the end of each year.

LO 1 42. **Calculating Present Values.** In September 2011, the Tennessee Titans signed running back Chris Johnson to a contract reportedly worth $56 million. Johnson's salary included a $10 million signing bonus to be paid immediately and $3 million in salary for 2011. The remaining salary was $8 million in 2012, $10 million in 2013, $8 million in 2014 and 2015, and $9 million in 2016. If the appropriate interest rate is 11 percent, what kind of deal did the running back scamper away with? Assume all payments other than the first $10 million are paid at the end of each year.

LO 4 43. **EAR versus APR.** You have just purchased a new warehouse. To finance the purchase, you've arranged for a 30-year mortgage loan for 80 percent of the $2,900,000 purchase price. The monthly payment on this loan will be $14,900. What is the APR on this loan? The EAR?

LO 1 44. **Annuity Values.** You are planning your retirement in 10 years. You currently have $120,000 in a bond account and $500,000 in a stock account. You plan to add $5,000 per year at the end of each of the next 10 years to your bond account. The stock account will earn a return of 10.5 percent and the bond account will earn a return of

7 percent. When you retire, you plan to withdraw an equal amount for each of the next 25 years at the end of each year and have nothing left. Additionally, when you retire you will transfer your money to an account that earns 6.25 percent. How much can you withdraw each year?

LO 4 **45. Calculating Annuities Due Interest Rates.** You have arranged for a loan on your new car that will require the first payment today. The loan is for $32,000, and the monthly payments are $620. If the loan will be paid off over the next 60 months, what is the APR of the loan?

LO 1 **46. Calculating Annuities Due.** Suppose you are going to receive $15,000 per year for five years. The appropriate interest rate is 8 percent.

    a. What is the present value of the payments if they are in the form of an ordinary annuity? What is the present value if the payments are an annuity due?

    b. Suppose you plan to invest the payments for five years. What is the future value if the payments are an ordinary annuity? What if the payments are an annuity due?

    c. Which has the higher present value, the ordinary annuity or annuity due? Which has the higher future value? Will this always be true?

LO 1 **47. Annuity and Perpetuity Values.** Mary is going to receive a 30-year annuity of $10,500. Nancy is going to receive a perpetuity of $10,500. If the appropriate interest rate is 7 percent, how much more is Nancy's cash flow worth?

LO 1 **48. Calculating Present Values.** A 6-year annuity of 12 $8,500 semiannual payments will begin 9 years from now, with the first payment coming 9.5 years from now. If the discount rate is 9 percent compounded semiannually, what is the value of this annuity five years from now? What is the value three years from now? What is the current value of the annuity?

LO 1 **49. Present Value and Multiple Cash Flows.** What is the present value of $2,150 per year, at a discount rate of 9 percent, if the first payment is received 6 years from now and the last payment is received 20 years from now?

LO 1 **50. Variable Interest Rates.** A 10-year annuity pays $1,900 per month, and payments are made at the end of each month. If the interest rate is 9 percent compounded monthly for the first four years, and 7 percent compounded monthly thereafter, what is the present value of the annuity?

LO 1 **51. Comparing Cash Flow Streams.** You have your choice of two investment accounts. Investment A is a 10-year annuity that features end-of-month $1,525 payments and has an interest rate of 7 percent compounded monthly. Investment B is an annually compounded lump-sum investment with an interest rate of 9 percent, also good for 10 years. How much money would you need to invest in B today for it to be worth as much as Investment A 10 years from now?

LO 1 **52. Calculating Present Value of a Perpetuity.** Given an interest rate of 5.75 percent per year, what is the value at Year 7 of a perpetual stream of $5,000 payments that begin at Year 20?

LO 4 **53. Calculating EAR.** A local finance company quotes an interest rate of 18 percent on one-year loans. So, if you borrow $20,000, the interest for the year will be $3,600. Because you must repay a total of $23,600 in one year, the finance company requires you to pay $23,600/12, or $1,966.67 per month over the next 12 months. Is the interest rate on this loan 18 percent? What rate would legally have to be quoted? What is the effective annual rate?

www.mhhe.com/rwj

162   **PART 3**   Valuation of Future Cash Flows

LO 1

54. Calculating Future Values. If today is Year 0, what is the future value of the following cash flows five years from now? What is the future value 10 years from now? Assume an interest rate of 6.9 percent per year.

Year	Cash Flow
2	$15,000
3	24,000
5	33,000

LO 3

55. Amortization with Equal Payments. Prepare an amortization schedule for a three-year loan of $75,000. The interest rate is 8 percent per year, and the loan calls for equal annual payments. How much interest is paid in the third year? How much total interest is paid over the life of the loan?

LO 3

56. Amortization with Equal Principal Payments. Rework Problem 55 assuming that the loan agreement calls for a principal reduction of $25,000 every year instead of equal annual payments.

Challenge
(Questions 57–60)

LO 4

57. Discount Interest Loans. This question illustrates what is known as *discount interest.* Imagine you are discussing a loan with a somewhat unscrupulous lender. You want to borrow $15,000 for one year. The interest rate is 14 percent. You and the lender agree that the interest on the loan will be .14 × $15,000 = $2,100. So, the lender deducts this interest amount from the loan up front and gives you $12,900. In this case, we say that the discount is $2,100. What's wrong here?

LO 1

58. Calculating Annuity Values. You are serving on a jury. A plaintiff is suing the city for injuries sustained after a freak street sweeper accident. In the trial, doctors testified that it will be five years before the plaintiff is able to return to work. The jury has already decided in favor of the plaintiff. You are the foreperson of the jury and propose that the jury give the plaintiff an award to cover the following: (a) The present value of two years' back pay. The plaintiff's annual salary for the last two years would have been $38,000 and $42,000, respectively. (b) The present value of five years' future salary. You assume the salary will be $45,000 per year. (c) $150,000 for pain and suffering. (d) $20,000 for court costs. Assume that the salary payments are equal amounts paid at the end of each month. If the interest rate you choose is an EAR of 7 percent, what is the size of the settlement? If you were the plaintiff, would you like to see a higher or lower interest rate?

LO 4

59. Calculating EAR with Points. You are looking at a one-year loan of $10,000. The interest rate is quoted as 12 percent plus two points. A *point* on a loan is simply 1 percent (one percentage point) of the loan amount. Quotes similar to this one are common with home mortgages. The interest rate quotation in this example requires the borrower to pay two points to the lender up front and repay the loan later with 10 percent interest. What rate would you actually be paying here?

LO 1

60. Future Value and Multiple Cash Flows. An insurance company is offering a new policy to its customers. Typically, the policy is bought by a parent or grandparent for a child at the child's birth. The details of the policy are as follows:

The purchaser (say, the parent) makes the following six payments to the insurance company:

First birthday:	$ 800
Second birthday:	$ 800
Third birthday:	$ 900
Fourth birthday:	$ 900
Fifth birthday:	$1,000
Sixth birthday:	$1,000

After the child's sixth birthday, no more payments are made. When the child reaches age 65, he or she receives $350,000. If the relevant interest rate is 10 percent for the first six years and 7 percent for all subsequent years, is the policy worth buying?

www.mhhe.com/rwj

WHAT'S ON THE WEB?

5.1 Annuity Future Value.   The St. Louis Federal Reserve Board has files listing historical interest rates on their website www.stlouisfed.org. Find the link for "FRED®" (Federal Reserve Economic Data). You will find listings for Moody's Seasoned Aaa Corporate Bond Yield and Moody's Seasoned Baa Corporate Bond Yield. (These rates are discussed in the next chapter.) If you invest $2,000 per year for the next 40 years at the most recent Aaa yield, how much will you have? What if you invest the same amount at the Baa yield?

5.2 Loan Payments.   Finding the time necessary until you pay off a loan is simple if you make equal payments each month. However, when paying off credit cards many individuals only make the minimum monthly payment, which is generally $10 or 2 percent to 3 percent of the balance, whichever is greater. You can find a credit card calculator at www.fincalc.com. You currently owe $10,000 on a credit card with a 17 percent interest rate and a minimum payment of $10 or 2 percent of your balance, whichever is greater. How soon will you pay off this debt if you make the minimum payment each month? How much total interest will you pay?

5.3 Annuity Payments.   Find the retirement calculator at www.moneychimp.com to answer the following question: Suppose you have $1,500,000 when you retire and want to withdraw an equal amount each year for the next 30 years. How much can you withdraw each year if you earn 7 percent? What if you can earn 9 percent?

5.4 Annuity Payments.   The St. Louis Federal Reserve Board has files listing historical interest rates on their website www.stlouisfed.org. Find the link for "FRED®" (Federal Reserve Economic Data). You will find a listing for the Bank Prime Loan Rate. The file lists the monthly prime rates since January 1949 (1949.01). What is the most recent prime rate? What is the highest prime rate over this period? If you buy a house for $150,000 at the current prime rate on a 30-year mortgage with monthly payments, how much are your payments? If you had purchased the house at the same price when the prime rate was at its highest, what would your monthly payments have been?

5.5 Loan Amortization.   Bankrate.com, located at www.bankrate.com, has a financial calculator that will prepare an amortization table based on your inputs. First, find the APR quoted on the website for a 30-year fixed rate mortgage. You want to buy a home for $200,000 on a 30-year mortgage with monthly payments at the rate quoted on the site. What percentage of your first month's payment is principal? What percentage of your last month's payment is principal? What is the total interest paid on the loan?

EXCEL *MASTER IT!* PROBLEM

This is a classic retirement problem. A friend is celebrating her birthday and wants to start saving for her anticipated retirement. She has the following years to retirement and retirement spending goals:

Years until retirement:	30
Amount to withdraw each year:	$90,000
Years to withdraw in retirement:	20
Interest rate:	8%

Because your friend is planning ahead, the first withdrawal will not take place until one year after she retires. She wants to make equal annual deposits into her account for her retirement fund.

a. If she starts making these deposits in one year and makes her last deposit on the day she retires, what amount must she deposit annually to be able to make the desired withdrawals at retirement?

b. Suppose your friend just inherited a large sum of money. Rather than making equal annual payments, she decided to make one lump-sum deposit today to cover her retirement needs. What amount does she have to deposit today?

c. Suppose your friend's employer will contribute to the account each year as part of the company's profit-sharing plan. In addition, your friend expects a distribution from a family trust several years from now. What amount must she deposit annually now to be able to make the desired withdrawals at retirement?

Employer's annual contribution:	$1,500
Years until trust fund distribution:	20
Amount of trust fund distribution:	$25,000

CHAPTER CASE
S&S AIR'S MORTGAGE

Mark Sexton and Todd Story, the owners of S&S Air, Inc., were impressed by the work Chris had done on financial planning. Using Chris's analysis, and looking at the demand for light aircraft, they have decided that their existing fabrication equipment is sufficient, but it is time to acquire a bigger manufacturing facility. Mark and Todd have identified a suitable structure that is currently for sale, and they believe they can buy and refurbish it for about $35 million. Mark, Todd, and Chris are now ready to meet with Christie Vaughan, the loan officer for First United National Bank. The meeting is to discuss the mortgage options available to the company to finance the new facility.

Christie begins the meeting by discussing a 30-year mortgage. The loan would be repaid in equal monthly installments. Because of the previous relationship between S&S Air and the bank, there would be no closing costs for the loan. Christie states that the APR of the loan would be 6.1 percent. Todd asks if a shorter mortgage loan is available. Christie says that the bank does have a 20-year mortgage available at the same APR.

Mark decides to ask Christie about a "smart loan" he discussed with a mortgage broker when he was refinancing his home loan. A smart loan works as follows: Every two weeks a mortgage payment is made that is exactly one-half of the traditional monthly mortgage payment. Christie informs him that the bank does have smart loans. The APR of the smart loan would be the same as the APR of the traditional loan. Mark nods his head. He then states this is the best mortgage option available to the company since it saves interest payments.

Christie agrees with Mark, but then suggests that a bullet loan, or balloon payment, would result in the greatest interest savings. At Todd's prompting, she goes on to explain a bullet loan. The monthly payments of a bullet loan would be calculated using a 30-year traditional mortgage. In this case, there would be a 5-year bullet. This would mean that the company would make the mortgage payments for the traditional 30-year mortgage for the first five years, but immediately after the company makes the 60th payment, the bullet payment would be due. The bullet payment is the remaining principal of the loan. Chris then asks how the bullet payment is calculated. Christie tells him that the remaining principal can be calculated using an amortization table, but it is also the present value of the remaining 25 years of mortgage payments for the 30-year mortgage.

Todd has also heard of an interest-only loan and asks if this loan is available and what the terms would be. Christie says that the bank offers an interest-only loan with a term of 10 years and an APR of 3.5 percent. She goes on to further explain the terms. The company would be responsible for making interest payments each month on the amount borrowed. No principal payments are required. At the end of the 10-year term, the company would repay the $35 million. However, the company can make principal payments at any time. The principal payments would work just like those on a traditional mortgage. Principal payments would reduce the principal of the loan and reduce the interest due on the next payment.

Mark and Todd are satisfied with Christie's answers, but they are still unsure of which loan they should choose. They have asked Chris to answer the following questions to help them choose the correct mortgage. ∎

QUESTIONS

1. What are the monthly payments for a 30-year traditional mortgage? What are the payments for a 20-year traditional mortgage?

2. Prepare an amortization table for the first six months of the traditional 30-year mortgage. How much of the first payment goes toward principal?

3. How long would it take for S&S Air to pay off the smart loan assuming 30-year traditional mortgage payments? Why is this shorter than the time needed to pay off the traditional mortgage? How much interest would the company save?

4. Assume S&S Air takes out a bullet loan under the terms described. What are the payments on the loan?

5. What are the payments for the interest-only loan?

6. Which mortgage is the best for the company? Are there any potential risks in this action?

www.mhhe.com/rwj

6 | Interest Rates and Bond Valuation

learning objectives

After studying this chapter, you should be able to:

LO 1 Identify important bond features and types of bonds.

LO 2 Describe bond values and why they fluctuate.

LO 3 Discuss bond ratings and what they mean.

LO 4 Evaluate the impact of inflation on interest rates.

LO 5 Explain the term structure of interest rates and the determinants of bond yields.

In modern history, about the safest investment available has been U.S. Treasury bonds. And low risk meant that U.S. Treasury bonds paid a lower return, or "yield," than other bonds. However, in February 2010, insurer Berkshire Hathaway issued bonds with a lower promised yield than Treasury bonds. Berkshire Hathaway was not alone: Proctor & Gamble, Johnson & Johnson, and Lowe's all were able to sell bonds with lower promised yields.

So what happened? Apparently, the bond market was saying that these four corporations had lower risk than the U.S. government. In August 2011, credit rating agency S&P agreed when it lowered the credit rating on U.S. Treasury bonds from the vaunted AAA. Other countries had similar experiences. About the same time, Japan's government debt was downgraded, and on a single day in January 2012, nine nations, including France, Spain, and Italy, received downgrades on their sovereign debt.

This chapter takes what we have learned about the time value of money and shows how it can be used to value one of the most common of all financial assets, a bond. It then discusses bond features, bond types, and the operation of the bond market.

What we will see is that bond prices depend critically on interest rates, so we will go on to discuss some very fundamental issues regarding interest rates. Clearly, interest rates are important to everybody because they underlie what businesses of all types—small and large—must pay to borrow money.

Our goal in this chapter is to introduce you to bonds. We begin by showing how the techniques we developed in Chapters 4 and 5 can be applied to bond valuation. From there, we go on to discuss bond features and how bonds are bought and sold. One important thing we learn is that bond values depend, in large part, on interest rates. We therefore close out the chapter with an examination of interest rates and their behavior.

BONDS AND BOND VALUATION

6.1

ExcelMaster
coverage online

When a corporation (or government) wishes to borrow money from the public on a long-term basis, it usually does so by issuing, or selling, debt securities that are generically called bonds. In this section, we describe the various features of corporate bonds and some of the terminology associated with bonds. We then discuss the cash flows associated with a bond and how bonds can be valued using our discounted cash flow procedure.

Bond Features and Prices

As we mentioned in our previous chapter, a bond is normally an interest-only loan, meaning that the borrower will pay the interest every period, but none of the principal will be repaid until the end of the loan. For example, suppose the Beck Corporation wants to borrow $1,000 for 30 years. The interest rate on similar debt issued by similar corporations is 12 percent. Beck will thus pay .12 × $1,000 = $120 in interest every year for 30 years. At the end of 30 years, Beck will repay the $1,000. As this example suggests, a bond is a fairly simple financing arrangement. There is, however, a rich jargon associated with bonds, so we will use this example to define some of the more important terms.

In our example, the $120 regular interest payments that Beck promises to make are called the bond's **coupons**. Because the coupon is constant and paid every year, the type of bond we are describing is sometimes called a *level coupon bond*. The amount that will be repaid at the end of the loan is called the bond's **face value** or **par value**. As in our example, this par value is usually $1,000 for corporate bonds, and a bond that sells for its par value is called a *par value bond*. Government bonds frequently have much larger face, or par, values. Finally, the annual coupon divided by the face value is called the **coupon rate** on the bond; in this case, because $120/1,000 = 12%, the bond has a 12 percent coupon rate.

The number of years until the face value is paid is called the bond's time to **maturity**. A corporate bond will frequently have a maturity of 30 years when it is originally issued, but this varies. Once the bond has been issued, the number of years to maturity declines as time goes by.

Bond Values and Yields

As time passes, interest rates change in the marketplace. The cash flows from a bond, however, stay the same. As a result, the value of the bond will fluctuate. When interest rates rise, the present value of the bond's remaining cash flows declines, and the bond is worth less. When interest rates fall, the bond is worth more.

To determine the value of a bond at a particular point in time, we need to know the number of periods remaining until maturity, the face value, the coupon, and the market interest rate for bonds with similar features. This interest rate required in the market on a bond is called the bond's **yield to maturity (YTM)**. This rate is sometimes called the bond's *yield* for short. Given all this information, we can calculate the present value of the cash flows as an estimate of the bond's current market value.

coupon
Stated interest payment made on a bond.

face value
The principal amount of a bond that is repaid at the end of the term. Also, par value.

coupon rate
The annual coupon divided by the face value of a bond.

maturity
Date on which the principal amount of a bond is paid.

yield to maturity (YTM)
The rate required in the market on a bond.

FIGURE 6.1	**Cash flows for Xanth Co. bond**

As shown, the Xanth bond has an annual coupon of $80 and a face, or par, value of $1,000 paid at maturity in 10 years.

For example, suppose the Xanth (pronounced "zanth") Co. were to issue a bond with 10 years to maturity. The Xanth bond has an annual coupon of $80. Similar bonds have a yield to maturity of 8 percent. Based on our preceding discussion, the Xanth bond will pay $80 per year for the next 10 years in coupon interest. In 10 years, Xanth will pay $1,000 to the owner of the bond. The cash flows from the bond are shown in Figure 6.1. What would this bond sell for?

As illustrated in Figure 6.1, the Xanth bond's cash flows have an annuity component (the coupons) and a lump sum (the face value paid at maturity). We thus estimate the market value of the bond by calculating the present value of these two components separately and adding the results together. First, at the going rate of 8 percent, the present value of the $1,000 paid in 10 years is:

Present value = $1,000/1.08^{10} = $1,000/2.1589 = $463.19

Second, the bond offers $80 per year for 10 years; the present value of this annuity stream is:

Annuity present value = $80 × (1 − 1/1.08^{10})/.08
= $80 × (1 − 1/2.1589)/.08
= $80 × 6.7101
= $536.81

We can now add the values for the two parts together to get the bond's value:

Total bond value = $463.19 + 536.81 = $1,000

This bond sells for exactly its face value. This is not a coincidence. The going interest rate in the market is 8 percent. Considered as an interest-only loan, what interest rate does this bond have? With an $80 coupon, this bond pays exactly 8 percent interest only when it sells for $1,000.

To illustrate what happens as interest rates change, suppose that a year has gone by. The Xanth bond now has nine years to maturity. If the interest rate in the market has risen to 10 percent, what will the bond be worth? To find out, we repeat the present value calculations with 9 years instead of 10, and a 10 percent yield instead of an 8 percent yield. First, the present value of the $1,000 paid in nine years at 10 percent is:

Present value = $1,000/1.10^{9} = $1,000/2.3579 = $424.10

Second, the bond now offers $80 per year for nine years; the present value of this annuity stream at 10 percent is:

Annuity present value = $80 × (1 − 1/1.10^{9})/.10
= $80 × (1 − 1/2.3579)/.10
= $80 × 5.7590
= $460.72

We can now add the values for the two parts together to get the bond's value:

Total bond value = $424.10 + 460.72 = **$884.82**

Therefore, the bond should sell for about $885. In the vernacular, we say that this bond, with its 8 percent coupon, is priced to yield 10 percent at $885.

The Xanth Co. bond now sells for less than its $1,000 face value. Why? The market interest rate is 10 percent. Considered as an interest-only loan of $1,000, this bond only pays 8 percent, its coupon rate. Because this bond pays less than the going rate, investors are only willing to lend something less than the $1,000 promised repayment. Because the bond sells for less than face value, it is said to be a *discount bond*.

The only way to get the interest rate up to 10 percent is to lower the price to less than $1,000 so that the purchaser, in effect, has a built-in gain. For the Xanth bond, the price of $885 is $115 less than the face value, so an investor who purchased and kept the bond would get $80 per year and would have a $115 gain at maturity as well. This gain compensates the lender for the below-market coupon rate.

Another way to see why the bond is discounted by $115 is to note that the $80 coupon is $20 below the coupon on a newly issued par value bond, based on current market conditions. The bond would be worth $1,000 only if it had a coupon of $100 per year. In a sense, an investor who buys and keeps the bond gives up $20 per year for nine years. At 10 percent, this annuity stream is worth:

Annuity present value = **$20 × (1 − 1/1.10⁹)/.10**
$$= \textbf{\$20} \times \textbf{5.7590}$$
$$= \textbf{\$115.18}$$

This is just the amount of the discount.

What would the Xanth bond sell for if interest rates had dropped by 2 percent instead of rising by 2 percent? As you might guess, the bond would sell for more than $1,000. Such a bond is said to sell at a *premium* and is called a *premium bond*.

This case is just the opposite of that of a discount bond. The Xanth bond now has a coupon rate of 8 percent when the market rate is only 6 percent. Investors are willing to pay a premium to get this extra coupon amount. In this case, the relevant discount rate is 6 percent, and there are nine years remaining. The present value of the $1,000 face amount is:

Present value = **$1,000/1.06⁹** = **$1,000/1.6895** = $591.89

The present value of the coupon stream is:

Annuity present value = **$80 × (1 − 1/1.06⁹)/.06**
$$= \textbf{\$80} \times \textbf{(1} - \textbf{1/1.6895)/.06}$$
$$= \textbf{\$80} \times \textbf{6.8017}$$
$$= \$544.14$$

We can now add the values for the two parts together to get the bond's value:

Total bond value = $591.89 + 544.14 = **$1,136.03**

Total bond value is therefore about $136 in excess of par value. Once again, we can verify this amount by noting that the coupon is now $20 too high, based on current market conditions. The present value of $20 per year for nine years at 6 percent is:

Annuity present value = **$20 × (1 − 1/1.06⁹)/.06**
$$= \textbf{\$20} \times \textbf{6.8017}$$
$$= \textbf{\$136.03}$$

This is just as we calculated.

A good bond site to visit is bonds.yahoo.com, which has loads of useful information.

Based on our examples, we can now write the general expression for the value of a bond. If a bond has (1) a face value of F paid at maturity, (2) a coupon of C paid per period, (3) t periods to maturity, and (4) a yield of r per period, its value is:

$$\text{Bond value} = C \times [1 - 1/(1 + r)^t]/r + F/(1 + r)^t$$

$$\text{Bond value} = \begin{array}{c} \text{Present value} \\ \text{of the coupons} \end{array} + \begin{array}{c} \text{Present value} \\ \text{of the face amount} \end{array} \qquad \text{[6.1]}$$

EXAMPLE | **6.1**

SEMIANNUAL COUPONS

In practice, bonds issued in the United States usually make coupon payments twice a year. So, if an ordinary bond has a coupon rate of 14 percent, then the owner will get a total of $140 per year, but this $140 will come in two payments of $70 each. Suppose we are examining such a bond. The yield to maturity is quoted at 16 percent.

Bond yields are quoted like APRs; the quoted rate is equal to the actual rate per period multiplied by the number of periods. In this case, with a 16 percent quoted yield and semiannual payments, the true yield is 8 percent per six months. The bond matures in seven years. What is the bond's price? What is the effective annual yield on this bond?

Based on our discussion, we know that the bond will sell at a discount because it has a coupon rate of 7 percent every six months when the market requires 8 percent every six months. So, if our answer is equal to or exceeds $1,000, we know that we have made a mistake.

To get the exact price, we first calculate the present value of the bond's face value of $1,000 paid in seven years. This seven-year period has 14 periods of six months each. At 8 percent per period, the value is:

$$\text{Present value} = \$1,000/1.08^{14} = \$1,000/2.9372 = \$340.46$$

The coupons can be viewed as a 14-period annuity of $70 per period. At an 8 percent discount rate, the present value of such an annuity is:

$$\begin{aligned}
\text{Annuity present value} &= \$70 \times (1 - 1/1.08^{14})/.08 \\
&= \$70 \times (1 - .3405)/.08 \\
&= \$70 \times 8.2442 \\
&= \$577.10
\end{aligned}$$

The total present value gives us what the bond should sell for:

$$\text{Total present value} = \$340.46 + 577.10 = \$917.56$$

To calculate the effective yield on this bond, note that 8 percent every six months is equivalent to:

$$\text{Effective annual rate} = (1 + .08)^2 - 1 = 16.64\%$$

The effective yield, therefore, is 16.64 percent.

Online bond calculators are available at www.smartmoney.com; interest rate information is available at money.cnn.com/data/bonds and www.bankrate.com.

As we have illustrated in this section, bond prices and interest rates always move in opposite directions. When interest rates rise, a bond's value, like any other present value, will decline. Similarly, when interest rates fall, bond values rise. Even if we are considering a bond that is riskless in the sense that the borrower is certain to make all the payments, there is still risk in owning a bond. We discuss this next.

Interest Rate Risk

The risk that arises for bond owners from fluctuating interest rates is called *interest rate risk*. How much interest rate risk a bond has depends on how sensitive its price is to interest rate changes. This sensitivity directly depends on two things: the time to maturity and

FIGURE 6.2

Interest rate risk and time to maturity

Value of a Bond with a 10 Percent Coupon Rate for Different Interest Rates and Maturities

Interest Rate	Time to Maturity	
	1 Year	30 Years
5%	$1,047.62	$1,768.62
10	1,000.00	1,000.00
15	956.52	671.70
20	916.67	502.11

the coupon rate. As we will see momentarily, you should keep the following in mind when looking at a bond:

1. All other things being equal, the longer the time to maturity, the greater the interest rate risk.

2. All other things being equal, the lower the coupon rate, the greater the interest rate risk.

We illustrate the first of these two points in Figure 6.2. As shown, we compute and plot prices under different interest rate scenarios for 10 percent coupon bonds with maturities of 1 year and 30 years. Notice how the slope of the line connecting the prices is much steeper for the 30-year maturity bond than it is for the 1-year maturity bond. This steepness tells us that a relatively small change in interest rates will lead to a substantial change in the bond's value. In comparison, the one-year bond's price is relatively insensitive to interest rate changes.

Intuitively, we can see that the reason that longer-term bonds have greater interest rate sensitivity is that a large portion of a bond's value comes from the $1,000 face amount. The present value of this amount isn't greatly affected by a small change in interest rates if the amount is to be received in one year. Even a small change in the interest rate, however, once it is compounded for 30 years, can have a significant effect on the present value. As a result, the present value of the face amount will be much more volatile with a longer-term bond.

The other thing to know about interest rate risk is that, like most things in finance and economics, it increases at a decreasing rate. In other words, if we compared a 10-year bond to a 1-year bond, we would see that the 10-year bond has much greater interest rate risk. However, if you were to compare a 20-year bond to a 30-year bond, you would find that the 30-year bond has somewhat greater interest rate risk because it has a longer maturity, but the difference in the risk would be fairly small.

The reason that bonds with lower coupons have greater interest rate risk is easy to understand. As we discussed earlier, the value of a bond depends on the present value of its

Visit **investorguide.com** to learn more about bonds.

coupons and the present value of the face amount. If two bonds with different coupon rates have the same maturity, then the value of the one with the lower coupon is proportionately more dependent on the face amount to be received at maturity. As a result, all other things being equal, its value will fluctuate more as interest rates change. Put another way, the bond with the higher coupon has a larger cash flow early in its life, so its value is less sensitive to changes in the discount rate.

Bonds are usually not issued with maturities longer than 30 years. However, low interest rates have led to the issuance of bonds with much longer maturities. In the 1990s, Walt Disney issued "Sleeping Beauty" bonds with a 100-year maturity. Similarly, BellSouth (now known as AT&T), Coca-Cola, and Dutch banking giant ABN AMRO all issued bonds with 100-year maturities. These companies wanted to lock in the historically low interest rates for a *long* time. The current record holder for corporations appears to be Republic National Bank, which sold bonds with 1,000 years to maturity. Before these fairly recent issues, it appears the last time 100-year bonds were issued was in May 1954 by the Chicago and Eastern Railroad. And low interest rates in recent years have led to more 100-year bonds. For example, in December 2011, the California Institute of Technology, renowned for its math and science prowess, issued $350 million in 100-year bonds with a record low yield of 4.744 percent.

We can illustrate the effect of interest rate risk using the 100-year BellSouth issue. The following table provides some basic information on this issue, along with its prices on December 31, 1995, May 6, 2008, and January 24, 2011.

Maturity	Coupon Rate	Price on 12/31/95	Price on 5/6/08	Percentage Change in Price 1995–2008	Price on 1/24/11	Percentage Change in Price 2005–2011
2095	7.00%	$1,000.00	$1,008.40	+.84%	$702.95	−30.3%

Several things emerge from this table. First, interest rates apparently fell between December 31, 1995, and May 6, 2008 (why?). After that, however, they rose (why?). The bond's price first gained .84 percent and then lost 30.3 percent. These swings illustrate that longer-term bonds have significant interest rate risk.

Finding the Yield to Maturity: More Trial and Error

Frequently, we will know a bond's price, coupon rate, and maturity date, but not its yield to maturity. For example, suppose we are interested in a six-year, 8 percent coupon bond. A broker quotes a price of $955.14. What is the yield on this bond?

We've seen that the price of a bond can be written as the sum of its annuity and lump-sum components. Knowing that there is an $80 coupon for six years and a $1,000 face value, we can say that the price is:

$$\$955.14 = \$80 \times [1 - 1/(1 + r)^6]/r + 1{,}000/(1 + r)^6$$

where r is the unknown discount rate, or yield to maturity. We have one equation here and one unknown, but we cannot solve for r explicitly. The only way to find the answer is to use trial and error (or, better yet, a spreadsheet or financial calculator).

This problem is essentially identical to the one we examined in the last chapter when we tried to find the unknown interest rate on an annuity. However, finding the rate (or yield) on a bond is even more complicated because of the $1,000 face amount.

We can speed up the trial-and-error process by using what we know about bond prices and yields. In this case, the bond has an $80 coupon and is selling at a discount. We thus know that the yield is greater than 8 percent. If we compute the price at 10 percent:

$$\text{Bond value} = \$80 \times (1 - 1/1.10^6)/.10 + 1,000/1.10^6$$
$$= \$80 \times 4.3553 + 1,000/1.7716$$
$$= \$912.89$$

Current market rates are available at www.bankrate.com.

At 10 percent, the value we calculate is lower than the actual price, so 10 percent is too high. The true yield must be somewhere between 8 and 10 percent. At this point, it's "plug and chug" to find the answer. You would probably want to try 9 percent next. If you did, you would see that this is in fact the bond's yield to maturity.

A bond's yield to maturity should not be confused with its **current yield**, which is simply a bond's annual coupon divided by its price. In the example we just worked, the bond's annual coupon was $80, and its price was $955.14. Given these numbers, we see that the current yield is $80/955.14 = 8.38$ percent, which is less than the yield to maturity of 9 percent. The reason the current yield is too low is that it only considers the coupon portion of your return; it doesn't consider the built-in gain from the price discount. For a premium bond, the reverse is true, meaning that current yield would be higher because it ignores the built-in loss.

current yield
A bond's annual coupon divided by its price.

Our discussion of bond valuation is summarized in Table 6.1.

CURRENT EVENTS EXAMPLE 6.2

A bond has a quoted price of $1,080.42. It has a face value of $1,000, a semiannual coupon of $30, and a maturity of five years. What is its current yield? What is its yield to maturity? Which is bigger? Why?

Notice that this bond makes semiannual payments of $30, so the annual payment is $60. The current yield is thus $60/1,080.42 = 5.55$ percent. To calculate the yield to maturity, refer back to Example 6.1. Now, in this case, the bond pays $30 every six months and it has 10 six-month periods until maturity. So, we need to find r as follows:

$$\$1,080.42 = \$30 \times [1 - 1/(1 + r)^{10}]/r + 1,000/(1 + r)^{10}$$

After some trial and error, we find that r is equal to 2.1 percent. But, the tricky part is that this 2.1 percent is the yield per *six months*. We have to double it to get the yield to maturity, so the yield to maturity is 4.2 percent, which is less than the current yield. The reason is that the current yield ignores the built-in loss of the premium between now and maturity.

I. Finding the value of a bond
  Bond value $= C \times [1 - 1/(1 + r)^t]/r + F/(1 + r)^t$
  where
  C = Coupon paid each period
  r = Rate per period
  t = Number of periods
  F = Bond's face value

II. Finding the yield on a bond
  Given a bond value, coupon, time to maturity, and face value, it is possible to find the implicit discount rate, or yield to maturity, by trial and error only. To do this, try different discount rates in the formula above until the calculated bond value equals the given bond value. Remember that increasing the rate *decreases* the bond value.

TABLE 6.1

Summary of bond valuation

174   **PART 4**   Valuing Stocks and Bonds

EXAMPLE 6.3

BOND YIELDS

You're looking at two bonds identical in every way except for their coupons and, of course, their prices. Both have 12 years to maturity. The first bond has a 10 percent coupon rate and sells for $935.08. The second has a 12 percent coupon rate. What do you think it would sell for?

Because the two bonds are very similar, they will be priced to yield about the same rate. We first need to calculate the yield on the 10 percent coupon bond. Proceeding as before, we know that the yield must be greater than 10 percent because the bond is selling at a discount. The bond has a fairly long maturity of 12 years. We've seen that long-term bond prices are relatively sensitive to interest rate changes, so the yield is probably close to 10 percent. A little trial and error reveals that the yield is actually 11 percent:

$$\text{Bond value} = \$100 \times (1 - 1/1.11^{12})/.11 + 1{,}000/1.11^{12}$$
$$= \$100 \times 6.4924 + 1{,}000/3.4985$$
$$= \$649.24 + 285.84$$
$$= \$935.08$$

With an 11 percent yield, the second bond will sell at a premium because of its $120 coupon. Its value is:

$$\text{Bond value} = \$120 \times (1 - 1/1.11^{12})/.11 + 1{,}000/1.11^{12}$$
$$= \$120 \times 6.4924 + 1{,}000/3.4985$$
$$= \$779.08 + 285.84$$
$$= \$1{,}064.92$$

CALCULATOR HINTS

How to Calculate Bond Prices and Yields Using a Financial Calculator

Many financial calculators have fairly sophisticated built-in bond valuation routines. However, these vary quite a lot in implementation, and not all financial calculators have them. As a result, we will illustrate a simple way to handle bond problems that will work on just about any financial calculator.

To begin, of course, we first remember to clear out the calculator! Next, for Example 6.3, we have two bonds to consider, both with 12 years to maturity. The first one sells for $935.08 and has a 10 percent coupon rate. To find its yield, we can do the following:

Enter	12		100	−935.08	1,000
	N	**I/Y**	**PMT**	**PV**	**FV**
Solve for		11			

Notice that here we have entered both a future value of $1,000, representing the bond's face value, and a payment of 10 percent of $1,000, or $100, per year, representing the bond's annual coupon. Also notice that we have a negative sign on the bond's price, which we have entered as the present value.

For the second bond, we now know that the relevant yield is 11 percent. It has a 12 percent coupon and 12 years to maturity, so what's the price? To answer, we just enter the relevant values and solve for the present value of the bond's cash flows:

Enter	12	11	120		1,000
	N	**I/Y**	**PMT**	**PV**	**FV**
Solve for				−1064.92	

(continued)

There is an important detail that comes up here. Suppose we have a bond with a price of $902.29, 10 years to maturity, and a coupon rate of 6 percent. As we mentioned earlier, most bonds actually make semiannual payments. Assuming that this is the case for the bond here, what's the bond's yield? To answer, we need to enter the relevant numbers like this:

Enter	20		30	−902.29	1,000
	N	**I/Y**	**PMT**	**PV**	**FV**
Solve for		3.7			

Notice that we entered $30 as the payment because the bond actually makes payments of $30 every six months. Similarly, we entered 20 for N because there are actually 20 six-month periods. When we solve for the yield, we get 3.7 percent, but the tricky thing to remember is that this is the yield *per six months*, so we have to double it to get the right answer: $2 \times 3.7 = 7.4$ percent, which would be the bond's reported yield.

How to Calculate Bond Prices and Yields Using a Spreadsheet

SPREADSHEET STRATEGIES

Like financial calculators, most spreadsheets have fairly elaborate routines available for calculating bond values and yields; many of these routines involve details that we have not discussed. However, setting up a simple spreadsheet to calculate prices or yields is straightforward, as our next two spreadsheets show:

	A	B	C	D	E	F	G	H
1								
2	Using a spreadsheet to calculate bond yields							
3								
4	Suppose we have a bond with 22 years to maturity, a coupon rate of 8 percent, and a price of							
5	$960.17. If the bond makes semiannual payments, what is its yield to maturity?							
6								
7	Settlement date:	1/1/00						
8	Maturity date:	1/1/22						
9	Annual coupon rate:	.08						
10	Bond price (% of par):	96.017						
11	Face value (% of par):	100						
12	Coupons per year:	2						
13	Yield to maturity:	.084						
14								
15	The formula entered in cell B13 is = YIELD(B7,B8,B9,B10,B11,B12); notice that face value and bond							
16	price are entered as a percentage of face value.							
17								

(continued)

	A	B	C	D	E	F	G	H
1								
2	Using a spreadsheet to calculate bond values							
3								
4	Suppose we have a bond with 22 years to maturity, a coupon rate of 8 percent, and a yield to							
5	maturity of 9 percent. If the bond makes semiannual payments, what is its price today?							
6								
7	Settlement date:	1/1/00						
8	Maturity date:	1/1/22						
9	Annual coupon rate:	.08						
10	Yield to maturity:	.09						
11	Face value (% of par):	100						
12	Coupons per year:	2						
13	Bond price (% of par):	**90.49**						
14								
15	The formula entered in cell B13 is =PRICE(B7,B8,B9,B10,B11,B12); notice that face value and bond							
16	price are entered as a percentage of face value.							
17								

In our spreadsheets, notice that we had to enter two dates, a settlement date and a maturity date. The settlement date is just the date you actually pay for the bond, and the maturity date is the day the bond actually matures. In most of our problems, we don't explicitly have these dates, so we have to make them up. For example, since our bond has 22 years to maturity, we just picked 1/1/2000 (January 1, 2000) as the settlement date and 1/1/2022 (January 1, 2022) as the maturity date. Any two dates would do as long as they were exactly 22 years apart, but these are particularly easy to work with. Finally, notice that we had to enter the coupon rate and yield to maturity in annual terms and then explicitly provide the number of coupon payments per year.

CONCEPT QUESTIONS

6.1a   What are the cash flows associated with a bond?

6.1b   What is the general expression for the value of a bond?

6.1c   Is it true that the only risk associated with owning a bond is that the issuer will not make all the payments? Explain.

6.2

MORE ON BOND FEATURES

ExcelMaster
coverage online

In this section, we continue our discussion of corporate debt by describing in some detail the basic terms and features that make up a typical long-term corporate bond. We discuss additional issues associated with long-term debt in subsequent sections.

Securities issued by corporations may be classified roughly as *equity securities* and *debt securities*. At the crudest level, a debt represents something that must be repaid; it is the result of borrowing money. When corporations borrow, they generally promise to make regularly scheduled interest payments and to repay the original amount borrowed (that is, the principal). The person or firm making the loan is called the *creditor,* or *lender.* The corporation borrowing the money is called the *debtor,* or *borrower.*

From a financial point of view, the main differences between debt and equity are the following:

1. Debt is not an ownership interest in the firm. Creditors generally do not have voting power.

2. The corporation's payment of interest on debt is considered a cost of doing business and is fully tax deductible. Dividends paid to stockholders are *not* tax deductible.

3. Unpaid debt is a liability of the firm. If it is not paid, the creditors can legally claim the assets of the firm. This action can result in liquidation or reorganization, two of the possible consequences of bankruptcy. Thus, one of the costs of issuing debt is the possibility of financial failure. This possibility does not arise when equity is issued.

Information for bond investors can be found at www. investinginbonds. com.

Is It Debt or Equity?

Sometimes it is not clear if a particular security is debt or equity. For example, suppose a corporation issues a perpetual bond with interest payable solely from corporate income if and only if earned. Whether or not this is really a debt is hard to say and is primarily a legal and semantic issue. Courts and taxing authorities would have the final say.

Corporations are very adept at creating exotic, hybrid securities that have many features of equity but are treated as debt. Obviously, the distinction between debt and equity is very important for tax purposes. So, one reason that corporations try to create a debt security that is really equity is to obtain the tax benefits of debt and the bankruptcy benefits of equity.

As a general rule, equity represents an ownership interest, and it is a residual claim. This means that equity holders are paid after debt holders. As a result of this, the risks and benefits associated with owning debt and equity are different. To give just one example, note that the maximum reward for owning a debt security is ultimately fixed by the amount of the loan, whereas there is no upper limit to the potential reward from owning an equity interest.

Long-Term Debt: The Basics

Ultimately, all long-term debt securities are promises made by the issuing firm to pay principal when due and to make timely interest payments on the unpaid balance. Beyond this, there are a number of features that distinguish these securities from one another. We discuss some of these features next.

The maturity of a long-term debt instrument is the length of time the debt remains outstanding with some unpaid balance. Debt securities can be short term (with maturities of one year or less) or long term (with maturities of more than one year).[1] Short-term debt is sometimes referred to as *unfunded debt*.[2]

Debt securities are typically called *notes, debentures,* or *bonds.* Strictly speaking, a bond is a secured debt. However, in common usage, the word *bond* refers to all kinds of secured and unsecured debt. We will therefore continue to use the term generically to refer to long-term debt.

The two major forms of long-term debt are public issue and private issue. We concentrate on public-issue bonds. Most of what we say about them holds true for private-issue, long-term debt as well. The main difference between public-issue and private-issue debt

---

[1] There is no universally agreed-upon distinction between short-term and long-term debt. In addition, people often refer to intermediate-term debt, which has a maturity of more than 1 year and less than 3 to 5, or even 10, years.

[2] The word *funding* is part of the jargon of finance. It generally refers to the long term. Thus, a firm planning to "fund" its debt requirements may be replacing short-term debt with long-term debt.

Information on individual bonds can be found at www.bondsonline. com.

is that the latter is directly placed with a lender and not offered to the public. Because this is a private transaction, the specific terms are up to the parties involved.

There are many other dimensions to long-term debt, including such things as security, call features, sinking funds, ratings, and protective covenants. The following table illustrates these features for a bond issued by Macy's on January 15, 2012. If some of these terms are unfamiliar, have no fear. We will discuss them all presently.

Features of a Macy's bond		
Term		**Explanation**
Amount of issue	$550 million	The company issued $550 million worth of bonds.
Date of issue	01/15/2012	The bonds were sold on 01/15/2012.
Maturity	01/15/2022	The bonds mature on 01/15/2022.
Face value	$2,000	The denomination of the bonds is $2,000.
Annual coupon	3.875	Each bondholder will receive $77.50 per bond per year (3.875% of face value).
Offer price	99.189	The offer price will be 99.189% of the $2,000 face value, or $1,983.78, per bond.
Coupon payment dates	01/15, 07/15	Coupons of $77.50/2 = $38.75 will be paid on these dates.
Security	None	The bonds are not secured by specific assets.
Sinking fund	None	The bonds have no sinking fund.
Call provision	At any time	The bonds do not have a deferred call.
Call price	Treasury rate plus 0.35%.	The bonds have a "make whole" call price.
Rating	Moody's Baa3 S&P BBB−	The bonds have moderate credit risk at the bottom of investment grade.

Many of these features will be detailed in the bond indenture, so we discuss this first.

The Indenture

indenture

The written agreement between the corporation and the lender detailing the terms of the debt issue.

The **indenture** is the written agreement between the corporation (the borrower) and its creditors. It is sometimes referred to as the *deed of trust*.[3] Usually, a trustee (a bank, perhaps) is appointed by the corporation to represent the bondholders. The trust company must (1) make sure the terms of the indenture are obeyed, (2) manage the sinking fund (described in the following pages), and (3) represent the bondholders in default, that is, if the company defaults on its payments to them.

The bond indenture is a legal document. It can run several hundred pages and generally makes for very tedious reading. It is an important document, however, because it generally includes the following provisions:

1. The basic terms of the bonds.
2. The total amount of bonds issued.
3. A description of property used as security.
4. The repayment arrangements.
5. The call provisions.
6. Details of the protective covenants.

We discuss these features next.

---

[3] The term *loan agreement* or *loan contract* is usually used for privately placed debt and term loans.

Terms of a Bond   Corporate bonds usually have a face value (that is, a denomination) of $1,000, although par values of $2,000 like the Macy's bond have become fairly common. This is called the *principal value*, and it is stated on the bond certificate. So, if a corporation wanted to borrow $1 million, 1,000 bonds would have to be sold. The par value (that is, initial accounting value) of a bond is almost always the same as the face value, and the terms are used interchangeably in practice.

Corporate bonds are usually in **registered form**. For example, the indenture might read as follows:

> Interest is payable semiannually on July 1 and January 1 of each year to the person in whose name the bond is registered at the close of business on June 15 or December 15, respectively.

registered form
The form of bond issue in which the registrar of the company records ownership of each bond; payment is made directly to the owner of record.

This means that the company has a registrar who will record the ownership of each bond and record any changes in ownership. The company will pay the interest and principal directly to the owner of record. Long ago, corporate bonds (and other types) had attached "coupons." To obtain an interest payment, the owner had to separate a coupon from the bond certificate and send it to the company registrar (the paying agent).

Alternatively, the bond could be in **bearer form**. This means that the certificate is the basic evidence of ownership, and the corporation will "pay the bearer." Ownership is not otherwise recorded, and, as with a registered bond with attached coupons, the holder of the bond certificate detaches the coupons and sends them to the company to receive payment.

bearer form
The form of bond issue in which the bond is issued without record of the owner's name; payment is made to whomever holds the bond.

There are two drawbacks to bearer bonds. First, they are difficult to recover if they are lost or stolen. Second, because the company does not know who owns its bonds, it cannot notify bondholders of important events. Bearer bonds were once the dominant type, but they are now much less common (in the United States) than registered bonds.

Security   Debt securities are classified according to the collateral and mortgages used to protect the bondholder.

Collateral is a general term that frequently means securities (for example, bonds and stocks) that are pledged as security for payment of debt. For example, collateral trust bonds often involve a pledge of common stock held by the corporation. However, the term *collateral* is commonly used to refer to any asset pledged on a debt.

Mortgage securities are secured by a mortgage on the real property of the borrower. The property involved is usually real estate, for example, land or buildings. The legal document that describes the mortgage is called a *mortgage trust indenture* or *trust deed*. A "blanket" mortgage pledges all the real property owned by the company.[4]

Bonds frequently represent unsecured obligations of the company. A **debenture** is an unsecured bond, for which no specific pledge of property is made. The term **note** is generally used for such instruments if the maturity of the unsecured bond is less than 10 or so years when the bond is originally issued. Debenture holders only have a claim on property not otherwise pledged, in other words, the property that remains after mortgages and collateral trusts are taken into account.

debenture
An unsecured debt, usually with a maturity of 10 years or more.

note
An unsecured debt, usually with a maturity of under 10 years.

The terminology that we use here and elsewhere in this chapter is standard in the United States. Outside the United States, these same terms can have different meanings.

---

[4] Real property includes land and things "affixed thereto." It does not include cash or inventories.

For example, bonds issued by the British government ("gilts") are called treasury "stock." Also, in the United Kingdom, a debenture is a *secured* obligation.

At the current time, almost all public bonds issued in the United States by industrial and financial companies are debentures. However, most utility and railroad bonds are secured by a pledge of assets.

Seniority   In general terms, *seniority* indicates preference in position over other lenders, and debts are sometimes labeled as *senior* or *junior* to indicate seniority. Some debt is *subordinated,* as in, for example, a subordinated debenture.

In the event of default, holders of subordinated debt must give preference to other specified creditors. Usually, this means that the subordinated lenders will be paid off only after the specified creditors have been compensated. However, debt cannot be subordinated to equity.

Repayment   Bonds can be repaid at maturity, at which time the bondholder will receive the stated, or face, value of the bond, or they may be repaid in part or in entirety before maturity. Early repayment in some form is more typical and is often handled through a sinking fund.

A **sinking fund** is an account managed by the bond trustee for the purpose of repaying the bonds. The company makes annual payments to the trustee, who then uses the funds to retire a portion of the debt. The trustee does this by either buying up some of the bonds in the market or calling in a fraction of the outstanding bonds. This second option is discussed in the next section.

There are many different kinds of sinking fund arrangements, and the details would be spelled out in the indenture. For example:

1. Some sinking funds start about 10 years after the initial issuance.
2. Some sinking funds establish equal payments over the life of the bond.
3. Some high-quality bond issues establish payments to the sinking fund that are not sufficient to redeem the entire issue. As a consequence, there is the possibility of a large "balloon payment" at maturity.

The Call Provision   A **call provision** allows the company to repurchase, or "call," part or all of the bond issue at stated prices over a specific period. Corporate bonds are usually callable.

Generally, the call price is above the bond's stated value (that is, the par value). The difference between the call price and the stated value is the **call premium**. The amount of the call premium usually becomes smaller over time. One arrangement is to initially set the call premium equal to the annual coupon payment and then make it decline to zero as the call date moves closer to the time of maturity.

Call provisions are not usually operative during the first part of a bond's life. This makes the call provision less of a worry for bondholders in the bond's early years. For example, a company might be prohibited from calling its bonds for the first 10 years. This is a **deferred call provision**. During this period of prohibition, the bond is said to be **call protected**.

In just the last few years, use of a new type of call provision, a "make-whole" call, has become very widespread in the corporate bond market. With such a feature, bondholders receive exactly what the bonds are worth if they are called. When bondholders don't suffer a loss in the event of a call, they are made whole.

To determine the make-whole call price, we calculate the present value of the remaining interest and principal payments at a rate specified in the indenture. For example,

The Securities Industry and Financial Markets Association (SIFMA) website is www.sifma.org.

sinking fund
An account managed by the bond trustee for early bond redemption.

call provision
An agreement giving the corporation the option to repurchase the bond at a specific price prior to maturity.

call premium
The amount by which the call price exceeds the par value of the bond.

deferred call provision
A call provision prohibiting the company from redeeming the bond prior to a certain date.

call protected bond
A bond that currently cannot be redeemed by the issuer.

looking at our Macy's issue, we see that the discount rate is "Treasury rate plus .35%." What this means is that we determine the discount rate by first finding a U.S. Treasury issue with the same maturity. We calculate the yield to maturity on the Treasury issue and then add on an additional .35 percent to get the discount rate we use.

Notice that, with a make-whole call provision, the call price is higher when interest rates are lower and vice versa (why?). Also notice that, as is common with a make-whole call, the Macy's issue does not have a deferred call feature. Why might investors not be too concerned about the absence of this feature?

Protective Covenants   A **protective covenant** is that part of the indenture or loan agreement that limits certain actions a company might otherwise wish to take during the term of the loan. Protective covenants can be classified into two types: negative covenants and positive (or affirmative) covenants.

A *negative covenant* is a "thou shalt not" type of covenant. It limits or prohibits actions that the company might take. Here are some typical examples:

1. The firm must limit the amount of dividends it pays according to some formula.
2. The firm cannot pledge any assets to other lenders.
3. The firm cannot merge with another firm.
4. The firm cannot sell or lease any major assets without approval by the lender.
5. The firm cannot issue additional long-term debt.

A *positive covenant* is a "thou shalt" type of covenant. It specifies an action that the company agrees to take or a condition the company must abide by. Here are some examples:

1. The company must maintain its working capital at or above some specified minimum level.
2. The company must periodically furnish audited financial statements to the lender.
3. The firm must maintain any collateral or security in good condition.

This is only a partial list of covenants; a particular indenture may feature many different ones.

> **protective covenant**
> A part of the indenture limiting certain actions that might be taken during the term of the loan, usually to protect the lender.

> Want detailed information on the amount and terms of the debt issued by a particular firm? Check out the firm's latest financial statements by searching SEC filings at www.sec.gov.

CONCEPT QUESTIONS

6.2a   What are the distinguishing features of debt as compared to equity?

6.2b   What is the indenture? What are protective covenants? Give some examples.

6.2c   What is a sinking fund?

BOND RATINGS

6.3

Firms frequently pay to have their debt rated. The two leading bond-rating firms are Moody's and Standard and Poor's (S&P). The debt ratings are an assessment of the credit worthiness of the corporate issuer. The definitions of creditworthiness used by Moody's and S&P are based on how likely the firm is to default and the protection creditors have in the event of a default.

It is important to recognize that bond ratings are concerned *only* with the possibility of default. Earlier, we discussed interest rate risk, which we defined as the risk of a change in the value of a bond resulting from a change in interest rates. Bond ratings do not address this issue. As a result, the price of a highly rated bond can still be quite volatile.

Bond ratings are constructed from information supplied by the corporation. The rating classes and some information concerning them are shown in the following table.

	Investment-Quality Bond Ratings				Low-Quality, Speculative, and/or "Junk" Bond Ratings					
	High Grade		Medium Grade		Low Grade		Very Low Grade			
Standard & Poor's	AAA	AA	A	BBB	BB	B	CCC	CC	C	D
Moody's	Aaa	Aa	A	Baa	Ba	B	Caa	Ca	C	

Moody's	S&P	
Aaa	AAA	Debt rated Aaa and AAA has the highest rating. Capacity to pay interest and principal is extremely strong.
Aa	AA	Debt rated Aa and AA has a very strong capacity to pay interest and repay principal. Together with the highest rating, this group constitutes the high-grade bond class.
A	A	Debt rated A has a strong capacity to pay interest and repay principal, although it is somewhat more susceptible to the adverse effects of changes in circumstances and economic conditions than debt in higher-rated categories.
Baa	BBB	Debt rated Baa and BBB is regarded as having an adequate capacity to pay interest and repay principal. Whereas it normally exhibits adequate protection parameters, adverse economic conditions or changing circumstances are more likely to lead to a weakened capacity to pay interest and repay principal for debt in this category than in higher-rated categories. These bonds are medium-grade obligations.
Ba; B Caa Ca C	BB; B CCC CC C	Debt rated in these categories is regarded, on balance, as predominantly speculative with respect to capacity to pay interest and repay principal in accordance with the terms of the obligation. BB and Ba indicate the lowest degree of speculation, and Ca, CC, and C the highest degree of speculation. Although such debt is likely to have some quality and protective characteristics, these are outweighed by large uncertainties or major risk exposures to adverse conditions. Issues rated C by Moody's are typically in default.
	D	Debt rated D is in default, and payment of interest and/or repayment of principal is in arrears.

Note: At times, both Moody's and S&P use adjustments (called notches) to these ratings. S&P uses plus and minus signs: A+ is the strongest A rating and A− the weakest. Moody's uses a 1, 2, or 3 designation, with 1 being the highest.

Want to know what criteria are commonly used to rate corporate and municipal bonds? Go to www.standardandpoors.com, www.moodys.com, or www.fitchinv.com.

The highest rating a firm's debt can have is AAA or Aaa, and such debt is judged to be the best quality and to have the lowest degree of default risk. For example, the 100-year BellSouth issue we discussed earlier was rated AAA. This rating is not awarded very often: As of 2012, only four nonfinancial U.S. companies had AAA ratings. AA or Aa ratings indicate very good quality debt and are much more common. The lowest rating is D, for debt that is in default.

Beginning in the 1980s, a growing part of corporate borrowing has taken the form of low-grade, or "junk," bonds. If these low-grade corporate bonds are rated at all, they are rated below investment grade by the major rating agencies. Investment-grade bonds are bonds rated at least BBB by S&P or Baa by Moody's.

Some bonds are called "crossover" or "5B" bonds. The reason is that they are rated triple-B (or Baa) by one rating agency and double-B (or Ba) by another, a "split rating." For example, in January 2012, brokerage firm Charles Schwab issued $400 million worth of bonds that were rated Baa2 by Moody's and BBB+ by S&P, but BB+ by Fitch (the third-largest bond-rating firm).

A bond's credit rating can change as the issuer's financial strength improves or deteriorates. For example, in 2011, S&P downgraded Tokyo Electric Power, one of the most active bond issuers in Japan, from investment grade to junk bond status. Bonds that drop into junk territory from above are called "fallen angels." Why was Tokyo Electric Power downgraded? The reason given by S&P was the long-term costs from the crisis at the Fukushima Daiichi nuclear plant, which suffered a radiation leak after the 2011 tsunami. One estimate of the future liabilities to offset payments to displaced residents and businesses was $130 billion.

Credit ratings are important because defaults really do occur, and, when they do, investors can lose heavily. For example, in 2000, AmeriServe Food Distribution, Inc., which supplied restaurants such as Burger King with everything from burgers to giveaway toys, defaulted on $200 million in junk bonds. After the default, the bonds traded at just 18 cents on the dollar, leaving investors with a loss of more than $160 million.

Even worse in AmeriServe's case, the bonds had been issued only four months earlier, thereby making AmeriServe an NCAA champion. While that might be a good thing for a college basketball team such as the University of Kentucky Wildcats, in the bond market it means "No Coupon At All," and it's not a good thing for investors.

CONCEPT QUESTIONS

6.3a   What is a junk bond?

6.3b   What does a bond rating say about the risk of fluctuations in a bond's value resulting from interest rate changes?

SOME DIFFERENT TYPES OF BONDS

6.4

Thus far, we have considered only "plain vanilla" corporate bonds. In this section, we briefly look at bonds issued by governments and also at bonds with unusual features.

Government Bonds

The biggest borrower in the world—by a wide margin—is everybody's favorite family member, Uncle Sam. In early 2012, the total debt of the U.S. government was over $15.3 *trillion,* or about $50,000 per U.S. citizen (and growing rapidly). When the government wishes to borrow money for more than one year, it sells what are known as Treasury notes and bonds to the public (in fact, it does so every month). Currently, Treasury notes and bonds have original maturities ranging from 2 to 10 years. Treasury bonds have longer maturities, extending out as far as 30 years.

Most U.S. Treasury issues are just ordinary coupon bonds. Some older issues are callable, and a very few have some unusual features. There are two important things to keep in mind, however. First, U.S. Treasury issues, unlike essentially all other bonds, have no default risk because (we hope) the Treasury can always come up with the money to make the payments. Second, Treasury issues are exempt from state income taxes (though not federal income taxes). In other words, the coupons you receive on a Treasury note or bond are only taxed at the federal level.

State and local governments also borrow money by selling notes and bonds. Such issues are called *municipal* notes and bonds, or just "munis." Unlike Treasury issues, munis have varying degrees of default risk, and, in fact, they are rated much like corporate issues. Also, they are almost always callable. The most intriguing thing about munis

If you're nervous about the level of debt piled up by the U.S. government, don't go to www.publicdebt.treas.gov or to www.brillig.com/debt_clock! Learn all about government bonds at www.ny.frb.org.

is that their coupons are exempt from federal income taxes (and state income taxes in some cases), which makes them very attractive to high-income, high-tax bracket investors.

Because of the enormous tax break they receive, the yields on municipal bonds are much lower than the yields on taxable bonds. For example, in early 2012, long-term, high-quality corporate bonds were yielding about 4.5 percent. At the same time, long-term, high-quality munis were yielding about 3.0 percent. Suppose an investor was in a 30 percent tax bracket. All else being the same, would this investor prefer an Aa corporate bond or an Aa municipal bond?

To answer, we need to compare the *aftertax* yields on the two bonds. Ignoring state and local taxes, the muni pays 3.0 percent on both a pretax and an aftertax basis. The corporate issue pays 4.5 percent before taxes, but it only pays $.045 \times (1 - .30) = .032$, or 3.2 percent, once we account for the 30 percent tax bite. Given this, the yields are quite close.

| **EXAMPLE 6.4** | **TAXABLE VERSUS MUNICIPAL BONDS** |

Suppose taxable bonds are currently yielding 8 percent, while at the same time, munis of comparable risk and maturity are yielding 6 percent. Which is more attractive to an investor in a 40 percent tax bracket? What is the break-even tax rate? How do you interpret this rate?

For an investor in a 40 percent tax bracket, a taxable bond yields $8 \times (1 - .40) = 4.8$ percent after taxes, so the muni is much more attractive. The break-even tax rate is the tax rate at which an investor would be indifferent between a taxable and a nontaxable issue. If we let t^* stand for the break-even tax rate, then we can solve for it as follows:

$$.08 \times (1 - t^*) = .06$$
$$1 - t^* = .06/.08 = .75$$
$$t^* = .25$$

Thus, an investor in a 25 percent tax bracket would make 6 percent after taxes from either bond.

Zero Coupon Bonds

zero coupon bond
A bond that makes no coupon payments and thus is initially priced at a deep discount.

A bond that pays no coupons at all must be offered at a price that is much lower than its stated value. Such bonds are called **zero coupon bonds**, or just *zeroes*.[5]

Suppose the Eight-Inch Nails (EIN) Company issues a $1,000 face value, five-year zero coupon bond. The initial price is set at $508.35. Even though no interest payments are made on the bond, zero coupon bond calculations use semiannual periods to be consistent with coupon bond calculations. Using semiannual periods, it is straightforward to verify that, at this price, the bond yields 14 percent to maturity. The total interest paid over the life of the bond is $1,000 - 508.35 = $491.65.

For tax purposes, the issuer of a zero coupon bond deducts interest every year even though no interest is actually paid. Similarly, the owner must pay taxes on interest accrued every year, even though no interest is actually received.

---

[5] A bond issued with a very low coupon rate (as opposed to a zero coupon rate) is an original-issue discount (OID) bond.

Year	Beginning Value	Ending Value	Implicit Interest Expense	Straight-line Interest Expense
1	$508.35	$ 582.01	$ 73.66	$ 98.33
2	582.01	666.34	84.33	98.33
3	666.34	762.90	96.56	98.33
4	762.90	873.44	110.54	98.33
5	873.44	1,000.00	126.56	98.33
Total			$491.65	$491.65

TABLE 6.2

Interest expense for EIN's zeroes

The way in which the yearly interest on a zero coupon bond is calculated is governed by tax law. Before 1982, corporations could calculate the interest deduction on a straight-line basis. For EIN, the annual interest deduction would have been $491.65/5 = $98.33 per year.

Under current tax law, the implicit interest is determined by amortizing the loan. We do this by first calculating the bond's value at the beginning of each year. For example, after one year, the bond will have four years until maturity, so it will be worth $1,000/1.07^8 = $582.01; the value in two years will be $1,000/1.07^6 = $666.34; and so on. The implicit interest each year is simply the change in the bond's value for the year. The values and interest expenses for the EIN bond are listed in Table 6.2.

Notice that under the old rules, zero coupon bonds were more attractive for corporations because the deductions for interest expense were larger in the early years (compare the implicit interest expense with the straight-line expense).

Under current tax law, EIN could deduct $73.66 in interest paid the first year, and the owner of the bond would pay taxes on $73.66 of taxable income (even though no interest was actually received). This second tax feature makes taxable zero coupon bonds less attractive to individuals. However, they are still a very attractive investment for tax-exempt investors with long-term dollar-denominated liabilities, such as pension funds, because the future dollar value is known with relative certainty.

Some bonds are zero coupon bonds for only part of their lives. For example, at one time, General Motors had a debenture outstanding that matured on March 15, 2036. For the first 20 years, no coupon payments were scheduled, but 20 years into the bond's life, it was to begin paying coupons at a rate of 7.75 percent per year, payable semiannually.

Another good bond market site is **money.cnn.com**.

Floating-Rate Bonds

The conventional bonds we have talked about in this chapter have fixed-dollar obligations because the coupon rate is set as a fixed percentage of the par value. Similarly, the principal is set equal to the par value. Under these circumstances, the coupon payment and principal are completely fixed.

With *floating-rate bonds (floaters)*, the coupon payments are adjustable. The adjustments are tied to an interest rate index such as the Treasury bill interest rate or the 30-year Treasury bond rate. The value of a floating-rate bond depends on exactly how the coupon payment adjustments are defined. In most cases, the coupon adjusts with a lag to some base rate. For example, suppose a coupon rate adjustment is made on June 1. The adjustment might be based on the simple average of Treasury bond yields during the previous three months.

In addition, the majority of floaters have the following features:

1. The holder has the right to redeem the note at par on the coupon payment date after some specified amount of time. This is called a *put* provision, and it is discussed in the following section.

2. The coupon rate has a floor and a ceiling, meaning that the coupon is subject to a minimum and a maximum. In this case, the coupon rate is said to be "capped," and the upper and lower rates are sometimes called the *collar*.

> Official information on U.S. inflation-indexed bonds is at www.treasurydirect. gov.

A particularly interesting type of floating-rate bond is an *inflation-linked* bond. Such bonds have coupons that are adjusted according to the rate of inflation (the principal amount may be adjusted as well). The U.S. Treasury began issuing such bonds in January of 1997. The issues are sometimes called "TIPS," or Treasury Inflation Protection Securities. Other countries, including Canada, Israel, and Britain, have issued similar securities.

Other Types of Bonds

Many bonds have unusual, or exotic, features. Unfortunately, there are far too many variations for us to cover in detail here. We therefore focus on only a few of the more common types.

Structured notes are bonds that are based on stocks, bonds, commodities, or currencies. One particular type of structured note has a return based on a stock market index. At expiration, if the stock index has declined, the bond returns the principal. However, if the stock index has increased, the bond will return a portion of the stock index return, say 80 percent. Another type of structured note will return twice the stock index return, but with the potential for loss of principal.

A *convertible bond* can be swapped for a fixed number of shares of stock anytime before maturity at the holder's option. Convertibles are relatively common, but the number has been decreasing in recent years.

A *put bond* allows the *holder* to force the issuer to buy the bond back at a stated price. The put feature is therefore just the reverse of the call provision and is a relatively new development.

A given bond may have many unusual features. For example, two recent types of exotic bonds include CoCo bonds, which have a coupon payment, and NoNo bonds, which are zero coupon bonds. CoCo and NoNo bonds are contingent convertible, puttable, callable, subordinated bonds. The contingent convertible clause is similar to the normal conversion feature, except the contingency feature must be met. For example, a contingency feature may require that the company stock trade at 110 percent of the conversion price for 20 out of 30 days. Valuing a bond of this sort can be quite complex, and the yield to maturity calculation is often meaningless. The nearby *Finance Matters* box provides some more examples of exotic bonds.

CONCEPT QUESTIONS

6.4a   Why might an income bond be attractive to a corporation with volatile cash flows? Can you think of a reason why income bonds are not more popular?

6.4b   What do you think would be the effect of a put feature on a bond's coupon? How about a convertibility feature? Why?

◀ For the latest news on the topics covered in this chapter, scan here"

FINANCE MATTERS

Exotic Bonds

Bonds come in many flavors. The unusual types are called "exotics" and can range from the fairly simple to the truly esoteric. Take the case of mortgage-backed securities (MBSs). MBSs are a type of securitized financial instrument. In securitization, cash flows from financial assets are pooled together into securities, and the securities are sold to investors. There was about $45 billion in mortgage-backed securities issued in 2011, a major decline from the record $234 billion issued in 2007, but a big increase from the $3.4 billion issued in 2009. With an MBS, banks or mortgage brokers who originate mortgages sell the mortgages to a trust. The trust pools the mortgages and sells bonds to investors. Bondholders receive payments based on the mortgage payments made by homeowners. During 2008, problems with MBSs skyrocketed due to the precipitous drop in real estate values and the sharply increased default rates on the underlying mortgages.

The reverse convertible is a relatively new type of structured note. One type generally offers a high coupon rate, but the redemption at maturity can be paid in cash at par value or paid in shares of stock. For example, one recent General Motors (GM) reverse convertible had a coupon rate of 16 percent, which is a very high coupon rate in today's interest rate environment. However, at maturity, if GM's stock declined sufficiently, bondholders would receive a fixed number of

GM shares that were worth less than par value. So, while the income portion of the bond return would be high, the potential loss in par value could easily erode the extra return.

CAT bonds are issued to cover insurance companies against natural catastrophes. The type of natural catastrophe is outlined in the bond. For example, about 30 percent of all CAT bonds protect against a North Atlantic hurricane. The way these issues are structured is that the borrowers can suspend payment temporarily (or even permanently) if they have significant hurricane-related losses. These CAT bonds may seem like pretty risky investments, but, to date, only two such bonds have not made their scheduled payments, courtesy of the massive destruction caused by Hurricane Katrina and the 2011 Japanese tsunami.

Perhaps the most unusual bond (and certainly the most ghoulish) is the "death bond." Companies such as Stone Street Financial purchase life insurance policies from individuals who are expected to die within the next 10 years. They then sell bonds that are paid off from the life insurance proceeds received when the policyholders die. The return on the bonds to investors depends on how long the policyholders live. A major risk is that if medical treatment advances quickly, it will raise the life expectancy of the policyholders, thereby decreasing the return to the bondholder.

BOND MARKETS

Bonds are bought and sold in enormous quantities every day. You may be surprised to learn that the trading volume in bonds on a typical day is many, many times larger than the trading volume in stocks (by trading volume, we simply mean the amount of money that changes hands). Here is a finance trivia question: What is the largest securities market in the world? Most people would guess the New York Stock Exchange. In fact, the largest securities market in the world in terms of trading volume is the U.S. Treasury market.

ExcelMaster
coverage online

How Bonds Are Bought and Sold

As we mentioned all the way back in Chapter 1, most trading in bonds takes place over the counter, or OTC. Recall that this means that there is no particular place where buying and selling occur. Instead, dealers around the country (and around the world) stand ready to buy and sell. The various dealers are connected electronically.

One reason the bond markets are so big is that the number of bond issues far exceeds the number of stock issues. There are two reasons for this. First, a corporation would

188   PART 4   Valuing Stocks and Bonds

typically have only one common stock issue outstanding (there are exceptions to this that we discuss in our next chapter). However, a single large corporation could easily have a dozen or more note and bond issues outstanding. Beyond this, federal, state, and local borrowing is simply enormous. For example, even a small city would usually have a wide variety of notes and bonds outstanding, representing money borrowed to pay for things like roads, sewers, and schools. When you think about how many small cities there are in the United States, you begin to get the picture!

Because the bond market is almost entirely OTC, it has historically had little or no *transparency*. A financial market is transparent if it is possible to easily observe its prices and trading volume. On the New York Stock Exchange, for example, it is possible to see the price and quantity for every single transaction. In contrast, in the bond market, it is usually not possible to observe either. Transactions are privately negotiated between parties, and there is little or no centralized reporting of transactions.

Although the total volume of trading in bonds far exceeds that in stocks, only a very small fraction of the total bond issues that exist actually trade on a given day. This fact, combined with the lack of transparency in the bond market, means that getting up-to-date prices on individual bonds is often difficult or impossible, particularly for smaller corporate or municipal issues. Instead, a variety of sources of estimated prices exist and are very commonly used.

Bond Price Reporting

To learn more about TRACE, visit www.finra.org.

In 2002, transparency in the corporate bond market began to improve dramatically. Under new regulations, corporate bond dealers are now required to report trade information through what is known as the Trade Reporting and Compliance Engine (TRACE). A nearby *Work the Web* box shows how to get TRACE prices.

As we mentioned before, the U.S. Treasury market is the largest securities market in the world. As with bond markets in general, it is an OTC market, so there is limited transparency. However, unlike the situation with bond markets in general, trading in Treasury issues, particularly recently issued ones, is very heavy. Each day, representative prices for outstanding Treasury issues are reported.

To purchase newly issued corporate bonds, go to www.internotes.com.

Figure 6.3 shows a portion of the daily Treasury note and bond listings from *The Wall Street Journal* online. The only difference between a Treasury note and a Treasury bond is that notes have 10 years or less to maturity at the time of issuance. The entry that begins "05/15/2030" is highlighted. Reading from left to right, the "05/15/2030" tells us that the bond's maturity is May 15, 2030. The 6.250 is the bond's coupon rate. Treasury bonds all make semiannual payments and have a face value of $1,000, so this bond will pay $31.25 per six months until it matures.

bid price
The price a dealer is willing to pay for a security.

The next two pieces of information are the **bid** and **asked prices**. In general, in any OTC or dealer market, the bid price represents what a dealer is willing to pay for a security, and the asked price (or just "ask" price) is what a dealer is willing to take for it. The difference between the two prices is called the **bid-ask spread** (or just "spread"), and it represents the dealer's profit.

asked price
The price a dealer is willing to take for a security.

Treasury prices are quoted as a percentage of face value. The bid price, or what a dealer is willing to pay for the bond, on the 05/15/2030 bond is 150.7188. With a $1,000 face value, this quote represents $1,507.188. The asked price, or the price at which the dealer is willing to sell the bond, is 150.7500, or $1,507.500.

bid-ask spread
The difference between the bid price and the asked price.

The next number quoted is the change in the asked price from the previous day, measured as a percentage of face value, so this issue's asked price rose by .8906 percent, or

WORK THE WEB

Bond quotes have become more available with the rise of the web. One site where you can find current bond prices (from TRACE) is cxa.marketwatch.com/finra/BondCenter. We went to the site and entered "Dell" for the well-known computer manufacturer. We found a total of 14 bond issues outstanding. Below you will see the information we pulled up.

◄ To get updated data, scan here.

Include in Watchlist	Bond Symbol	Issuer Name	Coupon	Maturity	Callable	Ratings			Last Sale	
						Moody's	S&P	Fitch	Price	Yield
☐	DELL.GJ	DELL INC	3.38	06/15/2012	Yes	A2	A-	A	100.750	1.344
☐	DELL.GF	DELL INC	4.70	04/15/2013	Yes	A2	A-	A	104.909	0.606
☐	DELL.GL	DELL INC	1.40	09/10/2013	Yes	A2	A-	A	101.161	0.672
☐	DELL.GO	DELL INC	2.10	04/01/2014	Yes	A2	A-	A	102.421	0.967
☐	DELL.GP	DELL INC	-	04/01/2014	No	A2	A-	A	99.900	-
☐	DELL.GI	DELL INC	5.63	04/15/2014	Yes	A2	A-	A	110.335	0.882
☐	DELL.GM	DELL INC	2.30	09/10/2015	Yes	A2	A-	A	103.650	1.261
☐	DELL.GQ	DELL INC	3.10	04/01/2016	Yes	A2	A-	A	107.522	1.241
☐	DELL.GG	DELL INC	5.65	04/15/2018	Yes	A2	A-	A	117.210	2.625
☐	DELL.GK	DELL INC	5.88	06/15/2019	Yes	A2	A-	A	119.774	2.878
☐	DELL.GR	DELL INC	4.63	04/01/2021	Yes	A2	A-	A	110.750	3.258
☐	DELL.GB	DELL INC	7.10	04/15/2028	Yes	A2	A-	A	125.898	4.784
☐	DELL.GH	DELL INC	6.50	04/15/2038	Yes	A2	A-	A	125.300	4.793
☐	DELL.GN	DELL INC	5.40	09/10/2040	Yes	A2	A-	A	108.702	4.834

Most of the information is self-explanatory. The price and yield columns show the price and yield to maturity of the issues based on their most recent sales. If you need more information about a particular issue, clicking on it will give you more details such as coupon dates and call dates.

Questions

1. Go to this website and find the last bond shown above. When was this bond issued? What was the size of the bond issue? What were the yield to maturity and price when the bond was issued?
2. When you search for Chevron bonds (CVX), you will find bonds for several companies listed. Why do you think Chevron has bonds issued with different corporate names?

$8.906, in value from the previous day. Finally, the last number reported is the yield to maturity, based on the asked price. Notice that this is a premium bond because it sells for more than its face value. Not surprisingly, its yield to maturity (2.713 percent) is less than its coupon rate (6.25 percent).

The Federal Reserve Bank of St. Louis maintains dozens of online files containing macroeconomic data as well as rates on U.S. Treasury issues. Go to **research.stlouisfed. org/fred2/.**

FIGURE 6.3

Sample *Wall Street Journal* U.S. Treasury note and bond prices

U.S. Treasury Quotes
TREASURY NOTES & BONDS

Treasury note and bond data are representative over-the-counter quotations as of 3 p.m. Eastern time.

Maturity	Coupon	Bid	Asked	Chg	Asked Yield
11/30/2012	3.375	102.7266	102.7969	.0000	0.062
12/15/2012	1.125	100.8672	100.9063	.0234	0.102
4/15/2014	1.250	102.2422	102.2734	.1172	0.223
8/15/2015	10.625	135.8906	135.9375	.2031	0.426
5/31/2016	1.750	104.7656	104.7969	.4375	0.629
5/15/2017	8.750	140.9375	140.9688	.5313	0.835
6/30/2017	2.500	108.1250	108.1563	.4844	0.955
10/31/2018	1.750	102.5781	102.6250	.5469	1.342
2/15/2020	8.500	153.0156	153.0625	.7969	1.485
8/15/2021	8.125	155.1094	155.1563	.6719	1.812
11/15/2021	2.000	99.9063	99.9531	.4844	2.005
8/15/2022	7.250	149.7188	149.7500	.7188	1.998
11/15/2022	7.625	153.9219	153.9531	.7031	2.035
2/15/2026	6.000	141.3906	141.4375	.8750	2.488
8/15/2027	6.375	148.2344	148.2813	.8750	2.585
8/15/2029	6.125	147.8125	147.8438	.9063	2.688
5/15/2030	6.250	150.7188	150.7500	.8906	2.713
2/15/2031	5.375	138.5781	138.6250	.8281	2.756
2/15/2036	4.500	126.2500	126.2813	.5938	2.964
2/15/2037	4.750	130.8750	130.9219	.5469	2.988
5/15/2037	5.000	135.5156	135.5625	.5469	2.987
5/15/2039	4.250	122.0781	122.1250	.4219	3.050
8/15/2039	4.500	126.8906	126.9375	.5781	3.048
11/15/2039	4.375	124.5156	124.5469	.5781	3.058
2/15/2040	4.625	129.3281	129.3594	.4219	3.058
5/15/2040	4.375	124.6094	124.6406	.6719	3.066
8/15/2040	3.875	114.7813	114.8594	.4531	3.088
11/15/2041	3.125	99.5000	99.5625	.0938	3.148

Source: www.wsj.com, 01/27/2012.

To buy Treasury bonds directly from the government, go to www.treasurydirect.gov.

Current and historical Treasury yield information is available at www.treasurydirect.gov.

The very last ordinary bond listed, in this case the 11/15/2041, is often called the "bell-wether" bond. This bond's yield is the one that is usually reported in the evening news. So, for example, when you hear that long-term interest rates rose, what is really being said is that the yield on this bond went up (and its price went down).

If you examine the yields on the various issues in Figure 6.3, you will clearly see that they vary by maturity. Why this occurs and what it might mean is one of the things we discuss in our next section.

EXAMPLE 6.5

TREASURY QUOTES

Locate the Treasury issue in Figure 6.3 maturing in August 2015. What is its coupon rate? What is its bid price? What was the *previous day's* asked price?

The bond listed as 8/15/2015 is the one we seek. Its coupon rate is 10.625 percent of face value. The bid price is 135.8906, or 135.8906 percent of face value. The ask price is 135.9375, which is up by .2031 from the previous day. This means that the ask price on the previous day was equal to 135.9375 − .2031 = 135.7344.

A Note on Bond Price Quotes If you buy a bond between coupon payment dates, the price you pay is usually more than the price you are quoted. The reason is that standard convention in the bond market is to quote prices net of "accrued interest," meaning that accrued interest is deducted to arrive at the quoted price. This quoted price is called the clean price. The price you actually pay, however, includes the accrued interest. This price is the dirty price, also known as the "full" or "invoice" price.

An example is the easiest way to understand these issues. Suppose you buy a bond with a 12 percent annual coupon, payable semiannually. You actually pay $1,080 for this bond, so $1,080 is the dirty, or invoice, price. Further, on the day you buy it, the next coupon is due in four months, so you are between coupon dates. Notice that the next coupon will be $60.

The accrued interest on a bond is calculated by taking the fraction of the coupon period that has passed, in this case two months out of six, and multiplying this fraction by the next coupon, $60. So, the accrued interest in this example is $2/6 \times \$60 = \$20$. The bond's quoted price (i.e., its clean price) would be $1,080 - 20 = $1,060.

clean price
The price of a bond net of accrued interest; this is the price that is typically quoted.

dirty price
The price of a bond including accrued interest, also known as the *full* or *invoice price*. This is the price the buyer actually pays.

CONCEPT QUESTIONS

6.5a Why do we say bond markets may have little or no transparency?

6.5b In general, what are bid and ask prices?

6.5c What is the difference between a bond's clean price and dirty price?

INFLATION AND INTEREST RATES

6.6

So far, we haven't considered the role of inflation in our various discussions of interest rates, yields, and returns. Because this is an important consideration, we consider the impact of inflation next.

Real versus Nominal Rates

In examining interest rates, or any other financial market rates such as discount rates, bond yields, rates of return, and required returns, it is often necessary to distinguish between real rates and nominal rates. Nominal rates are called "nominal" because they have not been adjusted for inflation. Real rates are rates that have been adjusted for inflation.

To see the effect of inflation, suppose prices are currently rising by 5 percent per year. In other words, the rate of inflation is 5 percent. An investment is available that will be worth $115.50 in one year. It costs $100 today. Notice that with a present value of $100 and a future value in one year of $115.50, this investment has a 15.5 percent rate of return. In calculating this 15.5 percent return, we did not consider the effect of inflation, however, so this is the nominal return.

What is the impact of inflation here? To answer, suppose pizzas cost $5 apiece at the beginning of the year. With $100, we can buy 20 pizzas. Because the inflation rate is 5 percent, pizzas will cost 5 percent more, or $5.25, at the end of the year. If we take the investment, how many pizzas can we buy at the end of the year? Measured in pizzas, what is the rate of return on this investment?

Our $115.50 from the investment will buy us $115.50/5.25 = 22 pizzas. This is up from 20 pizzas, so our pizza rate of return is 10 percent. What this illustrates is that even though the nominal return on our investment is 15.5 percent, our buying power goes up by

real rates
Interest rates or rates of return that have been adjusted for inflation.

nominal rates
Interest rates or rates of return that have not been adjusted for inflation.

only 10 percent because of inflation. Put another way, we are really only 10 percent richer. In this case, we say that the real return is 10 percent.

Alternatively, we can say that with 5 percent inflation, each of the 115.50 nominal dollars we get is worth 5 percent less in real terms, so the real dollar value of our investment in a year is:

$115.50/1.05 = $110

What we have done is to *deflate* the $115.50 by 5 percent. Because we give up $100 in current buying power to get the equivalent of $110, our real return is again 10 percent. Now that we have removed the effect of future inflation, this $110 is said to be measured in current dollars.

The difference between nominal and real rates is important and bears repeating:

> **The nominal rate on an investment is the percentage change in the number of dollars you have.**
>
> **The real rate on an investment is the percentage change in how much you can buy with your dollars, in other words, the percentage change in your buying power.**

The Fisher Effect

Fisher effect

The relationship between nominal returns, real returns, and inflation.

Our discussion of real and nominal returns illustrates a relationship often called the **Fisher effect** (after the great economist Irving Fisher). Because investors are ultimately concerned with what they can buy with their money, they require compensation for inflation. Let R stand for the nominal rate and r stand for the real rate. The Fisher effect tells us that the relationship between nominal rates, real rates, and inflation can be written as:

$$1 + R = (1 + r) \times (1 + h)$$ [6.2]

where h is the inflation rate.

In the preceding example, the nominal rate was 15.50 percent, and the inflation rate was 5 percent. What was the real rate? We can determine it by plugging in these numbers:

$$1 + .1550 = (1 + r) \times (1 + .05)$$
$$1 + r = 1.1550/1.05 = 1.10$$
$$r = 10\%$$

This real rate is the same as we had before. If we take another look at the Fisher effect, we can rearrange things a little as follows:

$$1 + R = (1 + r) \times (1 + h)$$
$$R = r + h + r \times h$$ [6.3]

What this tells us is that the nominal rate has three components. First, there is the real rate on the investment, r. Next, there is the compensation for the decrease in the value of the money originally invested because of inflation, h. The third component represents compensation for the fact that the dollars earned on the investment are also worth less because of the inflation.

This third component is usually small, so it is often dropped. The nominal rate is then approximately equal to the real rate plus the inflation rate:

$$R \approx r + h$$ [6.4]

THE FISHER EFFECT | EXAMPLE | 6.6

If investors require a 10 percent real rate of return, and the inflation rate is 8 percent, what must the approximate nominal rate be? The exact nominal rate?

First of all, the nominal rate is approximately equal to the sum of the real rate and the inflation rate: 10% + 8% = 18%. From the Fisher effect, we have:

$$1 + R = (1 + r) \times (1 + h)$$
$$= 1.10 \times 1.08$$
$$= 1.1880$$

Therefore, the nominal rate will actually be closer to 19 percent.

It is important to note that financial rates, such as interest rates, discount rates, and rates of return, are almost always quoted in nominal terms. To remind you of this, we will henceforth use the symbol R instead of r in most of our discussions about such rates.

CONCEPT QUESTIONS

6.6a What is the difference between a nominal and a real return? Which is more important to a typical investor?

6.6b What is the Fisher effect?

DETERMINANTS OF BOND YIELDS

6.7

We are now in a position to discuss the determinants of a bond's yield. As we will see, the yield on any particular bond is a reflection of a variety of factors, some common to all bonds and some specific to the issue under consideration.

ExcelMaster
coverage online

The Term Structure of Interest Rates

At any point in time, short-term and long-term interest rates will generally be different. Sometimes short-term rates are higher, sometimes lower. Figure 6.4 gives us a long-range perspective on this by showing over two centuries of short- and long-term interest rates. As shown, through time, the difference between short- and long-term rates has ranged from essentially zero to up to several percentage points, both positive and negative.

The relationship between short- and long-term interest rates is known as the **term structure of interest rates**. To be a little more precise, the term structure of interest rates tells us what *nominal* interest rates are on *default-free, pure discount* bonds of all maturities. These rates are, in essence, "pure" interest rates because they involve no risk of default and a single, lump-sum future payment. In other words, the term structure tells us the pure time value of money for different lengths of time.

When long-term rates are higher than short-term rates, we say that the term structure is upward sloping, and when short-term rates are higher, we say it is downward sloping. The term structure can also be "humped." When this occurs, it is usually because rates increase at first, but then begin to decline as we look at longer- and longer-term rates. The most common shape of the term structure, particularly in modern times, is upward sloping, but the degree of steepness has varied quite a bit.

term structure of interest rates
The relationship between nominal interest rates on default-free, pure discount securities and time to maturity; that is, the pure time value of money.

| FIGURE 6.4 | U.S. interest rates: 1800–2011 |

Source: Adapted from Jeremy J. Siegel, *Stocks for the Long Run*, 3rd ed., © McGraw-Hill, 2004, as updated by the authors.

What determines the shape of the term structure? There are three basic components. The first two are the ones we discussed in our previous section: the real rate of interest and the rate of inflation. The real rate of interest is the compensation investors demand for forgoing the use of their money. You can think of it as the pure time value of money after adjusting for the effects of inflation.

The real rate of interest is the basic component underlying every interest rate, regardless of the time to maturity. When the real rate is high, all interest rates will tend to be higher, and vice versa. Thus, the real rate doesn't really determine the shape of the term structure; instead, it mostly influences the overall level of interest rates.

In contrast, the prospect of future inflation very strongly influences the shape of the term structure. Investors thinking about loaning money for various lengths of time recognize that future inflation erodes the value of the dollars that will be returned. As a result, investors demand compensation for this loss in the form of higher nominal rates. This extra compensation is called the **inflation premium**.

inflation premium
The portion of a nominal interest rate that represents compensation for expected future inflation.

If investors believe that the rate of inflation will be higher in the future, then long-term nominal interest rates will tend to be higher than short-term rates. Thus, an upward-sloping term structure may be a reflection of anticipated increases in inflation. Similarly, a downward-sloping term structure probably reflects the belief that inflation will be falling in the future.

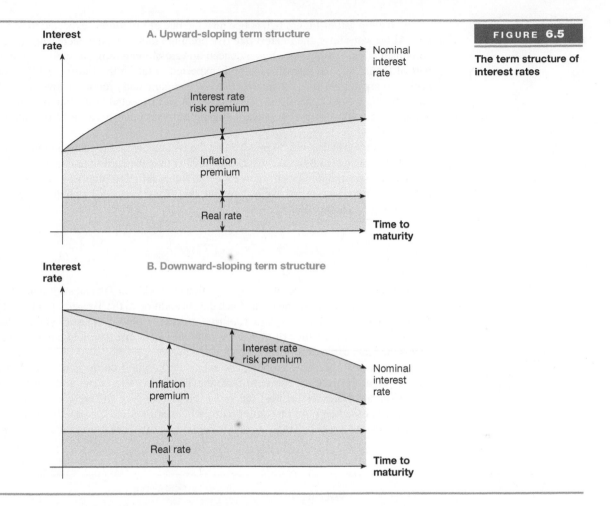

FIGURE **6.5**

**The term structure of
interest rates**

The third, and last, component of the term structure has to do with interest rate risk. As we discussed earlier in the chapter, longer-term bonds have much greater risk of loss resulting from changes in interest rates than do shorter-term bonds. Investors recognize this risk, and they demand extra compensation in the form of higher rates for bearing it. This extra compensation is called the **interest rate risk premium**. The longer the term to maturity, the greater is the interest rate risk, so the interest rate risk premium increases with maturity. However, as we discussed earlier, interest rate risk increases at a decreasing rate, so the interest rate risk premium does as well.[6]

Putting the pieces together, we see that the term structure reflects the combined effect of the real rate of interest, the inflation premium, and the interest rate risk premium. Figure 6.5 shows how these can interact to produce an upward-sloping term structure (in the top part of Figure 6.5) or a downward-sloping term structure (in the bottom part).

interest rate risk premium
The compensation investors demand for bearing interest rate risk.

---

[6] In days of old, the interest rate risk premium was called a "liquidity" premium. Today, the term *liquidity premium* has an altogether different meaning, which we explore in our next section. Also, the interest rate risk premium is sometimes called a maturity risk premium. Our terminology is consistent with the modern view of the term structure.

196   **PART 4**   Valuing Stocks and Bonds

In the top part of Figure 6.5, notice how the rate of inflation is expected to rise gradually. At the same time, the interest rate risk premium increases at a decreasing rate, so the combined effect is to produce a pronounced upward-sloping term structure. In the bottom part of Figure 6.5, the rate of inflation is expected to fall in the future, and the expected decline is enough to offset the interest rate risk premium and produce a downward-sloping term structure. Notice that if the rate of inflation was expected to decline by only a small amount, we could still get an upward-sloping term structure because of the interest rate risk premium.

We assumed in drawing Figure 6.5 that the real rate would remain the same. Actually, expected future real rates could be larger or smaller than the current real rate. Also, for simplicity, we used straight lines to show expected future inflation rates as rising or declining, but they do not necessarily have to look like this. They could, for example, rise and then fall, leading to a humped yield curve.

Bond Yields and the Yield Curve: Putting It All Together

Treasury yield curve
A plot of the yields on Treasury notes and bonds relative to maturity.

Going back to Figure 6.3, recall that we saw that the yields on Treasury notes and bonds of different maturities are not the same. Each day, in addition to the Treasury prices and yields shown in Figure 6.3, *The Wall Street Journal* provides a plot of Treasury yields relative to maturity. This plot is called the **Treasury yield curve** (or just the yield curve). Figure 6.6 shows the yield curve drawn from the yields in Figure 6.3.

As you probably now suspect, the shape of the yield curve is a reflection of the term structure of interest rates. In fact, the Treasury yield curve and the term structure of interest rates are almost the same thing. The only difference is that the term structure is based on pure discount bonds, whereas the yield curve is based on coupon bond yields. As a result, Treasury yields depend on the three components that underlie

---

FIGURE 6.6

The Treasury yield curve

Treasury Yield Curve
January 27, 2012

Online yield curve information is available at www.bloomberg.com/markets.

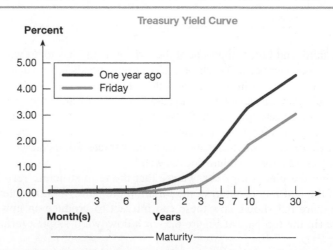

the term structure: the real rate, expected future inflation, and the interest rate risk premium.

Treasury notes and bonds have three important features that we need to remind you of: They are default-free, they are taxable, and they are highly liquid. This is not true of bonds in general, so we need to examine what additional factors come into play when we look at bonds issued by corporations or municipalities.

The first thing to consider is credit risk, that is, the possibility of default. Investors recognize that issuers other than the Treasury may or may not make all the promised payments on a bond, so they demand a higher yield as compensation for this risk. This extra compensation is called the **default risk premium**. Earlier in the chapter, we saw how bonds were rated based on their credit risk. What you will find if you start looking at bonds of different ratings is that lower-rated bonds have higher yields.

An important thing to recognize about a bond's yield is that it is calculated assuming that all the promised payments will be made. As a result, it is really a promised yield, and it may or may not be what you will earn. In particular, if the issuer defaults, your actual yield will be lower, probably much lower. This fact is particularly important when it comes to junk bonds. Thanks to a clever bit of marketing, such bonds are now commonly called high-yield bonds, which has a much nicer ring to it; but now you recognize that these are really high–*promised* yield bonds.

Next, recall that we discussed earlier how municipal bonds are free from most taxes and, as a result, have much lower yields than taxable bonds. Investors demand the extra yield on a taxable bond as compensation for the unfavorable tax treatment. This extra compensation is the **taxability premium**.

Finally, bonds have varying degrees of liquidity. As we discussed earlier, there are an enormous number of bond issues, most of which do not trade on a regular basis. As a result, if you wanted to sell quickly, you would probably not get as good a price as you could otherwise. Investors prefer liquid assets to illiquid ones, so they demand a **liquidity premium** on top of all the other premiums we have discussed. As a result, all else being the same, less liquid bonds will have higher yields than more liquid bonds.

> **default risk premium**
> The portion of a nominal interest rate or bond yield that represents compensation for the possibility of default.

> Check out the "living yield curve" at www.smartmoney.com.

> **taxability premium**
> The portion of a nominal interest rate or bond yield that represents compensation for unfavorable tax status.

> **liquidity premium**
> The portion of a nominal interest rate or bond yield that represents compensation for lack of liquidity.

Conclusion

If we combine all of the things we have discussed regarding bond yields, we find that bond yields represent the combined effect of no fewer than six things. The first is the real rate of interest. On top of the real rate are five premiums representing compensation for (1) expected future inflation, (2) interest rate risk, (3) default risk, (4) taxability, and (5) lack of liquidity. As a result, determining the appropriate yield on a bond requires careful analysis of each of these effects.

CONCEPT QUESTIONS

6.7a What is the term structure of interest rates? What determines its shape?

6.7b What is the Treasury yield curve?

6.7c What are the six components that make up a bond's yield?

198   **PART 4**   Valuing Stocks and Bonds

SUMMARY AND CONCLUSIONS

◀ Think you've mastered the material? Scan here to take a chapter quiz.

This chapter has explored bonds and bond yields. We saw that:

1. Determining bond prices and yields is an application of basic discounted cash flow principles.
2. Bond values move in the direction opposite that of interest rates, leading to potential gains or losses for bond investors.
3. Bonds have a variety of features spelled out in a document called the indenture.
4. Bonds are rated based on their default risk. Some bonds, such as Treasury bonds, have no risk of default, whereas so-called junk bonds have substantial default risk.
5. A wide variety of bonds exist, many of which contain exotic, or unusual, features.
6. Almost all bond trading is OTC, with little or no market transparency. As a result, bond price and volume information can be difficult to find.
7. Bond yields reflect the effect of six different things: the real rate and five premiums that investors demand as compensation for inflation, interest rate risk, default risk, taxability, and lack of liquidity.

In closing, we note that bonds are a vital source of financing to governments and corporations of all types. Bond prices and yields are a rich subject, and our one chapter, necessarily, touches on only the most important concepts and ideas. There is a great deal more we could say, but, instead, we will move on to stocks in our next chapter.

 connect POP QUIZ!
|FINANCE

Can you answer the following questions? If your class is using *Connect Finance,* log on to the Self-Quiz and Study feature in the Library tab to see if you know the answers to these and other questions, check out the study tools, and find out what topics require additional practice!

Section 6.1 Suppose you buy an 8.3 percent annual coupon bond for $915. The bond has 10 years to maturity. What rate of return do you expect to earn on your investment?

Section 6.2 What item found in an indenture agreement grants a firm the right to repurchase bonds prior to their maturity at a stated price?

Section 6.3 Do bond ratings consider default risk?

Section 6.4 A taxable bond yields 7.5 percent while a muni bond yields 5.48 percent. What is the break-even tax rate?

Section 6.5 A 5 percent, semiannual coupon bond has a clean price of $900. What is the dirty price if the bond paid its last coupon payment two months ago?

Section 6.6 If Treasury bills are currently paying 5.9 percent and the inflation rate is 2.5 percent, what is the approximate and the exact real rate of interest?

Section 6.7 The term structure of interest rates is based on what?

CHAPTER REVIEW AND SELF-TEST PROBLEMS

6.1 **Bond Values.** A Microgates Industries bond has a 10 percent coupon rate and a $1,000 face value. Interest is paid semiannually, and the bond has 20 years to maturity. If investors require a 12 percent yield, what is the bond's value? What is the effective annual yield on the bond? (See Problem 6.)

6.2 **Yields.** A Macrohard Corp. bond carries an 8 percent coupon, paid semiannually. The par value is $1,000, and the bond matures in six years. If the bond currently sells for $911.37, what is its yield to maturity? What is the effective annual yield? (See Problem 18.)

■ Answers to Chapter Review and Self-Test Problems

6.1 Because the bond has a 10 percent coupon yield and investors require a 12 percent return, we know that the bond must sell at a discount. Notice that, because the bond pays interest semiannually, the coupons amount to $100/2 = $50 every six months. The required yield is 12%/2 = 6% every six months. Finally, the bond matures in 20 years, so there are a total of 40 six-month periods.

The bond's value is thus equal to the present value of $50 every six months for the next 40 six-month periods, plus the present value of the $1,000 face amount:

$$\text{Bond value} = \$50 \times (1 - 1/1.06^{40})/.06 + 1,000/1.06^{40}$$
$$= \$50 \times 15.04630 + 1,000/10.2857$$
$$= \$849.54$$

Notice that we discounted the $1,000 back 40 periods at 6 percent per period, rather than 20 years at 12 percent. The reason is that the effective annual yield on the bond is $1.06^2 - 1 = 12.36\%$, not 12 percent. We thus could have used 12.36 percent per year for 20 years when we calculated the present value of the $1,000 face amount, and the answer would have been the same.

6.2 The present value of the bond's cash flows is its current price, $911.37. The coupon is $40 every six months for 12 periods. The face value is $1,000. So, the bond's yield is the unknown discount rate in the following:

$$\$911.37 = \$40 \times [1 - 1/(1 + r)^{12}]/r + 1,000/(1 + r)^{12}$$

The bond sells at a discount. Because the coupon rate is 8 percent, the yield must be something in excess of that.

If we were to solve this by trial and error, we might try 12 percent (or 6 percent per six months):

$$\text{Bond value} = \$40 \times (1 - 1/1.06^{12})/.06 + 1,000/1.06^{12}$$
$$= \$832.32$$

This is less than the actual value, so our discount rate is too high. We now know that the yield is somewhere between 8 and 12 percent. With further trial and error (or a little machine assistance), the yield works out to be 10 percent, or 5 percent every six months.

By convention, the bond's yield to maturity would be quoted as $2 \times 5\% = 10\%$. The effective yield is thus $1.05^2 - 1 = 10.25\%$.

CRITICAL THINKING AND CONCEPTS REVIEW

LO 1   6.1   **Treasury Bonds.**   Is it true that a U.S. Treasury security is risk-free?

LO 2   6.2   **Interest Rate Risk.**   Which has greater interest rate risk, a 30-year Treasury bond or a 30-year BB corporate bond?

LO 1   6.3   **Treasury Pricing.**   With regard to bid and ask prices on a Treasury bond, is it possible for the bid price to be higher? Why or why not?

LO 2   6.4   **Yield to Maturity.**   Treasury bid and ask quotes are sometimes given in terms of yields, so there would be a bid yield and an ask yield. Which do you think would be larger? Explain.

LO 1   6.5   **Call Provisions.**   A company is contemplating a long-term bond issue. It is debating whether or not to include a call provision. What are the benefits to the company from including a call provision? What are the costs? How do these answers change for a put provision?

LO 1   6.6   **Coupon Rate.**   How does a bond issuer decide on the appropriate coupon rate to set on its bonds? Explain the difference between the coupon rate and the required return on a bond.

LO 4   6.7   **Real and Nominal Returns.**   Are there any circumstances under which an investor might be more concerned about the nominal return on an investment than the real return?

LO 3   6.8   **Bond Ratings.**   Companies pay rating agencies such as Moody's and S&P to rate their bonds, and the costs can be substantial. However, companies are not required to have their bonds rated in the first place; doing so is strictly voluntary. Why do you think they do it?

LO 3   6.9   **Bond Ratings.**   Often, junk bonds are not rated. Why?

LO 3   6.10   **Crossover Bonds.**   Looking back at the crossover bonds we discussed in the chapter, why do you think split ratings such as these occur?

LO 1   6.11   **Municipal Bonds.**   Why is it that municipal bonds are not taxed at the federal level, but are taxable across state lines? Why is it that U.S. Treasury bonds are not taxable at the state level? (You may need to dust off the history books for this one.)

LO 1   6.12   **Treasury Market.**   All Treasury bonds are relatively liquid, but some are more liquid than others. Take a look back at Figure 6.3. Which issues appear to be the most liquid? The least liquid?

LO 3   6.13   **Rating Agencies.**   Several years ago, a controversy erupted regarding bond-rating agencies when some agencies began to provide unsolicited bond ratings. Why do you think this is controversial?

LO 1   6.14   **Bonds as Equity.**   The 100-year bonds we discussed in the chapter have something in common with junk bonds. Critics charge that, in both cases, the issuers are really selling equity in disguise. What are the issues here? Why would a company want to sell "equity in disguise"?

LO 2   6.15   **Bond Prices versus Yields.**

a.   What is the relationship between the price of a bond and its YTM?

b.   Explain why some bonds sell at a premium over par value while other bonds sell at a discount. What do you know about the relationship between the coupon rate and the YTM for premium bonds? What about for discount bonds? For bonds selling at par value?

c.   What is the relationship between the current yield and YTM for premium bonds? For discount bonds? For bonds selling at par value?

QUESTIONS AND PROBLEMS

Select problems are available in McGraw-Hill *Connect*. Please see the packaging options section of the preface for more information.

LO 2　**1.**　**Interpreting Bond Yields.**　Is the yield to maturity on a bond the same thing as the required return? Is YTM the same thing as the coupon rate? Suppose today a 10 percent coupon bond sells at par. Two years from now, the required return on the same bond is 8 percent. What is the coupon rate on the bond now? The YTM?

Basic
(Questions 1–14)

LO 2　**2.**　**Interpreting Bond Yields.**　Suppose you buy a 7 percent coupon, 20-year bond today when it's first issued. If interest rates suddenly rise to 15 percent, what happens to the value of your bond? Why?

LO 2　**3.**　**Bond Prices.**　Lycan, Inc., has 6 percent coupon bonds on the market that have 9 years left to maturity. The bonds make annual payments. If the YTM on these bonds is 8 percent, what is the current bond price?

LO 2　**4.**　**Bond Yields.**　The Timberlake-Jackson Wardrobe Co. has 7 percent coupon bonds on the market with nine years left to maturity. The bonds make annual payments. If the bond currently sells for $1,038.50, what is its YTM?

LO 2　**5.**　**Coupon Rates.**　Merton Enterprises has bonds on the market making annual payments, with 12 years to maturity, and selling for $963. At this price, the bonds yield 7.5 percent. What must the coupon rate be on Merton's bonds?

LO 2　**6.**　**Bond Prices.**　App Store Co. issued 20-year bonds one year ago at a coupon rate of 6.1 percent. The bonds make semiannual payments. If the YTM on these bonds is 5.3 percent, what is the current bond price?

LO 2　**7.**　**Bond Yields.**　Crossfade Co. issued 15-year bonds two years ago at a coupon rate of 6.9 percent. The bonds make semiannual payments. If these bonds currently sell for 94 percent of par value, what is the YTM?

LO 2　**8.**　**Coupon Rates.**　Volbeat Corporation has bonds on the market with 10.5 years to maturity, a YTM of 8.4 percent, and a current price of $945. The bonds make semiannual payments. What must the coupon rate be on the bonds?

LO 4　**9.**　**Calculating Real Rates of Return.**　If Treasury bills are currently paying 4.1 percent and the inflation rate is 1.6 percent, what is the approximate real rate of interest? The exact real rate?

LO 4　**10.**　**Inflation and Nominal Returns.**　Suppose the real rate is 2.8 percent and the inflation rate is 3.4 percent. What rate would you expect to see on a Treasury bill?

LO 4　**11.**　**Nominal and Real Returns.**　An investment offers a total return of 14 percent over the coming year. Bill Bernanke thinks the total real return on this investment will be only 10 percent. What does Bill believe the inflation rate will be over the next year?

LO 4　**12.**　**Nominal versus Real Returns.**　Say you own an asset that had a total return last year of 15 percent. If the inflation rate last year was 2.5 percent, what was your real return?

LO 2　**13.**　**Using Treasury Quotes.**　Locate the Treasury issue in Figure 6.3 maturing in August 2029. What is its coupon rate? What is the dollar bid price for a $1,000 par value bond? What was the *previous day's* asked price for a $1,000 par value bond?

LO 2　**14.**　**Using Treasury Quotes.**　Locate the Treasury bond in Figure 6.3 maturing in February 2037. Is this a premium or a discount bond? What is its current yield? What is its yield to maturity? What is the bid-ask spread for a $1,000 par value bond?

LO 2　**15.**　**Bond Price Movements.**　Bond X is a premium bond making annual payments. The bond has a coupon rate of 9 percent, a YTM of 7 percent, and has 13 years to maturity. Bond Y is a discount bond making annual payments. This bond has a coupon rate of 7 percent, a YTM of 9 percent, and also has 13 years to maturity. What are the prices of these bonds today? If interest rates remain

Intermediate
(Questions 15–30)

unchanged, what do you expect the prices of these bonds to be in one year? In three years? In eight years? In 12 years? In 13 years? What's going on here? Illustrate your answers by graphing bond prices versus time to maturity.

LO 2   16.   Interest Rate Risk. Both Bond Bill and Bond Ted have 7 percent coupons, make semiannual payments, and are priced at par value. Bond Bill has 3 years to maturity, whereas Bond Ted has 20 years to maturity. If interest rates suddenly rise by 2 percent, what is the percentage change in the price of Bond Bill? Of Bond Ted? If rates were to suddenly fall by 2 percent instead, what would the percentage change in the price of Bond Bill be then? Of Bond Ted? Illustrate your answers by graphing bond prices versus YTM. What does this problem tell you about the interest rate risk of longer-term bonds?

LO 2   17.   Interest Rate Risk. Bond J has a coupon rate of 4 percent. Bond S has a coupon rate of 14 percent. Both bonds have 10 years to maturity, make semiannual payments, and have a YTM of 8 percent. If interest rates suddenly rise by 2 percent, what is the percentage price change of these bonds? What if rates suddenly fall by 2 percent instead? What does this problem tell you about the interest rate risk of lower-coupon bonds?

LO 2   18.   Bond Yields. PK Software has 7.5 percent coupon bonds on the market with 22 years to maturity. The bonds make semiannual payments and currently sell for 97 percent of par. What is the current yield on PK's bonds? The YTM? The effective annual yield?

LO 2   19.   Bond Yields. BDJ Co. wants to issue new 25-year bonds for some much-needed expansion projects. The company currently has 7.8 percent coupon bonds on the market that sell for $1,125, make semiannual payments, and mature in 20 years. What coupon rate should the company set on its new bonds if it wants them to sell at par?

LO 2   20.   Accrued Interest. You purchase a bond with an invoice price of $1,043. The bond has a coupon rate of 6.8 percent, semiannual coupons, and there are five months to the next coupon date. What is the clean price of the bond?

LO 2   21.   Accrued Interest. You purchase a bond with a coupon rate of 5.9 percent, semiannual coupons, and a clean price of $957. If the next coupon payment is due in two months, what is the invoice price?

LO 2   22.   Using Bond Quotes. Suppose the following bond quote for IOU Corporation appears in the financial page of today's newspaper. Assume the bond has a face value of $1,000, and the current date is April 15, 2013. What is the yield to maturity of the bond? What is the current yield?

Company (Ticker)	Coupon	Maturity	Last Price	Last Yield	EST Vol (000s)
IOU (IOU)	9.75	Apr 15, 2027	86.352	??	1,827

LO 2   23.   Zero Coupon Bonds. Suppose your company needs to raise $30 million and you want to issue 20-year bonds for this purpose. Assume the required return on your bond issue will be 7.5 percent, and you're evaluating two issue alternatives: a

7.5 percent semiannual coupon bond and a zero coupon bond. Your company's tax rate is 35 percent.

a. How many of the coupon bonds would you need to issue to raise the $30 million? How many of the zeroes would you need to issue?

b. In 20 years, what will your company's repayment be if you issue the coupon bonds? What if you issue the zeroes?

c. Based on your answers in (a) and (b), why would you ever want to issue the zeroes? To answer, calculate the firm's aftertax cash outflows for the first year under the two different scenarios. Assume that the IRS amortization rules apply for the zero coupon bonds.

LO 2   **24.   Finding the Maturity.**   You've just found a 10 percent coupon bond on the market that sells for par value. What is the maturity on this bond (Warning: possible trick question)?

Use the following Treasury bond quotes to answer Questions 25–27. To calculate the number of years until maturity, assume that it is currently May 2013.

Rate	Maturity Mo/Yr	Bid	Asked	Chg	Ask Yld
??	May 18	103.5362	103.8235	+.3204	2.18
5.850	May 23	104.1762	104.3850	+.4513	??
6.125	May 36	??	??	+.6821	3.87

LO 2   **25.   Bond Yields.**   In the table, find the Treasury bond that matures in May 2023. What is your yield to maturity if you buy this bond?

LO 2   **26.   Bond Prices.**   In the table, find the Treasury bond that matures in May 2036. What is the asked price of this bond in dollars? If the bid-ask spread for this bond is .0628, what is the bid price in dollars?

LO 2   **27.   Coupon Rates.**   Find the Treasury bond that matures in May 2018. What is the coupon rate for this bond?

Use the following corporate bond quotes to answer Questions 28–30. To calculate the number of years until maturity, assume that it is currently January 15, 2013.

Company (Ticker)	Coupon	Maturity	Last Price	Last Yield	EST $ Vol (000's)
Xenon, Inc. (XIC)	5.400	Jan 15, 2020	94.183	??	57,362
Kenny Corp. (KCC)	7.125	Jan 15, 2017	??	6.02	48,941
Williams Co. (WICO)	??	Jan 15, 2026	94.735	6.85	43,802

LO 2   **28.   Bond Yields.**   What is the yield to maturity for the bond issued by Xenon, Inc.?

LO 2   **29.   Bond Prices.**   What price would you expect to pay for the Kenny Corp. bond? What is the bond's current yield?

LO 2   **30.   Coupon Rates.**   What is the coupon rate for the Williams Co. bond?

LO 2   **31.   Components of Bond Returns.**   Bond P is a premium bond with a coupon rate of 9 percent. Bond D is a discount bond with a 5 percent coupon rate. Both bonds make annual payments, have a YTM of 7 percent, and have five years to maturity. What is the current yield for bond P? For bond D? If interest rates

Challenge
(Questions 31–32)

www.mhhe.com/rwj

remain unchanged, what is the expected capital gains yield over the next year for bond P? For bond D? Explain your answers and the interrelationships among the various types of yields.

LO 2

32.   Holding Period Yield.   The YTM on a bond is the interest rate you earn on your investment if interest rates don't change. If you actually sell the bond before it matures, your realized return is known as the *holding period yield* (HPY).

   a.   Suppose that today you buy an annual coupon bond with a coupon rate of 7 percent for $875. The bond has 10 years to maturity. What rate of return do you expect to earn on your investment?

   b.   Two years from now, the YTM on your bond has declined by 1 percent, and you decide to sell. What price will your bond sell for? What is the HPY on your investment? Compare this yield to the YTM when you first bought the bond. Why are they different?

WHAT'S ON THE WEB?

6.1 Bond Quotes.   You can find current bond prices at cxa.marketwatch.com/finra/MarketData/Default.aspx. You want to find the bond prices and yields for bonds issued by Pfizer. Enter the ticker symbol "PFE" to do a search. What is the shortest maturity bond issued by Pfizer that is outstanding? What is the longest maturity bond? What is the credit rating for Pfizer's bonds? Do all of the bonds have the same credit rating? Why do you think this is?

6.2 Yield Curves.   You can find information regarding the most current bond yields at money.cnn.com. Go there and graph the yield curve for U.S. Treasury bonds. What is the general shape of the yield curve? What does this imply about expected future inflation? Now graph the yield curve for AAA-, AA-, and A-rated corporate bonds. Is the corporate yield curve the same shape as the Treasury yield curve? Why or why not?

6.3 Default Premiums.   The St. Louis Federal Reserve Board has files listing historical interest rates on their website www.stlouisfed.org. Find your way to the "FRED" data, then "Interest Rates." You will find listings for Moody's Seasoned Aaa Corporate Bond Yield and Moody's Seasoned Baa Corporate Bond Yield. A default premium can be calculated as the difference between the Aaa bond yield and the Baa bond yield. Calculate the default premium using these two bond indexes for the most recent 36 months. Is the default premium the same for every month? Why do you think this is?

EXCEL *MASTER IT*! PROBLEM

In an earlier worksheet, we discussed the difference between yield to maturity and yield to call. There is another yield that is commonly quoted, the yield to worst. The yield to worst is the lowest potential yield that can be received on a bond without the issuer actually defaulting. Yield to worst is calculated on all possible call dates. It is assumed that prepayment occurs if the bond has a call provision. The yield to worst will be the lowest of yield to maturity or yield to call. The yield to worst may be the same as yield to maturity but never higher. Of course, with a traditional callable bond that has a call premium, the call premium can decline over time.

A company has the following bond outstanding. The bond is callable every year on May 1, the anniversary date of the bond. The bond has a deferred call with three years left. The call premium on the first call date is one year's interest. The call premium will decline by 10 percent of the original call premium for 10 years. Eleven years from today, the call premium will be zero. Given the following information, what is the yield to worst for this bond?

Current date:	5/1/2013
Maturity date:	2/1/2032
Price (percent of par):	104.5%
Coupon rate:	10.00%
Par value (percent of par):	100%
Coupons per year:	2

Call date	Call premium
5/1/2015	$100
5/1/2016	90
5/1/2017	80
5/1/2018	70
5/1/2019	60
5/1/2020	50
5/1/2021	40
5/1/2022	30
5/1/2023	20
5/1/2024	10

CHAPTER CASE

FINANCING S&S AIR'S EXPANSION PLANS WITH A BOND ISSUE

Mark Sexton and Todd Story, the owners of S&S Air, have decided to expand their operations. They instructed their newly hired financial analyst, Chris Guthrie, to enlist an underwriter to help sell $20 million in new 10-year bonds to finance construction. Chris has entered into discussions with Renata Harper, an underwriter from the firm of Crowe & Mallard, about which bond features S&S Air should consider and what coupon rate the issue will likely have.

Although Chris is aware of the bond features, he is uncertain as to the costs and benefits of some features, so he isn't clear on how each feature would affect the coupon rate of the bond issue. You are Renata's assistant, and she has asked you to prepare a memo to Chris describing the effect of each of the following bond features on the coupon rate of the bond. She would also like you to list any advantages or disadvantages of each feature.

QUESTIONS

1. The security of the bond, that is, whether the bond has collateral.

2. The seniority of the bond.

3. The presence of a sinking fund.

4. A call provision with specified call dates and call prices.

5. A deferred call accompanying the above call provision.

6. A make-whole call provision.

7. Any positive covenants. Also, discuss several possible positive covenants S&S Air might consider.

8. Any negative covenants. Also, discuss several possible negative covenants S&S Air might consider.

9. A conversion feature (note that S&S Air is not a publicly traded company).

10. A floating rate coupon.

www.mhhe.com/rwj

Equity Markets and Stock Valuation

7

When the stock market closed on January 30, 2012, the common stock of McGraw-Hill, publisher of fine-quality college textbooks, was going for $46.31 per share. On that same day, public utility Southern Company closed at $45.07, while DIRECTV closed at $44.91. Because the stock prices of these three companies were so similar, you might expect that they would be offering similar dividends to their stockholders, but you would be wrong. In fact, the Southern Company's annual dividend was $1.89, McGraw-Hill's was $1.02, and DIRECTV was paying no dividend at all!

As we will see in this chapter, the dividends currently being paid are one of the primary factors we look at when we attempt to value common stocks. However, it is obvious from looking at DIRECTV that current dividends are not the end of the story, so this chapter explores dividends, stock values, and the connection between the two.

Going back to Chapter 1, we see that the goal of financial management is to maximize stock prices, so an understanding of what determines share values is obviously a key concern. When a corporation has publicly held stock, its shares will often be bought and sold on one or more of the major stock exchanges, so we will examine how stocks are traded. We will also see that the shareholders in a corporation have certain rights, and that just how these rights are allocated can have a significant impact on corporate control and governance.

learning objectives

After studying this chapter, you should be able to:

LO 1 Assess how stock prices depend on future dividends and dividend growth.

LO 2 Identify the different ways corporate directors are elected to office.

LO 3 Explain how the stock markets work.

PART 4   Valuing Stocks and Bonds

In our previous chapter, we introduced you to bonds and bond valuation. In this chapter, we turn to the other major source of financing for corporations, common and preferred stock. We first describe the cash flows associated with a share of stock and then go on to develop a very famous result, the dividend growth model. From there, we move on to examine various important features of common and preferred stock, focusing on shareholder rights. We close out the chapter with a discussion of how shares of stock are traded and how stock prices and other important information are reported in the financial press.

7.1 COMMON STOCK VALUATION

ExcelMaster
coverage online

A share of common stock is more difficult to value in practice than a bond, for at least three reasons. First, with common stock, not even the promised cash flows are known in advance. Second, the life of the investment is essentially forever, since common stock has no maturity. Third, there is no way to easily observe the rate of return that the market requires. Nonetheless, as we will see, there are cases in which we can come up with the present value of the future cash flows for a share of stock and thus determine its value.

Cash Flows

Imagine that you are considering buying a share of stock today. You plan to sell the stock in one year. You somehow know that the stock will be worth $70 at that time. You predict that the stock will also pay a $10 per share dividend at the end of the year. If you require a 25 percent return on your investment, what is the most you would pay for the stock? In other words, what is the present value of the $10 dividend along with the $70 ending value at 25 percent?

If you buy the stock today and sell it at the end of the year, you will have a total of $80 in cash. At 25 percent:

Present value = ($10 + 70)/1.25 = $64

Therefore, $64 is the value you would assign to the stock today.

More generally, let P_0 be the current price of the stock, and assign P_1 to be the price in one period. If D_1 is the cash dividend paid at the end of the period, then:

$$P_0 = (D_1 + P_1)/(1 + R) \qquad\qquad [7.1]$$

where R is the required return in the market on this investment.

Notice that we really haven't said much so far. If we wanted to determine the value of a share of stock today (P_0), we would first have to come up with the value in one year (P_1). This is even harder to do, so we've only made the problem more complicated.

What is the price in one period, P_1? We don't know in general. Instead, suppose we somehow knew the price in two periods, P_2. Given a predicted dividend in two periods, D_2, the stock price in one period would be:

$$P_1 = (D_2 + P_2)/(1 + R)$$

If we were to substitute this expression for P_1 into our expression for P_0, we would have:

$$P_0 = \frac{D_1 + P_1}{1 + R} = \frac{D_1 + \dfrac{D_2 + P_2}{1 + R}}{1 + R}$$

$$= \frac{D_1}{(1 + R)^1} + \frac{D_2}{(1 + R)^2} + \frac{P_2}{(1 + R)^2}$$

Now we need to get a price in two periods. We don't know this either, so we can procrastinate again and write:

$$P_2 = (D_3 + P_3)/(1 + R)$$

If we substitute this back in for P_2, we have:

$$P_0 = \frac{D_1}{(1+R)^1} + \frac{D_2}{(1+R)^2} + \frac{P_2}{(1+R)^2}$$

$$= \frac{D_1}{(1+R)^1} + \frac{D_2}{(1+R)^2} + \frac{\dfrac{D_3 + P_3}{1+R}}{(1+R)^2}$$

$$= \frac{D_1}{(1+R)^1} + \frac{D_2}{(1+R)^2} + \frac{D_3}{(1+R)^3} + \frac{P_3}{(1+R)^3}$$

You should start to notice that we can push the problem of coming up with the stock price off into the future forever. It is important to note that no matter what the stock price is, the present value is essentially zero if we push the sale of the stock far enough away. What we are eventually left with is the result that the current price of the stock can be written as the present value of the dividends beginning in one period and extending out forever:

$$P_0 = \frac{D_1}{(1+R)^1} + \frac{D_2}{(1+R)^2} + \frac{D_3}{(1+R)^3} + \frac{D_4}{(1+R)^4} + \frac{D_5}{(1+R)^5} + \cdots$$

We have illustrated here that the price of the stock today is equal to the present value of all of the future dividends. How many future dividends are there? In principle, there can be an infinite number. This means that we still can't compute a value for the stock because we would have to forecast an infinite number of dividends and then discount them all. In the next section, we consider some special cases in which we can get around this problem.

GROWTH STOCKS

EXAMPLE | 7.1

You might be wondering about shares of stock in companies such as eBay that currently pay no dividends. Small, growing companies frequently plow back everything and thus pay no dividends. Are such shares worth nothing? It depends. When we say that the value of the stock is equal to the present value of the future dividends, we don't rule out the possibility that some number of those dividends are zero. They just can't *all* be zero.

Imagine a company that has a provision in its corporate charter that prohibits the paying of dividends now or ever. The corporation never borrows any money, never pays out any money to stockholders in any form whatsoever, and never sells any assets. Such a corporation couldn't really exist because the IRS wouldn't like it, and the stockholders could always vote to amend the charter if they wanted to. If it did exist, however, what would the stock be worth?

The stock would be worth absolutely nothing. Such a company is a financial "black hole." Money goes in, but nothing valuable ever comes out. Because nobody would ever get any return on this investment, the investment has no value. This example is a little absurd, but it illustrates that when we speak of companies that don't pay dividends, what we really mean is that they are not *currently* paying dividends.

Some Special Cases

There are a few very useful special circumstances under which we can come up with a value for the stock. What we have to do is make some simplifying assumptions about the pattern of future dividends. The cases we consider are the following: (1) the dividend has a zero growth rate, (2) the dividend grows at a constant rate, and (3) the dividend grows at a nonconstant rate. Finally, we examine stock pricing using multiples.

Zero Growth The case of zero growth is one we've already seen. A share of common stock in a company with a constant dividend is much like a share of preferred stock. From Chapter 5 (Example 5.7), we know that the dividend on a share of preferred stock has zero growth and thus is constant through time. For a zero-growth share of common stock, this implies that:

$$D_1 = D_2 = D_3 = D = \textbf{constant}$$

So, the value of the stock is:

$$P_0 = \frac{D}{(1 + R)^1} + \frac{D}{(1 + R)^2} + \frac{D}{(1 + R)^3} + \frac{D}{(1 + R)^4} + \frac{D}{(1 + R)^5} + \cdots$$

Because the dividend is always the same, the stock can be viewed as an ordinary perpetuity with a cash flow equal to D every period. The per-share value is thus given by:

$$P_0 = D/R \qquad\qquad\qquad [7.2]$$

where R is the required return.

For example, suppose the Paradise Prototyping Company has a policy of paying a $10 per-share dividend every year. If this policy is to be continued indefinitely, what is the value of a share of stock if the required return is 20 percent? The stock in this case amounts to an ordinary perpetuity, so the stock is worth $10/.20 = $50 per share.

Constant Growth Suppose we know that the dividend for some company always grows at a steady rate. Call this growth rate g. If we let D_0 be the dividend just paid, then the next dividend, D_1, is:

$$D_1 = D_0 \times (1 + g)$$

The dividend in two periods is:

$$\begin{aligned} D_2 &= D_1 \times (1 + g) \\ &= [D_0 \times (1 + g)] \times (1 + g) \\ &= D_0 \times (1 + g)^2 \end{aligned}$$

We could repeat this process to come up with the dividend at any point in the future. In general, from our discussion of compound growth in Chapter 4, we know that the dividend t periods into the future, D_t, is given by:

$$D_t = D_0 \times (1 + g)^t$$

An asset with cash flows that grow at a constant rate forever is called a *growing perpetuity*. As we will see momentarily, there is a simple expression for determining the value of such an asset.

The assumption of steady dividend growth might strike you as peculiar. Why would the dividend grow at a constant rate? The reason is that, for many companies, steady growth in dividends is an explicit goal. This subject falls under the general heading of dividend policy, so we will defer further discussion of it to a later chapter.

Students who are interested in equity valuation techniques should check out the Motley Fool at www.fool.com/ School/Earnings-BasedValuations.htm.

DIVIDEND GROWTH   EXAMPLE   7.2

The Hedless Corporation has just paid a dividend of $3 per share. The dividend of this company grows at a steady rate of 8 percent per year. Based on this information, what will the dividend be in five years?

Here we have a $3 current amount that grows at 8 percent per year for five years. The future amount is thus:

$3 × 1.08⁵ = $3 × 1.4693 = $4.41

The dividend will therefore increase by $4.41 − $3 = $1.41 over the coming five years.

If the dividend grows at a steady rate, then we have replaced the problem of forecasting an infinite number of future dividends with the problem of coming up with a single growth rate, a considerable simplification. In this case, if we take D_0 to be the dividend just paid and g to be the constant growth rate, the value of a share of stock can be written as:

$$P_0 = \frac{D_1}{(1+R)^1} + \frac{D_2}{(1+R)^2} + \frac{D_3}{(1+R)^3} + \cdots$$

$$= \frac{D_0(1+g)^1}{(1+R)^1} + \frac{D_0(1+g)^2}{(1+R)^2} + \frac{D_0(1+g)^3}{(1+R)^3} + \cdots$$

As long as the growth rate, g, is less than the discount rate, R, the present value of this series of cash flows can be written very simply as:

$$P_0 = \frac{D_0 \times (1+g)}{R-g} = \frac{D_1}{R-g} \qquad [7.3]$$

This elegant result goes by a lot of different names. We will call it the **dividend growth model**. By any name, it is very easy to use. To illustrate, suppose D_0 is $2.30, R is 13 percent, and g is 5 percent. The price per share in this case is:

$$P_0 = D_0 \times (1+g)/(R-g)$$
$$= \$2.30 \times 1.05/(.13 - .05)$$
$$= \$2.415/.08$$
$$= \$30.19$$

dividend growth model
A model that determines the current price of a stock as its dividend next period divided by the discounted rate less the dividend growth rate.

We can actually use the dividend growth model to get the stock price at any point in time, not just today. In general, the price of the stock as of time t is:

$$P_t = \frac{D_t \times (1+g)}{R-g} = \frac{D_{t+1}}{R-g} \qquad [7.4]$$

In our example, suppose we are interested in the price of the stock in five years, P_5. We first need the dividend at Time 5, D_5. Because the dividend just paid is $2.30 and the growth rate is 5 percent per year, D_5 is:

$$D_5 = \$2.30 \times 1.05^5 = \$2.30 \times 1.2763 = \$2.935$$

From the dividend growth model, we get that the price of the stock in five years is:

$$P_5 = \frac{D_5 \times (1+g)}{R-g} = \frac{\$2.935 \times 1.05}{.13 - .05} = \frac{\$3.0822}{.08} = \$38.53$$

EXAMPLE	7.3

GORDON GROWTH COMPANY

The next dividend for the Gordon Growth Company will be $4 per share. Investors require a 16 percent return on companies such as Gordon. Gordon's dividend increases by 6 percent every year. Based on the dividend growth model, what is the value of Gordon's stock today? What is the value in four years?

The only tricky thing here is that the next dividend, D_1, is given as $4, so we won't multiply this by $(1 + g)$. With this in mind, the price per share is given by:

$$P_0 = D_1/(R - g)$$
$$= \$4/(.16 - .06)$$
$$= \$4/.10$$
$$= \$40$$

Because we already have the dividend in one year, we know that the dividend in four years is equal to $D_1 \times (1 + g)^3 = \$4 \times 1.06^3 = \$4.764$. The price in four years is therefore:

$$P_4 = D_4 \times (1 + g)/(R - g)$$
$$= \$4.764 \times 1.06/(.16 - .06)$$
$$= \$5.05/.10$$
$$= \$50.50$$

Notice in this example that P_4 is equal to $P_0 \times (1 + g)^4$

$$P_4 = \$50.50 = \$40 \times 1.06^4 = P_0 \times (1 + g)^4$$

To see why this is so, notice first that:

$$P_4 = D_5/(R - g)$$

However, D_5 is just equal to $D_1 \times (1 + g)^4$, so we can write P_4 as:

$$P_4 = D_1 \times (1 + g)^4/(R - g)$$
$$= [D_1/(R - g)] \times (1 + g)^4$$
$$= P_0 \times (1 + g)^4$$

This last example illustrates that the dividend growth model makes the implicit assumption that the stock price will grow at the same constant rate as the dividend. This really isn't too surprising. What it tells us is that if the cash flows on an investment grow at a constant rate through time, so does the value of that investment.

You might wonder what would happen with the dividend growth model if the growth rate, g, were greater than the discount rate, R. It looks like we would get a negative stock price because $R - g$ would be less than zero. This is not what would happen.

Instead, if the constant growth rate exceeds the discount rate, then the stock price is infinitely large. Why? If the growth rate is bigger than the discount rate, then the present value of the dividends keeps on getting bigger and bigger. Essentially, the same is true if the growth rate and the discount rate are equal. In both cases, the simplification that allows us to replace the infinite stream of dividends with the dividend growth model is "illegal," so the answers we get from the dividend growth model are nonsense unless the growth rate is less than the discount rate.

Finally, the expression we came up with for the constant growth case will work for any growing perpetuity, not just dividends on common stock. If C_1 is the next cash flow on a growing perpetuity, then the present value of the cash flows is given by:

Present value = $C_1/(R - g)$ = $C_0(1 + g)/(R - g)$

Notice that this expression looks like the result for an ordinary perpetuity except that we have $R - g$ on the bottom instead of just R.

Nonconstant Growth   The last case we consider is nonconstant growth. The main reason to consider this case is to allow for "supernormal" growth rates over some finite length of time. As we discussed earlier, the growth rate cannot exceed the required return indefinitely, but it certainly could do so for some number of years. To avoid the problem of having to forecast and discount an infinite number of dividends, we will require that the dividends start growing at a constant rate sometime in the future.

For a simple example of nonconstant growth, consider the case of a company that is currently not paying dividends. You predict that, in five years, the company will pay a dividend for the first time. The dividend will be $.50 per share. You expect that this dividend will then grow at a rate of 10 percent per year indefinitely. The required return on companies such as this one is 20 percent. What is the price of the stock today?

To see what the stock is worth today, we first find out what it will be worth once dividends are paid. We can then calculate the present value of that future price to get today's price. The first dividend will be paid in five years, and the dividend will grow steadily from then on. Using the dividend growth model, we can say that the price in four years will be:

$$P_4 = D_4 \times (1 + g)/(R - g)$$
$$= D_5 /(R - g)$$
$$= \$.50/(.20 - .10)$$
$$= \$5$$

If the stock will be worth $5 in four years, then we can get the current value by discounting this price back four years at 20 percent:

$$P_0 = \$5/1.20^4 = \$5/2.0736 = \$2.41$$

The stock is therefore worth $2.41 today.

The problem of nonconstant growth is only slightly more complicated if the dividends are not zero for the first several years. For example, suppose that you have come up with the following dividend forecasts for the next three years:

Year	Expected Dividend
1	$1.00
2	$2.00
3	$2.50

After the third year, the dividend will grow at a constant rate of 5 percent per year. The required return is 10 percent. What is the value of the stock today?

In dealing with nonconstant growth, a time line can be very helpful. Figure 7.1 illustrates one for this problem. The important thing to notice is when constant growth starts. As we've shown, for this problem, constant growth starts at Time 3. This means that we can use our constant growth model to determine the stock price at Time 3, P_3. By far the most

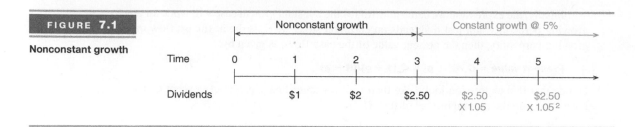

FIGURE 7.1		Nonconstant growth	Constant growth @ 5%

Nonconstant growth

Time	0	1	2	3	4	5
Dividends		$1	$2	$2.50	$2.50 X 1.05	$2.50 X 1.05²

common mistake in this situation is to incorrectly identify the start of the constant growth phase and, as a result, calculate the future stock price at the wrong time.

As always, the value of the stock is the present value of all the future dividends. To calculate this present value, we first have to compute the present value of the stock price three years down the road, just as we did before. We then have to add in the present value of the dividends that will be paid between now and then. So, the price in three years is:

$$P_3 = D_3 \times (1 + g)/(R - g)$$
$$= \$2.50 \times 1.05/(.10 - .05)$$
$$= \$52.50$$

We can now calculate the total value of the stock as the present value of the first three dividends plus the present value of the price at time 3, P_3.

$$P_0 = \frac{D_1}{(1 + R)^1} + \frac{D_2}{(1 + R)^2} + \frac{D_3}{(1 + R)^3} + \frac{P_3}{(1 + R)^3}$$
$$= \frac{\$1}{1.10} + \frac{2}{1.10^2} + \frac{2.50}{1.10^3} + \frac{52.50}{1.10^3}$$
$$= \$.91 + 1.65 + 1.88 + 39.44$$
$$= \$43.88$$

The value of the stock today is thus $43.88.

EXAMPLE 7.4

SUPERNORMAL GROWTH

Chain Reaction, Inc., has been growing at a phenomenal rate of 30 percent per year because of its rapid expansion and explosive sales. You believe that this growth rate will last for three more years and that the rate will then drop to 10 percent per year. If the growth rate then remains at 10 percent indefinitely, what is the total value of the stock? Total dividends just paid were $5 million, and the required return is 20 percent.

Chain Reaction's situation is an example of supernormal growth. It is unlikely that a 30 percent growth rate can be sustained for any extended length of time. To value the equity in this company, we first need to calculate the total dividends over the supernormal growth period:

Year	Total Dividends (in millions)
1	$5.00 × 1.3 = $ 6.500
2	6.50 × 1.3 = 8.450
3	8.45 × 1.3 = 10.985

The price at Time 3 can be calculated as:

$$P_3 = D_3 \times (1 + g)/(R - g)$$

(continued)

where g is the long-run growth rate. So we have:

$$P_3 = \$10.985 \times 1.10/(.20 - .10) = \$120.835$$

To determine the value today, we need the present value of this amount plus the present value of the total dividends:

$$
\begin{aligned}
P_0 &= \frac{D_1}{(1 + R)^1} + \frac{D_2}{(1 + R)^2} + \frac{D_3}{(1 + R)^3} + \frac{P_3}{(1 + R)^3} \\
&= \frac{\$6.50}{1.20} + \frac{8.45}{1.20^2} + \frac{10.985}{1.20^3} + \frac{120.835}{1.20^3} \\
&= \$5.42 + 5.87 + 6.36 + 69.93 \\
&= \$87.58
\end{aligned}
$$

The total value of the stock today is thus $87.58 million. If there were, for example, 20 million shares, then the stock would be worth $87.58/20 = $4.38 per share.

Components of the Required Return

Thus far, we have taken the required return, or discount rate, R, as given. We will have quite a bit to say on this subject in Chapters 10 and 11. For now, we want to examine the implications of the dividend growth model for this required return. Earlier, we calculated P_0 as:

$$P_0 = D_1/(R - g)$$

If we rearrange this to solve for R, we get:

$$R - g = D_1/P_0$$
$$R = D_1/P_0 + g \qquad \text{[7.5]}$$

This tells us that the total return, R, has two components. The first of these, D_1/P_0, is called the **dividend yield**. Because this is calculated as the expected cash dividend divided by the current price, it is conceptually similar to the current yield on a bond.

The second part of the total return is the growth rate, g. We know that the dividend growth rate is also the rate at which the stock price grows (see Example 7.3). Thus, this growth rate can be interpreted as the **capital gains yield**, that is, the rate at which the value of the investment grows.[1]

To illustrate the components of the required return, suppose we observe a stock selling for $20 per share. The next dividend will be $1 per share. You think that the dividend will grow by 10 percent per year more or less indefinitely. What return does this stock offer you if this is correct?

The dividend growth model calculates the total return as:

$$R = \text{Dividend yield} + \text{Capital gains yield}$$
$$R = D_1/P_0 + g$$

In this case, the total return works out to be:

$$
\begin{aligned}
R &= \$1/20 + 10\% \\
&= 5\% + 10\% \\
&= 15\%
\end{aligned}
$$

This stock, therefore, has a required return of 15 percent.

dividend yield
A stock's expected cash dividend divided by its current price.

capital gains yield
The dividend growth rate, or the rate at which the value of an investment grows.

---

[1] Here and elsewhere, we use the term *capital gains* a little loosely. For the record, a capital gain (or loss) is, strictly speaking, something defined by the IRS. For our purposes, it would be more accurate (but less common) to use the term *price appreciation* instead of *capital gain*.

We can verify this answer by calculating the price in one year, P_1, using 15 percent as the required return. Based on the dividend growth model, this price is:

$$P_1 = D_1 \times (1 + g)/(R - g)$$
$$= \$1 \times 1.10/(.15 - .10)$$
$$= \$1.10/.05$$
$$= \$22$$

Notice that this $22 is $20 × 1.1, so the stock price has grown by 10 percent, as it should. If you pay $20 for the stock today, you will get a $1 dividend at the end of the year, and you will have a $22 − 20 = $2 gain. Your dividend yield is thus $1/20 = 5%. Your capital gains yield is $2/20 = 10%, so your total return would be 5% + 10% = 15%.

To get a feel for actual numbers in this context, consider that, according to the 2012 Value Line *Investment Survey*, Hershey Food's dividends were expected to grow by 8 percent over the next 5 or so years, compared to an historical growth rate of 9.5 percent over the preceding 10 years. In 2012, the projected dividend for the coming year was given as $1.50. The stock price at that time was about $61 per share. What is the return investors require on Hershey? Here, the dividend yield is about 2.5 percent and the capital gains yield is 8 percent, giving a total required return of 10.5 percent on Hershey stock.

Stock Valuation Using Multiples

An obvious problem with our dividend-based approach to stock valuation is that many companies don't pay dividends. What do we do in such cases? A common approach is to make use of the PE ratio, which we defined in Chapter 3 as the ratio of a stock's price per share to its earnings per share (EPS) over the previous year. The idea here is to have some sort of benchmark or reference PE ratio, which we then multiply by earnings to come up with a price:

$$\text{Price at time } t = P_t = \text{Benchmark PE ratio} \times \text{EPS}_t \qquad [7.6]$$

The benchmark PE ratio could come from one of several possible sources. It could be based on similar companies (perhaps an industry average or median), or it could be based on a company's own historical values. For example, suppose we are trying to value Inactivision, Inc., a video game developer known for its hit *Slack Ops* series. Inactivision does not pay dividends, but after studying the industry, you feel that a PE ratio of 20 is appropriate for a company like this one. Total earnings over the four most recent quarters combined are $2 per share, so you think the stock should sell for 20 × $2 = $40. You might view it as an attractive purchase if it is going for less than $40, but not attractive if it sells for more than $40.

Security analysts spend a lot of time forecasting future earnings, particularly for the coming year. A PE ratio that is based on estimated future earnings is called a *forward* PE ratio. For example, suppose you felt that Inactivision's earnings for the coming year were going to be $2.50, reflecting the growing popularity of the company's *World of Slackcraft* massively multiplayer online role-playing game (MMORPG). In this case, if the current stock price is $40, the forward PE ratio is $40/$2.50 = 16.

Finally, notice that your benchmark PE of 20 applies to earnings over the previous year. If earnings over the coming year turn out to be $2.50, then the stock price one year from today should be 20 × $2.50 = $50. Forecast prices such as this one are often called *target* prices.

Often we will be interested in valuing newer companies that both don't pay dividends and are not yet profitable, meaning that earnings are negative. What do we do then? One

TABLE 7.1

Summary of stock valuation

I. The general case
In general, the price today of a share of stock, P_0, is the present value of all of its future dividends, $D_1, D_2, D_3, \ldots$:

$$P_0 = \frac{D_1}{(1 + R)^1} + \frac{D_2}{(1 + R)^2} + \frac{D_3}{(1 + R)^3} + \cdots$$

where R is the required return.

II. Constant growth case
If the dividend is constant and equal to D, then the price can be written as:

$$P_0 = \frac{D}{R}$$

If the dividend grows at a steady rate, g, then the price can be written as:

$$P_0 = \frac{D_1}{R - g}$$

This result is called the *dividend growth model.*

III. Nonconstant Growth
If the dividend grows steadily after t periods, then the price can be written as:

$$P_0 = \frac{D_1}{(1 + R)^1} + \frac{D_2}{(1 + R)^2} + \cdots + \frac{D_t}{(1 + R)^t} + \frac{P_t}{(1 + R)^t}$$

where

$$P_t = \frac{D_t \times (1 + g)}{(R - g)}$$

IV. Valuation Using Multiples
For stocks that don't pay dividends (or have erratic dividend growth rates), we can value them using the PE ratio and/or the price-sales ratio:

P_t = Benchmark PE ratio $\times$ EPS$_t$
P_t = Benchmark price-sales ratio $\times$ Sales per share$_t$

V. The required return, R, can be written as the sum of two things:
$R = D_1/P_0 + g$

where D_1/P_0 is the *dividend yield* and g is the *capital gains yield* (which is the same thing as the growth rate in dividends for the steady growth case).

answer is to use the price-sales ratio, which we also introduced in Chapter 3. As the name suggests, this ratio is the price per share on the stock divided by sales per share. You use this ratio just like you use the PE ratio, except you use sales per share instead of earnings per share. As with PE ratios, price-sales ratios vary depending on company age and industry. Typical values are in the .8–2.0 range, but they can be much higher for younger, faster-growing companies.

For future reference, our discussion of stock valuation techniques is summarized in Table 7.1.

CONCEPT QUESTIONS

7.1a What are the relevant cash flows for valuing a share of common stock?

7.1b Does the value of a share of stock depend on how long you expect to keep it?

7.1c What is the value of a share of stock when the dividend grows at a constant rate?

7.1d What is a "target price" on a stock? How is it determined?

7.2

SOME FEATURES OF COMMON AND PREFERRED STOCK

In discussing common stock features, we focus on shareholder rights and dividend payments. For preferred stock, we explain what "preferred" means, and we also debate whether preferred stock is really debt or equity.

Common Stock Features

common stock
Equity without priority for dividends or in bankruptcy.

The term **common stock** means different things to different people, but it is usually applied to stock that has no special preference either in paying dividends or in bankruptcy.

Shareholder Rights   The conceptual structure of the corporation assumes that shareholders elect directors who, in turn, hire management to carry out their directives. Shareholders, therefore, control the corporation through the right to elect the directors. Generally, only shareholders have this right.

Directors are elected each year at an annual meeting. Although there are exceptions (discussed in a moment), the general idea is "one share, one vote" (*not* one share*holder,* one vote). Corporate democracy is thus very different from our political democracy. With corporate democracy, the "golden rule" prevails absolutely.[2]

Directors are elected at an annual shareholders' meeting by a vote of the holders of a majority of shares who are present and entitled to vote. However, the exact mechanism for electing directors differs across companies. The most important difference is whether shares must be voted cumulatively or voted straight.

To illustrate the two different voting procedures, imagine that a corporation has two shareholders: Smith with 20 shares and Jones with 80 shares. Both want to be a director. Jones does not want Smith, however. We assume that there are a total of four directors to be elected.

cumulative voting
A procedure in which a shareholder may cast all votes for one member of the board of directors.

The effect of **cumulative voting** is to permit minority participation.[3] If cumulative voting is permitted, the total number of votes that each shareholder may cast is determined first. This is usually calculated as the number of shares (owned or controlled) multiplied by the number of directors to be elected.

With cumulative voting, the directors are elected all at once. In our example, this means that the top four vote-getters will be the new directors. Individual shareholders can distribute votes however they wish.

Will Smith get a seat on the board? If we ignore the possibility of a five-way tie, then the answer is yes. Smith will cast $20 \times 4 = 80$ votes, and Jones will cast $80 \times 4 = 320$ votes. If Smith gives all his votes to himself, he is assured of a directorship. The reason is that Jones can't divide 320 votes among four candidates in such a way as to give all of them more than 80 votes, so Smith will finish fourth at worst.

In general, if there are N directors up for election, then $1/(N + 1)$ percent of the stock plus one share will guarantee you a seat. In our current example, this is $1/(4 + 1) = 20\%$ (plus one share). So, the more seats that are up for election at one time, the easier (and cheaper) it is to win one.

straight voting
A procedure in which a shareholder may cast all votes for each member of the board of directors.

With **straight voting** the directors are elected one at a time. Each time, Smith can cast 20 votes and Jones can cast 80. As a consequence, Jones will elect all of the candidates. The only way to guarantee a seat is to own 50 percent plus one share. This also guarantees that you will win every seat, so it's really all or nothing.

---

[2] The golden rule: Whoever has the gold makes the rules.

[3] By minority participation, we mean participation by shareholders with relatively small amounts of stock.

BUYING THE ELECTION | EXAMPLE | 7.5

Stock in JRJ Corporation sells for $20 per share and features cumulative voting. There are 10,000 shares outstanding. If three directors are up for election, how much does it cost to ensure yourself a seat on the board?

The question here is how many shares of stock it will take to get a seat. The answer is 2,501, so the cost is 2,501 × $20 = $50,020. Why 2,501? Because there is no way the remaining 7,499 votes can be divided among three people to give all of them more than 2,501 votes. For example, suppose two people receive 2,502 votes and the first two seats. A third person can receive at most 10,000 − 2,502 − 2,502 − 2,501 = 2,495, so the third seat is yours. Verify that we arrived at 2,501 using the formula described earlier.

As we've illustrated, straight voting can "freeze out" minority shareholders; that is the reason many states have mandatory cumulative voting. In states where cumulative voting is mandatory, devices have been worked out to minimize its impact.

Many companies have staggered elections for directors. With staggered elections, only a fraction of the directorships are up for election at a particular time. Thus, if only two directors are up for election at any one time, it will take $1/(2 + 1) = 33.33\%$ of the stock plus one share to guarantee a seat. Staggered boards are often called "classified" boards because directors are placed into different classes with terms that expire at different times. In recent years, corporations have come under pressure to "declassify" their boards, meaning that all directors would stand for election every year, and many have done so.

Overall, staggering has two basic effects:

1. Staggering makes it more difficult for a minority to elect a director when there is cumulative voting because there are fewer directors to be elected at one time.

2. Staggering makes takeover attempts less likely to be successful because it makes it more difficult to vote in a majority of new directors.

We should note that staggering may serve a beneficial purpose. It provides "institutional memory," that is, continuity on the board of directors. This may be important for corporations with significant long-range plans and projects.

Proxy Voting   A proxy is the grant of authority by a shareholder to someone else to vote the shareholder's shares. For convenience, much of the voting in large public corporations is actually done by proxy.

As we have seen, with straight voting, each share of stock has one vote. The owner of 10,000 shares has 10,000 votes. Large companies have hundreds of thousands or even millions of shareholders. Shareholders can come to the annual meeting and vote in person, or they can transfer their right to vote to another party.

Obviously, management always tries to get as many proxies as possible transferred to it. However, if shareholders are not satisfied with management, an "outside" group of shareholders can try to obtain votes via proxy. They can vote by proxy in an attempt to replace management by electing enough directors. The resulting battle is called a *proxy fight*.

proxy
A grant of authority by a shareholder allowing another individual to vote that shareholder's shares.

Classes of Stock   Some firms have more than one class of common stock. Often, the classes are created with unequal voting rights. The Ford Motor Company, for example, has Class B common stock, which is not publicly traded (it is held by Ford family interests and trusts). This class has about 40 percent of the voting power, even though it represents less than 10 percent of the total number of shares outstanding.

There are many other cases of corporations with different classes of stock. For example, Google, the Web search company, has two classes of common stock, A and B. The Class A shares are held by the public, and each share has one vote. The Class B shares are held by company insiders, and each Class B share has 10 votes. As a result, Google's founders and managers control the company. The CEO of cable TV giant Comcast, Brian Roberts, owns about .4 percent of the company's equity, but he has a third of all the votes thanks to the creation of a special class of stock.

In principle, the New York Stock Exchange does not allow companies to create classes of publicly traded common stock with unequal voting rights. Exceptions (e.g., Ford) appear to have been made. In addition, many non-NYSE companies have dual classes of common stock.

A primary reason for creating dual or multiple classes of stock has to do with control of the firm. If such stock exists, management of a firm can raise equity capital by issuing nonvoting or limited-voting stock while maintaining control.

The subject of unequal voting rights is controversial in the United States, and the idea of one share, one vote has a strong following and a long history. Interestingly, however, shares with unequal voting rights are quite common in the United Kingdom and elsewhere around the world.

Other Rights   The value of a share of common stock in a corporation is directly related to the general rights of shareholders. In addition to the right to vote for directors, shareholders usually have the following rights:

1. The right to share proportionally in dividends paid.
2. The right to share proportionally in assets remaining after liabilities have been paid in a liquidation.
3. The right to vote on stockholder matters of great importance, such as a merger. Voting is usually done at the annual meeting or a special meeting.

In addition, shareholders sometimes have the right to share proportionally in any new stock sold. This is called the *preemptive right*.

Essentially, a preemptive right means that a company that wishes to sell stock must first offer it to the existing stockholders before offering it to the general public. The purpose is to give stockholders the opportunity to protect their proportionate ownership in the corporation.

dividends

Payments by a corporation to shareholders, made in either cash or stock.

Dividends   A distinctive feature of corporations is that they have shares of stock on which they are authorized by law to pay dividends to their shareholders. **Dividends** paid to shareholders represent a return on the capital directly or indirectly contributed to the corporation by the shareholders. The payment of dividends is at the discretion of the board of directors.

Some important characteristics of dividends include the following:

1. Unless a dividend is declared by the board of directors of a corporation, it is not a liability of the corporation. A corporation cannot default on an undeclared dividend. As a consequence, corporations cannot become bankrupt because of nonpayment of dividends. The amount of the dividend and even whether it is paid are decisions based on the business judgment of the board of directors.
2. The payment of dividends by the corporation is not a business expense. Dividends are not deductible for corporate tax purposes. In short, dividends are paid out of the corporation's aftertax profits.
3. Dividends received by individual shareholders are taxable. However, corporations that own stock in other corporations are permitted to exclude 70 percent of the dividend amounts they receive and are taxed only on the remaining 30 percent.[4]

---

[4] For the record, the 70 percent exclusion applies when the recipient owns less than 20 percent of the outstanding stock in a corporation. If a corporation owns more than 20 percent but less than 80 percent, the exclusion is 80 percent. If more than 80 percent is owned, the corporation can file a single "consolidated" return, and the exclusion is effectively 100 percent.

Preferred Stock Features

Preferred stock differs from common stock because it has preference over common stock in the payment of dividends and in the distribution of corporation assets in the event of liquidation. *Preference* means only that the holders of the preferred shares must receive a dividend (in the case of an ongoing firm) before holders of common shares are entitled to anything.

Preferred stock is a form of equity from a legal and tax standpoint. It is important to note, however, that holders of preferred stock sometimes have no voting privileges.

> **preferred stock**
> Stock with dividend priority over common stock, normally with a fixed dividend rate, sometimes without voting rights.

Stated Value Preferred shares have a stated liquidating value, usually $100 per share. The cash dividend is described in terms of dollars per share. For example, General Motors "$5 preferred" easily translates into a dividend yield of 5 percent of stated value.

Cumulative and Noncumulative Dividends A preferred dividend is *not* like interest on a bond. The board of directors may decide not to pay the dividends on preferred shares, and their decision may have nothing to do with the current net income of the corporation.

Dividends payable on preferred stock are either *cumulative* or *noncumulative*; most are cumulative. If preferred dividends are cumulative and are not paid in a particular year, they will be carried forward as an *arrearage*. Usually, both the accumulated (past) preferred dividends and the current preferred dividends must be paid before the common shareholders can receive anything.

Unpaid preferred dividends are *not* debts of the firm. Directors elected by the common shareholders can defer preferred dividends indefinitely. However, in such cases, common shareholders must also forgo dividends. In addition, holders of preferred shares are often granted voting and other rights if preferred dividends have not been paid for some time. For example, at one point, US Airways had failed to pay dividends on one of its preferred stock issues for six quarters. As a consequence, the holders of the shares were allowed to nominate two people to represent their interests on the airline's board. Because preferred stockholders receive no interest on the accumulated dividends, some have argued that firms have an incentive to delay paying preferred dividends, but, as we have seen, this may mean sharing control with preferred stockholders.

Is Preferred Stock Really Debt? A good case can be made that preferred stock is really debt in disguise, a kind of equity bond. Preferred shareholders are only entitled to receive a stated dividend, and, if the corporation is liquidated, preferred shareholders are only entitled to the stated value of their preferred shares. Often, preferred stocks carry credit ratings much like those of bonds. Furthermore, preferred stock is sometimes convertible into common stock, and preferred stocks are often callable.

In addition, in recent years, many new issues of preferred stock have had obligatory sinking funds. The existence of such a sinking fund effectively creates a final maturity because it means that the entire issue will ultimately be retired. For these reasons, preferred stock seems to be a lot like debt. However, for tax purposes, preferred dividends are treated like common stock dividends.

CONCEPT QUESTIONS

7.2a What is a proxy?

7.2b What rights do stockholders have?

7.2c Why is preferred stock called preferred?

ExcelMaster
coverage online

7.3

THE STOCK MARKETS

Back in Chapter 1, we very briefly mentioned that shares of stock are bought and sold on various stock exchanges, the two most important of which are the New York Stock Exchange and the NASDAQ. From our earlier discussion, recall that the stock market consists of a **primary market** and a **secondary market**. In the primary, or new-issue, market, shares of stock are first brought to the market and sold to investors. In the secondary market, existing shares are traded among investors.

In the primary market, companies sell securities to raise money. We will discuss this process in detail in a later chapter. We therefore focus mainly on secondary-market activity in this section. We conclude with a discussion of how stock prices are quoted in the financial press.

Dealers and Brokers

Because most securities transactions involve dealers and brokers, it is important to understand exactly what is meant by the terms *dealer* and *broker*. A **dealer** maintains an inventory and stands ready to buy and sell at any time. In contrast, a **broker** brings buyers and sellers together, but does not maintain an inventory. Thus, when we speak of used car dealers and real estate brokers, we recognize that the used car dealer maintains an inventory, whereas the real estate broker does not.

In the securities markets, a dealer stands ready to buy securities from investors wishing to sell them and sell securities to investors wishing to buy them. Recall from our previous chapter that the price the dealer is willing to pay is called the bid price. The price at which the dealer will sell is called the ask price (sometimes called the asked, offered, or offering price). The difference between the bid and ask prices is called the spread, and it is the basic source of dealer profits.

Dealers exist in all areas of the economy, not just the stock markets. For example, your local college bookstore is probably both a primary- and a secondary-market textbook dealer. If you buy a new book, this is a primary-market transaction. If you buy a used book, this is a secondary-market transaction, and you pay the store's ask price. If you sell the book back, you receive the store's bid price, often half of the ask price. The bookstore's spread is the difference between the two prices.

In contrast, a securities broker arranges transactions between investors, matching investors wishing to buy securities with investors wishing to sell securities. The distinctive characteristic of security brokers is that they do not buy or sell securities for their own accounts. Facilitating trades by others is their business.

Organization of the NYSE

The New York Stock Exchange, or NYSE, popularly known as the Big Board, recently celebrated its bicentennial. It has occupied its current location on Wall Street since the turn of the twentieth century. Measured in terms of dollar volume of activity and the total value of shares listed, it is the largest stock market in the world.

Members   Historically, the NYSE had 1,366 exchange **members**. Prior to 2006, the exchange members were said to own "seats" on the exchange, and, collectively, the members of the exchange were also the owners. For this and other reasons, seats were valuable and were bought and sold fairly regularly. Seat prices reached a record $4 million in 2005.

primary market
The market in which new securities are originally sold to investors.

secondary market
The market in which previously issued securities are traded among investors.

dealer
An agent who buys and sells securities from inventory.

broker
An agent who arranges security transactions among investors.

member
As of 2006, a member is the owner of a trading license on the NYSE.

In 2006, all of this changed when the NYSE became a publicly owned corporation called NYSE Group, Inc. Naturally, its stock is listed on the NYSE. Now, instead of purchasing seats, exchange members must purchase trading licenses, the number of which is limited to 1,366. In 2012, a license would set you back a cool $40,000—per year. Having a license entitles you to buy and sell securities on the floor of the exchange. Different members play different roles in this regard.

In April 2007, the NYSE completed a merger with Euronext to form the NYSE Euronext. The Euronext exchange was formed in 2000 and included markets in Belgium, France, Ireland, the Netherlands, Luxembourg, Portugal, and the United Kingdom. With the merger completed, the NYSE Euronext became the world's first global exchange, with trading occurring over 21 hours each business day. Further expansion occurred in 2008 when NYSE Euronext merged with the American Stock Exchange.

NYSE Euronext operates a number of markets (including four stock markets in the United States alone), but the NYSE is the biggest and best-known, so we will focus on it here. As we briefly describe how the NYSE operates, keep in mind that other markets owned by NYSE Euronext may function differently. What makes the NYSE somewhat unique is that it is a *hybrid market*. In a hybrid market, trading takes place both electronically and face-to-face.

With electronic trading, orders to buy and orders to sell are submitted to the exchange. Orders are compared by a computer and whenever there is a match, the orders are executed with no human intervention. Most trades on the NYSE occur this way. For orders that are not handled electronically, the NYSE relies on its license holders. There are three different types of license holders, **designated market makers (DMMs)**, **floor brokers**, and **supplemental liquidity providers (SLPs)**, and we now discuss the role played by each.

The DMMs, formerly known as "specialists," act as dealers in particular stocks. Typically, each stock on the NYSE is assigned to a single DMM. As a dealer, a DMM maintains a two-sided market, meaning that the DMM continually posts and updates bid and ask prices. By doing so, the DMM ensures that there is always a buyer or seller available, thereby promoting market liquidity.

The job of a floor broker is to execute trades for customers, with an emphasis on getting the best price possible. Floor brokers are generally employees of large brokerage firms such as Merrill Lynch, the wealth management division of Bank of America. The interaction between floor brokers and DMMs is the key to nonelectronic trading on the NYSE. We discuss this interaction in detail in just a moment.

The SLPs are essentially investment firms that agree to be active participants in stocks assigned to them. Their job is to regularly make a one-sided market (i.e., offering to either buy or sell). They trade purely for their own accounts (using their own money), so they do not represent customers. They are given a small rebate on their buys and sells, thereby encouraging them to be more aggressive. The NYSE's goal is to generate as much liquidity as possible, which makes it easier for ordinary investors to quickly buy and sell at prevailing prices. Unlike DMMs and floor brokers, SLPs do not operate on the floor of the stock exchange.

Operations   Now that we have a basic idea of how the NYSE is organized and who the major players are, we turn to the question of how trading actually takes place. Fundamentally, the business of the NYSE is to attract and process **order flow**. The term *order flow* means the flow of customer orders to buy and sell stocks. The customers of the NYSE are the millions of individual investors and tens of thousands of institutional investors who place their orders to buy and sell shares in NYSE-listed companies. The NYSE has been quite successful in attracting order flow. Currently, it is common for more than one billion shares to change hands in a single day.

---

designated market maker (DMM)
NYSE members who act as dealers in particular stocks. Formerly known as "specialists."

floor brokers
NYSE members who execute customer buy and sell orders.

supplemental liquidity providers (SLPs)
Investment firms that are active participants in stocks assigned to them. Their job is to make a one-sided market (i.e., offering to either buy or sell). They trade purely for their own accounts

order flow
The flow of customer orders to buy and sell securities.

224   **PART 4**   Valuing Stocks and Bonds

Floor Activity   It is quite likely that you have seen footage of the NYSE trading floor on television, or you may have visited the NYSE and viewed exchange floor activity from the visitors' gallery (it's worth the trip). Either way, you would have seen a big room, about the size of a basketball gym. This big room is called, technically, "the Big Room." There are a couple of other, smaller rooms that you normally don't see, one of which is called "the Garage" because that is literally what it was before it was taken over for trading.

On the floor of the exchange are a number of stations. These stations have multiple counters with numerous terminal screens above and on the sides. People operate behind and in front of the counters in relatively stationary positions.

Other people move around on the exchange floor. In all, you may be reminded of worker ants moving around an ant colony. It is natural to wonder: What are all those people doing down there (and why are so many wearing funny-looking coats)?

DMM's post
A fixed place on the exchange floor where the DMM operates.

As an overview of exchange floor activity, here is a quick look at what goes on. Each of the counters is a **DMM's post**. DMMs normally operate in front of their posts to monitor and manage trading in the stocks assigned to them. Clerical employees working for the DMMs operate behind the counter. Moving from the many workstations lining the walls of the exchange out to the exchange floor and back again are swarms of floor brokers, receiving customer orders, walking out to DMMs' posts where the orders can be executed, and returning to confirm order executions and receive new customer orders.

To better understand activity on the NYSE trading floor, imagine yourself as a floor broker. Your clerk has just handed you an order to sell 2,000 shares of Walmart for a customer of the brokerage company that employs you. The customer wants to sell the stock at the best possible price as soon as possible. You immediately walk (running violates exchange rules) to the DMM's post where Walmart stock is traded.

Take a virtual field trip to the New York Stock Exchange at www.nyse.com.

As you approach the DMM's post where Walmart is traded, you check the terminal screen for information on the current market price. The screen reveals that the last executed trade was at $25.63, and that the DMM is bidding $25.50 per share. You could immediately sell to the DMM at $25.50, but that would be too easy.

Instead, as the customer's representative, you are obligated to get the best possible price. It is your job to "work" the order, and your job depends on providing satisfactory order execution service. So, you look around for another broker who represents a customer who wants to buy Walmart stock. Luckily, you quickly find another broker at the DMM's post with an order to buy 2,000 shares. Noticing that the dealer is asking $25.76 per share, you both agree to execute your orders with each other at a price of $25.63. This price is halfway between the DMM's bid and ask prices, and it saves each of your customers $.13 × 2,000 = $260 as compared to dealing at the posted prices.

For a very actively traded stock, there may be many buyers and sellers around the DMM's post, and most of the trading will be done directly between brokers. This is called trading in the "crowd." In such cases, the DMM's responsibility is to maintain order and to make sure that all buyers and sellers receive a fair price. In other words, the DMM essentially functions as a referee.

More often, however, there will be no crowd at the DMM's post. Going back to our Walmart example, suppose you are unable to quickly find another broker with an order to buy 2,000 shares. Because you have an order to sell immediately, you may have no choice but to sell to the DMM at the bid price of $25.50. In this case, the need to execute an order quickly takes priority, and the DMM provides the liquidity necessary to allow immediate order execution.

Finally, note that colored coats are worn by many of the people on the floor of the exchange. The color of the coat indicates the person's job or position. Clerks, runners, visitors, exchange officials, and so on wear particular colors to identify themselves. Also, things can get a little hectic on a busy day, with the result that good clothing doesn't last long; the cheap coats offer some protection.

NASDAQ Operations

In terms of the number of companies listed and, on many days, the number of shares traded, the NASDAQ is even bigger than the NYSE. As we mentioned in Chapter 1, the somewhat odd name is derived from the acronym *NASDAQ,* which stood for National Association of Securities Dealers Automated Quotations system; but NASDAQ is now a name in its own right.

Introduced in 1971, the NASDAQ market is a computer network of securities dealers who disseminate timely security price quotes to NASDAQ subscribers. These dealers act as market makers for securities listed on the NASDAQ. As market makers, NASDAQ dealers post bid and asked prices at which they accept sell and buy orders, respectively. With each price quote, they also post the number of stock shares that they obligate themselves to trade at their quoted prices.

Not to be outdone by the NYSE, the NASDAQ completed a merger in May 2007 when it finalized its deal to buy the OMX, which controlled seven Nordic and Baltic stock exchanges. Since the merger, the NASDAQ is officially the NASDAQ OMX Group, although it is still often referred to as simply NASDAQ.

Unlike the NYSE DMM system, NASDAQ relies on multiple market makers for actively traded stocks. Thus, there are two key differences between the NYSE and NASDAQ: (1) NASDAQ is a computer network and has no physical location where trading takes place and (2) NASDAQ has a multiple market maker system rather than a DMM system. Notice that there is no direct trading in the crowd as there may be on the NYSE.

About 2,800 companies are listed on the NASDAQ system, with an average of about a dozen market makers for each security. Traditionally, shares of stock in smaller companies were listed on the NASDAQ, and there was a tendency for companies to move from the NASDAQ to the NYSE once they became large enough. Today, however, giant companies such as Amazon, Microsoft, and Intel have chosen to remain on the NASDAQ.

The NASDAQ network operates with three levels of information access. Level 1 is designed to provide a timely, accurate source of price quotations. These prices are freely available over the Internet.

Level 2 allows users to view price quotes from all NASDAQ market makers. In particular, this level allows access to **inside quotes**. Inside quotes are the highest bid quotes and the lowest asked quotes for a NASDAQ-listed security. Level 2 is now available on the Web, sometimes for a small fee. Level 3 is for the use of market makers only. This access level allows NASDAQ dealers to enter or change their price quote information.

The NASDAQ is actually made up of three separate markets: the NASDAQ Global Select Market, the NASDAQ Global Market, and the NASDAQ Capital Market. As the market for NASDAQ's larger and more actively traded securities, the Global Select Market lists about 1,600 companies (as of early 2012), including some of the best-known companies in the world, such as Microsoft and Intel. The Global Market companies are somewhat smaller in size, and NASDAQ lists about 800 of these companies. Finally, the smallest companies listed on NASDAQ are in the NASDAQ Capital Market; about 400 are currently listed. Of course, as Capital Market companies become more established, they may move up to the Global Market or Global Select Market.

ECNs   In a very important development in the late 1990s, the NASDAQ system was opened to so-called **electronic communications networks (ECNs)**. ECNs are basically

How big is the bid-ask spread on your favorite NASDAQ stock? Check out the latest quotes at money.cnn.com!

NASDAQ (www.nasdaq.com) has a *great* website; check it out!

inside quotes
The highest bid quotes and the lowest ask quotes for a security.

electronic communications networks (ECNs)
Websites that allow investors to trade directly with one another.

websites that allow investors to trade directly with one another. Investor buy and sell orders placed on ECNs are transmitted to the NASDAQ and displayed along with market maker bid and ask prices. Thus, the ECNs open up the NASDAQ by essentially allowing individual investors, not just market makers, to enter orders. As a result, the ECNs act to increase liquidity and competition. Our nearby *Work the Web* box describes one ECN, BATS Trading (www.batstrading.com), and contains important information about ECN "order books." Be sure to read it.

Of course, the NYSE and NASDAQ are not the only places stocks are traded. See our nearby *Finance Matters* box for a discussion of somewhat wilder markets.

Stock Market Reporting

Like so many other things, stock price reporting has largely migrated to the web. You can get up-to-the-minute prices on stocks from many online servers, along with plenty of information about a stock. Below you will see a stock quote from finance.yahoo.com for famed motorcycle manufacturer Harley-Davidson (HOG) from January 30, 2012.

Harley-Davidson, Inc. Common St (HOG) - NYSE   + Add to Portfolio   Like 84

44.09 ↓0.25(0.56%) 1:47PM EST - Nasdaq Real Time Price

Prev Close:	44.34	Day's Range:	43.45 - 44.37
Open:	43.89	52wk Range:	31.50 - 46.88
Bid:	44.01 x 1200	Volume:	908,587
Ask:	44.02 x 400	Avg Vol (3m):	1,950,070
1y Target Est:	46.31	Market Cap:	10.11B
Beta:	2.4	P/E (ttm):	17.26
Next Earnings Date:	N/A	EPS (ttm):	2.55
		Div & Yield:	0.50 (1.10%)

In the upper left, we have a recent trade price of $44.09. Based on that price, the stock had fallen by $.25 during the day, or .56 percent. In the box below, more information is provided. For example, the "Prev Close" is the closing price from the previous trading day, and "Open" is the first price of the current day. The high price for this day so far, shown in "Day's Range," was $44.37, and the low price was $43.45. About 909,000 shares of Harley-Davidson had traded, relative to an average volume over the last three months of 1.96 million shares. As always, the bid and ask are the highest price someone was willing to pay and the lowest price someone was willing to take. For example, 44.01 × 1200 tells you that someone was willing to pay $44.01 for 1,200 shares. The "×" is read as "by." You can also see the number of shares at the ask price. The 52-week range gives the highest and lowest stock prices over the past 52 weeks.

And there is even more information in the quote. "Beta" is an important number. We will have lots more to say about it in a later chapter. Because Harley-Davidson, like most dividend-paying companies, actually pays dividends quarterly, the dividend shown of $.50 is the last quarterly dividend multiplied by four. The dividend yield is the annual dividend divided by the stock price. Harley-Davidson's EPS for the past year was $2.55. The PE ratio shown is calculated using the current stock price divided by the last 12 months' earnings. The "1y Target Est" is the projected price next year based on analysts' estimates. Finally, we are shown the "Market Cap" (market capitalization, or total value of Harley-Davidson's stock).

WORK THE WEB

You can actually watch trading taking place on the web by visiting www.batstrading.com. The BATS Exchange is somewhat unique in that the "order book," meaning the list of all buy and sell orders, is public in real time. As shown, we have captured a sample of the order book for Intel (INTC). On the top in blue are sell orders (asks); buy orders (bids) are in green on the bottom. All orders are "limit" orders, which means the customer has specified the most he or she will pay (for buy orders) or the least he or she will accept (for sell orders). The inside quotes (the highest bid, or buy, and the lowest ask, or sell) in the market are shown in bold face.

◀ To get updated data, scan here.

Book Viewer   BZX   BYX

BATS   INTC   Go

INTEL CORP COM

Orders Accepted   Total Volume
150,457   3,591,697

| TOP OF BOOK | | LAST 10 TRADES | | |
SHARES	PRICE	TIME	PRICE	SHARES
11,410	26.7100	13:32:45	26.6650	100
10,360	26.7000	13:32:41	26.6650	100
9,884	26.6900	13:32:41	26.6650	100
13,277	26.6800	13:31:57	26.6650	100
5,828	**26.6700**	13:31:43	26.6600	200
10,594	**26.6600**	13:31:43	26.6600	600
13,807	26.6500	13:31:42	26.6700	100
19,360	26.6400	13:31:42	26.6700	1
10,513	26.6300	13:31:42	26.6700	3
13,210	26.6200	13:31:42	26.6700	96

(ASKS — top five rows; BIDS — bottom five rows)

If you visit the site, you can see trading take place as orders are entered and executed. Notice that on this particular day, about 3.6 million shares of Intel had traded on BATS. At that time, the inside quotes for Intel were 10,594 shares bid at $26.66 and 5,828 shares offered at $26.67. This is not the entire order book for Intel as there are more buy orders below $26.62 and more sell orders above $26.71.

Questions
1. *Go to www.batstrading.com and look up the order book for Microsoft (MSFT). What are the inside quotes for Microsoft?*
2. *Go to www.batstrading.com. This website shows the 25 most active stocks. Looking down through this list, what are the bid-ask spreads for these stocks?*

FINANCE MATTERS

◄ For the latest news on the topics covered in this chapter, scan here"

The Wild, Wild West of Stock Trading

Where do companies go when they can't (or don't want to) meet the listing requirements of the larger stock markets? Two options are the Over-the-Counter Bulletin Board (OTCBB) and the Pink Sheets. These two electronic markets are part of the Wild, Wild West of stock trading. The somewhat odd names have simple explanations. The OTCBB began as an electronic bulletin board that was created to facilitate OTC trading in nonlisted stocks. The name "Pink Sheets" just reflects the fact that, at one time, prices for such stocks were quoted on pink sheets of paper.

The well-known markets such as the NASDAQ and the NYSE have relatively strict listing requirements. If a company fails to meet these requirements, it can be delisted. The OTCBB and the Pink Sheets, on the other hand, have no listing

the OTCBB tend to have large trading volumes when they do trade, but the dollar amount is quite a bit lower than larger exchanges. For example, by the end of this same trading day, Bank of America (BAC) was the most active stock on NYSE, trading about 229 million shares. Adarna Energy traded about 163 million shares. If we assume the average price was $0.00015 per share, then the total dollar volume for the day was a whopping $24,480 or so. In contrast, about $1.62 billion worth of Bank of America stock was traded.

The Pink Sheets (www.pinksheets.com) is operated by a privately owned company. To be listed on the Pink Sheets, a company just has to find a market maker willing to trade in the company's stock. Companies list on the Pink Sheets for

Market Statistics

Data delayed 15-20 minutes

OTCBB ▼   Vol Actives ▼   [GO]

Name	Symbol	Last Price		Chg	% Chg	Open	High	Low	Volume
Adarna Energy Corp..	ADRN	0.0001	▼	-0.0001	-50.00%	0.0002	0.0002	0.0001	163.20 m
Attitude Drinks Inc NEW	ATTD	0.0056	△	0.0013	30.23%	0.0049	0.0065	0.0036	79.73 m
Evcarco Inc	EVCA	0.0003	△	0.0001	50.00%	0.0002	0.0003	0.0001	58.42 m
AlumiFuel Power Corp.	AFPW	0.0012	▼	-0.0001	-7.69%	0.0013	0.0013	0.001	38.14 m
CoroWare Inc.	COWI	0.0001	—	0.00	0.00%	0.0002	0.0002	0.0001	36.92 m
Team Nation Holdings Corp.	TEMN	0.0004	△	0.0001	33.33%	0.0002	0.0004	0.0002	33.22 m
SavWatt USA Inc.	SAVW	0.0002	—	0.00	0.00%	0.0002	0.0002	0.0001	26.65 m
Medisafe 1 Technologies Corp. Common	MFTH	0.028	△	0.013	86.67%	0.0311	0.036	0.025	26.45 m
Genta Inc.	GNTA	0.002	—	0.00	0.00%	0.0021	0.0022	0.0019	26.25 m
Next 1 Interactive Inc.	NXOI	0.002	▼	-0.0001	-4.76%	0.0021	0.0025	0.002	24.45 m

◄ To get updated data, scan here.

requirements. The OTCBB does require that companies file financial statements with the SEC (or other relevant agency), but the Pink Sheets does not.

Stocks traded on these markets often have very low prices and are frequently referred to as "penny stocks," "microcaps," or even "nanocaps." Relatively few brokers do any research on these companies, so information is often spread through word of mouth or the Internet, not the most reliable of sources. In fact, for many stocks, these markets often look like big electronic rumor mills and gossip factories. To get a feel for what trading looks like, we captured a typical screen from the OTCBB website (www.otcbb.com) above.

First, let's look at the returns. Adarna Energy Corp. had a return on this day of *negative* 50 percent! Of course, the loss occurred because the stock price dropped by $0.0001. The stock price of Medisafe 1 Technologies Corp. increased almost 87 percent as its price rose by $0.013. Stocks on

various reasons. Small companies that do not wish to meet listing requirements are one type. Foreign companies often list on the Pink Sheets because they do not prepare their financial statements according to GAAP, a requirement for listing on U.S. stock exchanges. There are many companies that were formerly listed on bigger stock markets that were either delisted involuntarily or chose to "go dark" for various reasons, including, as we discussed in Chapter 1, the costs associated with Sarbox compliance.

All in all, the OTCBB and Pink Sheets can be pretty wild places to trade. Low stock prices allow huge percentage returns on small stock price movements. Be advised, however, that attempts at manipulation and fraud are commonplace. Also, stocks on these markets are often very thinly traded, meaning there is little volume. It is not unusual for a stock listed on either market to have no trades on a given day. Even two or three days in a row without a trade in a particular stock is not uncommon.

CONCEPT QUESTIONS

7.3a What is the difference between a securities broker and a securities dealer?

7.3b Which is bigger, the bid price or the ask price? Why?

7.3c What are the four types of members of the New York Stock Exchange, or NYSE?

7.3d How does NASDAQ differ from the NYSE?

SUMMARY AND CONCLUSIONS

This chapter has covered the basics of stocks and stock valuation. The key points include:

◄ Think you've mastered the material? Scan here to take a chapter quiz.

1. The cash flows from owning a share of stock come in the form of future dividends. We saw that in certain special cases it is possible to calculate the present value of all the future dividends and thus come up with a value for the stock.

2. As the owner of shares of common stock in a corporation, you have various rights, including the right to vote to elect corporate directors. Voting in corporate elections can be either cumulative or straight. Most voting is actually done by proxy, and a proxy battle breaks out when competing sides try to gain enough votes to have their candidates for the board elected.

3. In addition to common stock, some corporations have issued preferred stock. The name stems from the fact that preferred stockholders must be paid first, before common stockholders can receive anything. Preferred stock has a fixed dividend.

4. The two biggest stock markets in the United States are the NYSE and the NASDAQ. We discussed the organization and operation of these two markets, and we saw how stock price information is reported.

This chapter completes Part 4 of our book. By now, you should have a good grasp of what we mean by present value. You should also be familiar with how to calculate present values, loan payments, and so on. In Part 5, we cover capital budgeting decisions. As you will see, the techniques you have learned in Chapters 4–7 form the basis for our approach to evaluating business investment decisions.

 connect POP QUIZ!

|FINANCE

Can you answer the following questions? If your class is using *Connect Finance*, log on to the Self-Quiz and Study feature in the Library tab to see if you know the answers to these and other questions, check out the study tools, and find out what topics require additional practice!

Section 7.1 Bruer, Inc. is expected to maintain a constant 5.55 percent growth rate in its dividends, indefinitely. If the company has a dividend yield of 4.05 percent, what is the required return on the company's stock?

Section 7.2 True or false: For tax purposes, preferred stock is considered a form of equity.

CHAPTER REVIEW AND SELF-TEST PROBLEMS

7.1.   Dividend Growth and Stock Valuation.   The Brigapenski Co. has just paid a cash dividend of $2 per share. Investors require a 16 percent return from investments such as this. If the dividend is expected to grow at a steady 8 percent per year, what is the current value of the stock? What will the stock be worth in five years? (See Problem 1.)

7.2.   Required Returns.   Suppose we observe a stock selling for $40 per share. The next dividend will be $1 per share, and you think the dividend will grow at 12 percent per year forever. What is the dividend yield in this case? The capital gains yield? The total required return? (See Problem 3.)

■ Answers to Chapter Review and Self-Test Problems

7.1.   The last dividend, D_0, was $2. The dividend is expected to grow steadily at 8 percent. The required return is 16 percent. Based on the dividend growth model, we can say that the current price is:

$$
\begin{aligned}
P_0 &= D_1/(R - g) \\
&= D_0 \times (1 + g)/(R - g) \\
&= \$2 \times 1.08/(.16 - .08) \\
&= \$2.16/.08 \\
&= \$27
\end{aligned}
$$

We could calculate the price in five years by calculating the dividend in five years and then using the growth model again. Alternatively, we could recognize that the stock price will increase by 8 percent per year and calculate the future price directly. We'll do both. First, the dividend in five years will be:

$$
\begin{aligned}
D_5 &= D_0 \times (1 + g)^5 \\
&= \$2 \times 1.08^5 \\
&= \$2.9387
\end{aligned}
$$

The price in five years would therefore be:

$$
\begin{aligned}
P_5 &= D_5 \times (1 + g)/(R - g) \\
&= \$2.9387 \times 1.08/.08 \\
&= \$3.1738/.08 \\
&= \$39.67
\end{aligned}
$$

Once we understand the dividend model, however, it's easier to notice that:

$$
\begin{aligned}
P_5 &= P_0 \times (1 + g)^5 \\
&= \$27 \times 1.08^5 \\
&= \$27 \times 1.4693 \\
&= \$39.67
\end{aligned}
$$

Notice that both approaches yield the same price in five years.

7.2.   The dividend yield is the next dividend, D_1, divided by the current price, P_0, or $1/40 = 2.5\%$. The capital gains yield is the same as the dividend growth rate, 12 percent. The total required return is the sum of the two, $2.5\% + 12\% = 14.5\%$.

CRITICAL THINKING AND CONCEPTS REVIEW

LO 1   **7.1. Stock Valuation.** Why does the value of a share of stock depend on dividends?

LO 1   **7.2. Stock Valuation.** A substantial percentage of the companies listed on the NYSE and the NASDAQ don't pay dividends, but investors are nonetheless willing to buy shares in them. How is this possible given your answer to the previous question?

LO 1   **7.3. Dividend Policy.** Referring to the previous questions, under what circumstances might a company choose not to pay dividends?

LO 1   **7.4 Dividend Growth Model.** Under what two assumptions can we use the dividend growth model presented in the chapter to determine the value of a share of stock? Comment on the reasonableness of these assumptions.

LO 1   **7.5. Common versus Preferred Stock.** Suppose a company has a preferred stock issue and a common stock issue. Both have just paid a $2 dividend. Which do you think will have a higher price, a share of the preferred or a share of the common?

LO 1   **7.6. Dividend Growth Model.** Based on the dividend growth model, what are the two components of the total return on a share of stock? Which do you think is typically larger?

LO 1   **7.7. Growth Rate.** In the context of the dividend growth model, is it true that the growth rate in dividends and the growth rate in the price of the stock are identical?

LO 1   **7.8. Dividends and Earnings.** Is it possible for a company to pay dividends when it has a negative net income for the year? Could this happen for longer periods?

LO 2   **7.9. Corporate Ethics.** Is it unfair or unethical for corporations to create classes of stock with unequal voting rights?

LO 2   **7.10. Voting Rights.** Some companies, such as Google, have created classes of stock with little or no voting rights at all. Why would investors buy such stock?

LO 2   **7.11. Stock Valuation.** Evaluate the following statement: Managers should not focus on the current stock value because doing so will lead to an overemphasis on short-term profits at the expense of long-term profits.

LO 1   **7.12. Constant Dividend Growth Model.** In the constant dividend growth model, what is the highest reasonable growth rate for a stock's dividend?

LO 3   **7.13. Voting Rights.** In the chapter, we mentioned that many companies have been under pressure to declassify their boards of directors. Why would investors want a board to be declassified? What are the advantages of a classified board?

LO 3   **7.14. Price Ratio Valuation.** What are the difficulties in using the PE ratio to value stock?

QUESTIONS AND PROBLEMS   Select problems are available in McGraw-Hill Connect. Please see the packaging options section of the preface for more information.

LO 1   **1. Stock Values.** Anton, Inc., just paid a dividend of $1.95 per share on its stock. The dividends are expected to grow at a constant rate of 4.1 percent per year, indefinitely. If investors require a return of 10.2 percent on this stock, what is the current price? What will the price be in three years? In 15 years?   **Basic** (Questions 1–14)

LO 1   **2. Stock Values.** The next dividend payment by Wyatt, Inc., will be $2.30 per share. The dividends are anticipated to maintain a growth rate of 4.5 percent forever. If the stock currently sells for $39.85 per share, what is the required return?

LO 1 3. **Stock Values.**   For the company in the previous problem, what is the dividend yield? What is the expected capital gains yield?

LO 1 4. **Stock Values.**   Nofal Corporation will pay a $3.65 per share dividend next year. The company pledges to increase its dividend by 5.1 percent per year, indefinitely. If you require a return of 12 percent on your investment, how much will you pay for the company's stock today?

LO 1 5. **Stock Valuation.**   Raffalovich, Inc., is expected to maintain a constant 4.9 percent growth rate in its dividends, indefinitely. If the company has a dividend yield of 5.7 percent, what is the required return on the company's stock?

LO 1 6. **Stock Valuation.**   Suppose you know that a company's stock currently sells for $58 per share and the required return on the stock is 12 percent. You also know that the total return on the stock is evenly divided between capital gains yield and dividend yield. If it's the company's policy to always maintain a constant growth rate in its dividends, what is the current dividend per share?

LO 1 7. **Stock Valuation.**   Bui Corp. pays a constant $12 dividend on its stock. The company will maintain this dividend for the next nine years and will then cease paying dividends forever. If the required return on this stock is 10 percent, what is the current share price?

LO 1 8. **Valuing Preferred Stock.**   Rabie, Inc., has an issue of preferred stock outstanding that pays a $3.80 dividend every year, in perpetuity. If this issue currently sells for $78.45 per share, what is the required return?

LO 2 9. **Voting Rights.**   After successfully completing your corporate finance class, you feel the next challenge ahead is to serve on the board of directors of Schenkel Enterprises. Unfortunately, you will be the only individual voting for you. If Schenkel has 350,000 shares outstanding and the stock currently sells for $37, how much will it cost you to buy a seat if the company uses straight voting? Assume that Schenkel uses cumulative voting and there are four seats in the current election; how much will it cost you to buy a seat now?

LO 1 10. **Growth Rates.**   The stock price of Webber Co. is $68. Investors require an 11 percent rate of return on similar stocks. If the company plans to pay a dividend of $3.85 next year, what growth rate is expected for the company's stock price?

LO 1 11. **Valuing Preferred Stock.**   E-Eyes.com has a new issue of preferred stock it calls 20/20 preferred. The stock will pay a $20 dividend per year, but the first dividend will not be paid until 20 years from today. If you require a return of 8 percent on this stock, how much should you pay today?

LO 1 12. **Stock Valuation.**   Alexander Corp. will pay a dividend of $2.72 next year. The company has stated that it will maintain a constant growth rate of 4.5 percent a year forever. If you want a return of 12 percent, how much will you pay for the stock? What if you want a return of 8 percent? What does this tell you about the relationship between the required return and the stock price?

LO 2 13. **Stock Valuation and PE Ratio.**   The Sleeping Flower Co. has earnings of $1.75 per share. The benchmark PE for company is 18. What stock price would you consider appropriate? What if the benchmark PE were 21?

LO 2 14. **Stock Valuation and PS Ratio.**   TwitterMe, Inc., is a new company and currently has negative earnings. The company's sales are $1.2 million and there are 130,000 shares outstanding. If the benchmark price-sales ratio is 5.2, what is your estimate of an appropriate stock price? What if the price-sales ratio were 4.6?

LO 1 15. **Nonconstant Growth.** Metallica Bearings, Inc., is a young start-up company. No dividends will be paid on the stock over the next nine years, because the firm needs to plow back its earnings to fuel growth. The company will then pay a dividend of $15 per share 10 years from today and will increase the dividend by 5 percent per year thereafter. If the required return on this stock is 14 percent, what is the current share price?

Intermediate (Questions 15–30)

LO 1 16. **Nonconstant Dividends.** Hot Wings, Inc., has an odd dividend policy. The company has just paid a dividend of $4 per share and has announced that it will increase the dividend by $5 per share for each of the next four years, and then never pay another dividend. If you require a return of 12 percent on the company's stock, how much will you pay for a share today?

LO 1 17. **Nonconstant Dividends.** Apocalyptica Corporation is expected to pay the following dividends over the next four years: $3, $10, $15, and $3.08. Afterwards, the company pledges to maintain a constant 5 percent growth rate in dividends, forever. If the required return on the stock is 11 percent, what is the current share price?

LO 1 18. **Supernormal Growth.** Yang Corp. is growing quickly. Dividends are expected to grow at a rate of 25 percent for the next three years, with the growth rate falling off to a constant 6 percent thereafter. If the required return is 13 percent and the company just paid a $2.50 dividend, what is the current share price?

LO 1 19. **Negative Growth.** Antiques 'R' Us is a mature manufacturing firm. The company just paid a dividend of $11.45 but management expects to reduce the payout by 4.5 percent per year, indefinitely. If you require a return of 11 percent on this stock, what will you pay for a share today?

LO 1 20. **Finding the Dividend.** Gontier Corporation stock currently sells for $53.95 per share. The market requires a return of 12 percent on the firm's stock. If the company maintains a constant 5.5 percent growth rate in dividends, what was the most recent dividend per share paid on the stock?

You've collected the following information from your favorite financial website. Use it to answer Questions 21–25 (the 52-week Hi and Lo are the highest and lowest stock prices over the previous 52 weeks).

| 52-Week Price | | | | | | |
Hi	Lo	Stock (Div)	Div Yld %	PE Ratio	Close Price	Net Chg
36.99	13.09	Arch Coal 0.44	3.0	20.0	14.53	0.25
42.81	32.90	Laclede Group 1.66	4.0	14.2	41.60	−0.31
194.90	151.71	IBM 3.00	1.6	14.7	192.37	1.91
41.86	23.44	JCPenney 0.80	1.9	45.8	41.77	0.35
29.92	22.82	Tootsie Roll 0.32	1.3	33.9	??	−0.19

LO 3 21. **Dividend Yield.** Find the quote for the Laclede Group. Assume that the dividend is constant. What was the highest dividend yield over the past year? What was the lowest dividend yield over the past year?

LO 1 22. **Stock Valuation.** According to the 2012 Value Line *Investment Survey*, the growth rate in dividends for IBM for the next five years is expected to be 12.5 percent. Suppose IBM meets this growth rate in dividends for the next five years and then the dividend growth rate falls to 5 percent indefinitely. Assume investors require a return of 11 percent on IBM stock. Is the stock priced correctly? What factors could affect your answer?

www.mhhe.com/rwj

LO 1 **23. Stock Valuation.** According to the 2012 Value Line *Investment Survey,* the growth rate in dividends for Arch Coal for the previous 10 years has been 3.5 percent. If investors feel this growth rate will continue, what is the required return for Arch Coal stock?

LO 1 **24. Negative Growth.** According to the 2012 Value Line *Investment Survey,* the growth rate in dividends for JCPenney for the previous 10 years has been –7.5 percent. If investors feel this growth rate will continue, what is the required return for JCPenney stock? Does this number make sense? What are some of the potential reasons for the negative growth in dividends?

LO 1 **25. Stock Quotes.** Using the dividend yield, calculate the closing price for Tootsie Roll on this day. The actual closing price for Tootsie Roll was $24.48. Why is your closing price different? The Value Line *Investment Survey* projects a 5.5 percent dividend growth rate for Tootsie Roll. What is the required return for the stock using the dividend discount model and the actual stock price?

LO 2 **26. Stock Valuation and PE.** Sully Corp. currently has an EPS of $2.35, and the benchmark PE for the company is 21. Earnings are expected to grow at 7 percent per year.

    a. What is your estimate of the current stock price?

    b. What is the target stock price in one year?

    c. Assuming the company pays no dividends, what is the implied return on the company's stock over the next year? What does this tell you about the implicit stock return using PE valuation?

LO 2 **27. Stock Valuation and PE.** You have found the following historical information for the Daniela Company:

	Year 1	Year 2	Year 3	Year 4
Stock price	$49.50	$58.12	$67.34	$60.25
EPS	2.40	2.58	2.71	2.85

Earnings are expected to grow at 11 percent for the next year. Using the company's historical average PE as a benchmark, what is the target stock price in one year?

LO 2 **28. Stock Valuation and PE.** In the previous problem, we assumed that the stock had a single stock price for the year. However, if you look at stock prices over any year, you will find a high and low stock price for the year. Instead of a single benchmark PE ratio, we now have a high and low PE ratio for each year. We can use these ratios to calculate a high and a low stock price for the next year. Suppose we have the following information on a particular company:

	Year 1	Year 2	Year 3	Year 4
High price	$97.90	$121.50	$130.90	$147.53
Low price	72.73	88.84	69.52	116.05
EPS	7.18	8.93	10.01	11.40

Earnings are projected to grow at 6 percent over the next year. What are your high and low target stock prices over the next year?

LO 2

29. Stock Valuation and PE.   Davis, Inc., currently has an EPS of $2 and an earnings growth rate of 8 percent. If the benchmark PE ratio is 22, what is the target share price five years from now?

LO 2

30. PE and Terminal Stock Price.   In practice, a common way to value a share of stock when a company pays dividends is to value the dividends over the next five years or so, then find the "terminal" stock price using a benchmark PE ratio. Suppose a company just paid a dividend of $1.15. The dividends are expected to grow at 20 percent over the next five years. In five years, the estimated payout ratio is 40 percent and the benchmark PE ratio is 21. After five years, the earnings are expected to grow at 7 percent per year. What is the target stock price in five years? What is the stock price today assuming a required return of 12 percent on this stock?

LO 1

31. Capital Gains versus Income.   Consider four different stocks, all of which have a required return of 16 percent and a most recent dividend of $2.80 per share. Stocks W, X, and Y are expected to maintain constant growth rates in dividends for the foreseeable future of 8 percent, 0 percent, and −5 percent per year, respectively. Stock Z is a growth stock that will increase its dividend by 20 percent for the next two years and then maintain a constant 12 percent growth rate, thereafter. What is the dividend yield for each of these four stocks? What is the expected capital gains yield? Discuss the relationship among the various returns that you find for each of these stocks.

Challenge
(Questions 31–32)

LO 1

32. Stock Valuation.   Most corporations pay quarterly dividends on their common stock rather than annual dividends. Barring any unusual circumstances during the year, the board raises, lowers, or maintains the current dividend once a year and then pays this dividend out in equal quarterly installments to its shareholders.

    a. Suppose a company currently pays an annual dividend of $3.20 on its common stock in a single annual installment, and management plans on raising this dividend by 6 percent per year indefinitely. If the required return on this stock is 12 percent, what is the current share price?

    b. Now suppose the company in (a) actually pays its annual dividend in equal quarterly installments; thus, the company has just paid a dividend of $.80 per share, as it has for the previous three quarters. What is your value for the current share price now? (*Hint:* Find the equivalent annual end-of-year dividend for each year.) Comment on whether you think this model of stock valuation is appropriate.

7.1 Dividend Discount Model.   According to the 2012 Value Line *Investment Survey,* the dividend growth rate for ExxonMobil (XOM) is 7 percent. Find the current stock price quote and dividend information at finance.yahoo.com. If this dividend growth rate is correct, what is the required return for ExxonMobil? Does this number make sense to you?

WHAT'S ON THE WEB?

7.2 Stock Quotes.   What is the most expensive publicly traded stock in the United States? Go to finance.yahoo.com and enter BRKA (for Berkshire Hathaway Class A). What is the current price per share? What is the 52-week high and low? How many shares trade on an average day? How many shares have traded today?

7.3 Supernormal Growth.   You are interested in buying stock in Coca-Cola (KO). You believe that the dividends will grow at 15 percent for the next four years and level off at 6 percent thereafter. Using the most recent dividend on finance.yahoo.com, if you want a 12 percent return, how much should you be willing to pay for a share of stock?

7.4 Market Operations.   How does a stock trade take place? Go to www.nyse.com to find out. Describe the process of a trade on the NYSE.

www.mhhe.com/rwj

EXCEL *MASTER IT!* PROBLEM

In practice, the use of the dividend discount model is refined from the method we presented in the textbook. Many analysts will estimate the dividend for the next five years and then estimate a perpetual growth rate at some point in the future, typically 10 years. Rather than have the dividend growth fall dramatically from the fast growth period to the perpetual growth period, linear interpolation is applied. That is, the dividend growth is projected to fall by an equal amount each year. For example, if the high growth period is 15 percent for the next five years and the dividends are expected to fall to a 5 percent perpetual growth rate five years later, the dividend growth rate would decline by 2 percent each year.

The Value Line *Investment Survey* provides information for investors. Below, you will find information for IBM found in the 2012 edition of Value Line:

2011 dividend:	$2.90
Five-year dividend growth rate:	12.5%

a. Assume that the perpetual growth rate of 5 percent begins 10 years from now and use linear interpolation between the high growth rate and perpetual growth rate. Construct a table that shows the dividend growth rate and dividend each year. What is the stock price at Year 10? What is the stock price today?

b. Instead of applying the constant dividend growth model to find the stock price in the future, analysts will often combine the dividend discount method with price ratio valuation, often with the PE ratio. Remember that the PE ratio is the price per share divided by the earnings per share. So, if we know what the PE ratio is, we can solve for the stock price. Suppose we also have the following information about IBM:

Payout ratio:	30%
PE at constant growth rate:	15

c. Use the PE ratio to calculate the stock price when IBM reaches a perpetual growth rate in dividends. Now supply the value of the stock today by finding the present value of the dividends during the supernormal growth rate and the price you calculated using the PE ratio.

d. How sensitive is the current stock price to changes in PE ratio when the stock reaches the perpetual growth rate? Graph the current stock price against the PE ratio in 10 years to find out.

CHAPTER CASE
STOCK VALUATION AT RAGAN, INC.

Ragan, Inc., was founded nine years ago by brother and sister Carrington and Genevieve Ragan. The company manufactures and installs commercial heating, ventilation, and cooling (HVAC) units. Ragan, Inc., has experienced rapid growth because of a proprietary technology that increases the energy efficiency of its units. The company is equally owned by Carrington and Genevieve. The original partnership agreement between the siblings gave each 50,000 shares of stock. In the event either wished to sell stock, the shares first had to be offered to the other at a discounted price.

Although neither sibling wants to sell, they have decided they should value their holdings in the company. To get started, they have gathered the following information about their main competitors:

Expert HVAC Corporation's negative earnings per share were the result of an accounting write-off last year. Without the write-off, earnings per share for the company would have been $.54.

Last year, Ragan, Inc., had an EPS of $4.85 and paid a dividend to Carrington and Genevieve of $75,000 each. The company also had a return on equity of 17 percent. The siblings believe that 14 percent is an appropriate required return for the company.

Ragan, Inc. — Competitors					
	EPS	Div.	Stock Price	ROE	R
Arctic Cooling, Inc.	$.84	$.39	$17.83	16.00%	10.00%
National Heating & Cooling	1.34	.65	19.23	14.00	13.00
Expert HVAC Corp.	−.55	.43	18.14	15.00	12.00
Industry Average	$.54	$.49	$18.40	15.00	11.67

QUESTIONS

1. Assuming the company continues its current growth rate, what is the value per share of the company's stock?

2. To verify their calculations, Carrington and Genevieve have hired Josh Schlessman as a consultant. Josh was previously an equity analyst and covered the HVAC industry. Josh has examined the company's financial statements, as well as those of its competitors. Although Ragan, Inc., currently has a technological advantage, his research indicates that other companies are investigating methods to improve efficiency. Given this, Josh believes that the company's technological advantage will last only for the next five years. After that period, the company's growth will likely slow to the industry growth average. Additionally, Josh believes that the required return used by the company is too high. He believes the industry average required return is more appropriate. Under this growth rate assumption, what is your estimate of the stock price?

www.mhhe.com/rwj

8 Net Present Value and Other Investment Criteria

learning objectives

After studying this chapter, you should be able to:

LO 1 Summarize the payback rule and some of its shortcomings.

LO 2 Discuss accounting rates of return and some of the problems with them.

LO 3 Explain the internal rate of return criterion and its associated strengths and weaknesses.

LO 4 Evaluate proposed investments by using the net present value criterion.

LO 5 Apply the modified internal rate of return.

LO 6 Calculate the profitability index and understand its relation to net present value.

Is there green in green? General Electric (GE) thinks so. Through its "Ecomagination" program, the company planned to double research and development spending on green products. In fact, GE has already committed over $5 billion to its Ecomagination program and announced it would invest another $10 billion from 2011 to 2015.

With products such as a hybrid railroad locomotive (described as a 200-ton, 6,000-horsepower "Prius on rails"), GE's green initiative seems to be paying off. Revenue from the company's green products was $18 billion in 2011, with a target of $20 billion in 2012. Further, revenues from Ecomagination products were growing twice as fast as the company's other revenues. GE's internal commitment to reduced energy consumption through green "Treasure Hunts" saved it more than $100 million, and, by 2010, the company had reduced water consumption by 30 percent relative to its 2006 baseline, another considerable cost savings.

While GE was in part motivated by the desire to go green, from a financial perspective the decision only makes sense if the company *makes* some green. Given that GE plans to spend about $2 billion per year on such undertakings, it is obviously a major financial decision, and the risks and rewards must be carefully weighed. In this chapter, we discuss the basic tools used in making such decisions.

This chapter introduces you to the practice of capital budgeting. Back in Chapter 1, we saw that increasing the value of the stock in a company is the goal of financial management. Thus, what we need to learn is how to tell whether a particular investment will achieve that or not. This chapter considers a variety of techniques that are actually used in practice. More importantly, it shows how many of these techniques can be misleading, and it explains why the net present value approach is the right one.

In Chapter 1, we identified the three key areas of concern to the financial manager. The first of these was the following: What long-term investments should we make? We called this the *capital budgeting decision*. In this chapter, we begin to deal with the issues that arise in answering this question.

The process of allocating, or budgeting, capital is usually more involved than just deciding whether or not to buy a particular fixed asset. We will frequently face broader issues like whether or not we should launch a new product or enter a new market. Decisions such as these will determine the nature of a firm's operations and products for years to come, primarily because fixed asset investments are generally long-lived and not easily reversed once they are made.

For these reasons, the capital budgeting question is probably the most important issue in corporate finance. How a firm chooses to finance its operations (the capital structure question) and how a firm manages its short-term operating activities (the working capital question) are certainly issues of concern, but it is the fixed assets that define the business of the firm. Airlines, for example, are airlines because they operate airplanes, regardless of how they finance them.

Any firm possesses a huge number of possible investments. Each possible investment is an option available to the firm. Some options are valuable and some are not. The essence of successful financial management, of course, is learning to identify which are which. With this in mind, our goal in this chapter is to introduce you to the techniques used to analyze potential business ventures to decide which are worth undertaking.

We present and compare several different procedures used in practice. Our primary goal is to acquaint you with the advantages and disadvantages of the various approaches. As we shall see, the most important concept in this area is the idea of net present value. We consider this next.

NET PRESENT VALUE

8.1

In Chapter 1, we argued that the goal of financial management is to create value for the stockholders. The financial manager must therefore examine a potential investment in light of its likely effect on the price of the firm's shares. In this section, we describe a widely used procedure for doing this, the net present value approach.

ExcelMaster
coverage online

The Basic Idea

An investment is worth undertaking if it creates value for its owners. In the most general sense, we create value by identifying an investment worth more in the marketplace than it costs us to acquire. How can something be worth more than it costs? It's a case of the whole being worth more than the cost of the parts.

For example, suppose you buy a run-down house for $25,000 and spend another $25,000 on painters, plumbers, and so on to get it fixed up. Your total investment is $50,000. When the work is completed, you place the house back on the market and find that it's worth $60,000. The market value ($60,000) exceeds the cost ($50,000) by $10,000. What you have done here is to act as a manager and bring together some fixed assets (a house), some labor (plumbers, carpenters, and others), and some materials (carpeting, paint, and so on). The net result is that you have created $10,000 in value. Put another way, this $10,000 is the *value added* by management.

With our house example, it turned out *after the fact* that $10,000 in value was created. Things thus worked out very nicely. The real challenge, of course, would have been to somehow

240   **PART 5**   Capital Budgeting

identify *ahead of time* whether or not investing the necessary $50,000 was a good idea in the first place. This is what capital budgeting is all about, namely, trying to determine whether a proposed investment or project will be worth more than it costs once it is in place.

For reasons that will be obvious in a moment, the difference between an investment's market value and its cost is called the **net present value** of the investment, abbreviated **NPV**. In other words, net present value is a measure of how much value is created or added today by undertaking an investment. Given our goal of creating value for the stockholders, the capital budgeting process can be viewed as a search for investments with positive net present values.

net present value (NPV)
The difference between an investment's market value and its cost.

With our run-down house, you can probably imagine how we would go about making the capital budgeting decision. We would first look at what comparable, fixed-up properties were selling for in the market. We would then get estimates of the cost of buying a particular property, fixing it up, and bringing it to market. At this point, we have an estimated total cost and an estimated market value. If the difference is positive, then this investment is worth undertaking because it has a positive estimated net present value. There is risk, of course, because there is no guarantee that our estimates will turn out to be correct.

As our example illustrates, investment decisions are greatly simplified when there is a market for assets similar to the investment we are considering. Capital budgeting becomes much more difficult when we cannot observe the market price for at least roughly comparable investments. The reason is that we are then faced with the problem of estimating the value of an investment using only indirect market information. Unfortunately, this is precisely the situation the financial manager usually encounters. We examine this issue next.

Estimating Net Present Value

Imagine we are thinking of starting a business to produce and sell a new product, say, organic fertilizer. We can estimate the start-up costs with reasonable accuracy because we know what we will need to buy to begin production. Would this be a good investment? Based on our discussion, you know that the answer depends on whether or not the value of the new business exceeds the cost of starting it. In other words, does this investment have a positive NPV?

This problem is much more difficult than our "fixer-upper" house example, because entire fertilizer companies are not routinely bought and sold in the marketplace; so it is essentially impossible to observe the market value of a similar investment. As a result, we must somehow estimate this value by other means.

Based on our work in Chapters 4 and 5, you may be able to guess how we will go about estimating the value of our fertilizer business. We will first try to estimate the future cash flows we expect the new business to produce. We will then apply our basic discounted cash flow procedure to estimate the present value of those cash flows. Once we have this estimate, we then estimate NPV as the difference between the present value of the future cash flows and the cost of the investment. As we mentioned in Chapter 5, this procedure is often called **discounted cash flow,** or **DCF, valuation.**

discounted cash flow (DCF) valuation
The process of valuing an investment by discounting its future cash flows.

To see how we might go about estimating NPV, suppose we believe the cash revenues from our fertilizer business will be $20,000 per year, assuming everything goes as expected. Cash costs (including taxes) will be $14,000 per year. We will wind down the business in eight years. The plant, property, and equipment will be worth $2,000 as salvage at that time. The project costs $30,000 to launch. We use a 15 percent discount rate on new projects such as this one. Is this a good investment? If there are 1,000 shares of stock outstanding, what will be the effect on the price per share from taking the investment?

From a purely mechanical perspective, we need to calculate the present value of the future cash flows at 15 percent. The net cash inflow will be $20,000 cash income less $14,000 in costs per year for eight years. These cash flows are illustrated in Figure 8.1.

Time (years)	0	1	2	3	4	5	6	7	8
Initial cost	−$30								
Inflows		$20	$20	$20	$20	$20	$20	$20	$20
Outflows		− 14	− 14	− 14	− 14	− 14	− 14	− 14	− 14
Net inflow		$ 6	$ 6	$ 6	$ 6	$ 6	$ 6	$ 6	$ 6
Salvage									2
Net cash flow	−$30	$ 6	$ 6	$ 6	$ 6	$ 6	$ 6	$ 6	$ 8

FIGURE 8.1

Project cash flows ($000)

As Figure 8.1 suggests, we effectively have an eight-year annuity of $20,000 − 14,000 = $6,000 per year along with a single lump-sum inflow of $2,000 in eight years. Calculating the present value of the future cash flows thus comes down to the same type of problem we considered in Chapter 5. The total present value is:

Present value = $6,000 × (1 − 1/1.15^8)/.15 + 2,000/1.15^8
= $6,000 × 4.4873 + 2,000/3.0590
= $26,924 + 654
= $27,578

When we compare this to the $30,000 estimated cost, the NPV is:

NPV = −$30,000 + 27,578 = −$2,422

Therefore, this is *not* a good investment. Based on our estimates, taking it would *decrease* the total value of the stock by $2,422. With 1,000 shares outstanding, our best estimate of the impact of taking this project is a loss of value of $2,422/1,000 = $2.422 per share.

Our fertilizer example illustrates how NPV estimates can be used to determine whether or not an investment is desirable. From our example, notice that if the NPV is negative, the effect on share value will be unfavorable. If the NPV were positive, the effect would be favorable. As a consequence, all we need to know about a particular proposal for the purpose of making an accept-reject decision is whether the NPV is positive or negative.

Given that the goal of financial management is to increase share value, our discussion in this section leads us to the *net present value rule:*

> **An investment should be accepted if the net present value is positive and rejected if it is negative.**

In the unlikely event that the net present value turned out to be exactly zero, we would be indifferent between taking the investment and not taking it.

Two comments about our example are in order. First and foremost, it is not the rather mechanical process of discounting the cash flows that is important. Once we have the cash flows and the appropriate discount rate, the required calculations are fairly straightforward. The task of coming up with the cash flows and the discount rate in the first place is much more challenging. We will have much more to say about this in our next chapter. For the remainder of this chapter, we take it as given that we have estimates of the cash revenues and costs and, where needed, an appropriate discount rate.

The second thing to keep in mind about our example is that the −$2,422 NPV is an estimate. Like any estimate, it can be high or low. The only way to find out the true NPV would be to place the investment up for sale and see what we could get for it. We generally won't be doing this, so it is important that our estimates be reliable. Once again, we will have more to say about this later. For the rest of this chapter, we will assume that the estimates are accurate.

EXAMPLE 8.1

USING THE NPV RULE

Suppose we are asked to decide whether or not a new consumer product should be launched. Based on projected sales and costs, we expect that the cash flows over the five-year life of the project will be $2,000 in the first two years, $4,000 in the next two, and $5,000 in the last year. It will cost about $10,000 to begin production. We use a 10 percent discount rate to evaluate new products. What should we do here?

Given the cash flows and discount rate, we can calculate the total value of the product by discounting the cash flows back to the present:

$$\text{Present value} = \$2,000/1.1 + 2,000/1.1^2 + 4,000/1.1^3 + 4,000/1.1^4 + 5,000/1.1^5$$

$$= \$1,818 + 1,653 + 3,005 + 2,732 + 3,105$$

$$= \$12,313$$

The present value of the expected cash flows is $12,313, but the cost of getting those cash flows is only $10,000, so the NPV is $12,313 − 10,000 = $2,313. This is positive; so, based on the net present value rule, we should take on the project.

SPREADSHEET STRATEGIES

Calculating NPVs with a Spreadsheet

Spreadsheets and financial calculators are commonly used to calculate NPVs. The procedures used by various financial calculators are too different for us to illustrate here, so we will focus on using a spreadsheet (financial calculators are covered in Appendix D). Examining the use of spreadsheets in this context also allows us to issue an important warning. Let's rework Example 8.1:

	A	B	C	D	E	F	G	H
1								
2	Using a spreadsheet to calculate net present values							
3								
4	From Example 8.1, the project's cost is $10,000. The cash flows are $2,000 per year for the first two							
5	years, $4,000 per year for the next two, and $5,000 in the last year. The discount rate is							
6	10 percent; what's the NPV?							
7								
8		Year	Cash flow					
9		0	−$10,000	Discount rate =		10%		
10		1	2,000					
11		2	2,000		NPV =	$2,102.72	(*wrong* answer)	
12		3	4,000		NPV =	$2,312.99	(*right* answer)	
13		4	4,000					
14		5	5,000					
15								
16	The formula entered in cell F11 is = NPV(F9,C9:C14). This gives the wrong answer because the							
17	NPV function actually calculates present values, not net present values.							
18								
19	The formula entered in cell F12 is = NPV(F9,C10:C14) + C9. This gives the right answer because the							
20	NPV function is used to calculate the present value of the cash flows and then the initial cost is							
21	subtracted to calculate the answer. Notice that we added cell C9 because it is already negative.							

As we have seen in this section, estimating NPV is one way of assessing the profitability of a proposed investment. It is certainly not the only way profitability is assessed, and we now turn to some alternatives. As we will see, when compared to NPV, each of the ways of assessing profitability that we examine is flawed in some key way; so, NPV is the preferred approach in principle, if not always in practice.

In our nearby *Spreadsheet Strategies* box, we rework Example 8.1. Notice that we have provided two answers. By comparing the answers to that found in Example 8.1, we see that the first answer is wrong even though we used the spreadsheet's NPV formula. What happened is that the "NPV" function in our spreadsheet is actually a PV function; unfortunately, one of the original spreadsheet programs many years ago got the definition wrong, and subsequent spreadsheets have copied it! Our second answer shows how to use the formula properly.

The example here illustrates the danger of blindly using calculators or computers without understanding what is going on; we shudder to think of how many capital budgeting decisions in the real world are based on incorrect use of this particular function. We will see another example of something that can go wrong with a spreadsheet later in the chapter.

CONCEPT QUESTIONS

8.1a   What is the net present value rule?

8.1b   If we say an investment has an NPV of $1,000, what exactly do we mean?

THE PAYBACK RULE

8.2

It is very common in practice to talk of the payback on a proposed investment. Loosely, the *payback* is the length of time it takes to recover our initial investment, or "get our bait back." Because this idea is widely understood and used, we will examine it in some detail.

Defining the Rule

ExcelMaster
coverage online

We can illustrate how to calculate a payback with an example. Figure 8.2 below shows the cash flows from a proposed investment. How many years do we have to wait until the accumulated cash flows from this investment equal or exceed the cost of the investment? As Figure 8.2 indicates, the initial investment is $50,000. After the first year, the firm has recovered $30,000, leaving $20,000 outstanding. The cash flow in the second year is exactly $20,000, so this investment "pays for itself" in exactly two years. Put another way, the **payback period** (or just payback) is two years. If we require a payback of, say, three years or less, then this investment is acceptable. This illustrates the *payback period rule:*

payback period
The amount of time required for an investment to generate cash flows sufficient to recover its initial cost.

> Based on the payback rule, an investment is acceptable if its calculated payback period is less than some prespecified number of years.

FIGURE 8.2

Net project cash flows

Year	0	1	2	3	4
	−$50,000	$30,000	$20,000	$10,000	$5,000

In our example, the payback works out to be exactly two years. This won't usually happen, of course. When the numbers don't work out exactly, it is customary to work with fractional years. For example, suppose the initial investment is $60,000, and the cash flows are $20,000 in the first year and $90,000 in the second. The cash flows over the first two years are $110,000, so the project obviously pays back sometime in the second year. After the first year, the project has paid back $20,000, leaving $40,000 to be recovered. To figure out the fractional year, note that this $40,000 is $40,000/90,000 = 4/9 of the second year's cash flow. Assuming that the $90,000 cash flow is paid uniformly throughout the year, the payback would thus be 1⁴⁄₉ years.

EXAMPLE | 8.2

CALCULATING PAYBACK

The projected cash flows from a proposed investment are:

Year	Cash Flow
1	$100
2	200
3	500

This project costs $500. What is the payback period for this investment?

The initial cost is $500. After the first two years, the cash flows total $300. After the third year, the total cash flow is $800, so the project pays back sometime between the end of year 2 and the end of year 3. Since the accumulated cash flows for the first two years are $300, we need to recover $200 in the third year. The third-year cash flow is $500, so we will have to wait $200/500 = .40 years to do this. The payback period is thus 2.4 years, or about two years and five months.

Now that we know how to calculate the payback period on an investment, using the payback period rule for making decisions is straightforward. A particular cutoff time is selected, say, two years, and all investment projects that have payback periods of two years or less are accepted, and all of those that pay back in more than two years are rejected.

Table 8.1 illustrates cash flows for five different projects. The figures shown as the Year 0 cash flows are the cost of the investment. We examine these to indicate some peculiarities that can, in principle, arise with payback periods.

The payback for the first project, A, is easily calculated. The sum of the cash flows for the first two years is $70, leaving us with $100 − 70 = $30 to go. Since the cash flow in the third year is $50, the payback occurs sometime in that year. When we compare the $30 we need to the $50 that will be coming in, we get $30/50 = .60; so, payback will occur 60 percent of the way into the year. The payback period is thus 2.6 years.

TABLE 8.1	Year	A	B	C	D	E
Expected cash flowa for projects A through E	0	−$100	−$200	−$200	−$200	−$ 50
	1	30	40	40	100	100
	2	40	20	20	100	− 50,000,000
	3	50	10	10	− 200	
	4	60		130	200	

Project B's payback is also easy to calculate: It *never* pays back because the cash flows never total up to the original investment. Project C has a payback of exactly four years because it supplies the $130 that B is missing in Year 4. Project D is a little strange. Because of the negative cash flow in Year 3, you can easily verify that it has two different payback periods, two years and four years. Which of these is correct? Both of them; the way the payback period is calculated doesn't guarantee a single answer. Finally, Project E is obviously unrealistic, but it does pay back in six months, thereby illustrating the point that a rapid payback does not guarantee a good investment.

Analyzing the Rule

When compared to the NPV rule, the payback period rule has some rather severe shortcomings. First, the payback period is calculated by simply adding up the future cash flows. There is no discounting involved, so the time value of money is completely ignored. The payback rule also fails to consider risk differences. The payback would be calculated the same way for both very risky and very safe projects.

Perhaps the biggest problem with the payback period rule is coming up with the right cutoff period, because we don't really have an objective basis for choosing a particular number. Put another way, there is no economic rationale for looking at payback in the first place, so we have no guide as to how to pick the cutoff. As a result, we end up using a number that is arbitrarily chosen.

Suppose we have somehow decided on an appropriate payback period, say two years or less. As we have seen, the payback period rule ignores the time value of money for the first two years. More seriously, cash flows after the second year are ignored entirely. To see this, consider the two investments, Long and Short, in Table 8.2. Both projects cost $250. Based on our discussion, the payback on Long is $2 + \$50/100 = 2.5$ years, and the payback on Short is $1 + \$150/200 = 1.75$ years. With a cutoff of two years, Short is acceptable and Long is not.

Is the payback period rule giving us the right decisions? Maybe not. Suppose again that we require a 15 percent return on this type of investment. We can calculate the NPV for these two investments as:

NPV(Short) = −$250 + 100/1.15 + 200/1.15² = −$11.81
NPV(Long) = −$250 + 100 × (1 − 1/1.15⁴)/.15 = $35.50

Now we have a problem. The NPV of the shorter-term investment is actually negative, meaning that taking it diminishes the value of the shareholders' equity. The opposite is true for the longer-term investment—it increases share value.

Our example illustrates two primary shortcomings of the payback period rule. First, by ignoring time value, we may be led to take investments (like Short) that actually are worth less than they cost. Second, by ignoring cash flows beyond the cutoff, we may be led to reject profitable long-term investments (like Long). More generally, using a payback period rule will tend to bias us towards shorter-term investments.

Year	Long	Short
0	−$250	−$250
1	100	100
2	100	200
3	100	0
4	100	0

TABLE 8.2

Investment projected cash flows

Redeeming Qualities of the Rule

Despite its shortcomings, the payback period rule is often used by large and sophisticated companies when they are making relatively minor decisions. There are several reasons for this. The primary reason is that many decisions simply do not warrant detailed analysis because the cost of the analysis would exceed the possible loss from a mistake. As a practical matter, an investment that pays back rapidly and has benefits extending beyond the cutoff period probably has a positive NPV.

Small investment decisions are made by the hundreds every day in large organizations. Moreover, they are made at all levels. As a result, it would not be uncommon for a corporation to require, for example, a two-year payback on all investments of less than $10,000. Investments larger than this are subjected to greater scrutiny. The requirement of a two-year payback is not perfect for reasons we have seen, but it does exercise some control over expenditures and thus has the effect of limiting possible losses.

In addition to its simplicity, the payback rule has two other positive features. First, because it is biased towards short-term projects, it is biased towards liquidity. In other words, a payback rule tends to favor investments that free up cash for other uses more quickly. This could be very important for a small business; it would be less so for a large corporation. Second, the cash flows that are expected to occur later in a project's life are probably more uncertain. Arguably, a payback period rule adjusts for the extra riskiness of later cash flows, but it does so in a rather draconian fashion—by ignoring them altogether.

We should note here that some of the apparent simplicity of the payback rule is an illusion. The reason is that we still must come up with the cash flows first, and, as we discuss above, this is not at all easy to do. Thus, it would probably be more accurate to say that the *concept* of a payback period is both intuitive and easy to understand.

Summary of the Rule

To summarize, the payback period is a kind of "break-even" measure. Because time value is ignored, you can think of the payback period as the length of time it takes to break even in an accounting sense, but not in an economic sense. The biggest drawback to the payback period rule is that it doesn't ask the right question. The relevant issue is the impact an investment will have on the value of our stock, not how long it takes to recover the initial investment.

Nevertheless, because it is so simple, companies often use it as a screen for dealing with the myriad of minor investment decisions they have to make. There is certainly nothing wrong with this practice. Like any simple rule of thumb, there will be some errors in using it, but it wouldn't have survived all this time if it weren't useful. Now that you understand the rule, you can be on the alert for those circumstances under which it might lead to problems. To help you remember, the following table lists the pros and cons of the payback period rule:

Advantages and Disadvantages of the Payback Period Rule	
Advantages	**Disadvantages**
1. Easy to understand.	1. Ignores the time value of money.
2. Adjusts for uncertainty of later cash flows.	2. Requires an arbitrary cutoff point.
3. Biased toward liquidity.	3. Ignores cash flows beyond the cutoff date.
	4. Biased against long-term projects, such as research and development, and new projects.

CONCEPT QUESTIONS

8.2a   In words, what is the payback period? The payback period rule?

8.2b   Why do we say that the payback period is, in a sense, an accounting break-even measure?

THE AVERAGE ACCOUNTING RETURN

8.3

Another attractive, but flawed, approach to making capital budgeting decisions involves the **average accounting return (AAR)**. There are many different definitions of the AAR. However, in one form or another, the AAR is always defined as:

Some measure of average accounting profit
Some measure of average accounting value

The specific definition we will use is:

Average net income
Average book value

To see how we might calculate this number, suppose we are deciding whether or not to open a store in a new shopping mall. The required investment in improvements is $500,000. The store would have a five-year life because everything reverts to the mall owners after that time. The required investment would be 100 percent depreciated (straight-line) over five years, so the depreciation would be $500,000/5 = $100,000 per year. The tax rate is 25 percent. Table 8.3 contains the projected revenues and expenses. Based on these figures, net income in each year is also shown.

To calculate the average book value for this investment, we note that we started out with a book value of $500,000 (the initial cost) and ended up at $0. The average book value during the life of the investment is thus ($500,000 + 0)/2 = $250,000. As long as we use straight-line depreciation and a zero salvage value, the average investment will always be one-half of the initial investment.[1]

average accounting return (AAR)
An investment's average net income divided by its average book value.

ExcelMaster
coverage online

	Year 1	Year 2	Year 3	Year 4	Year 5
Revenue	$433,333	$450,000	$266,667	$200,000	$133,333
Expenses	200,000	150,000	100,000	100,000	100,000
Earnings before depreciation	$233,333	$300,000	$166,667	$100,000	$ 33,333
Depreciation	100,000	100,000	100,000	100,000	100,000
Earnings before taxes	$133,333	$200,000	$ 66,667	$ 0	−$ 66,667
Taxes (25%)	33,333	50,000	16,667	0	− 16,667
Net income	$100,000	$150,000	$ 50,000	$ 0	−$ 50,000

TABLE 8.3

Projected yearly revenues and costs for average accounting return

$$\text{Average net income} = \frac{(\$100,000 + \$150,000 + \$50,000 + 0 - 50,000)}{5} = \$50,000$$

$$\text{Average book value} = \frac{\$500,000 + 0}{2} = \$250,000$$

---

[1] We could, of course, calculate the average of the six book values directly. In thousands, we would have ($500 + 400 + 300 + 200 + 100 + 0)/6 = $250.

Looking at Table 8.3, we see that net income is $100,000 in the first year, $150,000 in the second year, $50,000 in the third year, $0 in Year 4, and −$50,000 in Year 5. The average net income, then, is:

$$[\$100{,}000 + 150{,}000 + 50{,}000 + 0 + (-50{,}000)]/5 = \$50{,}000$$

The average accounting return is:

$$\text{AAR} = \frac{\textbf{Average net income}}{\textbf{Average book value}} = \frac{\$50{,}000}{250{,}000} = 20\%$$

If the firm has a target AAR less than 20 percent, then this investment is acceptable; otherwise, it is not. The *average accounting return rule* is thus:

Based on the average accounting return rule, a project is acceptable if its average accounting return exceeds a target average accounting return.

As we will see next, this rule has a number of problems.

You should recognize the chief drawback to the AAR immediately. Above all else, the AAR is not a rate of return in any meaningful economic sense. Instead, it is the ratio of two accounting numbers, and it is not comparable to the returns offered, for example, in financial markets.[2]

One of the reasons the AAR is not a true rate of return is that it ignores time value. When we average figures that occur at different times, we are treating the near future and the more distant future the same way. There was no discounting involved when we computed the average net income, for example.

The second problem with the AAR is similar to the problem we had with the payback period rule concerning the lack of an objective cutoff period. Since a calculated AAR is really not comparable to a market return, the target AAR must somehow be specified. There is no generally agreed-upon way to do this. One way of doing it is to calculate the AAR for the firm as a whole and use this as a benchmark, but there are lots of other ways as well.

The third, and perhaps worst, flaw in the AAR is that it doesn't even look at the right things. Instead of cash flow and market value, it uses net income and book value. These are both poor substitutes. As a result, an AAR doesn't tell us what the effect on share price will be from taking an investment, so it doesn't tell us what we really want to know.

Does the AAR have any redeeming features? About the only one is that it almost always can be computed. The reason is that accounting information will almost always be available, both for the project under consideration and for the firm as a whole. We hasten to add that once the accounting information is available, we can always convert it to cash flows, so even this is not a particularly important fact. The AAR is summarized in the table that follows:

Advantages and Disadvantages of the Average Accounting Return	
Advantages	**Disadvantages**
1. Easy to calculate.	1. Not a true rate of return; time value of money is ignored.
2. Needed information will usually be available.	2. Uses an arbitrary benchmark cutoff rate.
	3. Based on accounting net income and book values, not cash flows and market values.

---

[2] The AAR is closely related to the return on assets, or ROA, discussed in Chapter 3. In practice, the AAR is sometimes computed by first calculating the ROA for each year and then averaging the results. This produces a number that is similar, but not identical, to the one we computed.

8.3a   What is an average accounting rate of return, or AAR?

8.3b   What are the weaknesses of the AAR rule?

THE INTERNAL RATE OF RETURN

We now come to the most important alternative to NPV, the **internal rate of return**, universally known as the **IRR**. As we will see, the IRR is closely related to NPV. With the IRR, we try to find a single rate of return that summarizes the merits of a project. Furthermore, we want this rate to be an "internal" rate in the sense that it only depends on the cash flows of a particular investment, not on rates offered elsewhere.

internal rate of return (IRR)
The discount rate that makes the NPV of an investment zero.

To illustrate the idea behind the IRR, consider a project that costs $100 today and pays $110 in one year. Suppose you were asked, "What is the return on this investment?" What would you say? It seems both natural and obvious to say that the return is 10 percent because, for every dollar we put in, we get $1.10 back. In fact, as we will see in a moment, 10 percent is the internal rate of return, or IRR, on this investment.

ExcelMaster
coverage online

Is this project with its 10 percent IRR a good investment? Once again, it would seem apparent that this is a good investment only if our required return is less than 10 percent. This intuition is also correct and illustrates the *IRR rule:*

> **Based on the IRR rule, an investment is acceptable if the IRR exceeds the required return. It should be rejected otherwise.**

Imagine that we wanted to calculate the NPV for our simple investment. At a discount rate of *R,* the NPV is:

$$NPV = -\$100 + 110/(1 + R)$$

Now, suppose we didn't know the discount rate. This presents a problem, but we could still ask how high the discount rate would have to be before this project was unacceptable. We know that we are indifferent between taking and not taking this investment when its NPV is just equal to zero. In other words, this investment is *economically* a break-even proposition when the NPV is zero because value is neither created nor destroyed. To find the break-even discount rate, we set NPV equal to zero and solve for *R:*

$$NPV = 0 = -\$100 + 110/(1 + R)$$
$$\$100 = \$110/(1 + R)$$
$$1 + R = \$110/100 = 1.10$$
$$R = 10\%$$

This 10 percent is what we already have called the return on this investment. What we have now illustrated is that the internal rate of return on an investment (or just "return" for short) is the discount rate that makes the NPV equal to zero. This is an important observation, so it bears repeating:

> **The IRR on an investment is the required return that results in a zero NPV when it is used as the discount rate.**

The fact that the IRR is simply the discount rate that makes the NPV equal to zero is important because it tells us how to calculate the returns on more complicated investments. As we have seen, finding the IRR turns out to be relatively easy for a single-period investment. However, suppose you were now looking at an investment with the cash flows shown in Figure 8.3. As illustrated, this investment costs $100 and has a cash flow of $60 per year for two years, so it's only slightly more complicated than our single-period example. However, if you were asked for the return on this investment, what would you say? There doesn't seem to be any obvious answer (at least to us). However, based on what we now know, we can set the NPV equal to zero and solve for the discount rate:

$$\text{NPV} = 0 = -\$100 + 60/(1 + \text{IRR}) + 60/(1 + \text{IRR})^2$$

Unfortunately, the only way to find the IRR in general is by trial and error, either by hand or by calculator. This is precisely the same problem that came up in Chapter 5 when we found the unknown rate for an annuity and in Chapter 6 when we found the yield to maturity on a bond. In fact, we now see that, in both of those cases, we were finding an IRR.

In this particular case, the cash flows form a two-period, $60 annuity. To find the unknown rate, we can try some different rates until we get the answer. If we were to start with a 0 percent rate, the NPV would obviously be $120 − 100 = $20. At a 10 percent discount rate, we would have:

$$\text{NPV} = -\$100 + 60/1.1 + 60/1.1^2 = \$4.13$$

Now, we're getting close. We can summarize these and some other possibilities as shown in Table 8.4. From our calculations, the NPV appears to be zero between 10 percent and 15 percent, so the IRR is somewhere in that range. With a little more effort, we can find that the IRR is about 13.1 percent. So, if our required return is less than 13.1 percent, we would take this investment. If our required return exceeds 13.1 percent, we would reject it.

By now, you have probably noticed that the IRR rule and the NPV rule appear to be quite similar. In fact, the IRR is sometimes simply called the *discounted cash flow,* or *DCF, return.* The easiest way to illustrate the relationship between NPV and IRR is to plot the numbers we calculated in Table 8.4. We put the different NPVs on the vertical axis, or *y*-axis, and the discount rates on the horizontal axis, or *x*-axis. If we had a very large number of points, the resulting picture would be a smooth curve called a

FIGURE 8.3			
Project cash flows			

TABLE 8.4	Discount Rate	NPV
NPV at different	0%	$20.00
discount rates	5	11.56
	10	4.13
	15	− 2.46
	20	− 8.33

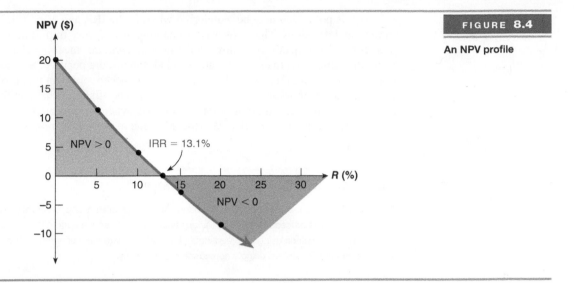

FIGURE 8.4

An NPV profile

net present value profile. Figure 8.4 illustrates the NPV profile for this project. Beginning with a 0 percent discount rate, we have $20 plotted directly on the *y*-axis. As the discount rate increases, the NPV declines smoothly. Where will the curve cut through the *x*-axis? This will occur where the NPV is just equal to zero, so it will happen right at the IRR of 13.1 percent.

In our example, the NPV rule and the IRR rule lead to identical accept-reject decisions. We will accept an investment using the IRR rule if the required return is less than 13.1 percent. As Figure 8.4 illustrates, however, the NPV is positive at any discount rate less than 13.1 percent, so we would accept the investment using the NPV rule as well. The two rules are equivalent in this case.

net present value profile
A graphical representation of the relationship between an investment's NPV and various discount rates.

CALCULATING THE IRR

EXAMPLE 8.3

A project has a total up-front cost of $435.44. The cash flows are $100 in the first year, $200 in the second year, and $300 in the third year. What's the IRR? If we require an 18 percent return, should we take this investment?

We'll describe the NPV profile and find the IRR by calculating some NPVs at different discount rates. You should check our answers for practice. Beginning with 0 percent, we have:

Discount Rate	NPV
0%	$164.56
5	100.36
10	46.15
15	.00
20	−39.61

The NPV is zero at 15 percent, so 15 percent is the IRR. If we require an 18 percent return, then we should not take the investment. The reason is that the NPV is negative at 18 percent (verify that it is −$24.47). The IRR rule tells us the same thing in this case. We shouldn't take this investment because its 15 percent return is below our required 18 percent return.

At this point, you may be wondering whether the IRR and NPV rules always lead to identical decisions. The answer is yes as long as two very important conditions are met. First, the project's cash flows must be *conventional,* meaning that the first cash flow (the initial investment) is negative and all the rest are positive. Second, the project must be *independent,* meaning that the decision to accept or reject this project does not affect the decision to accept or reject any other. The first of these conditions is typically met, but the second often is not. In any case, when one or both of these conditions are not met, problems can arise. We discuss some of these in a moment.

SPREADSHEET STRATEGIES

Calculating IRRs with a Spreadsheet

Because IRRs are so tedious to calculate by hand, financial calculators and, especially, spreadsheets are generally used. The procedures used by various financial calculators are too different for us to illustrate here, so we will focus on using a spreadsheet (financial calculators are covered in Appendix D). As the following example illustrates, using a spreadsheet is very easy:

	A	B	C	D	E	F	G	H
1								
2	Using a spreadsheet to calculate internal rates of return							
3								
4	Suppose we have a four-year project that costs $500. The cash flows over the four-year life will be							
5	$100, $200, $300, and $400. What is the IRR?							
6								
7		Year	Cash flow					
8		0	−$500					
9		1	100		IRR =	27.3%		
10		2	200					
11		3	300					
12		4	400					
13								
14								
15	The formula entered in cell F9 is = IRR(C8:C12). Notice that the Year 0 cash flow has a negative sign,							
16	representing the initial cost of the project.							
17								

Problems with the IRR

The problems with the IRR come about when the cash flows are not conventional or when we are trying to compare two or more investments to see which is best. In the first case, surprisingly, the simple question "What's the return?" can become very difficult to answer. In the second case, the IRR can be a misleading guide.

Nonconventional Cash Flows   Suppose we have a strip-mining project that requires a $60 investment. Our cash flow in the first year will be $155. In the second year, the mine is depleted, but we have to spend $100 to restore the terrain. As Figure 8.5 illustrates, both the first and third cash flows are negative.

Year 0	1	2
−$60	+$155	−$100

FIGURE 8.5

Project cash flows

To find the IRR on this project, we can calculate the NPV at various rates:

Discount Rate	NPV
0%	−$5.00
10	−1.74
20	−.28
30	.06
40	−.31

The NPV appears to be behaving in a very peculiar fashion here. First, as the discount rate increases from 0 percent to 30 percent, the NPV starts out negative and becomes positive. This seems backward because the NPV is rising as the discount rate rises. It then starts getting smaller and becomes negative again. What's the IRR? To find out, we draw the NPV profile in Figure 8.6.

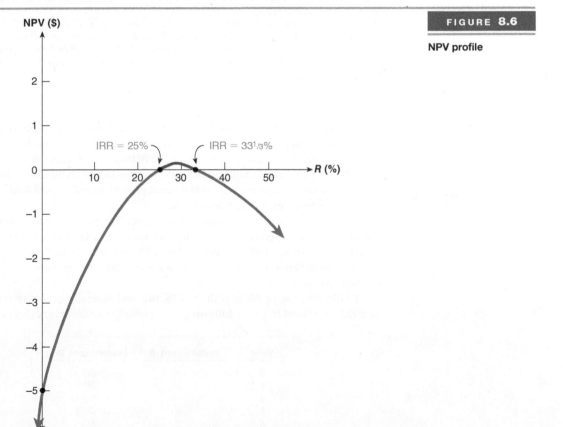

FIGURE 8.6

NPV profile

In Figure 8.6, notice that the NPV is zero when the discount rate is 25 percent, so this is the IRR. Or is it? The NPV is also zero at 33⅓ percent. Which of these is correct? The answer is both or neither; more precisely, there is no unambiguously correct answer. This is the **multiple rates of return** problem. Many computer spreadsheet packages aren't aware of this problem and just report the first IRR that is found. Others report only the smallest positive IRR, even though this answer is no better than any other. For example, if you enter this problem in our spreadsheet above, it will simply report that the IRR is 25 percent.

multiple rates of return
The possibility that more than one discount rate makes the NPV of an investment zero.

In our current example, the IRR rule breaks down completely. Suppose our required return was 10 percent. Should we take this investment? Both IRRs are greater than 10 percent, so, by the IRR rule, maybe we should. However, as Figure 8.6 shows, the NPV is negative at any discount rate less than 25 percent, so this is not a good investment. When should we take it? Looking at Figure 8.6 one last time, we see that the NPV is positive only if our required return is between 25 percent and 33⅓ percent.

The moral of the story is that when the cash flows aren't conventional, strange things can start to happen to the IRR. This is not anything to get upset about, however, because the NPV rule, as always, works just fine. This illustrates that, oddly enough, the obvious question "What's the rate of return?" may not always have a good answer.

EXAMPLE 8.4

WHAT'S THE IRR?

You are looking at an investment that requires you to invest $51 today. You'll get $100 in one year, but you must pay out $50 in two years. What is the IRR on this investment?

You're on the alert now to the nonconventional cash flow problem, so you probably wouldn't be surprised to see more than one IRR. However, if you start looking for an IRR by trial and error, it will take you a long time. The reason is that there is no IRR. The NPV is negative at every discount rate, so we shouldn't take this investment under any circumstances. What's the return on this investment? Your guess is as good as ours.

Mutually Exclusive Investments   Even if there is a single IRR, another problem can arise concerning **mutually exclusive investment decisions**. If two investments, X and Y, are mutually exclusive, then taking one of them means that we cannot take the other. Two projects that are not mutually exclusive are said to be independent. For example, if we own one corner lot, then we can build a gas station or an apartment building, but not both. These are mutually exclusive alternatives.

mutually exclusive investment decisions
A situation where taking one investment prevents the taking of another.

Thus far, we have asked whether or not a given investment is worth undertaking. There is a related question, however, that comes up very often: Given two or more mutually exclusive investments, which one is the best? The answer is simple enough: The best one is the one with the largest NPV. Can we also say that the best one has the highest return? As we show, the answer is no.

To illustrate the problem with the IRR rule and mutually exclusive investments, consider the cash flows from the following two mutually exclusive investments:

Year	Investment A	Investment B
0	−$100	−$100
1	50	20
2	40	40
3	40	50
4	30	60

The IRR for A is 24 percent, and the IRR for B is 21 percent. Since these investments are mutually exclusive, we can only take one of them. Simple intuition suggests that Investment A is better because of its higher return. Unfortunately, simple intuition is not always correct.

To see why Investment A is not necessarily the better of the two investments, we've calculated the NPV of these investments for different required returns:

Discount Rate	NPV (A)	NPV (B)
0%	$60.00	$70.00
5	43.13	47.88
10	29.06	29.79
15	17.18	14.82
20	7.06	2.31
25	−1.63	−8.22

The IRR for A (24 percent) is larger than the IRR for B (21 percent). However, if you compare the NPVs, you'll see that which investment has the higher NPV depends on our required return. B has greater total cash flow, but it pays back more slowly than A. As a result, it has a higher NPV at lower discount rates.

In our example, the NPV and IRR rankings conflict for some discount rates. If our required return is 10 percent, for instance, then B has the higher NPV and is thus the better of the two, even though A has the higher IRR. If our required return is 15 percent, then there is no ranking conflict: A is better.

The conflict between the IRR and NPV for mutually exclusive investments can be illustrated by plotting their NPV profiles as we have done in Figure 8.7. In Figure 8.7, notice

FIGURE 8.7

NPV profiles for mutually exclusive investments

that the NPV profiles cross at 11.1 percent. Notice also that at any discount rate less than 11.1 percent, the NPV for B is higher. In this range, taking B benefits us more than taking A, even though A's IRR is higher. At any rate greater than 11.1 percent, Investment A has the greater NPV.

This example illustrates that whenever we have mutually exclusive projects, we shouldn't rank them based on their returns. More generally, anytime we are comparing investments to determine which is best, IRRs can be misleading. Instead, we need to look at the relative NPVs to avoid the possibility of choosing incorrectly. Remember, we're ultimately interested in creating value for the shareholders, so the option with the higher NPV is preferred, regardless of the relative returns.

If this seems counterintuitive, think of it this way. Suppose you have two investments. One has a 10 percent return and makes you $100 richer immediately. The other has a 20 percent return and makes you $50 richer immediately. Which one do you like better? We would rather have $100 than $50, regardless of the returns, so we like the first one better.

As we saw from Figure 8.7, the crossover rate for Investment A and Investment B is 11.1 percent. You might be wondering how we got this number. Actually, the calculation is fairly easy. We begin by subtracting the cash flows from one project from the cash flows of the second project. In this case, we will subtract Investment B from Investment A. Doing so, we get:

Year	Investment A	Investment B	Cash Flow Difference (A – B)
0	–$100	–$100	$ 0
1	50	20	30
2	40	40	0
3	40	50	–10
4	30	60	–30

Now all we have to do is calculate the IRR for these differential cash flows, which works out to be 11.1 percent. Verify for yourself that if you subtract Investment A's cash flows from Investment B's cash flows the crossover rate is still 11.1 percent, so it doesn't matter which one you subtract from which.

Redeeming Qualities of the IRR

Despite its flaws, the IRR is very popular in practice, more so than even the NPV. It probably survives because it fills a need that the NPV does not. In analyzing investments, people in general, and financial analysts in particular, seem to prefer talking about rates of return rather than dollar values.

In a similar vein, the IRR also appears to provide a simple way of communicating information about a proposal. One manager might say to another, "Remodeling the clerical wing has a 20 percent return." This may somehow be simpler than saying, "At a 10 percent discount rate, the net present value is $4,000."

Finally, under certain circumstances, the IRR may have a practical advantage over the NPV. We can't estimate the NPV unless we know the appropriate discount rate, but we can still estimate the IRR. Suppose we didn't know the required return on an investment, but we found, for example, that it had a 40 percent return. We would probably be inclined to take it since it is very unlikely that the required return would be that high. The advantages and disadvantages of the IRR are summarized on the next page.

Advantages and Disadvantages of the Internal Rate of Return	
Advantages	**Disadvantages**
1. Closely related to NPV, often leading to identical decisions.	1. May result in multiple answers with nonconventional cash flows.
2. Easy to understand and communicate.	2. May lead to incorrect decisions in comparisons of mutually exclusive investments.

The Modified Internal Rate of Return (MIRR)

To address some of the problems that can crop up with the standard IRR, it is often proposed that a modified version be used. As we will see, there are several different ways of calculating a modified IRR, or MIRR, but the idea is to modify the cash flows first and then calculate IRR using the modified cash flows.

To illustrate, let's go back to the cash flows in Figure 8.5: −$60, +$155, and −$100. As we saw, there are two IRRs, 25 percent and 33⅓ percent. We next illustrate three different MIRRs, all of which have the property that only one answer will result, thereby eliminating the multiple IRR problem.

Method 1: The Discounting Approach   With the discounting approach, the idea is to discount all negative cash flows back to the present at the required return and add them to the initial cost. Then, calculate the IRR. Because only the first modified cash flow is negative, there will be only one IRR. The discount rate used might be the required return, or it might be some other exernally supplied rate. We will use the project's required return.

If the required return on the project is 20 percent, then the modified cash flows look like this:

Time 0: $-\$60 + \frac{-\$100}{1.20^2} = -\$129.44$

Time 1:   +$155

Time 2:   +$0

If you calculate the MIRR now, you should get 19.74 percent.

Method 2: The Reinvestment Approach   With the reinvestment approach, we compound *all* cash flows (positive and negative) except the first out to the end of the project's life and then calculate the IRR. In a sense, we are "reinvesting" the cash flows and not taking them out of the project until the very end. The rate we use could be the required return on the project, or it could be a separately specified "reinvestment rate." We will use the project's required return. When we do, here are the modified cash flows:

Time 0:   −$60

Time 1:   +0

Time 2: $-\$100 + (\$155 \times 1.2) = \$86$

The MIRR on this set of cash flows is 19.72 percent, or a little lower than we got using the discounting approach.

Method 3: The Combination Approach   As the name suggests, the combination approach blends our first two methods. Negative cash flows are discounted back to the present, and positive cash flows are compounded to the end of the project. In practice, different discount or compounding rates might be used, but we will again stick with the project's required return.

With the combination approach, the modified cash flows are as follows:

Time 0: $-\$60 + \dfrac{-\$100}{1.20^2} = -\$129.44$

Time 1: $+0$

Time 2: $\$155 \times 1.2 = \$186$

See if you don't agree that the MIRR is 19.87, the highest of the three.

MIRR or IRR: Which Is Better?

MIRRs are controversial. At one extreme are those who claim that MIRRs are superior to IRRs, period. For example, by design, they clearly don't suffer from the multiple rate of return problem.

At the other end, detractors say that MIRR should stand for "meaningless internal rate of return." As our example makes clear, one problem with MIRRs is that there are different ways of calculating them, and there is no clear reason to say one of our three methods is better than any other. The differences are small with our simple cash flows, but they could be much larger for a more complex project. Further, it's not clear how to interpret an MIRR. It may look like a rate of return; but it's a rate of return on a modified set of cash flows, not the project's actual cash flows.

We're not going to take sides. However, notice that calculating an MIRR requires discounting, compounding, or both, which leads to two obvious observations. First, if we have the relevant discount rate, why not calculate the NPV and be done with it? Second, because an MIRR depends on an externally supplied discount (or compounding) rate, the answer you get is not truly an "internal" rate of return, which, by definition, depends on only the project's cash flows.

We *will* take a stand on one issue that frequently comes up in this context. The value of a project does not depend on what the firm does with the cash flows generated by that project. A firm might use a project's cash flows to fund other projects, to pay dividends, or to buy an executive jet. It doesn't matter: How the cash flows are spent in the future does not affect their value today. As a result, there is generally no need to consider reinvestment of interim cash flows.

CONCEPT QUESTIONS

8.4a   Under what circumstances will the IRR and NPV rules lead to the same accept-reject decisions? When might they conflict?

8.4b   Is it generally true that an advantage of the IRR rule over the NPV rule is that we don't need to know the required return to use the IRR rule?

8.5   THE PROFITABILITY INDEX

profitability index (PI)

The present value of an investment's future cash flows divided by its initial cost. Also, benefit-cost ratio.

Another method used to evaluate projects involves the **profitability index (PI)**, or benefit-cost ratio. This index is defined as the present value of the future cash flows divided by the initial investment. So, if a project costs $200 and the present value of its future cash flows is $220, the profitability index value would be $220/200 = 1.10. Notice that the NPV for this investment is $20, so it is a desirable investment.

More generally, if a project has a positive NPV, then the present value of the future cash flows must be bigger than the initial investment. The profitability index would thus be bigger than 1.00 for a positive NPV investment and less than 1.00 for a negative NPV investment.

How do we interpret the profitability index? In our example, the PI was 1.10. This tells us that, per dollar invested, $1.10 in value or $.10 in NPV results. The profitability index thus measures "bang for the buck," that is, the value created per dollar invested. For this reason, it is often proposed as a measure of performance for government or other not-for-profit investments. Also, when capital is scarce, it may make sense to allocate it to those projects with the highest PIs.

The PI is obviously very similar to the NPV. However, consider an investment that costs $5 and has a $10 present value and an investment that costs $100 with a $150 present value. The first of these investments has an NPV of $5 and a PI of 2. The second has an NPV of $50 and a PI of 1.50. If these are mutually exclusive investments, then the second one is preferred, even though it has a lower PI. This ranking problem is very similar to the IRR ranking problem we saw in the previous section. In all, there seems to be little reason to rely on the PI instead of the NPV. Our discussion of the PI is summarized below:

ExcelMaster
coverage online

Advantages and Disadvantages of the Profitability Index	
Advantages	**Disadvantages**
1. Closely related to NPV, generally leading to identical decisions.	1. May lead to incorrect decisions in comparisons of mutually exclusive investments.
2. Easy to understand and communicate.	
3. May be useful when available investment funds are limited.	

CONCEPT QUESTIONS

8.5a   What does the profitability index measure?

8.5b   How would you state the profitability index rule?

THE PRACTICE OF CAPITAL BUDGETING

8.6

Given that NPV seems to be telling us directly what we want to know, you might be wondering why there are so many other procedures and why alternative procedures are commonly used. Recall that we are trying to make an investment decision and that we are frequently operating under considerable uncertainty about the future. We can only *estimate* the NPV of an investment in this case. The resulting estimate can be very "soft," meaning that the true NPV might be quite different.

Because the true NPV is unknown, the astute financial manager seeks clues to assess whether the estimated NPV is reliable. For this reason, firms would typically use multiple criteria for evaluating a proposal. For example, suppose we have an investment with a positive estimated NPV. Based on our experience with other projects, this one appears to have a short payback and a very high AAR. In this case, the different indicators seem to agree that it's "all systems go." Put another way, the payback and the AAR are consistent with the conclusion that the NPV is positive.

On the other hand, suppose we had a positive estimated NPV, a long payback, and a low AAR. This could still be a good investment, but it looks like we need to be much more careful in making the decision since we are getting conflicting signals. If the estimated NPV is based on projections in which we have little confidence, then further analysis is probably in order. We will consider how to go about this analysis in more detail in the next chapter.

Large firms often have huge capital budgets. For example, for 2012, ExxonMobil announced that it expected to have about $37 billion in capital outlays during the year, up from $36.8 billion in 2011. In fact, ExxonMobil was expected to spend $37 billion per year for several years beyond 2012. About the same time, competitor Chevron announced that its capital budget for 2012 would be $32.7 billion, down slightly from $33 billion in 2011. Other companies with large capital spending budgets were Walmart, which projected capital spending of about $13 to $14 billion for 2012, and McDonald's, which projected capital spending of about $2.9 billion to open 1,325 outlets in 2012.

Large-scale capital spending is often an industrywide occurrence. For example, in 2012, capital spending in the semiconductor industry was expected to be $51.7 billion. This tidy sum actually represented a 20 percent decrease compared to 2011. But on a brighter note, capital spending was expected to increase to $61.6 billion in 2013.

According to information released by the Census Bureau in 2011, capital investment for the economy as a whole was $1.090 trillion in 2009, $1.375 trillion in 2008, and $1.355 trillion in 2007. The totals for the three years therefore exceeded $3.8 trillion! Given the sums at stake, it is not too surprising that careful analysis of capital expenditures is something at which successful businesses seek to become adept.

There have been a number of surveys conducted asking firms what types of investment criteria they actually use. Table 8.5 summarizes the results of several of these. The first part of the table is a historical comparison looking at the primary capital budgeting techniques used by large firms through time. In 1959, only 19 percent of the firms surveyed used either IRR or NPV, and 68 percent used either payback periods or accounting returns. It is clear that, by the 1980s, IRR and NPV had become the dominant criteria.

TABLE 8.5	**Capital budgeting techniques in practice**

A. Historical Comparison of the Primary Use of Various Capital Budgeting Techniques							
	1959	**1964**	**1970**	**1975**	**1977**	**1979**	**1981**
Payback period	34%	24%	12%	15%	9%	10%	5.0%
Average accounting return (AAR)	34	30	26	10	25	14	10.7
Internal rate of return (IRR)	19	38	57	37	54	60	65.3
Net present value (NPV)	—	—	—	26	10	14	16.5
IRR or NPV	19	38	57	63	64	74	81.8

B. Percentage of CFOs Who Always or Almost Always Use a Given Technique in 1999				
Capital Budgeting Technique	**Percentage Always or Almost Always Use**	**Average Score Scale is 4 (always) to 0 (never)**		
		Overall	**Large Firms**	**Small Firms**
Internal rate of return	76%	3.09	3.41	2.87
Net present value	75	3.08	3.42	2.83
Payback period	57	2.53	2.25	2.72
Accounting rate of return	20	1.34	1.25	1.41
Profitability index	12	0.83	0.75	0.88

Sources: J. R. Graham and C. R. Harvey, "The Theory and Practice of Corporate Finance: Evidence from the Field," *Journal of Financial Economics,* May–June 2001, pp. 187–244; J. S. Moore and A. K. Reichert, "An Analysis of the Financial Management Techniques Currently Employed by Large U.S. Corporations," *Journal of Business Finance and Accounting,* Winter 1983, pp. 623–45; M. T. Stanley and S. B. Block, "A Survey of Multinational Capital Budgeting," *The Financial Review,* March 1984, pp. 36–51.

Panel B of Table 8.5 summarizes the results of a 1999 survey of chief financial officers (CFOs) at both large and small firms in the United States. A total of 392 CFOs responded. What is shown is the percentage of CFOs who always or almost always use the various capital budgeting techniques we described in this chapter. Not surprisingly, IRR and NPV are the two most widely used techniques, particularly at larger firms. However, over half of the respondents always, or almost always, use the payback criterion as well. In fact, among smaller firms, payback is used just about as much as NPV and IRR. Less commonly used are accounting rates of return and the profitability index. For quick reference, these criteria are briefly summarized in Table 8.6.

CONCEPT QUESTIONS

8.6a   What are the most commonly used capital budgeting procedures?

8.6b   Since NPV is conceptually the best tool for capital budgeting, why do you think multiple measures are used in practice?

TABLE 8.6   **Summary of investment criteria**

I.   Discounted cash flow criteria

    A. *Net present value (NPV).* The NPV of an investment is the difference between its market value and its cost. The NPV rule is to take a project if its NPV is positive. NPV is frequently estimated by calculating the present value of the future cash flows (to estimate market value) and then subtracting the cost. NPV has no serious flaws; it is the preferred decision criterion.

    B. *Internal rate of return (IRR).* The IRR is the discount rate that makes the estimated NPV of an investment equal to zero; it is sometimes called the *discounted cash flow (DCF) return.* The IRR rule is to take a project when its IRR exceeds the required return. IRR is closely related to NPV, and it leads to exactly the same decisions as NPV for conventional, independent projects. When project cash flows are not conventional, there may be no IRR or there may be more than one. More seriously, the IRR cannot be used to rank mutually exclusive projects; the project with the highest IRR is not necessarily the preferred investment.

    C. *Modified internal rate of return (MIRR).* The MIRR is a modification to the IRR. A project's cash flows are modified by (1) discounting the negative cash flows back to the present; (2) compounding all cash flows to the end of the project's life; or (3) combining (1) and (2). An IRR is then computed on the modified cash flows. MIRRs are guaranteed to avoid the multiple rate of return problem. But, it is unclear how to interpret them, and they are not truly "internal" because they depend on externally supplied discounting or compounding rates.

    D. *Profitability index (PI).* The PI, also called the *benefit-cost ratio,* is the ratio of present value to cost. The PI rule is to take an investment if the index exceeds 1. The PI measures the present value of an investment per dollar invested. It is quite similar to NPV, but, like IRR, it cannot be used to rank mutually exclusive projects. However, it is sometimes used to rank projects when a firm has more positive NPV investments than it can currently finance.

II.   Payback criteria

    A. *Payback period.* The payback period is the length of time until the sum of an investment's cash flows equals its cost. The payback period rule is to take a project if its payback is *less* than some cutoff. The payback period is a flawed criterion primarily because it ignores risk, the time value of money, and cash flows beyond the cutoff point.

III.   Accounting criteria

    A. *Average accounting return (AAR).* The AAR is a measure of accounting profit relative to book value. It is *not* related to the IRR, but it is similar to the accounting return on assets (ROA) measure in Chapter 3. The AAR rule is to take an investment if its AAR exceeds a benchmark AAR. The AAR is seriously flawed for a variety of reasons, and it has little to recommend it.

SUMMARY AND CONCLUSIONS

◀ Think you've mastered the material? Scan here to take a chapter quiz.

This chapter has covered the different criteria used to evaluate proposed investments. The five criteria, in the order in which we discussed them, are:

1. Net present value (NPV)
2. Payback period
3. Average accounting return (AAR)
4. Internal rate of return (IRR)
5. Modified internal rate of return (MIRR)
6. Profitability index (PI)

We illustrated how to calculate each of these and discussed the interpretation of the results. We also described the advantages and disadvantages of each of them. Ultimately, a good capital budgeting criterion must tell us two things. First, is a particular project a good investment? Second, if we have more than one good project, but we can only take one of them, which one should we take? The main point of this chapter is that only the NPV criterion can always provide the correct answer to both questions.

For this reason, NPV is one of the two or three most important concepts in finance, and we will refer to it many times in the chapters ahead. When we do, keep two things in mind: (1) NPV is always just the difference between the market value of an asset or project and its cost and (2) the financial manager acts in the shareholders' best interests by identifying and taking positive NPV projects.

Finally, we noted that NPVs can't normally be observed in the market; instead, they must be estimated. Because there is always the possibility of a poor estimate, financial managers use multiple criteria for examining projects. These other criteria provide additional information about whether a project truly has a positive NPV.

 connect POP QUIZ!
|FINANCE

Can you answer the following questions? If your class is using *Connect Finance,* log on to the Self-Quiz and Study feature in the Library tab to see if you know the answers to these and other questions, check out the study tools, and find out what topics require additional practice!

Section 8.2 An investment project provides cash inflows of $1,000 per year for eight years. What is the project payback period if the initial cost is $3,550?

Section 8.3 What will increase the average accounting return for a proposed project, all else held constant?

CHAPTER REVIEW AND SELF-TEST PROBLEMS

8.1 Investment Criteria. This problem will give you some practice calculating NPVs and paybacks. A proposed overseas expansion has the following cash flows:

Year	Cash Flow
0	−$100
1	50
2	40
3	40
4	15

Calculate the payback and NPV at a required return of 15 percent. (See Problem 21.)

8.2 Mutually Exclusive Investments. Consider the following two mutually exclusive investments. Calculate the IRR for each. Under what circumstances will the IRR and NPV criteria rank the two projects differently? (See Problem 8.)

Year	Investment A	Investment B
0	−$100	−$100
1	50	70
2	70	75
3	40	10

8.3 Average Accounting Return. You are looking at a three-year project with a projected net income of $1,000 in Year 1, $2,000 in Year 2, and $4,000 in Year 3. The cost is $9,000, which will be depreciated straight-line to zero over the three-year life of the project. What is the average accounting return, or AAR? (See Problem 4.)

■ Answers to Chapter Review and Self-Test Problems

8.1 In the table below, we have listed the cash flows and their discounted values (at 15 percent).

	Cash Flow	
Year	Undiscounted	Discounted (at 15%)
1	$ 50	$ 43.48
2	40	30.25
3	40	26.30
4	15	8.58
Total	$145	$108.61

Recall that the initial investment is $100. Examining the undiscounted cash flows, we see that the payback occurs between Years 2 and 3. The cash flows for the first two years are $90 total, so, going into the third year, we are short by $10. The total cash flow in Year 3 is $40, so the payback is 2 + $10/40 = 2.25 years.

Looking at the discounted cash flows, we see that the sum is $108.61, so the NPV is $8.61.

8.2 To calculate the IRR, we might try some guesses as in the following table:

Discount Rate	NPV(A)	NPV(B)
0%	$60.00	$55.00
10	33.36	33.13
20	13.43	16.20
30	− 1.91	2.78
40	−13.99	− 8.09

Several things are immediately apparent from our guesses. First, the IRR on A must be just a little less than 30 percent (why?). With some more effort, we find that it's 28.61 percent. For B, the IRR must be a little more than 30 percent (again, why?); it works out to be 32.37 percent. Also, notice that at 10 percent, the NPVs are very close, indicating that the NPV profiles cross in that vicinity. Verify that the NPVs are the same at 10.61 percent.

Now, the IRR for B is always higher. As we've seen, A has the larger NPV for any discount rate less than 10.61 percent, so the NPV and IRR rankings will conflict in that range. Remember, if there's a conflict, we will go with the higher NPV. Our decision rule is thus very simple: Take A if the required return is less than 10.61 percent, take B if the required return is between 10.61 percent and 32.37 percent (the IRR on B), and take neither if the required return is more than 32.37 percent.

8.3 Here we need to calculate the ratio of average net income to average book value to get the AAR. Average net income is:

Average net income = ($1,000 + 2,000 + 4,000)/3
= $2,333.33

Average book value is:

Average book value = $9,000/2 = $4,500

So, the average accounting return is:

AAR = $2,333.33/4,500 = 51.85%

This is an impressive return. Remember, however, that it isn't really a rate of return like an interest rate or an IRR, so the size doesn't tell us a lot. In particular, our money is probably not going to grow at 51.85 percent per year, sorry to say.

CRITICAL THINKING AND CONCEPTS REVIEW

LO 4 **LO 1** 8.1. **Payback Period and Net Present Value.** If a project with conventional cash flows has a payback period less than its life, can you definitively state the algebraic sign of the NPV? Why or why not?

LO 4 8.2. **Net Present Value.** Suppose a project has conventional cash flows and a positive NPV. What do you know about its payback? Its profitability index? Its IRR? Explain.

LO 1   8.3.   **Payback Period.**   Concerning payback:

   a.   Describe how the payback period is calculated and describe the information this measure provides about a sequence of cash flows. What is the payback criterion decision rule?

   b.   What are the problems associated with using the payback period as a means of evaluating cash flows?

   c.   What are the advantages of using the payback period to evaluate cash flows? Are there any circumstances under which using payback might be appropriate? Explain.

LO 2   8.4.   **Average Accounting Return.**   Concerning AAR:

   a.   Describe how the average accounting return is usually calculated and describe the information this measure provides about a sequence of cash flows. What is the AAR criterion decision rule?

   b.   What are the problems associated with using the AAR as a means of evaluating a project's cash flows? What underlying feature of AAR is most troubling to you from a financial perspective? Does the AAR have any redeeming qualities?

LO 4   8.5.   **Net Present Value.**   Concerning NPV:

   a.   Describe how NPV is calculated and describe the information this measure provides about a sequence of cash flows. What is the NPV criterion decision rule?

   b.   Why is NPV considered to be a superior method of evaluating the cash flows from a project? Suppose the NPV for a project's cash flows is computed to be $2,500. What does this number represent with respect to the firm's shareholders?

LO 3   8.6.   **Internal Rate of Return.**   Concerning IRR:

   a.   Describe how the IRR is calculated, and describe the information this measure provides about a sequence of cash flows. What is the IRR criterion decision rule?

   b.   What is the relationship between IRR and NPV? Are there any situations in which you might prefer one method over the other? Explain.

   c.   Despite its shortcomings in some situations, why do most financial managers use IRR along with NPV when evaluating projects? Can you think of a situation in which IRR might be a more appropriate measure to use than NPV? Explain.

LO 6   8.7.   **Profitability Index.**   Concerning the profitability index:

   a.   Describe how the profitability index is calculated and describe the information this measure provides about a sequence of cash flows. What is the profitability index decision rule?

   b.   What is the relationship between the profitability index and the NPV? Are there any situations in which you might prefer one method over the other? Explain.

LO 3   **LO 1**   8.8.   **Payback and Internal Rate of Return.**   A project has perpetual cash flows of C per period, a cost of I, and a required return of R. What is the relationship between the project's payback and its IRR? What implications does your answer have for long-lived projects with relatively constant cash flows?

266   **PART 5**   Capital Budgeting

LO 4   **8.9.   International Investment Projects.**   In October 2011, automobile manufacturer Daimler AG announced plains to invest $350 million to manufacture an entirely new Mercedes-Benz model at its Alabama plant. Daimler AG apparently felt that it would be better able to compete and create value with U.S-based facilities. Other companies such as Fuji Film and Swiss chemical company Lonza have reached similar conclusions and taken similar actions. What are some of the reasons that foreign manufacturers of products as diverse as automobiles, film, and chemicals might arrive at this same conclusion?

LO 4   **8.10.   Capital Budgeting Problems.**   What are some of the difficulties that might come up in actual applications of the various criteria we discussed in this chapter? Which one would be the easiest to implement in actual applications? The most difficult?

LO 4   **8.11.   Capital Budgeting in Not-for-Profit Entities.**   Are the capital budgeting criteria we discussed applicable to not-for-profit corporations? How should such entities make capital budgeting decisions? What about the U.S. government? Should it evaluate spending proposals using these techniques?

LO 3   **8.12.   Internal Rate of Return.**   In a previous chapter, we discussed the yield to maturity (YTM) of a bond. In what ways are the IRR and the YTM similar? How are they different?

LO 5   **8.13.   Modified Internal Rate of Return.**   One of the less flattering interpretations of the acronym MIRR is "meaningless internal rate of return." Why do you think this term is applied to MIRR?

LO 4   **8.14.   Net Present Value.**   It is sometimes stated that "the net present value approach assumes reinvestment of the intermediate cash flows at the required return." Is this claim correct? To answer, suppose you calculate the NPV of a project in the usual way. Next, suppose you do the following:

    a.   Calculate the future value (as of the end of the project) of all the cash flows other than the initial outlay assuming they are reinvested at the required return, producing a single future value figure for the project.

    b.   Calculate the NPV of the project using the single future value calculated in the previous step and the initial outlay. It is easy to verify that you will get the same NPV as in your original calculation only if you use the required return as the reinvestment rate in the previous step.

LO 3   **8.15.   Internal Rate of Return.**   It is sometimes stated that "the internal rate of return approach assumes reinvestment of the intermediate cash flows at the internal rate of return." Is this claim correct? To answer, suppose you calculate the IRR of a project in the usual way. Next, suppose you do the following:

    a.   Calculate the future value (as of the end of the project) of all the cash flows other than the initial outlay assuming they are reinvested at the IRR, producing a single future value figure for the project.

    b.   Calculate the IRR of the project using the single future value calculated in the previous step and the initial outlay. It is easy to verify that you will get the same IRR as in your original calculation only if you use the IRR as the reinvestment rate in the previous step.

QUESTIONS AND PROBLEMS

Select problems are available in McGraw-Hill *Connect*. Please see the packaging options section of the preface for more information.

LO 1   **1. Calculating Payback.**   What is the payback period for the following set of cash flows?

Basic
(Questions 1–22)

Year	Cash Flow
0	−$5,900
1	2,000
2	2,700
3	1,500
4	900

LO 1   **2. Calculating Payback.**   An investment project provides cash inflows of $875 per year for eight years. What is the project payback period if the initial cost is $3,200? What if the initial cost is $4,600? What if it is $7,900?

LO 1   **3. Calculating Payback.**   Global Toys Inc., imposes a payback cutoff of three years for its international investment projects. If the company has the following two projects available, should it accept either of them?

Year	Cash Flow (A)	Cash Flow (B)
0	−$55,000	−$ 95,000
1	19,000	18,000
2	27,000	26,000
3	24,000	28,000
4	9,000	260,000

LO 2   **4. Calculating AAR.**   You're trying to determine whether or not to expand your business by building a new manufacturing plant. The plant has an installation cost of $14 million, which will be depreciated straight-line to zero over its four-year life. If the plant has projected net income of $1,253,000, $1,935,000, $1,738,000, and $1,310,000 over these four years, what is the project's average accounting return (AAR)?

LO 3   **5. Calculating IRR.**   A firm evaluates all of its projects by applying the IRR rule. If the required return is 11 percent, should the firm accept the following project?

Year	Cash Flow
0	−$153,000
1	78,000
2	67,000
3	49,000

LO 4   **6. Calculating NPV.**   For the cash flows in the previous problem, suppose the firm uses the NPV decision rule. At a required return of 9 percent, should the firm accept this project? What if the required return was 21 percent?

LO 3 **LO 4**   **7. Calculating NPV and IRR.**   A project that provides annual cash flows of $1,930 for eight years costs $7,700 today. Is this a good project if the required return is 8 percent? What if it's 24 percent? At what discount rate would you be indifferent between accepting the project and rejecting it?

LO 3   **8. Calculating IRR.**   What is the IRR of the following set of cash flows?

Year	Cash Flow
0	−$27,000
1	11,400
2	16,300
3	9,400

LO 4   **9. Calculating NPV.**   For the cash flows in the previous problem, what is the NPV at a discount rate of zero percent? What if the discount rate is 10 percent? If it is 20 percent? If it is 30 percent?

LO 3 **LO 4**   **10. NPV versus IRR.**   Romboski, LLC, has identified the following two mutually exclusive projects:

Year	Cash Flow (A)	Cash Flow (B)
0	−$65,000	−$65,000
1	34,000	19,000
2	27,000	25,000
3	21,000	29,000
4	17,000	34,000

a.   What is the IRR for each of these projects? If you apply the IRR decision rule, which project should the company accept? Is this decision necessarily correct?

b.   If the required return is 11 percent, what is the NPV for each of these projects? Which project will you choose if you apply the NPV decision rule?

c.   Over what range of discount rates would you choose Project A? Project B? At what discount rate would you be indifferent between these two projects? Explain.

LO 3 **LO 4**   **11. NPV versus IRR.**   Consider the following two mutually exclusive projects:

Year	Cash Flow (X)	Cash Flow (Y)
0	−$19,000	−$19,000
1	10,800	6,840
2	8,630	9,410
3	5,210	9,300

Sketch the NPV profiles for X and Y over a range of discount rates from zero to 25 percent. What is the crossover rate for these two projects?

LO 3   **12. Problems with IRR.**   Howell Petroleum, Inc., is trying to evaluate a generation project with the following cash flows:

Year	Cash Flow
0	−$31,000,000
1	48,000,000
2	−7,000,000

a. If the company requires a 10 percent return on its investments, should it accept this project? Why?

b. Compute the IRR for this project. How many IRRs are there? If you apply the IRR decision rule, should you accept the project or not? What's going on here?

LO 6   **13. Calculating Profitability Index.**   What is the profitability index for the following set of cash flows if the relevant discount rate is 10 percent? What if the discount rate is 15 percent? If it is 22 percent?

Year	Cash Flow
0	−$31,000
1	17,300
2	15,200
3	10,600

LO 6   **14. Problems with Profitability Index.**   The Matterhorn Corporation is trying to choose between the following two mutually exclusive design projects:

Year	Cash Flow (I)	Cash Flow (II)
0	−$65,000	−$24,000
1	24,000	8,000
2	29,000	14,500
3	36,000	12,800

a. If the required return is 11 percent and the company applies the profitability index decision rule, which project should the firm accept?

b. If the company applies the NPV decision rule, which project should it take?

c. Explain why your answers in (a) and (b) are different.

.01 **LO 3**   **15. Comparing Investment Criteria.**   Consider the following two mutually
.04 **LO 6**   exclusive projects:

Year	Cash Flow (A)	Cash Flow (B)
0	−$365,000	−$40,000
1	38,000	20,300
2	47,000	15,200
3	62,000	14,100
4	455,000	11,200

Whichever project you choose, if any, you require a return of 13 percent on your investment.

a. If you apply the payback criterion, which investment will you choose? Why?

b. If you apply the NPV criterion, which investment will you choose? Why?

c. If you apply the IRR criterion, which investment will you choose? Why?

d. If you apply the profitability index criterion, which investment will you choose? Why?

e. Based on your answers in (a) through (d), which project will you finally choose? Why?

LO 3 **LO 4**   **16. NPV and IRR.**   Kerron Company is presented with the following two mutually exclusive projects. The required return for both projects is 15 percent.

Year	Project M	Project N
0	−$125,000	−$310,000
1	57,000	135,000
2	64,000	161,000
3	59,000	129,000
4	34,000	92,000

   a.   What is the IRR for each project?

   b.   What is the NPV for each project?

   c.   Which, if either, of the projects should the company accept?

LO 4 **LO 6**   **17. NPV and Profitability Index.**   Dahlia Manufacturing has the following two possible projects. The required return is 12 percent.

Year	Project Y	Project Z
0	−$31,000	−$60,000
1	14,000	24,000
2	12,400	23,000
3	14,800	22,000
4	10,400	21,000

   a.   What is the profitability index for each project?

   b.   What is the NPV for each project?

   c.   Which, if either, of the projects should the company accept?

LO 3   **18. Crossover Point.**   Handy Enterprises has gathered projected cash flows for two projects. At what interest rate would the company be indifferent between the two projects? Which project is better if the required return is above this interest rate? Why?

Year	Project I	Project J
0	−$215,000	−$215,000
1	104,000	75,000
2	93,000	86,000
3	79,000	96,000
4	72,000	105,000

LO 1 **LO 3**   **19. Payback Period and IRR.**   Suppose you have a project with a payback period exactly equal to the life of the project. What do you know about the IRR of the project? Suppose that the payback period is never. What do you know about the IRR of the project now?

LO 4   **20. NPV and Discount Rates.**   An investment has an installed cost of $673,658. The cash flows over the four-year life of the investment are projected to be $228,701, $281,182, $219,209, and $190,376. If the discount rate is zero, what is the NPV? If the discount rate is infinite, what is the NPV? At what discount rate is the NPV just equal to zero? Sketch the NPV profile for this investment based on these three points.

1 **LO 4** **21. NPV and Payback Period.** Kaleb Konstruction, Inc., has the following mutually exclusive projects available. The company has historically used a three-year cutoff for projects. The required return is 10 percent.

Year	Project F	Project G
0	−$150,000	−$235,000
1	78,000	54,000
2	54,000	72,000
3	68,000	103,000
4	60,000	139,000
5	54,000	156,000

    a. Calculate the payback period for both projects.

    b. Calculate the NPV for both projects.

    c. Which project, if any, should the company accept?

LO 5 **22. MIRR.** Chamberlain Corp. is evaluating a project with the following cash flows:

Year	Cash Flow
0	−$19,500
1	7,930
2	9,490
3	8,970
4	7,210
5	−3,980

The company uses an interest rate of 10 percent on all of its projects. Calculate the MIRR of the project using all three methods.

LO 5 **23. MIRR.** Suppose the company in the previous problem uses a discount rate of 11 percent and a reinvestment rate of 8 percent on all of its projects. Calculate the MIRR of the project using all three methods with these rates.

Intermediate
(Questions 23–27)

LO 4 **24. Crossover and NPV.** Seether, Inc., has the following two mutually exclusive projects available.

Year	Project R	Project S
0	−$55,000	−$76,000
1	21,000	20,000
2	22,000	20,000
3	19,000	35,000
4	12,000	30,000
5	9,000	10,000

What is the crossover rate for these two projects? What is the NPV of each project at the crossover rate?

LO 3 **25. Calculating IRR.** A project has the following cash flows:

Year	Cash Flow
0	$75,000
1	−43,000
2	−37,000

What is the IRR for this project? If the required return is 10 percent, should the firm accept the project? What is the NPV of this project? What is the NPV of the project if the required return is 0 percent? 24 percent? What is going on here? Sketch the NPV profile to help you with your answer.

LO 4   **LO 6**

26. NPV and the Profitability Index.   If we define the NPV index as the ratio of NPV to cost, what is the relationship between this index and the profitability index?

LO 1   **LO 4**
LO 6

27. Cash Flow Intuition.   A project has an initial cost of I, has a required return of R, and pays C annually for N years.

a.   Find C in terms of I and N such that the project has a payback period just equal to its life.

b.   Find C in terms of I, N, and R such that this is a profitable project according to the NPV decision rule.

c.   Find C in terms of I, N, and R such that the project has a benefit-cost ratio of 2.

Challenge
(Questions 28–30)

LO 4

28. NPV Valuation.   The Yurdone Corporation wants to set up a private cemetery business. According to the CFO, Barry M. Deep, business is "looking up." As a result, the cemetery project will provide a net cash inflow of $109,000 for the firm during the first year, and the cash flows are projected to grow at a rate of 5.1 percent per year forever. The project requires an initial investment of $1,425,000.

a.   If Yurdone requires a return of 12 percent on such undertakings, should the cemetery business be started?

b.   The company is somewhat unsure about the assumption of a 5.1 percent growth rate in its cash flows. At what constant growth rate would the company just break even if it still required a return of 12 percent on its investment?

LO 3

29. Problems with IRR.   Ashwood Corp. has a project with the following cash flows:

Year	Cash Flow
0	$35,000
1	−27,000
2	29,000

What is the IRR of the project? What is happening here?

LO 3   **LO 4**

30. NPV and IRR.   Anderson International Limited is evaluating a project in Erewhon. The project will create the following cash flows:

Year	Cash Flow
0	−$690,000
1	243,000
2	175,000
3	256,000
4	231,000

All cash flows will occur in Erewhon and are expressed in dollars. In an attempt to improve its economy, the Erewhonian government has declared that all cash flows created by a foreign company are "blocked" and must be reinvested with the government for one year. The reinvestment rate for these funds is 4 percent. If Anderson uses a required return of 10 percent on this project, what are the NPV and IRR of the project? Is the IRR you calculated the MIRR of the project? Why or why not?

8.1 Net Present Value. You have a project that has an initial cash outflow of $-\$20,000$ and cash inflows of $6,000, $5,000, $4,000, and $3,000, respectively, for the next four years. Go to www.datadynamica.com and find the IRR calculator. Enter the cash flows. If the required return is 12 percent, what is the IRR of the project? The NPV?

8.2 Internal Rate of Return. Using the online calculator from the previous problem, find the IRR for a project with cash flows of $-\$500$, $1,200, and $-\$400$. What is going on here?

CHAPTER CASE
BULLOCK GOLD MINING

Seth Bullock, the owner of Bullock Gold Mining, is evaluating a new gold mine in South Dakota. Dan Dority, the company's geologist, has just finished his analysis of the mine site. He has estimated that the mine would be productive for eight years, after which the gold would be completely mined. Dan has taken an estimate of the gold deposits to Alma Garrett, the company's financial officer. Alma has been asked by Seth to perform an analysis of the new mine and present her recommendation on whether the company should open the new mine.

Alma has used the estimates provided by Dan to determine the revenues that could be expected from the mine. She has also projected the expense of opening the mine and the annual operating expenses. If the company opens the mine, it will cost $650 million today, and it will have a cash outflow of $72 million nine years from today in costs associated with closing the mine and reclaiming the area surrounding it. The expected cash flows each year from the mine are shown in the table on this page. Bullock Mining has a 12 percent required return on all of its gold mines.

Year	Cash Flow
0	−$650,000,000
1	80,000,000
2	121,000,000
3	162,000,000
4	221,000,000
5	210,000,000
6	154,000,000
7	108,000,000
8	86,000,000
9	−72,000,000

QUESTIONS

1. Construct a spreadsheet to calculate the payback period, internal rate of return, modified internal rate of return, and net present value of the proposed mine.

2. Based on your analysis, should the company open the mine?

3. Bonus question: Most spreadsheets do not have a built-in formula to calculate the payback period. Write a VBA script that calculates the payback period for a project.

Making Capital Investment Decisions

9

In early 2011, the Disney movie *Mars Needs Moms* hit Earthly theaters with a splat. As one critic said, "Mars may need moms, but Earth needs good movies, and this isn't one of them." Others were equally harsh, saying things like "It's an interplanetary clunker" and "The whole fiasco turns out to be an excuse to let Seth Green play a (redubbed) little boy."

Looking at the numbers, Disney spent close to $150 million making the movie, plus millions more for marketing and distribution. Unfortunately for Disney, *Mars Needs Moms* never reached orbit, pulling in only $39 million worldwide. In fact, about 4 of 10 movies lose at theaters, though DVD sales often help in the final tally. Of course, there are movies that do quite well. Also in 2011, *Harry Potter and the Deathly Hallows: Part 2* raked in about $1.33 billion worldwide at a production cost of about $125 million.

Obviously, Disney didn't *plan* to lose $150 or so million on *Mars Needs Moms,* but it happened. As the box office crash of *Mars Needs Moms* shows, projects don't always go as companies think they will. This chapter explores how this can happen and what companies can do to analyze and possibly avoid these situations.

In broader terms, this chapter follows up on our previous one by delving more deeply into capital budgeting. We have two main tasks. First, recall that in the last chapter, we saw that cash flow estimates are the critical input into a net present value analysis, but we didn't say very much about where these cash flows come from; so, we will now examine this question in some detail. Our second goal is to learn how to critically examine NPV estimates and, in particular, how to evaluate the sensitivity of NPV estimates to assumptions made about the uncertain future.

learning objectives

After studying this chapter, you should be able to:

LO 1 Determine the relevant cash flows for a proposed investment.

LO 2 Analyze a project's projected cash flows.

LO 3 Evaluate an estimated NPV.

276   **PART 5**   Capital Budgeting

So far, we've covered various parts of the capital budgeting decision. Our task in this chapter is to start bringing these pieces together. In particular, we will show you how to "spread the numbers" for a proposed investment or project and, based on those numbers, make an initial assessment about whether or not the project should be undertaken.

In the discussion that follows, we focus on the process of setting up a discounted cash flow analysis. From the last chapter, we know that the projected future cash flows are the key element in such an evaluation. Accordingly, we emphasize working with financial and accounting information to come up with these figures.

In evaluating a proposed investment, we pay special attention to deciding what information is relevant to the decision at hand and what information is not. As we shall see, it is easy to overlook important pieces of the capital budgeting puzzle. We also describe how to go about evaluating the results of our discounted cash flow analysis.

9.1   PROJECT CASH FLOWS: A FIRST LOOK

The effect of taking a project is to change the firm's overall cash flows today and in the future. To evaluate a proposed investment, we must consider these changes in the firm's cash flows and then decide whether or not they add value to the firm. The first (and most important) step, therefore, is to decide which cash flows are relevant and which are not.

Relevant Cash Flows

What is a relevant cash flow for a project? The general principle is simple enough: A relevant cash flow for a project is a change in the firm's overall future cash flow that comes about as a direct consequence of the decision to take that project. Because the relevant cash flows are defined in terms of changes in, or increments to, the firm's existing cash flow, they are called the **incremental cash flows** associated with the project.

incremental cash flows
The difference between a firm's future cash flows with a project and those without the project.

The concept of incremental cash flow is central to our analysis, so we will state a general definition and refer back to it as needed:

> The incremental cash flows for project evaluation consist of *any and all* changes in the firm's future cash flows that are a direct consequence of taking the project.

This definition of incremental cash flows has an obvious and important corollary: Any cash flow that exists regardless of whether or *not* a project is undertaken is *not* relevant.

The Stand-Alone Principle

stand-alone principle
The assumption that evaluation of a project may be based on the project's incremental cash flows.

In practice, it would be very cumbersome to actually calculate the future total cash flows to the firm with and without a project, especially for a large firm. Fortunately, it is not really necessary to do so. Once we identify the effect of undertaking the proposed project on the firm's cash flows, we need only focus on the project's resulting incremental cash flows. This is called the **stand-alone principle**.

What the stand-alone principle says is that, once we have determined the incremental cash flows from undertaking a project, we can view that project as a kind of "minifirm" with its own future revenues and costs, its own assets, and, of course, its own cash flows. We will then be primarily interested in comparing the cash flows from this minifirm to the cost of acquiring it. An important consequence of this approach is that we will be evaluating the proposed project purely on its own merits, in isolation from any other activities or projects.

CONCEPT QUESTIONS

9.1a   What are the relevant incremental cash flows for project evaluation?

9.1b   What is the stand-alone principle?

INCREMENTAL CASH FLOWS

9.2

We are concerned here only with those cash flows that are incremental and that result from a project. Looking back at our general definition, it seems easy enough to decide whether a cash flow is incremental or not. Even so, there are a few situations where mistakes are easy to make. In this section, we describe some of these common pitfalls and how to avoid them.

Sunk Costs

A **sunk cost**, by definition, is a cost we have already paid or have already incurred the liability to pay. Such a cost cannot be changed by the decision today to accept or reject a project. Put another way, the firm will have to pay this cost no matter what. Based on our general definition of incremental cash flow, such a cost is clearly not relevant to the decision at hand. So, we will always be careful to exclude sunk costs from our analysis.

sunk cost
A cost that has already been incurred and cannot be recouped and therefore should not be considered in an investment decision.

That a sunk cost is not relevant seems obvious given our discussion. Nonetheless, it's easy to fall prey to the sunk cost fallacy. For example, suppose General Milk Company hires a financial consultant to help evaluate whether or not a line of chocolate milk should be launched. When the consultant turns in the report, General Milk objects to the analysis because the consultant did not include the hefty consulting fee as a cost of the chocolate milk project.

Who is correct? By now, we know that the consulting fee is a sunk cost because the consulting fee must be paid whether or not the chocolate milk line is actually launched (this is an attractive feature of the consulting business).

Opportunity Costs

When we think of costs, we normally think of out-of-pocket costs, namely, those that require us to actually spend some amount of cash. An **opportunity cost** is slightly different; it requires us to give up a benefit. A common situation arises where a firm already owns some of the assets a proposed project will be using. For example, we might be thinking of converting an old rustic cotton mill we bought years ago for $100,000 into "upmarket" condominiums.

opportunity cost
The most valuable alternative that is given up if a particular investment is undertaken.

If we undertake this project, there will be no direct cash outflow associated with buying the old mill since we already own it. For purposes of evaluating the condo project, should we then treat the mill as "free"? The answer is no. The mill is a valuable resource used by the project. If we didn't use it here, we could do something else with it. Like what? The obvious answer is that, at a minimum, we could sell it. Using the mill for the condo complex thus has an opportunity cost: We give up the valuable opportunity to do something else with it.[1]

---

[1] Economists sometimes use the acronym *TANSTAAFL*, which is short for "There ain't no such thing as a free lunch," to describe the fact that only very rarely is something truly free.

There is another issue here. Once we agree that the use of the mill has an opportunity cost, how much should the condo project be charged? Given that we paid $100,000, it might seem that we should charge this amount to the condo project. Is this correct? The answer is no, and the reason is based on our discussion concerning sunk costs.

The fact that we paid $100,000 some years ago is irrelevant. That cost is sunk. At a minimum, the opportunity cost that we charge the project is what the mill would sell for today (net of any selling costs) because this is the amount that we give up by using it instead of selling it.

Side Effects

Remember that the incremental cash flows for a project include all the changes in the *firm's* future cash flows. It would not be unusual for a project to have side, or spillover, effects, both good and bad. For example, if the Innovative Motors Company (IMC) introduces a new car, some of the sales might come at the expense of other IMC cars. This is called **erosion**, and the same general problem could occur for any multiline consumer product producer or seller.[2] In this case, the cash flows from the new line should be adjusted downward to reflect lost profits on other lines.

In accounting for erosion, it is important to recognize that any sales lost as a result of our launching a new product might be lost anyway because of future competition. Erosion is only relevant when the sales would not otherwise be lost.

erosion

The cash flows of a new project that come at the expense of a firm's existing projects.

Net Working Capital

Normally, a project will require that the firm invest in net working capital in addition to long-term assets. For example, a project will generally need some amount of cash on hand to pay any expenses that arise. In addition, a project will need an initial investment in inventories and accounts receivable (to cover credit sales). Some of this financing will be in the form of amounts owed to suppliers (accounts payable), but the firm will have to supply the balance. This balance represents the investment in net working capital.

It's easy to overlook an important feature of net working capital in capital budgeting. As a project winds down, inventories are sold, receivables are collected, bills are paid, and cash balances can be drawn down. These activities free up the net working capital originally invested. So, the firm's investment in project net working capital closely resembles a loan. The firm supplies working capital at the beginning and recovers it towards the end.

Financing Costs

In analyzing a proposed investment, we will not include interest paid or any other financing costs such as dividends or principal repaid, because we are interested in the cash flow generated by the assets of the project. As we mentioned in Chapter 2, interest paid, for example, is a component of cash flow to creditors, not cash flow from assets.

More generally, our goal in project evaluation is to compare the cash flow from a project to the cost of acquiring that project in order to estimate NPV. The particular mixture of debt and equity a firm actually chooses to use in financing a project is a managerial variable and primarily determines how project cash flow is divided between owners and creditors. This is not to say that financing arrangements are unimportant. They are just something to be analyzed separately. We will cover this in later chapters.

---

[2] More colorfully, erosion is sometimes called *piracy* or *cannibalism*.

Other Issues

There are some other things to watch out for. First, we are only interested in measuring cash flow. Moreover, we are interested in measuring it when it actually occurs, not when it accrues in an accounting sense. Second, we are always interested in *aftertax* cash flow since taxes are definitely a cash outflow. In fact, whenever we write "incremental cash flows," we mean aftertax incremental cash flows. Remember, however, that aftertax cash flow and accounting profit, or net income, are entirely different things.

CONCEPT QUESTIONS

9.2a   What is a sunk cost? An opportunity cost?

9.2b   Explain what erosion is and why it is relevant.

9.2c   Explain why interest paid is not a relevant cash flow for project evaluation.

PRO FORMA FINANCIAL STATEMENTS AND PROJECT CASH FLOWS

9.3

The first thing we need when we begin evaluating a proposed investment is a set of pro forma, or projected, financial statements. Given these, we can develop the projected cash flows from the project. Once we have the cash flows, we can estimate the value of the project using the techniques we described in the previous chapter.

ExcelMaster
coverage online

Getting Started: Pro Forma Financial Statements

Pro forma financial statements are a convenient and easily understood means of summarizing much of the relevant information for a project. To prepare these statements, we will need estimates of quantities such as unit sales, the selling price per unit, the variable cost per unit, and total fixed costs. We will also need to know the total investment required, including any investment in net working capital.

To illustrate, suppose we think we can sell 50,000 cans of shark attractant per year at a price of $4.00 per can. It costs us about $2.50 per can to make the attractant, and a new product such as this one typically has only a three-year life (perhaps because the customer base dwindles rapidly). We require a 20 percent return on new products.

Fixed costs for the project, including such things as rent on the production facility, will run $12,000 per year. Further, we will need to invest a total of $90,000 in manufacturing equipment. For simplicity, we will assume that this $90,000 will be 100 percent depreciated over the three-year life of the project. Furthermore, the cost of removing the equipment will roughly equal its actual value in three years, so it will be essentially worthless on a market value basis as well. Finally, the project will require an initial $20,000 investment in net working capital. As usual, the tax rate is 34 percent.

In Table 9.1, we organize these initial projections by first preparing the pro forma income statement for each of the three years. Once again, notice that we have *not* deducted any interest expense. This will always be so. As we described earlier, interest paid is a financing expense, not a component of operating cash flow.

We can also prepare a series of abbreviated balance sheets that show the capital requirements for the project as we've done in Table 9.2. Here we have net working capital

pro forma financial statements
Financial statements projecting future years' operations.

TABLE 9.1		
Projected income statement, shark attractant project, Years 1–3	Sales (50,000 units at $4.00/unit)	$200,000
	Variable costs ($2.50/unit)	125,000
	Gross profit	$ 75,000
	Fixed costs	12,000
	Depreciation ($90,000/3)	30,000
	EBIT	$ 33,000
	Taxes (34%)	11,220
	Net income	$ 21,780

TABLE 9.2		Year			
		0	1	2	3
Projected capital requirements, shark attractant project	Net working capital	$ 20,000	$20,000	$20,000	$20,000
	Net fixed assets	90,000	60,000	30,000	0
	Total investment	$110,000	$80,000	$50,000	$20,000

of $20,000 in each year. Fixed assets are $90,000 at the start of the project's life (Year 0), and they decline by the $30,000 in depreciation each year, ending up at zero. Notice that the total investment given here for future years is the total book, or accounting, value, not market value.

At this point, we need to start converting this accounting information into cash flows. We consider how to do this next.

Project Cash Flows

To develop the cash flows from a project, we need to recall (from Chapter 2) that cash flow from assets has three components: operating cash flow, capital spending, and additions to net working capital. To evaluate a project, or minifirm, we need to arrive at estimates for each of these.

Once we have estimates of the components of cash flow, we will calculate cash flow for our minifirm just as we did in Chapter 2 for an entire firm:

> **Project cash flow = Project operating cash flow**
> **− Project change in net working capital**
> **− Project capital spending**

We consider these components next.

Project Operating Cash Flow   To determine the operating cash flow associated with a project, we first need to recall the definition of operating cash flow:

> **Operating cash flow = Earnings before interest and taxes**
> **+ Depreciation**
> **− Taxes**

To illustrate the calculation of operating cash flow, we will use the projected information from the shark attractant project. For ease of reference, Table 9.3 repeats the income statement.

Sales	$200,000	**TABLE 9.3**
Variable costs	125,000	
Fixed costs	12,000	**Projected income**
Depreciation	30,000	**statement, shark**
EBIT	$ 33,000	**attractant project,**
Taxes (34%)	11,220	**Years 1–3**
Net income	$ 21,780	

EBIT	$33,000	**TABLE 9.4**
Depreciation	+30,000	
Taxes	−11,220	**Projected operating**
Operating cash flow	$51,780	**cash flow, shark**
		attractant project

	Year				
	0	**1**	**2**	**3**	**TABLE 9.5**
Operating cash flow		$51,780	$51,780	$51,780	**Projected total**
Change in NWC	−$ 20,000			+20,000	**cash flows, shark**
Capital spending	−90,000				**attractant project**
Total project cash flow	−$110,000	$51,780	$51,780	$71,780	

Given the income statement in Table 9.3, calculating the operating cash flow is very straightforward. As we see in Table 9.4, projected operating cash flow for the shark attractant project is $51,780.

Project Net Working Capital and Capital Spending We next need to take care of the fixed asset and net working capital requirements. Based on our balance sheets above, the firm must spend $90,000 up front for fixed assets and invest an additional $20,000 in net working capital. The immediate outflow is thus $110,000. At the end of the project's life, the fixed assets will be worthless (the salvage value will be zero), but the firm will recover the $20,000 that was tied up in working capital. This will lead to a $20,000 cash *inflow* in the last year.

On a purely mechanical level, notice that whenever we have an investment in net working capital, that same investment has to be recovered; in other words, the same number needs to appear at some time in the future with the opposite sign.

Projected Total Cash Flow and Value

Given the information we've accumulated, we can finish the preliminary cash flow analysis as illustrated in Table 9.5.

Now that we have cash flow projections, we are ready to apply the various criteria we discussed in the last chapter. First, the NPV at the 20 percent required return is:

$$\text{NPV} = -\$110,000 + 51,780/1.2 + 51,780/1.2^2 + 71,780/1.2^3$$
$$= \$10,648$$

So, based on these projections, the project creates over $10,000 in value and should be accepted. Also, the return on this investment obviously exceeds 20 percent (since the NPV is positive at 20 percent). After some trial and error, we find that the IRR works out to be about 25.8 percent.

In addition, if required, we could go ahead and calculate the payback and the average accounting return, or AAR. Inspection of the cash flows shows that the payback on this project is just a little over two years (verify that it's about 2.1 years).

From the last chapter, we know that the AAR is average net income divided by average book value. The net income each year is $21,780. The average (in thousands) of the four book values (from Table 9.2) for a total investment is ($110 + 80 + 50 + 20)/4 = $65, so the AAR is $21,780/65,000 = 33.51 percent. We've already seen that the return on this investment (the IRR) is about 26 percent. The fact that the AAR is larger illustrates again why the AAR cannot be meaningfully interpreted as the return on a project.

The Tax Shield Approach

A useful variation on our basic definition of operating cash flow (OCF) is the *tax shield* approach. The tax shield definition of OCF is:

$$\text{OCF} = (\text{Sales} - \text{Costs}) \times (1 - T_c) + \text{Depreciation} \times T_c$$

where T_C is the corporate tax rate. Assuming that $T_C = 34\%$, the OCF works out to be:

$$\text{OCF} = (\$200{,}000 - 137{,}000) \times .66 + 30{,}000 \times .34$$
$$= \$41{,}580 + 10{,}200$$
$$= \$51{,}780$$

This is just as we had before.

This approach views OCF as having two components. The first part is what the project's cash flow would be if there were no depreciation expense. In this case, this would-have-been cash flow is $41,580.

depreciation tax shield

The tax saving that results from the depreciation deduction, calculated as depreciation multiplied by the corporate tax rate.

The second part of OCF in this approach is the depreciation deduction multiplied by the tax rate. This is called the **depreciation tax shield**. We know that depreciation is a non-cash expense. The only cash flow effect of deducting depreciation is to reduce our taxes, a benefit to us. At the current 34 percent corporate tax rate, every dollar in depreciation expense saves us 34 cents in taxes. So, in our example, the $30,000 depreciation deduction saves us $30,000 × .34 = $10,200 in taxes.

The tax shield approach will always give the same answer as our basic approach, so you might wonder why we bother. The answer is that it is sometimes a little simpler to use, particularly for projects that involve cost-cutting.

CONCEPT QUESTIONS

9.3a   What is the definition of project operating cash flow? How does this differ from net income?

9.3b   In the shark attractant project, why did we add back the firm's net working capital investment in the final year?

9.3c   What is the "depreciation tax shield"?

MORE ON PROJECT CASH FLOW

In this section, we take a closer look at some aspects of project cash flow. In particular, we discuss project net working capital in more detail. We then examine current tax laws regarding depreciation.

A Closer Look at Net Working Capital

In calculating operating cash flow, we did not explicitly consider the fact that some of our sales might be on credit. Also, we may not have actually paid some of the costs shown. In either case, the cash flow has not yet occurred. We show here that these possibilities are not a problem as long as we don't forget to include additions to net working capital in our analysis. This discussion thus emphasizes the importance and the effect of doing so.

Suppose during a particular year of a project we have the following simplified income statement:

Sales	$500
Costs	310
Net income	$190

Depreciation and taxes are zero. No fixed assets are purchased during the year. Also, to illustrate a point, we assume that the only components of net working capital are accounts receivable and payable. The beginning and ending amounts for these accounts are:

	Beginning of Year	**End of Year**	**Change**
Accounts receivable	$880	$910	+$30
Accounts payable	550	605	+ 55
Net working capital	$330	$305	−$25

Based on this information, what is total cash flow for the year? We can first just mechanically apply what we have been discussing to come up with the answer. Operating cash flow in this particular case is the same as EBIT since there are no taxes or depreciation and thus equals $190. Also, notice that net working capital actually *declined* by $25, so the change in net working capital is negative. This just means that $25 was freed up during the year. There was no capital spending, so the total cash flow for the year is:

Total cash flow = Operating cash flow − Change in NWC − Capital spending
= $190 − (−25) − 0
= $215

Now, we know that this $215 total cash flow has to be "dollars in" less "dollars out" for the year. We could therefore ask a different question: What were cash revenues for the year? Also, what were cash costs?

To determine cash revenues, we need to look more closely at net working capital. During the year, we had sales of $500. However, accounts receivable rose by $30 over the same time period. What does this mean? The $30 increase tells us that sales exceeded collections by $30. In other words, we haven't yet received the cash from $30 of the $500 in sales. As a result, our cash inflow is $500 − 30 = $470. In general, cash inflow is sales minus the increase in accounts receivable.

Cash outflows can be similarly determined. We show costs of $310 on the income statement, but accounts payable increased by $55 during the year. This means that we have not yet paid $55 of the $310, so cash costs for the period are just $310 − 55 = $255. In other words, in this case, cash costs equal costs less the increase in accounts payable.

Putting this information together, cash inflows less cash outflows is $470 − 255 = $215, just as we had before. Notice that:

Cash flow = Cash inflow − Cash outflow

$$= (\$500 - 30) - (310 - 55)$$
$$= (\$500 - 310) - (30 - 55)$$
$$= \textbf{Operating cash flow} - \textbf{Change in NWC}$$
$$= \$190 - (-25)$$
$$= \$215$$

More generally, this example illustrates that including net working capital changes in our calculations has the effect of adjusting for the discrepancy between accounting sales and costs and actual cash receipts and payments.

EXAMPLE 9.1

CASH COLLECTIONS AND COSTS

For the year just completed, the Combat Wombat Telestat Co. (CWT) reports sales of $998 and costs of $734. You have collected the following beginning and ending balance sheet information:

	Beginning	Ending
Accounts receivable	$100	$110
Inventory	100	80
Accounts payable	100	70
Net working capital	$100	$120

Based on these figures, what are cash inflows? Cash outflows? What happened to each account? What is net cash flow?

Sales were $998, but receivables rose by $10. So, cash collections were $10 less than sales, or $988. Costs were $734, but inventories fell by $20. This means that we didn't replace $20 worth of inventory, so costs are actually overstated by this amount. Also, payables fell by $30. This means that, on a net basis, we actually paid our suppliers $30 more than we received from them, resulting in a $30 understatement of costs. Adjusting for these events, cash costs are $734 − 20 + 30 = $744. Net cash flow is $988 − 744 = $244.

Finally, notice that net working capital increased by $20 overall. We can check our answer by noting that the original accounting sales less costs of $998 − 734 is $264. In addition, CWT spent $20 on net working capital, so the net result is a cash flow of $264 − 20 = $244, as we calculated.

Depreciation

Accelerated Cost Recovery System (ACRS)

Depreciation method under U.S. tax law allowing for the accelerated write-off of property under various classifications.

As we note elsewhere, accounting depreciation is a noncash deduction. As a result, depreciation has cash flow consequences only because it influences the tax bill. The way that depreciation is computed for tax purposes is thus the relevant method for capital investment decisions. Not surprisingly, the procedures are governed by tax law. We now discuss some specifics of the depreciation system enacted by the Tax Reform Act of 1986. This system is a modification of the **Accelerated Cost Recovery System (ACRS)** instituted in 1981.

Class	Examples	
3-year	Equipment used in research	
5-year	Autos, computers	
7-year	Most industrial equipment	

TABLE 9.6

Modified ACRS property classes

Year	Property Class		
	3-Year	5-Year	7-Year
1	33.33%	20.00%	14.29%
2	44.45	32.00	24.49
3	14.81	19.20	17.49
4	7.41	11.52	12.49
5		11.52	8.93
6		5.76	8.92
7			8.93
8			4.46

TABLE 9.7

Modified ACRS depreciation allowances

Modified ACRS (MACRS) Depreciation   Calculating depreciation is normally very mechanical. While there are a number of *ifs, ands,* and *buts* involved, the basic idea is that every asset is assigned to a particular class. An asset's class establishes its life for tax purposes. Once an asset's tax life is determined, we compute the depreciation for each year by multiplying the cost of the asset by a fixed percentage. The expected salvage value (what we think the asset will be worth when we dispose of it) and the actual expected economic life (how long we expect the asset to be in service) are not explicitly considered in the calculation of depreciation.

Some typical depreciation classes are described in Table 9.6, and associated percentages (rounded to two decimal places) are shown in Table 9.7. Remember that land cannot be depreciated.

To illustrate how depreciation is calculated, we consider an automobile costing $12,000. Autos are normally classified as five-year property. Looking at Table 9.7, we see that the relevant figure for the first year of a five-year asset is 20 percent. The depreciation in the first year is thus $12,000 \times .20 = \$2,400$. The relevant percentage in the second year is 32 percent, so the depreciation in the second year is $12,000 \times .32 = \$3,840$, and so on. We can summarize these calculations as follows:

Year	MACRS Percentage	Depreciation	
1	20.00%	$.2000 \times \$12,000 =$	$ 2,400.00
2	32.00	$.3200 \times 12,000 =$	3,840.00
3	19.20	$.1920 \times 12,000 =$	2,304.00
4	11.52	$.1152 \times 12,000 =$	1,382.40
5	11.52	$.1152 \times 12,000 =$	1,382.40
6	5.76	$.0576 \times 12,000 =$	691.20
	100.00%		$12,000.00

	Year	Beginning Book Value	Depreciation	Ending Book Value
TABLE 9.8	1	$12,000.00	$2,400.00	$9,600.00
	2	9,600.00	3,840.00	5,760.00
MACRS book values	3	5,760.00	2,304.00	3,456.00
	4	3,456.00	1,382.40	2,073.60
	5	2,073.60	1,382.40	691.20
	6	691.20	691.20	0.00

Notice that the MACRS percentages sum up to 100 percent. As a result, we write off 100 percent of the cost of the asset, or $12,000 in this case.

Book Value versus Market Value   In calculating depreciation under current tax law, the economic life and future market value of the asset are not an issue. As a result, the book value of an asset can differ substantially from its actual market value. For example, with our $12,000 car, book value after the first year is $12,000 less the first year's depreciation of $2,400, or $9,600. The remaining book values are summarized in Table 9.8. After six years, the book value of the car is zero.

Suppose we wanted to sell the car after five years. Based on historical averages, it will be worth, say, 25 percent of the purchase price, or .25 × $12,000 = $3,000. If we actually sold it for this, then we would have to pay taxes at the ordinary income tax rate on the difference between the sale price of $3,000 and the book value of $691.20. For a corporation in the 34 percent bracket, the tax liability is .34 × $2,308.80 = $784.99.

The reason that taxes must be paid in this case is that the difference in market value and book value is "excess" depreciation, and it must be "recaptured" when the asset is sold. What this means is that, as it turns out, we overdepreciated the asset by $3,000 − 691.20 = $2,308.80. Since we deducted $2,308.80 too much in depreciation, we paid $784.99 too little in taxes, and we simply have to make up the difference.

Notice that this is *not* a tax on a capital gain. As a general (albeit rough) rule, a capital gain only occurs if the market price exceeds the original cost. However, what is and what is not a capital gain is ultimately up to taxing authorities, and the specific rules can be very complex. We will ignore capital gains taxes for the most part.

Finally, if the book value exceeds the market value, then the difference is treated as a loss for tax purposes. For example, if we sell the car after two years for $4,000, then the book value exceeds the market value by $1,760. In this case, a tax saving of .34 × $1,760 = $598.40 occurs.

EXAMPLE 9.2

MACRS DEPRECIATION

The Staple Supply Co. has just purchased a new computerized information system with an installed cost of $160,000. The computer is treated as five-year property. What are the yearly depreciation allowances? Based on historical experience, we think that the system will be worth only $10,000 when we get rid of it in four years. What are the tax consequences of the sale? What is the total aftertax cash flow from the sale?

The yearly depreciation allowances are calculated by just multiplying $160,000 by the five-year percentages in Table 9.7:

(continued)

Year	MACRS Percentage	Depreciation	Ending Book Value
1	20.00%	.2000 × $160,000 = $ 32,000	$128,000
2	32.00	.3200 × 160,000 = 51,200	76,800
3	19.20	.1920 × 160,000 = 30,720	46,080
4	11.52	.1152 × 160,000 = 18,432	27,648
5	11.52	.1152 × 160,000 = 18,432	9,216
6	5.76	.0576 × 160,000 = 9,216	0
	100.00%	$160,000	

Notice that we have also computed the book value of the system as of the end of each year. The book value at the end of Year 4 is $27,648. If we sell the system for $10,000 at that time, we will have a loss of $17,648 (the difference) for tax purposes. This loss, of course, is like depreciation because it isn't a cash expense.

What really happens? Two things. First: We get $10,000 from the buyer. Second: We save .34 × $17,648 = $6,000 in taxes. So, the total aftertax cash flow from the sale is a $16,000 cash inflow.

An Example: The Majestic Mulch and Compost Company (MMCC)

At this point, we want to go through a somewhat more involved capital budgeting analysis. Keep in mind as you read that the basic approach here is exactly the same as that in the shark attractant example above. We have only added some more "real-world" detail (and a lot more numbers).

MMCC is investigating the feasibility of a new line of power mulching tools aimed at the growing number of home composters. Based on exploratory conversations with buyers for large garden shops, it projects unit sales as follows:

Year	Unit Sales
1	3,000
2	5,000
3	6,000
4	6,500
5	6,000
6	5,000
7	4,000
8	3,000

The new power mulcher will be priced to sell at $120 per unit to start. When the competition catches up after three years, however, MMCC anticipates that the price will drop to $110.

The power mulcher project will require $20,000 in net working capital at the start. Subsequently, total net working capital at the end of each year will be about 15 percent of sales for that year. The variable cost per unit is $60, and total fixed costs are $25,000 per year.

It will cost about $800,000 to buy the equipment necessary to begin production. This investment is primarily in industrial equipment and thus qualifies as seven-year MACRS property. The equipment will actually be worth about 20 percent of its cost in eight years, or .20 × $800,000 = $160,000. The relevant tax rate is 34 percent, and the required return is 15 percent. Based on this information, should MMCC proceed?

TABLE 9.9	Year	Unit Price	Unit Sales	Revenues
Projected revenues, power mulcher project	1	$120	3,000	$360,000
	2	120	5,000	600,000
	3	120	6,000	720,000
	4	110	6,500	715,000
	5	110	6,000	660,000
	6	110	5,000	550,000
	7	110	4,000	440,000
	8	110	3,000	330,000

TABLE 9.10	Year	MACRS Percentage	Depreciation	Ending Book Value
Annual depreciation, power mulcher project	1	14.29%	$.1429 \times \$800,000 = \$114,320$	$685,680
	2	24.49	$.2449 \times 800,000 = 195,920$	489,760
	3	17.49	$.1749 \times 800,000 = 139,920$	349,840
	4	12.49	$.1249 \times 800,000 = 99,920$	249,920
	5	8.93	$.0893 \times 800,000 = 71,440$	178,480
	6	8.92	$.0892 \times 800,000 = 71,360$	107,120
	7	8.93	$.0893 \times 800,000 = 71,440$	35,680
	8	4.46	$.0446 \times 800,000 = 35,680$	0
		100.00%	$800,000	

TABLE 9.11   Pro forma income statements, power mulcher project

	Year							
	1	**2**	**3**	**4**	**5**	**6**	**7**	**8**
Unit price	$ 120	$ 120	$ 120	$ 110	$ 110	$ 110	$ 110	$ 110
Unit sales	3,000	5,000	6,000	6,500	6,000	5,000	4,000	3,000
Revenues	$360,000	$600,000	$720,000	$715,000	$660,000	$550,000	$440,000	$330,000
Variable costs	180,000	300,000	360,000	390,000	360,000	300,000	240,000	180,000
Fixed costs	25,000	25,000	25,000	25,000	25,000	25,000	25,000	25,000
Depreciation	114,320	195,920	139,920	99,920	71,440	71,360	71,440	35,680
EBIT	$ 40,680	$ 79,080	$195,080	$200,080	$203,560	$153,640	$103,560	$ 89,320
Taxes (34%)	13,831	26,887	66,327	68,027	69,210	52,238	35,210	30,369
Net income	$ 26,849	$ 52,193	$128,753	$132,053	$134,350	$101,402	$ 68,350	$ 58,951

Operating Cash Flows   There is a lot of information here that we need to organize. The first thing we can do is calculate projected sales. Sales in the first year are projected at 3,000 units at $120 apiece, or $360,000 total. The remaining figures are shown in Table 9.9.

Next, we compute the depreciation on the $800,000 investment in Table 9.10. With this information, we can prepare the pro forma income statements, as shown in Table 9.11. From here, computing the operating cash flows is straightforward. The results are illustrated in the first part of Table 9.13 (on page 290).

Year	Revenues	Net Working Capital	Cash Flow
0		$ 20,000	−$20,000
1	$360,000	54,000	−34,000
2	600,000	90,000	−36,000
3	720,000	108,000	−18,000
4	715,000	107,250	750
5	660,000	99,000	8,250
6	550,000	82,500	16,500
7	440,000	66,000	16,500
8	330,000	49,500	16,500

TABLE 9.12

Changes in net working capital, power mulcher project

Changes in NWC   Now that we have the operating cash flows, we need to determine the changes in NWC. By assumption, net working capital requirements change as sales change. In each year, we will generally either add to or recover some of our project net working capital. Recalling that NWC starts out at $20,000 and then rises to 15 percent of sales, we can calculate the amount of NWC for each year as illustrated in Table 9.12.

As illustrated, during the first year, net working capital grows from $20,000 to .15 × $360,000 = $54,000. The increase in net working capital for the year is thus $54,000 − 20,000 = $34,000. The remaining figures are calculated the same way.

Remember that an increase in net working capital is a cash outflow, so we use a negative sign in this table to indicate an additional investment that the firm makes in net working capital. A positive sign represents net working capital returning to the firm. Thus, for example, $16,500 in NWC flows back to the firm in Year 6. Over the project's life, net working capital builds to a peak of $108,000 and declines from there as sales begin to drop off.

We show the result for changes in net working capital in the second part of Table 9.13. Notice that at the end of the project's life there is $49,500 in net working capital still to be recovered. Therefore, in the last year, the project returns $16,500 of NWC during the year and then returns the remaining $49,500 at the end of the year for a total of $66,000.

Capital Spending   Finally, we have to account for the long-term capital invested in the project. In this case, we invest $800,000 at Year 0. By assumption, this equipment will be worth $160,000 at the end of the project. It will have a book value of zero at that time. As we discussed above, this $160,000 excess of market value over book value is taxable, so the aftertax proceeds will be $160,000 × (1 − .34) = $105,600. These figures are shown in the third part of Table 9.13.

Total Cash Flow and Value   We now have all the cash flow pieces, and we put them together in Table 9.14. In addition to the total project cash flows, we have calculated the cumulative cash flows. At this point, it's essentially plug-and-chug to calculate the net present value, internal rate of return, and payback.

If we sum the discounted cash flows and the initial investment, the net present value (at 15 percent) works out to be $65,485. This is positive; so, based on these preliminary projections, the power mulcher project is acceptable. The internal, or DCF, rate of return is greater than 15 percent since the NPV is positive. It works out to be 17.24 percent, again, indicating that the project is acceptable.

Looking at the cumulative cash flows, we see that the project has almost paid back after four years since the cumulative cash flow is almost zero at that time. As indicated, the fractional year works out to be $17,322/214,040 = .08, so the payback is 4.08 years. We can't say whether or not this is good since we don't have a benchmark for MMCC. This is the usual problem with payback periods.

TABLE 9.13 Projected cash flows, power mulcher project

					Year				
	0	1	2	3	4	5	6	7	8
I. Operating Cash Flow									
EBIT		$ 40,680	$ 79,080	$195,080	$200,080	$203,560	$153,640	$103,560	$ 89,320
Depreciation		114,320	195,920	139,920	99,920	71,440	71,360	71,440	35,680
Taxes		– 13,831	– 26,887	– 66,327	– 68,027	– 69,210	– 52,238	– 35,210	– 30,369
Operating cash flow		$141,169	$248,113	$268,673	$231,973	$205,790	$172,762	$139,790	$ 94,631
II. Net Working Capital									
Initial NWC	–$ 20,000								
Increases in NWC		–$ 34,000	–$ 36,000	–$ 18,000	$ 750	$ 8,250	$ 16,500	$ 16,500	$ 16,500
NWC recovery									49,500
Changes in NWC	–$ 20,000	–$ 34,000	–$ 36,000	–$ 18,000	$ 750	$ 8,250	$ 16,500	$ 16,500	$ 66,000
III. Capital Spending									
Initial outlay	–$800,000								
Aftertax salvage									$105,600
Capital spending	–$800,000								$105,600

TABLE 9.14 Projected total cash flows, power mulcher project

					Year				
	0	1	2	3	4	5	6	7	8
Operating cash flow		$141,169	$248,113	$268,673	$231,973	$205,790	$172,762	$139,790	$ 94,631
Changes in NWC	–$ 20,000	– 34,000	– 36,000	– 18,000	750	8,250	16,500	16,500	66,000
Capital spending	– 800,000								105,600
Total project cash flow	–$820,000	$107,169	$212,113	$250,673	$232,723	$214,040	$189,262	$156,290	$266,231
Cumulative cash flow	–$820,000	–$712,831	–$500,718	–$250,046	–$ 17,323	$196,717	$385,979	$542,269	$808,500

Net present value (15%) = $65,485
Internal rate of return = 17.24%
Payback = 4.08 years

Conclusion

This completes our preliminary DCF analysis. Where do we go from here? If we have a great deal of confidence in our projections, then there is no further analysis to be done. We should begin production and marketing immediately. It is unlikely that this will be the case. It is important to remember that the result of our analysis is an estimate of NPV, and we will usually have less than complete confidence in our projections. This means we have more work to do. In particular, we will almost surely want to spend some time evaluating the quality of our estimates. We will take up this subject in the next several sections.

CONCEPT QUESTIONS

9.4a   Why is it important to consider changes in net working capital in developing cash flows? What is the effect of doing so?

9.4b   How is depreciation calculated for fixed assets under current tax law? What effect do expected salvage value and estimated economic life have on the calculated depreciation deduction?

EVALUATING NPV ESTIMATES

9.5

As we discussed in Chapter 8, an investment has a positive net present value if its market value exceeds its cost. Such an investment is desirable because it creates value for its owner. The primary problem in identifying such opportunities is that most of the time we can't actually observe the relevant market value. Instead, we estimate it. Having done so, it is only natural to wonder whether or not our estimates are at least close to the true values. We consider this question next.

The Basic Problem

Suppose we are working on a preliminary DCF analysis along the lines we described in previous sections. We carefully identify the relevant cash flows, avoiding such things as sunk costs, and we remember to consider working capital requirements. We add back any depreciation; we account for possible erosion; and we pay attention to opportunity costs. Finally, we double-check our calculations, and, when all is said and done, the bottom line is that the estimated NPV is positive.

Now what? Do we stop here and move on to the next proposal? Probably not. The fact that the estimated NPV is positive is definitely a good sign, but, more than anything, this tells us that we need to take a closer look.

If you think about it, there are two circumstances under which a discounted cash flow analysis could lead us to conclude that a project has a positive NPV. The first possibility is that the project really does have a positive NPV. That's the good news. The bad news is the second possibility: A project may appear to have a positive NPV because our estimate is inaccurate.

Notice that we could also err in the opposite way. If we conclude that a project has a negative NPV when the true NPV is positive, then we lose a valuable opportunity.

FINANCE MATTERS

◄ For the latest news on the topics covered in this chapter, scan here.

When Things Go Wrong . . .

If you think about it, the decision by a company to acquire another company is a capital budgeting decision. One important difference, however, is that an acquisition may be more expensive than a typical project, and possibly much more expensive. Of course, as with any other project, acquisitions can fail. When they do, the losses can be huge.

For example, in April 2010, HP announced that it was acquiring Palm, Inc., for $1.2 billion. HP stated that its global scale and financial strength, combined with Palm's webOS operating system, would allow HP to enter the $100 billion mobile device market. Of course, the merger did not go as planned. For example, HP debuted its webOS TouchPad tablet on July 1, 2011. About eight weeks later, with sales lagging behind projections, HP dropped the price on the tablet from the original $499 price to $99. Finally, in November 2011, less than two years after the acquisition, HP announced that it would write off its investment in Palm for $3.3 billion, almost three times the acquisition price.

In another example, consider Bank of America's (BOA) 2008 purchase of Countrywide Financial for $2.5 billion. Countrywide became the symbol for loose lending and risky mortgage practices when housing markets began to falter in 2007. In the middle of 2011, BOA reached an agreement to pay $14 billion to settle claims related to Countrywide

mortgages. This payment brought the total losses attributable to Countrywide to $30 billion, and BOA faced even more costs. Countrywide borrowers were suing BOA and five other mortgage servicers over foreclosure procedures. That lawsuit was expected to cost between $5 billion and $20 billion.

One of the largest acquisitions in U.S. history was America Online's (AOL) purchase of Time Warner in 2001. AOL purchased Time Warner under the assumption that AOL was part of the "new economy" and primed for fast growth. Time Warner was the "old" communications company, owning cable stations and a music label, among other things. But things didn't work as well as planned. Infighting among employees from the two companies hurt production and morale. In 2002, accounting irregularities were uncovered at AOL, and, as a result of the acquisition costs, the company was saddled with massive debt. To make matters worse, AOL began to lose customers and money. Although AOL was the acquirer, and once dominant partner, things got so bad at AOL that the company changed its name back to Time Warner. To cap things off, in 2002, Time Warner wrote off a stunning $54 billion in assets associated with the acquisition, which was at the time the largest such write-off in history.

Forecasting Risk

The key inputs into a DCF analysis are projected future cash flows. If these projections are seriously in error, then we have a classic GIGO, or garbage-in, garbage-out, system. In this case, no matter how carefully we arrange the numbers and manipulate them, the resulting answer can still be grossly misleading. This is the danger in using a relatively sophisticated technique like DCF. It is sometimes easy to get caught up in number crunching and forget the underlying nuts-and-bolts economic reality.

forecasting risk
The possibility that errors in projected cash flows will lead to incorrect decisions. Also *estimation risk.*

The possibility that we will make a bad decision because of errors in the projected cash flows is called **forecasting risk** (or *estimation risk*). Because of forecasting risk, there is the danger that we will think a project has a positive NPV when it really does not. How is this possible? It occurs if we are overly optimistic about the future, and, as a result, our projected cash flows don't realistically reflect the possible future cash flows. Our nearby *Finance Matters* box shows what can happen in such cases.

So far, we have not explicitly considered what to do about the possibility of errors in our forecasts, so our goal is to develop some tools that will be useful in identifying areas where potential errors exist and where they might be especially damaging. In one form or another, we will be trying to assess the economic "reasonableness" of our estimates. We will also be wondering how much damage will be done by errors in those estimates.

Sources of Value

The first line of defense against forecasting risk is simply to ask: What is it about this investment that leads to a positive NPV? We should be able to point to something specific as the source of value. For example, if the proposal under consideration involved a new product, then we might ask questions such as the following: Are we certain that our new product is significantly better than that of the competition? Can we truly manufacture at lower cost, or distribute more effectively, or identify undeveloped market niches, or gain control of a market?

These are just a few of the potential sources of value. There are many others. A key factor to keep in mind is the degree of competition in the market. It is a basic principle of economics that positive NPV investments will be rare in a highly competitive environment. Therefore, proposals that appear to show significant value in the face of stiff competition are particularly troublesome, and the likely reaction of the competition to any innovations must be closely examined.

The point to remember is that positive NPV investments are probably not all that common, and the number of positive NPV projects is almost certainly limited for any given firm. If we can't articulate some sound economic basis for thinking ahead of time that we have found something special, then the conclusion that our project has a positive NPV should be viewed with some suspicion.

CONCEPT QUESTIONS

9.5a   What is forecasting risk? Why is it a concern for the financial manager?

9.5b   What are some potential sources of value in a new project?

SCENARIO AND OTHER WHAT-IF ANALYSES

9.6

Our basic approach to evaluating cash flow and NPV estimates involves asking what-if questions. Accordingly, we discuss some organized ways of going about a what-if analysis. Our goal in doing so is to assess the degree of forecasting risk and to identify those components most critical to the success or failure of an investment.

ExcelMaster
coverage online

Getting Started

We are investigating a new project. Naturally, the first thing we do is estimate NPV based on our projected cash flows. We will call this the *base case*. Now, however, we recognize the possibility of error in those cash flow projections. After completing the base case, we thus wish to investigate the impact of different assumptions about the future on our estimates.

One way to organize this investigation is to put an upper and lower bound on the various components of the project. For example, suppose we forecast sales at 100 units per year. We know this estimate may be high or low, but we are relatively certain it is not off by more than 10 units in either direction. We would thus pick a lower bound of 90 and an upper bound of 110. We go on to assign such bounds to any other cash flow components we are unsure about.

When we pick these upper and lower bounds, we are not ruling out the possibility that the actual values could be outside this range. What we are saying, loosely speaking, is that it is unlikely that the true average (as opposed to our estimated average) of the possible values is outside this range.

An example is useful to illustrate the idea here. The project under consideration costs $200,000, has a five-year life, and has no salvage value. Depreciation is straight-line to zero. The required return is 12 percent, and the tax rate is 34 percent. In addition, we have compiled the following information:

	Base Case	Lower Bound	Upper Bound
Unit sales	6,000	5,500	6,500
Price per unit	$80	$75	$85
Variable cost per unit	$60	$58	$62
Fixed costs per year	$50,000	$45,000	$55,000

With this information, we can calculate the base-case NPV by first calculating net income:

Sales	$480,000
Variable costs	360,000
Fixed costs	50,000
Depreciation	40,000
EBIT	$ 30,000
Taxes (34%)	10,200
Net income	$ 19,800

Operating cash flow is thus $30,000 + 40,000 − 10,200 = $59,800 per year. At 12 percent, the five-year annuity factor is 3.6048, so the base-case NPV is:

Base-case NPV = −$200,000 + 59,800 × 3.6048

= $15,567

Thus, the project looks good so far.

Scenario Analysis

scenario analysis
The determination of what happens to NPV estimates when we ask what-if questions.

The basic form of what-if analysis is called **scenario analysis**. What we do is investigate the changes in our NPV estimates that result from asking questions like: "What if unit sales realistically should be projected at 5,500 units instead of 6,000?"

Once we start looking at alternative scenarios, we might find that most of the plausible ones result in positive NPVs. In this case, we have some confidence in proceeding with the project. If a substantial percentage of the scenarios look bad, then the degree of forecasting risk is high and further investigation is in order.

There are a number of possible scenarios we could consider. A good place to start is with the worst-case scenario. This will tell us the minimum NPV of the project. If this is positive, we will be in good shape. While we are at it, we will go ahead and determine the other extreme, the best case. This puts an upper bound on our NPV.

To get the worst case, we assign the least favorable value to each item. This means *low* values for items such as units sold and price per unit and *high* values for costs. We do the reverse for the best case. For our project, these values would be:

	Worst Case	Best Case
Unit sales	5,500	6,500
Price per unit	$75	$85
Variable cost per unit	$62	$58
Fixed costs	$55,000	$45,000

With this information, we can calculate the net income and cash flows under each scenario (check these for yourself):

Scenario	Net Income	Cash Flow	Net Present Value	IRR
Base case	$19,800	$59,800	$15,567	15.1%
Worst case*	−15,510	24,490	−111,719	−14.4
Best case	59,730	99,730	159,504	40.9

* We assume a tax credit is created in our worst-case scenario.

What we learn is that under the worst scenario, the cash flow is still positive at $24,490. That's good news. The bad news is that the return is −14.4 percent in this case, and the NPV is −$111,719. Since the project costs $200,000, we stand to lose a little more than half of the original investment under the worst possible scenario. The best case offers an attractive 41 percent return.

The terms *best case* and *worst case* are very commonly used, and we will stick with them, but we should note that they are somewhat misleading. The absolutely best thing that could happen would be something absurdly unlikely, such as launching a new diet soda and subsequently learning that our (patented) formulation also just happens to cure the common cold. Of course, on rare occasions, things do go very, very wrong. For example, in April 2010, BP's Gulf of Mexico oil rig *Deepwater Horizon* caught fire and sank following an explosion, leading to a massive oil spill. The leak was finally stopped in July after releasing over 200 million gallons of crude oil into the Gulf. BP's costs associated with the disaster are expected to exceed $40 billion, perhaps by a wide margin. As an example of some of the costs, in March 2011, BP stated that it paid $14 billion responding to the spill and had earlier created a $20 billion fund to compensate those affected by the spill. The company was also near a settlement in a class action lawsuit that would cost another $7.8 billion. Nonetheless, our point is that in assessing the reasonableness of an NPV estimate, we need to stick to cases that are reasonably likely to occur.

Instead of *best* and *worst*, then, it is probably more accurate to say *optimistic* and *pessimistic*. In broad terms, if we were thinking about a reasonable range for, say, unit sales, then what we call the best case would correspond to something near the upper end of that range. The worst case would simply correspond to the lower end.

As we have mentioned, there are an unlimited number of different scenarios that we could examine. At a minimum, we might want to investigate two intermediate cases by going halfway between the base amounts and the extreme amounts. This would give us five scenarios in all, including the base case.

Beyond this point, it is hard to know when to stop. As we generate more and more possibilities, we run the risk of "paralysis of analysis." The difficulty is that no matter how many scenarios we run, all we can learn are possibilities, some good and some bad. Beyond that, we don't get any guidance as to what to do. Scenario analysis is thus useful in telling us what can happen and in helping us gauge the potential for disaster, but it does not tell us whether or not to take the project.

Sensitivity Analysis

Sensitivity analysis is a variation on scenario analysis that is useful in pinpointing the areas where forecasting risk is especially severe. The basic idea with a sensitivity analysis is to freeze all of the variables except one and then see how sensitive our estimate of NPV is to

sensitivity analysis
Investigation of what happens to NPV when only one variable is changed.

changes in that one variable. If our NPV estimate turns out to be very sensitive to relatively small changes in the projected value of some component of project cash flow, then the forecasting risk associated with that variable is high.

To illustrate how sensitivity analysis works, we go back to our base case for every item except unit sales. We can then calculate cash flow and NPV using the largest and smallest unit sales figures.

Scenario	Unit Sales	Cash Flow	Net Present Value	IRR
Base case	6,000	$59,800	$15,567	15.1%
Worst case	5,500	53,200	−8,226	10.3
Best case	6,500	66,400	39,357	19.7

The results of our sensitivity analysis for unit sales can be illustrated graphically as in Figure 9.1. Here we place NPV on the vertical axis and unit sales on the horizontal axis. When we plot the combinations of unit sales versus NPV, we see that all possible combinations fall on a straight line. The steeper the resulting line is, the greater is the sensitivity of the estimated NPV to the projected value of the variable being investigated.

By way of comparison, we now freeze everything except fixed costs and repeat the analysis:

Scenario	Fixed Costs	Cash Flow	Net Present Value	IRR
Base case	$50,000	$59,800	$15,567	15.1%
Worst case	55,000	56,500	3,670	12.7
Best case	45,000	63,100	27,461	17.4

What we see here is that, given our ranges, the estimated NPV of this project is more sensitive to projected unit sales than it is to projected fixed costs. In fact, under the worst case for fixed costs, the NPV is still positive.

FIGURE **9.1**

Sensitivity analysis for unit sales

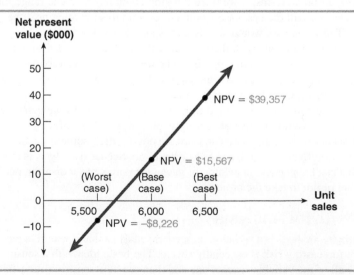

As we have illustrated, sensitivity analysis is useful in pinpointing those variables that deserve the most attention. If we find that our estimated NPV is especially sensitive to a variable that is difficult to forecast (such as unit sales), then the degree of forecasting risk is high. We might decide that further market research would be a good idea in this case.

Because sensitivity analysis is a form of scenario analysis, it suffers from the same drawbacks. Sensitivity analysis is useful for pointing out where forecasting errors will do the most damage, but it does not tell us what to do about possible errors.

CONCEPT QUESTIONS

9.6a   What are scenario and sensitivity analyses?

9.6b   What are the drawbacks to what-if analyses?

ADDITIONAL CONSIDERATIONS IN CAPITAL BUDGETING

9.7

Our final task for this chapter is a brief discussion of two additional considerations in capital budgeting: managerial options and capital rationing. Both of these can be very important in practice, but, as we will see, explicitly dealing with either of them is difficult.

Managerial Options and Capital Budgeting

In our capital budgeting analysis thus far, we have more or less ignored the possibility of future managerial actions. Implicitly, we have assumed that once a project is launched, its basic features cannot be changed. For this reason, we say that our analysis is *static* (as opposed to dynamic).

In reality, depending on what actually happens in the future, there will always be ways to modify a project. We will call these opportunities **managerial options**. Because they involve real (as opposed to financial) assets, such options are often called "real" options. There are a great number of these options. The way a product is priced, manufactured, advertised, and produced can all be changed, and these are just a few of the possibilities. We discuss some of the most important managerial options in the next few sections.

managerial options
Opportunities that managers can exploit if certain things happen in the future. Also known as "real" options.

Contingency Planning   The various what-if procedures in this chapter have another use. We can also view them as primitive ways of exploring the dynamics of a project and investigating managerial options. What we think about in this case are some of the possible futures that could come about and what actions we might take if they do.

For example, we might find that a project fails to break even when sales drop below 10,000 units. This is a fact that is interesting to know, but the more important thing is to then go on and ask "What actions are we going to take if this actually occurs?" This is called **contingency planning**, and it amounts to an investigation of some of the managerial options implicit in a project.

contingency planning
Taking into account the managerial options implicit in a project.

There is no limit to the number of possible futures, or contingencies, that we could investigate. However, there are some broad classes, and we consider these next.

The option to expand   One particularly important option we have not explicitly addressed is the option to expand. If we truly find a positive NPV project, then there is an

298 **PART 5** Capital Budgeting

obvious consideration: Can we expand the project or repeat it to get an even larger NPV? Our static analysis implicitly assumes that the scale of the project is fixed.

For example, if the sales demand for a particular product were to greatly exceed expectations, we might investigate increasing production. If this were not feasible for some reason, then we could always increase cash flow by raising the price. Either way, the potential cash flow is higher than we have indicated because we have implicitly assumed that no expansion or price increase is possible. Overall, because we ignore the option to expand in our analysis, we *underestimate* NPV (all other things being equal).

The option to abandon At the other extreme, the option to scale back or even abandon a project is also quite valuable. For example, if a project does not even cover its own expenses, we might be better off if we just abandoned it. Our DCF analysis implicitly assumes that we would keep operating even in this case.

In reality, if sales demand were significantly below expectations, we might be able to sell off some capacity or put it to another use. Maybe the product or service could be redesigned or otherwise improved. Regardless of the specifics, we once again *underestimate* NPV if we assume that the project must last for some fixed number of years, no matter what happens in the future.

The option to wait Implicitly, we have treated proposed investments as if they were "go or no-go" decisions. Actually, there is a third possibility. The project can be postponed, perhaps in hope of more favorable conditions. We call this the option to wait.

For example, suppose an investment costs $120 and has a perpetual cash flow of $10 per year. If the discount rate is 10 percent, then the NPV is $10/.10 − 120 = −$20, so the project should not be undertaken now. However, this does not mean that we should forget about the project forever, because in the next period, the appropriate discount rate could be different. If it fell to, say, 5 percent, then the NPV would be $10/.05 − 120 = $80, and we would take the project.

More generally, as long as there is some possible future scenario under which a project has a positive NPV, then the option to wait is valuable.

To illustrate some of these ideas, consider the case of Euro Disney. The deal to open Euro Disney occurred in 1987, and the park opened its doors outside of Paris in 1992. Disney's management thought Europeans would go goofy over the new park, but trouble soon began. The number of visitors never met expectations, in part because the company priced tickets too high. Disney also decided not to serve alcohol in a country that was accustomed to wine with meals. French labor inspectors fought Disney's strict dress codes, and so on.

After several years of operations, the park began serving wine in its restaurants, lowered ticket prices, and made other adjustments. In other words, management exercised its option to reformulate the product. The park began to make a small profit. Then, the company exercised the option to expand by adding a "second gate," which was another theme park next to Euro Disney named Walt Disney Studios. The second gate was intended to encourage visitors to extend their stays. But the new park flopped. The reasons ranged from high ticket prices, attractions geared toward Hollywood rather than European filmmaking, labor strikes in Paris, and a summer heat wave.

By the summer of 2003, Euro Disney was close to bankruptcy again. Executives discussed a variety of options. These options ranged from letting the company go broke (the option to abandon) to pulling the Disney name from the park. In 2005, the company finally agreed to a restructuring with the help of the French government.

After all the changes made at Euro Disney, the park gained momentum for several years, almost breaking even in 2008. In 2011, the resort posted revenues that were 5 percent higher than the previous year as it experienced a record 15.6 million visitors. However, the net loss for the year was €63.9 million.

Disney hopes to leverage the lessons learned in its other theme parks around the world. As of 2011, Hong Kong Disneyland had a total of 31 million visitors in its five years of existence. The park lost about $30.5 million in 2011, an improvement from the $92 million loss in 2010. And in April 2011, the groundbreaking occurred on a new $4.4 billion theme park in Shanghai that would be opened in late 2015.

The whole idea of managerial options was summed up aptly by Jay Rasulo, the overseer of Disney's theme parks, when he said: "One thing we know for sure is that you never get it 100 percent right the first time. We open every one of our parks with the notion that we're going to add content."

Strategic Options Companies sometimes undertake new projects just to explore possibilities and evaluate potential future business strategies. This is a little like testing the water by sticking a toe in before diving. Such projects are difficult to analyze using conventional DCF methods because most of the benefits come in the form of strategic options, that is, options for future, related business moves. Projects that create such options may be very valuable, but that value is difficult to measure. Research and development, for example, is an important and valuable activity for many firms precisely because it creates options for new products and procedures.

strategic options
Options for future, related business products or strategies.

To give another example, a large manufacturer might decide to open a retail outlet as a pilot study. The primary goal is to gain some market insight. Because of the high start-up costs, this one operation won't break even. However, based on the sales experience from the pilot, we can then evaluate whether or not to open more outlets, to change the product mix, to enter new markets, and so on. The information gained and the resulting options for actions are all valuable, but coming up with a reliable dollar figure is probably not feasible.

Conclusion We have seen that incorporating options into capital budgeting analysis is not easy. What can we do about them in practice? The answer is that we can only keep them in the back of our minds as we work with the projected cash flows. We will tend to underestimate NPV by ignoring options. The damage might be small for a highly structured, very specific proposal, but it might be great for an exploratory one.

Capital Rationing

Capital rationing is said to exist when we have profitable (positive NPV) investments available but we can't get the needed funds to undertake them. For example, as division managers for a large corporation, we might identify $5 million in excellent projects, but find that, for whatever reason, we can spend only $2 million. Now what? Unfortunately, for reasons we will discuss, there may be no truly satisfactory answer.

capital rationing
The situation that exists if a firm has positive NPV projects but cannot obtain the necessary financing.

Soft Rationing The situation we have just described is soft rationing. This occurs when, for example, different units in a business are allocated some fixed amount of money each year for capital spending. Such an allocation is primarily a means of controlling and keeping track of overall spending. The important thing about soft rationing is that the corporation as a whole isn't short of capital; more can be raised on ordinary terms if management so desires.

soft rationing
The situation that occurs when units in a business are allocated a certain amount of financing for capital budgeting.

If we face soft rationing, the first thing to do is try and get a larger allocation. Failing that, one common suggestion is to generate as large a net present value as possible within the existing budget. This amounts to choosing those projects with the largest benefit-cost ratio (profitability index).

Strictly speaking, this is the correct thing to do only if the soft rationing is a one-time event; that is, it won't exist next year. If the soft rationing is a chronic problem, then something is amiss. The reason goes all the way back to Chapter 1. Ongoing soft rationing means we are constantly bypassing positive NPV investments. This contradicts our goal of the firm. If we are not trying to maximize value, then the question of which projects to take becomes ambiguous because we no longer have an objective goal in the first place.

hard rationing
The situation that occurs when a business cannot raise financing for a project under any circumstances.

Hard Rationing   With **hard rationing**, a business cannot raise capital for a project under any circumstances. For large, healthy corporations, this situation probably does not occur very often. This is fortunate because with hard rationing, our DCF analysis breaks down, and the best course of action is ambiguous.

The reason DCF analysis breaks down has to do with the required return. Suppose we say that our required return is 20 percent. Implicitly, we are saying that we will take a project with a return that exceeds this. However, if we face hard rationing, then we are not going to take a new project no matter what the return on that project is, so the whole concept of a required return is ambiguous. About the only interpretation we can give this situation is that the required return is so large that no project has a positive NPV in the first place.

Hard rationing can occur when a company experiences financial distress, meaning that bankruptcy is a possibility. Also, a firm may not be able to raise capital without violating a pre-existing contractual agreement. We discuss these situations in greater detail in a later chapter.

CONCEPT QUESTIONS

9.7a   Why do we say that our standard discounted cash flow analysis is static?

9.7b   What are managerial options in capital budgeting? Give some examples.

9.7c   What is capital rationing? What types are there? What problems does capital rationing create for discounted cash flow analysis?

SUMMARY AND CONCLUSIONS

◄ Think you've mastered the material? Scan here to take a chapter quiz.

www.mhhe.com/rwj

This chapter has described how to go about putting together a discounted cash flow analysis and evaluating the results. In it, we covered:

1. The identification of relevant project cash flows. We discussed project cash flows and described how to handle some issues that often come up, including sunk costs, opportunity costs, financing costs, net working capital, and erosion.

2. Preparing and using pro forma, or projected, financial statements. We showed how pro forma financial statement information is useful in coming up with projected cash flows.

3. The use of scenario and sensitivity analysis. These tools are widely used to evaluate the impact of assumptions made about future cash flows and NPV estimates.

4. Additional issues in capital budgeting. We examined the managerial options implicit in many capital budgeting situations. We also discussed the capital rationing problem.

The discounted cash flow analysis we've covered here is a standard tool in the business world. It is a very powerful tool, so care should be taken in its use. The most important thing is to get the cash flows identified in a way that makes economic sense. This chapter gives you a good start on learning to do this.

connect POP QUIZ!
|FINANCE

Can you answer the following questions? If your class is using *Connect Finance,* log on to the Self-Quiz and Study feature in the Library tab to see if you know the answers to these and other questions, check out the study tools, and find out what topics require additional practice!

Section 9.1 Winnebagel Corp. currently sells 29,200 motor homes per year at $79,000 each and 8,200 luxury motor coaches per year at $121,000 each. The company wants to introduce a new portable camper to fill out its product line; it hopes to sell 24,200 of these campers per year at $25,000 each. An independent consultant has determined that if Winnebagel introduces the new campers, it should boost the sales of its existing motor homes by 3,800 units per year and reduce the sales of its motor coaches by 970 units per year. What is the amount to use as the annual sales figure when evaluating this project?

Section 9.2 Better Carpets currently sells the Roseland brand of carpets and is considering adding the Bloomington line of carpets to its offerings. Betters Carpets feels that it can sell $328,000 of Bloomington carpets per year but by doing so will lose $87,000 of Roseland carpet sales per year. Which one of the following terms best describes the $87,000?

Section 9.3 A proposed new investment has projected sales of $827,000. Variable costs are 57 percent of sales, and fixed costs are $187,110; depreciation is $92,000. Assume a tax rate of 40 percent. What is the projected net income?

Section 9.4 Consider an asset that costs $966,000 and is depreciated straight-line to zero over its 10-year tax life. The asset is to be used in a seven-year project; at the end of the project, the asset can be sold for $136,800. If the relevant tax rate is 35 percent, what is the aftertax cash flow from the sale of this asset?

Section 9.5 Marti erroneously determined that a project had a positive NPV when it fact it did not. The error was caused by Marti's incorrect projection of the cash inflows for the project. What type of risk does this example illustrate?

Section 9.6 Automatic Transmissions, Inc., has the following estimates for its new gear assembly project: price = $1,230 per unit; variable cost = $450 per unit; fixed costs = $4.96 million; quantity = 86,000 units. Suppose the company believes all of its estimates are accurate only to within ±20 percent. What values should the company use for the four variables given here when it performs its best-case and worst-case scenario analysis?

Section 9.7 If Kathy ignores the option to abandon when analyzing a project, what will result?

www.mhhe.com/rwj

CHAPTER REVIEW AND SELF-TEST PROBLEMS

9.1 **Calculating Operating Cash Flow.**   Mater Pasta, Inc., has projected a sales volume of $1,432 for the second year of a proposed expansion project. Costs normally run 70 percent of sales, or about $1,002 in this case. The depreciation expense will be $80, and the tax rate is 34 percent. What is the operating cash flow? (See Problem 9.)

9.2 **Scenario Analysis.**   A project under consideration costs $500,000, has a five-year life, and has no salvage value. Depreciation is straight-line to zero. The required return is 15 percent, and the tax rate is 34 percent. Sales are projected at 400 units per year. Price per unit is $3,000, variable cost per unit is $1,900, and fixed costs are $250,000 per year. No net working capital is required.

Suppose you think the unit sales, price, variable cost, and fixed cost projections are accurate to within 5 percent. What are the upper and lower bounds for these projections? What is the base-case NPV? What are the best- and worst-case scenario NPVs? (See Problem 19.)

■ Answers to Chapter Review and Self-Test Problems

9.1   First, we can calculate the project's EBIT, its tax bill, and its net income.

$$\text{EBIT} = \$1,432 - 1,002 - 80 = \$350$$
$$\text{Taxes} = \$350 \times .34 = \$119$$
$$\text{Net income} = \$350 - 119 = \$231$$

With these numbers, operating cash flow is:

$$\text{OCF} = \text{EBIT} + \text{Depreciation} - \text{Taxes}$$
$$= \$350 + 80 - 119$$
$$= \$311$$

9.2   We can summarize the relevant information as follows:

	Base Case	Lower Bound	Upper Bound
Unit sales	400	380	420
Price per unit	$3,000	$2,850	$3,150
Variable cost per unit	$1,900	$1,805	$1,995
Fixed costs	$250,000	$237,500	$262,500

The depreciation is $100,000 per year, and the tax rate is 34 percent, so we can calculate the cash flows under each scenario. Remember that we assign high costs and low prices and volume under the worst case and just the opposite for the best case.

Scenario	Unit Sales	Price	Variable Costs	Fixed Costs	Cash Flow
Base case	400	$3,000	$1,900	$250,000	$159,400
Best case	420	3,150	1,805	237,500	250,084
Worst case	380	2,850	1,995	262,500	75,184

At 15 percent, the five-year annuity factor is 3.35216, so the NPVs are:

Base-case NPV = −$500,000 + 159,400 × 3.35216 = $34,334

Best-case NPV = −$500,000 + 250,084 × 3.35216 = $338,320

Worst-case NPV = −$500,000 + 75,184 × 3.35216 = −$247,972

CRITICAL THINKING AND CONCEPTS REVIEW

LO 1   **9.1**   **Opportunity Cost.**   In the context of capital budgeting, what is an opportunity cost?

LO 1   **9.2**   **Depreciation.**   Given the choice, would a firm prefer to use MACRS depreciation or straight-line depreciation? Why?

LO 1   **9.3**   **Net Working Capital.**   In our capital budgeting examples, we assumed that a firm would recover all of the working capital it invested in a project. Is this a reasonable assumption? When might it not be valid?

LO 1   **9.4**   **Stand-Alone Principle.**   Suppose a financial manager is quoted as saying, "Our firm uses the stand-alone principle. Because we treat projects like minifirms in our evaluation process, we include financing costs because they are relevant at the firm level." Critically evaluate this statement.

LO 1   **9.5**   **Cash Flow and Depreciation.**   "When evaluating projects, we're only concerned with the relevant incremental aftertax cash flows. Therefore, because depreciation is a noncash expense, we should ignore its effects when evaluating projects." Critically evaluate this statement.

LO 1   **9.6**   **Capital Budgeting Considerations.**   A major college textbook publisher has an existing finance textbook. The publisher is debating whether or not to produce an "essentialized" version, meaning a shorter (and lower-priced) book. What are some of the considerations that should come into play?

To answer the next three questions, refer to the following example. In 2003, Porsche unveiled its new sports-utility vehicle (SUV), the Cayenne. With a price tag of over $40,000, the Cayenne goes from zero to 62 mph in 9.7 seconds. Porsche's decision to enter the SUV market was in response to the runaway success of other high-priced SUVs such as the Mercedes-Benz M-class. Vehicles in this class had generated years of very high profits. The Cayenne certainly spiced up the market, and Porsche subsequently introduced the Cayenne Turbo S, which goes from zero to 60 mph in 4.8 seconds and has a top speed of 168 mph. The price tag for the Cayenne Turbo S? Over $107,000 in 2012.

Some analysts questioned Porsche's entry into the luxury SUV market. The analysts were concerned not only that Porsche was a late entry into the market, but also that the introduction of the Cayenne would damage Porsche's reputation as a maker of high-performance automobiles.

LO 1   **9.7**   **Erosion.**   In evaluating the Cayenne, would you consider the possible damage to Porsche's reputation?

LO 1   **9.8**   **Capital Budgeting.**   Porsche was one of the last manufacturers to enter the sports-utility vehicle market. Why would one company decide to proceed with a product when other companies, at least initially, decide not to enter the market?

LO 1   **9.9**   **Capital Budgeting.**   In evaluating the Cayenne, what do you think Porsche needs to assume regarding the substantial profit margins that exist in this market? Is it likely they will be maintained as the market becomes more competitive, or will Porsche be able to maintain the profit margin because of its image and the performance of the Cayenne?

www.mhhe.com/rwj

LO 2 9.10 **Sensitivity Analysis and Scenario Analysis.** What is the essential difference between sensitivity analysis and scenario analysis?

LO 1 9.11 **Marginal Cash Flows.** A co-worker claims that looking at all this marginal this and incremental that is just a bunch of nonsense and states: "Listen, if our average revenue doesn't exceed our average cost, then we will have a negative cash flow, and we will go broke!" How do you respond?

LO 1 9.12 **Capital Rationing.** Going all the way back to Chapter 1, recall that we saw that partnerships and proprietorships can face difficulties when it comes to raising capital. In the context of this chapter, the implication is that small businesses will generally face what problem?

LO 2 9.13 **Forecasting Risk.** What is forecasting risk? In general, would the degree of forecasting risk be greater for a new product or a cost-cutting proposal? Why?

LO 2 9.14 **Options and NPV.** What is the option to abandon? The option to expand? Explain why we tend to underestimate NPV when we ignore these options.

QUESTIONS AND PROBLEMS

Select problems are available in McGraw-Hill Connect. Please see the packaging options section of the preface for more information.

Basic
(Questions 1–20)

LO 1 1. **Relevant Cash Flows.** Kenny, Inc., is looking at setting up a new manufacturing plant in South Park. The company bought some land six years ago for $7.5 million in anticipation of using it as a warehouse and distribution site, but the company has since decided to rent facilities elsewhere. The land would net $10.3 million if it were sold today. The company now wants to build its new manufacturing plant on this land; the plant will cost $24 million to build, and the site requires $975,000 worth of grading before it is suitable for construction. What is the proper cash flow amount to use as the initial investment in fixed assets when evaluating this project? Why?

LO 1 2. **Relevant Cash Flows.** Winnebagel Corp. currently sells 28,000 motor homes per year at $73,000 each and 7,000 luxury motor coaches per year at $115,000 each. The company wants to introduce a new portable camper to fill out its product line; it hopes to sell 29,000 of these campers per year at $18,500 each. An independent consultant has determined that if Winnebagel introduces the new campers, it should boost the sales of its existing motor homes by 2,500 units per year and reduce the sales of its motor coaches by 750 units per year. What is the amount to use as the annual sales figure when evaluating this project? Why?

LO 2 3. **Calculating Projected Net Income.** A proposed new investment has projected sales of $750,000. Variable costs are 55 percent of sales, and fixed costs are $182,500; depreciation is $86,000. Prepare a pro forma income statement assuming a tax rate of 35 percent. What is the projected net income?

LO 2 4. **Calculating OCF.** Consider the following income statement:

Sales	$657,900
Costs	352,900
Depreciation	97,500
EBIT	?
Taxes (35%)	?
Net income	?

Fill in the missing numbers and then calculate the OCF. What is the depreciation tax shield?

LO 2   **5. Calculating Depreciation.**   A piece of newly purchased industrial equipment costs $870,000 and is classified as seven-year property under MACRS. Calculate the annual depreciation allowances and end-of-the-year book values for this equipment.

LO 2   **6. Calculating Salvage Value.**   Consider an asset that costs $635,000 and is depreciated straight-line to zero over its eight-year tax life. The asset is to be used in a five-year project; at the end of the project, the asset can be sold for $125,000. If the relevant tax rate is 35 percent, what is the aftertax cash flow from the sale of this asset?

LO 2   **7. Calculating Salvage Value.**   An asset used in a four-year project falls in the five-year MACRS class for tax purposes. The asset has an acquisition cost of $6,400,000 and will be sold for $1,530,000 at the end of the project. If the tax rate is 34 percent, what is the aftertax salvage value of the asset?

LO 2   **8. Calculating Project OCF.**   Rolston Music Company is considering the sale of a new sound board used in recording studios. The new board would sell for $26,400, and the company expects to sell 1,500 per year. The company currently sells 1,850 units of its existing model per year. If the new model is introduced, sales of the existing model will fall to 1,520 units per year. The old board retails for $22,300. Variable costs are 55 percent of sales, depreciation on the equipment to produce the new board will be $1,975,000 per year, and fixed costs are $2,400,000 per year. If the tax rate is 38 percent, what is the annual OCF for the project?

LO 2   **9. Calculating Project OCF.**   Cochrane, Inc., is considering a new three-year expansion project that requires an initial fixed asset investment of $1,860,000. The fixed asset will be depreciated straight-line to zero over its three-year tax life, after which time it will be worthless. The project is estimated to generate $1,950,000 in annual sales, with costs of $1,060,000. If the tax rate is 35 percent, what is the OCF for this project?

LO 2   **10. Calculating Project NPV.**   In the previous problem, suppose the required return on the project is 14 percent. What is the project's NPV?

LO 2   **11. Calculating Project Cash Flow from Assets.**   In the previous problem, suppose the project requires an initial investment in net working capital of $150,000, and the fixed asset will have a market value of $175,000 at the end of the project. What is the project's Year 0 net cash flow? Year 1? Year 2? Year 3? What is the new NPV?

LO 2   **12. NPV and Modified ACRS.**   In the previous problem, suppose the fixed asset actually falls into the three-year MACRS class. All the other facts are the same. What is the project's Year 1 net cash flow now? Year 2? Year 3? What is the new NPV?

LO 2   **13. Project Evaluation.**   Kolby's Korndogs is looking at a new sausage system with an installed cost of $735,000. This cost will be depreciated straight-line to zero over the project's five-year life, at the end of which the sausage system can be scrapped for $105,000. The sausage system will save the firm $204,000 per year in pretax operating costs, and the system requires an initial investment in net working capital of $35,000. If the tax rate is 34 percent and the discount rate is 8 percent, what is the NPV of this project?

LO 2   **14. Project Evaluation.**   Your firm is contemplating the purchase of a new $480,000 computer-based order entry system. The system will be depreciated straight-line to zero over its five-year life. It will be worth $30,000 at the end of that time. You will save $145,000 before taxes per year in order processing costs, and you will be able to reduce working capital by $35,000 at the beginning of the project. Working capital will revert back to normal at the end of the project. If the tax rate is 35 percent, what is the IRR for this project?

LO 2   **15. Project Evaluation.**   In the previous problem, suppose your required return on the project is 10 percent and your pretax cost savings are $155,000 per year. Will you accept the project? What if the pretax cost savings are only $125,000 per year?

LO 3   **16. Scenario Analysis.**   Automatic Transmissions, Inc., has the following estimates for its new gear assembly project: price = $860 per unit; variable cost = $320 per unit; fixed costs = $3.4 million; quantity = 60,000 units. Suppose the company believes all of its estimates are accurate only to within ±15 percent. What values should the company use for the four variables given here when it performs its best-case scenario analysis? What about the worst-case scenario?

LO 3   **17. Sensitivity Analysis.**   For the company in the previous problem, suppose management is most concerned about the impact of its price estimate on the project's profitability. How could you address this concern for Automatic Transmissions? Describe how you would calculate your answer. What values would you use for the other forecast variables?

LO 3   **18. Sensitivity Analysis.**   We are evaluating a project that costs $1,675,000, has a six-year life, and has no salvage value. Assume that depreciation is straight-line to zero over the life of the project. Sales are projected at 91,000 units per year. Price per unit is $35.95, variable cost per unit is $21.40, and fixed costs are $775,000 per year. The tax rate is 35 percent, and we require a return of 11 percent on this project.

   a.   Calculate the base-case cash flow and NPV. What is the sensitivity of NPV to changes in the sales figure? Explain what your answer tells you about a 500-unit decrease in projected sales.

   b.   What is the sensitivity of OCF to changes in the variable cost figure? Explain what your answer tells you about a $1 decrease in estimated variable costs.

LO 3   **19. Scenario Analysis.**   In the previous problem, suppose the projections given for price, quantity, variable costs, and fixed costs are all accurate to within ±10 percent. Calculate the best-case and worst-case NPV figures.

LO 2   **20. Calculating Project Cash Flows and NPV.**   Pappy's Potato has come up with a new product, the Potato Pet (they are freeze-dried to last longer). Pappy's paid $120,000 for a marketing survey to determine the viability of the product. It is felt that Potato Pet will generate sales of $725,000 per year. The fixed costs associated with this will be $187,000 per year, and variable costs will amount to 20 percent of sales. The equipment necessary for production of the Potato Pet will cost $835,000 and will be depreciated in a straight-line manner for the four years of the product life (as with all fads, it is felt the sales will end quickly). This is the only initial cost for the production. Pappy's is in a 40 percent tax bracket and has a required return of 13 percent. Calculate the payback period, NPV, and IRR.

Intermediate
(Questions 21–24)

LO 2   **21. Cost-Cutting Proposals.**   CSM Machine Shop is considering a four-year project to improve its production efficiency. Buying a new machine press for $545,000 is estimated to result in $197,000 in annual pretax cost savings. The press falls in the MACRS five-year class, and it will have a salvage value at the end of the project of $70,000. The press also requires an initial investment in spare parts inventory of $21,000, along with an additional $3,000 in inventory for each succeeding year of the project. If the shop's tax rate is 34 percent and its discount rate is 11 percent, should the company buy and install the machine press?

LO 3 **22. Sensitivity Analysis.**   Consider a three-year project with the following information: initial fixed asset investment = $730,000; straight-line depreciation to zero over the five-year life; zero salvage value; price = $40.30; variable costs = $32.80; fixed costs = $345,000; quantity sold = 90,000 units; tax rate = 34 percent. How sensitive is OCF to changes in quantity sold?

LO 2 **23. Project Analysis.**   You are considering a new product launch. The project will cost $875,000, have a four-year life, and have no salvage value; depreciation is straight-line to zero. Sales are projected at 190 units per year; price per unit will be $19,200, variable cost per unit will be $15,100, and fixed costs will be $345,000 per year. The required return on the project is 11 percent, and the relevant tax rate is 35 percent.

    a.   Based on your experience, you think the unit sales, variable cost, and fixed cost projections given here are probably accurate to within ±10 percent. What are the best and worst cases for these projections? What is the base-case NPV? What are the best-case and worst-case scenarios?

    b.   Evaluate the sensitivity of your base-case NPV to changes in fixed costs.

LO 2 **24. Project Analysis.**   McGilla Golf has decided to sell a new line of golf clubs. The clubs will sell for $750 per set and have a variable cost of $360 per set. The company has spent $150,000 for a marketing study that determined the company will sell 72,000 sets per year for seven years. The marketing study also determined that the company will lose sales of 8,500 sets per year of its high-priced clubs. The high-priced clubs sell at $1,100 and have variable costs of $540. The company will also increase sales of its cheap clubs by 11,000 sets per year. The cheap clubs sell for $360 and have variable costs of $125 per set. The fixed costs each year will be $13,900,000. The company has also spent $1,000,000 on research and development for the new clubs. The plant and equipment required will cost $28,700,000 and will be depreciated on a straight-line basis. The new clubs will also require an increase in net working capital of $2,100,000 that will be returned at the end of the project. The tax rate is 40 percent, and the cost of capital is 14 percent. Calculate the payback period, the NPV, and the IRR.

LO 2 **25. Project Evaluation.**   Aguilera Acoustics, Inc. (AAI), projects unit sales for a new seven-octave voice emulation implant as follows:

Year	Unit Sales
1	87,500
2	105,000
3	119,000
4	108,000
5	92,000

Challenge
(Questions 25–26)

Production of the implants will require $1,500,000 in net working capital to start and additional net working capital investments each year equal to 15 percent of the projected sales increase for the following year. Total fixed costs are $1,450,000 per year, variable production costs are $230 per unit, and the units are priced at $355 each. The equipment needed to begin production has an installed cost of $24,000,000. Because the implants are intended for professional singers, this equipment is considered industrial machinery and thus qualifies as seven-year MACRS property. In five years, this equipment can be sold for about 20 percent of its acquisition cost. AAI is in the 35 percent marginal tax bracket and has a required return on all its projects of 18 percent. Based on these preliminary project estimates, what is the NPV of the project? What is the IRR?

LO 2   26. **Calculating Required Savings.**   A proposed cost-saving device has an installed cost of $585,000. The device will be used in a five-year project but is classified as three-year MACRS property for tax purposes. The required initial net working capital investment is $45,000, the marginal tax rate is 35 percent, and the project discount rate is 12 percent. The device has an estimated Year 5 salvage value of $65,000. What level of pretax cost savings do we require for this project to be profitable?

CHAPTER CASE
CONCH REPUBLIC ELECTRONICS

Conch Republic Electronics is a midsized electronics manufacturer located in Key West, Florida. The company president is Shelly Couts, who inherited the company. The company originally repaired radios and other household appliances when it was founded over 70 years ago. Over the years, the company has expanded, and it is now a reputable manufacturer of various specialty electronic items. Jay McCanless, a recent MBA graduate, has been hired by the company in its finance department.

One of the major revenue-producing items manufactured by Conch Republic is a smart phone. Conch Republic currently has one smart phone model on the market and sales have been excellent. The smart phone is a unique item in that it comes in a variety of tropical colors and is preprogrammed to play Jimmy Buffett music. However, as with any electronic item, technology changes rapidly, and the current smart phone has limited features in comparison with newer models. Conch Republic spent $750,000 to develop a prototype for a new smart phone that has all the features of the existing one but adds new features

such as wifi tethering. The company has spent a further $200,000 for a marketing study to determine the expected sales figures for the new smart phone.

Conch Republic can manufacture the new smart phone for $205 each in variable costs. Fixed costs for the operation are estimated to run $5.1 million per year. The estimated sales volume is 64,000, 106,000, 87,000, 78,000, and 54,000 per year for the next five years, respectively. The unit price of the new smart phone will be $485. The necessary equipment can be purchased for $34.5 million and will be depreciated on a seven-year MACRS schedule. It is believed the value of the equipment in five years will be $5.5 million.

Net working capital for the smart phones will be 20 percent of sales and will occur with the timing of the cash flows for the year (i.e., there is no initial outlay for NWC). Changes in NWC will thus first occur in Year 1 with the first year's sales. Conch Republic has a 35 percent corporate tax rate and a required return of 12 percent.

Shelly has asked Jay to prepare a report that answers the following questions:

QUESTIONS

1. What is the payback period of the project?
2. What is the profitability index of the project?
3. What is the IRR of the project?
4. What is the NPV of the project?
5. How sensitive is the NPV to changes in the price of the new smart phone?
6. How sensitive is the NPV to changes in the quantity sold?

7. Should Conch Republic produce the new smart phone?
8. Suppose Conch Republic loses sales on other models because of the introduction of the new model. How would this affect your analysis?

www.mhhe.com/rwj

10 | Some Lessons from Capital Market History

learning objectives

After studying this chapter, you should be able to:

LO 1 Calculate the return on an investment.

LO 2 Discuss the historical returns on various important types of investments.

LO 3 Explain the historical risks on various important types of investments.

LO 4 Assess the implications of market efficiency.

With the S&P 500 returning about 2 percent and the NASDAQ Composite Index down about 1 percent in 2011, stock market performance overall was not very good. However, investors in software company eGain Communications had to be happy about the 412 percent gain in that stock, and investors in semiconductor company Silicon Motion Technology had to feel at least semigood following that company's 382 percent gain. On the other hand, investors in First Solar were probably not too sunny about that stock's 74 percent decline during the year, while stock in Alpha Natural Resources dropped 66 percent. These examples show that there were tremendous potential profits to be made during 2011, but there was also the risk of losing money—and lots of it. So what should you, as a stock market investor, expect when you invest your own money? In this chapter, we study more than eight decades of market history to find out.

This chapter and the next take us into new territory: the relation between risk and return. As you will see, this chapter has a lot of very practical information for anyone thinking of investing in financial assets such as stocks and bonds. For example, suppose you were to start investing in stocks today. Do you think your money would grow at an average rate of 5 percent per year? Or 10 percent? Or 20 percent? This chapter gives you an idea of what to expect (the answer may surprise you). The chapter also shows how risky certain investments can be, and it gives you the tools to think about risk in an objective way.

Thus far, we haven't had much to say about what determines the required return on an investment. In one sense, the answer is very simple: The required return depends on the risk of the investment. The greater the risk, the greater is the required return.

Having said this, we are left with a somewhat more difficult problem. How can we measure the amount of risk present in an investment? Put another way, what does it mean to say that one investment is riskier than another? Obviously, we need to define what we mean by risk if we are going to answer these questions. This is our task in the next two chapters.

From the last several chapters, we know that one of the responsibilities of the financial manager is to assess the value of proposed investments. In doing this, it is important that we first look at what financial investments have to offer. At a minimum, the return we require from a proposed nonfinancial investment must be at least as large as what we can get from buying financial assets of similar risk.

Our goal in this chapter is to provide a perspective on what capital market history can tell us about risk and return. The most important thing to get out of this chapter is a feel for the numbers. What is a high return? What is a low one? More generally, what returns should we expect from financial assets and what are the risks from such investments? This perspective is essential for understanding how to analyze and value risky investment projects.

We start our discussion of risk and return by describing the historical experience of investors in the U.S. financial markets. In 1931, for example, the stock market lost 43 percent of its value. Just two years later, the stock market gained 54 percent. In more recent memory, the market lost about 25 percent of its value on October 19, 1987, alone, and stocks lost almost 40 percent in 2008. What lessons, if any, can financial managers learn from such shifts in the stock market? We will explore the last half century (and then some) of market history to find out.

Not everyone agrees on the value of studying history. On the one hand, there is philosopher George Santayana's famous comment "Those who cannot remember the past are condemned to repeat it." On the other hand, there is industrialist Henry Ford's equally famous comment "History is more or less bunk." Nonetheless, perhaps everyone would agree with the following observation from Mark Twain: "October. This is one of the peculiarly dangerous months to speculate in stocks in. The others are July, January, September, April, November, May, March, June, December, August, and February."

There are two central lessons that emerge from our study of market history. First: There is a reward for bearing risk. Second: The greater the potential reward is, the greater is the risk. To understand these facts about market returns, we devote much of this chapter to reporting the statistics and numbers that make up the modern capital market history of the United States. In the next chapter, these facts provide the foundation for our study of how financial markets put a price on risk.

RETURNS

We wish to discuss historical returns on different types of financial assets. The first thing we need to do, then, is to briefly discuss how to calculate the return from investing.

Dollar Returns

If you buy an asset of any sort, your gain (or loss) from that investment is called your *return on investment*. This return will usually have two components. First: You may receive some

ExcelMaster
coverage online

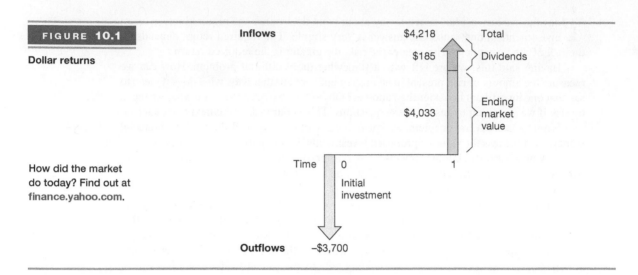

FIGURE 10.1

Dollar returns

How did the market do today? Find out at finance.yahoo.com.

cash directly while you own the investment. This is called the income component of your return. Second: The value of the asset you purchase will often change. In this case, you have a capital gain or capital loss on your investment.[1]

To illustrate, suppose the Video Concept Company has several thousand shares of stock outstanding. You purchased some of these shares of stock in the company at the beginning of the year. It is now year-end, and you want to determine how well you have done on your investment.

First, over the year, a company may pay cash dividends to its shareholders. As a stockholder in Video Concept Company, you are a part owner of the company. If the company is profitable, it may choose to distribute some of its profits to shareholders (we discuss the details of dividend policy in a later chapter). So, as the owner of some stock, you will receive some cash. This cash is the income component from owning the stock.

In addition to the dividend, the other part of your return is the capital gain or capital loss on the stock. This part arises from changes in the value of your investment. For example, consider the cash flows illustrated in Figure 10.1. At the beginning of the year, the stock is selling for $37 per share. If you buy 100 shares, you have a total outlay of $3,700. Suppose, over the year, the stock pays a dividend of $1.85 per share. By the end of the year, then, you will have received income of:

Dividend = $1.85 × 100 = $185

Also, the value of the stock rises to $40.33 per share by the end of the year. Your 100 shares are worth $4,033, so you have a capital gain of:

Capital gain = ($40.33 − 37) × 100 = $333

On the other hand, if the price had dropped to, say, $34.78, you would have had a capital loss of:

Capital loss = ($34.78 − 37) × 100 = −$222

Notice that a capital loss is the same thing as a negative capital gain.

---

[1] As we mentioned in an earlier chapter, strictly speaking, what is and what is not a capital gain (or loss) is determined by the IRS. We thus use the terms loosely.

The total dollar return on your investment is the sum of the dividend and the capital gain:

Total dollar return = Dividend income + Capital gain (or loss)   [10.1]

In our first example, the total dollar return is thus given by:

Total dollar return = $185 + 333 = $518

Notice that, if you sold the stock at the end of the year, the total amount of cash you would have would be your initial investment plus the total return. In the preceding example, then:

$$\begin{aligned} \textbf{Total cash if stock is sold} &= \textbf{Initial investment + Total return} \\ &= \textbf{\$3,700 + 518} \\ &= \textbf{\$4,218} \end{aligned}$$ [10.2]

As a check, notice that this is the same as the proceeds from the sale of the stock plus the dividends:

$$\begin{aligned} \textbf{Proceeds from stock sale + Dividends} &= \textbf{\$40.33} \times \textbf{100 + 185} \\ &= \textbf{\$4,033 + 185} \\ &= \textbf{\$4,218} \end{aligned}$$

Suppose you hold on to your Video Concept stock and don't sell it at the end of the year. Should you still consider the capital gain as part of your return? Isn't this only a "paper" gain and not really a return if you don't sell the stock?

The answer to the first question is a strong yes, and the answer to the second is an equally strong no. The capital gain is every bit as much a part of your return as the dividend, and you should certainly count it as part of your return. That you actually decided to keep the stock and not sell (you don't "realize" the gain) is irrelevant because you could have converted it to cash if you had wanted to. Whether you choose to do so or not is up to you.

After all, if you insisted on converting your gain to cash, you could always sell the stock at year-end and immediately reinvest by buying the stock back. There is no net difference between doing this and just not selling (assuming, of course, that there are no tax consequences from selling the stock). Again, the point is that whether you actually cash out and buy sodas (or whatever) or reinvest by not selling doesn't affect the return you earn.

Percentage Returns

It is usually more convenient to summarize information about returns in percentage terms, rather than dollar terms, because that way your return doesn't depend on how much you actually invest. The question we want to answer is this: How much do we get for each dollar we invest?

To answer this question, let P_t be the price of the stock at the beginning of the year and let D_{t+1} be the dividend paid on the stock during the year. Consider the cash flows in Figure 10.2. These are the same as those in Figure 10.1, except that we have now expressed everything on a per-share basis.

In our example, the price at the beginning of the year was $37 per share and the dividend paid during the year on each share was $1.85. As we discussed in Chapter 7, expressing the dividend as a percentage of the beginning stock price results in the dividend yield:

$$\begin{aligned} \textbf{Dividend yield} &= D_{t+1}/P_t \\ &= \textbf{\$1.85/37 = .05 = 5\%} \end{aligned}$$

This says that, for each dollar we invest, we get five cents in dividends.

Go to
www.smartmoney.
com/marketmap
for a cool Java applet
that shows today's
returns by market
sector.

FIGURE 10.2

Dollar returns per share

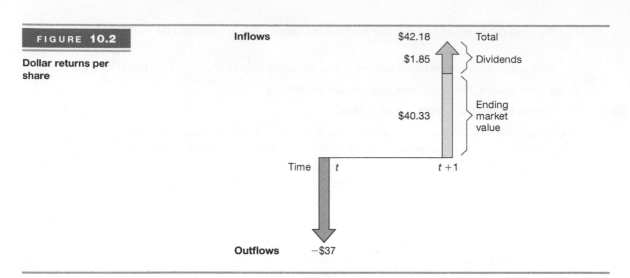

The second component of our percentage return is the capital gains yield. Recall (from Chapter 7) that this is calculated as the change in the price during the year (the capital gain) divided by the beginning price:

Capital gains yield $= (P_{t+1} - P_t)/P_t$

$= (\$40.33 - 37)/37$

$= \$3.33/37$

$= 9\%$

So, per dollar invested, we get nine cents in capital gains.

Putting it together, per dollar invested, we get 5 cents in dividends and 9 cents in capital gains; so, we get a total of 14 cents. Our percentage return is 14 cents on the dollar, or 14 percent.

To check this, notice that we invested \$3,700 and ended up with \$4,218. By what percentage did our \$3,700 increase? As we saw, we picked up \$4,218 − 3,700 = \$518. This is a \$518/3,700 = 14% increase.

To give a more concrete example, stock in McDonald's, the famous hamburger chain, began 2011 at \$76.76 per share. McDonald's paid dividends of \$2.53 during 2011, and the stock price at the end of the year was \$100.33. What was the return on McDonald's for the year? For practice, see if you agree that the answer is 34 percent. Of course, negative returns occur as well. For example, again in 2011, JPMorgan's stock price at the beginning of the year was \$42.42 per share, and dividends of \$.80 were paid. The stock ended the year at \$33.25 per share. Verify that the loss was 19.73 percent for the year.

EXAMPLE 10.1

CALCULATING RETURNS

Suppose you buy some stock for \$25 per share. At the end of the year, the price is \$35 per share. During the year, you get a \$2 dividend per share. This is the situation illustrated in Figure 10.3. What is the dividend yield? The capital gains yield? The percentage return? If your total investment was \$1,000, how much do you have at the end of the year?

Your \$2 dividend per share works out to a dividend yield of:

Dividend yield $= D_{t+1}/P_t$

$= \$2/25 = .08 = 8\%$

The per-share capital gain is $10, so the capital gains yield is:

$$\text{Capital gains yield} = (P_{t+1} - P_t)/P_t$$
$$= (\$35 - 25)/25$$
$$= \$10/25$$
$$= 40\%$$

The total percentage return is thus 48 percent.

If you had invested $1,000, you would have had $1,480 at the end of the year, representing a 48 percent increase. To check this, note that your $1,000 would have bought you $1,000/25 = 40 shares. Your 40 shares would then have paid you a total of 40 × $2 = $80 in cash dividends. Your $10 per share gain would have given you a total capital gain of $10 × 40 = $400. Add these together, and you get the $480 increase.

FIGURE 10.3

Cash flow—an investment example

CONCEPT QUESTIONS

10.1a What are the two parts of total return?

10.1b Why are unrealized capital gains or losses included in the calculation of returns?

10.1c What is the difference between a dollar return and a percentage return? Why are percentage returns more convenient?

THE HISTORICAL RECORD

10.2

Roger Ibbotson and Rex Sinquefield conducted a famous set of studies dealing with rates of return in U.S. financial markets.[2] They presented year-to-year historical rates of return on five important types of financial investments. The returns can be interpreted as what you would have earned if you had held portfolios of the following:

ExcelMaster
coverage online

1. Large-company stocks. The large-company stock portfolio is based on the Standard & Poor's 500 index, which contains 500 of the largest companies (in terms of total market value of outstanding stock) in the United States.

---

[2] R. G. Ibbotson and R. A. Sinquefield, *Stocks, Bonds, Bills, and Inflation* [SBBI] (Charlottesville, VA: Financial Analysis Research Foundation, 1982).

For more on market history, visit www.globalfinancialdata.com where you can download free sample data.

2. **Small-company stocks.** This is a portfolio composed of stock of smaller companies, where "small" corresponds to the smallest 20 percent of the companies listed on the New York Stock Exchange, again as measured by market value of outstanding stock.

3. **Long-term corporate bonds.** This is a portfolio of high-quality bonds with 20 years to maturity.

4. **Long-term U.S. government bonds.** This is a portfolio of U.S. government bonds with 20 years to maturity.

5. **U.S. Treasury bills.** This is based on Treasury bills (T-bills for short) with a one-month maturity.

These returns are not adjusted for inflation or taxes; thus, they are nominal, pretax returns.

In addition to the year-to-year returns on these financial instruments, the year-to-year percentage change in the consumer price index (CPI) is also computed. This is a commonly used measure of inflation, so we can calculate real returns using this as the inflation rate.

A First Look

Go to www.bigcharts.com to see both intraday and long-term charts.

Before looking closely at the different portfolio returns, we take a look at the big picture. Figure 10.4 shows what happened to $1 invested in these different portfolios at the beginning of 1926. The growth in value for each of the different portfolios over the 86-year period ending in 2011 is given separately (the long-term corporate bonds are omitted). Notice that to get everything on a single graph, some modification in scaling is used. As is commonly done with financial series, the vertical axis is scaled such that equal distances measure equal percentage (as opposed to dollar) changes in values.

Looking at Figure 10.4, we see that the small-company, or "small-cap" (short for small-capitalization), investment did the best overall. Every dollar invested grew to a remarkable $15,532.07 over the 86 years. The larger common stock portfolio did less well; a dollar invested in it grew to $3,045.22.

At the other end, the T-bill portfolio grew to only $20.56. This is even less impressive when we consider the inflation over this period. As illustrated, the increase in the price level was such that $12.59 is needed just to replace the original $1.

Given the historical record, why would anybody buy anything other than small-cap stocks? If you look closely at Figure 10.4, you will probably see the answer. The T-bill portfolio and the long-term government bond portfolio grew more slowly than did the stock portfolios, but they also grew much more steadily. The small stocks ended up on top, but, as you can see, they grew quite erratically at times. For example, the small stocks were the worst performers for about the first 10 years and had a smaller return than long-term government bonds for almost 15 years.

A Closer Look

To illustrate the variability of the different investments, Figures 10.5 through 10.8 plot the year-to-year percentage returns in the form of vertical bars drawn from the horizontal axis. The height of the bar tells us the return for the particular year. For example, looking at the long-term government bonds (Figure 10.7), we see that the largest historical return (40.35 percent) occurred in 1982. This was a good year for bonds. In comparing these charts, notice the differences in the vertical axis scales. With these differences in mind, you

| FIGURE **10.4** | A $1 investment in different types of portfolios: 1925–2011 (year-end 1925 = $1) |

can see how predictably the Treasury bills (Figure 10.7) behaved compared to the small stocks (Figure 10.6).

The returns shown in these bar graphs are sometimes very large. Looking at the graphs, we see, for example, that the largest single-year return was a remarkable 143 percent for

FIGURE 10.5

Year-to-year total returns on large-company stocks: 1926–2011

FIGURE 10.6

Year-to-year total returns on small-company stocks: 1926–2011

the small-cap stocks in 1933. In the same year, the large-company stocks "only" returned 53 percent. In contrast, the largest Treasury bill return was 15 percent in 1981. For future reference, the actual year-to-year returns for the S&P 500, long-term government bonds, Treasury bills, and the CPI are shown in Table 10.1.

TABLE 10.1 Year-to-year total returns: 1926–2011

Year	Large-Company Stocks	Long-Term Government Bonds	U.S. Treasury Bills	Consumer Price Index
1926	11.14%	7.90%	3.30%	-1.12%
1927	37.13	10.36	3.15	-2.26
1928	43.31	-1.37	4.05	-1.16
1929	-8.91	5.23	4.47	0.58
1930	-25.26	5.80	2.27	-6.40
1931	-43.86	-8.04	1.15	-9.32
1932	-8.85	14.11	0.88	-10.27
1933	52.88	0.31	0.52	0.76
1934	-2.34	12.98	0.27	1.52
1935	47.22	5.88	0.17	2.99
1936	32.80	8.22	0.17	1.45
1937	-35.26	-0.13	0.27	2.86
1938	33.20	6.26	0.06	-2.78
1939	-0.91	5.71	0.04	0.00
1940	-10.08	10.34	0.04	0.71
1941	-11.77	-8.66	0.14	9.93
1942	21.07	2.67	0.34	9.03
1943	25.76	2.50	0.38	2.96
1944	19.69	2.88	0.38	2.30
1945	36.46	5.17	0.38	2.25
1946	-8.18	4.07	0.38	18.13
1947	5.24	-1.15	0.62	8.84
1948	5.10	2.10	1.06	2.99
1949	18.06	7.02	1.12	-2.07
1950	30.58	-1.44	1.22	5.93
1951	24.55	-3.53	1.56	6.00
1952	18.50	1.82	1.75	0.75
1953	-1.10	-0.88	1.87	0.75
1954	52.40	7.89	0.93	-0.74
1955	31.43	-1.03	1.80	0.37
1956	6.63	-3.14	2.66	2.99
1957	-10.85	5.25	3.28	2.90
1958	43.34	-6.70	1.71	1.76
1959	11.90	-1.35	3.48	1.73
1960	0.48	7.74	2.81	1.36
1961	26.81	3.02	2.40	0.67
1962	-8.78	4.63	2.82	1.33
1963	22.69	1.37	3.23	1.64
1964	16.36	4.43	3.62	0.97
1965	12.36	1.40	4.06	1.92
1966	-10.10	-1.61	4.94	3.46
1967	23.94	-6.38	4.39	3.04
1968	11.00%	5.33%	5.49%	4.72%
1969	-8.47	-7.45	6.90	6.20
1970	3.94	12.24	6.50	5.57
1971	14.30	12.67	4.36	3.27
1972	18.99	9.15	4.23	3.41
1973	-14.69	-12.66	7.29	8.71
1974	-26.47	-3.28	7.99	12.34
1975	37.23	4.67	5.87	6.94
1976	23.93	18.34	5.07	4.86
1977	-7.16	2.31	5.45	6.70
1978	6.57	-2.07	7.64	9.02
1979	18.61	-2.76	10.56	13.29
1980	32.50	-5.91	12.10	12.52
1981	-4.92	-0.16	14.60	8.92
1982	21.55	49.99	10.94	3.83
1983	22.56	-2.11	8.99	3.79
1984	6.27	16.53	9.90	3.95
1985	31.73	39.03	7.71	3.80
1986	18.67	32.51	6.09	1.10
1987	5.25	-8.09	5.88	4.43
1988	16.61	8.71	6.94	4.42
1989	31.69	22.15	8.44	4.65
1990	-3.10	5.44	7.69	6.11
1991	30.46	20.04	5.43	3.06
1992	7.62	8.09	3.48	2.90
1993	10.08	22.32	3.03	2.75
1994	1.32	-11.46	4.39	2.67
1995	37.58	37.28	5.61	2.54
1996	22.96	-2.59	5.14	3.32
1997	33.36	17.70	5.19	1.70
1998	28.58	19.22	4.86	1.61
1999	21.04	-12.76	4.80	2.68
2000	-9.10	22.16	5.98	3.39
2001	-11.89	5.30	3.33	1.55
2002	-22.10	14.08	1.61	2.38
2003	28.68	1.62	1.03	1.88
2004	10.88	10.34	1.43	3.26
2005	4.91	10.35	3.30	3.42
2006	15.79	0.28	4.97	2.54
2007	5.49	10.85	4.52	4.08
2008	-37.00	39.46	1.24	0.09
2009	26.46	-25.61	.15	2.72
2010	15.06	7.73	.14	1.50
2011	2.11	35.75	.06	2.96

Source: Author calculations based on data from *Global Financial Data* and other sources.

320   **PART 6**   Risk and Return

Year-to-year total returns on bonds and bills: 1926–2011

Long-term government bonds

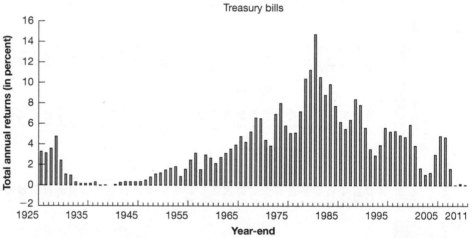

Treasury bills

CONCEPT QUESTIONS

10.2a   With 20-20 hindsight, what was the best investment for the period 1926–1935?

10.2b   Why doesn't everyone just buy small stocks as investments?

10.2c   What was the smallest return observed over the 86 years for each of these investments? Approximately when did it occur?

10.2d   About how many times did large stocks (common stocks) return more than 30 percent? How many times did they return less than −20 percent?

10.2e   What was the longest "winning streak" (years without a negative return) for large stocks? For long-term government bonds?

10.2f   How often did the T-bill portfolio have a negative return?

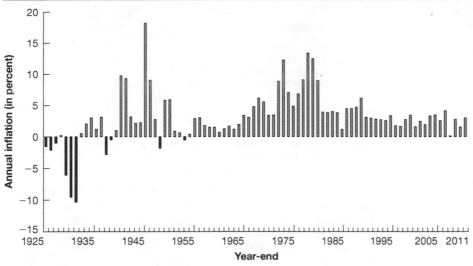

FIGURE **10.8**

Year-to-year inflation:
1926–2011

Source: Stocks, Bonds, Bills, and Inflation Yearbook™, Morningstar, Inc., Chicago (annually updates work by Roger G. Ibbotson and Rex A. Sinquefield). All rights reserved.

AVERAGE RETURNS: THE FIRST LESSON

ExcelMaster
coverage online

10.3

As you've probably begun to notice, the history of capital market returns is too complicated to be of much use in its undigested form. We need to begin summarizing all these numbers. Accordingly, we discuss how to go about condensing the detailed data. We start out by calculating average returns.

Calculating Average Returns

The obvious way to calculate the average returns on the different investments in Table 10.1 is simply to add up the yearly returns and divide by 86. The result is the historical average of the individual values.

For example, if you add up the returns for the large-company common stocks for the 86 years, you will get about 10.15. The average annual return is thus $10.15/86 = .118 = 11.8\%$. You interpret this 11.8 percent just like any other average. If you picked a year at random from the 86-year history and you had to guess what the return in that year was, the best guess would be 11.8 percent.

Average Returns: The Historical Record

Table 10.2 shows the average returns for the investments we have discussed. As shown, in a typical year, the small stocks increased in value by 16.5 percent. Notice also how much larger the stock returns are than the bond returns.

These averages are, of course, nominal since we haven't worried about inflation. Notice that the average inflation rate was 3.1 percent per year over this 86-year span. The nominal return on U.S. Treasury bills was 3.6 percent per year. The average real return on Treasury bills was thus approximately .5 percent per year; so, the real return on T-bills has been quite low historically.

At the other extreme, small stocks had an average real return of about $16.5\% - 3.1\% = 13.4\%$, which is relatively large. If you remember the Rule of 72 (Chapter 4), then you recall that a quick back-of-the-envelope calculation tells us that 13.4 percent real growth doubles your buying power about every five years. Notice also that the real value of the large stock portfolio increased by 8.7 percent in a typical year.

TABLE 10.2		
Average annual returns: 1926–2011	**Investment**	**Average Return**
	Large stocks	11.8%
	Small stocks	16.5
	Long-term corporate bonds	6.4
	Long-term government bonds	6.1
	U.S. Treasury bills	3.6
	Inflation	3.1

Source: Stocks, Bonds, Bills, and Inflation Yearbook™, Morningstar, Inc., Chicago (annually updates work by Roger G. Ibbotson and Rex A. Sinquefield). All rights reserved.

TABLE 10.3			
Average annual returns and risk premiums: 1926–2011	**Investment**	**Average Return**	**Risk Premium**
	Large stocks	11.8%	8.2%
	Small stocks	16.5	12.9
	Long-term corporate bonds	6.4	2.8
	Long-term government bonds	6.1	2.5
	U.S. Treasury bills	3.6	—

Source: Stocks, Bonds, Bills, and Inflation Yearbook™, Morningstar, Inc., Chicago (annually updates work by Roger G. Ibbotson and Rex A. Sinquefield). All rights reserved.

Risk Premiums

Now that we have computed some average returns, it seems logical to see how they compare with each other. Based on our discussion above, one such comparison involves government-issued securities. These are free of much of the variability we see in, for example, the stock market.

The government borrows money by issuing bonds. These bonds come in different forms. The ones we will focus on are Treasury bills. These have the shortest time to maturity of the different government bonds. Because the government can always raise taxes to pay its bills, this debt is virtually free of any default risk over its short life. Thus, we will call the rate of return on such debt the *risk-free return,* and we will use it as a kind of benchmark.

A particularly interesting comparison involves the virtually risk-free return on T-bills and the very risky return on common stocks. The difference between these two returns can be interpreted as a measure of the *excess return* on the average risky asset (assuming the stock of a large U.S. corporation has about average risk compared to all risky assets).

risk premium

The excess return required from an investment in a risky asset over that required from a risk-free investment.

We call this the "excess" return since it is the additional return we earn by moving from a relatively risk-free investment to a risky one. Because it can be interpreted as a reward for bearing risk, we will call it a **risk premium**.

From Table 10.2, we can calculate the risk premiums for the different investments. We report only the nominal risk premium in Table 10.3 because there is only a slight difference between the historical nominal and real risk premiums.

The risk premium on T-bills is shown as zero in the table because we have assumed that they are riskless.

The First Lesson

Looking at Table 10.3, we see that the average risk premium earned by a typical large common stock is $11.8\% - 3.6\% = 8.2\%$. This is a significant reward. The fact that it exists historically is an important observation, and it is the basis for our first lesson: Risky assets, on average, earn a risk premium. Put another way: There is a reward for bearing risk.

Why is this so? Why, for example, is the risk premium for small stocks so much larger than the risk premium for large stocks? More generally, what determines the relative sizes of the risk premiums for the different assets? The answers to these questions are at the heart of modern finance, and the next chapter is devoted to them. For now, part of the answer can be found by looking at the historical variability of the returns of these different investments. So, to get started, we now turn our attention to measuring variability in returns.

CONCEPT QUESTIONS

10.3a What do we mean by excess return and risk premium?

10.3b What was the real (as opposed to nominal) risk premium on the common stock portfolio?

10.3c What was the nominal risk premium on corporate bonds? The real risk premium?

10.3d What is the first lesson from capital market history?

THE VARIABILITY OF RETURNS: THE SECOND LESSON

10.4

We have already seen that the year-to-year returns on common stocks tend to be more volatile than the returns on, say, long-term government bonds. We now discuss measuring this variability so we can begin examining the subject of risk.

Frequency Distributions and Variability

ExcelMaster
coverage online

To get started, we can draw a *frequency distribution* for the common stock returns like the one in Figure 10.9. What we have done here is to count up the number of times the annual return on the large stock portfolio falls within each 10 percent range. For example, in Figure 10.9, the height of 14 in the range 20 percent to 30 percent means that 14 of the 86 annual returns were in that range. Notice also that the returns are very concentrated between −10 and 40 percent.

What we need to do now is to actually measure the spread in returns. We know, for example, that the return on small stocks in a typical year was 16.5 percent. We now want to know how far the actual return deviates from this average in a typical year. In other words, we need a

---

				2010			
				2006			
			2011	2004	2009		
		2000	2007	1988	2003	1997	
		1990	2005	1986	1999	1995	
		1981	1994	1979	1998	1991	
		1977	1993	1972	1996	1989	
		1969	1992	1971	1983	1985	
		1962	1987	1968	1982	1980	
		1953	1984	1965	1976	1975	
		1946	1978	1964	1967	1955	
	2001	1940	1970	1959	1963	1950	
	1973	1939	1960	1952	1961	1945	
	2002	1966	1934	1956	1949	1951	1938	1958
2008	1974	1957	1932	1948	1944	1943	1936	1935	1954
1931	1937	1930	1941	1929	1947	1926	1942	1927	1928	1933

```
−80 −70 −60 −50 −40 −30 −20 −10  0  10  20  30  40  50  60  70  80  90
```

Percent

FIGURE 10.9

Frequency distribution of returns on common stocks: 1926–2011

PRINCIPLES OF FINANCE Finance 301

variance

The average squared difference between the actual return and the average return.

standard deviation

The positive square root of the variance.

measure of how volatile the return is. The **variance** and its square root, the **standard deviation**, are the most commonly used measures of volatility. We describe how to calculate them next.

The Historical Variance and Standard Deviation

The variance essentially measures the average squared difference between the actual returns and the average return. The bigger this number is, the more the actual returns tend to differ from the average return. Also, the larger the variance or standard deviation is, the more spread out the returns will be.

The way we will calculate the variance and standard deviation depends on the specific situation. In this chapter, we are looking at historical returns; so, the procedure we describe here is the correct one for calculating the *historical* variance and standard deviation. If we were examining projected future returns, then the procedure would be different. We describe this procedure in the next chapter.

To illustrate how we calculate the historical variance, suppose a particular investment had returns of 10 percent, 12 percent, 3 percent, and −9 percent over the last four years. The average return is $(.10 + .12 + .03 − .09)/4 = 4\%$. Notice that the return is never actually equal to 4 percent. Instead, the first return deviates from the average by $.10 − .04 = .06$, the second return deviates from the average by $.12 − .04 = .08$, and so on. To compute the variance, we square each of these deviations, add up the squares, and divide the result by the number of returns less 1, or 3 in this case. This information is summarized in the following table:

For an easy-to-read review of basic stats, check out www.robertniles.com/stats.

Year	(1) Actual Return	(2) Average Return	(3) Deviation (1) − (2)	(4) Squared Deviation
1	.10	.04	.06	.0036
2	.12	.04	.08	.0064
3	.03	.04	−.01	.0001
4	−.09	.04	−.13	.0169
Totals	.16		.00	.0270

In the first column, we write down the four actual returns. In the third column, we calculate the difference between the actual returns and the average by subtracting out 4 percent. Finally, in the fourth column, we square the numbers in Column 3 to get the squared deviations from the average.

The variance can now be calculated by dividing .0270, the sum of the squared deviations, by the number of returns less 1. Let Var(R), or σ^2 (read this as "sigma squared"), stand for the variance of the return:

Var(R) = σ^2 = .027/(4 − 1) = .009

The standard deviation is the square root of the variance. So, if SD(R), or σ, stands for the standard deviation of the return:

SD(R) = σ = $\sqrt{.009}$ = .09487

The square root of the variance is used because the variance is measured in "squared" percentages and thus is hard to interpret. The standard deviation is an ordinary percentage, so the answer here could be written as 9.487 percent.

In the table above, notice that the sum of the deviations is equal to zero. This will always be the case, and it provides a good way to check your work. In general, if we have T historical returns, where T is some number, we can write the historical variance as:

$$\text{Var}(R) = \frac{1}{T-1}[(R_1 - \bar{R})^2 + \cdots + (R_T - \bar{R})^2] \qquad \text{[10.3]}$$

This formula tells us to do just what we did above: Take each of the T individual returns (R_1, R_2, . . .) and subtract the average return, $\overline{R}$; square the results, and add up all these squares; and finally, divide this total by the number of returns less 1 ($T - 1$). The standard deviation is always the square root of $\text{Var}(R)$. Standard deviations are a widely used measure of volatility. Our nearby *Work the Web* box gives a real-world example.

WORK THE WEB

Standard deviations are widely reported for mutual funds. For example, the Fidelity Magellan Fund is a large mutual fund. How volatile is it? To find out, we went to www.morningstar.com, entered the ticker symbol FMAGX, and hit the "Ratings & Risk" link. Here is what we found:

◄ To get updated data, scan here.

MPT Statistics FMAGX

| 3-Year | 5-Year | 10-Year | 15-Year |

3-Year Trailing	Index	R-Squared	Beta	Alpha	Treynor Ratio	Currency
vs. Best-Fit Index						
FMAGX	Russell Mid Cap Growth TR USD	97.09	1.04	-8.90	--	USD
vs. Standard Index						
FMAGX	S&P 500 TR	91.64	1.22	-5.48	-2.25	USD
Category: LG	S&P 500 TR	91.70	1.00	-0.11	2.78	USD
06/30/2011						

Volatility Measures FMAGX

| 3-Year | 5-Year | 10-Year | 15-Year |

3-Year Trailing	Standard Deviation	Mean	Sharpe Ratio	Sortino Ratio	Bear Market Percentile Rank
FMAGX	27.11	-2.47	0.04	0.05	--
S&P 500 TR	21.21	3.34	0.25	0.34	--
Category: LG	22.20	3.02	0.23	0.32	--

The standard deviation for the Fidelity Magellan Fund is 27.11 percent. When you consider the average stock has a standard deviation of about 50 percent, this seems like a low number. The reason for the low standard deviation has to do with the power of diversification, a topic we discuss in the next chapter. The mean is the average return, so over the last three years, investors in the Magellan Fund lost 2.47 percent per year. Also under the Volatility Measures section, you will see the Sharpe ratio. The Sharpe ratio is calculated as the risk premium of the asset divided by the standard deviation. As such, it is a measure of return to the level of risk taken (as measured by standard deviation). The "beta" for the Fidelity Magellan Fund is 1.22. We will have more to say about this number—lots more—in the next chapter.

Questions

1. Go to the Morningstar website at www.morningstar.com. What does the Bear Market Decile Rank measure?
2. Get a quote for the Fidelity Magellan fund at Morningstar. What are the five sectors that have the highest percentage investment for this fund? What are the five stocks with the highest percentage investment?

EXAMPLE 10.2

CALCULATING THE VARIANCE AND STANDARD DEVIATION

Suppose the Supertech Company and the Hyperdrive Company have experienced the following returns in the last four years:

Year	Supertech Returns	Hyperdrive Returns
2009	−.20	.05
2010	.50	.09
2011	.30	−.12
2012	.10	.20

What are the average returns? The variances? The standard deviations? Which investment was more volatile?

To calculate the average returns, we add up the returns and divide by 4. The results are:

Supertech average return $= \overline{R} = .70/4 = .175$

Hyperdrive average return $= \overline{R} = .22/4 = .055$

To calculate the variance for Supertech, we can summarize the relevant calculations as follows:

Year	(1) Actual Return	(2) Average Return	(3) Deviation (1) − (2)	(4) Squared Deviation
2009	−.20	.175	−.375	.140625
2010	.50	.175	.325	.105625
2011	.30	.175	.125	.015625
2012	.10	.175	−.075	.005625
Totals	.70		.000	.267500

Since there are four years of returns, we calculate the variance by dividing .2675 by $(4 − 1) = 3$:

	Supertech	Hyperdrive
Variance (σ^2)	.2675/3 = .0892	.0529/3 = .0176
Standard deviation (σ)	$\sqrt{.0892} = .2987$	$\sqrt{.0176} = .1327$

For practice, verify that you get the same answer as we do for Hyperdrive. Notice that the standard deviation for Supertech, 29.87 percent, is a little more than twice Hyperdrive's 13.27 percent; Supertech was thus the more volatile investment.

The Historical Record

Figure 10.10 summarizes much of our discussion of capital market history so far. It displays average returns, standard deviations, and frequency distributions of annual returns on a common scale. In Figure 10.10, notice, for example, that the standard deviation for the small-stock portfolio (32.5 percent per year) is more than 10 times larger than the T-bill portfolio's standard deviation (3.1 percent per year). We will return to these figures momentarily.

FIGURE 10.10	Historical average returns, standard deviations, and frequency distributions: 1926–2011		

Series	Arithmetic Mean (%)	Standard Deviation (%)	Distribution (%)
Small-company stocks	16.5	32.5	
Large-company stocks	11.8	20.3	
Long-term corporate bonds	6.4	8.4	
Long-term government bonds	6.1	9.8	
Intermediate-term government bonds	5.5	5.7	
U.S. Treasury bills	3.6	3.1	
Inflation	3.1	4.2	

* The 1933 small-company stocks total return was 142.9 percent.

Source: Stocks, Bonds, Bills, and Inflation Yearbook™, Morningstar, Inc., Chicago (annually updates work by Roger G. Ibbotson and Rex A. Sinquefield). All rights reserved.

Normal Distribution

For many different random events in nature, a particular frequency distribution, the **normal distribution** (or *bell curve*), is useful for describing the probability of ending up in a given range. For example, the idea behind "grading on a curve" comes from the fact that exam scores often resemble a bell curve.

Figure 10.11 illustrates a normal distribution and its distinctive bell shape. As you can see, this distribution has a much cleaner appearance than the actual return distributions illustrated in Figure 10.10. Even so, like the normal distribution, the actual distributions do appear to be at least roughly mound-shaped and symmetric. When this is true, the normal distribution is often a very good approximation.

Also, keep in mind that the distributions in Figure 10.10 are based on only 86 yearly observations, while Figure 10.11 is, in principle, based on an infinite number. So, if we

normal distribution
A symmetric, bell-shaped frequency distribution that is completely defined by its average and standard deviation.

328   **PART 6**   Risk and Return

328

FIGURE 10.11

The normal distribution
Illustrated returns are based on the historical return and standard deviation for a portfolio of large common stocks.

had been able to observe returns for, say, 1,000 years, we might have filled in a lot of the irregularities and ended up with a much smoother picture. For our purposes, it is enough to observe that the returns are at least roughly normally distributed.

The usefulness of the normal distribution stems from the fact that it is completely described by the average and the standard deviation. If you have these two numbers, then there is nothing else to know. For example, with a normal distribution, the probability that we end up within one standard deviation of the average is about ⅔. The probability that we end up within two standard deviations is about 95 percent. Finally, the probability of being more than three standard deviations away from the average is less than 1 percent. These ranges and the probabilities are illustrated in Figure 10.11.

To see why this is useful, recall from Figure 10.10 that the standard deviation of returns on the large common stocks is 20.3 percent. The average return is 11.8 percent. So, assuming that the frequency distribution is at least approximately normal, the probability that the return in a given year is in the range of −8.5 percent to 32.1 percent (11.8 percent plus or minus one standard deviation, 20.3 percent) is about ⅔. This range is illustrated in Figure 10.11. In other words, there is about one chance in three that the return will be *outside* this range. This literally tells you that, if you buy stocks in large companies, you should expect to be outside this range in one year out of every three. This reinforces our earlier observations about stock market volatility. However, there is only a 5 percent chance (approximately) that we would end up outside the range of −28.8 percent to 52.4 percent (11.8 percent plus or minus 2 × 20.3%). These points are also illustrated in Figure 10.11.

The Second Lesson

Our observations concerning the year-to-year variability in returns are the basis for our second lesson from capital market history. On average, bearing risk is handsomely rewarded, but, in a given year, there is a significant chance of a dramatic change in value. Thus, our second lesson is this: The greater the potential reward, the greater is the risk.

Thus far in this chapter, we have emphasized the year-to-year variability in returns. We should note that even day-to-day movements can exhibit considerable volatility. For example, on September 17, 2001, the Dow Jones Industrial Average (DJIA) plummeted 684.81 points, or 7.13 percent. By historical standards, it was one of the worst days ever for the 30 stocks that comprise the DJIA (as well as for a majority of stocks in the market). Still, while the drop was the largest decrease in the DJIA ever in terms of points, it actually wasn't quite in the top 12 largest one-day percentage decreases in history, as illustrated in the following table:

Top 12 One-Day Percentage Changes in the Dow Jones Industrial Average		
1	October 19, 1987	−22.61
2	October 28, 1929	−12.82
3	October 29, 1929	−11.73
4	November 6, 1929	−9.92
5	December 18, 1899	−8.72
6	August 12, 1932	−8.40
7	March 14, 1907	−8.29
8	October 26, 1987	−8.04
9	October 15, 2008	−7.87
10	July 21, 1933	−7.84
11	October 18, 1937	−7.75
12	December 1, 2008	−7.70

Source: http://online.wsj.com/mdc/public/page/2_3047-djia_alltime.html.

This discussion also highlights the importance of looking at returns in terms of percentages rather than dollar amounts or index points. For example, as we noted before, the biggest one-day loss in terms of points was on September 17, 2001, when the DJIA declined by 685 points. The second worst was the 554-point drop of October 27, 1997. In contrast, the 5.57-point drop in the DJIA on December 18, 1899, marked the fifth worst day in the history of the index, but a 5.6-point loss in the DJIA in today's market would hardly be noticed. This is precisely why we relied on percentage returns when we examined market history in this chapter.[3]

2008: The Bear Growled and Investors Howled

To reinforce our point concerning stock market volatility, consider that just a few short years ago, 2008 entered the record books as one of the worst years for stock market investors in U.S. history. How bad was it? As shown in several exhibits in the chapter (e.g., Table 10.1), the widely followed S&P 500 index plunged 37 percent. Of the 500 stocks in the index, 485 were down for the year.

Over the period 1926–2011, only the year 1931 had a lower return than 2008 (−44 percent versus −37 percent). Making matters worse, the downdraft continued with a further decline of 8.43 percent in January 2009. In all, from November 2007 (when the decline began) through March 2009 (when it ended), the S&P 500 lost 50 percent of its value.

Figure 10.12 shows the month-by-month performance of the S&P 500 during 2008. As indicated, returns were negative in 8 of the 12 months. Most of the damage occurred in the fall, with investors losing almost 17 percent in October alone. Small stocks fared no better. They also fell 37 percent for the year (with a 21 percent drop in October), their worst performance since losing 58 percent in 1937.

As Figure 10.12 suggests, stock prices were highly volatile during the year. Oddly, the S&P had 126 up days and 126 down days (remember the markets are closed weekends and holidays). Of course, the down days were much worse on average. To see how

---

[3] By the way, as you may have noticed, what's kind of weird is that 6 of the 12 worst days in the history of the DJIA occurred in October, including the top 3. We have no clue as to why. Furthermore, looking back at the Mark Twain quote near the beginning of the chapter, how do you suppose he knew? Sounds like a case for *CSI: Wall Street.*

FIGURE 10.12

S&P 500 Monthly
Returns: 2008

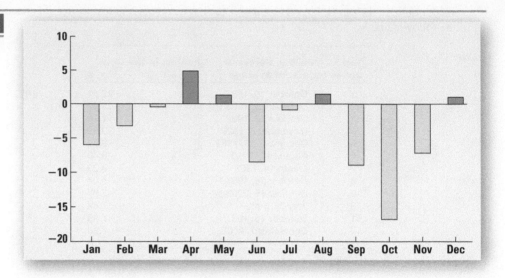

extraordinary volatility was in 2008, consider that there were 18 days during which the value of the S&P changed by more than five percent. There were only 17 such moves between 1956 and 2007!

The drop in stock prices was a global phenomenon, and many of the world's major markets were off by much more than the S&P. China, India, and Russia, for example, all experienced declines of more than 50 percent. Tiny Iceland saw share prices drop by more than 90 percent for the year. Trading on the Icelandic exchange was temporarily suspended on October 9. In what has to be a modern record for a single day, stocks fell by 76 percent when trading resumed on October 14.

Were there any bright spots in 2008 for U.S. investors? The answer is yes because, as stocks tanked, bonds soared, particularly U.S. Treasury bonds. In fact, long-term Treasuries gained 40 percent, while shorter-term Treasury bonds were up 13 percent. Long-term corporate bonds did less well, but still managed to finish in positive territory, up 9 percent. These returns were especially impressive considering that the rate of inflation, as measured by the CPI, was essentially zero.

Of course, stock prices can be volatile in both directions. From March 2009 through February 2011, a period of about 700 days, the S&P 500 doubled in value. This climb was the fastest doubling since 1936 when the S&P did it in just 500 days. So, what lessons should investors take away from this very recent, and very turbulent, bit of capital market history? First, and most obviously, stocks have significant risk! But there is a second, equally important lesson. Depending on the mix, a diversified portfolio of stocks and bonds might have suffered in 2008, but the losses would have been much smaller than those experienced by an all-stock portfolio. In other words, diversification matters, a point we will examine in detail in our next chapter.

Using Capital Market History

Based on the discussion in this section, you should begin to have an idea of the risks and rewards from investing. For example, in early 2012, Treasury bills were paying about .1 percent. Suppose we had an investment that we thought had about the same risk as a

FINANCE MATTERS

◄ For the latest news on the topics covered in this chapter, scan here.

The Super Guide to Investing

Every year, in late January or early February, about 90 million people in the United States watch television for a prediction of how well the stock market is going to do in the upcoming year. So you missed it this year? Maybe not. The stock market predictor we're talking about is the Super Bowl!

The Super Bowl indicator has become one of the more famous (or infamous) indicators of stock market performance. Here's how it works. In the 1960s, the original National Football League (NFL) and the upstart American Football League (AFL) were fighting for dominance. The Super Bowl indicator says that if a team from the original AFL wins the Super Bowl, the market posts a negative return for the year, and, if a team from the original NFL wins, the market will post a gain for the year.

So are you ready to bet the ranch on the Super Bowl indicator? Maybe that's not a super idea. Between 1997 and 2011, the Super Bowl indicator has only been right seven out of 14 years. Of course, you could follow the second Super Bowl indicator. When there are 50 points or more scored in the game, the stock market had an average return of 24 percent. When 39 points or fewer are scored, the average market return is only 5.3 percent.

Not all teams can accurately predict the stock market. For example, the New York Giants, an original NFL team, won three titles in 1987, 1991, and 2008. The market return after a Giants victory has averaged –0.5 percent per year. Much of this poor performance can be attributed to 2008 when the Giants won and the market dropped by about 37 percent.

In good (or bad) news for the stock market, the Giants won again in 2012, so the market should be up for the year. Was it?

For those of you who like horse racing, there is the Triple Crown Winner indicator. According to this indicator, if a horse wins the Kentucky Derby, Preakness, and Belmont Stakes, better known as the Triple Crown, the stock market will fall dramatically. However, when you consider that the youngest of these races, the Kentucky Derby, began in 1875 and to date there have only been 11 Triple Crown winners, what do you do in the 100+ years when there is no Triple Crown winner?

So you want more predictors? How about the hemline indicator, also known as the "bull markets and bare knees" indicator? Through much of the nineteenth century, long skirts dominated women's fashion, and the stock market experienced many bear markets. In the 1920s, flappers revealed their knees and the stock market boomed. Even the stock market crash of October 1987 was predicted by hemlines. During the 1980s, miniskirts flourished, but by October 1987 a fashion shift had women wearing longer skirts.

These are only three examples of what are known as "technical" trading rules. There are lots of others. How seriously should you take them? That's up to you, but our advice is to keep in mind that life is full of odd coincidences. Just because a bizarre stock market predictor seems to have worked well in the past doesn't mean that it's going to work in the future.

---

portfolio of large-firm common stocks. At a minimum, what return would this investment have to offer for us to be interested?

From Table 10.3, the risk premium on larger common stocks has been 8.2 percent historically, so a reasonable estimate of our required return would be this premium plus the T-bill rate, 8.2% + .1% = 8.3%. If we were thinking of starting a new business, then the risks of doing so might resemble those of investing in small-company stocks. In this case, the risk premium is 12.9 percent, so we might require more like 13 percent from such an investment at a minimum.

We will discuss the relationship between risk and required return in more detail in the next chapter. For now, you should notice that a projected internal rate of return, or IRR, on a risky investment in the 10 percent to 20 percent range isn't particularly outstanding. It depends on how much risk there is. This, too, is an important lesson from capital market history.

The discussion in this section shows that there is much to be learned from capital market history. As the accompanying *Finance Matters* box describes, capital market history also provides some odd coincidences.

EXAMPLE 10.3

INVESTING IN GROWTH STOCKS

The term *growth stock* is frequently a euphemism for small-company stock. Are such invest-ments suitable for "widows and orphans"? Before answering, you should consider the historical volatility. For example, from the historical record, what is the approximate probability that you will actually lose 16 percent or more of your money in a single year if you buy a portfolio of such companies?

Looking back at Figure 10.10, we see that the average return on small stocks is 16.5 percent, and the standard deviation is 32.5 percent. Assuming that the returns are approximately normal, there is about a $1/3$ probability that you will experience a return outside the range of -16 percent to 49 percent (16.5% ± 32.5%).

Because the normal distribution is symmetric, the odds of being above or below this range are equal. There is thus a $1/6$ chance (half of $1/3$) that you will lose more than 16.6 percent. So, you should expect this to happen once in every six years, on average. Such investments can thus be very volatile, and they are not well suited for those who cannot afford the risk.

More on the Stock Market Risk Premium

As we have discussed, the historical stock market risk premium has been substantial. In fact, based on standard economic models, it has been argued that the historical risk premium is *too* big and is thus an overestimate of what is likely to happen in the future.

Of course, any time we use the past to predict the future, there is the danger that the past period we observe isn't representative of what the future will hold. For example, in this chapter, we studied the period 1926–2011. Perhaps investors got lucky over this pe-riod and earned particularly high returns. Data from earlier years is available, though it is not of the same quality. With that caveat in mind, researchers have traced returns back to 1802, and the risk premiums seen in the pre-1926 era are perhaps a little smaller, but not dramatically so.

Another possibility is that the U.S. stock market experience was unusually good. Investors in at least some other major countries did not do as well because their finan-cial markets were nearly or completely wiped out because of revolution, war, and/or hy-perinflation. A recent study addresses this issue by examining data from 1900–2010 for 17 countries.

Figure 10.13 shows the historical average stock market risk premium for all 17 coun-tries over the 111-year period. Looking at the numbers, the U.S. risk premium is the 7th highest at 7.2 percent (which differs from our earlier estimate because of the differing time periods examined). The overall average risk premium is 6.9 percent. These numbers make it clear that U.S. investors did well, but not exceptionally so relative to investors in many other countries.

So, is the U.S. stock market risk premium estimated from 1926–2011 too high? The evidence seems to suggest that the answer is "maybe a little." One thing we haven't stressed so far is that even with 111 years of data, the average risk premium is still not measured with great precision. From a statistical standpoint, the standard error associated with the U.S. estimated risk premium of 7.2 percent is about 2 percent.[4] So, even one standard error range covers 5.2 to 9.2 percent.

---

[4] Recall from basic "sadistics" that the standard error of a sample mean is the sample standard deviation divided by the square root of the sample size. In our case, the standard deviation over the 1900–2010 period (not shown) was 19.8 percent, so the standard error is $.198/\sqrt{111} = .019$.

CHAPTER **10**   Some Lessons from Capital Market History

| FIGURE **10.13** | Stock market risk premiums for 17 countries: 1900–2010 |

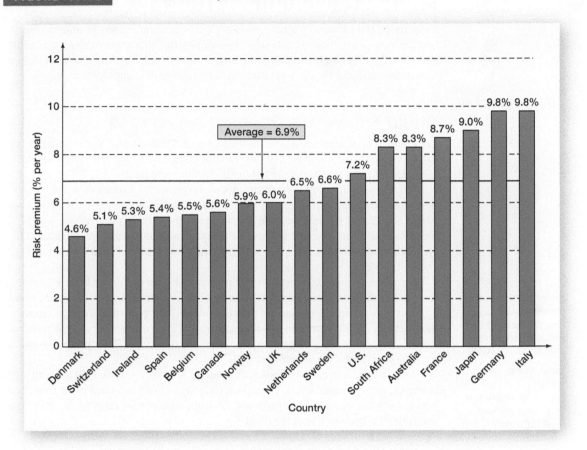

Source: Based on information in Elroy Dimson, Paul Marsh, and Michael Staunton, "The Worldwide Equity Premium: A Smaller Puzzle," in Handbook of the *Equity Risk Premium,* Rajnish Mehra, ed. (Elsevier: 2007). Updates by the authors.

CONCEPT QUESTIONS

10.4a In words, how do we calculate a variance? A standard deviation?

10.4b With a normal distribution, what is the probability of ending up more than one standard deviation below the average?

10.4c Assuming that long-term corporate bonds have an approximately normal distribution, what is the approximate probability of earning 14.6 percent or more in a given year? With T-bills, approximately what is this probability?

10.4d What is the second lesson from capital market history?

10.5   MORE ON AVERAGE RETURNS

ExcelMaster
coverage online

Thus far in this chapter, we have looked closely at simple average returns. But there is another way of computing an average return. The fact that average returns are calculated two different ways leads to some confusion, so our goal in this section is to explain the two approaches and also the circumstances under which each is appropriate.

Arithmetic versus Geometric Averages

Let's start with a simple example. Suppose you buy a particular stock for $100. Unfortunately, the first year you own it, it falls to $50. The second year you own it, it rises back to $100, leaving you where you started (no dividends were paid).

What was your average return on this investment? Common sense seems to say that your average return must be exactly zero since you started with $100 and ended with $100. But if we calculate the returns year-by-year, we see that you lost 50 percent the first year (you lost half of your money). The second year, you made 100 percent (you doubled your money). Your average return over the two years was thus $(-50\% + 100\%)/2 = 25\%$!

So which is correct, 0 percent or 25 percent? The answer is that both are correct: They just answer different questions. The 0 percent is called the **geometric average return**. The 25 percent is called the **arithmetic average return**. The geometric average return answers the question *"What was your average compound return per year over a particular period?"* The arithmetic average return answers the question *"What was your return in an average year over a particular period?"*

geometric average return

The average compound return earned per year over a multiyear period.

arithmetic average return

The return earned in an average year over a multiyear period.

Notice that, in previous sections, the average returns we calculated were all arithmetic averages, so we already know how to calculate them. What we need to do now is (1) learn how to calculate geometric averages and (2) learn the circumstances under which one average is more meaningful than the other.

Calculating Geometric Average Returns

First, to illustrate how we calculate a geometric average return, suppose a particular investment had annual returns of 10 percent, 12 percent, 3 percent, and -9 percent over the last four years. The geometric average return over this four-year period is calculated as $(1.10 \times 1.12 \times 1.03 \times .91)^{1/4} - 1 = 3.66\%$. In contrast, the average arithmetic return we have been calculating is $(.10 + .12 + .03 - .09)/4 = 4.0\%$.

In general, if we have T years of returns, the geometric average return over these T years is calculated using this formula:

$$\text{Geometric average return} = [(1 + R_1) \times (1 + R_2) \times \cdots \times (1 + R_T)]^{1/T} - 1 \qquad [10.4]$$

This formula tells us that four steps are required:

1. Take each of the T annual returns $R_1, R_2, \ldots, R_T$ and add a one to each (after converting them to decimals!).
2. Multiply all the numbers from step 1 together.
3. Take the result from step 2 and raise it to the power of $1/T$.
4. Finally, subtract one from the result of step 3. The result is the geometric average return.

CALCULATING THE GEOMETRIC AVERAGE RETURN

EXAMPLE 10.4

Calculate the geometric average return for the S&P 500 using the returns given below. To do so, convert percentages to decimal returns, add one, and then calculate their product:

S&P 500 Returns	Product
11.14%	1.1114
37.13	×1.3713
43.31	×1.4331
−8.91	× .9109
−25.26	× .7474
	1.4870

Notice that the number 1.4870 is what our investment is worth after five years if we started with a one dollar investment. The geometric average return is then calculated as:

Geometric average return = $1.4870^{1/5} - 1 = 0.0826$, or 8.26%

Thus the geometric average return is about 8.26 percent in this example. Here is a tip: If you are using a financial calculator, you can put $1 in as the present value, $1.4870 as the future value, and 5 as the number of periods. Then, solve for the unknown rate. You should get the same answer we did.

One thing you may have noticed in our examples thus far is that the geometric average returns seem to be smaller. It turns out that this will always be true (as long as the returns are not all identical, in which case the two "averages" would be the same). To illustrate, Table 10.4 shows the arithmetic averages and standard deviations from Figure 10.10, along with the geometric average returns.

As shown in Table 10.4, the geometric averages are all smaller, but the magnitude of the difference varies quite a bit. The reason is that the difference is greater for more volatile investments. In fact, there is a useful approximation. Assuming all the numbers are expressed in decimals (as opposed to percentages), the geometric average return is approximately equal to the arithmetic average return minus half the variance. For example, looking at the large-company stocks, the arithmetic average is .118 and the standard deviation is .203, implying that the variance is .0412. The approximate geometric average is thus $.118 - \frac{.0412}{2} = .097$, which is about the same as the actual value.

Series	Average Return		Standard Deviation
	Geometric	Arithmetic	
Large-company stocks	9.8%	11.8%	20.3%
Small-company stocks	11.9	16.5	32.5
Long-term corporate bonds	6.1	6.4	8.4
Long-term government bonds	5.7	6.1	9.8
Intermediate-term government bonds	5.4	5.5	5.7
U.S. Treasury bills	3.6	3.6	3.1
Inflation	3.0	3.1	4.2

TABLE 10.4

Geometric versus arithmetic average returns: 1926–2011

MORE GEOMETRIC AVERAGES

Take a look back at Figure 10.4. There, we showed the value of a $1 investment after 86 years. Use the value for the large-company stock investment to check the geometric average in Table 10.4.

In Figure 10.4, the large-company investment grew to $3,045.22 over 86 years. The geometric average return is thus:

Geometric average return = $3{,}045.22^{1/86} - 1 = .098$, or 9.8%

This 9.8% is the value shown in Table 10.4. For practice, check some of the other numbers in Table 10.4 the same way.

Arithmetic Average Return or Geometric Average Return?

When we look at historical returns, the difference between the geometric and arithmetic average returns isn't too hard to understand. To put it slightly differently, the geometric average tells you what you actually earned per year on average, compounded annually. The arithmetic average tells you what you earned in a typical year. You should use whichever one answers the question you want answered.

A somewhat trickier question concerns which average return to use when forecasting future wealth levels, and there's a lot of confusion on this point among analysts and financial planners. First, let's get one thing straight: If you *know* the true arithmetic average return, then this is what you should use in your forecast. So, for example, if you know the arithmetic return is 10 percent, then your best guess of the value of a $1,000 investment in 10 years is the future value of $1,000 at 10 percent for 10 years, or $2,593.74.

The problem we face, however, is that we usually only have *estimates* of the arithmetic and geometric returns, and estimates have errors. In this case, the arithmetic average return is probably too high for longer periods and the geometric average is probably too low for shorter periods. So, you should regard long-run projected wealth levels calculated using arithmetic averages as optimistic. Short-run projected wealth levels calculated using geometric averages are probably pessimistic.

As a practical matter, if you are using averages calculated over a long period of time (such as the 86 years we use) to forecast up to a decade or so into the future, then you should use the arithmetic average. If you are forecasting a few decades into the future (such as you might do for retirement planning), then you should just split the difference between the arithmetic and geometric average returns. Finally, if for some reason you are doing very long forecasts covering many decades, use the geometric average.

This concludes our discussion of geometric versus arithmetic averages. One last note: In the future, when we say "average return," we mean arithmetic unless we explicitly say otherwise.

CONCEPT QUESTIONS

10.5a If you wanted to forecast what the stock market is going to do over the next year, should you use an arithmetic or geometric average?

10.5b If you wanted to forecast what the stock market is going to do over the next century, should you use an arithmetic or geometric average?

CAPITAL MARKET EFFICIENCY

10.6

Capital market history suggests that the market values of stocks and bonds can fluctuate widely from year to year. Why does this occur? At least part of the answer is that prices change because new information arrives, and investors reassess asset values based on that information.

The behavior of market prices has been extensively studied. A question that has received particular attention is whether prices adjust quickly and correctly when new information arrives. A market is said to be *efficient* if this is the case. To be more precise, in an **efficient capital market**, current market prices fully reflect available information. By this we simply mean that, based on available information, there is no reason to believe that the current price is too low or too high.

The concept of market efficiency is a rich one, and much has been written about it. A full discussion of the subject goes beyond the scope of our study of business finance. However, because the concept figures so prominently in studies of market history, we briefly describe the key points here.

efficient capital market
Market in which security prices reflect available information.

Price Behavior in an Efficient Market

To illustrate how prices behave in an efficient market, suppose the F-Stop Camera Corporation (FCC) has, through years of secret research and development, developed a camera whose autofocusing system will double the speed of those now available. FCC's capital budgeting analysis suggests that launching the new camera is a highly profitable move; in other words, the NPV appears to be positive and substantial. The key assumption thus far is that FCC has not released any information about the new system, so the fact of its existence is "inside" information only.

Now, consider a share of stock in FCC. In an efficient market, its price reflects what is known about FCC's current operations and profitability, and it reflects market opinion about FCC's potential for future growth and profits. The value of the new autofocusing system is not reflected, however, because the market is unaware of its existence.

If the market agrees with FCC's assessment of the value of the new project, FCC's stock price will rise when the decision to launch is made public. For example, assume the announcement is made in a press release on Wednesday morning. In an efficient market, the price of shares in FCC will adjust quickly to this new information. Investors should not be able to buy the stock on Wednesday afternoon and make a profit on Thursday. This would imply that it took the stock market a full day to realize the implication of the FCC press release. If the market is efficient, the price of shares of FCC stock on Wednesday afternoon will already reflect the information contained in the Wednesday morning press release.

Figure 10.14 presents three possible stock price adjustments for FCC. In the figure, Day 0 represents the announcement day. As illustrated, before the announcement, FCC's stock sells for $140 per share. The NPV per share of the new system is, say, $40, so the new price will be $180 once the value of the new project is fully reflected.

The solid line in Figure 10.14 represents the path taken by the stock price in an efficient market. In this case, the price adjusts immediately to the new information and no further changes in the price of the stock take place. The broken line in Figure 10.14 depicts a delayed reaction. Here, it takes the market eight days or so to fully absorb the information. Finally, the dotted line illustrates an overreaction and subsequent adjustment to the correct price.

The broken line and the dotted line in Figure 10.14 illustrate paths that the stock price might take in an inefficient market. If, for example, stock prices don't adjust immediately to new information (the broken line), then buying stock immediately following the release of new information and then selling it several days later would be a positive NPV activity because the price is too low for several days after the announcement.

| FIGURE 10.14 | Reaction of stock price to new information in efficient and inefficient markets |

Efficient market reaction: The price instantaneously adjusts to and fully reflects new information; there is no tendency for subsequent increases and decreases.

Delayed reaction: The price partially adjusts to the new information; eight days elapse before the price completely reflects the new information.

Overreaction and correction: The price overadjusts to the new information; it overshoots the new price and subsequently corrects.

The Efficient Markets Hypothesis

efficient markets hypothesis (EMH)
The hypothesis that actual capital markets, such as the NYSE, are efficient.

The **efficient markets hypothesis (EMH)** asserts that well-organized capital markets, such as the NYSE, are efficient markets, at least as a practical matter. In other words, an advocate of the EMH might argue that while inefficiencies may exist, they are relatively small and not common.

If a market is efficient, then there is a very important implication for market participants: All investments in an efficient market are *zero* NPV investments. The reason is not complicated. If prices are neither too low nor too high, then the difference between the market value of an investment and its cost is zero; hence, the NPV is zero. As a result, in an efficient market, investors get exactly what they pay for when they buy securities, and firms receive exactly what their stocks and bonds are worth when they sell them.

What makes a market efficient is competition among investors. Many individuals spend their entire lives trying to find mispriced stocks. For any given stock, they study what has happened in the past to the stock's price and its dividends. They learn, to the extent possible, what a company's earnings have been, how much it owes to creditors, what taxes it pays, what businesses it is in, what new investments are planned, how sensitive it is to changes in the economy, and so on.

Not only is there a great deal to know about any particular company, there is a powerful incentive for knowing it, namely, the profit motive. If you know more about some company than other investors in the marketplace, you can profit from that knowledge by investing in the company's stock if you have good news and by selling it if you have bad news.

Look under the "contents" link at www. investorhome.com for more info on the EMH.

The logical consequence of all this information being gathered and analyzed is that mispriced stocks will become fewer and fewer. In other words, because of competition among investors, the market will become increasingly efficient. A kind of equilibrium comes into being where there is just enough mispricing around for those who are best at identifying it to make a living at it. For most other investors, the activity of information gathering and analysis will not pay.[5]

---

[5] The idea behind the EMH can be illustrated by the following short story: A student was walking down the hall with her finance professor when they both saw a $20 bill on the ground. As the student bent down to pick it up, the professor shook her head slowly and, with a look of disappointment on her face, said patiently to the student, "Don't bother. If it were really there, someone else would have picked it up already." The moral of the story reflects the logic of the efficient markets hypothesis: If you think you have found a pattern in stock prices or a simple device for picking winners, you probably have not.

FINANCE MATTERS

◄ For the latest news on the topics covered in this chapter, scan here.

Can the Pros Beat the Market?

2011 was a good year for investors in the Vitus Small Cap Sustainable Growth fund, which posted a gain of 18.8 percent for the year, the highest return for any stock mutual fund. In an industry where literally millions of dollars are at stake for mutual fund managers, it would seem that mutual funds should be able to consistently outperform the market. Unfortunately for investors, during 2011, only 20 percent of large-stock mutual funds outperformed the S&P 500 index for the year. And just so you don't think this was a strange year for mutual funds, only 36 percent outperformed the S&P 500 in 2010.

Other facts point to the difficulty that mutual funds have in beating the market. For example, over the past 50 years, the stock market had an average return of 13.5 percent, while the average mutual fund returned 11.8 percent. And during the past five years, only 11 percent of mutual fund managers had a performance each year that was in the top half of the funds in its respective category. This underperformance is not limited to mutual funds managers. The *Hulbert Financial Digest*, which tracks the performance of investment letters, reported that 80 percent of investment letters underperformed the stock market over the long term.

One thing we know for sure is that past performance is no predictor of future returns. For example, in July 1994, the American Century Giftrust fund had been the best performing mutual fund for the previous 10 years, with an average annual return above 20 percent. But the next 10 years weren't as kind to the investors in this fund. The average annual return for 1994 to 2004 was 2.87 percent, which was lower than U.S. Treasury bills during the same period. Following the old saying "What goes up, must come down," other funds have had similar stories. The Van Wagoner Emerging Growth Fund returned 291.2 percent in 1999, only to lose 59.7 percent and 64.6 percent the next two years. Similarly, the Oppenheimer Enterprise Fund gained 105.75 percent in 1999, but lost 40.6 percent in 2000, followed by two more years of double-digit losses.

Sometimes we see proposed evidence showing that mutual fund managers collectively can beat the market. Consider 2005, when the S&P 500 gained about 3 percent. Diversified U.S. stock funds averaged 7 percent for the year, so it appears at first glance that mutual fund managers outperform the market. However, in 2008, only 42 percent of all managers outperformed the market, with an average return about 1 percent lower than the market return. Over the years, the track record of the pros is relatively clear: More often than not, they underperform. In fact, based on historical averages, about 70 percent of all managers will underperform in a typical year.

The inability of the pros to consistently beat the market doesn't prove that markets are efficient. The evidence does, however, lend some credence to the semistrong form version of market efficiency. Plus, it adds to a growing body of evidence that tends to support a basic premise: While it may be possible to outperform the market for relatively short periods of time, it is very difficult to do so consistently over the long haul.

Having said this, the accompanying *Finance Matters* box indicates just how hard it is for *anybody* to "beat the market."

Some Common Misconceptions about the EMH

No idea in finance has attracted as much attention as that of efficient markets, and not all of the attention has been flattering. Rather than rehash the arguments here, we will be content to observe that some markets are more efficient than others. For example, financial markets on the whole are probably much more efficient than real asset markets.

Having said this, it is the case that much of the criticism of the EMH is misguided because it is based on a misunderstanding of what the hypothesis says and what it doesn't say. For example, when the notion of market efficiency was first publicized and debated in the popular financial press, it was often characterized by words to the effect that "throwing darts at the financial page will produce a portfolio that can be expected to do as well as any managed by professional security analysts."

Confusion over statements of this sort has often led to a failure to understand the implications of market efficiency. For example, sometimes it is wrongly argued that market efficiency means that it doesn't matter how you invest your money because the efficiency of the market will protect you from making a mistake. However, a random dart-thrower might wind up with all of the darts sticking into one or two high-risk stocks that deal in genetic engineering. Would you really want all of your money in two such stocks?

What efficiency does imply is that the price a firm will obtain when it sells a share of its stock is a "fair" price in the sense that it reflects the value of that stock given the information available about the firm. Shareholders do not have to worry that they are paying too much for a stock with a low dividend or some other sort of characteristic because the market has already incorporated that characteristic into the price. We sometimes say the information has been "priced in."

The concept of efficient markets can be explained further by replying to a frequent objection. It is sometimes argued that the market cannot be efficient because stock prices fluctuate from day to day. If the prices are right, the argument goes, then why do they change so much and so often? From our discussion above, we can see that these price movements are in no way inconsistent with efficiency. Investors are bombarded with information every day. The fact that prices fluctuate is, at least in part, a reflection of that information flow. In fact, the absence of price movements in a world that changes as rapidly as ours would suggest inefficiency.

The Forms of Market Efficiency

It is common to distinguish between three forms of market efficiency. Depending on the degree of efficiency, we say that markets are either *weak form efficient, semistrong form efficient,* or *strong form efficient.* The difference between these forms relates to what information is reflected in prices.

We start with the extreme case. If the market is strong form efficient, then *all* information of *every* kind is reflected in stock prices. In such a market, there is no such thing as inside information. Therefore, in our FCC example above, we apparently were assuming that the market was not strong form efficient.

Casual observation, particularly in recent years, suggests that inside information does exist and it can be valuable to possess. Whether it is lawful or ethical to use that information is another issue. In any event, we conclude that private information about a particular stock may exist that is not currently reflected in the price of the stock. For example, prior knowledge of a takeover attempt could be very valuable.

The second form of efficiency, semistrong efficiency, is the most controversial. If a market is semistrong form efficient, then all *public* information is reflected in the stock price. The reason this form is controversial is that it implies that security analysts who try to identify mispriced stocks using, for example, financial statement information are wasting their time because that information is already reflected in the current price.

The third form of efficiency, weak form efficiency, suggests that, at a minimum, the current price of a stock reflects its own past prices. In other words, studying past prices in an attempt to identify mispriced securities is futile if the market is weak form efficient. While this form of efficiency might seem rather mild, it implies that searching for patterns in historical prices that are useful in identifying mispriced stocks will not work (this practice, known as "technical" analysis, is quite common).

What does capital market history say about market efficiency? Here again, there is great controversy. At the risk of going out on a limb, the evidence does seem to tell us three things. First: Prices do appear to respond very rapidly to new information, and the response is at least not grossly different from what we would expect in an efficient market. Second: The future of market prices, particularly in the short run, is very difficult to predict based on publicly available information. Third: If mispriced stocks do exist, then there is no obvious means of identifying them. Put another way: Simpleminded schemes based on public information will probably not be successful.

CONCEPT QUESTIONS

10.6a What is an efficient market?

10.6b What are the forms of market efficiency?

SUMMARY AND CONCLUSIONS

This chapter has explored the subject of capital market history. Such history is useful because it tells us what to expect in the way of returns from risky assets. We summed up our study of market history with two key lessons:

◄ Think you've mastered the material? Scan here to take a chapter quiz.

1. Risky assets, on average, earn a risk premium. There is a reward for bearing risk.
2. The greater the potential reward from a risky investment, the greater is the risk.

These lessons have significant implications for the financial manager. We will be considering these implications in the chapters ahead.

We also discussed the concept of market efficiency. In an efficient market, prices adjust quickly and correctly to new information. Consequently, asset prices in efficient markets are rarely too high or too low. How efficient capital markets (such as the NYSE) are is a matter of debate, but, at a minimum, they are probably much more efficient than most real asset markets.

connect POP QUIZ!

|FINANCE

Can you answer the following questions? If your class is using *Connect Finance,* log on to the Self-Quiz and Study feature in the Library tab to see if you know the answers to these and other questions, check out the study tools, and find out what topics require additional practice!

Section 10.1 Suppose a stock had an initial price of $119 per share, paid a dividend of $3.20 per share during the year, and had an ending share price of $150. Compute the percentage total return.

Section 10.3 You've observed the following returns on Staverosky Corporation's stock over the past five years: 24.3 percent, 13.2 percent, 29.4 percent, 2.1 percent, and 21.1 percent. The average inflation rate over this period was 3.21 percent and the average T-bill rate over the period was 4.3 percent. What was the average real return on the stock?

Section 10.4 Suppose the returns on long-term government bonds are normally distributed. Assume long-term government bonds have a mean return of 5.6 percent and a standard deviation of 9.3 percent. What is the approximate probability that your return on these bonds will be less than −3.7 percent in a given year?

Section 10.5 You've observed the following returns on Staverosky Corporation's stock over the past five years: 24.3 percent, 13.2 percent, 29.4 percent, 2.1 percent, and 21.1 percent. What was the arithmetic average return on the stock over this five-year period?

Section 10.6 What characterizes an efficient capital market's reaction to new information?

www.mhhe.com/rwj

CHAPTER REVIEW AND SELF-TEST PROBLEMS

10.1   Recent Return History.   Use Table 10.1 to calculate the average return over the years 1997–2001 for large-company stocks, long-term government bonds, and Treasury bills. (See Problem 9.)

10.2   More Recent Return History.   Calculate the standard deviations using information from Problem 10.1. Which of the investments was the most volatile over this period? (See Problem 7.)

■ Answers to Chapter Review and Self-Test Problems

10.1   We calculate the averages as follows:

	Actual Returns and Averages		
Year	Large-Company Stocks	Long-Term Government Bonds	Treasury Bills
1997	0.3336	0.1770	0.0519
1998	0.2858	0.1922	0.0486
1999	0.2104	−0.1276	0.0480
2000	−0.0910	0.2216	0.0598
2001	−0.1189	0.0530	0.0333
Average:	0.1240	0.1032	0.0483

10.2   We first need to calculate the deviations from the average returns. Using the averages from Problem 1, we get:

	Deviations from Average Returns		
Year	Large-Company Stocks	Long-Term Government Bonds	Treasury Bills
1997	0.2096	0.0738	0.0036
1998	0.1618	0.0890	0.0003
1999	0.0864	−0.2308	−0.0003
2000	−0.2150	0.1184	0.0115
2001	−0.2429	−0.0502	−0.0150
Total:	0.0000	0.0000	0.0000

We square these deviations and calculate the variances and standard deviations:

	Squared Deviations from Average Returns		
Year	Large-Company Stocks	Long-Term Government Bonds	Treasury Bills
1997	0.043941	0.0054	0.000013
1998	0.026186	0.0079	0.000000
1999	0.007468	0.0533	0.000000
2000	0.046216	0.0140	0.000132
2001	0.058991	0.0025	0.000226
Variance:	0.0457	0.0208	0.0001
Standard deviation:	0.2138	0.1442	0.0096

To calculate the variances, we added up the squared deviations and divided by 4, the number of returns less 1. Notice that the stocks had substantially greater volatility with a larger average return. Once again, such investments are risky, particularly over short periods of time.

CRITICAL THINKING AND CONCEPTS REVIEW

LO 3   **10.1   Investment Selection.**   Given that eGain Communications was up by 412 percent for 2011, why didn't all investors hold eGain Communications?

LO 3   **10.2   Investment Selection.**   Given that First Solar was down by 74 percent for 2011, why did some investors hold the stock? Why didn't they sell out before the price declined so sharply?

LO 3   **10.3   Risk and Return.**   We have seen that over long periods of time, stock investments have tended to substantially outperform bond investments. However, it is not at all uncommon to observe investors with long horizons holding entirely bonds. Are such investors irrational?

LO 4   **10.4   Market Efficiency Implications.**   Explain why a characteristic of an efficient market is that investments in that market have zero NPVs.

LO 4   **10.5   Efficient Markets Hypothesis.**   A stock market analyst is able to identify mispriced stocks by comparing the average price for the last 10 days to the average price for the last 60 days. If this is true, what do you know about the market?

LO 4   **10.6   Semistrong Efficiency.**   If a market is semistrong form efficient, is it also weak form efficient? Explain.

LO 4   **10.7   Efficient Markets Hypothesis.**   What are the implications of the efficient markets hypothesis for investors who buy and sell stocks in an attempt to "beat the market"?

LO 4   **10.8   Stocks versus Gambling.**   Critically evaluate the following statement: Playing the stock market is like gambling. Such speculative investing has no social value, other than the pleasure people get from this form of gambling.

LO 4   **10.9   Efficient Markets Hypothesis.**   There are several celebrated investors and stock pickers frequently mentioned in the financial press who have recorded huge returns on their investments over the past two decades. Is the success of these particular investors an invalidation of the EMH? Explain.

LO 4   **10.10   Efficient Markets Hypothesis.**   For each of the following scenarios, discuss whether profit opportunities exist from trading in the stock of the firm under the conditions that (1) the market is not weak form efficient, (2) the market is weak form but not semistrong form efficient, (3) the market is semistrong form but not strong form efficient, and (4) the market is strong form efficient.

a.   The stock price has risen steadily each day for the past 30 days.

b.   The financial statements for a company were released three days ago, and you believe you've uncovered some anomalies in the company's inventory and cost control reporting techniques that are causing the firm's true liquidity strength to be understated.

c.   You observe that the senior management of a company has been buying a lot of the company's stock on the open market over the past week.

QUESTIONS AND PROBLEMS

 Select problems are available in McGraw-Hill *Connect.* Please see the packaging options section of the preface for more information.

Basic
(Questions 1–18)

LO 1 **1. Calculating Returns.**   Suppose a stock had an initial price of $61 per share, paid a dividend of $1.40 per share during the year, and had an ending share price of $69. Compute the percentage total return. What was the dividend yield? The capital gains yield?

LO 1 **2. Calculating Returns.**   Rework Problem 1 assuming the ending share price is $54.

LO 1 **3. Calculating Dollar Returns.**   You purchased 250 shares of a particular stock at the beginning of the year at a price of $68.12. The stock paid a dividend of $.85 per share, and the stock price at the end of the year was $76.45. What was your dollar return on this investment?

LO 1 **4. Calculating Returns.**   Suppose you bought a bond with a coupon rate of 7.5 percent one year ago for $941. The bond sells for $949 today.

    a.   Assuming a $1,000 face value, what was your total dollar return on this investment over the past year?

    b.   What was your total nominal rate of return on this investment over the past year?

    c.   If the inflation rate last year was 4 percent, what was your total real rate of return on this investment?

LO 2 **5. Nominal versus Real Returns.**   What was the arithmetic average annual return on large-company stocks from 1926 through 2011:

    a.   In nominal terms?

    b.   In real terms?

LO 2 **6. Bond Returns.**   What is the historical real return on long-term government bonds? On long-term corporate bonds?

LO 1 **7. Calculating Returns and Variability.**   Using the following returns, calculate the average returns, the variances, and the standard deviations for X and Y.

	Returns	
Year	**X**	**Y**
1	14%	32%
2	−21	−5
3	17	17
4	9	−12
5	23	45

LO 2 **8. Risk Premiums.**   Refer to Table 10.1 in the text and look at the period from 1973 through 1978.

    a.   Calculate the arithmetic average returns for large-company stocks and T-bills over this time period.

    b.   Calculate the standard deviation of the returns for large-company stocks and T-bills over this time period.

    c.   Calculate the observed risk premium in each year for the large-company stocks versus the T-bills. What was the arithmetic average risk premium over this period? What was the standard deviation of the risk premium over this period?

d.   Is it possible for the risk premium to be negative before an investment is undertaken? Can the risk premium be negative after the fact? Explain.

LO 1   **9. Calculating Returns and Variability.**   You've observed the following returns on Doyscher Corporation's stock over the past five years: −12 percent, 21 percent, 27 percent, 6 percent, and 17 percent.

a.   What was the arithmetic average return on the stock over this five-year period?

b.   What was the variance of the returns over this period? The standard deviation?

LO 1   **10. Calculating Real Returns and Risk Premiums.**   For Problem 9, suppose the average inflation rate over this period was 3.2 percent and the average T-bill rate over the period was 4.3 percent.

a.   What was the average real return on the stock?

b.   What was the average nominal risk premium on the stock?

LO 1   **11. Calculating Real Rates.**   Given the information in Problem 10, what was the average real risk-free rate over this time period? What was the average real risk premium?

LO 2   LO 3   **12. Effects of Inflation.**   Look at Table 10.1 and Figure 10.7 in the text. When were T-bill rates at their highest over the period from 1926 through 2011? Why do you think they were so high during this period? What relationship underlies your answer?

LO 1   **13. Calculating Returns.**   You purchased a zero-coupon bond one year ago for $176.38. The market interest rate is now 9 percent. If the bond had 20 years to maturity when you originally purchased it, what was your total return for the past year?

LO 1   **14. Calculating Returns.**   You bought a share of 4.5 percent preferred stock for $96.18 last year. The market price for your stock is now $98.21. What is your total return for last year?

LO 1   **15. Calculating Returns.**   You bought a stock three months ago for $34.18 per share. The stock paid no dividends. The current share price is $35.07. What is the APR of your investment? The EAR?

LO 1   **16. Calculating Real Returns.**   Refer to Table 10.1. What was the average real return for Treasury bills from 1926 through 1932?

LO 3   **17. Return Distributions.**   Refer back to Figure 10.10. What range of returns would you expect to see 68 percent of the time for long-term corporate bonds? What about 95 percent of the time?

LO 3   **18. Return Distributions.**   Refer back to Figure 10.10. What range of returns would you expect to see 68 percent of the time for large-company stocks? What about 95 percent of the time?

LO 1   **19. Calculating Returns and Variability.**   You find a certain stock that had returns of 11 percent, −15 percent, 32 percent, and 8 percent for four of the last five years. If the average return of the stock over this period was 10 percent, what was the stock's return for the missing year? What is the standard deviation of the stock's returns?

Intermediate
(Questions 19–26)

LO 1   **20. Arithmetic and Geometric Returns.**   A stock has had returns of −26 percent, 6 percent, 34 percent, −5 percent, 28 percent, and 19 percent over the last six years. What are the arithmetic and geometric returns for the stock?

www.mhhe.com/rwj

346   **PART 6**   Risk and Return

LO 1   **21. Arithmetic and Geometric Returns.**   A stock has had the following year-end prices and dividends:

Year	Price	Dividend
1	$ 99.15	—
2	107.11	$1.60
3	91.65	2.00
4	127.16	2.20
5	162.15	2.60
6	192.60	3.00

What are the arithmetic and geometric returns for the stock?

LO 2 **LO 3**   **22. Calculating Returns.**   Refer to Table 10.1 in the text and look at the period from 1973 through 1980.

    a.   Calculate the average return for Treasury bills and the average annual inflation rate (consumer price index) for this period.

    b.   Calculate the standard deviation of Treasury bill returns and inflation over this time period.

    c.   Calculate the real return for each year. What is the average real return for Treasury bills?

    d.   Many people consider Treasury bills to be risk-free. What does this tell you about the potential risks of Treasury bills?

LO 1   **23. Calculating Investment Returns.**   You bought one of Rocky Mountain Manufacturing Co.'s 8 percent coupon bonds one year ago for $1,032.15. These bonds make annual payments and mature nine years from now. Suppose you decide to sell your bonds today, when the required return on the bonds is 7.2 percent. If the inflation rate was 3.5 percent over the past year, what would be your total real return on investment?

LO 3   **24. Using Return Distributions.**   Suppose the returns on long-term government bonds are normally distributed. Based on the historical record, what is the approximate probability that your return on these bonds will be less than −3.7 percent in a given year? What range of returns would you expect to see 95 percent of the time? What range would you expect to see 99 percent of the time?

LO 3   **25. Using Return Distributions.**   Assuming that the returns from holding small-company stocks are normally distributed, what is the approximate probability that your money will double in value in a single year? What about triple in value?

LO 3   **26. Distributions.**   In the previous problem, what is the probability that the return is less than −100 percent (think)? What are the implications for the distribution of returns?

LO 3   **27. Using Probability Distributions.**   Suppose the returns on large-company stocks are normally distributed. Based on the historical record, use the NORMDIST function in Excel® to determine the probability that in any given year you will lose money by investing in common stock.

Challenge
(Question 27–28)

LO 3   28. **Using Probability Distributions.**   Suppose the returns on long-term corporate bonds and T-bills are normally distributed. Based on the historical record, use the NORMDIST function in Excel® to answer the following questions:

    a.   What is the probability that in any given year, the return on long-term corporate bonds will be greater than 10 percent? Less than 0 percent?

    b.   What is the probability that in any given year, the return on T-bills will be greater than 10 percent? Less than 0 percent?

    c.   In 1979, the return on long-term corporate bonds was – 4.18 percent. How likely is it that such a low return will recur at some point in the future? T-bills had a return of 10.56 percent in this same year. How likely is it that such a high return on T-bills will recur at some point in the future?

Historical Interest Rates.   Go to the St. Louis Federal Reserve website at www.stlouisfed.org and find the "FRED®" link and the "Interest Rates" link. You will find a list of links for different historical interest rates. Follow the "10-Year Treasury Constant Maturity Rate" link and you will find the monthly 10-year Treasury note interest rates. Calculate the average annual 10-year Treasury interest rate for 2011 and 2012. Compare this number to the long-term government bond returns and the U.S. Treasury bill returns found in Table 10.1. How does the 10-year Treasury interest rate compare to these numbers? Do you expect this relationship to always hold? Why or why not?

WHAT'S ON THE WEB?

www.mhhe.com/rwj

EXCEL *MASTER IT!* PROBLEM

As we have seen, over the 1926–2011 period, small-company stocks had the highest return and the highest risk, while U.S. Treasury bills had the lowest return and the lowest risk. While we certainly hope you have an 86-year holding period, it is likely your investment will be for fewer years. One way risk and return is examined over shorter investment periods is by using rolling returns and standard deviations. Suppose you have a series of annual returns, and you want to calculate a 3-year rolling average return. You would calculate the first rolling average at Year 3 using the returns for the first 3 years. The next rolling average would be calculated using the returns from Years 2, 3, and 4, and so on.

    a.   Using the annual returns for large-company stocks and Treasury bills, calculate both the 5- and 10-year rolling average return and standard deviation.

    b.   Over how many 5-year periods did Treasury bills outperform large-company stocks? How many 10-year periods?

    c.   Over how many 5-year periods did Treasury bills have a larger standard deviation than large-company stocks? Over how many 10-year periods?

    d.   Graph the rolling 5-year and 10-year average returns for large-company stocks and Treasury bills.

    e.   What conclusions do you draw from the above results?

CHAPTER CASE
A JOB AT S&S AIR

You recently graduated from college, and your job search led you to S&S Air. Since you felt the company's business was headed skyward, you accepted the job offer. As you are finishing your employment paperwork, Chris Guthrie, who works in the finance department, stops by to inform you about the company's new 401(k) plan.

A 401(k) is a type of retirement plan offered by many companies. A 401(k) is tax deferred, which means that any deposits you make into the plan are deducted from your current income, so no current taxes are paid on the money. For example, assume your salary will be $30,000 per year. If you contribute $1,500 to the 401(k) plan, you will pay taxes only on $28,500 in income. No taxes will be due on any capital gains or plan income while you are invested in the plan, but you will pay taxes when you withdraw the money at retirement. You can contribute up to 15 percent of your salary to the plan. As is common, S&S Air also has a five percent match program. This means that the company will match your contribution dollar-for-dollar up to five percent of your salary, but you must contribute to get the match.

The 401(k) plan has several options for investments, most of which are mutual funds. As you know, a mutual fund is a portfolio of assets. When you purchase shares in a mutual fund, you are actually purchasing partial ownership of the fund's assets, similar to purchasing shares of stock in a company. The return of the fund is the weighted average of the return of the assets owned by the fund, minus any expenses. The largest expense is typically the management fee paid to the fund manager, who makes all of the investment decisions for the fund. S&S Air uses Arias Financial Services as its 401(k) plan administrator.

Chris Guthrie then explains that the retirement investment options offered for employees are as follows:

1. *Company Stock*. One option is stock in S&S Air. The company is currently privately held. The price you would pay for the stock is based on an annual appraisal, less a 20 percent discount. When you interviewed with the owners, Mark Sexton and Todd Story, they informed you that the company stock was expected to be publicly sold in three to five years. If you needed to sell the stock before it became publicly traded, the company would buy it back at the then-current appraised value.

2. *Arias S&P 500 Index Fund*. This mutual fund tracks the S&P 500. Stocks in the fund are weighted exactly the same as they are in the S&P 500. This means that the fund's return is approximately the return of the S&P 500, minus expenses. With an index fund, the manager is not required to research stocks and make investment decisions, so fund expenses are usually low. The Arias S&P 500 Index Fund charges expenses of 0.20 percent of assets per year.

3. *Arias Small-Cap Fund*. This fund primarily invests in small capitalization stocks. As such, the returns of the fund are more volatile. The fund can also invest 10 percent of its assets in companies based outside the United States. This fund charges 1.70 percent of assets in expenses per year.

4. *Arias Large-Company Stock Fund*. This fund invests primarily in large capitalization stocks of companies based in the United States. The fund is managed by Melissa Arias and has outperformed the market in six of the last eight years. The fund charges 1.50 percent in expenses.

5. *Arias Bond Fund*. This fund invests in long-term corporate bonds issued by U.S. domiciled companies. The fund is restricted to investments in bonds with an investment grade credit rating. This fund charges 1.40 percent in expenses.

6. *Arias Money Market Fund*. This fund invests in short-term, high credit quality debt instruments, which include Treasury bills. As such, the return on money market funds is only slightly higher than the return on Treasury bills. Because of the credit quality and short-term nature of the investments, there is only a very slight risk of negative return.The fund charges 0.60 percent in expenses.

QUESTIONS

1. What advantages/disadvantages do the mutual funds offer compared to company stock for your retirement investing?

2. Notice that, for every dollar you invest, S&S Air also invests a dollar. What return on your investment does this represent? What does your answer suggest about matching programs?

3. Assume you decide you should invest at least part of your money in large capitalization stocks of companies based in the United States. What are the advantages and disadvantages of choosing the Arias Large-Company Stock Fund compared to the Arias S&P 500 Index Fund?

4. The returns of the Arias Small-Cap Fund are the most volatile of all the mutual funds offered in the

401 (k) plan. Why would you ever want to invest in this fund? When you examine the expenses of the mutual funds, you will notice that this fund also has the highest expenses. Will this affect your decision to invest in this fund?

5. A measure of risk-adjusted performance that is often used in practice is the Sharpe ratio. The Sharpe ratio is calculated as the risk premium of an asset divided by its standard deviation.

The standard deviations and returns for the funds over the past 10 years are listed below. Assuming a risk-free rate of 4 percent, calculate the Sharpe ratio for each of these. In broad terms, what do you suppose the Sharpe ratio is intended to measure?

	10-year Annual Return	Standard Deviation
Arias S&P 500 Index Fund	9.15%	19.35%
Arias Small-Cap Fund	14.05	26.82
Arias Large-Company Stock Fund	9.53	23.82
Arias Bond Fund	8.73	11.45

www.mhhe.com/rwj

11 | Risk and Return

In February 2012, Humana, Hewlett-Packard, and Johnson Controls joined a host of other companies in announcing operating results. As you might expect, news such as this tends to move stock prices. Health care company Humana announced that net income rose to $199 million compared to $107.3 million in the same quarter the previous year. Its quarterly EPS of $1.20 was precisely what analysts had estimated for the company. Surprisingly, the stock price fell about 5.4 percent on the news. Technology giant Hewlett-Packard announced that its net income for the most recent quarter was $1.5 billion, a 44 percent decline from the previous year. Total revenue dropped by 7 percent as all the company's three divisions saw a sales decline. The company's stock rose 1.3 percent on the announcement. And Johnson Controls, the building efficiency and power solutions company, announced record sales and earnings, but its stock price fell by 9 percent.

Two of these announcements seem positive, yet the stock price fell. The other announcement seems to be negative, yet the stock price rose. So when is good news really good news? The answer is fundamental to understanding risk and return, and—the good news is—this chapter explores it in detail.

This chapter continues the discussion we began in the previous chapter. We've seen pretty clearly that some investments have greater risks than others. We now begin to drill down a bit to investigate one of the most fundamental problems in finance: Just what is risk? What we will learn is that risk is not always what it seems, and the reward for bearing risk is more subtle than we have indicated so far. Understanding how risks are rewarded is important for everyone in business for the simple reason that business is risky, and only businesses that manage risk wisely will survive over the long haul.

In our last chapter, we learned some important lessons from capital market history. Most important, there is a reward, on average, for bearing risk. We called this reward a *risk premium.* The second lesson is that this risk premium is larger for riskier investments. This chapter explores the economic and managerial implications of this basic idea.

Thus far, we have concentrated mainly on the return behavior of a few large portfolios. We need to expand our consideration to include individual assets. Specifically, we have two tasks to accomplish. First, we have to define risk and then discuss how to measure it. We then must quantify the relationship between an asset's risk and its required return.

When we examine the risks associated with individual assets, we find there are two types of risk: systematic and unsystematic. This distinction is crucial because, as we will see, systematic risk affects almost all assets in the economy, at least to some degree, while unsystematic risk affects at most a small number of assets. We then develop the principle of diversification, which shows that highly diversified portfolios will tend to have almost no unsystematic risk.

The principle of diversification has an important implication: To a diversified investor, only systematic risk matters. It follows that in deciding whether or not to buy a particular individual asset, a diversified investor will only be concerned with that asset's systematic risk. This is a key observation, and it allows us to say a great deal about the risks and returns on individual assets. In particular, it is the basis for a famous relationship between risk and return called the *security market line,* or SML. To develop the SML, we introduce the equally famous "beta" coefficient, one of the centerpieces of modern finance. Beta and the SML are key concepts because they supply us with at least part of the answer to the question of how to go about determining the required return on an investment.

EXPECTED RETURNS AND VARIANCES

11.1

In our previous chapter, we discussed how to calculate average returns and variances using historical data. We now begin to discuss how to analyze returns and variances when the information we have concerns future possible returns and their probabilities.

Expected Return

We start with a straightforward case. Consider a single period of time, say, a year. We have two stocks, L and U, which have the following characteristics: Stock L is expected to have a return of 25 percent in the coming year. Stock U is expected to have a return of 20 percent for the same period.

In a situation like this, if all investors agreed on the expected returns, why would anyone want to hold Stock U? After all, why invest in one stock when the expectation is that another will do better? Clearly, the answer must depend on the risk of the two investments. The return on Stock L, although it is *expected* to be 25 percent, could actually turn out to be higher or lower.

For example, suppose the economy booms. In this case, we think Stock L will have a 70 percent return. If the economy enters a recession, we think the return will be −20 percent. In this case, we say that there are two *states of the economy,* which means that these are the only two possible situations. This setup is oversimplified, of course, but it allows us to illustrate some key ideas without a lot of computation.

Suppose we think a boom and a recession are equally likely to happen, for a 50–50 chance of each. Table 11.1 illustrates the basic information we have described and some additional information about Stock U. Notice that Stock U earns 30 percent if there is a recession and 10 percent if there is a boom.

352   PART 6   Risk and Return

TABLE 11.1		Probability of	Security Returns if State Occurs	
States of the economy and stock returns	**State of Economy**	**State of Economy**	**Stock L**	**Stock U**
	Recession	.5	−20%	30%
	Boom	.5	70	10
		1.0		

TABLE 11.2			Stock L		Stock U	
Calculation of expected return	**(1) State of Economy**	**(2) Probability of State of Economy**	**(3) Rate of Return if State Occurs**	**(4) Product (2) × (3)**	**(5) Rate of Return if State Occurs**	**(6) Product (2) × (5)**
	Recession	.5	−.20	−.10	.30	.15
	Boom	.5	.70	.35	.10	.05
		1.0		$E(R_L) = .25$		$E(R_U) = .20$

Obviously, if you buy one of these stocks, say Stock U, what you earn in any particular year depends on what the economy does during that year. However, suppose the probabilities stay the same through time. If you hold U for a number of years, you'll earn 30 percent about half the time and 10 percent the other half. In this case, we say that your **expected return** on Stock U, $E(R_U)$, is 20 percent:

expected return
Return on a risky asset expected in the future

$$E(R_U) = .50 \times 30\% + .50 \times 10\% = 20\%$$

In other words, you should expect to earn 20 percent from this stock, on average.

For Stock L, the probabilities are the same, but the possible returns are different. Here we lose 20 percent half the time, and we gain 70 percent the other half. The expected return on L, $E(R_L)$, is thus 25 percent:

$$E(R_L) = .50 \times -20\% + .50 \times 70\% = 25\%$$

Table 11.2 illustrates these calculations.

In our previous chapter, we defined the risk premium as the difference between the return on a risky investment and that on a risk-free investment, and we calculated the historical risk premiums on some different investments. Using our projected returns, we can calculate the *projected*, or *expected, risk premium* as the difference between the expected return on a risky investment and the certain return on a risk-free investment.

For example, suppose risk-free investments are currently offering 8 percent. We will say that the risk-free rate, which we label as R_f, is 8 percent. Given this, what is the projected risk premium on Stock U? On Stock L? Since the expected return on Stock U, $E(R_U)$, is 20 percent, the projected risk premium is:

$$\begin{aligned}
\text{Risk premium} &= \text{Expected return} - \text{Risk-free rate} \\
&= E(R_U) - R_f \\
&= 20\% - 8\% \\
&= 12\%
\end{aligned} \quad [11.1]$$

Similarly, the risk premium on Stock L is $25\% - 8\% = 17\%$.

In general, the expected return on a security or other asset is simply equal to the sum of the possible returns multiplied by their probabilities. So, if we had 100 possible returns, we would multiply each one by its probability and then add the results up. The result would be the expected return. The risk premium would then be the difference between this expected return and the risk-free rate.

UNEQUAL PROBABILITIES

EXAMPLE 11.1

Look again at Tables 11.1 and 11.2. Suppose you thought a boom would occur only 20 percent of the time instead of 50 percent. What are the expected returns on Stocks U and L in this case? If the risk-free rate is 10 percent, what are the risk premiums?

The first thing to notice is that a recession must occur 80 percent of the time $(1 - .20 = .80)$ since there are only two possibilities. With this in mind, we see that Stock U has a 30 percent return in 80 percent of the years and a 10 percent return in 20 percent of the years. To calculate the expected return, we again just multiply the possibilities by the probabilities and add up the results:

$$E(R_U) = .80 \times 30\% + .20 \times 10\% = 26\%$$

Table 11.3 summarizes the calculations for both stocks. Notice that the expected return on L is −2 percent.

The risk premium for Stock U is $26\% - 10\% = 16\%$ in this case. The risk premium for Stock L is negative: $-2\% - 10\% = -12\%$. This is a little odd, but, for reasons we discuss later, it is not impossible.

Calculating the Variance

To calculate the variances of the returns on our two stocks, we first determine the squared deviations from the expected returns. We then multiply each possible squared deviation by its probability. We add these up, and the result is the variance. The standard deviation, as always, is the square root of the variance.

To illustrate, Stock U above has an expected return of $E(R_U) = 20\%$. In a given year, it will actually return either 30 percent or 10 percent. The possible deviations are thus $30\% - 20\% = 10\%$ and $10\% - 20\% = -10\%$. In this case, the variance is:

$$\text{Variance} = \sigma_U^2 = .50 \times (10\%)^2 + .50 \times (-10\%)^2 = .01$$

(1) State of Economy	(2) Probability of State of Economy	Stock L		Stock U		**TABLE 11.3**
		(3) Rate of Return if State Occurs	(4) Product (2) × (3)	(5) Rate of Return if State Occurs	(6) Product (2) × (5)	Calculation of expected return
Recession	.8	−.20	−.16	.30	.24	
Boom	.2	.70	.14	.10	.02	
	1.0		$E(R_L) = -.02$		$E(R_U) = .26$	

TABLE 11.4	(1) State of Economy	(2) Probability of State of Economy	(3) Return Deviation from Expected Return	(4) Squared Return Deviation from Expected Return	(5) Product (2) × (4)
Calculation of variance					
	Stock L				
	Recession	.5	$-.20 - .25 = -.45$	$-.45^2 = .2025$	.10125
	Boom	.5	$.70 - .25 = .45$	$.45^2 = .2025$	.10125
		1.0			$\sigma_L^2 = .2025$
	Stock U				
	Recession	.5	$.30 - .20 = .10$	$.10^2 = .01$	.00500
	Boom	.5	$.10 - .20 = -.10$	$-.10^2 = .01$	.00500
		1.0			$\sigma_U^2 = .0100$

The standard deviation is the square root of this:

$$\text{Standard deviation} = \sigma_U = \sqrt{.01} = .10 = 10\%$$

Table 11.4 summarizes these calculations for both stocks. Notice that Stock L has a much larger variance.

When we put the expected return and variability information for our two stocks together, we have:

	Stock L	Stock U
Expected return, $E(R)$	25%	20%
Variance, σ^2	.2025	.0100
Standard deviation, σ	45%	10%

Stock L has a higher expected return, but U has less risk. You could get a 70 percent return on your investment in L, but you could also lose 20 percent. Notice that an investment in U will always pay at least 10 percent.

Which of these two stocks should you buy? We can't really say; it depends on your personal preferences. We can be reasonably sure, however, that some investors would prefer L to U and some would prefer U to L.

You've probably noticed that the way we calculated expected returns and variances here is somewhat different from the way we did it in the last chapter. The reason is that, in Chapter 10, we were examining actual historical returns, so we estimated the average return and the variance based on some actual events. Here, we have projected *future* returns and their associated probabilities, so this is the information with which we must work.

EXAMPLE 11.2

MORE UNEQUAL PROBABILITIES

Going back to Example 11.1, what are the variances on the two stocks once we have unequal probabilities? The standard deviations?

(continued)

We can summarize the needed calculations as follows:

(1) State of Economy	(2) Probability of State of Economy	(3) Return Deviation from Expected Return	(4) Squared Return Deviation from Expected Return	(5) Product (2) × (4)
Stock L				
Recession	.80	$-.20 - (-.02) = -.18$	.0324	.02592
Boom	.20	$.70 - (-.02) = \ .72$	.5184	.10368
				$\sigma_L^2 = .12960$
Stock U				
Recession	.80	$.30 - .26 = \ .04$	.0016	.00128
Boom	.20	$.10 - .26 = -.16$	.0256	.00512
				$\sigma_U^2 = .00640$

Based on these calculations, the standard deviation for L is $\sigma_L = \sqrt{.1296} = .36$, or 36%. The standard deviation for U is much smaller; $\sigma_U = \sqrt{.0064} = .08$, or 8%.

CONCEPT QUESTIONS

11.1a   How do we calculate the expected return on a security?

11.1b   In words, how do we calculate the variance of the expected return?

PORTFOLIOS

11.2

Thus far in this chapter, we have concentrated on individual assets considered separately. However, most investors actually hold a **portfolio** of assets. All we mean by this is that investors tend to own more than just a single stock, bond, or other asset. Given that this is so, portfolio return and portfolio risk are of obvious relevance. Accordingly, we now discuss portfolio expected returns and variances.

portfolio
Group of assets such as stocks and bonds held by an investor.

Portfolio Weights

There are many equivalent ways of describing a portfolio. The most convenient approach is to list the percentages of the total portfolio's value that are invested in each portfolio asset. We call these percentages the **portfolio weights**.

For example, if we have $50 in one asset and $150 in another, then our total portfolio is worth $200. The percentage of our portfolio in the first asset is $50/200 = .25. The percentage of our portfolio in the second asset is $150/200, or .75. Our portfolio weights are thus .25 and .75. Notice that the weights have to add up to 1.00 since all of our money is invested somewhere.[1]

portfolio weight
Percentage of a portfolio's total value in a particular asset.

Portfolio Expected Returns

Let's go back to Stocks L and U. You put half your money in each. The portfolio weights are obviously .50 and .50. What is the pattern of returns on this portfolio? The expected return?

---

[1] Some of it could be in cash, of course, but we would then just consider the cash to be one of the portfolio assets.

356   **PART 6**   Risk and Return

TABLE 11.5	(1) State of Economy	(2) Probability of State of Economy	(3) Portfolio Return if State Occurs	(4) Product (2) × (3)
Expected return on an equally weighted portfolio of Stock L and Stock U	Recession	.50	.50 × −20% + .50 × 30% = 5%	.025
	Boom	.50	.50 × 70% + .50 × 10% = 40%	.200
		1.00		$E(R_p) = \overline{.225}$

To answer these questions, suppose the economy actually enters a recession. In this case, half your money (the half in L) loses 20 percent. The other half (the half in U) gains 30 percent. Your portfolio return, R_p, in a recession will thus be:

$$R_p = .50 \times -20\% + .50 \times 30\% = 5\%$$

Table 11.5 summarizes the remaining calculations. Notice that when a boom occurs, your portfolio will return 40 percent:

$$R_p = .50 \times 70\% + .50 \times 10\% = 40\%$$

As indicated in Table 11.5, the expected return on your portfolio, $E(R_p)$, is 22.5 percent.

We can save ourselves some work by calculating the expected return more directly. Given these portfolio weights, we could have reasoned that we expect half of our money to earn 25 percent (the half in L) and half of our money to earn 20 percent (the half in U). Our portfolio expected return is thus:

$$E(R_p) = .50 \times E(R_L) + .50 \times E(R_U)$$
$$= .50 \times 25\% + .50 \times 20\%$$
$$= 22.5\%$$

This is the same portfolio expected return we had before.

This method of calculating the expected return on a portfolio works no matter how many assets there are in the portfolio. Suppose we had n assets in our portfolio, where n is any number. If we let x_i stand for the percentage of our money in Asset i, then the expected return is:

$$E(R_p) = x_1 \times E(R_1) + x_2 \times E(R_2) + \cdots + x_n \times E(R_n) \qquad \text{[11.2]}$$

This says that the expected return on a portfolio is a straightforward combination of the expected returns on the assets in that portfolio. This seems somewhat obvious, but, as we will examine next, the obvious approach is not always the right one.

EXAMPLE 11.3 **PORTFOLIO EXPECTED RETURN**

Suppose we have the following projections on three stocks:

State of Economy	Probability of State	Returns		
		Stock A	**Stock B**	**Stock C**
Boom	.40	10%	15%	20%
Bust	.60	8	4	0

(continued)

We want to calculate portfolio expected returns in two cases. First: What would be the expected return on a portfolio with equal amounts invested in each of the three stocks? Second: What would be the expected return if half of the portfolio were in A, with the remainder equally divided between B and C?

From our earlier discussions, the expected returns on the individual stocks are (check these for practice):

$E(R_A) = 8.8\%$

$E(R_B) = 8.4\%$

$E(R_C) = 8.0\%$

If a portfolio has equal investments in each asset, the portfolio weights are all the same. Such a portfolio is said to be *equally weighted.* Since there are three stocks in this case, the weights are all equal to ⅓. The portfolio expected return is thus:

$E(R_P) = ⅓ × 8.8\% + ⅓ × 8.4\% + ⅓ × 8.0\% = 8.4\%$

In the second case, verify that the portfolio expected return is 8.5 percent.

Portfolio Variance

From our discussion above, the expected return on a portfolio that contains equal investments in Stocks U and L is 22.5 percent. What is the standard deviation of return on this portfolio? Simple intuition might suggest that half of the money has a standard deviation of 45 percent and the other half has a standard deviation of 10 percent, so the portfolio's standard deviation might be calculated as:

$\sigma_P = .50 × 45\% + .50 × 10\% = 27.5\%$

Unfortunately, this approach is completely incorrect!

Let's see what the standard deviation really is. Table 11.6 summarizes the relevant calculations. As we see, the portfolio's variance is about .031, and its standard deviation is less than we thought—it's only 17.5 percent. What is illustrated here is that the variance on a portfolio is not generally a simple combination of the variances of the assets in the portfolio.

We can illustrate this point a little more dramatically by considering a slightly different set of portfolio weights. Suppose we put $^2/_{11}$ (about 18 percent) in L and the other $^9/_{11}$ (about 82 percent) in U. If a recession occurs, this portfolio will have a return of:

$R_P = ^2/_{11} × -20\% + ^9/_{11} × 30\% = 20.91\%$

If a boom occurs, this portfolio will have a return of:

$R_P = ^2/_{11} × 70\% + ^9/_{11} × 10\% = 20.91\%$

(1) State of Economy	(2) Probability of State of Economy	(3) Portfolio Return if State Occurs	(4) Squared Deviation from Expected Return	(5) Product (2) × (4)
Recession	.50	5%	$(.05 - .225)^2 = .030625$	.0153125
Boom	.50	40	$(.40 - .225)^2 = .030625$	.0153125
	1.00		$\sigma_P^2 = .030625$	
			$\sigma_P = \sqrt{.030625} = 17.5\%$	

TABLE 11.6

Variance on an equally weighted portfolio of Stock L and Stock U

Notice that the return is the same no matter what happens. No further calculations are needed: This portfolio has a zero variance. Apparently, combining assets into portfolios can substantially alter the risks faced by the investor. This is a crucial observation, and we will begin to explore its implications in the next section.

EXAMPLE 11.4

PORTFOLIO VARIANCE AND STANDARD DEVIATION

In Example 11.3, what are the standard deviations on the two portfolios? To answer, we first have to calculate the portfolio returns in the two states. We will work with the second portfolio, which has 50 percent in Stock A and 25 percent in each of Stocks B and C. The relevant calculations can be summarized as follows:

State of Economy	Probability of State	Returns			
		Stock A	Stock B	Stock C	Portfolio
Boom	.40	10%	15%	20%	13.75%
Bust	.60	8	4	0	5.00

The portfolio return when the economy booms is calculated as:

$$.50 \times 10\% + .25 \times 15\% + .25 \times 20\% = 13.75\%$$

The return when the economy goes bust is calculated the same way. The expected return on the portfolio is .085. The variance is thus:

$$\sigma^2 = .40 \times (.1375 - .085)^2 + .60 \times (.05 - .085)^2$$
$$= .0018375$$

The standard deviation is thus about 4.3 percent. For our equally weighted portfolio, verify that the standard deviation is about 5.4 percent.

CONCEPT QUESTIONS

11.2a What is a portfolio weight?

11.2b How do we calculate the expected return on a portfolio?

11.2c Is there a simple relationship between the standard deviation on a portfolio and the standard deviations of the assets in the portfolio?

11.3

ANNOUNCEMENTS, SURPRISES, AND EXPECTED RETURNS

Now that we know how to construct portfolios and evaluate their returns, we begin to describe more carefully the risks and returns associated with individual securities. Thus far, we have measured volatility by looking at the difference between the actual return on an asset or portfolio, R, and the expected return, E(R). We now look at why such deviations exist.

Expected and Unexpected Returns

To begin, for concreteness, we consider the return on the stock of a company called Flyers. What will determine this stock's return in, say, the coming year?

The return on any stock traded in a financial market is composed of two parts. First, the normal, or expected, return from the stock is the part of the return that shareholders in the market predict or expect. This return depends on the information shareholders have that bears on the stock, and it is based on the market's understanding today of the important factors that will influence the stock in the coming year.

The second part of the return on the stock is the uncertain, or risky, part. This is the portion that comes from unexpected information revealed within the year. A list of all possible sources of such information would be endless, but here are a few examples:

News about research on Flyers

Government figures released on gross domestic product (GDP).

The results from the latest arms control talks.

The news that Flyers's sales figures are higher than expected.

A sudden, unexpected drop in interest rates.

Based on this discussion, one way to express the return on Flyers stock in the coming year would be:

Total return = Expected return + Unexpected return
$$R = E(R) + U \tag{11.3}$$

where R stands for the actual total return in the year, $E(R)$ stands for the expected part of the return, and U stands for the unexpected part of the return. What this says is that the actual return, R, differs from the expected return, $E(R)$, because of surprises that occur during the year. In any given year, the unexpected return will be positive or negative, but, through time, the average value of U will be zero. This simply means that, on average, the actual return equals the expected return.

Announcements and News

We need to be careful when we talk about the effect of news items on the return. For example, suppose Flyers's business is such that the company prospers when GDP grows at a relatively high rate and suffers when GDP is relatively stagnant. In this case, in deciding what return to expect this year from owning stock in Flyers, shareholders either implicitly or explicitly must think about what GDP is likely to be for the year.

When the government actually announces GDP figures for the year, what will happen to the value of Flyers stock? Obviously, the answer depends on what figure is released. More to the point, however, the impact depends on how much of that figure is *new* information.

At the beginning of the year, market participants will have some idea or forecast of what the yearly GDP will be. To the extent that shareholders have predicted GDP, that prediction will already be factored into the expected part of the return on the stock, $E(R)$. On the other hand, if the announced GDP is a surprise, then the effect will be part of U, the unanticipated portion of the return.

As an example, suppose shareholders in the market had forecast that the GDP increase this year would be .5 percent. If the actual announcement this year is exactly .5 percent, the same as the forecast, then the shareholders don't really learn anything, and the announcement isn't news. There will be no impact on the stock price as a result. This is like receiving confirmation of something that you suspected all along; it doesn't reveal anything new.

A common way of saying that an announcement isn't news is to say that the market has already "discounted" the announcement. The use of the word *discount* here is different from the use of the term in computing present values, but the spirit is the same.

When we discount a dollar in the future, we say it is worth less to us because of the time value of money. When we say that we discount an announcement, or a news item, we mean that it has less of an impact on the market because the market already knew much of it.

For example, going back to Flyers, suppose the government announces that the actual GDP increase during the year has been 1.5 percent. Now shareholders have learned something, namely, that the increase is one percentage point higher than they had forecast. This difference between the actual result and the forecast, one percentage point in this example, is sometimes called the *innovation* or the *surprise*.

An announcement, then, can be broken into two parts, the anticipated, or expected, part and the surprise, or innovation:

$$\textbf{Announcement = Expected part + Surprise} \qquad [11.4]$$

The expected part of any announcement is the part of the information that the market uses to form the expectation, $E(R)$, of the return on the stock. The surprise is the news that influences the unanticipated return on the stock, U.

To take another example, if shareholders knew in January that the president of the firm was going to resign, the official announcement in February would be fully expected and would be discounted by the market. Because the announcement was expected before February, its influence on the stock would have taken place before February. The announcement itself will contain no surprise, and the stock's price shouldn't change at all when it is actually made.

The fact that only the unexpected, or surprise, part of an announcement matters explains why two companies can make similar announcements but experience different stock price reactions. For example, to open the chapter, we compared Humana, Hewlett-Packard, and Johnson Controls. In Humana's case, the company stated that its 2012 annual EPS would be $7.50 to $7.70. Unfortunately for shareholders, analysts had projected an EPS of $7.99. In Hewlett-Packard's case, much of the loss was expected by the market. In the earnings announcement, the new CEO, Meg Whitman, gave a sweeping description of the changes planned at the company, including cost-cutting measures aimed at directing more money toward innovation in new products. In Johnson Controls' case, even though the company had record earnings, the EPS was actually two cents lower than analysts' estimates. The company further warned about the next year because of the warmer than usual weather. For example, the company expected to ship fewer aftermarket car batteries to Walmart and Sears, and the demand for its York furnaces was expected to fall because of the end of the federal energy efficiency tax credit.

Our discussion of market efficiency in the previous chapter bears on this discussion. We are assuming that relevant information known today is already reflected in the expected return. This is identical to saying that the current price reflects relevant publicly available information. We are thus implicitly assuming that markets are at least reasonably efficient in the semistrong form sense.

Henceforth, when we speak of news, we will mean the surprise part of an announcement and not the portion that the market has expected and therefore already discounted.

CONCEPT QUESTIONS

11.3a   What are the two basic parts of a return?

11.3b   Under what conditions will an announcement have no effect on common stock prices?

RISK: SYSTEMATIC AND UNSYSTEMATIC

11.4

The unanticipated part of the return, that portion resulting from surprises, is the true risk of any investment. After all, if we always receive exactly what we expect, then the investment is perfectly predictable and, by definition, risk-free. In other words, the risk of owning an asset comes from surprises—unanticipated events.

There are important differences, though, among various sources of risk. Look back at our previous list of news stories. Some of these stories are directed specifically at Flyers, and some are more general. Which of the news items are of specific importance to Flyers?

Announcements about interest rates or GDP are clearly important for nearly all companies, whereas the news about Flyers's president, its research, or its sales is of specific interest to Flyers. We will distinguish between these two types of events, because, as we shall see, they have very different implications.

Systematic and Unsystematic Risk

The first type of surprise, the one that affects a large number of assets, we will label **systematic risk**. Because systematic risks have marketwide effects, they are sometimes called *market risks*.

systematic risk
A risk that influences a large number of assets. Also *market risk*.

The second type of surprise we will call **unsystematic risk**. An unsystematic risk is one that affects a single asset or a small group of assets. Because these risks are unique to individual companies or assets, they are sometimes called *unique* or *asset-specific risks*. We will use these terms interchangeably.

unsystematic risk
A risk that affects at most a small number of assets. Also *unique* or *asset-specific risk*.

As we have seen, uncertainties about general economic conditions, such as GDP, interest rates, or inflation, are examples of systematic risks. These conditions affect nearly all companies to some degree. An unanticipated increase, or surprise, in inflation, for example, affects wages and the costs of the supplies that companies buy; it affects the value of the assets that companies own; and it affects the prices at which companies sell their products. Forces such as these, to which all companies are susceptible, are the essence of systematic risk.

In contrast, the announcement of an oil strike by a company will primarily affect that company and, perhaps, a few others (such as primary competitors and suppliers). It is unlikely to have much of an effect on the world oil market, however, or on the affairs of companies not in the oil business, so this is an unsystematic event.

Systematic and Unsystematic Components of Return

The distinction between a systematic risk and an unsystematic risk is never really as exact as we make it out to be. Even the most narrow and peculiar bit of news about a company ripples through the economy. This is true because every enterprise, no matter how tiny, is a part of the economy. It's like the tale of a kingdom that was lost because one horse lost a shoe. This is mostly hairsplitting, however. Some risks are clearly much more general than others. We'll see some evidence on this point in just a moment.

The distinction between the types of risk allows us to break down the surprise portion, *U*, of the return on Flyers's stock into two parts. From before, we had the actual return broken down into its expected and surprise components:

$$R = E(R) + U$$

We now recognize that the total surprise for Flyers, *U*, has a systematic and an unsystematic component, so:

$$R = E(R) + \text{Systematic portion} + \text{Unsystematic portion} \qquad [11.5]$$

Because it is traditional, we will use the Greek letter epsilon, ϵ, to stand for the unsystematic portion. Since systematic risks are often called market risks, we will use the letter m to stand for the systematic part of the surprise. With these symbols, we can rewrite the total return:

$$R = E(R) + U$$
$$ = E(R) + m + \epsilon$$

The important thing about the way we have broken down the total surprise, U, is that the unsystematic portion, ϵ, is more or less unique to Flyers. For this reason, it is unrelated to the unsystematic portion of the return on most other assets. To see why this is important, we need to return to the subject of portfolio risk.

CONCEPT QUESTIONS

11.4a   What are the two basic types of risk?

11.4b   What is the distinction between the two types of risk?

11.5   DIVERSIFICATION AND PORTFOLIO RISK

We've seen earlier that portfolio risks can, in principle, be quite different from the risks of the assets that make up the portfolio. We now look more closely at the riskiness of an individual asset versus the risk of a portfolio of many different assets. We will once again examine some market history to get an idea of what happens with actual investments in U.S. capital markets.

The Effect of Diversification: Another Lesson from Market History

In our previous chapter, we saw that the standard deviation of the annual return on a portfolio of 500 large common stocks has historically been about 20 percent per year (see Figure 10.10, for example). Does this mean that the standard deviation of the annual return on a typical stock in that group of 500 is about 20 percent? As you might suspect by now, the answer is *no*. This is an extremely important observation.

For more on risk and diversification, visit www.investopedia.com/university.

To examine the relationship between portfolio size and portfolio risk, Table 11.7 illustrates typical average annual standard deviations for portfolios that contain different numbers of randomly selected NYSE securities.

In Column 2 of Table 11.7, we see that the standard deviation for a "portfolio" of one security is about 49 percent. What this means is that, if you randomly selected a single NYSE stock and put all your money into it, your standard deviation of return would typically be a substantial 49 percent per year. If you were to randomly select two stocks and invest half your money in each, your standard deviation would be about 37 percent on average, and so on.

The important thing to notice in Table 11.7 is that the standard deviation declines as the number of securities is increased. By the time we have 100 randomly chosen stocks, the portfolio's standard deviation has declined by about 60 percent, from 49 percent to about 20 percent. With 500 securities, the standard deviation is 19.27 percent, similar to the 20 percent we saw in our previous chapter for the large common stock portfolio. The small difference exists because the portfolio securities and time periods examined are not identical.

TABLE **11.7**

Standard deviations of annual portfolio returns

(1) Number of Stocks in Portfolio	(2) Average Standard Deviation of Annual Portfolio Returns	(3) Ratio of Portfolio Standard Deviation to Standard Deviation of a Single Stock
1	49.24%	1.00
2	37.36	.76
4	29.69	.60
6	26.64	.54
8	24.98	.51
10	23.93	.49
20	21.68	.44
30	20.87	.42
40	20.46	.42
50	20.20	.41
100	19.69	.40
200	19.42	.39
300	19.34	.39
400	19.29	.39
500	19.27	.39
1,000	19.21	.39

Sources: These figures are from Table 1 in Meir Statman, "How Many Stocks Make a Diversified Portfolio?" *Journal of Financial and Quantitative Analysis* 22 (September 1987), pp. 353–64. They were derived from E. J. Elton and M. J. Gruber, "Risk Reduction and Portfolio Size: An Analytical Solution," *Journal of Business* 50 (October 1977), pp. 415–37.

The Principle of Diversification

Figure 11.1 illustrates the point we've been discussing. What we have plotted is the standard deviation of return versus the number of stocks in the portfolio. Notice in Figure 11.1 that the benefit in terms of risk reduction from adding securities drops off as we add more and more. By the time we have 10 securities, most of the effect is already realized, and by the time we get to 30 or so, there is very little remaining benefit.

Figure 11.1 illustrates two key points. First: Some of the riskiness associated with individual assets can be eliminated by forming portfolios. The process of spreading an investment across assets (and thereby forming a portfolio) is called *diversification*. The **principle of diversification** tells us that spreading an investment across many assets will eliminate some of the risk. The green shaded area in Figure 11.1, labeled "diversifiable risk," is the part that can be eliminated by diversification.

The second point is equally important: There is a minimum level of risk that cannot be eliminated simply by diversifying. This minimum level is labeled "nondiversifiable risk" in Figure 11.1. Taken together, these two points are another important lesson from capital market history: Diversification reduces risk, but only up to a point. Put another way: Some risk is diversifiable and some is not.

principle of diversification
Spreading an investment across a number of assets will eliminate some, but not all, of the risk.

Diversification and Unsystematic Risk

From our discussion of portfolio risk, we know that some of the risk associated with individual assets can be diversified away and some cannot. We are left with an obvious question: Why is this so? It turns out that the answer hinges on the distinction we made earlier between systematic and unsystematic risk.

By definition, an unsystematic risk is one that is particular to a single asset or, at most, a small group. For example, if the asset under consideration is stock in a single company, the discovery of positive NPV projects such as successful new products and innovative

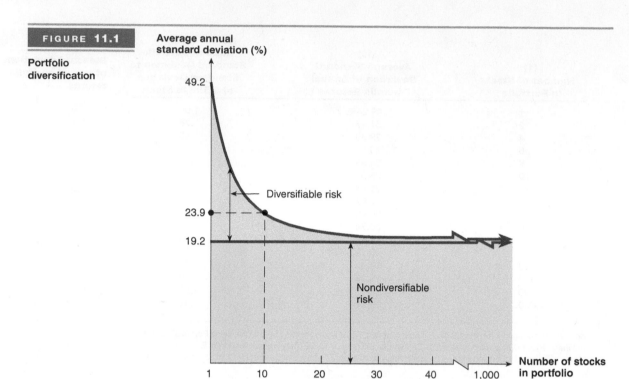

FIGURE 11.1

Portfolio diversification

cost savings will tend to increase the value of the stock. Unanticipated lawsuits, industrial accidents, strikes, and similar events will tend to decrease future cash flows and thereby reduce share values.

Here is the important observation: If we only held a single stock, then the value of our investment would fluctuate because of company-specific events. If we hold a large portfolio, on the other hand, some of the stocks in the portfolio will go up in value because of positive company-specific events and some will go down in value because of negative events. The net effect on the overall value of the portfolio will be relatively small, however, as these effects will tend to cancel each other out.

Now we see why some of the variability associated with individual assets is eliminated by diversification. When we combine assets into portfolios, the unique, or unsystematic, events—both positive and negative—tend to "wash out" once we have more than just a few assets.

This is an important point that bears restating:

> **Unsystematic risk is essentially eliminated by diversification, so a relatively large portfolio has almost no unsystematic risk.**

In fact, the terms *diversifiable risk* and *unsystematic risk* are often used interchangeably.

Diversification and Systematic Risk

We've seen that unsystematic risk can be eliminated by diversifying. What about systematic risk? Can it also be eliminated by diversification? The answer is no because, by definition, a systematic risk affects almost all assets to some degree. As a result, no matter how many assets we put into a portfolio, the systematic risk doesn't go away. Thus, for obvious reasons, the terms *systematic risk* and *nondiversifiable risk* are used interchangeably.

Because we have introduced so many different terms, it is useful to summarize our discussion before moving on. What we have seen is that the total risk of an investment, as measured by the standard deviation of its return, can be written as:

Total risk = Systematic risk + Unsystematic risk   [11.6]

Systematic risk is also called *nondiversifiable risk* or *market risk.* Unsystematic risk is also called *diversifiable risk, unique risk,* or *asset-specific risk.* For a well-diversified portfolio, the unsystematic risk is negligible. For such a portfolio, essentially all of the risk is systematic.

CONCEPT QUESTIONS

11.5a   What happens to the standard deviation of return for a portfolio if we increase the number of securities in the portfolio?

11.5b   What is the principle of diversification?

11.5c   Why is some risk diversifiable?

11.5d   Why can't systematic risk be diversified away?

SYSTEMATIC RISK AND BETA   **11.6**

The question that we now begin to address is this: What determines the size of the risk premium on a risky asset? Put another way: Why do some assets have a larger risk premium than other assets? The answer to these questions, as we discuss next, is also based on the distinction between systematic and unsystematic risk.

For more on beta, see money.cnn.com.

The Systematic Risk Principle

Thus far, we've seen that the total risk associated with an asset can be decomposed into two components: systematic and unsystematic risk. We have also seen that unsystematic risk can be essentially eliminated by diversification. The systematic risk present in an asset, on the other hand, cannot be eliminated by diversification.

Based on our study of capital market history, we know that there is a reward, on average, for bearing risk. However, we now need to be more precise about what we mean by risk. The **systematic risk principle** states that the reward for bearing risk depends only on the systematic risk of an investment. The underlying rationale for this principle is straightforward: Since unsystematic risk can be eliminated at virtually no cost (by diversifying), there is no reward for bearing it. Put another way: The market does not reward risks that are borne unnecessarily.

systematic risk principle
The expected return on a risky asset depends only on that asset's systematic risk.

The systematic risk principle has a remarkable and very important implication:

> **The expected return on an asset depends only on that asset's systematic risk.**

There is an obvious corollary to this principle: No matter how much total risk an asset has, only the systematic portion is relevant in determining the expected return (and the risk premium) on that asset.

TABLE 11.8	Company	Beta Coefficient (β_i)
	Costco	.48
Beta coefficients for selected companies	Amazon.com	.72
	Yum! Brands	.82
	Home Depot	.98
	Apple	1.04
	Google	1.13
	Starbucks	1.28
	eBay	1.36
	Citigroup	2.47

Sources: finance.yahoo.com, 2012.

Measuring Systematic Risk

beta coefficient

Amount of systematic risk present in a particular risky asset relative to that in an average risky asset.

Since systematic risk is the crucial determinant of an asset's expected return, we need some way of measuring the level of systematic risk for different investments. The specific measure we will use is called the **beta coefficient**, for which we will use the Greek symbol β. A beta coefficient, or beta for short, tells us how much systematic risk a particular asset has relative to an average asset. By definition, an average asset has a beta of 1.0 relative to itself. An asset with a beta of .50, therefore, has half as much systematic risk as an average asset; an asset with a beta of 2.0 has twice as much.

Table 11.8 contains the estimated beta coefficients for the stocks of some well-known companies. The range of betas in Table 11.8 is typical for stocks of large U.S. corporations. Betas outside this range occur, but they are less common. See our nearby *Work the Web* box to learn how to find betas online.

The important thing to remember is that the expected return, and thus the risk premium, on an asset depends only on its systematic risk. Since assets with larger betas have greater systematic risks, they will have greater expected returns. Thus, from Table 11.8, an investor who buys stock in Yum! Brands, with a beta of .82, should expect to earn less, on average, than an investor who buys stock in eBay, with a beta of about 1.36. To learn more about "real-world" betas, see the *Finance Matters* box on page 368.

EXAMPLE 11.5	**TOTAL RISK VERSUS BETA**

Consider the following information on two securities. Which has greater total risk? Which has greater systematic risk? Greater unsystematic risk? Which asset will have a higher risk premium?

	Standard Deviation	Beta
Security A	40%	.50
Security B	20	1.50

From our discussion in this section, Security A has greater total risk, but it has substantially less systematic risk. Since total risk is the sum of systematic and unsystematic risk, Security A must have greater unsystematic risk. Finally, from the systematic risk principle, Security B will have a higher risk premium and a greater expected return, despite the fact that it has less total risk.

WORK THE WEB

◄ To get updated data, scan here.

Suppose you want to find the beta for a company like apparel maker Liz Claiborne. One way is to go to the web. We went to finance.yahoo.com, found and entered the ticker symbol for Liz Claiborne (LIZ), and followed the "Key Statistics" link. Here is part of what we found:

Stock Price History	
Beta:	2.95
52-Week Change[3]:	119.37%
S&P500 52-Week Change[3]:	5.75%
52-Week High (Mar 9, 2012)[3]:	12.14
52-Week Low (Aug 19, 2011)[3]:	4.02
50-Day Moving Average[3]:	10.11
200-Day Moving Average[3]:	7.97

The reported beta for Liz Claiborne is 2.95, which means that Liz Claiborne has about 3 times the systematic risk of a typical stock. You would expect that the company's stock is a risky bet, and, looking at the other numbers, we agree. During 2011, Liz Claiborne reported a net loss of about $172 million and a negative book value of equity of about $109 million. So, the ROE for the company is about 158 percent, an extraordinarily good number. However, a closer look shows that the more Liz Claiborne loses, the higher its ROE becomes. Not a good situation! The reason is that Liz Claiborne has reported a loss every year from 2009 to 2011. In all, Liz Claiborne appears to be a good candidate for a high beta.

Questions
1. Has Liz Claiborne's ROE "improved" since this was written? Check out the current numbers on the website to see.
2. What growth rate are analysts projecting for Liz Claiborne? How does this growth rate compare to the industry?

Portfolio Betas

Earlier, we saw that the riskiness of a portfolio has no simple relationship to the risks of the assets in the portfolio. A portfolio beta, however, can be calculated just like a portfolio expected return. For example, looking again at Table 11.8, suppose you put half of your money in Home Depot and half in eBay. What would the beta of this combination be? Since Home Depot has a beta of .98 and eBay has a beta of 1.36, the portfolio's beta, β_p, would be:

$$\beta_p = .50 \times \beta_{Home\ Depot} + .50 \times \beta_{eBay}$$
$$= .50 \times .98 + .50 \times 1.36$$
$$= 1.17$$

In general, if we had a large number of assets in a portfolio, we would multiply each asset's beta by its portfolio weight and then add the results up to get the portfolio's beta.

Betas are easy to find on the web. Try finance.yahoo.com and money.cnn.com.

FINANCE MATTERS

 ◀ For the latest news on the topics covered in this chapter, scan here.

Beta, Beta, Who's Got the Beta?

Based on what we've studied so far, you can see that beta is a pretty important topic. You might wonder then, are all published betas created equal? Read on for a partial answer to this question.

We did some checking on betas and found some interesting results. The Value Line *Investment Survey* is one of the best-known sources for information on publicly traded companies. However, with the explosion of online investing, there has been a corresponding increase in the amount of investment information available online. We decided to compare the betas presented by Value Line to those reported by Yahoo! Finance (finance.yahoo.com) and CNN Money (money.cnn.com). What we found leads to an important note of caution.

Consider DuPont, the chemical company. Its beta reported on the Internet was 1.65, which is larger than Value Line's beta of 1.15. DuPont wasn't the only stock that showed a divergence in betas from different sources. In fact, for most of the technology companies we looked at, Value Line reported betas that were significantly lower than their online cousins. For example, the online beta for eBay was 1.36, but Value Line reported 1.10. The online beta for Adobe (maker of the ubiquitous Acrobat software) was 1.61 versus a Value Line beta of 1.20. Value Line's betas are not always lower. For example, the online beta for Yahoo! was .94, compared to Value Line's 1.00.

We also found some unusual, and even hard to believe, estimates for beta. Dollar General had a very low online beta

of .00, while Value Line reported Dollar General's beta as .60. The online estimate for Campbell Soup was .17, compared to Value Line's .55. Perhaps the most outrageous reported betas were the online betas for Constar International and Ghost Technology, with betas of 647.08 and –7,584.46 (notice the minus sign!), respectively. Value Line did not report a beta for these companies. How do you suppose we should interpret a beta of –7,584.46?

There are a few lessons to be learned from all of this. First, not all betas are created equal. Some are computed using weekly returns and some using daily returns. Some are computed using 60 months of stock returns; some consider more or less. Some betas are computed by comparing the stock to the S&P 500 index, while others use alternative indices. Finally, some reporting firms (including Value Line) make adjustments to raw betas to reflect information other than just the fluctuation in stock prices.

The second lesson is perhaps more subtle. We are interested in knowing what the betas of the stocks will be in the future, but betas have to be estimated using historical data. Anytime we use the past to predict the future, there is the danger of a poor estimate. As we will see later in the chapter (and in the next one), it is very unlikely that Constar International has a beta anything like 647.08 or that Ghost Technology has a beta of –7,584.46. Instead, the estimates are almost certainly poor ones. The moral of the story is that, as with any financial tool, beta is not a black box that should be taken without question.

EXAMPLE 11.6   **PORTFOLIO BETAS**

Suppose we had the following investments:

Security	Amount Invested	Expected Return	Beta
Stock A	$1,000	8%	.80
Stock B	2,000	12	.95
Stock C	3,000	15	1.10
Stock D	4,000	18	1.40

What is the expected return on this portfolio? What is the beta of this portfolio? Does this portfolio have more or less systematic risk than an average asset?

To answer, we first have to calculate the portfolio weights. Notice that the total amount invested is $10,000. Of this, $1,000/10,000 = 10% is invested in Stock A. Similarly, 20 percent is invested in

(continued)

Stock B, 30 percent is invested in Stock C, and 40 percent is invested in Stock D. The expected return, $E(R_P)$, is thus:

$$E(R_P) = .10 \times E(R_A) + .20 \times E(R_B) + .30 \times E(R_C) + .40 \times E(R_D)$$
$$= .10 \times 8\% + .20 \times 12\% + .30 \times 15\% + .40 \times 18\%$$
$$= 14.9\%$$

Similarly, the portfolio beta, β_P, is:

$$\beta_P = .10 \times \beta_A + .20 \times \beta_B + .30 \times \beta_C + .40 \times \beta_D$$
$$= .10 \times .80 + .20 \times .95 + .30 \times 1.10 + .40 \times 1.40$$
$$= 1.16$$

This portfolio thus has an expected return of 14.9 percent and a beta of 1.16. Since the beta is larger than 1.0, this portfolio has greater systematic risk than an average asset.

CONCEPT QUESTIONS

11.6a   What is the systematic risk principle?

11.6b   What does a beta coefficient measure?

11.6c   How do you calculate a portfolio beta?

11.6d   True or false: The expected return on a risky asset depends on that asset's total risk. Explain.

THE SECURITY MARKET LINE

11.7

We're now in a position to see how risk is rewarded in the marketplace. To begin, suppose that Asset A has an expected return of $E(R_A) = 20\%$ and a beta of $\beta_A = 1.6$. Furthermore, the risk-free rate is $R_f = 8\%$. Notice that a risk-free asset, by definition, has no systematic risk (or unsystematic risk), so a risk-free asset has a beta of 0.

Beta and the Risk Premium

Consider a portfolio made up of Asset A and a risk-free asset. We can calculate some different possible portfolio expected returns and betas by varying the percentages invested in these two assets. For example, if 25 percent of the portfolio is invested in Asset A, then the expected return is:

$$E(R_P) = .25 \times E(R_A) + (1 - .25) \times R_f$$
$$= .25 \times 20\% + .75 \times 8\%$$
$$= 11.0\%$$

Similarly, the beta on the portfolio, β_P, would be:

$$\beta_P = .25 \times \beta_A + (1 - .25) \times 0$$
$$= .25 \times 1.6$$
$$= .40$$

Notice that, since the weights have to add up to 1, the percentage invested in the risk-free asset is equal to 1 minus the percentage invested in Asset A.

370

One thing that you might wonder about is whether it is possible for the percentage invested in Asset A to exceed 100 percent. The answer is yes. The way this can happen is for the investor to borrow at the risk-free rate. For example, suppose an investor has $100 and borrows an additional $50 at 8 percent, the risk-free rate. The total investment in Asset A would be $150, or 150 percent of the investor's wealth. The expected return in this case would be:

$$E(R_p) = 1.50 \times E(R_A) + (1 - 1.50) \times R_f$$
$$= 1.50 \times 20\% - .50 \times 8\%$$
$$= 26.0\%$$

The beta on the portfolio would be:

$$\beta_p = 1.50 \times \beta_A + (1 - 1.50) \times 0$$
$$= 1.50 \times 1.6$$
$$= 2.4$$

We can calculate some other possibilities as follows:

Percentage of Portfolio in Asset A	Portfolio Expected Return	Portfolio Beta
0%	8%	.0
25	11	.4
50	14	.8
75	17	1.2
100	20	1.6
125	23	2.0
150	26	2.4

In Figure 11.2A, these portfolio expected returns are plotted against the portfolio betas. Notice that all the combinations fall on a straight line.

The Reward-to-Risk Ratio   What is the slope of the straight line in Figure 11.2A? As always, the slope of a straight line is equal to "the rise over the run." In this case, as we move out of the risk-free asset into Asset A, the beta increases from 0 to 1.6 (a "run" of 1.6). At the same time, the expected return goes from 8 percent to 20 percent, a "rise" of 12 percent. The slope of the line is thus 12%/1.6 = 7.50%.

Notice that the slope of our line is just the risk premium on Asset A, $E(R_A) - R_f$, divided by Asset A's beta, β_A:

$$\text{Slope} = \frac{E(R_A) - R_f}{\beta_A}$$
$$= \frac{20\% - 8\%}{1.6}$$
$$= 7.50\%$$

What this tells us is that Asset A offers a *reward-to-risk ratio* of 7.50 percent.[2] In other words, Asset A has a risk premium of 7.50 percent per "unit" of systematic risk.

---

[2] This ratio is sometimes called the *Treynor index,* after one of its originators.

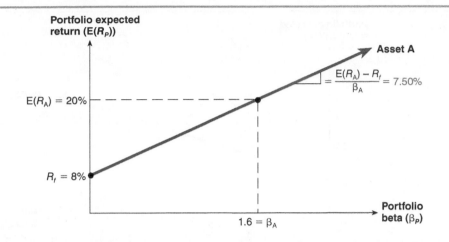

FIGURE 11.2A

FIGURE 11.2A

Portfolio expected returns and betas for Asset A

The Basic Argument

Now suppose we consider a second asset, Asset B. This asset has a beta of 1.2 and an expected return of 16 percent. Which investment is better, Asset A or Asset B? You might think that, once again, we really cannot say. Some investors might prefer A; some investors might prefer B. Actually, however, we can say: A is better because, as we shall demonstrate, B offers inadequate compensation for its level of systematic risk, at least relative to A.

To begin, we calculate different combinations of expected returns and betas for portfolios of Asset B and a risk-free asset just as we did for Asset A. For example, if we put 25 percent in Asset B and the remaining 75 percent in the risk-free asset, the portfolio's expected return would be:

$$E(R_p) = .25 \times E(R_B) + (1 - .25) \times R_f$$
$$= .25 \times 16\% + .75 \times 8\%$$
$$= 10.0\%$$

Similarly, the beta on the portfolio, β_P, would be:

$$\beta_P = .25 \times \beta_B + (1 - .25) \times 0$$
$$= .25 \times 1.2$$
$$= .30$$

Some other possibilities are as follows:

Percentage of Portfolio in Asset B	Portfolio Expected Return	Portfolio Beta
0%	8%	.0
25	10	.3
50	12	.6
75	14	.9
100	16	1.2
125	18	1.5
150	20	1.8

When we plot these combinations of portfolio expected returns and portfolio betas in Figure 11.2B, we get a straight line just as we did for Asset A.

FIGURE 11.2B

Portfolio expected
returns and betas for
Asset B

FIGURE 11.2C

Portfolio expected
returns and betas for
both assets

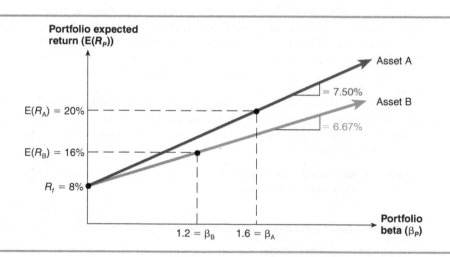

The key thing to notice is that when we compare the results for Assets A and B, as in Figure 11.2C, the line describing the combinations of expected returns and betas for Asset A is higher than the one for Asset B. What this tells us is that for any given level of systematic risk (as measured by β), some combination of Asset A and the risk-free asset always offers a larger return. This is why we were able to state that Asset A is a better investment than Asset B.

Another way of seeing that A offers a superior return for its level of risk is to note that the slope of our line for Asset B is:

$$\textbf{Slope} = \frac{E(R_B) - R_f}{\beta_B}$$

$$= \frac{16\% - 8\%}{1.2} = 6.67\%$$

Thus, Asset B has a reward-to-risk ratio of 6.67 percent, which is less than the 7.5 percent offered by Asset A.

The Fundamental Result   The situation we have described for Assets A and B cannot persist in a well-organized, active market, because investors would be attracted to Asset A and away from Asset B. As a result, Asset A's price would rise and Asset B's price would fall. Since prices and returns move in opposite directions, the result would be that A's expected return would decline and B's would rise.

This buying and selling would continue until the two assets plotted on exactly the same line, which means they would offer the same reward for bearing risk. In other words, in an active, competitive market, we must have that:

$$\frac{E(R_A) - R_f}{\beta_A} = \frac{E(R_B) - R_f}{\beta_B}$$

This is the fundamental relationship between risk and return.

Our basic argument can be extended to more than just two assets. In fact, no matter how many assets we had, we would always reach the same conclusion:

> **The reward-to-risk ratio must be the same for all the assets in the market.**

This result is really not so surprising. What it says, for example, is that, if one asset has twice as much systematic risk as another asset, its risk premium will simply be twice as large.

Since all of the assets in the market must have the same reward-to-risk ratio, they all must plot on the same line. This argument is illustrated in Figure 11.3. As shown, Assets A and B plot directly on the line and thus have the same reward-to-risk ratio. If an asset plotted above the line, such as C in Figure 11.3, its price would rise, and its expected return would fall until it plotted exactly on the line. Similarly, if an asset plotted below the line, such as D in Figure 11.3, its expected return would rise until it too plotted directly on the line.

The arguments we have presented apply to active, competitive, well-functioning markets. The financial markets, such as the NYSE, best meet these criteria. Other markets,

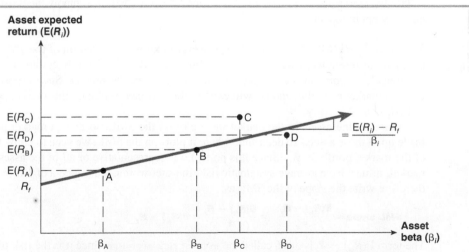

FIGURE 11.3

Expected returns and systematic risk

The fundamental relationship between beta and expected return is that all assets must have the same reward-to-risk ratio, $[E(R_i) - R_f]/\beta_i$. This means that they would all plot on the same straight line. Assets A and B are examples of this behavior. Asset C's expected return is too high; Asset D's is too low.

such as real asset markets, may or may not. For this reason, these concepts are most useful in examining financial markets. We will thus focus on such markets here. However, as we discuss in a later section, the information about risk and return gleaned from financial markets is crucial in evaluating the investments that a corporation makes in real assets.

EXAMPLE 11.7

BUY LOW, SELL HIGH

An asset is said to be *overvalued* if its price is too high given its expected return and risk. Suppose you observe the following situation:

Security	Expected Return	Beta
Fama Co.	14%	1.3
French Co.	10	.8

The risk-free rate is currently 6 percent. Is one of the two securities above overvalued relative to the other?

    To answer, we compute the reward-to-risk ratio for both. For Fama, this ratio is (14% − 6%)/ 1.3 = 6.15%. For French, this ratio is 5 percent. What we conclude is that French offers an insufficient expected return for its level of risk, at least relative to Fama. Since its expected return is too low, its price is too high. In other words, French is overvalued relative to Fama, and we would expect to see its price fall relative to Fama's. Notice that we could also say Fama is *undervalued* relative to French.

The Security Market Line

The line that results when we plot expected returns and beta coefficients is obviously of some importance, so it's time we gave it a name. This line, which we use to describe the relationship between systematic risk and expected return in financial markets, is usually called the **security market line**, or **SML**. After NPV, the SML is arguably the most important concept in modern finance.

security market line (SML)
Positively sloped straight line displaying the relationship between expected return and beta.

Market Portfolios   It will be very useful to know the equation of the SML. There are many different ways we could write it, but one way is particularly common. Suppose we consider a portfolio made up of all of the assets in the market. Such a portfolio is called a market portfolio, and we will express the expected return on this market portfolio as $E(R_M)$.

    Since all the assets in the market must plot on the SML, so must a market portfolio made up of those assets. To determine where it plots on the SML, we need to know the beta of the market portfolio, β_M. Since this portfolio is representative of all of the assets in the market, it must have average systematic risk. In other words, it has a beta of 1.0. We could therefore write the slope of the SML as:

$$\text{SML slope} = \frac{E(R_M) - R_f}{\beta_M} = \frac{E(R_M) - R_f}{1} = E(R_M) - R_f$$

market risk premium
Slope of the SML, the difference between the expected return on a market portfolio and the risk-free rate.

The term $E(R_M) - R_f$ is often called the **market risk premium** since it is the risk premium on a market portfolio.

The Capital Asset Pricing Model   To finish up, if we let $E(R_i)$ and β_i stand for the expected return and beta, respectively, on any asset in the market, then we know that asset must plot on the SML. As a result, we know that its reward-to-risk ratio is the same as the overall market's:

$$\frac{E(R_i) - R_f}{\beta_i} = E(R_M) - R_f$$

If we rearrange this, then we can write the equation for the SML as:

$$E(R_i) = R_f + [E(R_M) - R_f] \times \beta_i \qquad\qquad [11.7]$$

This result is identical to the famous **capital asset pricing model (CAPM)**.

What the CAPM shows is that the expected return for a particular asset depends on three things:

1. *The pure time value of money.* As measured by the risk-free rate, R_f, this is the reward for merely waiting for your money, without taking any risk.

2. *The reward for bearing systematic risk.* As measured by the market risk premium, $[E(R_M) - R_f]$, this component is the reward the market offers for bearing an average amount of systematic risk in addition to waiting.

3. *The amount of systematic risk.* As measured by β_i, this is the amount of systematic risk present in a particular asset, relative to an average asset.

capital asset pricing model (CAPM)
Equation of the SML showing the relationship between expected return and beta.

By the way, the CAPM works for portfolios of assets just as it does for individual assets. In an earlier section, we saw how to calculate a portfolio's β. To find the expected return on a portfolio, we simply use this β in the CAPM equation.

Figure 11.4 summarizes our discussion of the SML and the CAPM. As before, we plot expected return against beta. Now we recognize that, based on the CAPM, the slope of the SML is equal to the market risk premium, $[E(R_M) - R_f]$.

This concludes our presentation of concepts related to the risk-return trade-off. For future reference, Table 11.9 summarizes the various concepts in the order in which we discussed them.

FIGURE 11.4

The security market line, or SML

The slope of the security market line is equal to the market risk premium, i.e., the reward for bearing an average amount of systematic risk. The equation describing the SML can be written:

$$E(R_i) = R_f + [E(R_M) - R_f] \times \beta_i$$

which is the capital asset pricing model, or CAPM.

TABLE **11.9**	Summary of risk and return concepts

I. Total return

The *total return* on an investment has two components: the expected return and the unexpected return. The unexpected return comes about because of unanticipated events. The risk from investing stems from the possibility of an unanticipated event.

II. Total risk

The *total risk* of an investment is measured by the variance or, more commonly, the standard deviation of its return.

III. Systematic and unsystematic risks

Systematic risks (also called *market risks*) are unanticipated events that affect almost all assets to some degree because the effects are economywide. *Unsystematic risks* are unanticipated events that affect single assets or small groups of assets. Unsystematic risks are also called *unique or asset-specific risks*.

IV. The effect of diversification

Some, but not all, of the risk associated with a risky investment can be eliminated by diversification. The reason is that unsystematic risks, which are unique to individual assets, tend to wash out in a large portfolio, but systematic risks, which affect all of the assets in a portfolio to some extent, do not.

V. The systematic risk principle and beta

Because unsystematic risk can be freely eliminated by diversification, the *systematic risk principle* states that the reward for bearing risk depends only on the level of systematic risk. The level of systematic risk in a particular asset, relative to the average, is given by the beta of that asset.

VI. The reward-to-risk ratio and the security market line

The *reward-to-risk ratio* for Asset *i* is the ratio of its risk premium, $E(R_i) - R_f$, to its beta, β_i:

$$\frac{E(R_i) - R_f}{\beta_i}$$

In a well-functioning market, this ratio is the same for every asset. As a result, when asset expected returns are plotted against asset betas, all assets plot on the same straight line, called the *security market line* (SML).

VII. The capital asset pricing model

From the SML, the expected return on Asset *i* can be written:

$$E(R_i) = R_f + [E(R_M) - R_f] \times \beta_i$$

This is the *capital asset pricing model* (CAPM). The expected return on a risky asset thus has three components. The first is the pure time value of money, R_f; the second is the market risk premium, $[E(R_M) - R_f]$; and the third is the beta for that asset, β_i.

EXAMPLE **11.8**	**RISK AND RETURN**

Suppose the risk-free rate is 4 percent, the market risk premium is 7 percent, and a particular stock has a beta of 1.3. Based on the CAPM, what is the expected return on this stock? What would the expected return be if the beta were to double?

    With a beta of 1.3, the risk premium for the stock would be $1.3 \times 7\%$, or 9.1 percent. The risk-free rate is 4 percent, so the expected return is 13.1 percent. If the beta doubled to 2.6, the risk premium would double to 18.2 percent, so the expected return would be 22.2 percent.

CONCEPT QUESTIONS

11.7a   What is the fundamental relationship between risk and return in well-functioning markets?

11.7b   What is the security market line? Why must all assets plot directly on it in a well-functioning market?

11.7c   What is the capital asset pricing model, or CAPM? What does it tell us about the required return on a risky investment?

11.8

THE SML AND THE COST OF CAPITAL: A PREVIEW

Our goal in studying risk and return is twofold. First, risk is an extremely important consideration in almost all business decisions, so we want to discuss just what risk is and how it is rewarded in the market. Our second purpose is to learn what determines the appropriate discount rate for future cash flows. We briefly discuss this second subject now; we discuss it in more detail in Chapter 12.

The Basic Idea

The security market line tells us the reward for bearing risk in financial markets. At an absolute minimum, any new investment our firm undertakes must offer an expected return that is no worse than what the financial markets offer for the same risk. The reason for this is simply that our shareholders can always invest for themselves in the financial markets.

The only way we benefit our shareholders is by finding investments with expected returns that are superior to what the financial markets offer for the same risk. Such an investment will have a positive NPV. So, if we ask: "What is the appropriate discount rate?" the answer is that we should use the expected return offered in financial markets on investments with the same systematic risk.

In other words, to determine whether or not an investment has a positive NPV, we essentially compare the expected return on that new investment to what the financial market offers on an investment with the same beta. This is why the SML is so important; it tells us the "going rate" for bearing risk in the economy.

The Cost of Capital

The appropriate discount rate on a new project is the minimum expected rate of return an investment must offer to be attractive. This minimum required return is often called the **cost of capital** associated with the investment. It is called this because the required return is what the firm must earn on its capital investment in a project just to break even. It can thus be interpreted as the opportunity cost associated with the firm's capital investment.

cost of capital
The minimum required return on a new investment.

Notice that when we say an investment is attractive if its expected return exceeds what is offered in financial markets for investments of the same risk, we are effectively using the internal rate of return, or IRR, criterion that we developed and discussed in Chapter 8. The only difference is that now we have a much better idea of what determines the required return on an investment. This understanding will be critical when we discuss cost of capital and capital structure in Part Seven of our book.

CONCEPT QUESTIONS

11.8a   If an investment has a positive NPV, would it plot above or below the SML? Why?

11.8b   What is meant by the term *cost of capital?*

SUMMARY AND CONCLUSIONS

This chapter has covered the essentials of risk. Along the way, we have introduced a number of definitions and concepts. The most important of these is the security market line, or SML. The SML is important because it tells us the reward offered in financial markets for bearing risk. Once we know this, we have a benchmark against which we compare the returns expected from real asset investments to determine if they are desirable.

◀ Think you've mastered the material? Scan here to take a chapter quiz.

Because we have covered quite a bit of ground, it's useful to summarize the basic economic logic underlying the SML as follows:

1. Based on capital market history, there is a reward for bearing risk. This reward is the risk premium on an asset.

2. The total risk associated with an asset has two parts: systematic risk and unsystematic risk. Unsystematic risk can be freely eliminated by diversification (this is the principle of diversification), so only systematic risk is rewarded. As a result, the risk premium on an asset is determined by its systematic risk. This is the systematic risk principle.

3. An asset's systematic risk, relative to the average, can be measured by its beta coefficient, β_i. The risk premium on an asset is then given by its beta coefficient multiplied by the market risk premium, $[E(R_M) - R_f] \times \beta_i$.

4. The expected return on an asset, $E(R_i)$, is equal to the risk-free rate, R_f, plus the risk premium:

$$E(R_i) = R_f + [E(R_M) - R_f] \times \beta_i$$

This is the equation of the SML, and it is often called the *capital asset pricing model*, or CAPM.

This chapter completes our discussion of risk and return and concludes Part Six of our book. Now that we have a better understanding of what determines a firm's cost of capital for an investment, the next several chapters examine more closely how firms raise the long-term capital needed for investment.

 connect POP QUIZ!
|FINANCE

Can you answer the following questions? If your class is using *Connect Finance,* log on to the Self-Quiz and Study feature in the Library tab to see if you know the answers to these and other questions, check out the study tools, and find out what topics require additional practice!

Section 11.1 A portfolio is invested 14 percent in Stock G, 29 percent in Stock J, and 57 percent in Stock K. The expected returns on these stocks are 8.5 percent, 11.0 percent, and 16.4 percent, respectively. What is the portfolio's expected return?

Section 11.2 What are the portfolio weights for a portfolio that has 145 shares of Stock A that sell for $86 per share and 120 shares of Stock B that sell for $90 per share?

Section 11.4 Market risk generally refers to what type of risk?

Section 11.6 You own a stock portfolio invested 24 percent in Stock Q, 21 percent in Stock R, 44 percent in Stock S, and 11 percent in Stock T. The betas for these four stocks are 0.86, 0.92, 1.32, and 1.77, respectively. What is the portfolio beta?

Section 11.7 A stock has a beta of 1.19, the expected return on the market is 11.3 percent, and the risk-free rate is 4.80 percent. What must the expected return on this stock be?

CHAPTER REVIEW AND SELF-TEST PROBLEMS

11.1 Expected Return and Standard Deviation.   This problem will give you some practice calculating measures of prospective portfolio performance. There are two assets and three states of the economy:

(1) State of Economy	(2) Probability of State of Economy	(3) Stock A Rate of Return if State Occurs	(4) Stock B Rate of Return if State Occurs
Recession	.10	−.20	.30
Normal	.60	.10	.20
Boom	.30	.70	.50

What are the expected returns and standard deviations for these two stocks? (See Problem 7.)

11.2 Portfolio Risk and Return.   In the previous problem, suppose you have $20,000 total. If you put $6,000 in Stock A and the remainder in Stock B, what will be the expected return and standard deviation on your portfolio? (See Problem 10.)

11.3 Risk and Return.   Suppose you observe the following situation:

Security	Beta	Expected Return
Cooley, Inc.	1.6	19%
Moyer Co.	1.2	16

If the risk-free rate is 8 percent, are these securities correctly priced? What would the risk-free rate have to be if they are correctly priced? (See Problems 19, 20.)

11.4 CAPM.   Suppose the risk-free rate is 8 percent. The expected return on the market is 14 percent. If a particular stock has a beta of .60, what is its expected return based on the CAPM? If another stock has an expected return of 20 percent, what must its beta be? (See Problem 13.)

■ Answers to Chapter Review and Self-Test Problems

11.1   The expected returns are just the possible returns multiplied by the associated probabilities:

$$E(R_A) = .10 \times -.20 + .60 \times .10 + .30 \times .70 = 25\%$$
$$E(R_B) = .10 \times .30 + .60 \times .20 + .30 \times .50 = 30\%$$

The variances are given by the sums of the squared deviations from the expected returns multiplied by their probabilities:

$$\sigma_A^2 = .10 \times (-.20 - .25)^2 + .60 \times (.10 - .25)^2 + .30 \times (.70 - .25)^2$$
$$= .10 \times -.45^2 + .60 \times -.15^2 + .30 \times .45^2$$
$$= .10 \times .2025 + .60 \times .0225 + .30 \times .2025$$
$$= .0945$$
$$\sigma_B^2 = .10 \times (.30 - .30)^2 + .60 \times (.20 - .30)^2 + .30 \times (.50 - .30)^2$$
$$= .10 \times .00^2 + .60 \times -.10^2 + .30 \times .20^2$$
$$= .10 \times .00 + .60 \times .01 + .30 \times .04$$
$$= .0180$$

The standard deviations are thus:

$$\sigma_A = \sqrt{.0945} = 30.74\%$$
$$\sigma_B = \sqrt{.0180} = 13.42\%$$

11.2 The portfolio weights are $6,000/20,000 = .30$ and $14,000/20,000 = .70$. The expected return is thus:

$$E(R_P) = .30 \times E(R_A) + .70 \times E(R_B)$$
$$= .30 \times 25\% + .70 \times 30\%$$
$$= 28.50\%$$

Alternatively, we could calculate the portfolio's return in each of the states:

(1) State of Economy	(2) Probability of State of Economy	(3) Portfolio Return if State Occurs
Recession	.10	$.30 \times -.20 + .70 \times .30 = .15$
Normal	.60	$.30 \times .10 + .70 \times .20 = .17$
Boom	.30	$.30 \times .70 + .70 \times .50 = .56$

The portfolio's expected return is:

$$E(R_P) = .10 \times .15 + .60 \times .17 + .30 \times .56 = 28.50\%$$

This is the same as we had before.

The portfolio's variance is:

$$\sigma_P^2 = .10 \times (.15 - .285)^2 + .60 \times (.17 - .285)^2 + .30 \times (.56 - .285)^2$$
$$= .03245$$

So the standard deviation is $\sqrt{.03245} = 18.01\%$.

11.3 If we compute the reward-to-risk ratios, we get $(19\% - 8\%)/1.6 = 6.875\%$ for Cooley versus 6.67% for Moyer. Relative to that of Cooley, Moyer's expected return is too low, so its price is too high.

If they are correctly priced, then they must offer the same reward-to-risk ratio. The risk-free rate would have to be such that:

$$(19\% - R_f)/1.6 = (16\% - R_f)/1.2$$

With a little algebra, we find that the risk-free rate must be 7 percent:

$$(19\% - R_f) = (16\% - R_f)(1.6/1.2)$$
$$19\% - 16\% \times \tfrac{4}{3} = R_f - R_f \times \tfrac{4}{3}$$
$$R_f = 7\%$$

11.4 Since the expected return on the market is 14 percent, the market risk premium is $14\% - 8\% = 6\%$ (the risk-free rate is 8 percent). The first stock has a beta of .60, so its expected return is $8\% + .60 \times 6\% = 11.6\%$.

For the second stock, notice that the risk premium is $20\% - 8\% = 12\%$. Since this is twice as large as the market risk premium, the beta must be exactly equal to 2. We can verify this using the CAPM:

$$E(R_i) = R_f + [E(R_M) - R_f] \times \beta_i$$
$$20\% = 8\% + (14\% - 8\%) \times \beta_i$$
$$\beta_i = 12\%/6\% = 2.0$$

CRITICAL THINKING AND CONCEPTS REVIEW

LO 2 **11.1** **Diversifiable and Nondiversifiable Risks.** In broad terms, why is some risk diversifiable? Why are some risks nondiversifiable? Does it follow that an investor can control the level of unsystematic risk in a portfolio, but not the level of systematic risk?

LO 3 **11.2** **Information and Market Returns.** Suppose the government announces that, based on a just-completed survey, the growth rate in the economy is likely to be 2 percent in the coming year, as compared to 5 percent for the year just completed. Will security prices increase, decrease, or stay the same following this announcement? Does it make any difference whether or not the 2 percent figure was anticipated by the market? Explain.

LO 3 **11.3** **Systematic versus Unsystematic Risk.** Classify the following events as mostly systematic or mostly unsystematic. Is the distinction clear in every case?

    a. Short-term interest rates increase unexpectedly.

    b. The interest rate a company pays on its short-term debt borrowing is increased by its bank.

    c. Oil prices unexpectedly decline.

    d. An oil tanker ruptures, creating a large oil spill.

    e. A manufacturer loses a multimillion-dollar product liability suit.

    f. A Supreme Court decision substantially broadens producer liability for injuries suffered by product users.

LO 3 **11.4** **Systematic versus Unsystematic Risk.** Indicate whether the following events might cause stocks in general to change price, and whether they might cause Big Widget Corp.'s stock to change price.

    a. The government announces that inflation unexpectedly jumped by 2 percent last month.

    b. Big Widget's quarterly earnings report, just issued, generally fell in line with analysts' expectations.

    c. The government reports that economic growth last year was 3 percent, which generally agreed with most economists' forecasts.

    d. The directors of Big Widget die in a plane crash.

    e. Congress approves changes to the tax code that will increase the top marginal corporate tax rate. The legislation had been debated for the previous six months.

LO 1 **11.5** **Expected Portfolio Returns.** If a portfolio has a positive investment in every asset, can the expected return on the portfolio be greater than that on every asset in the portfolio? Can it be less than that on every asset in the portfolio? If you answer yes to one or both of these questions, give an example to support your answer.

LO 2 **11.6** **Diversification.** True or false: The most important characteristic in determining the expected return of a well-diversified portfolio is the variances of the individual assets in the portfolio. Explain.

LO 3 **11.7** **Portfolio Risk.** If a portfolio has a positive investment in every asset, can the standard deviation on the portfolio be less than that on every asset in the portfolio? What about the portfolio beta?

LO 4 **11.8** **Beta and CAPM.** Is it possible that a risky asset could have a beta of zero? Explain. Based on the CAPM, what is the expected return on such an asset? Is it possible that a risky asset could have a negative beta? What does the CAPM predict about the expected return on such an asset? Can you give an explanation for your answer?

LO 2   **11.9   Corporate Downsizing.**   In recent years, it has been common for companies to experience significant stock price changes in reaction to announcements of massive layoffs. Critics charge that such events encourage companies to fire longtime employees and that Wall Street is cheering them on. Do you agree or disagree?

LO 1   **11.10   Earnings and Stock Returns.**   As indicated by a number of examples in this chapter, earnings announcements by companies are closely followed by, and frequently result in, share price revisions. Two issues should come to mind. First: Earnings announcements concern past periods. If the market values stocks based on expectations of the future, why are numbers summarizing past performance relevant? Second: These announcements concern accounting earnings. Going back to Chapter 2, such earnings may have little to do with cash flow, so again, why are they relevant?

QUESTIONS AND PROBLEMS

LO 1

Basic
(Questions 1–24)

1. Determining Portfolio Weights.   What are the portfolio weights for a portfolio that has 135 shares of Stock A that sell for $71 per share and 95 shares of Stock B that sell for $84 per share?

LO 1   **2. Portfolio Expected Return.**   You own a portfolio that has $1,300 invested in Stock A and $2,100 invested in Stock B. If the expected returns on these stocks are 10 percent and 16 percent, respectively, what is the expected return on the portfolio?

LO 1   **3. Portfolio Expected Return.**   You own a portfolio that is 35 percent invested in Stock X, 45 percent in Stock Y, and 20 percent in Stock Z. The expected returns on these three stocks are 10 percent, 13 percent, and 15 percent, respectively. What is the expected return on the portfolio?

LO 1   **4. Portfolio Expected Return.**   You have $10,000 to invest in a stock portfolio. Your choices are Stock X with an expected return of 14 percent and Stock Y with an expected return of 11 percent. If your goal is to create a portfolio with an expected return of 12.4 percent, how much money will you invest in Stock X? In Stock Y?

LO 1   **5. Calculating Expected Return.**   Based on the following information, calculate the expected return.

State of Economy	Probability of State of Economy	Rate of Return if State Occurs
Recession	.30	−.08
Boom	.70	.19

LO 1   **6. Calculating Expected Return.**   Based on the following information, calculate the expected return.

State of Economy	Probability of State of Economy	Rate of Return if State Occurs
Recession	.20	−.09
Normal	.50	.11
Boom	.30	.30

LO 1

7. Calculating Returns and Standard Deviations. Based on the following information, calculate the expected return and standard deviation for the two stocks.

State of Economy	Probability of State of Economy	Rate of Return if State Occurs	
		Stock A	Stock B
Recession	.15	.02	−.30
Normal	.55	.10	.18
Boom	.30	.15	.31

LO 1

8. Calculating Expected Returns. A portfolio is invested 20 percent in Stock G, 35 percent in Stock J, and 45 percent in Stock K. The expected returns on these stocks are 9.2 percent, 12 percent, and 15.7 percent, respectively. What is the portfolio's expected return? How do you interpret your answer?

LO 1 LO 2

9. Returns and Standard Deviations. Consider the following information:

State of Economy	Probability of State of Economy	Rate of Return if State Occurs		
		Stock A	Stock B	Stock C
Boom	.75	.07	.01	.27
Bust	.25	.12	.19	−.05

a. What is the expected return on an equally weighted portfolio of these three stocks?

b. What is the variance of a portfolio invested 20 percent each in A and B and 60 percent in C?

LO 1 LO 2

10. Returns and Standard Deviations. Consider the following information:

State of Economy	Probability of State of Economy	Rate of Return if State Occurs		
		Stock A	Stock B	Stock C
Boom	.15	.35	.45	.33
Good	.50	.12	.10	.17
Poor	.25	.01	.02	−.05
Bust	.10	−.11	−.25	−.09

a. Your portfolio is invested 30 percent each in A and C and 40 percent in B. What is the expected return of the portfolio?

b. What is the variance of this portfolio? The standard deviation?

LO 3

11. Calculating Portfolio Betas. You own a stock portfolio invested 15 percent in Stock Q, 25 percent in Stock R, 40 percent in Stock S, and 20 percent in Stock T. The betas for these four stocks are .85, .91, 1.31, and 1.76, respectively. What is the portfolio beta?

LO 3

12. Calculating Portfolio Betas. You own a portfolio equally invested in a risk-free asset and two stocks. If one of the stocks has a beta of 1.42 and the total portfolio is equally as risky as the market, what must the beta be for the other stock in your portfolio?

LO 4

13. Using CAPM. A stock has a beta of 1.15, the expected return on the market is 10.9 percent, and the risk-free rate is 3.8 percent. What must the expected return on this stock be?

www.mhhe.com/rwj

LO 4   **14. Using CAPM.**   A stock has an expected return of 13.6 percent, the risk-free rate is 3.7 percent, and the market risk premium is 7.1 percent. What must the beta of this stock be?

LO 4   **15. Using CAPM.**   A stock has an expected return of 10.9 percent, its beta is .85, and the risk-free rate is 4.6 percent. What must the expected return on the market be?

LO 4   **16. Using CAPM.**   A stock has an expected return of 12.5 percent and a beta of 1.15, and the expected return on the market is 11.5 percent. What must the risk-free rate be?

LO 4   **17. Using CAPM.**   A stock has a beta of 1.15 and an expected return of 10.4 percent. A risk-free asset currently earns 3.8 percent.

  a.   What is the expected return on a portfolio that is equally invested in the two assets?

  b.   If a portfolio of the two assets has a beta of .7, what are the portfolio weights?

  c.   If a portfolio of the two assets has an expected return of 9 percent, what is its beta?

  d.   If a portfolio of the two assets has a beta of 2.3, what are the portfolio weights? How do you interpret the weights for the two assets in this case? Explain.

LO 4   **18. Using the SML.**   Asset W has an expected return of 12.1 percent and a beta of 1.18. If the risk-free rate is 3.7 percent, complete the following table for portfolios of Asset W and a risk-free asset. Illustrate the relationship between portfolio expected return and portfolio beta by plotting the expected returns against the betas. What is the slope of the line that results?

Percentage of Portfolio in Asset W	Portfolio Expected Return	Portfolio Beta
0%		
25		
50		
75		
100		
125		
150		

LO 4   **19. Reward-to-Risk Ratios.**   Stock Y has a beta of 1.25 and an expected return of 12.6 percent. Stock Z has a beta of .8 and an expected return of 9.9 percent. If the risk-free rate is 4.1 percent and the market risk premium is 7 percent, are these stocks correctly priced?

LO 4   **20. Reward-to-Risk Ratios.**   In the previous problem, what would the risk-free rate have to be for the two stocks to be correctly priced relative to each other?

LO 1   **21. Portfolio Returns.**   Using information from Table 10.2 on capital market history, determine the return on a portfolio that was equally invested in large-company stocks and long-term corporate bonds. What was the return on a portfolio that was equally invested in small stocks and Treasury bills?

LO 1   **22. Portfolio Expected Return.**   You have $250,000 to invest in a stock portfolio. Your choices are Stock H, with an expected return of 13.5 percent, and Stock L, with an expected return of 9.8 percent. If your goal is to create a portfolio with an expected return of 11.4 percent, how much money will you invest in Stock H? In Stock L?

LO 1   **23. Calculating Portfolio Weights.**   Stock J has a beta of 1.23 and an expected return of 13.25 percent, while Stock K has a beta of .8 and an expected return of 11.40 percent. You want a portfolio with the same risk as the market. How much will you invest in each stock? What is the expected return of your portfolio?

LO 1   **24. Calculating Portfolio Weights and Expected Return.**   You have a portfolio with the following:

Stock	Number of Shares	Price	Expected Return
W	550	$43	10%
X	625	29	15%
Y	350	94	11%
Z	700	51	14%

What is the expected return of your portfolio?

LO 2   **25. Portfolio Returns and Deviations.**   Consider the following information on a portfolio of three stocks:

Intermediate (Questions 25–27)

State of Economy	Probability of State of Economy	Stock A Rate of Return	Stock B Rate of Return	Stock C Rate of Return
Boom	.25	.02	.32	.60
Normal	.60	.10	.12	.20
Bust	.15	.16	−.11	−.35

a. If your portfolio is invested 40 percent each in A and B and 20 percent in C, what is the portfolio's expected return? The variance? The standard deviation?

b. If the expected T-bill rate is 3.75 percent, what is the expected risk premium on the portfolio?

LO 4   **26. CAPM.**   Using the CAPM, show that the ratio of the risk premiums on two assets is equal to the ratio of their betas.

LO 2   **27. Analyzing a Portfolio.**   You want to create a portfolio equally as risky as the market, and you have $500,000 to invest. Given this information, fill in the rest of the following table:

Asset	Investment	Beta
Stock A	$120,000	.80
Stock B	150,000	1.15
Stock C		1.40
Risk-free asset		

LO 1   **28. Analyzing a Portfolio.**   You have $100,000 to invest in either Stock D, Stock F, or a risk-free asset. You must invest all of your money. Your goal is to create a portfolio that has an expected return of 10.5 percent. If D has an expected return of 13.2 percent, F has an expected return of 9.5 percent, and the risk-free rate is 3.8 percent, and if you invest $50,000 in Stock D, how much will you invest in Stock F?

Challenge (Questions 28–30)

LO 4

29. SML.   Suppose you observe the following situation:

State of Economy	Probability of State	Return if State Occurs	
		Stock A	Stock B
Bust	.10	−.12	−.05
Normal	.65	.09	.10
Boom	.25	.35	.21

a.   Calculate the expected return on each stock.

b.   Assuming the capital asset pricing model holds and stock A's beta is greater than stock B's beta by .25, what is the expected market risk premium?

LO 3

30. Systematic versus Unsystematic Risk.   Consider the following information on Stocks I and II:

State of Economy	Probability of State of Economy	Rate of Return if State Occurs	
		Stock I	Stock II
Recession	.20	.02	−.20
Normal	.55	.32	.12
Irrational exuberance	.25	.18	.40

The market risk premium is 7 percent, and the risk-free rate is 4 percent. Which stock has the most systematic risk? Which one has the most unsystematic risk? Which stock is "riskier"? Explain.

WHAT'S ON THE WEB?

11.1 Expected Return.   You want to find the expected return for Honeywell using the CAPM. First, you need the market risk premium. Use the average large-company stock return in Table 10.3 to estimate the market risk premium. Next, go to money .cnn.com and find the current interest rate for three-month Treasury bills. Finally, go to finance.yahoo.com, enter the ticker symbol HON for Honeywell, and find the beta for Honeywell. What is the expected return for Honeywell using CAPM? What assumptions have you made to arrive at this number?

11.2 Portfolio Beta.   You have decided to invest in an equally weighted portfolio consisting of American Express, Procter & Gamble, Home Depot, and DuPont and need to find the beta of your portfolio. Go to finance.yahoo.com and find the ticker symbols for each of these companies. Next, find the beta for each company. What is the beta for your portfolio?

11.3 Beta.   Which stock has the highest and lowest betas? Go to finance.yahoo.com and locate the Stock Screener. Enter 0 as the maximum value. How many stocks have a beta less than zero? Which stock has the lowest beta? Go back to the screener and enter 3 as the minimum value. How many stocks have a beta greater than 3? What about greater than 4? Which stock has the highest beta?

CHAPTER CASE
THE BETA FOR FLIR SYSTEMS

Joey Moss, a recent finance graduate, has just begun his job with the investment firm of Covili and Wyatt. Paul Covili, one of the firm's founders, has been talking to Joey about the firm's investment portfolio.

As with any investment, Paul is concerned about the risk of the investment as well as the potential return. More specifically, because the company holds a diversified portfolio, Paul is concerned about the systematic risk of current and potential investments. One position the company currently holds is stock in FLIR Systems, Inc. (FLIR). FLIR Systems designs, manufactures, and markets thermal imaging and infrared camera systems. Although better known for its military applications, the company has divisions that design products for other applications such as automotive night vision, commercial products that require minute temperature difference measurements, recreational marine usage, and firefighting.

Covili and Wyatt currently uses a commercial data vendor for information about its positions. Because of this, Paul is unsure exactly how the numbers provided are calculated. The data provider considers its methods proprietary, and it will not disclose how stock betas and other information are calculated. Paul is uncomfortable with not knowing exactly how these numbers are being computed and also believes that it could be less expensive to calculate the necessary statistics in-house. To explore this question, Paul has asked Joey to do the following assignments:

QUESTIONS

1. Go to finance.yahoo.com and download the ending monthly stock prices for FLIR Systems (FLIR) for the last 60 months. Be sure to use the adjusted closing price to account for any stock splits and dividend payments. Next, download the ending value of the S&P 500 index over the same period. For the historical risk-free rate, go to the St. Louis Federal Reserve website (www.stlouisfed.org) and find the three-month Treasury bill constant maturity rate. Download this file. What are the monthly returns, average monthly returns, and standard deviations for FLIR Systems stock, the three-month Treasury bill, and the S&P 500 for this period?

2. Beta is often estimated by linear regression. A model often used is called the *market model,* which is:

$$R_t - R_{ft} = \alpha_i + \beta_i [R_{Mt} - R_{ft}] + \epsilon_t$$

In this regression, R_t is the return on the stock and R_{ft} is the risk-free rate for the same period. R_{Mt} is the return on a stock market index such as the S&P 500 index. α_i is the regression intercept, and β_i is the slope (and the stock's estimated beta). ϵ_t represents the residuals for the regression. What do you think is the motivation for this particular regression? The intercept, α_i, is often called *Jensen's alpha.* What does it measure? If an asset has a positive Jensen's alpha, where would it plot with respect to the SML? What is the financial interpretation of the residuals in the regression?

3. Use the market model to estimate the beta for FLIR Systems using the last 60 months of returns (the regression procedure in Excel is one easy way to do this). Plot the monthly returns on FLIR Systems against the index and also show the fitted line.

4. Compare your beta for FLIR Systems to the beta you find on finance.yahoo.com. How similar are they? Why might they be different?

12 | Cost of Capital

learning objectives

After studying this chapter, you should be able to:

LO 1 Determine a firm's cost of equity capital.

LO 2 Determine a firm's cost of debt.

LO 3 Determine a firm's overall cost of capital.

LO 4 Identify some of the pitfalls associated with a firm's overall cost of capital and what to do about them.

With over 95,000 employees on five continents, Germany-based BASF is a major international company. BASF operates in a variety of industries, including agriculture, oil and gas, chemicals, and plastics. In an attempt to increase value, BASF launched Vision 2020, a comprehensive plan that included all functions within the company and challenged and encouraged all employees to act in an entrepreneurial manner. The major financial component of the strategy was that the company expected to earn its weighted average cost of capital, or WACC, plus a premium. So, what exactly is the WACC?

The WACC is the minimum return a company needs to earn to satisfy all of its investors, including stockholders, bondholders, and preferred stockholders. In 2010, for example, BASF pegged its cost of capital at 9 percent and earned a company record premium of €3.9 billion over its target based on that number. In both 2011 and 2012, the company pegged its WACC at 11 percent. In this chapter, we learn how to compute a firm's cost of capital and find out what it means to the firm and its investors. We will also learn when to use the firm's cost of capital and, perhaps more important, when not to use it.

From our chapters on capital budgeting, we know that the discount rate, or required return, on an investment is a critical input. Thus far, however, we haven't discussed how to come up with that particular number, so it's time now to do so. This chapter brings together many of our earlier discussions dealing with stocks and bonds, capital budgeting, and risk and return. Our goal is to illustrate how firms go about determining the required return on a proposed investment. Understanding required returns is important to everyone because all proposed projects, whether they relate to marketing, management, accounting, or any other area, must offer returns in excess of their required returns to be acceptable.

Suppose you have just become the president of a large company and the first decision you face is whether to go ahead with a plan to renovate the company's warehouse distribution system. The plan will cost the company $50 million, and it is expected to save $12 million per year after taxes over the next six years.

This is a familiar problem in capital budgeting. To address it, you would determine the relevant cash flows, discount them, and, if the net present value is positive, take on the project; if the NPV is negative, you would scrap it. So far, so good; but what should you use as the discount rate?

From our discussion of risk and return, you know that the correct discount rate depends on the riskiness of the warehouse distribution system. In particular, the new project will have a positive NPV only if its return exceeds what the financial markets offer on investments of similar risk. We called this minimum required return the *cost of capital* associated with the project.[1]

Thus, to make the right decision as president, you must examine what the capital markets have to offer and use this information to arrive at an estimate of the project's cost of capital. Our primary purpose in this chapter is to describe how to go about doing this. There are a variety of approaches to this task, and a number of conceptual and practical issues arise.

One of the most important concepts we develop is that of the *weighted average cost of capital* (WACC). This is the cost of capital for the firm as a whole, and it can be interpreted as the required return on the overall firm. In discussing the WACC, we will recognize the fact that a firm will normally raise capital in a variety of forms and that these different forms of capital may have different costs associated with them.

We also recognize in this chapter that taxes are an important consideration in determining the required return on an investment, because we are always interested in valuing the aftertax cash flows from a project. We will therefore discuss how to incorporate taxes explicitly into our estimates of the cost of capital.

THE COST OF CAPITAL: SOME PRELIMINARIES

12.1

In Chapter 11, we developed the security market line, or SML, and used it to explore the relationship between the expected return on a security and its systematic risk. We concentrated on how the risky returns from buying securities looked from the viewpoint of, for example, a shareholder in the firm. This helped us understand more about the alternatives available to an investor in the capital markets.

In this chapter, we turn things around a bit and look more closely at the other side of the problem, which is how these returns and securities look from the viewpoint of the companies that issue the securities. The important fact to note is that the return an investor in a security receives is the cost of that security to the company that issued it.

Required Return versus Cost of Capital

When we say that the required return on an investment is, say, 10 percent, we usually mean that the investment will have a positive NPV only if its return exceeds 10 percent. Another way of interpreting the required return is to observe that the firm must earn 10 percent on

---

[1] The term *cost of money* is also used.

the investment just to compensate its investors for the use of the capital needed to finance the project. This is why we could also say that 10 percent is the cost of capital associated with the investment.

To illustrate the point further, imagine we are evaluating a risk-free project. In this case, how to determine the required return is obvious: We look at the capital markets and observe the current rate offered by risk-free investments, and we use this rate to discount the project's cash flows. Thus, the cost of capital for a risk-free investment is the risk-free rate.

If this project is risky, then, assuming that all the other information is unchanged, the required return is obviously higher. In other words, the cost of capital for this project, if it is risky, is greater than the risk-free rate, and the appropriate discount rate would exceed the risk-free rate.

We will henceforth use the terms *required return, appropriate discount rate,* and *cost of capital* more or less interchangeably because, as the discussion in this section suggests, they all mean essentially the same thing. The key fact to grasp is that the cost of capital associated with an investment depends on the risk of that investment. In other words, it's the use of the money, not the source, that matters. This is one of the most important lessons in corporate finance, so it bears repeating:

The cost of capital depends primarily on the use of the funds, not the source.

It is a common error to forget this crucial point and fall into the trap of thinking that the cost of capital for an investment depends primarily on how and where the capital is raised.

Financial Policy and Cost of Capital

We know that the particular mixture of debt and equity a firm chooses to employ—its capital structure—is a managerial variable. In this chapter, we will take the firm's financial policy as given. In particular, we will assume that the firm has a fixed debt-equity ratio that it maintains. This ratio reflects the firm's *target* capital structure. How a firm might choose that ratio is the subject of a later chapter.

From our discussion above, we know that a firm's overall cost of capital will reflect the required return on the firm's assets as a whole. Given that a firm uses both debt and equity capital, this overall cost of capital will be a mixture of the returns needed to compensate its creditors and its stockholders. In other words, a firm's cost of capital will reflect both its cost of debt capital and its cost of equity capital. We discuss these costs separately in the sections that follow.

CONCEPT QUESTIONS

12.1a What is the primary determinant of the cost of capital for an investment?

12.1b What is the relationship between the required return on an investment and the cost of capital associated with that investment?

THE COST OF EQUITY

We begin with the most difficult question on the subject of cost of capital: What is the firm's overall cost of equity? The reason this is a difficult question is that there is no way of directly observing the return that the firm's equity investors require on their investment. Instead, we must somehow estimate it. This section discusses two approaches to determining the cost of equity: the dividend growth model approach and the security market line, or SML, approach.

cost of equity
The return that equity investors require on their investment in the firm.

The Dividend Growth Model Approach

The easiest way to estimate the cost of equity capital is to use the dividend growth model we developed in Chapter 7. Recall that, under the assumption that the firm's dividend will grow at a constant rate, g, the price per share of the stock, P_0, can be written as:

ExcelMaster
coverage online

$$P_0 = \frac{D_0 \times (1 + g)}{R_E - g} = \frac{D_1}{R_E - g}$$

where D_0 is the dividend just paid and D_1 is the next period's projected dividend. Notice that we have used the symbol R_E (the E stands for *equity*) for the required return on the stock.

As we discussed in Chapter 7, we can rearrange this to solve for R_E as follows:

$$R_E = D_1/P_0 + g \qquad\qquad\qquad [12.1]$$

Since R_E is the return that the shareholders require on the stock, it can be interpreted as the firm's cost of equity capital.

Implementing the Approach   To estimate R_E using the dividend growth model approach, we obviously need three pieces of information: P_0, D_0, and g. Of these, for a publicly traded, dividend-paying company, the first two can be observed directly, so they are easily obtained.[2] Only the third component, the expected growth rate in dividends, must be estimated.

To illustrate how we estimate R_E, suppose Greater States Public Service, a large public utility, paid a dividend of $4 per share last year. The stock currently sells for $60 per share. You estimate that the dividend will grow steadily at 6 percent per year into the indefinite future. What is the cost of equity capital for Greater States?

Using the dividend growth model, we calculate that the expected dividend for the coming year, D_1, is:

$$D_1 = D_0 \times (1 + g)$$
$$= \$4 \times 1.06$$
$$= \$4.24$$

Given this, the cost of equity, R_E, is:

$$R_E = D_1/P_0 + g$$
$$= \$4.24/60 + .06$$
$$= 13.07\%$$

The cost of equity is thus 13.07%.

---

[2] Notice that if we have D_0 and g, we can simply calculate D_1 by multiplying D_0 by $(1 + g)$.

392   **PART 7**   Long-Term Financing

Estimating g   To use the dividend growth model, we must come up with an estimate for g, the growth rate. There are essentially two ways of doing this: (1) use historical growth rates or (2) use analysts' forecasts of future growth rates. Analysts' forecasts are available from a variety of sources. Naturally, different sources will have different estimates, so one approach might be to obtain multiple estimates and then average them.

Alternatively, we might observe dividends for the previous, say, five years, calculate the year-to-year growth rates, and average them. For example, suppose we observe the following for some company:

Year	Dividend
2009	$1.10
2010	1.20
2011	1.35
2012	1.40
2013	1.55

Aggregate growth estimates can be found at www.zacks.com /research/earnings.

We can calculate the percentage change in the dividend for each year as follows:

Year	Dividend	Dollar Change	Percentage Change
2009	$1.10	—	—
2010	1.20	$.10	9.09%
2011	1.35	.15	12.50
2012	1.40	.05	3.70
2013	1.55	.15	10.71

Notice that we calculated the change in the dividend on a year-to-year basis and then expressed the change as a percentage. Thus, in 2010, for example, the dividend rose from $1.10 to $1.20, for an increase of $.10. This represents a $.10/1.10 = 9.09% increase.

If we average the four growth rates, the result is (9.09 + 12.50 + 3.70 + 10.71)/4 = 9%, so we could use this as an estimate for the expected growth rate, g. Notice that this 9 percent growth rate we have calculated is a simple, or arithmetic average. Going back to Chapter 10, we also could calculate a geometric growth rate. Here, the dividend grows from $1.10 to $1.55 over a four-year period. What's the compound, or geometric growth rate? See if you don't agree that it's 8.95 percent; you can view this as a simple time value of money problem where $1.10 is the present value and $1.55 is the future value.

As usual, the geometric average (8.95 percent) is lower than the arithmetic average (9.00 percent), but the difference here is not likely to be of any practical significance. In general, if the dividend has grown at a relatively steady rate, as we assume when we use this approach, then it can't make much difference which way we calculate the average dividend growth rate.

Advantages and Disadvantages of the Approach   The primary advantage of the dividend growth model approach is its simplicity. It is both easy to understand and easy to use. However, there are a number of associated practical problems and disadvantages.

First and foremost, the dividend growth model is obviously only applicable to companies that pay dividends. This means that the approach is useless in many cases. Furthermore, even for companies that do pay dividends, the key underlying assumption is that the dividend grows at a constant rate. As our example above illustrates, this will never be *exactly* the case. More generally, the model is really only applicable to cases in which reasonably steady growth is likely to occur.

A second problem is that the estimated cost of equity is very sensitive to the estimated growth rate. For a given stock price, an upward revision of g by just one percentage point, for example, increases the estimated cost of equity by at least a full percentage point. Since D_1 will probably be revised upward as well, the increase will actually be somewhat larger than that.

Finally, this approach really does not explicitly consider risk. Unlike the SML approach (which we consider next), this one has no direct adjustment for the riskiness of the investment. For example, there is no allowance for the degree of certainty or uncertainty surrounding the estimated growth rate in dividends. As a result, it is difficult to say whether or not the estimated return is commensurate with the level of risk.[3]

The SML Approach

In Chapter 11, we discussed the security market line, or SML. Our primary conclusion was that the required or expected return on a risky investment depends on three things:

1. The risk-free rate, R_f
2. The market risk premium, $E(R_M) - R_f$
3. The systematic risk of the asset relative to average, which we called its beta coefficient, β

Using the SML, we can write the expected return on the company's equity, $E(R_E)$, as:

$$E(R_E) = R_f + \beta_E \times [E(R_M) - R_f]$$

where β_E is the estimated beta for the equity. To make the SML approach consistent with the dividend growth model, we will drop the Es denoting expectations and henceforth write the required return from the SML, R_E, as:

$$R_E = R_f + \beta_E \times (R_M - R_f) \qquad [12.2]$$

Implementing the Approach   To use the SML approach, we need a risk-free rate, R_f, an estimate of the market risk premium, $R_M - R_f$, and an estimate of the relevant beta, β_E. In Chapter 10, we saw that one estimate of the market risk premium is about 7 percent. U.S. Treasury bills are paying about .05 percent as this is being written, so we will use this as our risk-free rate. Beta coefficients for publicly traded companies are widely available.[4]

To illustrate, in Chapter 11, we saw that eBay had an estimated beta of 1.36 (Table 11.8). We could thus estimate eBay's cost of equity as:

Both betas and T-bill rates can be found at www.bloomberg.com.

$$
\begin{aligned}
R_{eBay} &= R_f + \beta_{eBay} \times (R_M - R_f) \\
&= .05\% + 1.36 \times 7\% \\
&= 9.57\%
\end{aligned}
$$

Thus, using the SML approach, eBay's cost of equity is about 9.6 percent.

---

[3] There is an implicit adjustment for risk because the current stock price is used. All other things being equal, the higher the risk, the lower is the stock price. Further, the lower the stock price, the greater is the cost of equity, again assuming that all the other information is the same.

[4] Beta coefficients can be estimated directly by using historical data. For a discussion of how to do this, see Chapters 10, 11, and 12 in S. A. Ross, R. W. Westerfield, and J. F. Jaffe, *Corporate Finance,* 10th ed. (Burr Ridge, Ill.: The McGraw-Hill Companies, 2013).

Advantages and Disadvantages of the Approach The SML approach has two primary advantages. First: It explicitly adjusts for risk. Second: It is applicable to companies other than just those with steady dividend growth. Thus, it may be useful in a wider variety of circumstances.

There are drawbacks, of course. The SML approach requires that two things be estimated, the market risk premium and the beta coefficient. To the extent that our estimates are poor, the resulting cost of equity will be inaccurate. For example, our estimate of the market risk premium, 7 percent, is based on about 100 years of returns on a particular portfolio of stocks. Using different time periods or different stocks could result in very different estimates.

Finally, as with the dividend growth model, we essentially rely on the past to predict the future when we use the SML approach. Economic conditions can change very quickly, so, as always, the past may not be a good guide to the future. In the best of all worlds, both approaches (dividend growth model and SML) are applicable and result in similar answers. If this happens, we might have some confidence in our estimates. We might also wish to compare the results to those for other, similar companies as a reality check.

EXAMPLE 12.1

THE COST OF EQUITY

Suppose stock in Alpha Air Freight has a beta of 1.2. The market risk premium is 8 percent, and the risk-free rate is 6 percent. Alpha's last dividend was $2 per share, and the dividend is expected to grow at 8 percent indefinitely. The stock currently sells for $30. What is Alpha's cost of equity capital?

We can start off by using the SML. Doing this, we find that the expected return on the common stock of Alpha Air Freight is:

$$R_E = R_f + \beta_E \times (R_M - R_f)$$
$$= 6\% + 1.2 \times 8\%$$
$$= 15.6\%$$

This suggests that 15.6 percent is Alpha's cost of equity. We next use the dividend growth model. The projected dividend is $D_0 \times (1 + g) = \$2 \times 1.08 = \$2.16$, so the expected return using this approach is:

$$R_E = D_1/P_0 + g$$
$$= \$2.16/30 + .08$$
$$= 15.2\%$$

Our two estimates are reasonably close, so we might just average them to find that Alpha's cost of equity is approximately 15.4 percent.

CONCEPT QUESTIONS

12.2a What do we mean when we say that a corporation's cost of equity capital is 16 percent?

12.2b What are two approaches to estimating the cost of equity capital?

12.3

THE COSTS OF DEBT AND PREFERRED STOCK

In addition to ordinary equity, firms use debt and, to a lesser extent, preferred stock to finance their investments. As we discuss next, determining the costs of capital associated with these sources of financing is much easier than determining the cost of equity.

ExcelMaster
coverage online

The Cost of Debt

The **cost of debt** is the return that the firm's creditors demand on new borrowing. In principle, we could determine the beta for the firm's debt and then use the SML to estimate the required return on debt just as we estimate the required return on equity. This isn't really necessary, however.

cost of debt
The return that lenders require on the firm's debt.

Unlike a firm's cost of equity, its cost of debt can normally be observed either directly or indirectly, because the cost of debt is simply the interest rate the firm must pay on new borrowing, and we can observe interest rates in the financial markets. For example, if the firm already has bonds outstanding, then the yield to maturity on those bonds is the market-required rate on the firm's debt.

Alternatively, if we knew that the firm's bonds were rated, say, AA, then we could simply find out what the interest rate on newly issued AA-rated bonds was. Either way, there is no need to actually estimate a beta for the debt since we can directly observe the rate we want to know.

There is one thing to be careful about, though. The coupon rate on the firm's outstanding debt is irrelevant here. That just tells us roughly what the firm's cost of debt was back when the bonds were issued, not what the cost of debt is today.[5] This is why we have to look at the yield on the debt in today's marketplace. For consistency with our other notation, we will use the symbol R_D for the cost of debt.

THE COST OF DEBT   **EXAMPLE 12.2**

Suppose the General Tool Company issued a 30-year, 7 percent bond eight years ago. The bond is currently selling for 96 percent of its face value, or $960. What is General Tool's cost of debt?

Going back to Chapter 6, we need to calculate the yield to maturity on this bond. Since the bond is selling at a discount, the yield is apparently greater than 7 percent, but not much greater, because the discount is fairly small. You can verify that the yield to maturity is about 7.37 percent, assuming annual coupons. General Tool's cost of debt, R_D, is thus 7.37 percent.

The Cost of Preferred Stock

Determining the *cost of preferred stock* is quite straightforward. As we discussed in Chapters 6 and 7, preferred stock has a fixed dividend paid every period forever, so a share of preferred stock is essentially a perpetuity. The cost of preferred stock, R_P, is thus:

$$R_P = D/P_0 \qquad\qquad [12.3]$$

where D is the fixed dividend and P_0 is the current price per share of the preferred stock. Notice that the cost of preferred stock is simply equal to the dividend yield on the preferred stock. Alternatively, preferred stocks are rated in much the same way as bonds, so the cost of preferred stock can be estimated by observing the required returns on other, similarly rated shares of preferred stock.

ALABAMA POWER'S COST OF PREFERRED STOCK   **EXAMPLE 12.3**

In 2012, Alabama Power had several issues of preferred stock that traded on the NYSE. One issue paid $1.325 annually per share and sold for $25.94 per share. Another paid $1.30 per share annually and sold for $25.95 per share. What was Alabama Power's cost of preferred stock?

(continued)

---

[5] The firm's cost of debt based on its historic borrowing is sometimes called the *embedded debt cost*.

Using the first issue, the cost of preferred stock was:

$R_P = D/P_0$

$= \$1.325/25.94$

$= .0511,$ or 5.11%

Using the second issue, the cost was:

$R_P = D/P_0$

$= \$1.30/25.95$

$= .0501,$ or 5.01%

So, Alabama Power's cost of preferred stock appears to have been just over 5 percent.

CONCEPT QUESTIONS

12.3a How can the cost of debt be calculated?

12.3b How can the cost of preferred stock be calculated?

12.3c Why is the coupon rate a bad estimate of a firm's cost of debt?

12.4   THE WEIGHTED AVERAGE COST OF CAPITAL

ExcelMaster
coverage online

Now that we have the costs associated with the main sources of capital the firm employs, we need to worry about the specific mix. As we mentioned above, we will take this mix, which is the firm's capital structure, as given for now. Also, we will focus mostly on debt and ordinary equity in this discussion.

The Capital Structure Weights

We will use the symbol E (for *equity*) to stand for the *market* value of the firm's equity. We calculate this by taking the number of shares outstanding and multiplying it by the price per share. Similarly, we will use the symbol D (for *debt*) to stand for the *market* value of the firm's debt. For long-term debt, we calculate this by multiplying the market price of a single bond by the number of bonds outstanding.

If there are multiple bond issues (as there normally would be), we repeat this calculation for each and then add up the results. If there is debt that is not publicly traded (because it is held by a life insurance company, for example), we must observe the yield on similar, publicly traded debt and then estimate the market value of the privately held debt using this yield as the discount rate. For short-term debt, the book (accounting) values and market values should be somewhat similar, so we might use the book values as estimates of the market values.

Finally, we will use the symbol V (for *value*) to stand for the combined market value of the debt and equity:

$$V = E + D \qquad [12.4]$$

If we divide both sides by V, we can calculate the percentages of the total capital represented by the debt and equity:

$$100\% = E/V + D/V \qquad [12.5]$$

These percentages can be interpreted just like portfolio weights, and they are often called the *capital structure weights*.

For example, if the total market value of a company's stock were calculated as $200 million and the total market value of the company's debt were calculated as $50 million, then the combined value would be $250 million. Of this total, $E/V = \$200/250 = 80\%$, so 80 percent of the firm's financing would be equity and the remaining 20 percent would be debt.

We emphasize here that the correct way to proceed is to use the *market* values of the debt and equity. Under certain circumstances, such as when considering a privately owned company, it may not be possible to get reliable estimates of these quantities. In this case, we might go ahead and use the accounting values for debt and equity. While this would probably be better than nothing, we would have to take the answer with a grain of salt.

Taxes and the Weighted Average Cost of Capital

There is one final issue we need to discuss. Recall that we are always concerned with aftertax cash flows. If we are determining the discount rate appropriate to those cash flows, then the discount rate also needs to be expressed on an aftertax basis.

As we discussed previously in various places in this book (and as we will discuss later), the interest paid by a corporation is deductible for tax purposes. Payments to stockholders, such as dividends, are not. What this means, effectively, is that the government pays some of the interest. Thus, in determining an aftertax discount rate, we need to distinguish between the pretax and the aftertax cost of debt.

To illustrate, suppose a firm borrows $1 million at 9 percent interest. The corporate tax rate is 34 percent. What is the aftertax interest rate on this loan? The total interest bill will be $90,000 per year. This amount is tax deductible, however, so the $90,000 interest reduces our tax bill by $.34 \times \$90,000 = \$30,600$. The aftertax interest bill is thus $90,000 − 30,600 = \$59,400$. The aftertax interest rate is thus $\$59,400/1$ million $= 5.94\%$.

Notice that, in general, the aftertax interest rate is simply equal to the pretax rate multiplied by 1 minus the tax rate. Thus, if we use the symbol T_C to stand for the corporate tax rate, then the aftertax rate that we use for the cost of debt can be written as $R_D \times (1 - T_C)$. For example, using the numbers above, we find that the aftertax interest rate is $9\% \times (1 - .34) = 5.94\%$.

Collecting together the various topics we have discussed in this chapter, we now have the capital structure weights along with the cost of equity and the aftertax cost of debt. To calculate the firm's overall cost of capital, we multiply the capital structure weights by the associated costs and add up the pieces. The result of this is the **weighted average cost of capital**, or **WACC**.

weighted average cost of capital (WACC)
The weighted average of the cost of equity and the aftertax cost of debt.

$$\text{WACC} = (E/V) \times R_E + (D/V) \times R_D \times (1 - T_C) \qquad [12.6]$$

This WACC has a very straightforward interpretation. It is the overall return the firm must earn on its existing assets to maintain the value of its stock. This is an important point, so it bears repeating:

> **The WACC is the overall return the firm must earn on its existing assets to maintain the value of its stock.**

The WACC is also the required return on any investments by the firm that have essentially the same risks as existing operations. So, if we were evaluating the cash flows from a proposed expansion of our existing operations, this is the discount rate we would use.

FINANCE MATTERS

◄ For the latest news on the topics covered in this chapter, scan here.

EVA: An Old Idea Moves into the Modern Age

You might not think of Briggs and Stratton, Coca-Cola, and Toys 'R' Us as having much in common. However, all three have linked their fortunes to a way of managing and measuring corporate performance that depends critically on the cost of capital. It goes by many names, but consulting firm Stern Stewart & Co., a well-known advocate, calls its particular flavor "economic value added," or EVA. Stockholder value added (SVA) is a common variant. Whatever the name, EVA and its cousins have become an important tool for corporate management since the mid-1990s.

Briefly stated, EVA is a method of measuring financial performance. To compute EVA, you must calculate your overall cost of capital. Then, you identify how much capital is tied up in your business. Next, you multiply the amount of capital by the cost of capital. The result is the amount, in dollars, you should be providing to your investors. Subtract out your actual operating cash flow, and the difference is a measure of EVA. A positive value means that you earned more than your cost of capital, thereby creating value, and vice versa (this is just a quick overview; for more detail visit www.eva.com).

Each year, Stern Stewart & Co. prepares the Stern Stewart 1000, a ranking of the 1,000 largest U.S. companies based on their respective EVAs. Over the history of the Stern Stewart 1000, several companies have shown consistently strong performances. For example, Microsoft, Intel, and ExxonMobil often appear near the top of the list. The list also has perennial poor performers, and some of the names may surprise you, for example, General Motors, Time Warner, Goodyear Tire & Rubber, and JDS Uniphase. Evidently, a well-known brand name does not always result in shareholder wealth.

One thing the Stern Stewart 1000 has done is to show the changing face of the economy. For instance, Intel, Dell

Computer, Cisco Systems, and eBay have all ranked rather well on the list. Consider that Intel is the oldest of these companies, having been publicly traded since 1971, while eBay has been publicly traded only since 1998. This highlights the dramatic impact of technology companies on the economy. Of course, not all technology-related companies have performed as well. For example, WebMD has appeared near the bottom of the list every year.

According to Bennett Stewart, one of the cofounders of Stern Stewart, EVA shows an important distinction between accounting income and economic profit. Accounting rules dictate that the interest expense a company incurs must be deducted from its reported profit, but those same rules forbid deducting a charge for the shareholders' funds used by a firm. In economic terms, equity capital is in fact a very costly financing source because shareholders bear the risk of being paid last, after all other stakeholders and investors are paid. But according to accountants, shareholder equity is essentially free. This oversight has dire practical consequences. For instance, it means that the profit figure accountants certify to be correct can conflict with the net present value decision rule. This conflict occurs when accounting rules lead to a focus on the accountant's bottom line rather than the more important question of whether a project's projected return exceeds its required return.

While EVA and its variants are sound in principle, they still have shortcomings. For one thing, they are typically computed using asset book values instead of market values. For another, they sometimes are based on accounting measures of income when cash flow would be a better choice. Nonetheless, potential problems aside, the concept of EVA focuses management attention on creating wealth for investors. That, in itself, makes EVA a worthwhile tool.

If a firm uses preferred stock in its capital structure, then our expression for the WACC needs a simple extension. If we define P/V as the percentage of the firm's financing that comes from preferred stock, then the WACC is simply:

$$\text{WACC} = (E/V) \times R_E + (P/V) \times R_P + (D/V) \times R_D \times (1 - T_c) \qquad [12.7]$$

where R_P is the cost of preferred stock.

The WACC is increasingly being used by corporations to evaluate financial performance. The accompanying *Finance Matters* box provides some details on how this is being done.

CALCULATING THE WACC

EXAMPLE 12.4

The B. B. Lean Co. has 1.4 million shares of stock outstanding. The stock currently sells for $20 per share. The firm's debt is publicly traded and was recently quoted at 93 percent of face value. It has a total face value of $5 million, and it is currently priced to yield 11 percent. The risk-free rate is 8 percent, and the market risk premium is 7 percent. You've estimated that Lean has a beta of .74. If the corporate tax rate is 34 percent, what is the WACC of Lean Co.?

We can first determine the cost of equity and the cost of debt. From the SML, the cost of equity is 8% + .74 × 7% = 13.18%. The total value of the equity is 1.4 million × $20 = $28 million. The pretax cost of debt is the current yield to maturity on the outstanding debt, 11 percent. The debt sells for 93 percent of its face value, so its current market value is .93 × $5 million = $4.65 million. The total market value of the equity and debt together is $28 + 4.65 = $32.65 million.

From here, we can calculate the WACC easily enough. The percentage of equity used by Lean to finance its operations is $28/32.65 = 85.76%. Since the weights have to add up to 1.0, the percentage of debt is 1.0 − .8576 = 14.24%. The WACC is thus:

$$\text{WACC} = (E/V) \times R_E + (D/V) \times R_D \times (1 - T_c)$$
$$= .8576 \times 13.18\% + .1424 \times 11\% \times (1 - .34)$$
$$= 12.34\%$$

B. B. Lean thus has an overall weighted average cost of capital of 12.34 percent.

Solving the Warehouse Problem and Similar Capital Budgeting Problems

Now we can use the WACC to solve the warehouse problem we posed at the beginning of the chapter. However, before we rush to discount the cash flows at the WACC to estimate NPV, we need to first make sure we are doing the right thing.

Going back to first principles, we need to find an alternative in the financial markets that is comparable to the warehouse renovation. To be comparable, an alternative must be of the same risk as the warehouse project. Projects that have the same risk are said to be in the same risk class.

The WACC for a firm reflects the risk and the target capital structure of the firm's existing assets as a whole. As a result, strictly speaking, the firm's WACC is the appropriate discount rate only if the proposed investment is a replica of the firm's existing operating activities.

In broader terms, whether or not we can use the firm's WACC to value the warehouse project depends on whether the warehouse project is in the same risk class as the firm. We will assume that this project is an integral part of the overall business of the firm. In such cases, it is natural to think that the cost savings will be as risky as the general cash flows of the firm, and the project will thus be in the same risk class as the overall firm. More generally, projects like the warehouse renovation that are intimately related to the firm's existing operations are often viewed as being in the same risk class as the overall firm.

We can now see what the president should do. Suppose the firm has a target debt-equity ratio of 1/3. From Chapter 3, we know that a debt-equity ratio of $D/E = 1/3$ implies that E/V is .75 and D/V is .25. Further suppose the cost of debt is 10 percent, and the cost of equity is 20 percent. Assuming a 34 percent tax rate, the WACC will then be:

$$\textbf{WACC} = \textbf{(E/V)} \times \textbf{\textit{R}}_E + \textbf{(D/V)} \times \textbf{\textit{R}}_D \times \textbf{(1 − \textit{T}}_c\textbf{)}$$
$$= \textbf{.75} \times \textbf{20\%} + \textbf{.25} \times \textbf{10\%} \times \textbf{(1 − .34)}$$
$$= \textbf{16.65\%}$$

TABLE 12.1
Summary of capital cost calculations

I. The cost of equity, R_E

A. Dividend growth model approach (from Chapter 7):

$$R_E = D_1/P_0 + g$$

where D_1 is the expected dividend in one period, g is the dividend growth rate, and P_0 is the current stock price.

B. SML approach (from Chapter 11):

$$R_E = R_f + \beta_E \times (R_M - R_f)$$

where R_f is the risk-free rate, R_M is the expected return on the overall market, and β_E is the systematic risk of the equity.

II. The cost of debt, R_D

A. For a firm with publicly held debt, the cost of debt can be measured as the yield to maturity on the outstanding debt. The coupon rate is irrelevant. Yield to maturity is covered in Chapter 6.

B. If the firm has no publicly traded debt, then the cost of debt can be measured as the yield to maturity on similarly rated bonds (bond ratings are discussed in Chapter 6).

III. The weighted average cost of capital, WACC

A. The firm's WACC is the overall required return on the firm as a whole. It is the appropriate discount rate to use for cash flows similar in risk to the overall firm.

B. The WACC is calculated as:

$$WACC = (E/V) \times R_E + (D/V) \times R_D \times (1 - T_C)$$

where T_C is the corporate tax rate, E is the *market* value of the firm's equity, D is the *market* value of the firm's debt, and $V = E + D$. Note that E/V is the percentage of the firm's financing (in market value terms) that is equity, and D/V is the percentage that is debt.

Recall that the warehouse project had a cost of $50 million and expected aftertax cash flows (the cost savings) of $12 million per year for six years. The NPV is thus:

$$NPV = -\$50 + \frac{12}{(1 + WACC)^1} + \cdots + \frac{12}{(1 + WACC)^6}$$

Since the cash flows are in the form of an ordinary annuity, we can calculate this NPV using 16.65 percent (the WACC) as the discount rate as follows:

$$NPV = -\$50 + 12 \times \frac{1 - [1/(1 + .1665)^6]}{.1665}$$

$$= -\$50 + 12 \times 3.6222$$

$$= -\$6.53 \text{ million}$$

Should the firm take on the warehouse renovation? The project has a negative NPV using the firm's WACC. This means that the financial markets offer superior projects in the same risk class (namely, the firm itself). The answer is clear: The project should be rejected. For future reference, our discussion of the WACC is summarized in Table 12.1. Our nearby *Finance Matters* box discusses a different use of the WACC.

Calculating the WACC for Eastman Chemical

In this section, we illustrate how to calculate the WACC for Eastman Chemical, a well-known chemical, plastics, and fiber producer. Our goal is to take you through, on a step-by-step basis, the process of finding and using the information needed using online sources. As you will see, there is a fair amount of detail involved, but the necessary information is, for the most part, readily available.

FINANCE MATTERS

◄ For the latest news on the topics covered in this chapter, scan here

The Cost of Capital, Texas Style

We have seen how the WACC is used in the corporate world. It is also used by state governments to value property for tax purposes. Property valuation can be tricky. The value of a home depends on what it could be sold for, which is not too hard to estimate, but how do you value an oil or gas field? For the Texas Comptroller of Public Accounts, the answer is to estimate the present value

12.56 percent and Murphy has the highest at 16.30 percent, but most other companies are in the 13 to 15 percent range. The average WACC for a company in this industry is 14.55 percent, with a standard deviation of 1.20 percent. When Texas uses this calculation, a two percent adjustment factor is added, plus any property-specific risk adjustment.

2011 Property Value Study: Discount Rate for Oil and Gas Properties

Table 1: Integrated Petroleum Companies' Financial Information Used for WACC Method

Company Name	Total Capital	Total Equity	Total Convertible Preferred Stock	Total Long-Term Debt	Equity % of Capital	Convertible Preferred Stock % of Capital	Long-Term Debt % of Capital	Beta Factor	After Income Tax Cost of Equity, %	Before Income Tax Cost of Equity, %	Cost of Convertible Preferred Stock %	Cost of Debt %	Before Income Tax WACC %
Anadarko	$52,263,592,000	$37,790,592,000	$0	$14,473,000,000	72.31	0.000	27.69	1.20	11.04	16.98	0.00	5.82	13.89
Apache	$53,742,567,399	$45,592,567,399	$55,000,000	$8,095,000,000	84.84	0.102	15.06	1.25	11.34	17.44	4.35	4.22	15.44
Chevron	$194,471,621,266	$183,182,621,266	$0	$11,289,000,000	94.20	0.000	5.80	0.90	9.24	14.21	0.00	3.18	13.57
Conoco Phillips	$120,091,121,493	$97,435,121,493	$0	$22,656,000,000	81.13	0.000	18.87	1.10	10.44	16.06	0.00	4.29	13.84
ExxonMobil	$376,291,480,000	$364,064,480,000	$0	$12,227,000,000	96.75	0.000	3.25	0.75	8.34	12.83	0.00	4.67	12.56
Hess	$31,383,103,740	$25,846,103,740	$0	$5,537,000,000	82.36	0.000	17.64	1.20	11.04	16.98	0.00	5.46	14.95
Marathon	$33,892,300,000	$26,291,300,000	$0	$7,601,000,000	77.57	0.000	22.43	1.25	11.34	17.44	0.00	4.55	14.55
Murphy	$15,315,274,396	$14,375,924,396	$0	$939,350,000	93.87	0.000	6.13	1.20	11.04	16.98	0.00	5.93	16.30
Occidental	$84,846,166,348	$79,735,166,348	$0	$5,111,000,000	93.98	0.000	6.02	1.15	10.74	16.52	0.00	5.47	15.85
TOTAL	$962,297,226,642	$874,313,876,642	$55,000,000	$87,928,350,000	777.00	0.102	122.90	10.00	94.53	145.43	4.35	43.58	130.94
ENTRIES					9	1	9	9	9	9	1	9	9
AVERAGE					86.33	0.102	13.66	1.11	10.50	16.16	4.35	4.84	14.55
STANDARD DEVIATION					8.69	0.034	8.69	0.17	1.04	1.60	1.45	0.90	1.20

of the future cash flows of the property. As you know by now, the cost of capital depends on the use of funds, not the source of funds. So, Texas calculates the WACC for companies in the oil industry and adjusts the industry average WACC for company-specific factors. The table above shows the state's calculations for integrated oil companies.

As you can see, the WACC numbers for the companies are similar. ExxonMobil has the lowest WACC at

Notice that the Texas Comptroller of Public Accounts calculated these numbers on a pretax, rather than aftertax, basis. In other words, the state did not account for the tax deductibility of interest payments in this calculation. The reason is that the state adjusts the cost of capital for taxes on a company-by-company basis.

Eastman's Cost of Equity   Our first stop is the stock price for Eastman, available at finance.yahoo.com (ticker: "EMN"). As of early 2012, here's what the screen looked like:

Eastman Chemical Company Common (EMN) - NYSE

53.74 ↓0.40(0.73%) 3:11PM EST - Nasdaq Real Time Price

Prev Close:	54.13	Day's Range:	53.71 - 54.61
Open:	54.34	52wk Range:	32.45 - 55.36
Bid:	53.88 x 300	Volume:	1,141,499
Ask:	53.89 x 200	Avg Vol (3m):	1,988,190
1y Target Est:	57.00	Market Cap:	7.38B
Beta:	2.31	P/E (ttm):	11.07
Next Earnings Date:	N/A	EPS (ttm):	4.86
		Div & Yield:	1.04 (1.90%)

We next looked under the "Key Statistics" link. Here is what we found:

Balance Sheet	
Total Cash (mrq):	777.00M
Total Cash Per Share (mrq):	5.68
Total Debt (mrq):	1.60B
Total Debt/Equity (mrq):	85.45
Current Ratio (mrq):	2.07
Book Value Per Share (mrq):	13.66
Cash Flow Statement	
Operating Cash Flow (ttm):	625.00M
Levered Free Cash Flow (ttm):	332.75M

Stock Price History	
Beta:	2.31
52-Week Change[3]:	11.26%
S&P500 52-Week Change[3]:	2.61%
52-Week High (Apr 29, 2011)[3]:	55.36
52-Week Low (Sep 22, 2011)[3]:	32.45
50-Day Moving Average[3]:	51.10
200-Day Moving Average[3]:	41.39
Share Statistics	
Avg Vol (3 month)[3]:	1,988,190
Avg Vol (10 day)[3]:	1,633,570
Shares Outstanding[5]:	136.92M
Float:	136.01M
% Held by Insiders[1]:	0.53%
% Held by Institutions[1]:	80.40%
Shares Short (as of Feb 15, 2012)[3]:	5.81M
Short Ratio (as of Feb 15, 2012)[3]:	2.40
Short % of Float (as of Feb 15, 2012)[3]:	4.10%
Shares Short (prior month)[3]:	2.01M

Dividends & Splits	
Forward Annual Dividend Rate[4]:	1.04
Forward Annual Dividend Yield[4]:	1.90%
Trailing Annual Dividend Yield[3]:	0.99
Trailing Annual Dividend Yield[3]:	1.80%
5 Year Average Dividend Yield[4]:	3.30%
Payout Ratio[4]:	20.00%
Dividend Date[3]:	Apr 1, 2012
Ex-Dividend Date[4]:	Mar 13, 2012
Last Split Factor (new per old)[2]:	2:1
Last Split Date[3]:	Oct 4, 2011

According to this screen, Eastman has 136.92 million shares of stock outstanding. The book value per share is $13.66, but the stock sells for $53.74. Total equity is therefore about $1.870 billion on a book value basis, but it is closer to $7.358 billion on a market value basis.

To estimate Eastman's cost of equity, we will assume a market risk premium of 7 percent, similar to what we saw in Chapter 10. Eastman's beta on Yahoo! is 2.31, which is more than twice as high as the beta of the average stock. This value seems high for this type of company, so we looked at the beta reported in Value Line. The beta reported there was a more reasonable 1.25, so we will use that number in our calculations According to the bond section of finance.yahoo.com, T-bills were paying about 0.05 percent. Using the CAPM to estimate the cost of equity, we find:

$$R_E = .0005 + 1.25(.07) = .0880, \text{ or } 8.80\%$$

Eastman has only paid dividends for a few years, so calculating the future growth rate for the dividend discount model is problematic. However, under the analysts' estimates link at finance.yahoo.com, we found the following:

Growth Est	EMN	Industry	Sector	S&P 500
Current Qtr.	-11.90%	21.70%	9.10%	13.40%
Next Qtr.	-2.20%	26.50%	15.80%	17.70%
This Year	6.40%	14.50%	19.40%	9.00%
Next Year	12.00%	-3.20%	9.60%	13.10%
Past 5 Years (per annum)	18.64%	N/A	N/A	N/A
Next 5 Years (per annum)	7.67%	13.55%	11.17%	10.38%
Price/Earnings (avg. for comparison categories)	11.16	17.08	13.03	14.31
PEG Ratio (avg. for comparison categories)	1.46	1.31	1.65	1.81

Analysts estimate the growth in earnings per share for the company will be 7.67 percent for the next five years. For now, we will use this growth rate in the dividend discount model to estimate the cost of equity; the link between earnings growth and dividends is discussed in a later chapter. The estimated cost of equity using the dividend discount model is thus:

$$R_E = \left(\frac{\$1.04(1 + .0767)}{\$53.74} \right) + .0767 = .0975, \text{ or } 9.75\%$$

Notice that the estimates for the cost of equity are quite different, probably due, at least in part, to the relatively high growth rate and dividend yield we used. In broader terms, remember that each method of estimating the cost of equity relies on different assumptions, so different estimates should not surprise us. If the estimates are different, there are two simple solutions. First, we could ignore one of the estimates. We would look at each estimate to see if one of them seemed too high or too low to be reasonable. Second, we could average the two estimates. Averaging the two estimates for Eastman's cost of equity gives us a cost of equity of 9.28 percent. Since this seems like a reasonable number, we will use it in calculating the cost of capital.

Eastman's Cost of Debt   Eastman has seven long-term bond issues that account for essentially all of its long-term debt. To calculate the cost of debt, we will have to combine these five issues. What we will do is compute a weighted average. We went to www.nasdbondinfo.com to find quotes on the bonds. We should note here that finding the yield to maturity for all of a company's outstanding bond issues on a single day is unusual. If you remember our previous discussion on bonds, the bond market is not as liquid as the stock market, and, on many days, individual bond issues may not trade. To find the book value of the bonds, we went to www.sec.gov and found the 10K report dated December 31, 2011, and filed with the SEC on February 22, 2012. The basic information is as follows:

Coupon Rate	Maturity	Book Value (face value, in millions)	Price (% of par)	Yield to Maturity
3.00%	2015	$250	103.513%	2.028%
6.30	2018	176	117.634	3.342
5.50	2019	250	114.180	3.390
4.50	2021	250	106.992	3.570
7.25	2024	243	121.530	4.843
7.625	2024	54	122.308	5.151
7.60	2027	222	126.478	5.051

To calculate the weighted average cost of debt, we take the percentage of the total debt represented by each issue and multiply by the yield on the issue. We then add to get the overall weighted average debt cost. We use both book values and market values here for comparison. The results of the calculations are as follows:

Coupon Rate	Book Value (face value, in millions)	Percentage of Total	Market Value (in millions)	Percentage of Total	Yield to Maturity	Book Values	Market Values
3.00%	$ 250	0.17	$ 258.78	0.16	2.03%	0.35%	0.32%
6.30	176	0.12	207.04	0.12	3.34	0.41	0.42
5.50	250	0.17	285.45	0.17	3.39	0.59	0.58
4.50	250	0.17	267.48	0.16	3.57	0.62	0.57
7.25	243	0.17	295.32	0.18	4.84	0.81	0.86
7.63	54	0.04	66.05	0.04	5.15	0.19	0.20
7.60	222	0.15	280.78	0.17	5.05	0.78	0.85
	$1,445	1.00	$1,660.89	1.00		3.74%	3.81%

As these calculations show, Eastman's cost of debt is 3.74 percent on a book value basis and 3.81 percent on a market value basis. Thus, for Eastman, whether market values or book values are used makes little difference. The reason is simply that the market values and book values are similar. This will often be the case and explains why companies frequently use book values for debt in WACC calculations. Also, Eastman has no preferred stock, so we don't need to consider a cost of preferred.

Eastman's WACC   We now have the various pieces necessary to estimate Eastman's WACC. First, we need to calculate the capital structure weights. On a book value basis, Eastman's equity and debt are worth $1.870 billion and $1.445 billion, respectively. The total value is $3.315 billion, so the equity and debt percentages are $1.870 billion/3.315 billion = .56 and $1.445 billion/3.315 billion = .44. Assuming a tax rate of 35 percent, Eastman's WACC is:

$$\text{WACC} = .56 \times 9.28\% + .44 \times 3.74\% \times (1 - .35)$$
$$= 6.29\%$$

Thus, using book value capital structure weights, we get about 6.29 percent for Eastman's WACC.

If we use market value weights, however, the WACC will be higher. To see why, notice that on a market value basis, Eastman's equity and debt are worth $7.358 billion and $1.661 billion, respectively. The capital structure weights are therefore $7.358 billion/9.019 billion = .82 and $1.661 billion/9.019 billion = .18, so the equity percentage is much higher. With these weights, Eastman's WACC is:

$$\text{WACC} = .82 \times 9.28\% + .18 \times 3.81\% \times (1 - .35)$$
$$= 8.02\%$$

Thus, using market value weights, we get 8.02 percent for Eastman's WACC, which is noticeably higher than the 6.29 percent WACC we got using book value weights.

As this example illustrates, using book values can lead to trouble, particularly if equity book values are used. Going back to Chapter 3, recall that we discussed the market-to-book ratio (the ratio of market value per share to book value per share). This ratio is often substantially bigger than 1. For Eastman, for example, verify that it's about 3.93, so book values significantly overstate the percentage of Eastman's financing that comes from debt.

In addition, if we were computing a WACC for a company that did not have publicly traded stock, we would try to come up with a suitable market-to-book ratio by looking at publicly traded companies, and we would then use this ratio to adjust the book value of the company under consideration. As we have seen, failure to do so can lead to significant underestimation of the WACC. See our nearby *Work the Web* box for more on the WACC.

WORK THE WEB

So how does our estimate of the WACC for Eastman compare to others? One place to find estimates for WACC is www.valuepro.net. We went there and found the following information for Eastman.

◄ To get updated data, scan here.

Online Valuation for EMN - 3 / 1 / 2012

Intrinsic Stock Value 150.49   Recalculate   Value Another Stock

Excess Return Period (yrs)	10	Depreciation Rate (% of Rev)	4.79
Revenues ($mil)	7178.0	Investment Rate (% of Rev)	4.16
Growth Rate (%)	13.5	Working Capital (% of Rev)	2.6
Net Oper. Profit Margin (%)	13.35	Short-Term Assets ($mil)	2354.0
Tax Rate (%)	34.103	Short-Term Liab. ($mil)	1250
Stock Price ($)	54.5300	Equity Risk Premium (%)	3
Shares Outstanding (mil)	137.6	Company Beta	1.3125
10-Yr Treasury Yield (%)	5	Value Debt Out. ($mil)	1445
Bond Spread Treasury (%)	1.5	Value Pref. Stock Out. ($mil)	0
Preferred Stock Yield (%)	7.5	Company WACC (%)	8.19

As you can see, ValuePro estimates the WACC for Eastman as 8.19 percent, which is about the same as our estimate of 8.02 percent. The methods used by this site are not identical to ours, but they are similar in the most important regards. However, notice that several important estimates differ. For example, ValuePro uses a market risk premium of 3 percent, while our estimate was 7 percent. Using our estimate of the market risk premium in the ValuePro website results in a WACC estimate of 12.59 percent, which is higher than our estimate. Visit the site to learn more if you are so inclined.

CONCEPT QUESTIONS

12.4a   How is the WACC calculated?

12.4b   Why do we multiply the cost of debt by $(1 - T_C)$ when we compute the WACC?

12.4c   Under what conditions is it correct to use the WACC to determine NPV?

12.5   DIVISIONAL AND PROJECT COSTS OF CAPITAL

As we have seen, using the WACC as the discount rate for future cash flows is only appropriate when the proposed investment is similar to the firm's existing activities. This is not as restrictive as it sounds. If we were in the pizza business, for example, and we were thinking of opening a new location, then the WACC would be the discount rate to use. The same would be true of a retailer thinking of a new store, a manufacturer thinking of expanding production, or a consumer products company thinking of expanding its markets.

Nonetheless, despite the usefulness of the WACC as a benchmark, there will clearly be situations where the cash flows under consideration have risks distinctly different from those of the overall firm. We consider how to cope with this problem next.

The SML and the WACC

When we are evaluating investments with risks that are substantially different from those of the overall firm, the use of the WACC will potentially lead to poor decisions. Figure 12.1 illustrates why.

FIGURE 12.1

The security market line, SML, and the weighted average cost of capital, WACC

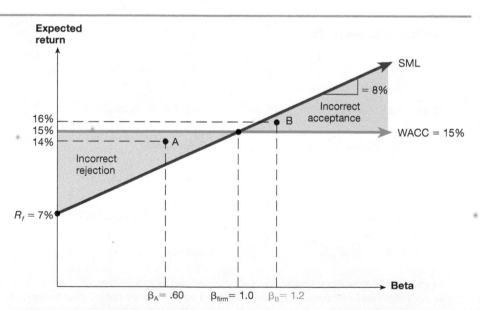

If a firm uses its WACC to make accept-reject decisions for all types of projects, it will have a tendency toward incorrectly accepting risky projects and incorrectly rejecting less risky projects.

In Figure 12.1, we have plotted an SML corresponding to a risk-free rate of 7 percent and a market risk premium of 8 percent. To keep things simple, we consider an all-equity company with a beta of 1. As we have indicated, the WACC and the cost of equity are exactly equal to 15 percent for this company since there is no debt.

Suppose our firm uses its WACC to evaluate all investments. This means that any investment with a return of greater than 15 percent will be accepted and any investment with a return of less than 15 percent will be rejected. We know from our study of risk and return, however, that a desirable investment is one that plots above the SML. As Figure 12.1 illustrates, using the WACC for all types of projects can result in the firm's incorrectly accepting relatively risky projects and incorrectly rejecting relatively safe ones.

For example, consider Point A. This project has a beta of $\beta_A = .60$ compared to the firm's beta of 1.0. It has an expected return of 14 percent. Is this a desirable investment? The answer is yes, because its required return is only:

Required return $= R_f + \beta_A \times (R_M - R_f)$

$\qquad\qquad\qquad = 7\% + .60 \times 8\%$

$\qquad\qquad\qquad = 11.8\%$

However, if we use the WACC as a cutoff, then this project will be rejected because its return is less than 15 percent. This example illustrates that a firm that uses its WACC as a cutoff will tend to reject profitable projects with risks less than those of the overall firm.

At the other extreme, consider Point B. This project has a beta of $\beta_B = 1.2$. It offers a 16 percent return, which exceeds the firm's cost of capital. This is not a good investment, however, because, given its level of systematic risk, its return is inadequate. Nonetheless, if we use the WACC to evaluate it, it will appear to be attractive. So the second error that will arise if we use the WACC as a cutoff is that we will tend to make unprofitable investments with risks greater than those of the overall firm. As a consequence, through time, a firm that uses its WACC to evaluate all projects will have a tendency to both accept unprofitable investments and become increasingly risky.

Divisional Cost of Capital

The same type of problem with the WACC can arise in a corporation with more than one line of business. Imagine, for example, a corporation that has two divisions, a regulated telephone company and an electronics manufacturing operation. The first of these (the phone operation) has relatively low risk; the second has relatively high risk.

In this case, the firm's overall cost of capital is really a mixture of two different costs of capital, one for each division. If the two divisions were competing for resources, and the firm used a single WACC as a cutoff, which division would tend to be awarded greater funds for investment?

The answer is that the riskier division would tend to have greater returns (ignoring the greater risk), so it would tend to be the "winner." The less glamorous operation might have great profit potential that would end up being ignored. Large corporations in the United States are aware of this problem, and many work to develop separate divisional costs of capital.

The Pure Play Approach

We've seen that using the firm's WACC inappropriately can lead to problems. How can we come up with the appropriate discount rates in such circumstances? Because we cannot observe the returns on these investments, there generally is no direct way of coming up with a beta, for example. Instead, what we must do is examine other investments outside the firm that are in the same risk class as the one we are considering and use the market-required returns on these investments as the discount rate. In other words, we will try to determine what the cost of capital is for such investments by trying to locate some similar investments in the marketplace.

For example, going back to our telephone division, suppose we want to come up with a discount rate to use for that division. What we can do is identify several other phone companies that have publicly traded securities. We might find that a typical phone company has a beta of .80, AA-rated debt, and a capital structure that is about 50 percent debt and 50 percent equity. Using this information, we could develop a WACC for a typical phone company and use this as our discount rate.

Alternatively, if we were thinking of entering a new line of business, we would try to develop the appropriate cost of capital by looking at the market-required returns on companies already in that business. In the language of Wall Street, a company that focuses only on a single line of business is called a *pure play*. For example, if you wanted to bet on the price of crude oil by purchasing common stocks, you would try to identify companies that dealt exclusively with this product since they would be the most affected by changes in the price of crude oil. Such companies would be called *pure plays* on the price of crude oil.

pure play approach
Use of a WACC that is unique to a particular project, based on companies in similar lines of business.

What we try to do here is to find companies that focus as exclusively as possible on the type of project in which we are interested. Our approach, therefore, is called the **pure play approach** to estimating the required return on an investment. To illustrate, suppose McDonald's decides to enter the personal computer and network server business with a line of machines called McPuters. The risks involved are quite different from those in the fast-food business. As a result, McDonald's would need to look at companies already in the personal computer business to compute a cost of capital for the new division. An obvious "pure play" candidate would be Dell, which is predominately in this line of business. IBM, on the other hand, would not be as good a choice because its primary focus is elsewhere, and it has many different product lines.

In Chapter 3, we discussed the subject of identifying similar companies for comparison purposes. The same problems we described there come up here. The most obvious one is that we may not be able to find any suitable companies. In this case, how to objectively determine a discount rate becomes a very difficult question. Even so, the important thing is to be aware of the issue so that we at least reduce the possibility of the kinds of mistakes that can arise when the WACC is used as a cutoff on all investments.

The Subjective Approach

Because of the difficulties that exist in objectively establishing discount rates for individual projects, firms often adopt an approach that involves making subjective adjustments to the overall WACC. To illustrate, suppose a firm has an overall WACC of 14 percent. It places all proposed projects into four categories as follows:

Category	Examples	Adjustment Factor	Discount Rate
High risk	New products	+6%	20%
Moderate risk	Cost savings, expansion of existing lines	+0	14
Low risk	Replacement of existing equipment	−4	10
Mandatory	Pollution control equipment	n/a	n/a

n/a = Not applicable.

The effect of this crude partitioning is to assume that all projects either fall into one of three risk classes or else are mandatory. In this last case, the cost of capital is irrelevant since the project must be taken. Of course, the firm's WACC may change through time as economic conditions change. As this happens, the discount rates for the different types of projects will also change.

Within each risk class, some projects will presumably have more risk than others, and the danger of incorrect decisions will still exist. Figure 12.2 illustrates this point. Comparing Figures 12.1 and 12.2, we see that similar problems exist, but the magnitude of the potential error is less with the subjective approach. For example, the project labeled "A" would be accepted if the WACC were used, but it is rejected once it is classified as a high risk investment. What this illustrates is that some risk adjustment, even if it is subjective, is probably better than no risk adjustment.

It would be better, in principle, to objectively determine the required return for each project separately. However, as a practical matter, it may not be possible to go much beyond subjective adjustments because either the necessary information is unavailable or else the cost and effort required are simply not worthwhile.

CONCEPT QUESTIONS

12.5a What are the likely consequences if a firm uses its WACC to evaluate all proposed investments?

12.5b What is the pure play approach to determining the appropriate discount rate? When might it be used?

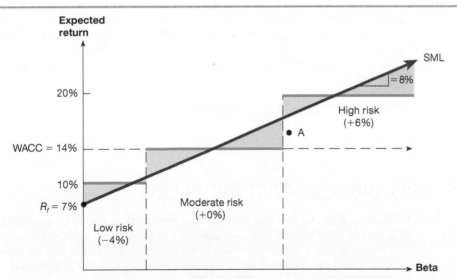

FIGURE 12.2

The security market line, SML, and the subjective approach

With the subjective approach, the firm places projects into one of several risk classes. The discount rate used to value the project is then determined by adding (for high risk) or subtracting (for low risk) an adjustment factor to or from the firm's WACC. This results in fewer incorrect decisions than if the firm simply used the WACC to make the decisions.

SUMMARY AND CONCLUSIONS

 ◄ Think you've mastered the material? Scan here to take a chapter quiz.

This chapter has discussed cost of capital. The most important concept is the weighted average cost of capital, or WACC, which we interpreted as the required rate of return on the overall firm. It is also the discount rate appropriate for cash flows that are similar in risk to the overall firm. We described how the WACC can be calculated, and we illustrated how it can be used in certain types of analysis.

We also pointed out situations in which it is inappropriate to use the WACC as the discount rate. To handle such cases, we described some alternative approaches to developing discount rates, such as the pure play approach.

 ≡connect POP QUIZ!
|FINANCE

Can you answer the following questions? If your class is using *Connect Finance,* log on to the Self-Quiz and Study feature in the Library tab to see if you know the answers to these and other questions, check out the study tools, and find out what topics require additional practice!

Section 12.1 The cost of capital for a project depends primarily on what?

Section 12.2 The Lo Tech Co. just issued a dividend of $3.10 per share on its common stock. The company is expected to maintain a constant 4 percent growth rate in its dividends indefinitely. If the stock sells for $43.90 a share, what is the company's cost of equity?

Section 12.3 You have $268,000 to invest in a stock portfolio. Your choices are Stock H, with an expected return of 14.3 percent, and Stock L, with an expected return of 11.9 percent. If your goal is to create a portfolio with an expected return of 12.90 percent, how much money will you invest in Stock H and in Stock L?

CHAPTER REVIEW AND SELF-TEST PROBLEMS

12.1   Calculating the Cost of Equity.   Suppose stock in Boone Corporation has a beta of .90. The market risk premium is 7 percent, and the risk-free rate is 8 percent. Boone's last dividend was $1.80 per share, and the dividend is expected to grow at 7 percent indefinitely. The stock currently sells for $25. What is Boone's cost of equity capital? (See Problem 1.)

12.2   Calculating the WACC.   In addition to the information in the previous problem, suppose Boone has a target debt-equity ratio of 50 percent. Its cost of debt is 8 percent, before taxes. If the tax rate is 34 percent, what is the WACC? (See Problem 10.)

■ Answers to Chapter Review and Self-Test Problems

12.1   We start off with the SML approach. Based on the information given, the expected return on Boone's common stock is:

$$R_E = R_f + \beta_E \times (R_M - R_f)$$
$$= 8\% + .9 \times 7\%$$
$$= 14.3\%$$

We now use the dividend growth model. The projected dividend is $D_0 \times (1 + g) =$ $\$1.80 \times 1.07 = \$1.926$, so the expected return using this approach is:

$$R_E = D_1/P_0 + g$$
$$= \$1.926/25 + .07$$
$$= 14.704\%$$

Since these two estimates, 14.3 percent and 14.7 percent, are fairly close, we will average them. Boone's cost of equity is approximately 14.5 percent.

12.2   Since the target debt-equity ratio is .50, Boone uses $.50 in debt for every $1.00 in equity. In other words, Boone's target capital structure is ⅓ debt and ⅔ equity. The WACC is thus:

$$WACC = (E/V) \times R_E + (D/V) \times R_D \times (1 - T_C)$$
$$= \tfrac{2}{3} \times 14.5\% + \tfrac{1}{3} \times 8\% \times (1 - .34)$$
$$= 11.427\%$$

CRITICAL THINKING AND CONCEPTS REVIEW

LO 3   **12.1**   **WACC.**   On the most basic level, if a firm's WACC is 12 percent, what does this mean?

LO 3   **12.2**   **Book Values versus Market Values.**   In calculating the WACC, if you had to use book values for either debt or equity, which would you choose? Why?

LO 4   **12.3**   **Project Risk.**   If you can borrow all the money you need for a project at 6 percent, doesn't it follow that 6 percent is your cost of capital for the project?

LO 4   **12.4**   **WACC and Taxes.**   Why do we use an aftertax figure for cost of debt but not for cost of equity?

LO 1   **12.5**   **DGM Cost of Equity Estimation.**   What are the advantages of using the dividend growth model (DGM) for determining the cost of equity capital? What are the disadvantages? What specific piece of information do you need to find the cost of equity using this model? What are some of the ways in which you could get an estimate of this number?

LO 1   **12.6**   **SML Cost of Equity Estimation.**   What are the advantages of using the SML approach to finding the cost of equity capital? What are the disadvantages? What are the specific pieces of information needed to use this method? Are all of these variables observable, or do they need to be estimated? What are some of the ways in which you could get these estimates?

LO 2   **12.7**   **Cost of Debt Estimation.**   How do you determine the appropriate cost of debt for a company? Does it make a difference if the company's debt is privately placed as opposed to being publicly traded? How would you estimate the cost of debt for a firm whose only debt issues are privately held by institutional investors?

www.mhhe.com/rwj

412   **PART 7** Long-Term Financing

LO 4 **12.8** **Cost of Capital.**   Suppose Tom O'Bedlam, president of Bedlam Products, Inc., has hired you to determine the firm's cost of debt and cost of equity capital.

   a. The stock currently sells for $50 per share, and the dividend per share will probably be about $5. Tom argues, "It will cost us $5 per share to use the stockholders' money this year, so the cost of equity is equal to 10 percent (=$5/50)." What's wrong with this conclusion?

   b. Based on the most recent financial statements, Bedlam Products' total liabilities are $8 million. Total interest expense for the coming year will be about $1 million. Tom therefore reasons, "We owe $8 million, and we will pay $1 million interest. Therefore, our cost of debt is obviously $1 million/ 8 million = 12.5%." What's wrong with this conclusion?

   c. Based on his own analysis, Tom is recommending that the company increase its use of equity financing, because "Debt costs 12.5 percent, but equity only costs 10 percent; thus equity is cheaper." Ignoring all the other issues, what do you think about the conclusion that the cost of equity is less than the cost of debt?

LO 4 **12.9** **Company Risk versus Project Risk.**   Both Dow Chemical Company, a large natural gas user, and Superior Oil, a major natural gas producer, are thinking of investing in natural gas wells near Houston. Both are all-equity–financed companies. Dow and Superior are looking at identical projects. They've analyzed their respective investments, which would involve a negative cash flow now and positive expected cash flows in the future. These cash flows would be the same for both firms. No debt would be used to finance the projects. Both companies estimate that their project would have a net present value of $1 million at an 18 percent discount rate and a −$1.1 million NPV at a 22 percent discount rate. Dow has a beta of 1.25, whereas Superior has a beta of .75. The expected risk premium on the market is 8 percent, and risk-free bonds are yielding 12 percent. Should either company proceed? Should both? Explain.

LO 4 **12.10** **Divisional Cost of Capital.**   Under what circumstances would it be appropriate for a firm to use different costs of capital for its different operating divisions? If the overall firm WACC were used as the hurdle rate for all divisions, would the riskier divisions or the more conservative divisions tend to get most of the investment projects? Why? If you were to try to estimate the appropriate cost of capital for different divisions, what problems might you encounter? What are two techniques you could use to develop a rough estimate for each division's cost of capital?

QUESTIONS AND PROBLEMS   ▓ connect   FINANCE

Basic
(Questions 1–20)

LO 1 **1. Calculating Cost of Equity.**   The Lo Tech Co. just issued a dividend of $1.80 per share on its common stock. The company is expected to maintain a constant 6 percent growth rate in its dividends indefinitely. If the stock sells for $41 a share, what is the company's cost of equity?

LO 1 **2. Calculating Cost of Equity.**   Halestorm Corporation's common stock has a beta of 1.15. If the risk-free rate is 3.9 percent and the expected return on the market is 12 percent, what is the company's cost of equity capital?

LO 1   3. **Calculating Cost of Equity.**   Stock in CDB Industries has a beta of .90. The market risk premium is 7 percent, and T-bills are currently yielding 3.5 percent. CDB's most recent dividend was $1.80 per share, and dividends are expected to grow at a 5 percent annual rate indefinitely. If the stock sells for $47 per share, what is your best estimate of CDB's cost of equity?

LO 1   4. **Estimating the DCF Growth Rate.**   Suppose Powers Ltd. just issued a dividend of $1.20 per share on its common stock. The company paid dividends of $.85, $.92, $.99, and $1.09 per share in the last four years. If the stock currently sells for $53, what is your best estimate of the company's cost of equity capital using arithmetic and geometric growth rates?

LO 1   5. **Calculating Cost of Preferred Stock.**   Sixth Fourth Bank has an issue of preferred stock with a $6.25 stated dividend that just sold for $108 per share. What is the bank's cost of preferred stock?

LO 2   6. **Calculating Cost of Debt.**   ICU Window, Inc., is trying to determine its cost of debt. The firm has a debt issue outstanding with seven years to maturity that is quoted at 108 percent of face value. The issue makes semiannual payments and has an embedded cost of 6.1 percent annually. What is ICU's pretax cost of debt? If the tax rate is 38 percent, what is the aftertax cost of debt?

LO 2   7. **Calculating Cost of Debt.**   Jiminy's Cricket Farm issued a 30-year, 6.5 percent semiannual bond 7 years ago. The bond currently sells for 107 percent of its face value. The company's tax rate is 35 percent.

    a.   What is the pretax cost of debt?

    b.   What is the aftertax cost of debt?

    c.   Which is more relevant, the pretax or the aftertax cost of debt? Why?

LO 2   8. **Calculating Cost of Debt.**   For the firm in Problem 7, suppose the book value of the debt issue is $105 million. In addition, the company has a second debt issue, a zero coupon bond with 10 years left to maturity; the book value of this issue is $75 million, and it sells for 62.5 percent of par. What is the total book value of debt? The total market value? What is the aftertax cost of debt now?

LO 3   9. **Calculating WACC.**   Mullineaux Corporation has a target capital structure of 75 percent common stock, 5 percent preferred stock, and 20 percent debt. Its cost of equity is 11.25 percent, the cost of preferred stock is 5.5 percent, and the cost of debt is 6.1 percent. The relevant tax rate is 35 percent.

    a.   What is Mullineaux's WACC?

    b.   The company president has approached you about Mullineaux's capital structure. He wants to know why the company doesn't use more preferred stock financing, since it costs less than debt. What would you tell the president?

LO 3   10. **Taxes and WACC.**   Benjamin Manufacturing has a target debt-equity ratio of .45. Its cost of equity is 12 percent, and its cost of debt is 7 percent. If the tax rate is 35 percent, what is the company's WACC?

LO 3   11. **Finding the Target Capital Structure.**   Fama's Llamas has a WACC of 8.65 percent. The company's cost of equity is 11 percent, and its cost of debt is 6 percent. The tax rate is 35 percent. What is Fama's target debt-equity ratio?

LO 4   12. **Book Value versus Market Value.**   Vedder, Inc., has 5 million shares of common stock outstanding. The current share price is $73, and the book value per share is $9. Vedder also has two bond issues outstanding. The first bond issue has a face value of $60 million, a coupon rate of 7 percent, and sells for 98 percent of par. The second issue has a face value of $40 million, a coupon rate of 6.5 percent, and sells for 97 percent of par. The first issue matures in 20 years, the second in 12 years.

    a. What are the company's capital structure weights on a book value basis?

    b. What are the company's capital structure weights on a market value basis?

    c. Which are more relevant, the book or market value weights? Why?

LO 3   **13. Calculating the WACC.** In Problem 12, suppose the most recent dividend was $2.85 and the dividend growth rate is 6 percent. Assume that the overall cost of debt is the weighted average of that implied by the two outstanding debt issues. Both bonds make semiannual payments. The tax rate is 35 percent. What is the company's WACC?

LO 3   **14. WACC.** Blue Bull, Inc., has a target debt-equity ratio of .55. Its WACC is 8.1 percent, and the tax rate is 35 percent.

    a. If the company's cost of equity is 11 percent, what is its pretax cost of debt?

    b. If the aftertax cost of debt is 3.8 percent, what is the cost of equity?

LO 3   **15. Finding the WACC.** Given the following information for Janicek Power Co., find the WACC. Assume the company's tax rate is 35 percent.

Debt:	8,500 7.2 percent coupon bonds outstanding, $1,000 par value, 25 years to maturity, selling for 118 percent of par; the bonds make semiannual payments.
Common stock:	225,000 shares outstanding, selling for $87 per share; beta is 1.15.
Preferred stock:	15,000 shares of 4.8 percent preferred stock outstanding, currently selling for $98 per share.
Market:	7 percent market risk premium and 3.1 percent risk-free rate.

LO 3   **16. Finding the WACC.** Organic Produce Corporation has 6.3 million shares of common stock outstanding, 350,000 shares of 5.8 percent preferred stock outstanding, and 150,000 of 7.1 percent semiannual bonds outstanding, par value $1,000 each. The common stock currently sells for $74 per share and has a beta of 1.09, the preferred stock currently sells for $107 per share, and the bonds have 20 years to maturity and sell for 109 percent of par. The market risk premium is 6.8 percent, T-bills are yielding 4.3 percent, and the firm's tax rate is 34 percent.

    a. What is the firm's market value capital structure?

    b. If the firm is evaluating a new investment project that has the same risk as the firm's typical project, what rate should the firm use to discount the project's cash flows?

LO 4   **17. SML and WACC.** An all-equity firm is considering the following projects:

Project	Beta	IRR
W	.80	10.2%
X	.90	11.4
Y	1.10	12.6
Z	1.35	15.1

The T-bill rate is 4 percent, and the expected return on the market is 12 percent.

a. Which projects have a higher expected return than the firm's 12 percent cost of capital?

b. Which projects should be accepted?

c. Which projects will be incorrectly accepted or rejected if the firm's overall cost of capital were used as a hurdle rate?

LO 3 **18. Calculating the WACC.** You are given the following information concerning Parrothead Enterprises:

Debt:	10,000 6.9 percent coupon bonds outstanding, with 15 years to maturity and a quoted price of 104. These bonds pay interest semiannually.
Common stock:	275,000 shares of common stock selling for $68.50 per share. The stock has a beta of .85 and will pay a dividend of $3.25 next year. The dividend is expected to grow by 5 percent per year indefinitely.
Preferred stock:	8,000 shares of 4.9 percent preferred stock selling at $94 per share.
Market:	12 percent expected return, risk-free rate of 3.5 percent, and a 35 percent tax rate.

Calculate the WACC for Parrothead Enterprises.

LO 3 **19. Calculating Capital Structure Weights.** Bennington Industrial Machines issued 155,000 zero coupon bonds four years ago. The bonds originally had 30 years to maturity with a yield to maturity of 5.9 percent. Interest rates have recently increased, and the bonds now have a yield to maturity of 6.7 percent. If the company has a $55 million market value of equity, what weight should it use for debt when calculating the cost of capital?

LO 3 **20. Calculating the WACC.** Gnomes R Us is considering a new project. The company has a debt-equity ratio of .65. The company's cost of equity is 13.2 percent, and the aftertax cost of debt is 5.1 percent. The firm feels that the project is riskier than the company as a whole and that it should use an adjustment factor of +3 percent. What is the WACC it should use for the project?

LO 4 **21. WACC and NPV.** Nally, Inc., is considering a project that will result in initial aftertax cash savings of $4.2 million at the end of the first year, and these savings will grow at a rate of 2.5 percent per year indefinitely. The firm has a target debt-equity ratio of .25, a cost of equity of 13.1 percent, and an aftertax cost of debt of 6.4 percent. The cost-saving proposal is somewhat riskier than the usual project the firm undertakes; management uses the subjective approach and applies an adjustment factor of +2 percent to the cost of capital for such risky projects. Under what circumstances should the company take on the project?

Intermediate
(Questions 21–23)

LO 2 **22. Calculating the Cost of Debt.** Ying Import has several bond issues outstanding, each making semiannual interest payments. The bonds are listed in the table below. If the corporate tax rate is 34 percent, what is the aftertax cost of the company's debt?

Bond	Coupon Rate	Price Quote	Maturity	Face Value
1	7.5%	105.0	5 years	$20,000,000
2	5.8	95.4	8 years	40,000,000
3	7.7	103.8	15½ years	45,000,000
4	8.1	105.7	25 years	60,000,000

LO 1

23. Calculating the Cost of Equity. Laverne Industries stock has a beta of 1.15. The company just paid a dividend of $.95, and the dividends are expected to grow at 4 percent. The expected return of the market is 11.5 percent, and Treasury bills are yielding 3.8 percent. The most recent stock price is $81.

a. Calculate the cost of equity using the dividend growth model method.

b. Calculate the cost of equity using the SML method.

c. Why do you think your estimates in (a) and (b) are so different?

LO 3

Challenge
(Questions 24–25)

24. WACC and NPV. Photochronograph Corporation (PC) manufactures time series photographic equipment. It is currently at its target debt-equity ratio of .45. It's considering building a new $55 million manufacturing facility. This new plant is expected to generate aftertax cash flows of $7.4 million in perpetuity. There are three financing options:

a. *A new issue of common stock:* The required return on the company's new equity is 15 percent.

b. *A new issue of 20-year bonds:* If the company issues these new bonds at an annual coupon rate of 7 percent, they will sell at par.

c. *Increased use of accounts payable financing:* Because this financing is part of the company's ongoing daily business, the company assigns it a cost that is the same as the overall firm WACC. Management has a target ratio of accounts payable to long-term debt of .15. (Assume there is no difference between the pretax and aftertax accounts payable cost.)

What is the NPV of the new plant? Assume that the company has a 35 percent tax rate.

LO 3

25. Project Evaluation. This is a comprehensive project evaluation problem bringing together much of what you have learned in this and previous chapters. Suppose you have been hired as a financial consultant to Defense Electronics, Inc. (DEI), a large, publicly traded firm that is the market share leader in radar detection systems (RDSs). The company is looking at setting up a manufacturing plant overseas to produce a new line of RDSs. This will be a five-year project. The company bought some land three years ago for $4.5 million in anticipation of using it as a toxic dump site for waste chemicals, but it built a piping system to safely discard the chemicals instead. If the land were sold today, the net proceeds would be $5 million after taxes. In five years, the land will be worth $5.3 million after taxes. The company wants to build its new manufacturing plant on this land; the plant will cost $15 million to build. The following market data on DEI's securities are current:

Debt:	40,000 6.2 percent coupon bonds outstanding, 25 years to maturity, selling for 95 percent of par; the bonds have a $1,000 par value each and make semiannual payments.
Common stock:	825,000 shares outstanding, selling for $97 per share; the beta is 1.15.
Preferred stock:	45,000 shares of 5.8 percent preferred stock outstanding, selling for $95 per share.
Market:	7 percent expected market risk premium; 3.8 percent risk-free rate.

DEI's tax rate is 34 percent. The project requires $825,000 in initial net working capital investment to get operational.

a. Calculate the project's Time 0 cash flow, taking into account all side effects.

b. The new RDS project is somewhat riskier than a typical project for DEI, primarily because the plant is being located overseas. Management has told you to use an adjustment factor of +2 percent to account for this increased riskiness. Calculate the appropriate discount rate to use when evaluating DEI's project.

c. The manufacturing plant has an eight-year tax life, and DEI uses straight-line depreciation. At the end of the project (i.e., the end of year 5), the plant can be scrapped for $2.1 million. What is the aftertax salvage value of this manufacturing plant?

d. The company will incur $3,500,000 in annual fixed costs. The plan is to manufacture 12,000 RDSs per year and sell them at $10,800 per machine; the variable production costs are $9,900 per RDS. What is the annual operating cash flow, OCF, from this project?

e. Finally, DEI's president wants you to throw all your calculations, all your assumptions, and everything else into a report for the chief financial officer; all he wants to know is what the RDS project's internal rate of return, IRR, and net present value, NPV, are. What will you report?

12.1 Cost of Equity. Go to finance.yahoo.com and look up the information for Allegheny Technologies (ATI), a metal manufacturing company in the S&P 500. You want to estimate the cost of equity for the company. First, find the current Treasury bill rate. Next, find the beta for Allegheny Technologies. Using the historical market risk premium, what is the estimated cost of equity for ATI using the CAPM? Now find the analysts' growth rate estimates for the next five years for the company. Using this growth rate in the dividend growth model, what is the estimated cost of equity? Now find the dividends paid by the company over the past five years and calculate the arithmetic and geometric growth rates in dividends. Using these growth rates, what is the estimated cost of equity? Looking at these four estimates, what cost of equity would you use for the company?

12.2 Cost of Debt. Go to www.nasdbondinfo.com and look up the outstanding bonds for Nike. Record the most recent price and YTM of each bond issue. Now go to www.sec.gov and find the most recent 10Q or 10K report filed by the company and find the book value of each bond issue. Assuming Nike's tax rate is 38 percent, what is the cost of debt using book value weights? What is the cost of debt using market value weights? Which of these numbers is more relevant?

WHAT'S ON THE WEB?

CHAPTER CASE
COST OF CAPITAL FOR HUBBARD COMPUTER, INC.

You have recently been hired by Hubbard Computer, Inc. (HCI), in its relatively new treasury management department. HCI was founded eight years ago by Bob Hubbard and currently operates 74 stores in the Southeast. HCI is privately owned by Bob and his family, and had sales of $97 million last year.

HCI primarily sells to in-store customers who come to the store and talk with a sales representative. The sales representative assists the customer in determining the type of computer and peripherals that are necessary for the individual customer's computing needs. After the order is taken, the customer pays for the order immediately, and the computer is made to fill the order. Delivery of the computer averages 15 days, and it is guaranteed in 30 days.

HCI's growth to date has been financed by its profits. When the company had sufficient capital, it would open a new store. Other than scouting locations, relatively little formal analysis has been used in its capital budgeting process. Bob has just read about capital budgeting techniques and has come to you for help. For starters, the company has never attempted to determine its cost of capital, and Bob would like you to perform the analysis. Since the company is privately owned, it is difficult to determine the cost of equity for the company. Bob wants you to use the pure play approach to estimating the cost of capital for HCI, and he has chosen Dell as a representative company. The following steps will allow you to calculate this estimate.

QUESTIONS

1. Most publicly traded corporations are required to submit quarterly (10Q) and annual reports (10K) to the SEC detailing the financial operations of the company over the past quarter or year, respectively. These corporate filings are available on the SEC website at www.sec.gov. Go to the SEC website and search for SEC filings made by Dell. Find the most recent 10Q or 10K and download the form. Look on the balance sheet to find the book value of debt and the book value of equity. If you look further down the report, you should find a section titled "Long-term Debt and Interest Rate Risk Management" that will provide a breakdown of Dell's long-term debt.

2. To estimate the cost of equity for Dell, go to finance.yahoo.com and enter the ticker symbol DELL. Follow the various links to answer the following questions: What is the most recent stock price listed for Dell? What is the market value of equity, or market capitalization? How many shares of stock does Dell have outstanding? What is the most recent annual dividend? Can you use the dividend discount model in this case? What is the beta for Dell? Now go back

   to finance.yahoo.com and find the "Bonds" link. What is the yield on 3-month Treasury bills? Using the historical market risk premium, what is the cost of equity for Dell using the CAPM?

3. You now need to calculate the cost of debt for Dell. Go to www.nasdbondinfo.com, enter Dell as the company and find the yield to maturity for each of Dell's bonds. What is the weighted average cost of debt for Dell using the book value weights and the market value weights? Does it make a difference in this case if you use book value weights or market value weights?

4. You now have all the necessary information to calculate the weighted average cost of capital for Dell. Calculate the weighted average cost of capital for Dell using book value weights and market value weights. Assume Dell has a 35 percent marginal tax rate. Which cost of capital number is more relevant?

5. You used Dell as a pure play company to estimate the cost of capital for HCI. Are there any potential problems with this approach in this situation?

Leverage and Capital Structure

13

What do Hostess, Eastman Kodak, and AMR, the parent company of American Airlines, have in common? In early 2012, all three companies were in bankruptcy. In fact, Hostess, the maker of the iconic Twinkie, was facing its second bankruptcy, having emerged from its previous one in 2009. This time around, the company listed about $860 million in debt, plus an additional liability of $944.2 million to its employee pension fund. At the same time, its assets were listed between $500 million and $1 billion. Kodak's bankruptcy was blamed on failing to leverage the company's digital camera innovations for fear of damaging its traditional film business. The company listed $5.1 billion in assets and $6.8 billion in debt. AMR cited fuel costs, increased competition, and labor costs in its bankruptcy filing. The company had lost $4.8 billion over the previous three and a half years, and it stated that its annual labor costs were $800 million per year higher than what they would be at competing airlines.

learning objectives

After studying this chapter, you should be able to:

LO 1 Discuss the effect of financial leverage.

LO 2 Analyze the impact of taxes and bankruptcy on capital structure choice.

LO 3 Identify the essentials of the bankruptcy process.

A firm's choice of how much debt it should have relative to equity is known as a capital structure decision. Such a choice has many implications for a firm and is far from being a settled issue in either theory or practice. In this chapter, we discuss the basic ideas underlying capital structures and how firms choose them.

A firm's capital structure is really just a reflection of its borrowing policy. Should we borrow a lot of money, or just a little? At first glance, it probably seems that debt is something to be avoided. After all, the more debt a firm has, the greater is the risk of bankruptcy. What we learn is that debt is really a double-edged sword, and, properly used, debt can be enormously beneficial to the firm.

A good understanding of the effects of debt financing is important simply because the role of debt is so misunderstood, and many firms (and individuals) are far too conservative in their use of debt. Having said this, we can also say that firms sometimes err in the opposite direction, becoming much too heavily indebted, with bankruptcy as the unfortunate consequence. Striking the right balance is what the capital structure issue is all about.

Thus far, we have taken the firm's capital structure as given. Debt-equity ratios don't just drop on firms from the sky, of course, so now it's time to wonder where they do come from. Going back to Chapter 1, we call decisions about a firm's debt-equity ratio *capital structure decisions*.[1]

For the most part, a firm can choose any capital structure that it wants. If management so desired, a firm could issue some bonds and use the proceeds to buy back some stock, thereby increasing the debt-equity ratio. Alternatively, it could issue stock and use the money to pay off some debt, thereby reducing the debt-equity ratio. Activities such as these that alter the firm's existing capital structure are called capital *restructurings*. In general, such restructurings take place whenever the firm substitutes one capital structure for another while leaving the firm's assets unchanged.

Since the assets of a firm are not directly affected by a capital restructuring, we can examine the firm's capital structure decision separately from its other activities. This means that a firm can consider capital restructuring decisions in isolation from its investment decisions. In this chapter, then, we will ignore investment decisions and focus on the long-term financing, or capital structure, question.

What we will see in this chapter is that capital structure decisions can have important implications for the value of the firm and its cost of capital. We will also find that important elements of the capital structure decision are easy to identify, but precise measures of these elements are generally not obtainable. As a result, we are only able to give an incomplete answer to the question of what the best capital structure might be for a particular firm at a particular time.

13.1   THE CAPITAL STRUCTURE QUESTION

How should a firm go about choosing its debt-equity ratio? Here, as always, we assume that the guiding principle is to choose the course of action that maximizes the value of a share of stock. However, when it comes to capital structure decisions, this is essentially the same thing as maximizing the value of the whole firm, and, for convenience, we will tend to frame our discussion in terms of firm value.

In Chapter 12, we discussed the concept of the firm's weighted average cost of capital, or WACC. You may recall that the WACC tells us that the firm's overall cost of capital is a weighted average of the costs of the various components of the firm's capital structure. When we described the WACC, we took the firm's capital structure as given. Thus, one important issue that we will want to explore in this chapter is what happens to the cost of capital when we vary the amount of debt financing, or the debt-equity ratio.

A primary reason for studying the WACC is that the value of the firm is maximized when the WACC is minimized. To see this, recall that the WACC is the discount rate appropriate for the firm's overall cash flows. Since values and discount rates move in opposite directions, minimizing the WACC will maximize the value of the firm's cash flows.

Thus, we will want to choose the firm's capital structure so that the WACC is minimized. For this reason, we will say that one capital structure is better than another if it results in a lower weighted average cost of capital. Further, we say that a particular

---

[1] It is conventional to refer to decisions regarding debt and equity as *capital structure decisions*. However, the term *financial structure* would be more accurate, and we use the terms interchangeably.

debt-equity ratio represents the *optimal capital structure* if it results in the lowest possible WACC. This optimal capital structure is sometimes called the firm's *target* capital structure as well.

CONCEPT QUESTIONS

13.1a   What is the relationship between the WACC and the value of the firm?

13.1b   What is an optimal capital structure?

THE EFFECT OF FINANCIAL LEVERAGE

13.2

ExcelMaster
coverage online

In this section, we examine the impact of financial leverage on the payoffs to stockholders. As you may recall, financial leverage refers to the extent to which a firm relies on debt. The more debt financing a firm uses in its capital structure, the more financial leverage it employs.

As we describe, financial leverage can dramatically alter the payoffs to shareholders in the firm. Remarkably, however, financial leverage may not affect the overall cost of capital. If this is true, then a firm's capital structure is irrelevant because changes in capital structure won't affect the value of the firm. We will return to this issue a little later.

The Impact of Financial Leverage

We start by illustrating how financial leverage works. For now, we ignore the impact of taxes. Also, for ease of presentation, we describe the impact of leverage in terms of its effects on earnings per share, EPS, and return on equity, ROE. These are, of course, accounting numbers and, as such, are not our primary concern. Using cash flows instead of these accounting numbers would lead to precisely the same conclusions, but a little more work would be needed. We discuss the impact of leverage on market values in a subsequent section.

Financial Leverage, EPS, and ROE: An Example   The Trans Am Corporation currently has no debt in its capital structure. The CFO, Ms. Morris, is considering a restructuring that would involve issuing debt and using the proceeds to buy back some of the outstanding equity. Table 13.1 presents both the current and proposed capital structures. As shown, the firm's assets have a market value of $8 million, and there are 400,000 shares outstanding. Because Trans Am is an all-equity firm, the price per share is $20.

The proposed debt issue would raise $4 million; the interest rate would be 10 percent. Since the stock sells for $20 per share, the $4 million in new debt would be used to purchase $4 million/20 = 200,000 shares, leaving 200,000 outstanding. After the restructuring, Trans Am would have a capital structure that was 50 percent debt, so the debt-equity ratio would be 1. Notice that, for now, we assume that the stock price will remain at $20.

To investigate the impact of the proposed restructuring, Ms. Morris has prepared Table 13.2, which compares the firm's current capital structure to the proposed capital

TABLE 13.1		Current	Proposed
Current and proposed capital structures for the Trans Am Corporation	Assets	$8,000,000	$8,000,000
	Debt	$0	$4,000,000
	Equity	$8,000,000	$4,000,000
	Debt-equity ratio	0	1
	Share price	$20	$20
	Shares outstanding	400,000	200,000
	Interest rate	10%	10%

TABLE 13.2

Capital structure scenarios for the Trans Am Corporation

Current Capital Structure: No Debt			
	Recession	Expected	Expansion
EBIT	$500,000	$1,000,000	$1,500,000
Interest	0	0	0
Net income	$500,000	$1,000,000	$1,500,000
ROE	6.25%	12.50%	18.75%
EPS	$1.25	$2.50	$3.75

Proposed Capital Structure: Debt = $4 million			
	Recession	Expected	Expansion
EBIT	$500,000	$1,000,000	$1,500,000
Interest	400,000	400,000	400,000
Net income	$100,000	$ 600,000	$1,100,000
ROE	2.50%	15.00%	27.50%
EPS	$.50	$3.00	$5.50

structure under three scenarios. The scenarios reflect different assumptions about the firm's EBIT. Under the expected scenario, EBIT is $1 million. In the recession scenario, EBIT falls to $500,000. In the expansion scenario, it rises to $1.5 million.

To illustrate some of the calculations in Table 13.2, consider the expansion case. EBIT is $1.5 million. With no debt (the current capital structure) and no taxes, net income is also $1.5 million. In this case, there are 400,000 shares worth $8 million total. EPS is therefore $1.5 million/400,000 = $3.75 per share. Also, since accounting return on equity, ROE, is net income divided by total equity, ROE is $1.5 million/8 million = 18.75 percent.[2]

With $4 million in debt (the proposed capital structure), things are somewhat different. Since the interest rate is 10 percent, the interest bill is $400,000. With EBIT of $1.5 million, interest of $400,000, and no taxes, net income is $1.1 million. Now there are only 200,000 shares worth $4 million total. EPS is therefore $1.1 million/200,000 = $5.5 per share versus the $3.75 per share that we calculated above. Furthermore, ROE is $1.1 million/4 million = 27.5 percent. This is well above the 18.75 percent we calculated for the current capital structure.

EPS versus EBIT The impact of leverage is evident in Table 13.2 when the effect of the restructuring on EPS and ROE is examined. In particular, the variability in both EPS

---

[2] ROE is discussed in some detail in Chapter 3.

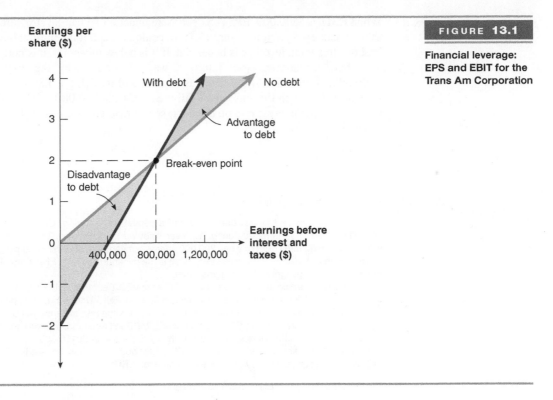

FIGURE 13.1

Financial leverage: EPS and EBIT for the Trans Am Corporation

and ROE is much larger under the proposed capital structure. This illustrates how financial leverage acts to magnify gains and losses to shareholders.

In Figure 13.1, we take a closer look at the effect of the proposed restructuring. This figure plots earnings per share, EPS, against earnings before interest and taxes, EBIT, for the current and proposed capital structures. The first line, labeled "No debt," represents the case of no leverage. This line begins at the origin, indicating that EPS would be zero if EBIT were zero. From there, every $400,000 increase in EBIT increases EPS by $1 (because there are 400,000 shares outstanding).

The second line represents the proposed capital structure. Here, EPS is negative if EBIT is zero. This follows because $400,000 of interest must be paid regardless of the firm's profits. Since there are 200,000 shares in this case, EPS is −$2 per share as shown. Similarly, if EBIT were $400,000, EPS would be exactly zero.

The important thing to notice in Figure 13.1 is that the slope of the line in this second case is steeper. In fact, for every $400,000 increase in EBIT, EPS rises by $2, so the line is twice as steep. This tells us that EPS is twice as sensitive to changes in EBIT because of the financial leverage employed.

Another observation to make in Figure 13.1 is that the lines intersect. At that point, EPS is exactly the same for both capital structures. To find this point, note that EPS is equal to EBIT/400,000 in the no-debt case. In the with-debt case, EPS is (EBIT − $400,000)/200,000. If we set these equal to each other, EBIT is:

$$\text{EBIT}/400{,}000 = (\text{EBIT} - \$400{,}000)/200{,}000$$
$$\text{EBIT} = 2 \times (\text{EBIT} - \$400{,}000)$$
$$\text{EBIT} = \$800{,}000$$

When EBIT is $800,000, EPS is $2 per share under either capital structure. This is labeled as the break-even point in Figure 13.1; we could also call it the indifference point. If EBIT is above this level, leverage is beneficial; if it is below this point, it is not.

There is another, more intuitive, way of seeing why the break-even point is $800,000. Notice that, if the firm has no debt and its EBIT is $800,000, its net income is also $800,000. In this case, the ROE is $800,000/8,000,000 = 10%. This is precisely the same as the interest rate on the debt, so the firm earns a return that is just sufficient to pay the interest.

EXAMPLE **13.1**

BREAK-EVEN EBIT

The MPD Corporation has decided in favor of a capital restructuring. Currently, MPD uses no-debt financing. Following the restructuring, however, debt will be $1 million. The interest rate on the debt will be 9 percent. MPD currently has 200,000 shares outstanding, and the price per share is $20. If the restructuring is expected to increase EPS, what is the minimum level for EBIT that MPD's management must be expecting? Ignore taxes in answering.

To answer, we calculate the break-even EBIT. At any EBIT above this, the increased financial leverage will increase EPS, so this will tell us the minimum level for EBIT. Under the old capital structure, EPS is simply EBIT/200,000. Under the new capital structure, the interest expense will be $1 million × .09 = $90,000. Furthermore, with the $1 million proceeds, MPD will repurchase $1 million/20 = 50,000 shares of stock, leaving 150,000 outstanding. EPS is thus (EBIT − $90,000)/150,000.

Now that we know how to calculate EPS under both scenarios, we set the two expressions for EPS equal to each other and solve for the break-even EBIT:

$$\text{EBIT}/200{,}000 = (\text{EBIT} - \$90{,}000)/150{,}000$$
$$\text{EBIT} = (\tfrac{4}{3}) \times (\text{EBIT} - \$90{,}000)$$
$$\text{EBIT} = \$360{,}000$$

Verify that, in either case, EPS is $1.80 when EBIT is $360,000. Management at MPD is apparently of the opinion that EPS will exceed $1.80.

Corporate Borrowing and Homemade Leverage

Based on Tables 13.1 and 13.2 and Figure 13.1, Ms. Morris draws the following conclusions:

1. The effect of financial leverage depends on the company's EBIT. When EBIT is relatively high, leverage is beneficial.

2. Under the expected scenario, leverage increases the returns to shareholders, as measured by both ROE and EPS.

3. Shareholders are exposed to more risk under the proposed capital structure since the EPS and ROE are much more sensitive to changes in EBIT in this case.

4. Because of the impact that financial leverage has on both the expected return to stockholders and the riskiness of the stock, capital structure is an important consideration.

The first three of these conclusions are clearly correct. Does the last conclusion necessarily follow? Surprisingly, the answer is no. As we discuss next, the reason is that shareholders can adjust the amount of financial leverage by borrowing and lending on

Proposed Capital Structure			
	Recession	**Expected**	**Expansion**
EPS	$ .50	$ 3.00	$ 5.50
Earnings for 100 shares	50.00	300.00	550.00
Net cost = 100 shares at $20 = $2,000			

Original Capital Structure and Homemade Leverage			
	Recession	**Expected**	**Expansion**
EPS	$ 1.25	$ 2.50	$ 3.75
Earnings for 200 shares	250.00	500.00	750.00
Less: Interest on $2,000 at 10%	200.00	200.00	200.00
Net earnings	$ 50.00	$300.00	$550.00
Net cost = 200 shares at $20 − Amount borrowed = $4,000 − 2,000 = $2,000			

TABLE 13.3

Proposed capital structure versus original capital structure with homemade leverage

their own. This use of personal borrowing to alter the degree of financial leverage is called **homemade leverage**.

We will now illustrate that it actually makes no difference whether or not Trans Am adopts the proposed capital structure, because any stockholder who prefers the proposed capital structure can simply create it using homemade leverage. To begin, the first part of Table 13.3 shows what will happen to an investor who buys $2,000 worth of Trans Am stock if the proposed capital structure is adopted. This investor purchases 100 shares of stock. From Table 13.2, EPS will either be $.50, $3, or $5.50, so the total earnings for 100 shares will either be $50, $300, or $550 under the proposed capital structure.

Now, suppose Trans Am does not adopt the proposed capital structure. In this case, EPS will be $1.25, $2.50, or $3.75. The second part of Table 13.3 demonstrates how a stockholder who prefers the payoffs under the proposed structure can create them using personal borrowing. To do this, the stockholder borrows $2,000 at 10 percent on his or her own. Our investor uses this amount, along with the original $2,000, to buy 200 shares of stock. As shown, the net payoffs are exactly the same as those for the proposed capital structure.

How did we know to borrow $2,000 to create the right payoffs? We are trying to replicate Trans Am's proposed capital structure at the personal level. The proposed capital structure results in a debt-equity ratio of 1. To replicate this capital structure at the personal level, the stockholder must borrow enough to create this same debt-equity ratio. Since the stockholder has $2,000 in equity invested, borrowing another $2,000 will create a personal debt-equity ratio of 1.

This example demonstrates that investors can always increase financial leverage themselves to create a different pattern of payoffs. It thus makes no difference whether or not Trans Am chooses the proposed capital structure.

homemade leverage
The use of personal borrowing to change the overall amount of financial leverage to which the individual is exposed.

UNLEVERING THE STOCK

EXAMPLE 13.2

In our Trans Am example, suppose management adopted the proposed capital structure. Further, suppose that an investor who owned 100 shares preferred the original capital structure. Show how this investor could "unlever" the stock to recreate the original payoffs.

(continued)

To create leverage, investors borrow on their own. To undo leverage, investors must loan out money. For Trans Am, the corporation borrowed an amount equal to half its value. The investor can unlever the stock by simply loaning out money in the same proportion. In this case, the investor sells 50 shares for $1,000 total and then loans out the $1,000 at 10 percent. The payoffs are calculated in the table below.

	Recession	Expected	Expansion
EPS (proposed structure)	$ .50	$ 3.00	$ 5.50
Earnings for 50 shares	25.00	150.00	275.00
Plus: Interest on $1,000 @ 10%	100.00	100.00	100.00
Total payoff	$125.00	$250.00	$375.00

These are precisely the payoffs the investor would have experienced under the original capital structure.

CONCEPT QUESTIONS

13.2a What is the impact of financial leverage on stockholders?

13.2b What is homemade leverage?

13.2c Why is Trans Am's capital structure irrelevant?

13.3   CAPITAL STRUCTURE AND THE COST OF EQUITY CAPITAL

ExcelMaster
coverage online

M&M Proposition I
The value of the firm is independent of its capital structure.

We have seen that there is nothing special about corporate borrowing because investors can borrow or lend on their own. As a result, whichever capital structure Trans Am chooses, the stock price will be the same. Trans Am's capital structure is thus irrelevant, at least in the simple world we have examined.

Our Trans Am example is based on a famous argument advanced by two Nobel laureates, Franco Modigliani and Merton Miller, whom we will henceforth call M&M. What we illustrated for the Trans Am Corporation is a special case of **M&M Proposition I.** M&M Proposition I states that it is completely irrelevant how a firm chooses to arrange its finances.

M&M Proposition I: The Pie Model

One way to illustrate M&M Proposition I is to imagine two firms that are identical on the left-hand side of the balance sheet. Their assets and operations are exactly the same. The right-hand sides are different because the two firms finance their operations differently. In this case, we can view the capital structure question in terms of a "pie" model. Why we choose this name is apparent in Figure 13.2. Figure 13.2 gives two possible ways of cutting up this pie between the equity slice, *E,* and the debt slice, *D:* 40%–60% and 60%–40%. However, the size of the pie in Figure 13.2 is the same for both firms because the value of the assets is the same. This is precisely what M&M Proposition I states: The size of the pie doesn't depend on how it is sliced.

FIGURE **13.2**

Two pie models of capital structure

FIGURE **13.3**

The cost of equity and the WACC: M&M Propositions I and II with no taxes

$R_E = R_A + (R_A - R_D) \times (D/E)$ by M&M Proposition II

$R_A = \text{WACC} = (E/V) \times R_E + (D/V) \times R_D$

where $V = D + E$

The Cost of Equity and Financial Leverage: M&M Proposition II

Although changing the capital structure of the firm may not change the firm's *total* value, it does cause important changes in the firm's debt and equity. We now examine what happens to a firm financed with debt and equity when the debt-equity ratio is changed. To simplify our analysis, we will continue to ignore taxes.

Based on our discussion in Chapter 12, if we ignore taxes, the weighted average cost of capital, WACC, is:

$$\text{WACC} = (E/V) \times R_E + (D/V) \times R_D$$

where $V = E + D$. We also saw that one way of interpreting the WACC is as the required return on the firm's overall assets. To remind us of this, we will use the symbol R_A to stand for the WACC and write:

$$R_A = (E/V) \times R_E + (D/V) \times R_D$$

If we rearrange this to solve for the cost of equity capital, we see that:

$$R_E = R_A + (R_A - R_D) \times (D/E) \qquad [13.1]$$

This is the famous **M&M Proposition II**, which tells us that the cost of equity depends on three things: the required rate of return on the firm's assets, R_A; the firm's cost of debt, R_D; and the firm's debt-equity ratio, D/E.

Figure 13.3 summarizes our discussion thus far by plotting the cost of equity capital, R_E, against the debt-equity ratio. As shown, M&M Proposition II indicates that the cost of

M&M Proposition II
A firm's cost of equity capital is a positive linear function of its capital structure.

equity, R_E, is given by a straight line with a slope of $(R_A - R_D)$. The y-intercept corresponds to a firm with a debt-equity ratio of zero, so $R_A = R_E$ in that case. Figure 13.3 shows that, as the firm raises its debt-equity ratio, the increase in leverage raises the risk of the equity and therefore the required return, or cost of equity (R_E).

Notice in Figure 13.3 that the WACC doesn't depend on the debt-equity ratio; it's the same no matter what the debt-equity ratio is. This is another way of stating M&M Proposition I: The firm's overall cost of capital is unaffected by its capital structure. As illustrated, the fact that the cost of debt is lower than the cost of equity is exactly offset by the increase in the cost of equity from borrowing. In other words, the change in the capital structure weights (E/V and D/V) is exactly offset by the change in the cost of equity (R_E), so the WACC stays the same.

EXAMPLE 13.3

THE COST OF EQUITY CAPITAL

The Ricardo Corporation has a weighted average cost of capital (ignoring taxes) of 12 percent. It can borrow at 8 percent. Assuming that Ricardo has a target capital structure of 80 percent equity and 20 percent debt, what is its cost of equity? What is the cost of equity if the target capital structure is 50 percent equity? Calculate the WACC, using your answers to verify that it is the same in both cases.

According to M&M Proposition II, the cost of equity, R_E, is:

$$R_E = R_A + (R_A - R_D) \times (D/E)$$

In the first case, the debt-equity ratio is .2/.8 = .25, so the cost of the equity is:

$$R_E = 12\% + (12\% - 8\%) \times .25$$
$$= 13\%$$

In the second case, verify that the debt-equity ratio is 1.0, so the cost of equity is 16 percent.

We can now calculate the WACC assuming that the percentage of equity financing is 80 percent, the cost of equity is 13 percent, and the tax rate is zero:

$$WACC = (E/V) \times R_E + (D/V) \times R_D$$
$$= .80 \times 13\% + .20 \times 8\%$$
$$= 12\%$$

In the second case, the percentage of equity financing is 50 percent and the cost of equity is 16 percent. The WACC is:

$$WACC = (E/V) \times R_E + (D/V) \times R_D$$
$$= .50 \times 16\% + .50 \times 8\%$$
$$= 12\%$$

As we calculated, the WACC is 12 percent in both cases.

Business and Financial Risk

M&M Proposition II shows that the firm's cost of equity can be broken down into two components. The first component, R_A, is the required return on the firm's overall assets, and it depends on the nature of the firm's operating activities. The risk inherent in a firm's operations is called the **business risk** of the firm's equity. Referring back to Chapter 11, we see that this business risk depends on the systematic risk of the firm's assets. The greater a firm's business risk, the greater R_A will be, and, all other things being the same, the greater will be the firm's cost of equity.

business risk

The equity risk that comes from the nature of the firm's operating activities.

The second component in the cost of equity, $(R_A - R_D) \times (D/E)$, is determined by the firm's financial structure. For an all-equity firm, this component is zero. As the firm begins to rely on debt financing, the required return on equity rises. This occurs because the debt financing increases the risks borne by the stockholders. This extra risk that arises from the use of debt financing is called the **financial risk** of the firm's equity.

The total systematic risk of the firm's equity thus has two parts: business risk and financial risk. The first part (the business risk) depends on the firm's assets and operations and is not affected by capital structure. Given the firm's business risk (and its cost of debt), the second part (the financial risk) is completely determined by financial policy. As we have illustrated, the firm's cost of equity rises when it increases its use of financial leverage because the financial risk of the equity increases while the business risk remains the same.

financial risk
The equity risk that comes from the financial policy (i.e., capital structure) of the firm.

CONCEPT QUESTIONS

13.3a   What does M&M Proposition I state?

13.3b   What are the three determinants of a firm's cost of equity?

13.3c   The total systematic risk of a firm's equity has two parts. What are they?

CORPORATE TAXES AND CAPITAL STRUCTURE

13.4

Debt has two distinguishing features that we have not taken into proper account. First, as we have mentioned in a number of places, interest paid on debt is tax deductible. This is good for the firm, and it may be an added benefit to debt financing. Second, failure to meet debt obligations can result in bankruptcy. This is not good for the firm, and it may be an added cost of debt financing. Since we haven't explicitly considered either of these two features of debt, we may get a different answer about capital structure once we do. Accordingly, we consider taxes in this section and bankruptcy in the next one.

We can start by considering what happens when we consider the effect of corporate taxes. To do this, we will examine two firms, Firm U (unlevered) and Firm L (levered). These two firms are identical on the left-hand side of the balance sheet, so their assets and operations are the same.

We assume that EBIT is expected to be $1,000 every year forever for both firms. The difference between the two firms is that Firm L has issued $1,000 worth of perpetual bonds on which it pays 8 percent interest each year. The interest bill is thus $.08 \times \$1,000 = \$80$ every year forever. Also, we assume that the corporate tax rate is 30 percent.

For our two firms, U and L, we can now calculate the following:

	Firm U	Firm L
EBIT	$1,000	$1,000
Interest	0	80
Taxable income	$1,000	$ 920
Taxes (30%)	300	276
Net income	$ 700	$ 644

The Interest Tax Shield

To simplify things, we will assume that depreciation is zero. We will also assume that capital spending is zero and that there are no additions to NWC. In this case, cash flow from assets is simply equal to EBIT − Taxes. For Firms U and L, we thus have:

Cash Flow from Assets	Firm U	Firm L
EBIT	$1,000	$1,000
−Taxes	300	276
Total	$ 700	$ 724

We immediately see that capital structure is now having some effect because the cash flows from U and L are not the same even though the two firms have identical assets.

To see what's going on, we can compute the cash flow to stockholders and bondholders.

Cash Flow	Firm U	Firm L
To stockholders	$700	$644
To bondholders	0	80
Total	$700	$724

What we are seeing is that the total cash flow to L is $24 more. This occurs because L's tax bill (which is a cash outflow) is $24 less. The fact that interest is deductible for tax purposes has generated a tax saving equal to the interest payment ($80) multiplied by the corporate tax rate (30 percent): $80 × .30 = $24. We call this tax saving the **interest tax shield**.

interest tax shield
The tax savings attained by a firm from the tax deductibility of interest expense.

Taxes and M&M Proposition I

Since the debt is perpetual, the same $24 shield will be generated every year forever. The aftertax cash flow to L will thus be the same $700 that U earns plus the $24 tax shield. Since L's cash flow is always $24 greater, Firm L is worth more than Firm U by the value of this $24 perpetuity.

Because the tax shield is generated by paying interest, it has the same risk as the debt, and 8 percent (the cost of debt) is therefore the appropriate discount rate. The value of the tax shield is thus:

$$\text{PV} = \frac{\$24}{.08} = \frac{.30 \times \$1,000 \times .08}{.08} = .30 \times \$1,000 = \$300$$

As our example illustrates, the present value of the interest tax shield can be written as:

$$\text{Present value of the interest tax shield} = (T_c \times D \times R_D)/R_D$$
$$= T_c \times D \quad \text{[13.2]}$$

We have now come up with another famous result, M&M Proposition I with corporate taxes. We have seen that the value of Firm L, V_L, exceeds the value of Firm U, V_U, by the

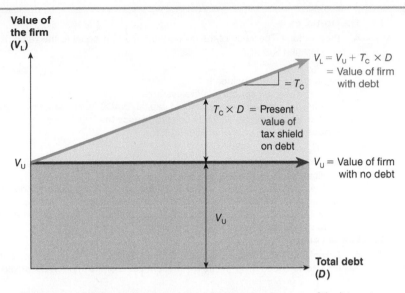

FIGURE **13.4**

M&M Proposition I with taxes

The value of the firm increases as total debt increases because of the interest tax shield. This is the basis of M&M Proposition I with taxes.

present value of the interest tax shield, $T_c \times D$. M&M Proposition I with taxes therefore states that:

$$V_L = V_U + T_c \times D \qquad\qquad [13.3]$$

The effect of borrowing in this case is illustrated in Figure 13.4. We have plotted the value of the levered firm, V_L, against the amount of debt, D. M&M Proposition I with corporate taxes implies that the relationship is given by a straight line with a slope of T_C.

In Figure 13.4, we have also drawn a horizontal line representing V_U. As is shown, the distance between the two lines is $T_C \times D$, the present value of the tax shield.

As Figure 13.4 indicates, the value of the firm goes up by $.30 for every $1 in debt. In other words, the NPV *per dollar* of debt is $.30. It is difficult to imagine why any corporation would not borrow to the absolute maximum under these circumstances.

Conclusion

The result of our analysis in this section is that, once we include taxes, capital structure definitely matters. However, we immediately reach the illogical conclusion that the optimal capital structure is 100 percent debt. Of course, we have not yet considered the impact of bankruptcy, so our story may change. For future reference, Table 13.4 contains a summary of the various M&M calculations and conclusions.

CONCEPT QUESTIONS

13.4a What is the relationship between the value of an unlevered firm and the value of a levered firm once we consider the effect of corporate taxes?

13.4b If we only consider the effect of taxes, what is the optimum capital structure?

TABLE 13.4
Modigliani and Miller summary

I. The no-tax case

   A. Proposition I: The value of the leveraged firm (V_L) is equal to the value of the unleveraged firm (V_U):

$$V_L = V_U$$

   B. Implications of Proposition I:

      1. A firm's capital structure is irrelevant.

      2. A firm's weighted average cost of capital, WACC, is the same no matter what mixture of debt and equity is used to finance the firm.

   C. Proposition II: The cost of equity, R_E, is:

$$R_E = R_A + (R_A - R_D) \times D/E$$

   where R_A is the WACC, R_D is the cost of debt, and D/E is the debt-equity ratio.

   D. Implications of Proposition II:

      1. The cost of equity rises as the firm increases its use of debt financing.

      2. The risk of the equity depends on two things: the riskiness of the firm's operations (*business risk*) and the degree of financial leverage (*financial risk*). Business risk determines R_A; financial risk is determined by D/E.

II. The tax case

   A. Proposition I with taxes: The value of the leveraged firm (V_L) is equal to the value of the unleveraged firm (V_U) plus the present value of the interest tax shield:

$$V_L = V_U + T_C \times D$$

   where T_C is the corporate tax rate and D is the amount of debt.

   B. Implications of Proposition I with taxes:

      1. Debt financing is highly advantageous, and, in the extreme, a firm's optimal capital structure is 100 percent debt.

      2. A firm's weighted average cost of capital, WACC, decreases as the firm relies more heavily on debt financing.

13.5   BANKRUPTCY COSTS

One limit to the amount of debt a firm might use comes in the form of *bankruptcy costs*. As the debt-equity ratio rises, so too does the probability that the firm will be unable to pay its bondholders what was promised to them. When this happens, ownership of the firm's assets is ultimately transferred from the stockholders to the bondholders.

In principle, a firm becomes bankrupt when the value of its assets equals the value of its debt. When this occurs, the value of equity is zero, and the stockholders turn over control of the firm to the bondholders. At this point, the bondholders hold assets whose value is exactly equal to what is owed on the debt. In a perfect world, there are no costs associated with this transfer of ownership, and the bondholders don't lose anything.

This idealized view of bankruptcy is not, of course, what happens in the real world. Ironically, it is expensive to go bankrupt. As we discuss, the costs associated with bankruptcy may eventually offset the tax-related gains from leverage.

Direct Bankruptcy Costs

direct bankruptcy costs

The costs that are directly associated with bankruptcy, such as legal and administrative expenses.

When the value of a firm's assets equals the value of its debt, then the firm is economically bankrupt in the sense that the equity has no value. However, the formal turning over of the assets to the bondholders is a *legal* process, not an economic one. There are legal and administrative costs to bankruptcy, and it has been remarked that bankruptcies are to lawyers what blood is to sharks.

Because of the expenses associated with bankruptcy, bondholders won't get all that they are owed. Some fraction of the firm's assets will "disappear" in the legal process of going bankrupt. These are the legal and administrative expenses associated with the bankruptcy proceeding. We call these costs **direct bankruptcy costs**.

Indirect Bankruptcy Costs

Because it is expensive to go bankrupt, a firm will spend resources to avoid doing so. When a firm is having significant problems in meeting its debt obligations, we say that it is experiencing financial distress. Some financially distressed firms ultimately file for bankruptcy, but most do not because they are able to recover or otherwise survive.

The costs of avoiding a bankruptcy filing incurred by a financially distressed firm are called **indirect bankruptcy costs**. We use the term **financial distress costs** to refer generically to the direct and indirect costs associated with going bankrupt and/or avoiding a bankruptcy filing.

The problems that come up in financial distress are particularly severe, and the financial distress costs are thus larger, when the stockholders and the bondholders are different groups. Until the firm is legally bankrupt, the stockholders control it. They, of course, will take actions in their own economic interests. Since the stockholders can be wiped out in a legal bankruptcy, they have a very strong incentive to avoid a bankruptcy filing.

The bondholders, on the other hand, are primarily concerned with protecting the value of the firm's assets and will try to take control away from the stockholders. They have a strong incentive to seek bankruptcy to protect their interests and keep stockholders from further dissipating the assets of the firm. The net effect of all this fighting is that a long, drawn-out, and potentially quite expensive legal battle gets started.

Meanwhile, as the wheels of justice turn in their ponderous way, the assets of the firm lose value because management is busy trying to avoid bankruptcy instead of running the business. Normal operations are disrupted, and sales are lost. Valuable employees leave, potentially fruitful programs are dropped to preserve cash, and otherwise profitable investments are not taken.

These are all indirect bankruptcy costs, or costs of financial distress. Whether or not the firm ultimately goes bankrupt, the net effect is a loss of value because the firm chose to use debt in its capital structure. It is this possibility of loss that limits the amount of debt that a firm will choose to use.

indirect bankruptcy costs
The costs of avoiding a bankruptcy filing incurred by a financially distressed firm.

financial distress costs
The direct and indirect costs associated with going bankrupt or experiencing financial distress.

CONCEPT QUESTIONS

13.5a What are direct bankruptcy costs?

13.5b What are indirect bankruptcy costs?

OPTIMAL CAPITAL STRUCTURE

13.6

Our previous two sections have established the basis for an optimal capital structure. A firm will borrow because the interest tax shield is valuable. At relatively low debt levels, the probability of bankruptcy and financial distress is low, and the benefit from debt outweighs the cost. At very high debt levels, the possibility of financial distress is a chronic, ongoing problem for the firm, so the benefit from debt financing may be more than offset by the financial distress costs. Based on our discussion, it would appear that an optimal capital structure exists somewhere in between these extremes.

The Static Theory of Capital Structure

The theory of capital structure that we have outlined is called the **static theory of capital structure**. It says that firms borrow up to the point where the tax benefit from an extra dollar in debt is exactly equal to the cost that comes from the increased probability of financial distress. We call this the static theory because it assumes that the firm is fixed in terms of its assets and operations, and it only considers possible changes in the debt-equity ratio.

static theory of capital structure
Theory that a firm borrows up to the point where the tax benefit from an extra dollar in debt is exactly equal to the cost that comes from the increased probability of financial distress.

FIGURE 13.5

The static theory of capital structure: The optimal capital structure and the value of the firm

According to the static theory, the gain from the tax shield on debt is offset by financial distress costs. An optimal capital structure exists that just balances the additional gain from leverage against the added financial distress costs.

The static theory is illustrated in Figure 13.5, which plots the value of the firm, V_L, against the amount of debt, D. In Figure 13.5, we have drawn lines corresponding to three different stories. The first is M&M Proposition I with no taxes. This is the horizontal line extending from V_U, and it indicates that the value of the firm is unaffected by its capital structure. The second case, M&M Proposition I with corporate taxes, is given by the upward-sloping straight line. These two cases are exactly the same as the ones we previously illustrated in Figure 13.4.

The third case in Figure 13.5 illustrates our current discussion: The value of the firm rises to a maximum and then declines beyond that point. This is the picture that we get from our static theory. The maximum value of the firm, V_L^*, is reached at a debt level of D^*, so this is the optimal amount of borrowing. Put another way, the firm's optimal capital structure is composed of D^*/V_L^* in debt and $(1 - D^*/V_L^*)$ in equity.

The final thing to notice in Figure 13.5 is that the difference between the value of the firm in our static theory and the M&M value of the firm with taxes is the loss in value from the possibility of financial distress. Also, the difference between the static theory value of the firm and the M&M value with no taxes is the gain from leverage, net of distress costs.

Optimal Capital Structure and the Cost of Capital

As we discussed earlier, the capital structure that maximizes the value of the firm is also the one that minimizes the cost of capital. With the help of Figure 13.6, we can illustrate this point and tie together our discussion of capital structure and cost of capital. As we have seen, there are essentially three cases. We will use the simplest of the three cases as a starting point and then build up to the static theory of capital structure. Along the way, we will pay particular attention to the connection between capital structure, firm value, and cost of capital.

Figure 13.6 illustrates the original Modigliani and Miller, M&M, no-tax, no-bankruptcy argument in Case I. This is the most basic case. In the top part, we have plotted the value

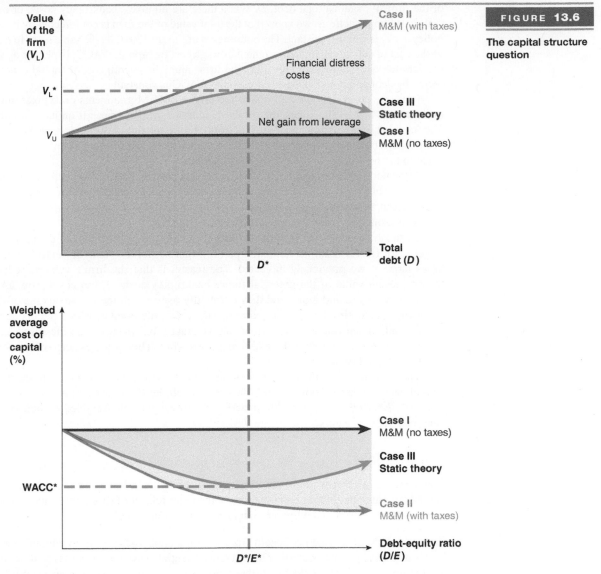

FIGURE **13.6**

The capital structure question

Case I
With no taxes or bankruptcy costs, the value of the firm and its weighted average cost of capital are not affected by capital structures.

Case II
With corporate taxes and no bankruptcy costs, the value of the firm increases and the weighted average cost of capital decreases as the amount of debt goes up.

Case III
With corporate taxes and bankruptcy costs, the value of the firm, V_L, reaches a maximum at D^*, the optimal amount of borrowing. At the same time, the weighted average cost of capital, WACC, is minimized at D^*/E^*.

of the firm, V_L, against total debt, D. When there are no taxes, bankruptcy costs, or other real-world imperfections, we know that the total value of the firm is not affected by its debt policy, so V_L is simply constant. The bottom part of Figure 13.6 tells the same story in terms of the cost of capital. Here, the weighted average cost of capital, WACC, is plotted against the debt-to-equity ratio, D/E. As with total firm value, the overall cost of capital is not affected by debt policy in this basic case, so the WACC is constant.

Next, we consider what happens to the original M&M arguments once taxes are introduced. As Case II illustrates, the firm's value now critically depends on its debt policy. The more the firm borrows, the more it is worth. From our earlier discussion, we know that this happens because interest payments are tax deductible, and the gain in firm value is just equal to the present value of the interest tax shield.

In the bottom part of Figure 13.6, notice how the WACC declines as the firm uses more and more debt financing. As the firm increases its financial leverage, the cost of equity does increase, but this increase is more than offset by the tax break associated with debt financing. As a result, the firm's overall cost of capital declines.

To finish our story, we include the impact of bankruptcy, or financial distress, costs to get Case III. As is shown in the top part of Figure 13.6, the value of the firm will not be as large as we previously indicated. The reason is that the firm's value is reduced by the present value of the potential future bankruptcy costs. These costs grow as the firm borrows more and more, and they eventually overwhelm the tax advantage of debt financing. The optimal capital structure occurs at D^*, the point at which the tax saving from an additional dollar in debt financing is exactly balanced by the increased bankruptcy costs associated with the additional borrowing. This is the essence of the static theory of capital structure.

The bottom part of Figure 13.6 presents the optimal capital structure in terms of the cost of capital. Corresponding to D^*, the optimal debt level, is the optimal debt-to-equity ratio, D^*/E^*. At this level of debt financing, the lowest possible weighted average cost of capital, **WACC***, occurs.

Capital Structure: Some Managerial Recommendations

The static model that we have described is not capable of identifying a precise optimal capital structure, but it does point out two of the more relevant factors: taxes and financial distress. We can draw some limited conclusions concerning these.

Taxes   First of all, the tax benefit from leverage is obviously only important to firms that are in a tax-paying position. Firms with substantial accumulated losses will get little value from the interest tax shield. Furthermore, firms that have substantial tax shields from other sources, such as depreciation, will get less benefit from leverage.

Also, not all firms have the same tax rate. The higher the tax rate, the greater the incentive to borrow.

Financial Distress   Firms with a greater risk of experiencing financial distress will borrow less than firms with a lower risk of financial distress. For example, all other things being equal, the greater the volatility in EBIT, the less a firm should borrow.

In addition, financial distress is more costly for some firms than for others. The costs of financial distress depend primarily on the firm's assets. In particular, financial distress costs will be determined by how easily ownership of those assets can be transferred.

For example, a firm with mostly tangible assets that can be sold without great loss in value will have an incentive to borrow more. For firms that rely heavily on intangibles, such as employee talent or growth opportunities, debt will be less attractive since these assets effectively cannot be sold.

13.6a Can you describe the trade-off that defines the static theory of capital structure?

13.6b What are the important factors in making capital structure decisions?

OBSERVED CAPITAL STRUCTURES

13.7

No two firms have identical capital structures. Nonetheless, there are some regular elements that we see when we start looking at actual capital structures. We discuss a few of these next.

The most striking thing we observe about capital structures, particularly in the United States, is that most corporations seem to have relatively low debt-equity ratios. In fact, most corporations use much less debt financing than equity financing. To illustrate, Table 13.5 presents median debt ratios and debt-equity ratios for various U.S. industries classified by SIC code (we discussed such codes in Chapter 3).

In Table 13.5, what is most striking is the wide variation across industries, ranging from essentially no debt for drug and computer companies to relatively heavy debt usage in the airline and cable television industries. Notice that these last two industries are the only ones for which more debt is used than equity, and most of the other industries rely far more heavily on equity than debt. This is true even though many of the companies in these industries pay substantial taxes. Table 13.5 makes it clear that corporations have not, in general, issued debt up to the point that tax shelters have been completely used up, and we conclude that there must be limits to the amount of debt corporations can use. Take a look at our nearby *Work the Web* box for more on actual capital structures.

Different industries have different operating characteristics in terms of, for example, EBIT volatility and asset types, and there does appear to be some connection between these characteristics and capital structure. Our story involving tax savings and financial distress costs undoubtedly supplies part of the reason, but, to date, there is no fully satisfactory theory that explains these regularities in capital structures.

TABLE 13.5

Capital structures for U.S. industries

Industry	Ratio of Debt to Total Capital(%)*	Ratio of Debt to Equity(%)	Number of Companies	SIC Code	Representative Companies
Electric utilities	48.54	94.31	33	491	American Electric Power, Southern Co.
Computer equipment	9.09	10.02	48	357	Apple, Cisco
Paper	27.75	38.40	24	26	Avery Dennison, Weyerhaeuser
Petroleum refining	32.27	47.65	18	29	Chevron, Sunoco
Airlines	63.92	177.19	10	4512	Delta, Southwest
Pay television	63.56	193.88	5	484	Dish Network, TiVo
Motor vehicles	17.77	21.60	25	371	Ford, Winnebago
Fabric apparel	15.86	18.84	14	23	Guess, Jones Apparel
Department stores	27.40	37.73	8	531	J.C. Penney, Macy's
Eating places	23.40	30.54	42	5812	McDonald's, Papa John's
Drugs	7.80	8.46	194	283	Merck, Pfizer
Steel works	19.96	24.95	9	331	Nucor, U.S. Steel

* Debt is the book value of preferred stock and long-term debt, including amounts due in one year. Equity is the market value of outstanding shares. Total capital is the sum of debt and equity. Median values are shown.

Source: Cost of Capital, 2010 Yearbook (Chicago: Morningstar, 2010).

WORK THE WEB

◀ To get
updated data,
scan here.

When it comes to capital structure, all companies (and industries) are not created equal. To illustrate, we looked up some capital structure information on American Electric Power (AEP) and Johnson & Johnson (JNJ) using the "Financials" area of www.reuters.com. American Electric Power's capital structure looks like this (note that leverage ratios are expressed as percentages on this site):

	Company	Industry	Sector
Quick Ratio (MRQ)	0.44	0.46	0.47
Current Ratio (MRQ)	0.63	0.57	0.58
LT Debt to Equity (MRQ)	102.86	81.71	74.90
Total Debt to Equity (MRQ)	123.88	93.53	86.16
Interest Coverage (TTM)	2.77	0.06	0.09

For every dollar of equity, American Electric Power has long-term debt of $1.0286 and total debt of $123.88. Compare this result to Johnson & Johnson:

	Company	Industry	Sector
Quick Ratio (MRQ)	2.11	1.79	1.52
Current Ratio (MRQ)	2.38	2.25	1.88
LT Debt to Equity (MRQ)	22.72	15.57	29.05
Total Debt to Equity (MRQ)	34.39	19.53	38.89
Interest Coverage (TTM)	49.70	2.51	2.52

For every dollar of equity, Johnson & Johnson has only $.2272 of long-term debt and total debt of $.3439. When we examine the industry and sector averages, the differences are again apparent. The electric utility industry on average has $.8171 of long-term and $.9353 of total debt for every dollar of equity. By comparison, the pharmaceutical industry on average has only $.1557 of long-term debt and $.1953 of total debt for every dollar of equity. Thus, we see that choice of capital structure is a management decision, but it is also clearly influenced by industry characteristics.

Questions

1. The ratios shown for these companies are based on March 2012 figures. Go to www. reuters.com and find the current long-term debt-to-equity and total debt-to-equity ratios for both American Electric Power (AEP) and Johnson & Johnson (JNJ). How have these ratios changed over this time?

2. Go to www.reuters.com and find the long-term debt-to-equity and total debt-to-equity ratios for Bank of America (BAC), Dell (DELL), and Chevron (CVX). Why do you think these three companies use such differing amounts of debt?

CONCEPT QUESTIONS

13.7a Do U.S. corporations rely heavily on debt financing?

13.7b What regularities do we observe in capital structures?

A QUICK LOOK AT THE BANKRUPTCY PROCESS

13.8

As we have discussed, one of the consequences of using debt is the possibility of financial distress, which can be defined in several ways:

1. *Business failure.* This term is usually used to refer to a situation in which a business has terminated with a loss to creditors, but even an all-equity firm can fail.
2. *Legal bankruptcy.* Firms or creditors bring petitions to a federal court for bankruptcy. **Bankruptcy** is a legal proceeding for liquidating or reorganizing a business.
3. *Technical insolvency.* Technical insolvency occurs when a firm is unable to meet its financial obligations.
4. *Accounting insolvency.* Firms with negative net worth are insolvent on the books. This happens when the total book liabilities exceed the book value of the total assets.

> **bankruptcy**
> A legal proceeding for liquidating or reorganizing a business.

We now very briefly discuss some of the terms and more relevant issues associated with bankruptcy and financial distress.

> The SEC has a good overview of the bankruptcy process in its "online publications" section of www.sec.gov.

Liquidation and Reorganization

Firms that cannot or choose not to make contractually required payments to creditors have two basic options: liquidation or reorganization. **Liquidation** means termination of the firm as a going concern, and it involves selling off the assets of the firm. The proceeds, net of selling costs, are distributed to creditors in order of established priority. **Reorganization** is the option of keeping the firm a going concern; it often involves issuing new securities to replace old securities. Liquidation or reorganization is the result of a bankruptcy proceeding. Which occurs depends on whether the firm is worth more "dead or alive."

> **liquidation**
> Termination of the firm as a going concern.

> **reorganization**
> Financial restructuring of a failing firm to attempt to continue operations as a going concern.

Bankruptcy Liquidation   Chapter 7 of the Federal Bankruptcy Reform Act of 1978 deals with "straight" liquidation. The following sequence of events is typical:

1. A petition is filed in a federal court. A corporation may file a voluntary petition, or involuntary petitions may be filed against the corporation by several of its creditors.
2. A trustee-in-bankruptcy is elected by the creditors to take over the assets of the debtor corporation. The trustee will attempt to liquidate the assets.
3. When the assets are liquidated, after payment of the bankruptcy administration costs, the proceeds are distributed among the creditors.
4. If any proceeds remain, after expenses and payments to creditors, they are distributed to the shareholders.

The distribution of the proceeds of the liquidation occurs according to the following priority list:

1. Administrative expenses associated with the bankruptcy.
2. Other expenses arising after the filing of an involuntary bankruptcy petition but before the appointment of a trustee.

3. Wages, salaries, and commissions.
4. Contributions to employee benefit plans.
5. Consumer claims.
6. Government tax claims.
7. Payment to unsecured creditors.
8. Payment to preferred stockholders.
9. Payment to common stockholders.

absolute priority rule (APR)
The rule establishing priority of claims in liquidation.

This priority list for liquidation is a reflection of the **absolute priority rule (APR)**. The higher a claim is on this list, the more likely it is to be paid. In many of these categories, there are various limitations and qualifications that we omit for the sake of brevity.

Two qualifications to this list are in order. The first concerns secured creditors. Such creditors are entitled to the proceeds from the sale of the security and are outside this ordering. However, if the secured property is liquidated and provides cash insufficient to cover the amount owed, the secured creditors join with unsecured creditors in dividing the remaining liquidated value. In contrast, if the secured property is liquidated for proceeds greater than the secured claim, the net proceeds are used to pay unsecured creditors and others. The second qualification to the APR is that, in reality, what happens, and who gets what in the event of bankruptcy, is subject to much negotiation, and, as a result, the APR is frequently not followed.

The American Bankruptcy Institute provides extensive information. See www.abiworld.org.

Bankruptcy Reorganization Corporate reorganization takes place under Chapter 11 of the Federal Bankruptcy Reform Act of 1978. The general objective of a proceeding under Chapter 11 is to plan to restructure the corporation with some provision for repayment of creditors. A typical sequence of events follows:

1. A voluntary petition can be filed by the corporation, or an involuntary petition can be filed by creditors.
2. A federal judge either approves or denies the petition. If the petition is approved, a time for filing proofs of claims is set.
3. In most cases, the corporation (the "debtor in possession") continues to run the business.
4. The corporation (and, in certain cases, the creditors) submits a reorganization plan.
5. Creditors and shareholders are divided into classes. A class of creditors accepts the plan if a majority of the class agrees to the plan.
6. After its acceptance by creditors, the plan is confirmed by the court.
7. Payments in cash, property, and securities are made to creditors and shareholders. The plan may provide for the issuance of new securities.
8. For some fixed length of time, the firm operates according to the provisions of the reorganization plan.

The corporation may wish to allow the old stockholders to retain some participation in the firm. Needless to say, this may involve some protest by the holders of unsecured debt.

To give you some idea of the costs associated with a bankruptcy, consider the case of Lehman Brothers, which filed for bankruptcy in September 2008. The company wanted to reorganize through the bankruptcy process, but complications arose almost from the bankruptcy filing date. Because of the complexity of many of Lehman's assets, unwinding and selling them was difficult and time-consuming. Eventually, Lehman exited bankruptcy about three and a half years later in March 2012. Some of the firms that were involved in the Lehman bankruptcy were Alvarez & Marsal, which billed about $512 million in fees; Weil, Gotshal & Manges, which billed $383 million; and Milbank Tweed Hadley & McCloy, which billed $133 million. In all, Lehman's bankruptcy costs were $1.6 *billion* in fees. The next largest bankruptcy fees appear to have been paid to those involved in energy giant Enron's bankruptcy. The fees in that case reached a mere $1 billion.

So-called prepackaged bankruptcies are a relatively new phenomenon. What happens is that the corporation secures the necessary approval of a bankruptcy plan from a majority of its creditors first, and then it files for bankruptcy. As a result, the company enters bankruptcy and reemerges almost immediately.

For example, in November 2004, Trump Hotels and Casinos filed for Chapter 11 bankruptcy. This was the second bankruptcy proceeding for the company. Fortunately for "The Donald," creditors didn't say "You're fired!" Under the terms of the deal, Trump's stake in the company was cut, but he stayed on as chairman of the board and CEO. He also received, among other things, a 25 percent stake in the Miss USA Pageant and four acres of land in Atlantic City. The then-current bondholders agreed to exchange their bonds for a combination of new bonds with a lower coupon rate, along with cash and stock. Unfortunately for The Donald, this was not his last experience with the bankruptcy process. In early 2009, Trump Hotels filed Chapter 11 bankruptcy for the third time, making it a "Chapter 33" bankruptcy.

In some cases, the bankruptcy procedure is needed to invoke the "cram-down" power of the bankruptcy court. Under certain circumstances, a class of creditors can be forced to accept a bankruptcy plan even if they vote not to approve it, hence the remarkably apt description "cram down."

In 2005, Congress passed the most significant overhaul of U.S. bankruptcy laws in the last 25 years, the Bankruptcy Abuse Prevention and Consumer Protection Act of 2005 (BAPCPA). Most of the changes were aimed at individual debtors, but corporations were also affected. Before BAPCPA, a bankrupt company had the exclusive right to submit reorganization plans to the bankruptcy court. It has been argued that this exclusivity is one reason some companies have remained in bankruptcy for so long. Under the new law, after 18 months, creditors can submit their own plan for the court's consideration. This change is likely to speed up bankruptcies and also lead to more "prepacks" (to learn about prepacks, see our nearby *Finance Matters* box).

One controversial change made by BAPCPA has to do with so-called key employee retention plans or KERPs. Strange as it may sound, bankrupt companies routinely give bonus payments to executives, even though the executives may be the same ones who led the company into bankruptcy in the first place. Such bonuses are intended to keep valuable employees from moving to more successful firms, but critics have argued they are often abused. The new law permits KERPs only if the employee in question actually has a job offer from another company.

Recently, Section 363 of the bankruptcy code has been in the news. In a traditional Chapter 11 filing, the bankruptcy plan is described to creditors and shareholders in a prospectus-like disclosure. The plan must then be approved by a vote involving the interested parties. A Section 363 bankruptcy is more like an auction. An initial bidder, known as a *stalking horse,* bids on all or part of the bankrupt company's assets. Other bidders are then invited into the process to determine the highest bid for the company's assets. The main advantage of a Section 363 bankruptcy is speed. Since a traditional bankruptcy requires the approval of interested parties, it is not uncommon for the process to take several years, while a Section 363 bankruptcy is generally much quicker. For example, in the middle of 2009, both General Motors and Chrysler sped through the bankruptcy process in less than 45 days with the help of Section 363 sales.

FINANCE MATTERS

◀ For the latest news on the topics covered in this chapter, scan here.

Bankruptcy, "Prepack" Style

On December 12, 2011, Lee Enterprises, which publishes 48 daily newspapers and provides infrastructure for over 1,500 online newspapers, filed for Chapter 11 reorganization under the U.S. Bankruptcy code. At the time of filing, the company had about $1 billion in debt. A firm in this situation could reasonably be expected to spend a year or more in bankruptcy. Not so with Lee Enterprises. The company exited bankruptcy on January 31, 2012. In bankruptcy, most companies shed debt from the balance sheet; however, in Lee's case the company lengthened the maturity of the debt, but at a cost. The interest rate on the debt jumped from 5.1 percent to 9.2 percent, and bondholders received 13 percent of the company's equity. Even though Lee Enterprises had a brief stay in bankruptcy, the all-time record belongs to Blue Bird, maker of the iconic yellow school buses. Blue Bird's stay in bankruptcy was *one day*!

Firms typically file for bankruptcy to seek protection from their creditors, essentially admitting that they cannot meet their financial obligations as they are then structured. Once in bankruptcy, the firm attempts to reorganize its operations and finances so that it can survive. A key to this process is that most of the creditors must ultimately give their approval to the restructuring plan. The time a firm spends in Chapter 11 depends on many things, but it usually depends most on the time it takes to get creditors to agree to a plan of reorganization.

Blue Bird was able to expedite its bankruptcy by filing a presolicited, or prepackaged, bankruptcy, often called a prepack. The idea is simple. Before filing for bankruptcy, the firm approaches its creditors with a plan for reorganization.

The two sides negotiate a settlement and agree on the details of how the firm's finances will be restructured. Then, the firm puts together the necessary paperwork for the bankruptcy court before filing for bankruptcy. A filing is a prepack if the firm essentially walks into court and, at the same time, files a reorganization plan complete with the documentation of its creditors' approval, which is exactly what Blue Bird did.

The key to the prepackaged reorganization process is that both sides have something to gain and something to lose. If bankruptcy is imminent, it may make sense for the creditors to expedite the process even though they are likely to take a financial loss in the restructuring. Blue Bird's bankruptcy was relatively painless for most of its creditors. Several different classes of creditors were involved. Bank loans were converted into senior secured notes and senior bondholders exchanged their bonds for new bonds with the same face value and terms. Of course, the old stockholders received nothing, and, in fact, had their shares canceled.

For a firm, operating in bankruptcy can be a difficult process. The bankruptcy court typically has a great deal of oversight over the firm's day-to-day operations, and putting together a reorganization plan to emerge from bankruptcy can be a tremendous drain on management time, time that would be better spent making the firm profitable again. Also, news that a firm is in bankruptcy can make skittish customers turn to competitors, endangering the future health of the firm. A prepack can't completely eliminate these problems, but by speeding up the bankruptcy process, it can reduce the headaches involved.

Financial Management and the Bankruptcy Process

Get the latest on bankruptcy at www.bankruptcydata.com.

It may seem a little odd, but the right to go bankrupt is very valuable. There are several reasons why this is true. First of all, from an operational standpoint, when a firm files for bankruptcy, there is an immediate "stay" on creditors, usually meaning that payments to creditors will cease, and creditors will have to await the outcome of the bankruptcy process to find out if and how much they will be paid. This stay gives the firm time to evaluate its options, and it prevents what is usually termed a "race to the courthouse steps" by creditors and others.

Beyond this, some bankruptcy filings are actually strategic actions intended to improve a firm's competitive position, and firms have filed for bankruptcy even though they were not insolvent at the time. Probably the most famous example is Continental Airlines. In 1983, following deregulation of the airline industry, Continental found itself competing with newly established airlines that had much lower labor costs. In response, Continental filed for reorganization under Chapter 11 even though it was not insolvent.

Continental argued that, based on pro forma data, it would become insolvent in the future, and a reorganization was therefore necessary. By filing for bankruptcy, Continental was able to terminate its existing labor agreements, lay off large numbers of workers, and slash wages for the remaining employees. In other words, at least in the eyes of critics, Continental essentially used the bankruptcy process as a vehicle for reducing labor costs. Congress has subsequently modified bankruptcy laws to make it more difficult, though not impossible, for companies to abrogate a labor contract through the bankruptcy process. For example, Delta Air Lines filed for bankruptcy in 2005, in part to renegotiate the contracts with its union employees.

Other famous examples of strategic bankruptcies exist. For example, Manville (then known as Johns-Manville) and Dow Corning filed for bankruptcies because of expected future losses resulting from litigations associated with asbestos and silicone breast implants, respectively. Similarly, in the then-largest ever bankruptcy, Texaco filed in 1987 after Pennzoil was awarded a $10.3 billion judgment against the company. Texaco later settled for $3.5 billion and emerged from bankruptcy. As of early 2012, the largest bankruptcies ever in terms of assets occurred less than two weeks apart in 2008. On September 15, 2008, the investment bank Lehman Brothers Holdings filed for bankruptcy. The company listed about $639 billion in assets. Then, on September 26, 2008, the giant savings bank Washington Mutual (or "WaMu" as it was better known) filed for bankruptcy with about $328 billion in assets. The 2003 bankruptcy filing of Italian dairy company Parmalat may have topped them both in terms of relative importance. This company, by itself, represented 1.5 percent of the Italian gross national product!

Agreements to Avoid Bankruptcy

When a firm defaults on an obligation, it can avoid a bankruptcy filing. Because the legal process of bankruptcy can be lengthy and expensive, it is often in everyone's best interest to devise a "workout" that avoids a bankruptcy filing. Much of the time, creditors can work with the management of a company that has defaulted on a loan contract. Voluntary arrangements to restructure, or "reschedule," the company's debt can be and often are made. This may involve *extension,* which postpones the date of payment, or *composition,* which allows a reduced payment.

CONCEPT QUESTIONS

13.8a   What is the APR (in connection with bankruptcy proceedings)?

13.8b   What is the difference between liquidation and reorganization?

SUMMARY AND CONCLUSIONS

The ideal mixture of debt and equity for a firm—its optimal capital structure—is the one that maximizes the value of the firm and minimizes the overall cost of capital. If we ignore taxes, financial distress costs, and any other imperfections, we find that there is no ideal mixture. Under these circumstances, the firm's capital structure is simply irrelevant.

If we consider the effect of corporate taxes, we find that capital structure matters a great deal. This conclusion is based on the fact that interest is tax deductible and thus generates a valuable tax shield. Unfortunately, we also find that the optimal capital structure is 100 percent debt, which is not something we observe in healthy firms.

We next introduced costs associated with bankruptcy, or, more generally, financial distress. These costs reduce the attractiveness of debt financing. We concluded that an optimal capital structure exists when the net tax saving from an additional dollar in interest just equals the increase in expected financial distress costs. This is the essence of the static theory of capital structure.

◀ Think you've mastered the material? Scan here to take a chapter quiz.

When we examine actual capital structures, we find two regularities. First, firms in the United States typically do not use great amounts of debt, but they pay substantial taxes. This suggests that there is a limit to the use of debt financing to generate tax shields. Second, there is wide variation in the use of debt across industries, suggesting that the nature of a firm's assets and operations is an important determinant of its capital structure.

 CONNECT POP QUIZ!   **connect** |FINANCE

Can you answer the following questions? If your class is using *Connect Finance,* log on to the Self-Quiz and Study feature in the Library tab to see if you know the answers to these and other questions, check out the study tools, and find out what topics require additional practice!

Section 13.3 Crosby Industries has a debt-equity ratio of 1.2. Its WACC is 11 percent, and its cost of debt is 5 percent. There is no corporate tax. What is Crosby's cost of equity capital?

Section 13.4 Cede & Co. can borrow at 12.25 percent. Cede currently has no debt, and the cost of equity is 15.50 percent. The current value of the firm is $679,000. The corporate tax rate is 40 percent. What will the value be if Cede borrows $228,000 and uses the proceeds to repurchase shares?

Section 13.5 What are indirect costs of bankruptcy?

Section 13.6 The static theory of capital structure is based on the theory that firms use leverage up to the point where the marginal value of what two things are equal?

Section 13.7 Do U.S. firms tend to totally offset their tax liabilities with their interest deductions?

Section 13.8 What would generally receive the lowest priority when the assets of a Chapter 7 bankruptcy firm are distributed?

CHAPTER REVIEW AND SELF-TEST PROBLEMS

13.1   EBIT and EPS. Suppose the GNR Corporation has decided in favor of a capital restructuring that involves increasing its existing $5 million in debt to $25 million. The interest rate on the debt is 12 percent and is not expected to change. The firm currently has one million shares outstanding, and the price per share is $40. If the restructuring is expected to increase the ROE, what is the minimum level for EBIT that GNR's management must be expecting? Ignore taxes in your answer. (See Problem 4.)

13.2   M&M Proposition II (no taxes). The Pro Bono Corporation has a WACC of 20 percent. Its cost of debt is 12 percent. If Pro Bono's debt-equity ratio is 2, what is its cost of equity capital? Ignore taxes in your answer. (See Problem 10.)

13.3   M&M Proposition I (with corporate taxes). Suppose TransGlobal Co. currently has no debt and its equity is worth $20,000. If the corporate tax rate is 30 percent, what will the value of the firm be if TransGlobal borrows $6,000 and uses the proceeds to buy up stock? (See Problem 14.)

■ Answers to Chapter Review and Self-Test Problems

13.1 To answer, we can calculate the break-even EBIT. At any EBIT above this, the increased financial leverage will increase EPS. Under the old capital structure, the interest bill is $5 million $\times$ .12 = $600,000. There are one million shares of stock, so, ignoring taxes, EPS is (EBIT − $600,000)/1 million.

Under the new capital structure, the interest expense will be $25 million $\times$ .12 = $3 million. Furthermore, the debt rises by $20 million. This amount is sufficient to repurchase $20 million/40 = 500,000 shares of stock, leaving 500,000 outstanding. EPS is thus (EBIT − $3 million)/500,000.

Now that we know how to calculate EPS under both scenarios, we set the two expressions for EPS equal to each other and solve for the break-even EBIT:

$$\text{(EBIT − \$600,000)/1 million = (EBIT − \$3 million) / 500,000}$$
$$\text{EBIT − \$600,000 = 2} \times \text{(EBIT − \$3 million)}$$
$$\text{EBIT = \$5,400,000}$$

Verify that, in either case, EPS is $4.80 when EBIT is $5.4 million.

13.2 According to M&M Proposition II (no taxes), the cost of equity is:

$$R_E = R_A + (R_A − R_D) \times (D/E)$$
$$= 20\% + (20\% − 12\%) \times 2$$
$$= 36\%$$

13.3 After the debt issue, TransGlobal will be worth the original $20,000 plus the present value of the tax shield. According to M&M Proposition I with taxes, the present value of the tax shield is $T_C \times D$, or .30 $\times$ $6,000 = $1,800, so the firm is worth $20,000 + 1,800 = $21,800.

CRITICAL THINKING AND CONCEPTS REVIEW

LO 1   **13.1 Business Risk versus Financial Risk.** Explain what is meant by business and financial risk. Suppose Firm A has greater business risk than Firm B. Is it true that Firm A also has a higher cost of equity capital? Explain.

LO 1   **13.2 M&M Propositions.** How would you answer in the following debate?

Q: Isn't it true that the riskiness of a firm's equity will rise if the firm increases its use of debt financing?

A: Yes, that's the essence of M&M Proposition II.

Q: And isn't it true that, as a firm increases its use of borrowing, the likelihood of default increases, which increases the risk of the firm's debt?

A: Yes.

Q: In other words, increased borrowing increases the risk of the equity *and* the debt?

A: That's right.

Q: Well, given that the firm uses only debt and equity financing, and given that the risk of both is increased by increased borrowing, does it not follow that increasing debt increases the overall risk of the firm and therefore decreases the value of the firm?

A: ??

LO 1   **13.3 Optimal Capital Structure.**   Is there an easily identifiable debt-equity ratio that will maximize the value of a firm? Why or why not?

LO 1   **13.4 Observed Capital Structures.**   Refer to the observed capital structures given in Table 13.5 of the text. What do you notice about the types of industries with respect to their average debt-equity ratios? Are certain types of industries more likely to be highly leveraged than others? What are some possible reasons for this observed segmentation? Do the operating results and tax history of the firms play a role? How about their future earnings prospects? Explain.

LO 1   **13.5 Financial Leverage.**   Why is the use of debt financing referred to as using financial "leverage"?

LO 1   **13.6 Homemade Leverage.**   What is homemade leverage?

LO 3   **13.7 Bankruptcy and Corporate Ethics.**   As mentioned in the text, some firms have filed for bankruptcy because of actual or likely litigation-related losses. Is this a proper use of the bankruptcy process?

LO 3   **13.8 Bankruptcy and Corporate Ethics.**   Firms sometimes use the threat of a bankruptcy filing to force creditors to renegotiate terms. Critics argue that in such cases, the firm is using bankruptcy laws "as a sword rather than a shield." Is this an ethical tactic?

LO 3   **13.9 Bankruptcy and Corporate Ethics.**   As mentioned in the text, Continental Airlines filed for bankruptcy, at least in part, as a means of reducing labor costs. Whether this move was ethical, or proper, was hotly debated. Give both sides of the argument.

LO 1   **13.10 Capital Structure Goal.**   What is the basic goal of financial management with regard to capital structure?

QUESTIONS AND PROBLEMS   Select problems are available in McGraw-Hill *Connect.* Please see the packaging options section of the preface for more information.

Basic
(Questions 1–13)

LO 1   **1. EBIT and Leverage.**   Kaelea, Inc., has no debt outstanding and a total market value of $125,000. Earnings before interest and taxes, EBIT, are projected to be $10,400 if economic conditions are normal. If there is strong expansion in the economy, then EBIT will be 20 percent higher. If there is a recession, then EBIT will be 35 percent lower. Kaelea is considering a $42,000 debt issue with a 6 percent interest rate. The proceeds will be used to repurchase shares of stock. There are currently 6,250 shares outstanding. Ignore taxes for this problem.

   a. Calculate earnings per share, EPS, under each of the three economic scenarios before any debt is issued. Also, calculate the percentage changes in EPS when the economy expands or enters a recession.

   b. Repeat part (*a*) assuming that Kaelea goes through with recapitalization. What do you observe?

LO 2   **2. EBIT, Taxes, and Leverage.**   Repeat parts (a) and (b) in Problem 1 assuming Kaelea has a tax rate of 35 percent.

LO 1   LO 2   **3. ROE and Leverage.**   Suppose the company in Problem 1 has a market-to-book ratio of 1.0.

   a. Calculate return on equity, ROE, under each of the three economic scenarios before any debt is issued. Also, calculate the percentage changes in ROE for economic expansion and recession, assuming no taxes.

b. Repeat part (a) assuming the firm goes through with the proposed recapitalization.

c. Repeat parts (a) and (b) of this problem assuming the firm has a tax rate of 35 percent.

LO 1   **4. Break-Even EBIT.** Kyle Corporation is comparing two different capital structures, an all-equity plan (Plan I) and a levered plan (Plan II). Under Plan I, Kyle would have 400,000 shares of stock outstanding. Under Plan II, there would be 260,000 shares of stock outstanding and $6,020,000 in debt outstanding. The interest rate on the debt is 10 percent, and there are no taxes.

   a. If EBIT is $1.3 million, which plan will result in the higher EPS?

   b. If EBIT is $2.1 million, which plan will result in the higher EPS?

   c. What is the break-even EBIT?

LO 1   **5. M&M and Stock Value.** In Problem 4, use M&M Proposition I to find the price per share of equity under each of the two proposed plans. What is the value of the firm?

LO 1   **LO 2**   **6. Break-Even EBIT and Leverage.** Cooke Co. is comparing two different capital structures. Plan I would result in 8,500 shares of stock and $361,000 in debt. Plan II would result in 12,000 shares of stock and $228,000 in debt. The interest rate on the debt is 10 percent.

   a. Ignoring taxes, compare both of these plans to an all-equity plan assuming that EBIT will be $61,000. The all-equity plan would result in 18,000 shares of stock outstanding. Which of the three plans has the highest EPS? The lowest?

   b. In part (a), what are the break-even levels of EBIT for each plan as compared to that for an all-equity plan? Is one higher than the other? Why?

   c. Ignoring taxes, when will EPS be identical for Plans I and II?

   d. Repeat parts (a), (b), and (c) assuming that the corporate tax rate is 35 percent. Are the break-even levels of EBIT different from before? Why or why not?

LO 1   **7. Leverage and Stock Value.** Ignoring taxes in Problem 6, what is the price per share of equity under Plan I? Plan II? What principle is illustrated by your answers?

LO 1   **8. Homemade Leverage.** FCOJ, Inc., a prominent consumer products firm, is debating whether or not to convert its all-equity capital structure to one that is 30 percent debt. Currently, there are 5,700 shares outstanding and the price per share is $55. EBIT is expected to remain at $18,600 per year forever. The interest rate on new debt is 8 percent, and there are no taxes.

   a. Melanie, a shareholder of the firm, owns 100 shares of stock. What is her cash flow under the current capital structure, assuming the firm has a dividend payout rate of 100 percent?

   b. What will Melanie's cash flow be under the proposed capital structure of the firm? Assume that she keeps all 100 of her shares.

   c. Suppose FCOJ does convert, but Melanie prefers the current all-equity capital structure. Show how she could unlever her shares of stock to recreate the original capital structure.

   d. Using your answer to part (c), explain why FCOJ's choice of capital structure is irrelevant.

LO 1   **9. Homemade Leverage.** Staal Enterprises is considering a change from its current capital structure. Staal currently has an all-equity capital structure and is considering a capital structure with 25 percent debt. There are currently 6,100 shares outstanding at a price per share of $60. EBIT is expected to remain constant at $38,000. The interest rate on new debt is 7 percent and there are no taxes.

a. Rebecca owns $18,000 worth of stock in the company. If the firm has a 100 percent payout, what is her cash flow?

b. What would her cash flow be under the new capital structure assuming that she keeps all of her shares?

c. Suppose the company does convert to the new capital structure. Show how Rebecca can maintain her current cash flow.

d. Under your answer to part (c), explain why Staal's choice of capital structure is irrelevant.

LO 1 **10. Calculating WACC.** Crosby Industries has a debt-equity ratio of 1.5. Its WACC is 8.5 percent, and its cost of debt is 6 percent. There is no corporate tax.

a. What is Crosby's cost of equity capital?

b. What would the cost of equity be if the debt-equity ratio were 2.0? What if it were 0.5? What if it were zero?

LO 1 **11. Calculating WACC.** Malkin Corp. has no debt but can borrow at 7 percent. The firm's WACC is currently 11 percent, and there is no corporate tax.

a. What is Malkin's cost of equity?

b. If the firm converts to 30 percent debt, what will its cost of equity be?

c. If the firm converts to 60 percent debt, what will its cost of equity be?

d. What is Malkin's WACC in part (b)? In part (c)?

LO 2 **12. M&M and Taxes.** Dupuis can borrow at 9 percent. Dupuis currently has no debt, and the cost of equity is 15 percent. The current value of the firm is $735,000. What will the value be if Dupuis borrows $220,000 and uses the proceeds to repurchase shares? The corporate tax rate is 35 percent.

LO 2 **13. Interest Tax Shield.** Fleury Co. has a 38 percent tax rate. Its total interest payment for the year just ended was $24 million. What is the interest tax shield? How do you interpret this amount?

LO 1 **14. M&M.** Neal Enterprises has no debt. Its current total value is $45 million. Ignoring taxes, what will the company's value be if it sells $16 million in debt? Suppose now that the company's tax rate is 40 percent. What will its overall value be if it sells $16 million in debt? Assume debt proceeds are used to repurchase equity.

Intermediate
(Questions 14–16)

LO 1 **15. M&M.** In the previous question, what is the debt-equity ratio in both cases?

LO 1 **16. M&M.** Kunitz Co. has no debt. Its cost of capital is 8.7 percent. Suppose Kunitz converts to a debt-equity ratio of 1.0. The interest rate on the debt is 6.3 percent. Ignoring taxes, what is the company's new cost of equity? What is its new WACC?

LO 2 **17. Firm Value.** Letang Corporation expects an EBIT of $19,750 every year forever. The company currently has no debt, and its cost of equity is 15 percent.

Challenge
(Questions 17–20)

a. What is the current value of the company?

b. Suppose the company can borrow at 10 percent. If the corporate tax rate is 35 percent, what will the value of the firm be if the company takes on debt equal to 50 percent of its unlevered value? What if it takes on debt equal to 100 percent of its unlevered value?

c. What will the value of the firm be if the company takes on debt equal to 50 percent of its levered value? What if the company takes on debt equal to 100 percent of its levered value?

LO 2

18. **Firm Value.** What is the cost of capital for a firm that is 100 percent debt financed? What is the value of the firm?

LO 2

19. **Cost of Equity and Leverage.** Assuming a world of corporate taxes only, show that the cost of equity, R_E, is as follows: $R_E = R_U + (R_U - R_D) \times (D/E) \times (1 - T_C)$.

LO 2

20. **Business and Financial Risk.** Assume a firm's debt is risk-free, so that the cost of debt equals the risk-free rate, R_f. Define β_A as the firm's *asset* beta—that is, the systematic risk of the firm's assets. Define β_E to be the beta of the firm's equity. Use the capital asset pricing model (CAPM) along with M&M Proposition II to show that $\beta_E = \beta_A \times (1 + D/E)$, where D/E is the debt-equity ratio. Assume the tax rate is zero.

13.1 **Capital Structure.** Go to reuters.com and enter the ticker symbol AMGN for Amgen, a biotechnology company. Find the long-term debt-to-equity and total debt-to-equity ratios. How does Amgen compare to the industry, sector, and S&P 500 in these areas? Now answer the same question for Edison International (EIX), the parent company of Southern California Edison, a utility company. How do the capital structures of Amgen and Edison International compare? Can you think of possible explanations for the difference between these two companies?

13.2 **Capital Structure.** Go to finance.yahoo.com and find the stock screener. Use the Java stock screener to answer the following questions. How many companies have debt-to-equity ratios greater than 2? Greater than 5? Greater than 10? What company has the highest debt-to-equity ratio? What is the ratio? Now find how many companies have a negative debt-to-equity ratio. What is the lowest debt-to-equity ratio? What does it mean if a company has a negative debt-to-equity ratio?

WHAT'S ON THE WEB?

www.mhhe.com/rwj

CHAPTER CASE
STEPHENSON REAL ESTATE RECAPITALIZATION

Stephenson Real Estate Company was founded 25 years ago by the current CEO, Robert Stephenson. The company purchases real estate, including land and buildings, and rents the property to tenants. The company has shown a profit every year for the past 18 years, and the shareholders are satisfied with the company's management. Prior to founding Stephenson Real Estate, Robert was the founder and CEO of a failed alpaca farming operation. The resulting bankruptcy made him extremely averse to debt financing. As a result, the company is entirely equity financed, with 9 million shares of common stock outstanding. The stock currently trades at $42.50 per share.

Stephenson is evaluating a plan to purchase a huge tract of land in the southeastern United States for $50 million. The land will subsequently be leased to tenant farmers. This purchase is expected to increase Stephenson's annual pretax earnings by $12 million in perpetuity. Kim Weyand, the company's new CFO, has been put in charge of the project. Kim has determined that the company's current cost of capital is 12.5 percent. She feels that the company would be more valuable if it included debt in its capital structure, so she is evaluating whether the company should issue debt to entirely finance the project. Based on some conversations with investment banks, she thinks that the company can issue bonds at par value with an 8 percent coupon rate. From her analysis, she also believes that a capital structure in the range of 70 percent equity/30 percent debt would be optimal. If the company goes beyond 30 percent debt, its bonds would carry a lower rating and a much higher coupon because the possibility of financial distress and the associated costs would rise sharply. Stephenson has a 40 percent corporate tax rate (state and federal).

www.mhhe.com/rwj

QUESTIONS

1. If Stephenson wishes to maximize its total market value, would you recommend that it issue debt or equity to finance the land purchase? Explain.

2. Construct Stephenson's market value balance sheet before it announces the purchase.

3. Suppose Stephenson decides to issue equity to finance the purchase.

   a. What is the net present value of the project?

   b. Construct Stephenson's market value balance sheet after it announces that the firm will finance the purchase using equity. What would be the new price per share of the firm's stock? How many shares will Stephenson need to issue to finance the purchase?

   c. Construct Stephenson's market value balance sheet after the equity issue but before the purchase has been made. How many

   shares of common stock does Stephenson have outstanding? What is the price per share of the firm's stock?

   d. Construct Stephenson's market value balance sheet after the purchase has been made.

4. Suppose Stephenson decides to issue debt to finance the purchase.

   a. What will the market value of the Stephenson Company be if the purchase is financed with debt?

   b. Construct Stephenson's market value balance sheet after both the debt issue and the land purchase. What is the price per share of the firm's stock?

5. Which method of financing maximizes the per-share stock price of Stephenson's equity?

Glossary

absolute priority rule (APR)   The rule establishing priority of claims in liquidation.

Accelerated Cost Recovery System (ACRS)   Depreciation method under U.S. tax law allowing for the accelerated write-off of property under various classifications.

accounts payable period   The time between receipt of inventory and payment for it.

accounts receivable financing   A secured short-term loan that involves either the assignment or factoring of receivables.

accounts receivable period   The time between sale of inventory and collection of the receivable.

agency problem   The possibility of conflict of interest between the owners and management of a firm.

aging schedule   A compilation of accounts receivable by the age of each account.

American Depositary Receipt (ADR)   A security issued in the United States representing shares of a foreign stock and allowing that stock to be traded in the United States.

annual percentage rate (APR)   The interest rate charged per period multiplied by the number of periods per year.

annuity   A level stream of cash flows for a fixed period of time.

annuity due   An annuity for which the cash flows occur at the beginning of the period.

arithmetic average return   The return earned in an average year over a particular period.

asked price   The price a dealer is willing to take for a security.

asset-specific risk   A risk that affects at most a small number of assets. Also *unique* or *unsystematic risk*.

average accounting return (AAR)   An investment's average net income divided by its average book value.

average tax rate   Total taxes paid divided by total taxable income.

balance sheet   Financial statement showing a firm's accounting value on a particular date.

bankruptcy   A legal proceeding for liquidating or reorganizing a business. Also, the transfer of some or all of a firm's assets to its creditors.

bearer form   A bond issued without record of the owner's name; payment is made to whomever holds the bond.

benefit-cost ratio   The present value of an investment's future cash flows divided by its initial cost. Also *profitability index.*

best efforts underwriting   The underwriter sells as much of the issue as possible, but can return any unsold shares to the issuer without financial responsibility.

beta coefficient   Amount of systematic risk present in a particular risky asset relative to that in an average risky asset.

bid-ask spread   The difference between the bid price and the asked price.

bid price   The price a dealer is willing to pay for a security.

broker   An agent who arranges security transactions among investors.

business risk   The equity risk that comes from the nature of the firm's operating activities.

call premium   The amount by which the call price exceeds the par value of the bond.

call protected bond   Bond during period in which it cannot be redeemed by the issuer.

call provision   Agreement giving the issuer the option to repurchase a bond at a specific price prior to maturity.

capital asset pricing model (CAPM)   Equation of the security market line showing the relationship between expected return and beta.

capital budgeting   The process of planning and managing a firm's long-term investments.

capital gains yield   The dividend growth rate, or the rate at which the value of an investment grows.

capital rationing   The situation that exists if a firm has positive net present value projects but cannot obtain the necessary financing.

capital structure   The mixture of debt and equity maintained by a firm.

captive finance company   A partially or wholly owned subsidiary that handles the credit function for the parent company.

carrying costs   Costs that rise with increases in the level of investment in current assets.

cash budget   A forecast of cash receipts and disbursements for the next planning period.

cash concentration   The practice of and procedures for moving cash from multiple banks into the firm's main accounts.

cash cycle   The time between cash disbursement and cash collection.

cash discount   A discount given to induce prompt payment. Also *sales discount.*

624   GLOSSARY

cash flow from assets   The total of cash flow to creditors and cash flow to stockholders, consisting of the following: operating cash flow, capital spending, and changes in net working capital.

cash flow to creditors   A firm's interest payments to creditors less net new borrowings.

cash flow to stockholders   Dividends paid out by a firm less net new equity raised.

cash flow time line   Graphical representation of the operating cycle and the cash cycle.

clean price   The price of a bond net of accrued interest; this is the price that is typically quoted.

clientele effect   Argument that stocks attract particular groups based on dividend yield and the resulting tax effects.

collection policy   Procedures followed by a firm in collecting accounts receivable.

commission brokers   NYSE members who execute orders to buy and sell stock transmitted to the exchange floor.

common-size statement   A standardized financial statement presenting all items in percentage terms. Balance sheet items are shown as a percentage of assets and income statement items as a percentage of sales.

common stock   Equity without priority for dividends or in bankruptcy.

compounding   The process of accumulating interest in an investment over time to earn more interest.

compound interest   Interest earned on both the initial principal and the interest reinvested from prior periods.

compound value   The amount an investment is worth after one or more periods. Also *future value*.

consol   A type of perpetuity.

contingency planning   Taking into account the managerial options implicit in a project.

controlled disbursement account   A disbursement practice under which the firm transfers an amount to a disbursing account that is sufficient to cover demands for payment.

corporation   A business created as a distinct legal entity owned by one or more individuals or entities.

cost of capital   The minimum required return on a new investment.

cost of debt   The return that lenders require on the firm's debt.

cost of equity   The return that equity investors require on their investment in the firm.

coupon   The stated interest payment made on a bond.

coupon rate   The annual coupon divided by the face value of a bond.

credit analysis   The process of determining the probability that customers will or will not pay.

credit cost curve   Graphical representation of the sum of the carrying costs and the opportunity costs of a credit policy.

credit instrument   The evidence of indebtedness.

credit period   The length of time for which credit is granted.

credit scoring   The process of quantifying the probability of default when granting consumer credit.

cross-rate   The implicit exchange rate between two currencies (usually non-U.S.) quoted in some third currency (usually the U.S. dollar).

cumulative voting   A procedure in which a shareholder may cast all votes for one member of the board of directors.

current yield   A bond's coupon payment divided by its closing price.

date of payment   Date that the dividend checks are mailed.

date of record   Date on which holders must be on record to receive a dividend.

dealer   An agent who buys and sells securities from inventory.

debenture   Unsecured debt, usually with a maturity of 10 years or more.

declaration date   Date on which the board of directors passes a resolution to pay a dividend.

default risk premium   The portion of a nominal interest rate or bond yield that represents compensation for the possibility of default.

deferred call provision   Bond call provision prohibiting the company from redeeming the bond prior to a certain date.

depreciation tax shield   The tax saving that results from the depreciation deduction, calculated as depreciation multiplied by the corporate tax rate.

designated market maker (DMM)   An NYSE member acting as a dealer in a small number of securities on the exchange floor; formerly known as a "specialist."

direct bankruptcy costs   The costs that are directly associated with bankruptcy, such as legal and administrative expenses.

dirty price   The price of a bond including accrued interest, also known as the *full* or *invoice price*. This is the price the buyer actually pays.

discount   Calculation of the present value of some future amount.

discounted cash flow (DCF) valuation   (a) Valuation calculating the present value of a future cash flow to determine its value today. (b) The process of valuing an investment by discounting its future cash flows.

discount rate   The rate used to calculate the present value of future cash flows.

distribution   Payment made by a firm to its owners from sources other than current or accumulated retained earnings.

dividend   Payment made out of a firm's earnings to its owners, in the form of either cash or stock.

dividend growth model   Model that determines the current price of a stock as its dividend next period divided by the discount rate less the dividend growth rate.

dividend yield   A stock's expected cash dividend divided by its current price.

DMM's post   A fixed place on the exchange floor where the DMM operates.

DuPont identity   Popular expression breaking ROE into three parts: operating efficiency, asset use efficiency, and financial leverage.

Dutch auction underwriting   The type of underwriting in which the offer price is set based on competitive bidding by investors. Also known as a *uniform price auction*.

economic order quantity (EOQ)   The restocking quantity that minimizes the total inventory costs.

effective annual rate (EAR)   The interest rate expressed as if it were compounded once per year.

efficient capital market   Market in which security prices reflect available information.

efficient markets hypothesis (EMH)   The hypothesis that actual capital markets, such as the New York Stock Exchange, are efficient.

electronic communications networks (ECNs)   Websites that allow investors to trade directly with one another.

erosion   The cash flows of a new project that come at the expense of a firm's existing projects.

estimation risk   The possibility that errors in projected cash flows will lead to incorrect decisions. Also *forecasting risk*.

Eurobonds   International bonds issued in multiple countries but denominated in a single currency (usually the issuer's currency).

Eurocurrency   Money deposited in a financial center outside the country whose currency is involved.

exchange rate   The price of one country's currency expressed in terms of another country's currency.

exchange rate risk   The risk related to having international operations in a world where relative currency values vary.

ex dividend date   Date two business days before the date of record, establishing those individuals entitled to a dividend.

expected return   Return on a risky asset expected in the future.

face value   The principal amount of a bond that is repaid at the end of the term. Also *par value*.

financial distress costs   The direct and indirect costs associated with going bankrupt or experiencing financial distress.

financial ratios   Relationships determined from a firm's financial information and used for comparison purposes.

financial risk   The equity risk that comes from the financial policy (i.e., capital structure) of the firm.

firm commitment underwriting   The underwriter buys the entire issue, assuming full financial responsibility for any unsold shares.

Fisher effect   The relationship among nominal returns, real returns, and inflation.

five Cs of credit   The five basic credit factors to be evaluated: character, capacity, capital, collateral, and conditions.

float   The difference between book cash and bank cash, representing the net effect of checks in the process of clearing.

floor brokers   NYSE members who execute customer buy and sell orders; sometimes called $2 brokers.

floor traders   NYSE members who trade for their own accounts, trying to anticipate temporary price fluctuations.

forecasting risk   The possibility that errors in projected cash flows will lead to incorrect decisions. Also *estimation risk*.

foreign bonds   International bonds issued in a single country, usually denominated in that country's currency.

foreign exchange market   The market in which one country's currency is traded for another's.

forward exchange rate   The agreed-upon exchange rate to be used in a forward trade.

forward trade   Agreement to exchange currency at some time in the future.

free cash flow   Another name for cash flow from assets.

future value (FV)   The amount an investment is worth after one or more periods. Also *compound value*.

general cash offer   An issue of securities offered for sale to the general public on a cash basis.

Generally Accepted Accounting Principles (GAAP)   The common set of standards and procedures by which audited financial statements are prepared.

geometric average return   The average compound return earned per year over a multiyear period.

gilts   British and Irish government securities.

Green Shoe provision   A contract provision giving the underwriter the option to purchase additional shares from the issuer at the offering price. Also *overallotment option*.

hard rationing   The situation that occurs when a business cannot raise financing for a project under any circumstances.

homemade leverage   The use of personal borrowing to change the overall amount of financial leverage to which an individual is exposed.

income statement   Financial statement summarizing a firm's performance over a period of time.

incremental cash flows   The difference between a firm's future cash flows with a project and those without the project.

indenture The written agreement between the corporation and the lender detailing the terms of the debt issue.

indirect bankruptcy costs The costs of avoiding a bankruptcy filing incurred by a financially distressed firm.

inflation premium The portion of a nominal interest rate that represents compensation for expected future inflation.

initial public offering (IPO) A company's first equity issue made available to the public. Also *unseasoned new issue*.

inside quotes The highest bid quotes and the lowest ask quotes for a security.

interest on interest Interest earned on the reinvestment of previous interest payments.

interest rate parity (IRP) The condition stating that the interest rate differential between two countries is equal to the percentage difference between the forward exchange rate and the spot exchange rate.

interest rate risk premium The compensation investors demand for bearing interest rate risk.

interest tax shield The tax savings attained by a firm from the tax deductibility of interest expense.

internal growth rate The maximum possible growth rate a firm can achieve without external financing of any kind.

internal rate of return (IRR) The discount rate that makes the net present value of an investment zero.

inventory loan A secured short-term loan to purchase inventory.

inventory period The time it takes to acquire and sell inventory.

invoice Bill for goods or services provided by the seller to the purchaser.

just-in-time (JIT) inventory A system for managing demand-dependent inventories that minimizes inventory holdings.

line of credit A formal (committed) or informal (noncommitted) prearranged, short-term bank loan.

liquidation Termination of the firm as a going concern.

liquidity premium The portion of a nominal interest rate or bond yield that represents compensation for lack of liquidity.

lockboxes Special post office boxes set up to intercept and speed up accounts receivable collections.

lockup agreement The part of the underwriting contract that specifies how long insiders must wait after an IPO before they can sell stock.

London Interbank Offer Rate (LIBOR) The rate most international banks charge one another for overnight Eurodollar loans.

M&M Proposition I The value of a firm is independent of its capital structure.

M&M Proposition II A firm's cost of equity capital is a positive linear function of its capital structure.

managerial options Opportunities that managers can exploit if certain things happen in the future. Also known as "real" options.

marginal tax rate Amount of tax payable on the next dollar earned.

market risk A risk that influences a large number of assets. Also *systematic risk*.

market risk premium Slope of the security market line; the difference between the expected return on a market portfolio and the risk-free rate.

materials requirements planning (MRP) A set of procedures used to determine inventory levels for demand-dependent inventory types, such as work-in-progress and raw materials.

maturity Specified date on which the principal amount of a bond is paid.

member The owner of a trading license on the NYSE.

multiple rates of return The possibility that more than one discount rate will make the net present value of an investment zero.

mutually exclusive investment decisions A situation where taking one investment prevents the taking of another.

net present value (NPV) The difference between an investment's market value and its cost.

net present value profile A graphical representation of the relationship between an investment's net present values and various discount rates.

net working capital Current assets less current liabilities.

nominal rates Interest rates or rates of return that have not been adjusted for inflation.

noncash items Expenses charged against revenues that do not directly affect cash flow, such as depreciation.

normal distribution A symmetric, bell-shaped frequency distribution that is completely defined by its average and standard deviation.

note Unsecured debt, usually with a maturity of under 10 years.

operating cash flow Cash generated from a firm's normal business activities.

operating cycle The time period between the acquisition of inventory and the collection of cash from receivables.

opportunity cost The most valuable alternative that is given up if a particular investment is undertaken.

order flow The flow of customer orders to buy and sell securities.

overallotment option A contract provision giving the underwriter the option to purchase additional shares from the issuer at the offering price. Also *Green Shoe provision*.

partnership A business formed by two or more individuals or entities.

par value The principal amount of a bond that is repaid at the end of the term. Also *face value*.

payback period The amount of time required for an investment to generate cash flows sufficient to recover its initial cost.

perpetuity An annuity in which the cash flows continue forever.

political risk Risk related to changes in value that arise because of political actions.

portfolio Group of assets such as stocks and bonds held by an investor.

portfolio weight Percentage of a portfolio's total value in a particular asset.

precautionary motive The need to hold cash as a safety margin to act as a financial reserve.

preferred stock Stock with dividend priority over common stock, normally with a fixed dividend rate, sometimes without voting rights.

present value (PV) The current value of future cash flows discounted at the appropriate discount rate.

primary market The market in which new securities are originally sold to investors.

principle of diversification Spreading an investment across a number of assets will eliminate some, but not all, of the risk.

private placements Loans, usually long-term in nature, provided directly by a limited number of investors.

profitability index (PI) The present value of an investment's future cash flows divided by its initial cost. Also *benefit-cost ratio*.

pro forma financial statements Financial statements projecting future years' operations.

prospectus A legal document describing details of the issuing corporation and the proposed offering to potential investors.

protective covenant A part of the indenture limiting certain actions that might be taken during the term of the loan, usually to protect the lender's interest.

proxy A grant of authority by a shareholder allowing another individual to vote his or her shares.

purchasing power parity (PPP) The idea that the exchange rate adjusts to keep purchasing power constant among currencies.

pure play approach Use of a weighted average cost of capital that is unique to a particular project, based on companies in similar lines of business.

quoted interest rate The interest rate expressed in terms of the interest payment made each period. Also *stated interest rate*.

real rates Interest rates or rates of return that have been adjusted for inflation.

real return Return adjusted for the effects of inflation.

red herring A preliminary prospectus distributed to prospective investors in a new issue of securities.

registered form The registrar of a company records who owns each bond, and bond payments are made directly to the owner of record.

registration statement A statement filed with the SEC that discloses all material information concerning the corporation making a public offering.

regular cash dividend Cash payment made by a firm to its owners in the normal course of business, usually quarterly.

reorganization Financial restructuring of a failing firm to attempt to continue operations as a going concern.

repurchase Refers to a firm's purchase of its own stock; an alternative to a cash dividend.

residual dividend approach Policy under which a firm pays dividends only after meeting its investment needs while maintaining a desired debt-equity ratio.

reverse split Stock split under which a firm's number of shares outstanding is reduced.

rights offer A public issue of securities in which securities are first offered to existing shareholders. Also known as *rights offering*.

risk premium The excess return required from an investment in a risky asset over that required from a risk-free investment.

sales discount A discount given to induce prompt payment. Also known as *cash discount*.

scenario analysis The determination of what happens to net present value estimates when we ask what-if questions.

seasoned equity offering (SEO) A new equity issue of securities by a company that has previously issued securities to the public.

secondary market The market in which previously issued securities are traded among investors.

security market line (SML) Positively sloped straight line displaying the relationship between expected return and beta.

sensitivity analysis Investigation of what happens to net present value when only one variable is changed.

shelf registration Registration permitted by SEC Rule 415, which allows a company to register all issues it expects to sell within two years at one time, with subsequent sales at any time within those two years.

shortage costs Costs that fall with increases in the level of investment in current assets.

simple interest Interest earned only on the original principal amount invested.

sinking fund An account managed by the bond trustee for early bond redemption.

soft rationing The situation that occurs when units in a business are allocated a certain amount of financing for capital budgeting.

sole proprietorship A business owned by a single individual.

speculative motive The need to hold cash to take advantage of additional investment opportunities, such as bargain purchases.

spot exchange rate The exchange rate on a spot trade.

spot trade An agreement to trade currencies based on the exchange rate today for settlement within two business days.

spread Compensation to the underwriter, determined by the difference between the underwriter's buying price and offering price.

stakeholder Someone other than a stockholder or creditor who potentially has a claim on the cash flows of the firm.

stand-alone principle The assumption that evaluation of a project may be based on the project's incremental cash flows.

standard deviation The positive square root of the variance.

Standard Industrial Classification (SIC) code U.S. government code used to classify a firm by its type of business operations.

stated interest rate The interest rate expressed in terms of the interest payment made each period. Also *quoted interest rate*.

static theory of capital structure Theory that a firm borrows up to the point where the tax benefit from an extra dollar in debt is exactly equal to the cost that comes from the increased probability of financial distress.

stock dividend Payment made by a firm to its owners in the form of stock, diluting the value of each share outstanding.

stock repurchase The purchase, by a corporation, of its own shares of stock; also known as *buyback*.

stock split An increase in a firm's shares outstanding without any change in owners' equity.

straight voting A procedure in which a shareholder may cast all votes for each member of the board of directors.

strategic options Options for future, related business products or strategies.

sunk cost A cost that has already been incurred and cannot be recouped and therefore should not be considered in an investment decision.

supplemental liquidity providers (SLPs) Investment firms that are active participants in stocks assigned to them. Their job is to make a one-sided market (i.e., offering to either buy or sell). They trade purely for their own accounts.

sustainable growth rate The maximum possible growth rate a firm can achieve without external equity financing while maintaining a constant debt-equity ratio.

swaps Agreements to exchange two securities or currencies.

syndicate A group of underwriters formed to share the risk and to help sell an issue.

systematic risk A risk that influences a large number of assets. Also *market risk*.

systematic risk principle The expected return on a risky asset depends only on that asset's systematic risk.

taxability premium The portion of a nominal interest rate or bond yield that represents compensation for unfavorable tax status.

term loans Direct business loans of, typically, one to five years.

terms of sale Conditions under which a firm sells its goods and services for cash or credit.

term structure of interest rates The relationship between nominal interest rates on default-free, pure discount securities and time to maturity; that is, the pure time value of money.

tombstone An advertisement announcing a public offering.

trading range Price range between highest and lowest prices at which a stock is typically traded.

transaction motive The need to hold cash to satisfy normal disbursement and collection activities associated with a firm's ongoing operations.

Treasury yield curve A plot of the yields on Treasury notes and bonds relative to maturity.

underwriters Investment firms that act as intermediaries between a company selling securities and the investing public.

unique risk A risk that affects at most a small number of assets. Also *unsystematic* or *asset-specific risk*.

unseasoned new issue A company's first equity issue made available to the public. Also *initial public offering*.

unsystematic risk A risk that affects at most a small number of assets. Also *unique* or *asset-specific risk*.

variance The average squared difference between the actual return and the average return.

venture capital (VC) Financing for new, often high-risk ventures.

weighted average cost of capital (WACC) The weighted average of the cost of equity and the aftertax cost of debt.

working capital A firm's short-term assets and liabilities.

yield to maturity (YTM) The rate required in the market on a bond.

zero-balance account A disbursement account in which the firm maintains a zero balance, transferring funds in from a master account only as needed to cover checks presented for payment.

zero coupon bond A bond that makes no coupon payments, and thus is initially priced at a deep discount.

Name Index

Subject Index

Note: **Boldface** entries and page numbers indicate defined terms.

The integrated solutions for Ross/Westerfield/Jordan's *Essentials of Corporate Finance 8e* have been specifically designed to help improve student performance, meaning that students are prepared for and engaged in class, and they can successfully solve problems and analyze the results. Whether accessing online homework, quizzes, and tests or utilizing an interactive eBook, McGraw-Hill's *Connect® Finance* provides a complete digital solution. *Connect's* seamless partnership with the text's content allows instructors and students to go beyond the print world and into the digital realm with complete confidence.

McGraw-Hill's adaptive learning component, **LearnSmart**, provides assignable modules that help students master core concepts and come to class more prepared.

McGraw-Hill's Finance Prep Courses are available for math, statistics, accounting, and economics. These courses are comprised of animated tutorial modules with quiz questions that save instructors time in class and get students up to speed on the basics, so they will be ready for more complex finance topics.

Guided Examples offer online student tutorials at the problem level. They present a similar problem using formulas, calculator, or Excel next to the homework problem to help students understand how to move forward.

In addition, **Interactive Applications** within *Connect* allow students to practice real business situations, encourage critical thinking, and reinforce key concepts, while applying what they have learned from the text.

PROVEN EFFECTIVE

FEATURES

McGraw-Hill LearnSmart™ is an adaptive learning program that identifies what an individual student knows and doesn't know. LearnSmart's adaptive learning path helps students learn faster, study more efficiently, and retain more knowledge.

LearnSmart™

Get Connected.

Guided Examples

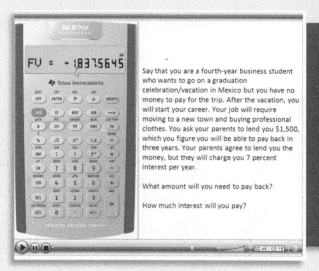

FU = -1837.5645

Say that you are a fourth-year business student who wants to go on a graduation celebration/vacation in Mexico but you have no money to pay for the trip. After the vacation, you will start your career. Your job will require moving to a new town and buying professional clothes. You ask your parents to lend you $1,500, which you figure you will be able to pay back in three years. Your parents agree to lend you the money, but they will charge you 7 percent interest per year.

What amount will you need to pay back?

How much interest will you pay?

Guided Examples provide students with narrated and animated video tutorials and step-by-step walkthroughs of exercises and examples from the text. Students appreciate the Guided Examples because they can learn to solve a problem when they get stuck doing their homework. There are multiple tutorials for each example, including a tutorial with decision points and walkthroughs using different calculators and Excel.

Finance Prep Courses

Do your students struggle with prerequisite material from accounting, math, statistics, and economics? With the Finance Prep Courses, students will view a video to refresh them on these topics, and then answer questions to test their understanding. You can either assign as homework or include for optional practice. This product gives you more time in class to cover finance topics, and ensures that students do not get left behind.

Get Engaged.

eBooks

Connect Plus includes a media-rich eBook that allows you to share your notes with your students. Your students can insert and review their own notes, highlight the text, search for specific information, and interact with media resources. Using an eBook with *Connect Plus* gives your students a complete digital solution that allows them to access their materials from any computer.

End-of-Chapter and Test

Connect Finance includes both static and algorithmic versions of end-of-chapter problems and static and algorithmic test bank questions.

Student Quick Tips

Use this Student Quick Tips guide for a quick and easy start with McGraw-Hill Connect. You'll get valuable tips on registering, doing assignments, and accessing resources, as well as information about the support center hours.

How to Access Connect using the Code Inside of your McGraw-Hill Create™ PRINT textbook.

NOTE: *If you are using an eBook, please see the next set of instructions below.*

Getting Started

TIP: You will need a 20 digit unique code which comes with the purchase of your McGraw-Hill Create™ print textbook. This code is **located on the inside back cover** of your printed textbook.

Registration and Sign In

1. Find the ISBN of your Create textbook. This can be found on Connect instructions page which is the last printed page of your book (begins with 978…)
2. Visit www.mcgrawhillcreate.com/shop
3. Search for the 13 digit ISBN found in step 1 (978XXXXXXXXXX).
4. The book should match your course (i.e. school, instructor, course name/number) and should say "Free With Access Code." Enter your unique 20 digit code found on the inside back cover of your textbook.
5. Register as a new user or sign-in if you already have a McGraw-Hill account

TIP: Remember this username and password as you will need it when you get to Connect

6. Open a new browser and go to the unique URL provided by your instructor
   (example: http://www.mcgrawhillconnect.com/class/instructorname_section_name)

> Sample of Connect Web Address
> http://www.mcgrawhillconnect.com/class/instructorname_section_name

7. Click the Register Now button and sign in using the same email address and password you created on the McGraw-Hill Bookstore (Step 5).

How to Access Connect Using the Code Inside of your McGraw-Hill Create™ eBOOK.

If you are viewing this page in your purchased Create ebook, then you only have a few more steps to complete your registration.

1. Open a new browser and go to the unique URL provided by your instructor
   (example: http://www.mcgrawhillconnect.com/class/instructorname_section_name)

> Sample of Connect Web Address
> http://www.mcgrawhillconnect.com/class/instructorname_section_name

2. Click the Register Now button and sign in using the same email address and password you created on the McGraw-Hill Bookstore when you purchased/accessed your eBook.

Trouble Logging In?

- Ensure you are using the same email address you used during registration

- If you have forgotten your password, click on the "Forgot Password?" link at your Instructor's Connect Course Web Address

- When logged into Connect, you can update your account information (e.g. email address, password, and security question/answer) by clicking on the *"My Account"* link located at the top-right corner

Home (Assignments)

TIP: If you are unable to begin an assignment, verify the following:

- The assignment is available (start and due dates)

- That you have not exceeded the maximum number of attempts

- That you have not achieved a score of 100%

- If your assignment contains questions that require manual grading, you will not be able to begin your next attempt until your instructor has graded those questions

TIP: Based on the assignment policy settings established by your Instructor, you may encounter the following limitations when working on your assignment(s):

- Ability to Print Assignment

- Timed assignments – once you begin a *"timed assignment,"* the timer will not stop by design

TIP: *"Save & Exit"* vs. *"Submit"* button

- If you are unable to complete your assignment in one sitting, utilize the *"Save & Exit"* button to save your work and complete it at a later time

- Once you have completed your assignment, utilize the *"Submit"* button in order for your assignment to be graded

Library

TIP: The *Library* section of your Connect account provides shortcuts to various resources.

- If you purchased ConnectPlus, you will see an *eBook* link, which can also be accessed from the section information widget of the *Home* tab

- *Recorded Lectures* can be accessed if your instructor is using *Tegrity Campus* to capture lectures. You may also access recorded lectures when taking an assignment by clicking on the projector icon in the navigation bar

- Many McGraw-Hill textbooks offer additional resources such as narrated slides and additional problems, which are accessible through the *Student Resources* link

Reports

TIP: Once you submit your assignment, you can view your available results in the *Reports* tab.

- If you see a dash (-) as your score, your instructor has either delayed or restricted your ability to see the assignment feedback

- Your instructor has the ability to limit the amount of information (e.g. questions, answers, scores) you can view for each submitted assignment

Need More Help?

CONTACT US ONLINE

Visit us at:

www.mcgrawhillconnect.com/support

Browse our support materials including tutorial videos and our searchable Connect knowledge base. If you cannot find an answer to your question, click on "Contact Us" button to send us an email.

GIVE US A CALL

Call us at:

1-800-331-5094

Our live support is available:

Mon-Thurs:	8 am – 11pm CT
Friday:	8 am – 6 pm CT
Sunday:	6 pm – 11 pm CT

Online Supplements

Connect Finance with LearnSmart One-Semester Online Access for Essentials of Corporate Finance, Eighth Edition

McGraw-Hill Connect is a digital teaching and learning environment that improves performance over a variety of critical outcomes. With Connect, instructors can deliver assignments, quizzes and tests easily online. Students can practice important skills at their own pace and on their own schedule.

HOW TO REGISTER

Using a _Print Book_?
To register and activate your Connect account, simply follow these easy steps:
1. **Go to the Connect course web address provided by your instructor or visit the Connect link set up on your instructor's course within your campus learning management system.**
2. **Click on the link to register.**
3. **When prompted, enter the Connect code found on the inside back cover of your book and click Submit. Complete the brief registration form that follows to begin using Connect.**

Using an _eBook_?
To register and activate your Connect account, simply follow these easy steps:
1. **Upon purchase of your eBook, you will be granted automatic access to Connect.**
2. **Go to the Connect course web address provided by your instructor or visit the Connect link set up on your instructor's course within your campus learning management system.**
3. **Sign in using the same email address and password you used to register on the eBookstore. Complete your registration and begin using Connect.**

Note: Access Code is for one use only. If you did not purchase this book new, the access code included in this book is no longer valid.

Need help? Visit mhhe.com/support